THE PAPERS OF

WOODROW WILSON

VOLUME 66

AUGUST 2-DECEMBER 23, 1920

SPONSORED BY THE WOODROW WILSON

FOUNDATION

AND PRINCETON UNIVERSITY

THE PAPERS OF

WOODROW WILSON

ARTHUR S. LINK, *EDITOR*

JOHN E. LITTLE, *ASSOCIATE EDITOR*

MANFRED F. BOEMEKE, *ASSOCIATE EDITOR*

L. KATHLEEN AMON, *ASSISTANT EDITOR*

PHYLLIS MARCHAND, *INDEXER*

Volume 66
August 2-December 23, 1920

PRINCETON, NEW JERSEY

PRINCETON UNIVERSITY PRESS

1992

INTRODUCTION

As this volume opens (August 2, 1920), the presidential campaign is about to get under way. Wilson has received the Democratic candidates, Cox and Roosevelt, at the White House on July 18 and given them his blessing, but he has neither the physical strength nor any strong desire to become involved in the contest, or even to have his subordinates do so. Thus, when Tumulty and Colby say that they want to join in the debate with Harding, the Republican candidate, Wilson imposes a stern rule of silence on them.

It is of course impossible for so combative a person as Wilson to sit quietly on the side lines. Tumulty leads Wilson into a personal quarrel with Senator Spencer of Missouri over what Wilson had said in Paris about the possible use of American military forces to preserve peace through the League of Nations. Bested in this controversy, Wilson acts maladroitly again by sending a letter with threatening overtones to Harding, asking whether it is true that the latter has been conducting unofficial diplomatic relations with the French government. Harding's dignified if curt reply ends all such Wilsonian forays into the contest.

On the single great issue of the campaign—American membership in the League of Nations—Wilson cannot remain silent. In a statement to the country on October 3, he says that the coming election will be "a genuine national referendum" on this issue. On October 27, just a week before the election, Wilson receives fifteen pro-League Republicans at the White House and, in his first speech since his breakdown, makes an eloquent plea for the fulfillment of what he calls the moral obligations of the United States. Finally, on October 29, he sends a message of commendation and encouragement to Cox. It is the first time that Wilson has publicly mentioned the Democratic candidate by name since the reception of the Democratic candidates at the White House.

Not many people heed Wilson's appeals, any more than they listen to Cox. The Republicans succeed in obfuscating not only the League issue, but all issues except Wilson and his record. On election day, November 2, the voters seemingly repudiate Wilson and all he stands for in a landslide majority for Harding and Coolidge. Much to the surprise of his intimates, Wilson accepts the verdict cheerfully in the confidence that the voters have only been momentarily misled and that the Republicans have, as he puts it, in fact committed suicide.

Meanwhile, the work of governing the United States has gone on, smoothly and efficiently on the whole. Wilson gains strength slowly but steadily during the summer and early autumn of 1920. He does not have the strength to write messages or letters concerning public policies and relies on Tumulty and members of his Cabinet to do this for him. Indeed, upon the few matters of domestic policy of any complexity that come up during these months, Wilson gratefully accepts the decisions of his advisers.

Wilson also generally follows the lead of his two principal advisers on foreign policy, Secretary of State Bainbridge Colby and Undersecretary Norman Davis, and relies upon them to draft the correspondence with other governments. But Wilson maintains daily oversight over the State Department and makes all important decisions. Hence, when the opportunity to enunciate a policy toward the now triumphant Soviet regime arises, Wilson lays down the fundamental principles and policy. Under his direction, Colby, Davis, and others draft the note which sets the policy of nonrecognition of the Soviet government and noninterference in Russian affairs by the United States Government which prevails until 1933. When Britain, France, and Italy agree to divide concessions in the former Ottoman Empire, Wilson cheers when Colby writes an eloquent defense of the basic open-door policies of the mandate system. Wilson plays an even more active role in a controversy now developing with Japan over the latter country's control of the Pacific Island of Yap, formerly under German sovereignty and now a strategic junction point of one of two transpacific cable routes. Wilson strongly supports Colby and the new head of the Latin American Division of the State Department, Sumner Welles, in plans to restore a large measure of self-government to the Dominican Republic, as well as Colby's and Davis' efforts to establish cordial relations with Mexico. On a few matters, Wilson takes a peremptory stand. He will not permit the State Department to have any official relations with the League of Nations (he even refuses to allow an American official to attend the first session of the Assembly of the League of Nations as an observer); he withdraws Americans from all commissions established by the Versailles Treaty; and he refuses to permit the State Department to send warships to Cuba, where civil war seems to impend.

As this volume ends, Wilson is awarded the Nobel Peace Prize for 1919; he and Mrs. Wilson are making plans for their retirement; and Tumulty and the departmental heads are winding up their respective affairs. The pall of the election results still lies heavily upon the Wilson circle, but the apotheosis of Woodrow Wilson has already begun, as personal friends and publicists begin to take stock of the Wilson presidency and its legacy.

We extend our sincere thanks to the persons who have given invaluable assistance in the preparation of this volume: Timothy Connelly, of the National Historical Publications and Records Commission, for continuing excellent research for documents and many of the photographs in this volume; John Whiteclay Chambers II, for the information that went into n. 1 to the extract from the Daniels Diary printed at August 21, 1920; John Milton Cooper, Jr., William H. Harbaugh, August Heckscher, Richard W. Leopold, and Betty Miller Unterberger of our Editorial Advisory Committee, for carefully reviewing the manuscript of this volume; and Alice Calaprice, our editor at Princeton University Press.

THE EDITORS

Princeton, New Jersey
September 30, 1991

CONTENTS

CONTENTS

Diplomatic, Military, and Naval Affairs

Personal Affairs

ILLUSTRATIONS

Following page 296

ABBREVIATIONS

A.E.F.	American Expeditionary Forces
AL	autograph letter
ALI	autograph letter initialed
ALS	autograph letter signed
AMP	Alexander Mitchell Palmer
ASB	Albert Sidney Burleson
BC	Bainbridge Colby
BMB	Bernard Mannes Baruch
CC	carbon copy
CCL	carbon copy of letter
CLSsh	Charles Lee Swem shorthand
DFH	David Franklin Houston
EBW	Edith Bolling Galt Wilson
EBWhw	Edith Bolling Galt Wilson handwriting, handwritten
EMH	Edward Mandell House
ENH	Edward Nash Hurley
FDR	Franklin Delano Roosevelt
FLP	Frank Lyon Polk
FR	*Papers Relating to the Foreign Relations of the United States*
Hw, hw	handwriting, handwritten
HSC	Homer Stillé Cummings
JD	Josephus Daniels
JPT	Joseph Patrick Tumulty
JRT	Jack Romagna typed
JRW	Joseph Ruggles Wilson
MS, MSS	manuscript, manuscripts
NDB	Newton Diehl Baker
NHD	Norman Hezekiah Davis
PPC	*Papers Relating to the Foreign Relations of the United States, The Paris Peace Conference, 1919*
RG	record group
RL	Robert Lansing
T	typed
TC	typed copy
TCL	typed copy of letter
TI	typed initialed
TL	typed letter
TLS	typed letter signed
TS	typed signed
TWG	Thomas Watt Gregory
WBW	William Bauchop Wilson
WGM	William Gibbs McAdoo
WW	Woodrow Wilson
WWhw	Woodrow Wilson handwriting, handwritten
WWhwL	Woodrow Wilson handwritten letter
WWsh	Woodrow Wilson shorthand
WWT	Woodrow Wilson typed

Following the National Union Catalog of the
Library of Congress

CtY	Yale University
CtY-D	Yale University Divinity School
DLC	Library of Congress
DNA	National Archives
FWpR	Rollins College
InNd	Notre Dame University
KyBB	Berea College
MiDbF	Ford Motor Company
MH	Harvard University
MH-BA	Harvard University Graduate School of Business Administration
MWC	Clark University
NcDad	Davidson College
NcU	University of North Carolina, Chapel Hill
NjP	Princeton University
NHpR	Franklin D. Roosevelt Library
NRU	University of Rochester
PPAmP	American Philosophical Society
RSB Coll., DLC	Ray Stannard Baker Collection of Wilsoniana, Library of Congress
SDR	State Department Records
TxHR	Rice University
TxU	University of Texas, Austin
UMWA	United Mine Workers of America
ViU	University of Virginia
VtU	University of Vermont
WC, NjP	Woodrow Wilson Collection, Princeton University
WP, DLC	Woodrow Wilson Papers, Library of Congress

SYMBOLS

[Nov. 3, 1920]	publication date of published writing; also date of document when date is not part of text
[*Dec. 2, 1920*]	composition date when publication date differs
[[Oct. 4, 1920]]	delivery date of speech when publication date differs
* * * * * * *	text deleted by author of document

THE PAPERS OF

WOODROW WILSON

VOLUME 66

AUGUST 2-DECEMBER 23, 1920

THE PAPERS OF
WOODROW WILSON

To James F. Griffin[1]

My dear Sir: [The White House] 2 August, 1920

I have your letter of July 20 in which you ask me whether Messrs. Scott Ferris and Thomas P. Gore are acceptable to me as candidates for the U. S. Senate.[2] I do not feel that I have the least right to decide for the people of Oklahoma who are acceptable candidates but if my opinion of these gentlemen is of interest to the voters of Oklahoma I feel gratified that it should be desired and herewith frankly state my estimate of at least one of these gentlemen. Mr. Gore has never been a sincere supporter of my administration. His course has always been incalculable and apparently governed by undisclosed motives which it was very difficult for those of us who were associated with him to assess or understand. Even when he has acted with his Democratic colleagues in the Senate upon important issues, he has created as many obstacles and set up as many objections as possible and has constantly embarrassed the course of action. His motives I cannot judge and do not feel at liberty to speculate upon.

T transcript (C. L. Swem Coll., NjP).
  [1] Of Pauls Valley, Oklahoma. We have been unable futher to identify him.
  [2] They were opponents in the Democratic primary campaign for the seat held by Gore.

To William Bauchop Wilson

My dear Mr. Secretary: The White House 2 August, 1920

Thank you for your letter of the thirty-first of July.[1] It brings very cheering news and the assurances you give of your own opinion as to what will happen among the striking miners has cheered me very much. You are always exceedingly helpful.

        Cordially and faithfully yours,   Woodrow Wilson

TLS (received from Mary A. Strohecker).
  [1] It is printed at that date in Vol. 65.

To John Llewellyn Lewis

My dear Mr. Lewis: [The White House] 2 August, 1920

Your action in response to my statement urging the striking miners to return to work[1] has gratified me very deeply indeed. It is the action of a patriotic citizen and a man of vision and prescience. I am glad that you feel as I do that in urging the men to return to work I was speaking in their interest as much as in the interest of the general public and of the industrial energy of the country.
                    Cordially and sincerely yours,   [Woodrow Wilson]

CCL (WP, DLC).
  [1] See J. L. Lewis to WW, July 31, 1920, Vol. 65.

Joseph Patrick Tumulty to Edith Bolling Galt Wilson

Dear Mrs. Wilson: The White House, 2 August, 1920.

I gave Dr. Axson a complete copy of Governor Cox's speech,[1] which one of the newspaper men handed me this morning. In my newspaper conference today, without pretending to give any impressions of my own, I found among the newspaper men that the Wilson admirers felt that Governor Cox had generously backed up the President's position on the League of Nations and that it was a good speech. Arthur Sinnott of the Newark News was especially warm in his praise of it. Of course, he criticized its literary texture, but said that the position he took on the League of Nations was honest and straightforward and in generous support of the President's attitude toward it.   Sincerely,   [Tumulty]

CCL (J. P. Tumulty Papers, DLC).
  [1] An advance copy of Cox's acceptance speech, which he was to deliver in Dayton, Ohio, on August 7.

From the Diary of Josephus Daniels

August Tuesday 3 1920

Cabinet. Payne & I told of our trip to Alaska.[1]

Palmer wanted his Fair Price Com. to fix a price for coal and prosecute all who charged more. They were all int. as buyers or producers. W.W. told Palmer that the Fed. Trade Com. was authorized to investigate & he would be wise to get that Board to make report instead of depending on voluntary & interests committees.

Palmer spoke of the growth of the Communist & Bolshevik sentiment & wanted to take action against it.

Colby brought up the suggestion that the President or Dept of

State make known the dangers of Bolshevist propaganda from Russia as obtained by State Dept. Suggested that John Spargo, who had written on autocratic bolshevism,[2] get out the facts. The President thought Duncan[3] (Labor Delegate to Russia) might be able to reach many. Colby to see Wilson.

After cabinet I talked of FDR's resignation & asked if President had any man in view for vacancy. No.

"I resent & deeply resent &c" he said.

Hw bound diary (J. Daniels Papers, DLC).
    [1] Daniels and John Barton Payne had gone to Alaska to inspect coal lands reserved for the United States Navy.
    [2] Spargo's books on this general theme were *Bolshevism: The Enemy of Political and Industrial Democracy* (New York and London, 1919); *The Psychology of Bolshevism* (New York and London, 1919); *Russia as an American Problem* (New York and London, 1920); and *"The Greatest Failure in All History": A Critical Examination of the Actual Workings of Bolshevism in Russia* (New York and London, 1920). As the titles imply, Spargo was strongly opposed to Bolshevism and believed that the United States had a vital stake, both political and economic, in the future of a free and democratic Russia. He had been an informal adviser on Russian affairs to Lansing and Colby since November 1919, and he had drafted and sent to Colby on July 31 a memorandum which was to serve as the basis of the diplomatic note on Poland and Russia printed as an Enclosure with BC to WW, Aug. 9, 1920. See Ronald Radosh, "John Spargo and Wilson's Russian Policy, 1920," *Journal of American History*, LII (Dec. 1965), 548-65, and Daniel M. Smith, *Aftermath of War: Bainbridge Colby and Wilsonian Diplomacy, 1920-1921* (Philadelphia, 1970), pp. 60-66.
    [3] James Duncan, first vice-president of the American Federation of Labor; labor representative on the Root Commission to Russia in 1917.

To Carl E. Moore,[1] with Enclosure

My dear Mr. Moore: [The White House] 3 August, 1920

I am happy to acknowledge the receipt of your letter of July 31,[2] inviting me to contribute a greeting to the souvenir edition of The Legionnaire, to be published while Cleveland is entertaining the Second Annual Convention of The American Legion. I enclose a greeting which I should be happy to have so used.

Cordially yours,   Woodrow Wilson

TLS (Letterpress Books, WP, DLC).
    [1] Newspaper reporter of Cleveland; chairman of the committee on printing, program, and publicity for the second annual convention of the American Legion to be held in Cleveland, September 27-29, 1920.
    [2] C. E. Moore to WW, July 31, 1920, TLS (WP, DLC). Wilson had sent this letter to Newton D. Baker, and Baker had returned it on August 3 saying that all of the men connected with *The Legionnaire* were responsible and prominent citizens of Cleveland. Baker had also enclosed a draft of the Enclosure. NDB to JPT, Aug. 3, 1920, TLS (WP, DLC). Wilson changed one word in the message sent to Moore: "privilege" for "blessing" at the end of the first sentence of the second paragraph.

ENCLOSURE

To the American Legion:

Years are now beginning to separate us from the days of trial and deeds of valor which marked America's participation in the World War. As the number of the years increases, the things you did in foreign fields will be seen in clearer perspective, and your heroic quality will be more and more apparent. The Nation sent you as its representatives and its champions; the fidelity with which you fought fittingly represented the faithfulness with which those at home labored and sacrificed in the same cause. The result of it all was a military victory in France and a moral victory in the world; the deeds of valor, the deeds of high-thinking, the deeds of righteous impulses together make a great tradition, and it will be good for all future generations to continue your practice of cherishing these memories and keeping them bright as an example and inspiration.

My own high privilege of leadership was a daily privilege. There was no need to urge; we all went forward as comrades to a great end, and we can survey the result with gratitude that America was permitted to make so great a contribution to righteousness among peoples and among nations.   Woodrow Wilson

TS MS (Letterpress Books, WP, DLC).

Four Letters from Joseph Patrick Tumulty

Dear Governor: The White House, 3 August, 1920

I can't tell you how much I appreciate the little note you wrote me on Friday,[1] offering me a judgeship in the Customs Court of Appeals. To be thought of in such a way cheers me more than anything that could happen, and it is an honor that I would not forego. You always know best how to do the pleasing and cheering thing.

I know you will expect me to think the matter over before giving a definite answer. I can probably make up my mind within the month. But, in the meantime, if you feel that you cannot in the public interest keep the position open, I hope you will feel free to name somebody else for it. This is only fair.

With affectionate appreciation,   Sincerely,   [Tumulty]

CCL (J. P. Tumulty Papers, DLC).
 [1] WW to JPT, July 30, 1920, Vol. 65.

Dear Governor: The White House, 3 August, 1920.

Certain members of the National Committee telephoned me from Chicago today and urged me to go to Dayton to attend the speech of acceptance ceremonies, saying it was their desire that the administration be represented there. Of course, I was non-committal. I do not wish to do anything without your advice.

Sincerely,   Tumulty

I think it w'd be all right <u>W.W.</u>

TLS (J. P. Tumulty Papers, DLC).

Dear Governor: The White House, 3 August 1920.

Secretary Alexander, before he left for Missouri, frankly told me that he would like to be appointed a member of the new Shipping Board. He thinks there is great constructive work to be done there, and that his experience as a member of the Committee in the House having to do with this bill would enable him to be of much service.

He told me that the matter was so delicate that he did not know how to approach it himself but that he understood you had heard of his desire to serve. I presume Judge Payne has already told you about him.   Sincerely yours,   Tumulty

TLS (WP, DLC).

Dear Governor: The White House 4 August, 1920.

If you decide to appoint Judge Alexander to the Shipping Board, a vacancy would be made in the Cabinet. I trust you will pardon the suggestion I make with reference to Mr. Homer Cummings as Judge Alexander's successor in the Cabinet. I do this without any suggestion from anyone.

No one is more deeply or unselfishly devoted to you. Every line of his great speech at the convention[1] breathes not only admiration but deep affection for you and the great principles for which you have stood. There is no doubt that without suggestion from any-one, he raised the level of the convention by his unswerving devotion to your ideals and the things accomplished by you. You will remember that when Mr. Lansing resigned I suggested Homer Cummings' name as Secretary of State,[2] but you turned away from the suggestion for the reason that he could better serve the party as chairman of the National Committee. He has been most un-kindly treated and I am sure your recognition of him at this time

would be fine acknowledgment of his high services to the party
and his devotion to you.   Sincerely,   [Tumulty]

CCL (J. P. Tumulty Papers, DLC).
   ¹ See HSC to WW, June 28, 1920 (second telegram of that date), n. 1, Vol. 65.
   ² JPT to EBW, Feb. 13, 1920, Vol. 64.

From Joseph Patrick Tumulty, with Enclosure

Dear Governor: The White House, 4 August 1920.
   I am sending you herewith Governor McCall's declination.
   I think you ought, in some way, to bring out in your reply to him
the fact that it is too bad that when the nation can take advantage
of such an offer of fine service as Governor McCall could render—
through his experience as a member of the Ways and Means Committee of the House—the action of a a [sic] few men in the Senate
can prevent its consummation.
                    Sincerely yours,   J P Tumulty

TLS (WP, DLC).

E N C L O S U R E

From Samuel Walker McCall

To the President   Winchester Massachusetts Aug 3. '20
   When you did me the wholly unsought honor of proposing to
appoint me as a member of the Tariff Com.¹ it seemed to me my
long experience on Ways & Means would fit me to render some
good service in an important field. Accordingly with my approval
you sent my name to the Senate. A month afterward that body adjourned without action upon many appointments including my
own. With regard to the recess appointment the tenure is uncertain & maybe very brief & I understand a member of this commission may not actively engage in any other business. While I should
be able to readjust my private affairs to meet this requirement if
the term were fixed & reasonable it would not be prudent I think
to withdraw from some private interests to enter on a tenure so
uncertain & which might be so short as not to permit me to render
any public service at all commensurate with the sacrifice I was
making. The circumstances in which I find myself fairly preclude
my entering upon the tenure of a recess appointment Let me add
that I am deeply sensible of the distinction conferred by your
thought of me in connection with an important public service.

I have been very glad to see the public evidence of your rapid recovery. With my heartiest wishes for your complete restoration to the best of health

I am　　　　　Very Respectfully Yours　　Samuel W McCall

ALS (WP, DLC).

¹ David John Lewis, a member of the United States Tariff Commission, had written to Tumulty on April 23, 1920, to suggest that either McCall or George Sutherland, former congressman and senator from Utah, would be suitable appointments to fill a vacancy on the commission. D. J. Lewis to JPT, April 23, 1920, TLS (WP, DLC). Wilson wrote the following note on this letter: "McCall is an excellent suggestion Please prepare a nomination W.W." Tumulty wrote to Lewis on May 3 to inform him that Wilson had asked McCall to accept the appointment. [JPT] to D. J. Lewis, May 3, 1920, CCL (WP, DLC). It was announced on May 5 that McCall had done so, and Wilson sent the nomination to the Senate on May 6. *New York Times*, May 6 and 7, 1920. Wilson made a recess appointment of McCall to the commission on June 9. *Ibid.*, June 10, 1920.

From Bainbridge Colby, with Enclosure

The President:　　　　　　　　　　Washington, August 4, 1920.

The undersigned, the Secretary of State, has the honor to lay before the President a copy of a note dated July 31, 1920, from the Minister of Poland at Washington, embodying the text of a cable message to the President from the Prime Minister of Poland.

The Secretary of State would be pleased to direct the delivery, through the American Legation at Warsaw, of such reply as the President may wish sent.

　　　　　　　　Respectfully submitted,　Bainbridge Colby

TLS (WP, DLC).

E N C L O S U R E

Kazimierz Lubomirski to Bainbridge Colby

Sir:　　　　　　　　　　　　Washington July 31, 1920.

I have the honor to submit the following cable received for the President of the United States, from the Prime Minister of Poland:

"Mr. President, Having assumed the office of Prime Minister of Poland at this momentous hour,¹ I hasten to renew to Your Excellency the expression of the Polish Government's deep and sincere gratitude for America's generous help and continuous sympathy extended to this country. Poland, for her part, not only has American welfare and American interest strongly at heart, but the entire Polish people consider Polish American friendship to be one of the greatest assets in the future prosperity of both countries. Let me add, Mr. President, that you having been the

most staunch promoter and defensor of Polish Independence are
at this hour of country's greatest need nearer and dearer than
ever to every Polish heart.   Witos."[2]

Accept, Sir, the renewed assurances of my highest consideration.   (Signed) Casimir Lubomirski
                                        Minister of Poland.

TCL (WP, DLC).
   [1] The Red Army was virtually at the gates of Warsaw when this telegram was sent.
   [2] Wincenty Witos.

To Scott Ferris

                          [The White House] 5 Aug, 1920

I sincerely congratulate you for I am sure the national interest
will be served by your nomination and election.[1]

T transcript (C. L. Swem Coll., NjP).
   [1] Ferris had defeated Gore by a vote of 106,454 to 80,243.

To Samuel Walker McCall

My dear Governor McCall: [The White House] 5 August, 1920

I am genuinely distressed that you find it impossible to take your
place upon the Tariff Commission. It does seem to me a serious
injury to the public interest that the action of a few Senators
should prevent the functioning of the Tariff Commission in the
way in which it was intended to function, that is to say, with intelligence and without partisan bias. It can function in that way only
through the membership of such men as yourself, whose experience and attitude in public affairs insure the right sort of public
spirit and public motive.

I do not want to urge you in any way that is unwelcome to you,
but I do beg that you will reconsider the matter, and I do so with
the sincere hope that you may render the Government services in
this matter which I am sure will be invaluable.

                    Cordially and sincerely yours,   [Woodrow Wilson]

CCL (WP, DLC).

To Ira Clemens[1]

                          [The White House] August 5, 1920.

It has been reported to me that part of the trouble at the mines
in Illinois and Indiana is due to the fact that some operators have

been asserting that the day men are entitled to a higher wage, and they would be willing to pay more, but for the fact that they are bound by the bituminous coal commission's award. It is not my purpose to change the award of the Commission, but if the operators and miners jointly agree that there are some inequalities in the award that ought to be adjusted, I can see no reason why they should not be permitted to adjust them. The statement contained in your telegram[2] that such a course would greatly increase the cost of coal and work further hardship upon the consuming public, does not appeal to me as sound. In view of the exorbitant prices that have been exacted from the public for spot coal during the past few months which have had no relation to the cost of production on present wage scale, I shall therefore call the Joint Scale Committee of the Central Competitive Field into conference as soon as I learn that the miners have returned to work, for the purpose of adjusting any inequalities which they may mutually agree should be adjusted.   Woodrow Wilson.[3]

T telegram (Letterpress Books, WP, DLC).
  [1] President of the Southwestern Interstate Coal Operators Association of Kansas City.
  [2] I. Clemens to WW, Aug. 1, 1920, T telegram (WP, DLC).
  [3] William B. Wilson had drafted this reply to Clemens. WBW to H. L. Kerwin, Aug. 3, 1920, T telegram, enclosed in H. L. Kerwin to JPT, Aug. 4, 1920, TLS, both in WP, DLC. The telegram was typed, Wilson wrote "OKeh W.W." on the copy, and it was then sent.

To Bainbridge Colby

My dear Mr. Secretary: The White House 5 August, 1920

Thank you for your letter enclosing the message to me from the Prime Minister of Poland. I would be very much indebted to you if you would instruct our representative at Warsaw as to the proper acknowledgment to make, for I am sure you can frame it as well as I could, if you will be so generous.[1]
                    Cordially and faithfully yours,   Woodrow Wilson

TLS (SDR, RG 59, 760c.61/318, DNA).
  [1] In his reply, Colby reiterated expressions of American friendship for Poland and commended the gallantry of the Polish army. However, he went on in a virtual condemnation of Polish conduct: the Polish invasion of Russia had stirred nationalistic feeling in that country, which had enabled the Soviets to undertake an invasion of Poland; the Polish government should declare that it would abstain from aggression against Russian territorial integrity, that its policy was not directed against the establishment of a strong and united Russia, and that, pending an agreement on its eastern frontier, Poland would remain within the boundary indicated by the peace conference; and Poland should exhibit "real moderation" in dealing with Soviet negotiators and insist upon only such terms as were essential to the security, full sovereignty, and territorial integrity of the Polish state. Colbto to the Chargé in Poland, Aug. 21, 1920, FR 1920, III, 391-92. Insofar as we know, Wilson never saw this telegram before it was sent.

From Bainbridge Colby, with Enclosure

My dear Mr. President: [Washington] August 5, 1920.

I send you herewith a full memorandum of an important exchange of views between Mr. Morris, our Ambassador to Japan, and the Japanese Ambassador to this country, relative to the California situation.[1]

I would greatly appreciate the guidance of your thought on any phase of this matter.

Very respectfully yours,   Bainbridge Colby

CCL (B. Colby Papers, DLC).
    [1] Morris had returned to the United States on June 20, 1920, and was then assigned to the State Department as a consultant on "certain Far Eastern questions, particularly the questions with Japan rising out of the alien land legislation in California." *New York Times*, Nov. 7, 1920. As it turned out, he never returned to Tokyo.

E N C L O S U R E

July 22, 1920.

MEMORANDUM OF CONVERSATION BETWEEN
AMBASSADOR MORRIS AND AMBASSADOR SHIDEHARA

I explained to Mr. Shidehara the tentative conclusions which I have reached as a result of my discussions with residents of California and Japanese representatives during my recent trip to San Francisco.

I told Mr. Shidehara that there was practically a unanimous determination on the part of the people of California to prevent all Asiatic immigration to California. I explained to him that in my judgment this was not primarily economic but that it arose from the fear of the people of California that the presence of a large body of unassimilable people would threaten them with a serious and persistent race problem. I said that there was a division of sentiment among those who had studied the question whether the Japanese people ever could assimilate with Western civilization. I further expressed my opinion that this question could only be determined by the test of experience and I saw in the California conditions a peculiar opportunity for such a test.

There were admittedly 85,000 Japanese already there and if we could allow two or three generations to pass without adding by immigration to that number we would then know how Japanese had blended into the economic and social structure of California life. I explained that the "Gentlemen's Agreement"[1] had not succeeded satisfactorily in preventing immigration during the past ten years. I believed that if arrangements could be made to provide for total exclusion in the future that we would thus establish the foundation for better treatment by Californians towards Japanese already there. I further told him that the initiative would in my judgment undoubtedly pass and that any effort on the part of the Japanese residents or the Federal Government to prevent its passage by propaganda or otherwise would only serve to accentuate the present antagonism. I had, I said, serious doubts as to the validity of the existing and proposed discriminatory legislation against Japanese residents,[2] in view of our Constitutional provisions and treaty obligations, and that I wished that question could be determined. I asked him to think over the following procedure to handle the problem for the immediate future.

First, to wait in the hope that a test of the validity of the Act of 1913[3] might be made in our courts so that we know whether we were discussing a real or fictitious situation.

Second, to begin immediate discussions of amendments to strengthen the "Gentlemen's Agreement" so that it would hereafter operate totally to exclude all Japanese. I pointed out that this procedure would accomplish the following results:

(1st) The pendency of a litigation in our courts would give Mr. Hara's[4] Cabinet the opportunity to explain that the legislation which was sure to pass by initiative and refereadum [referendum] was still undetermined as to its effect and in this way allay any possible resentment in Japan. (2nd), At the same time it would give a chance for so strengthening the "Gentlemen's Agreement" that if the Supreme Court should decide in the test case that the legislation of 1913 was valid, then the result of the negotiations of an amended "Gentlemen's Agreement" could be published and thus give ground for modifying the California laws. If, on the other hand, it was held not valid, the new and effective "Gentlemen's Agreement" would operate to prevent subsequent action by California.

I spoke at length and very frankly of the problem in its general aspects; that it represented the whole issue of contact between the West and the East and that it could only be approached in a broad and statesmanlike spirit. So long as it involved undetermined questions of assimilability, it was absolutely essential that we wait until time had solved these questions. In the meantime we must adjust our minds to the conclusion that the people of our Western coast would not permit any further additions to the population by immigration until time had determined these questions.

He replied:

First, that he agreed with me as to my conclusion about the feeling in California. He had always wished that the legality of the

legislation of 1913 had been tested; that the reason it had not was
that he, as Counselor in Washington then, consulted several eminent American Lawyers and was assured by them that the legislation could not be successfully attacked. I replied that this was not
the conclusion of some lawyers in California. He was inclined favorably to my suggestion that the question ought to be definitely
determined.

Second, as to my suggestion of strengthening by carefully
thought–out amendments the terms of the "Gentlemen's Agreement," he would admit that he had been earnestly working on that
for some time and had made a careful study of the provisions with
a view to determining what amendments could be made. He enu-
merated the various causes of the increase in population in spite of
the "Gentlemen's Agreement" and thought that some of them
could be remedied. He was quite prepared to discuss that general
problem seriously.

He asked me whether I believed that any good could come of the
international commission such as had been suggested by the conference held in Tokyo.[5] I told him that in my judgment that plan
was utterly impracticable; that our Government would never con-
sign a domestic question of immigration to an international commission and if any further reason were desired, I had no faith that
such a commission, if approved by the Government, could reach
any conclusions of this subject that could not be better reached by
diplomatic conversations. He said he was glad to hear me say that,
as he had advised his own Government exactly to that effect—that
the American Government would never consent to such a plan.

In conclusion I explained to him that I had not had an opportunity to report to my own Department on my general observations
in California, and I had no idea what their views would be, but
speaking entirely personally I thought that we should handle the
present situation thus:

First: to cooperate sympathetically in any effort that might be
made by Californians independently to test the validity of the 1913
legislation, and I admitted to him that I had so expressed myself to
Californians.

Second: to begin at once a discussion of the strengthening of the
"Gentlemen's Agreement," to hold any announcement of the result
until such time as any test case as to the validity of the legislation
might be determined, or it might be necessary, in order to neutral-
ize threatened Congressional action.

I pointed out in conclusion that whether the legislation was valid
or invalid, it seemed to me essential that our Governments should
agree on a larger understanding that meant total exclusion for a

sufficiently long period to test the assimilability of those Japanese already resident on the Pacific Coast.   R.S.M.

TS MS (SDR, RG 59, 811.5294/94, DNA).

[1] The agreement between the Japanese and American governments, embodied in an exchange of notes in 1907, in which the former promised not to issue passports to Japanese laborers bound for the continental United States.

[2] About this California initiative and the general agitation for exclusion of all Asiatics, see BC to WW, Oct. 4, 1920.

[3] That is, the California Alien Land law of 1913, which provided that only aliens "eligible to citizenship" might own land in the state.

[4] Takashi Hara, Japanese Prime Minister.

[5] A conference of Japanese and American businessmen, meeting in Tokyo in early April 1920, had proposed the establishment of a joint commission for solution of the California land dispute and allied questions. *New York Times*, April 5, 1920.

Irwin Hood Hoover to Cary Travers Grayson

My Dear Doctor.—   The White House Aug 5/20.

You have only been gone a couple of days and yet it seems a long time and I feel you would like a word from headquarters.

Everything is just as when you left and the distinguished patient really seems to be unusually well and in good spirits. The routine has been the same and the nurse says "the nights have been good" She spoke of having me send you a wire to that effect but I include it here instead.

One change of note is that the President & Mrs. Wilson went for a ride this afternoon in a horse drawn victoria. The touring car is being repaired so the President thought he would try the carriage. If appearances count for anything it was a great pleasure to him and a great success.

Your machine is jacked up in the White House garage as per last instructions thro Miller. I had them bring the key up to me, so there will be no question.

It may interest you to know, the Captain of the Mayflower, thro Mr. Tumulty, applied for permission to take the boat on a short cruise. It was denied him. "Nuf sed"

The weather has been just the same, cool and pleasant. The days long, especially with you away, for it is quite different, but whats the matter just so everything goes well.

Dr. Axson, too, seems in very good shape, he has been sitting in on the pictures during the morning, since you left, which I would think was a very good sign.

So it goes and if I knew what would interest you most I would write more. But with your vivid imagination and your recollections of recent days you just about know what goes on from hour to hour. Then all that is left to me is to so positively assure you that all is well, from both an professional and personal standpoint.

I shall write you again in time and before if I feel the necessity for doing so, but now, have a good time, win a good big stake and come back happy and well—   Faithfully   Hoover.

ALS (received from James Gordon Grayson and Cary T. Grayson, Jr.).

A News Report

[Aug. 7, 1920]

WILSON CONFERENCE DECIDES ON ANTI-LENINE, PRO-RUSSIA POLICY
U. S. Favors Assurance of Territorial Integrity.
By ALBERT W. FOX.

America's policy toward the Russian-Polish conflict and the bolshevik menace to Europe took definite form yesterday at a White House conference between President Wilson, Secretary of State Bainbridge Colby and Under Secretary Norman Davis. An important declaration made jointly by the allies and the United States or by the United States independently is looked for in the near future.[1]

The essence of the American policy, which is now the subject of cable code exchanges between Washington, London and Paris, may be summarized as follows:

First—America does not believe that the bolshevik menace can be removed by fighting or antagonizing the Russian nation.

Second—The President and the State Department favor a solemn declaration, by the allies and the United States together, or by the United States alone, that territory belonging to the Russians (excepting Finland and Poland) shall not be taken from the people of Russia and that such Russian territory as is now held by allied forces shall be regarded as simply held in trust to be delivered to the Russians when they are ready to receive it.

Third—Friendship toward Russia and willingness to assist the Russians should coincide with an unmistakable opposition to recognition of the present soviet government and all that bolshevism implies.

The President's conference with his diplomatic advisers lasted upward of an hour. The situation with particular regard to the bolshevik menace was reviewed, and attention is understood to have been devoted to the present Lloyd George policy, which does not meet the approval of the United States.

The situation is regarded as very grave but not hopeless. But it is admitted that if diplomacy blunders at this critical stage, Europe may be plunged into a war of great magnitude with bolshevism, the extent of which none can foresee. There never was a time when it was more important for statesmanship to follow the right course. . . .

Printed in the *Washington Post*, Aug. 7, 1920.
[1] Although Wilson called Fox a "skunk," presumably for writing this story, he did not deny its accuracy. See the Daniels Diary printed at Aug. 17, 1920. We see no reason to doubt its authenticity. Indeed, Fox must have seen a copy of the note on the Polish situation and the question of recognition of the Soviet government, printed as an Enclosure with BC to WW, Aug. 9, 1920, because Fox's description of the contents of that note was, for the most part, a good summary of it.

Fox's account of British plans for a pan-European war against the Soviet regime (which Fox discussed at some length in that portion of his story not printed), however, was greatly exaggerated. For the then current Anglo-French discussions of possible ways to end the Russian-Polish war and to normalize relations between the western powers and the Soviet government, see D. Lloyd George to WW, Aug. 5, 1920, printed as an Enclosure with BC to WW, Aug. 18, 1920, and n. 7 thereto.

To Josephus Daniels

My dear Daniels: The White House 7 August, 1920

I have your letter of August fifth repeating Doctor Matthews' request for an interview.[1] I am sorry to say I shall have to deny myself the pleasure of seeing him. I find that if I begin making appointments, the flood will descend upon me, and Doctor Matthews, with all his admirable qualities, is never brief.

            Cordially and faithfully yours,   Woodrow Wilson

P.S. I have not yet replied to Assistant Secretary's letter of resignation.[2] I will be very much obliged if you would formulate for me something to say in accepting the resignation.   W.W.

TLS (J. Daniels Papers, DLC).
[1] JD to WW, Aug. 5, 1920, TLS (WP, DLC). Daniels said that, when he had been in Seattle recently, he had had a "long talk" with the Rev. Dr. Mark Allison Matthews, pastor of the First Presbyterian Church of that city. Matthews had stated that he would arrive in Washington on August 16 and wanted an appointment with Wilson on that day or the next.
[2] That is, FDR to WW, July 24, 1920, Vol 65.

From Norman Hezekiah Davis

My dear Mr. President: [Washington] August 7, 1920.

In order that you may be kept abreast of the developments in the Mexican situation, I beg to inform you that no further conferences with Señor Fernando Iglesias Calderon, representing the de facto administration of De La Huerta, have been held since July 9. With the subjects touched upon at that time, you are already familiar. Following that conference, Señor Iglesias sent me a memorandum on it which contained a number of omissions and inaccuracies. Instead of attempting to point them out and correct them, I sent him a copy of my memorandum, dictated immediately after our conference. He acknowledged receipt of this on July 23, and suggested the addition of a phrase explanatory of and qualifying his statement that the present régime would recognize contracts made by previous recognized governments in Mexico; also that it would assume the responsibilities established by international law for damages caused to foreigners during a civil war. I replied on July 28 saying that, although our conversations have been entirely unofficial, I saw no objection to the addition of the qualifying statement mentioned.

His last note, dated July 30, reiterates "the earnest wishes by which my government and I personally are animated to further, for our mutual advantage, the settlement of all questions pending between Mexico and the United States, and also the firm purpose to examine those questions in the utmost sincerity and spirit of honest cooperation."

I have made no acknowledgment of his last note. I am of the opinion, however, that this is an opportune time to acquaint Señor Iglesias in considerable detail with the bases on which a resumption of official relations between the two governments may be made possible.   Faithfully yours,   [Norman H. Davis]

CCL (N. H. Davis Papers, DLC).

Hugh Leo Kerwin to Rudolph Forster

My dear Mr. Forster: Washington August 7, 1920.

As you remember, last Saturday, at the request of the President, the Secretary prepared a suggested call for a conference of the Joint Scale Committee of the Competitive Coal Fields, to be issued after the miners in Indiana and Illinois had returned to work. The Secretary communicated with the President, stating that he had prepared a tentative call, but would leave it here at the Department of Labor and when we had been informed that practically all of the miners had returned to work, we would send the suggested call over, together with the information from our Commissioners of Conciliation and other interested parties as to the time when the call should be issued.

We have been keeping in very close touch with the matter during the week, and I am taking the liberty of enclosing herewith two telegrams from President Lewis of the United Mine Workers, which will give you a clear insight into the exact situation.[1] We expect a detailed report late tonight or tomorrow from our Commissioners, and feel that we will be able to communicate with you definitely some time Monday, as we are hopeful that by that time practically all will have returned to their work in Illinois. So far as Indiana is concerned, practically 100 per cent of the miners are now at work. We will keep you informed.

Sincerely yours,   H. L. Kerwin[2]

TLS (WP, DLC).
[1] J. L. Lewis to Walter J. James, Washington representative of the United Mine Workers of America, Aug. 6, 1920, T telegram, and J. L. Lewis to H. L. Kerwin, Aug. 6, 1920, T telegram, both in WP, DLC. Lewis reported in the first telegram that all mine workers in Indiana and many in Illinois had returned to work and, in the second, that "advices" indicated that all Illinois miners would be back at work not later than August 9 or 10.
[2] Wilson wrote "Ackn & file W.W." on a summary (T MS, WP, DLC) of Kerwin's letter and Lewis' telegrams attached to it.

From Bainbridge Colby, with Enclosure

My dear Mr. President: Washington August 9, 1920.

The enclosed draft of a Note on the Polish situation[1] has certainly one outstanding weakness. It is impossible to say what we will *do*, if anything. It is also pretty long, but there is a reason for saying almost everything that it contains.

I hope you will not find it altogether inadequate.

Very respectfully yours,   Bainbridge Colby

Thank you. This seems to me excellent and sufficient <u>W.W.</u>

TLS (B. Colby Papers, DLC).
[1] About the drafting of this note, see the news report printed at Aug. 7, 1920; Smith, *Aftermath of War*, pp. 60-66; and Radosh, "John Spargo and Wilson's Russian Policy," pp. 554-60. The note was prompted by a conversation between the Secretary of the Italian embassy, Alessandro Mariani, and Norman Davis on August 5. Colby's note, addressed to Ambassador Avezzana, embodied the rationale for nonrecognition of the Soviet government that underlay American policy toward the Soviet Union until 1933.

E N C L O S U R E

Excellency: August 9, 1920.

The agreeable intimation, which you have conveyed to the State Department that the Italian Government would welcome a statement of the views of this Government on the situation presented by the Russian advance into Poland, deserves a prompt response, and I will attempt without delay, a definition of this Government's position not only as to the situation arising from Russian military

pressure upon Poland, but also as to certain cognate and insepa-
rable phases of the Russian question viewed more broadly.

This Government believes in a united, free and autonomous Polish State and the people of the United States are earnestly solicitous for the maintenance of Poland's political independence and
territorial integrity. From this attitude we will not depart, and the
policy of this Government will be directed to the employment of all
available means to render it effectual. The Government therefore
takes no exception to the effort apparently being made in some
quarters to arrange an armistice between Poland and Russia, but
it would not, at least for the present, participate in any plan for the
expansion of the armistice negotiations into a general European
conference which would in all probability involve two results, from
both of which this country strongly recoils, viz. the recognition of
the Bolshevist regime and a settlement of Russian problems almost
inevitably upon the basis of a dismemberment of Russia.

From the beginning of the Russian Revolution, in March, 1917,
to the present moment, the Government and the people of the
United States have followed its development with friendly solicitude and with profound sympathy for the efforts of the Russian
people to reconstruct their national life upon the broad basis of
Democratic self-government. The Government of the United
States, reflecting the spirit of its people, has at all times desired to
help the Russian people. In that spirit all its relations with Russia,
and with other nations in matters affecting the latter's interests,
have been conceived and governed.

The Government of the United States was the first government
to acknowledge the validity of the Revolution and give recognition
to the Provisional Government of Russia. Almost immediately
thereafter it became necessary for the United States to enter the
war against Germany and in that undertaking to become closely
associated with the Allied Nations, including, of course, Russia.
The war weariness of the masses of the Russian people was fully
known to this government and sympathetically comprehended.
Prudence, self-interest and loyalty to our associates made it desirable that we should give moral and material support to the Provisional Government, which was struggling to accomplish a two-fold
task, to carry on the war with vigor and, at the same time, to reor-
ganize the life of the nation and establish a stable government
based on popular sovereignty.

Quite independent of these motives, however, was the sincere
friendship of the Government and the people of the United States
for the great Russian nation. The friendship manifested by Russia
toward this nation in a time of trial and distress has left with us an

imperishable sense of gratitude. It was as a grateful friend that we sent to Russia an expert commission to aid in bringing about such a reorganization of the railroad transportation system of the country as would reinvigorate the whole of its economic life and so add to the well-being of the Russian people.

While deeply regretting the withdrawal of Russia from the war at a critical time, and the disastrous surrender at Brest-Litovsk, the United States has fully understood that the people of Russia were in no wise responsible.

The United States maintains unimpaired its faith in the Russian people, in their high character and their future. That they will overcome the existing anarchy, suffering and destitution we do not entertain the slightest doubt. The distressing character of Russia's transition has many historical parallels, and the United States is confident that restored, free and united Russia will again take a leading place in the world, joining with the other free nations in upholding peace and orderly justice.

Until that time shall arrive the United States feels that friendship and honor require that Russia's interests must be generously protected, and that, as far as possible, all decisions of vital importance to it, and especially those concerning its sovereignty over the territory of the former Russian Empire, be held in abeyance. By this feeling of friendship and honorable obligation to the great nation whose brave and heroic self-sacrifice contributed so much to the successful termination of the war, the Government of the United States was guided in its reply to the Lithuanian National Council, on October 15, 1919,[1] and in its persistent refusal to recognize the Baltic States as separate nations independent of Russia. The same spirit governed the President's note to the Supreme Council at San Remo, March 31, 1920, in which it was held, in particular with regard to the settlement in the Near East, that "no final decision should or can be made without the consent of Russia."[2]

In line with these important declarations of policy, the United States withheld its approval from the decision of the Supreme Council at Paris recognizing the independence of the socalled republics of Georgia and Azerbaijan, and so instructed its representative in Southern Russia, Rear-Admiral Newton A. McCully. Finally, while gladly giving recognition to the independence of Armenia, the Government of the United States has taken the position that the final determination of its boundaries must not be made without Russia's cooperation and agreement. Not only is Russia concerned because a considerable part of the territory of the new State of Armenia, when it shall be defined, formerly belonged to the Russian Empire: equally important is the fact that Armenia must have the good will and the protective friendship of Russia if it is to remain independent and free.

These illustrations show with what consistency the Government of the United States has been guided in its foreign policy by a loyal friendship for Russia. We are unwilling that while it is helpless in the grip of a non-representative government, whose only sanction is brutal force, Russia shall be weakened still further by a policy of dismemberment, conceived in other than Russian interests.

With the desire of the Allied Powers to bring about a peaceful solution of the existing difficulties in Europe, this Government is of course in hearty accord, and will support any justifiable steps to that end. It is unable to perceive, however, that a recognition of the Soviet regime would promote, much less accomplish this object, and it is therefore averse to any dealings with the Soviet regime beyond the most narrow boundaries to which a discussion of an armistice can be confined.

That the present rulers of Russia do not rule by the will or the consent of any considerable proportion of the Russian people is an incontestable fact. Although nearly two and a half years have passed since they seized the machinery of government, promising to protect the Constituent Assembly against alleged conspiracies against it, they have not yet permitted anything in the nature of a popular election. At the moment when the work of creating a democratic representative government based upon universal suffrage was nearing completion the Bolsheviki, although, in number, an inconsiderable minority of the people, by force and cunning seized the powers and machinery of government and have continued to use them with savage oppression to maintain themselves in power.

Without any desire to interfere in the internal affairs of the Russian people, or to suggest what kind of government they should have, the Government of the United States does express the hope that they will soon find a way to set up a government representing their free will and purpose. When that time comes, the United States will consider the measures of practical assistance which can be taken to promote the restoration of Russia, provided Russia has not taken itself wholly out of the pale of the friendly interest of other nations, by the pillage and oppression of the Poles.

It is not possible for the Government of the United States to recognize the present rulers of Russia as a government with which the relations common to friendly governments can be maintained. This conviction has nothing to do with any particular political or social structure which the Russian people themselves may see fit to embrace. It rests upon a wholly different set of facts. These facts, which none disputes, have convinced the Government of the United States, against its will, that the existing regime in Russia is based upon the negation of every principle of honor and good faith, and every usage and convention, underlying the whole structure of international law; the negation, in short, of every principle upon which it is possible to base harmonious and trustful relations, whether of nations or of individuals. The responsible leaders of the regime have frequently and openly boasted that they are willing to sign agreements and undertakings with foreign Powers while not having the slightest intention of observing such undertakings or carrying out such agreements. This attitude of disregard of obligations voluntarily entered into, they base upon the theory that no compact or agreement made with a non-Bolshevist government can have any moral force for them. They have not only avowed this as a doctrine, but have exemplified it in practice. Indeed, upon numerous occasions the responsible spokesmen of this Power, and its official agencies, have declared that it is their understanding that the very existence of Bolshevism in Russia, the maintenance of their own rule, depends, and must continue to depend, upon the occurrence of revolutions in all other great civilized nations, including the United States, which will overthrow and destroy their governments and set up Bolshevist rule in their stead. They have made it quite plain that they intend to use every means, including, of course, diplomatic agencies, to promote such revolutionary movements in other countries.

It is true that they have in various ways expressed their willingness to give "assurances" and "guarantees" that they will not abuse the privileges and immunities of diplomatic agencies by using them for this purpose. In view of their own declarations, already referred to, such assurances and guarantees cannot be very seriously regarded. Moreover, it is within the knowledge of the Government of the United States that the Bolshevist Government is itself subject to the control of a political faction, with extensive international ramifications through the Third Internationale, and that this body, which is heavily subsidized by the Bolshevist Government from the public revenues of Russia, has for its openly avowed aim the promotion of Bolshevist revolutions throughout the world. The leaders of the Bolsheviki have boasted that their promises of non–interference with other nations would in no wise bind the agents of this body. There is no room for reasonable doubt that such agents would receive the support and protection of any diplomatic agencies the Bolsheviki might have in other countries. Inevitably, therefore, the diplomatic service of the Bolshevist Government would become a channel for intrigues and the propaganda of revolt against the institutions and laws of countries, with whom it was at peace, which would be an abuse of friendship to which enlightened governments cannot subject themselves.

In the view of this Government, there cannot be any common ground upon which it can stand with a Power whose conceptions of international relations are so entirely alien to its own, so utterly repugnant to its moral sense. There can be no mutual confidence or trust, no respect even, if pledges are to be given and agreements made with a cynical repudiation of their obligations already in the mind of one of the parties. We cannot recognize, hold official relations with, or give friendly reception to the agents of, a government which is determined and bound to conspire against our institutions; whose diplomats will be the agitators of dangerous revolt; whose spokesmen say that they sign agreements with no intention of keeping them.

To summarize the position of this Government, I would say, therefore, in response to your Excellency's inquiry, that it would regard with satisfaction a declaration by the Allied and Associated Powers, that the territorial integrity and true boundaries of Russia shall be respected. These boundaries should properly include the whole of the former Russian Empire, with the exception of Finland proper, and ethnic Poland. The aspirations of these nations for independence are legitimate. Each was forcibly annexed and their liberation from oppressive alien rule involves no aggressions against Russia's territorial rights, and has received the sanction of the public opinion of all free peoples. Such a declaration presupposes the withdrawal of all foreign troops from the territory embraced by these boundaries, and in the opinion of this Government should be accompanied by the announcement that no transgression by Poland, Finland or any other Power, of the line so drawn and proclaimed will be permitted.

Thus only can the Bolshevist regime be deprived of its false, but effective, appeal to Russian nationalism and compelled to meet the inevitable challenge of reason and self-respect which the Russian people, secure from invasion and territorial violation, are sure to address to a social philosophy that degrades them and a tyranny that oppresses them.

The policy herein outlined will command the support of this Government.

Accept, Excellency, the renewed assurance of my highest consideration.[3]

T MS (B. Colby Papers, DLC).
[1] The note from the Lithuanian National Council, Washington, D. C., was Matthias J. Vinikas, chairman, executive committee, to RL, Oct. 4, 1919, TLS (SDR, RG 59,

860.M.01/27, DNA). It enclosed a pamphlet entitled LITHUANIA AGAINST POLAND: *An Appeal for Justice*. Both Vinikas' letter and the pamphlet appealed to the President, Congress, and all American citizens for protection against Polish aggression and for the immediate recognition of the Lithuanian government by the United States. M. J. Vinikas to WW, Oct. 3, 1919, TLS (SDR, RG 59, 860.M.01/25½, DNA), was a similar letter, which also enclosed a copy of the pamphlet.

Lansing's reply was RL to Lithuanian National Council, Oct. 15, 1919, CCL (SDR, RG 59, 860.M.01/30, DNA). Reiterating the policy of the United States Government toward the Baltic provinces of the former Russian Empire (excluding Finland, which was not a province, but a grand duchy), Lansing wrote:

"The question of the future status of Lithuania has been given careful consideration. As you are aware, the Government of the United States is traditionally sympathetic with the national aspirations of dependent peoples. On the other hand, it has been thought unwise and unfair to prejudice in advance of the establishment of orderly, constitutional government in Russia the principle of Russian unity as a whole.

"Accordingly, when the President, in common with the heads of the other principal Allied and Associated Governments, proffered Admiral Kolchak aid in bringing about in Russia a situation conducive to the establishment of orderly, constitutional government, it was especially stipulated, inter alia, that failing an immediate agreement between Lithuania and the new Russian Government, an arrangement would be made in consultation and cooperation with the League of Nations and that, pending such an arrangement Russia must agree to recognize Lithuania as autonomous and to confirm the relations which might exist between the local government of Lithuania and the Allied and Associated Governments. Copies of the note to Admiral Kolchak and his reply are enclosed for your information.

"It is believed that this arrangement assures the autonomous development of Lithuania, together with the other nationalities comprised within the former Russian Empire, and wisely leaves to a future adjustment the determination of the relations which shall exist between them and the new Russian Government.

"I am confident your Council will recognize the justice of this attitude."

[2] See the Enclosure printed with FLP to WW, March 22, 1920, Vol. 65.

[3] This note was sent verbatim as BC to Baron Avezzana, Aug. 10, 1920, TLS (SDR, RG 59, 760c.61/300b, DNA); it was published widely at the time, e.g., in the *New York Times*, Aug. 11, 1920, and is printed in *FR 1920*, III, 463-68.

From the Diary of Josephus Daniels

1920 Tuesday 10 August

Cabinet. I brought up Haiti & San Domingo & the propaganda to try to make people believe conditions were bad & the government was killing people & having a despotic government.[1] Colby said the Uraguay minister[2] had called to see him about it. Baker said the Governor of Porto Rico[3] had wanted to send surplus population to Santo Domingo. I suggested as answer to the criticisms that we ask Cong. Com on Insular Affairs to continue the study.

Shall Debs & others who have served 15 months sentence be pardoned. Palmer, Payne & I advocated it & Baker also. Burleson opposed & Colby doubted. In N. J., said the President the Governor is a member of the Board of Pardons. He cannot pardon by himself, but his vote is necessary to secure pardon. He said that with finality & that ended hope for Debs and the others

Burleson says Cox is sure to win.

Houston said GB had broken off negotiations with Treas officials about 5 mil pounds Engl owes us in open debt & said Lloyd George would take it up with Wilson. "I have had no com. with Lloyd George on any subject"   WW

¹ This discussion was prompted by a telegram and several articles published at this time. The telegram was Victor M. Lecastro and Emilia G. Godoy to WW, Aug. 10, 1920, T telegram (WP, DLC). These persons, who described themselves as "Dominican Journalists" of New York, pleaded with Wilson, "in the name of humanity and the principles pretexted by you to invade our country," to put a stop to the "burning[,] assassinating and violating our country" by United States troops.
A brief article appeared in the *New York Times*, Aug. 8, 1920, VIII, 20, which stated that the Press Club of Havana had sent a communication to the State Department asking that Wilson intervene in the case of Fabio Fiallo, the Dominican poet and patriot, who was on trial by United States military authorities. The article said also that the State Department had cabled to the Dominican Republic for a full report on the matter. Two more reports on Fiallo appeared in *ibid.*, Aug. 10 and 11, 1920, the second of which said that he faced a possible death sentence. As it turned out, he was soon released.
Finally, *The Nation* had begun a series of articles on alleged atrocities and mismanagement by the American occupation forces in Haiti, the first of which was Herbert J. Seligman, "The Conquest of Haiti," *The Nation*, CXI (July 10, 1920), 35-36. Later articles in the series were to be written by the American black author and poet, James Weldon Johnson. For citations and summaries of these articles, see John W. Blassingame, "The Press and American Intervention in Haiti and the Dominican Republic, 1904-1920," *Caribbean Studies*, IX (July 1969), 39-41.
² Jacobo Varela.
³ That is, Arthur Yager.

To Bainbridge Colby

My dear Mr. Secretary: The White House 10 August, 1920

The enclosed telegrams¹ deal with matters of so critical and international a character that I am sending them to you for your information, and I take this occasion to request that you consult with the Secretary of the Navy about the instructions he is to send to the naval officers in the Adriatic. Would it not be well for you to have a conversation, too, with the Italian Ambassador in the light of the situation disclosed in these dispatches about the necessity for combined plans of action?

Cordially and faithfully yours,   Woodrow Wilson

TLS (B. Colby Papers, DLC).
¹ Philip Andrews to Force Commander, July 25, 1920, T telegram (SDR, RG 59, 760H.65/85, DNA) and P. Andrews to Chief of Naval Operations, Aug. 7, 1920, T telegram (SDR, RG 59, 760H.65/91, DNA). Adm. Andrews, Commander of U. S. Naval Forces in the Eastern Mediterranean, sent these telegrams from his base in Spalato in Dalmatia. He was about to turn over to the Italians certain former Austrian warships interned in that port. The main question, he said, was whether he should remove his own small squadron from Spalato once the ships had been handed over. Yugoslav forces occupied and totally controlled Spalato, and there was a likely prospect of hostilities between the Italians and Yugoslavs if the Italians did not also withdraw their ships, which lay outside the port. Any aggressive action by the Italians, Andrews stated, would certainly bring on war at once. The only solution, Andrews advised, was for the Italian and American squadrons to withdraw at the same time; in light of the attitude of the local Italian commander, this could only be achieved by agreement between the United States and Italian governments.

To Thomas T. Brewster[1] and John Llewellyn Lewis[2]

Gentlemen: [The White House] August 10, 1920.

In a statement issued by me to the striking members of the United Mine Workers of America on July 30, 1920, requesting them to return to work, I said:

"In the consideration of the nation-wide wage scale involving many different classes of labor by the Bituminous Coal Commission in the limited time at its disposal some inequalities may have developed in the award that ought to be corrected. I can not, however, recommend any consideration of such inequalities as long as the mine workers continue on strike in violation of the terms of the award which they had accepted as their wage agreement for a definite length of time. I must therefore insist that the striking mine workers return to work, thereby demonstrating their good faith in keeping their contract. When I have learned that they have thus returned to work, I will invite the scale committees of the operators and miners to reconvene for the purpose of adjusting any such inequalities as they may mutually agree should be adjusted."[3]

I have been informed that in compliance with my request the striking miners have now resumed work, an action on their part which I desire to commend. In conformity, therefore, with the promise contained in my statement, I hereby request the members of the Joint Scale Committee of Operators and Miners of the Central Competitive Coal Field to meet in the city of Cleveland, Ohio, on Friday morning, August 13, 1920, for the purpose of considering any inequalities that may have occurred in the award of the Bituminous Coal Commission and the joint agreement growing out of the same and adjusting any and all such inequalities as the Joint Scale Committee may mutually agree should be adjusted.

Woodrow Wilson

TLS (WP, DLC).
[1] Chairman of the Coal Operators Association and of the Joint Scale Committee.
[2] William B. Wilson had drafted this letter in early August, and it was used without alteration, except for the date of the proposed meeting of the Joint Scale Committee, which was changed from August 10 to August 13. H. L. Kerwin to R. Forster, Aug. 10, 1920, TLS (WP, DLC).
[3] From WW to the members of the United Mine Workers, July 30, 1920, printed as Enclosure II with JPT to EBW, July 30, 1920, Vol. 65.

From Norman Hapgood

Dear Mr. President: Petersham Massachusetts August 10/20

For the first time, I think, I am departing from my principle of not writing to you except when some important matter demands it. This time I have no excuse except sentiment. In sending you a book I have just published[1] (which goes by this mail) my only reason is that not to send it would be a failure to mark the amount you have meant in my thought and feeling, and the amount you will continue to mean through many years.

As to whether the book contains anything worth your glancing at, that is another matter. The similarity between your fight for a League of Nations and George Washington's fight for a union of the thirteen states struck me forcibly. It is on pages 54-7. More about the League is on pages 246-253.

My treatment of the Russian question is long and documentary, but the conclusion is put briefly on pages XIII-XVII. To me it is the simplest as well as the most pregnant of outstanding questions: and I believe that if we bungle it, or in the handling of it are guided by our pride, we shall destroy the League and not improbably bring about a war against a combined Russia and Germany, with Turkey and India in eruption.

I am happy over Cox's behavior and have my heart in the campaign.

Many great things will happen before March 4th, and in the great things that happen after then all of us will listen for your voice.   Yours very sincerely   Norman Hapgood

ALS (WP, DLC).
    [1] Norman Hapgood, *The Advancing Hour* (New York, 1920). This book is in the Wilson Library, DLC.

From Josephus Daniels

My dear Mr. President: Washington. 12th of August 1920

I have received copy of the telegram which you sent[1] and I have telegraphed to the naval authorities at Santo Domingo for all the facts and when received I will furnish you the information.
                         Faithfully,   Josephus Daniels

TLS (WP, DLC).
    [1] That is, the telegram cited and summarized in n. 1 to the extract from the Daniels Diary printed at Aug. 10, 1920.

To Bainbridge Colby

My dear Mr. Secretary: The White House 12 August, 1920

Of course, we shall have to say to these gentlemen[1] that the United States is not a party to the Council to which they appeal in their memorial, but I must say that I am very sympathetic with their object and am wondering if there is any way in which we can assist them to attain it. While I was in Paris I had a visit from a most impressive person, a high ecclesiastic of the Greek Church who represented the Greeks of the Euxine Pontus[2] and he made a deep impression upon me. While we are participating in settling some part of the controversial matters connected with an independent Armenia, is there any door by which we can open an opportunity to the Greeks of the Euxine as an autonomous unit associated with the Armenian Republic?

       Cordially and faithfully yours,   Woodrow Wilson

TLS (SDR, RG 59, 763.72119/10374, DNA).

[1] Wilson enclosed Constantin-Jason G. Constantinides, president of the Pan-Pontic Congress, and Socrates Œconomos, president of the National League of the Euxine Pontus at Paris, to WW, July 10, 1920, TLS (SDR, RG 59, 763.72119/10374, DNA). The writers urged the Supreme Council, through Wilson, to consider the situation of the "unredeemed Greeks of the Euxine Pontus." The Euxine Pontus was the region surrounding the city of Trebizond (Trabzon, Turkey) on the southeastern shore of the Black Sea. The writers stated that the population of this area was predominately Greek in heritage. Representatives of the Euxine Pontus had several times petitioned the Paris Peace Conference to make the area an independent state, or at least an autonomous region within the new Armenian nation, but the conference had seen fit to do neither. The writers asserted that, at the present time, roving bands of Turkish "brigands and irregulars" threatened to destroy or drive out the Greek population of the area altogether. The Turkish peace treaty then under consideration in Paris, they said, made no special provision at all for the Euxine Pontus. Therefore, they requested that the Allied governments once again consider the question of independence or autonomy for the region.

[2] Archbishop Chrysanthos, Greek Metropolitan of Trebizond. His meeting with Wilson took place on May 16, 1919 (see the extract from the Grayson Diary printed at that date in Vol. 59). The Archbishop had led a delegation to Paris to petition the peace conference to recognize an independent "Republic of the Euxine Pontus." See Richard G. Hovannisian, *The Republic of Armenia* (2 vols. to date, Berkeley and Los Angeles, Calif., 1971–82), I, 279, n. 82; II, 528.

From the Shorthand Diary of Charles Lee Swem

13 August, 1920

This morning the President complained about the envelopes I sent over with his letters. He said that his paper wouldn't fit in the long #9 envelopes. I asked how they were folded and Mrs. Wilson told me she folded them lengthwise. I then showed how they should be folded in 3 folds beginning at the bottom. The President watched but said that it didn't matter, we would have to get special-size envelopes so that they could be put in the way Mrs. Wilson folded them. It's your life!

JRT transcript (WC, NjP) of CLSsh (C. L. Swem Coll., NjP).

To Seth M. Walker[1]

[The White House] August 13, 1920.

May I not in the interest of national harmony and vigor and of the establishment of the leadership of America in all liberal policies express the earnest hope that the House over which you preside will concur in the Suffrage Amendment.

Woodrow Wilson.

T telegram (Letterpress Books, WP, DLC).
  [1] Speaker of the Tennessee House of Representatives. This telegram was prompted by Carrie C. L. C. Catt to R. Forster, Aug. 13, 1920, T telegram (WP, DLC), and by a note from Tumulty (T MS, WP, DLC), saying that, since the receipt of Mrs. Catt's telegram, news had come that the Tennessee Senate had acted favorably on the Nineteenth Amendment.

To Norman Hapgood

My dear Hapgood: The White House 13 August, 1920

Thank you for sending me your book. I shall look forward with the greatest pleasure to reading it when I have time and strength to do it justice.

I am very glad indeed to know that you are interested in the campaign, and know it will mean a great deal to the campaigners.

With warmest personal regards,

Sincerely yours,   Woodrow Wilson

TLS (WC, NjP).

To Josephus Daniels

My dear Mr. Secretary: The White House 13 August, 1920

Sometime ago I was asked if it would be agreeable to me to have the Mayflower go out for a few days on a practice trip to get her new personnel in shape, and I asked that the trip be postponed.[1] I dare say that it would be advantageous to give the men the practice, and I am writing, therefore, to say that I hope you will feel at liberty to send her out if the trip can be so arranged that she is here at each week-end in case I should be able to use her.

Cordially and faithfully yours,   Woodrow Wilson

TLS (J. Daniels Papers, DLC).
[1] The earlier correspondence on this subject is R. E. Coontz to JPT, July 15, 1920, TLS; JPT to EBW, July 16, 1920, TL; Ralston S. Holmes to JPT, Aug. 4, 1920, TLS; and JPT to WW, Aug. 4, 1920, TLS, all WP, DLC. Both notes from Tumulty have WWhw notations which order postponement of the proposed voyages of the *Mayflower*. Commander Holmes was the commanding officer of the vessel.

From Josephus Daniels

My dear Mr. President: Washington. August 13, 1920.

I am enclosing you a letter I have received from General Logan Feland of the Marine Corps,[1] who won his spurs at Chateau Thierry and is an efficient Marine officer, and who is now at Haiti. Before sending him there, I told him of the policy of our Government; that it was kindness and helpfulness to the people, and I told him to write me frequently giving me the atmosphere as well as the official information.

I am sending a copy of this letter to the Secretary of State also.

Sincerely yours,   Josephus Daniels

TLS (WP, DLC).
[1] Brig. Gen. Logan Feland to JD, July 29, 1920, TCL (WP, DLC). Feland reported on a movement in the Dominican Republic to restore the full independence of the country. The leaders of this movement, characterized by Feland as "professional politicians and grafters," had begun a "lying abuse" of the American military government and all things American, a campaign "to teach the people a gospel of hatred towards us," and "open appeals to prepare to take up arms against us." Feland believed that only about one half of the inhabitants of the cities supported the movement and that most of the small farmers wished the Americans to remain, although he admitted that most Dominicans would say little openly on the subject. Feland recently had had arrested the newspapermen responsible for the most inflamatory agitation. Feland enclosed as a sample a translation (T MS, WP, DLC) of an editorial by one Flores Cabrera, dated July 14, 1920, and published in *Las Noticias* of Santo Domingo City. Feland characterized him as a "Venezuelan adventurer and agitator."

From Edward William Bok

My dear Mr. President: Camden Maine August 13 1920

Having no idea of your plans after your retirement from the Presidency, my suggestion may be entirely out of order. But I am sure you will allow for this lack of knowledge.

It is merely that if your plans include any public addresses, it may be in order to call your attention to our new venture here.[1] You know all about our beautiful and historic old Academy of Music. It was in danger of being turned into a motion picture house, and feeling that there are a few things in this world which must still be kept to their original purpose, thirty of the most prominent men of Philadelphia came together and leased the building for five years in order to keep it as a temple of music, and for civic expression, electing me President of the corporation. The opera and the Philadelphia Orchestra will play here as heretofore, but I am anxious, with the opportunity offered by our possession of the beautiful building, to have it stand as a sort of forum for the public good. At least, here is a theater managed by gentlemen! and not for commercial profit but for the public good.

It occurred to me that directly after your retirement from the Presidency, with a feeling for freer expression than now, you might perhaps consider the making of say one or two public addresses on the League of Nations before your successor in office began to function with regard to it. It might seem to you that such an opportunity might afford a full and clear explanation which would clear the atmosphere both for yourself and your friends,—and of course for the general public.

If there is any such thought in your mind, I would like you to consider the Academy in Philadelphia as a possible place for such an expression. We have just enlarged the auditorium so as to seat 3000 persons, and we can find room for 400 additional. My idea would be to make such an affair one of paid admissions, of course, with a honorarium to the speaker of one thousand dollars for each address.

Of course, as I say, your plans may be radically different from the line suggested: at the same time, I venture to make the suggestion in case by any chance such a thought was included in them.

I should think the very contemplation of a relief from the office would seem a pleasant thought to you, particularly when you must feel, as do some of us so strongly, that as Time goes on your vision is going to stand out in its largeness, and your work in all its greatness. It is only a question of time when the people will see: just at present they cannot & many will not.

It is already saddening in reading the letters of acceptance of both of the candidates to realize how great is going to be our loss in the dignity and expression of our state documents. And so Time will point to other losses.

Meanwhile, I can only hope that the reports of your gaining health and strength are true. Too bad you can't play golf these summer days!

With always continuing regard, believe me,

Faithfully & believingly yours   Edward W. Bok

May I ask a line to my summer home: Camden, Maine?

ALS (WP, DLC).
   [1] Bok wrote on the stationery of the president's office of the Academy of Music Corporation, Philadelphia.

George Creel to Edith Bolling Galt Wilson, with Enclosure

New York City August Thirteenth,
Nineteen Twenty.

Dear Mrs. Wilson:

I was so happy and proud to get the picture. Aside from my faith in the President and my deep admiration for him, there is a personal devotion to him that formed as a result of association.

On a separate sheet I am sending the outline of my proposition. I knew, as a matter of course, that he would shrink from any idea of commercialization, for the things with which he will deal are so big as to seem shamed by connection with money making. The fact remains, however, that money *will* be made from his work. There is no way by which he can give it to the people as a free gift. The question is, therefore, whether *he* will make it as a necessary provision for himself and his family or whether he will let these large amounts be made by publishers, newspaper proprietors and scores of middlemen unknown to him.

Under separate cover I am sending you a copy of my Irish book.[1]

With warm regards,   Always sincerely,   George Creel

TLS (EBW Papers, DLC).
[1] George Creel, *Ireland's Fight for Freedom, Setting Forth the High Lights of Irish History* (New York and London, 1919). This book is in the Wilson Library, DLC.

E N C L O S U R E

August Thirteenth, Nineteen Twenty.

I have served for seven years on the Executive Committee of the Authors League and have had five books published. This experience, together with some recent investigations, have convinced me that the publishing business is absolutely out of touch with energy and efficiency. It is not only that an unfair percentage is taken from the author, but the methods of distribution are such as to bar him from proper returns. In a country of one hundred and ten [million?] readers, a book that sells five thousand copies is supposed to have done very well.

The system of salesmanship is poor, but the trouble is over production. Before a book has had time to sell, it is pushed off the shelves by a new lot. Under this terrific pressure, book selling has broken down.

My idea is a compact organization for the *exclusive* handling of the President's literary output, developing 100 per cent distribution and return from (1) magazine articles, (2) books, (3) second serial rights, that is, publication of the books in newspapers after a certain time, and (4) publication in foreign countries.

The handling of magazine articles and second serial rights constitutes nothing more than a problem in skillful marketing to get the highest price.

With respect to foreign publication, I would send an expert to Europe to make the best arrangement in eeach [each] country. The Scandinavian rights, for instance, should net us an amount equal to twenty-five per cent of the American returns, and Czechoslovakia ought to do as well.

For this country, I would work out a plan of *direct selling* in addition to the regular book stores. I have tried it with my last three books, and even in the elementary stage, it has quadrupled sales.

The chief values of the plan are these: (1) a compact, expert organization concentrated upon a single product, (2) absolute centralization. Instead of dealing separately with publishers, magazine editors, syndicate people, foreign representatives, etc., the President deals directly and simply with one company that handles product and every form of by-product.

I am willing to enter into a contract to pay the President fifty per cent of *gross* receipts. Based upon one book a year, I will guarantee him a minimum return of $75,000 a year, and will pay him such amount in advance as he thinks fair.

T MS (EBW Papers, DLC).

From Newton Diehl Baker

My dear Mr. President: Washington. August 14, 1920.

In transmitting this record to you, I feel that I ought to make a word of personal explanation. I have concurred in the recommendation of the Judge Advocate General in favor of a commutation of the death penalty to life imprisonment. I am aware, however, of a deep-seated conviction against capital punishment and realize that I may be unconsciously influenced by it in some of my recommendations to you. In this case, my purely military advisers feel that the death penalty ought to be inflicted in support of military discipline in the Army since the offense consisted of the murder of a noncommissioned officer by a soldier. I have reached the other conclusion for this reason:

This particular soldier[1] was disciplined by the noncommissioned officer in question in a way perhaps not authorized by regulations. It seems clear that this infliction of discipline was, so far as the prisoner was concerned, regarded as a final act in a continuing series of harsh discipline for minor delinquencies which may or may not have been the truth, but the prisoner so felt it. Within ten minutes after the incident which caused the trouble, the prisoner, having in the meantime loaded his revolver, sought out the corporal and killed him.

If the shooting had taken place immediately upon the provocation it would, in law, have been a typical case of manslaughter due to the uncontrollable rage of the accused. That substantially ten minutes elapsed, raises the question as to whether enough time had been given for this man to cool off, recover from the original rage, and form a premeditated design to commit a deliberate murder. In my judgment, it is safer to take the other view. The man was evidently not of high-grade mentality, and there are dispositions in which rage smolders and accumulates, lasting for periods longer than ten minutes.

It is to be noted, too, that this murder was not the result of premeditation based upon any gain to the accused; that is to say, he did not form the design to murder his victim in order that he might rob him, or might be relieved from any embarrassment due to his presence. It was obviously the result of rage occasioned by fancied abuses.

Under these circumstances, I have concurred with the Judge Advocate General, and do now recommend that the commutation to life imprisonment be made.[2]

Respectfully yours,   Newton D. Baker

TLS (WP, DLC).
 [1] One Pvt. Devore Mumphrey.
 [2] A note typed on this letter says that Wilson commuted the sentence to life imprisonment at hard labor.

From Seth M. Walker

Nashville, Tennessee, August 14, 1920.

I have the profound honor to acknowledge your wire of August 13th. I do not attempt to express the views of other members of the lower house of Tennessee but speak for myself alone which on the Anthony Amendment are contrary to yours. You were too great to ask it and I do not believe that men of Tennessee will surrender honest convictions for political expediency or harmony.

Seth M. Walker.

T telegram (WP, DLC).

To Francis Xavier Dercum

My dear Doctor Dercum: [The White House] 15 August, 1920

Since Doctor Grayson is absent on a brief, well-earned vacation, I dare say it falls to me to report that the nurse, Sasseville, left us because he was unwilling to perform his duties in a proper spirit, declaring that he would not work with another nurse unless he were "put in full charge of the case," and he ended by becoming intolerably impertinent to Mrs. Wilson. I am very sorry if this incident should cause you any inconvenience.

Hoping that your visit to Narragansett is proving as refreshing as you wish, with warmest regards from us both,

Cordially and sincerely yours,   [Woodrow Wilson]

CCL (WP, DLC).

From Nathaniel Barksdale Dial[1] and Others

My dear Mr. President: Washington, D. C. August 16, 1920.

We desire to call to your attention the condition of the farmers in this country and ask your help.[2] For various reasons the growing crop has been and will be a very expensive one. Labor was scarce and high, fertilizers were high, and everything that goes into the making of a crop seems to be at excessive figures. Owing to the congested condition of the railroads, the money situation and the state of exchange, a great deal of the last crop has not been disposed of. Some time ago the War Finance Corporation ceased to take on new business. We now desire to ask you to authorize this corporation to resume active operations. We are not desiring the government to engage in business which the citizens should carry on. In ordinary times and under usual conditions we would not make the above request. A few months ago some of us mentioned the matter to the Secretary of the Treasury, but at that time he did not see the necessity of taking on new business. We called at his office again the other day, as we desired to present the matter to him again, since conditions had greatly changed within the last sixty days. Within this time, wheat has declined something like 60 cents per bushel, oats and corn in proportion, and cotton about 8 cents a pound.[3] In fact, all agricultural products are moving slowly—and this in the face of the harvest rapidly approaching.

During the war, the government ordered its supplies of cotton goods made out of the higher grades; furthermore, of course Germany and Austria, and even other countries, could not receive their usual amounts of American cotton. Therefore, there is a great quantity of off-grade staple in the South, for which there is practically no market. For example, low middling cotton is quoted at 10 cents a pound, or $50 a bale, under middling. The next grade is nearly $100 a bale under middling. At present it seems that the growing crop will be a very large one and perhaps prices will continue to decline.

During the war, the agricultural interests of this country did all they could to buy bonds and otherwise support the government in every financial way, with the expectation that the government would continue to aid them to market their crops to the best advantage until world conditions should become settled and normal. If it would require a bond issue to accomplish this, we certainly would not make the request. The loans desired are temporary and would soon be repaid. We are informed that there are about 153,000,000 spindles in the world and that a large majority of these are idle.

We understand that various European countries are exceedingly anxious to purchase our cotton and other agricultural products, but that it is essential that they shall receive some indulgence. The manufacturing interests of Czecho-Slovakia have been particularly called to our attention, as they desire to buy directly from our exporters, on credits endorsed by their banks and guaranteed by their government, and further agree to hold the product in trust for payment of the purchase money.

We are strongly of the opinion that the War Finance Corporation should resume operations, at least so far as agricultural products are concerned. The Corporation while operating did considerable business and more was being rapidly offered. Czecho-Slovakia especially was a very promising customer. We have been urged, by our constituents, and also by friends of some of the Central European countries, to present the urgency of this matter strongly to the President.

To our certain knowledge, a great number of farmers purchased bonds and they borrowed money from the banks to carry these, expecting to pay for them when they disposed of their cotton. You are doubtless aware, Mr. President, that the farmers lose annually millions of dollars because they have not had the opportunity of learning in its modern phases the complex art of marketing to the best advantage. By enabling foreign countries to purchase our surplus supplies, our warehouses will be relieved so that they will be prepared to handle the next crop and customers will be enabled to pay their obligations to the banks, thereby taking up their bonds, keeping these securities off the market and preventing them from being sacrificed. By this course every interest in this country and abroad would be benefited. Supplies will be placed where they are needed and many idle people of the world will be enabled in part at least to pay their obligations. By giving people employment, the spread of unrest and Bolshevism will be checked. We have been recently impressed more than ever with the fact that it takes both time and credit to restore a war-stricken world.

We know of no grander work than aiding farmers to make their employment successful. If some relief is not granted, many of them will face bankruptcy. Just the knowledge that other markets have been opened to their products will greatly stabilize conditions.

We respectfully urge your immediate consideration of this suggestion and believe that if you will authorize the measure proposed, great good will immediately follow.

Respectfully,   N. B. Dial
F. M. Simmons
Duncan U. Fletcher[4]

TLS (WP, DLC).

[1] Democratic senator from South Carolina. The other signers were Furnifold McLendel Simmons and Duncan Upshaw Fletcher, Democratic senators from North Carolina and Florida, respectively.

[2] This is a sample, albeit one of the most prominent ones, of a number of letters and telegrams to Wilson from southern congressmen and senators, state and local agricultural organizations, etc., appealing for federal assistance to support the cotton market.

[3] As it turned out, the price declines here cited turned out to be only the beginning of a steep fall in the prices of agricultural products which, by mid-1921, saw the price of wheat decrease to approximately 40 per cent of its highest price in 1920, corn to 32 per cent, and cotton to 34 per cent. See Arthur S. Link, "The Federal Reserve Policy and the Agricultural Depression of 1920-1921," *The Higher Realism of Woodrow Wilson, and Other Essays* (Nashville, Tenn., 1971), pp. 330-48, especially pp. 330-32.

[4] Tumulty sent this letter to Houston on August 19: JPT to DFH, Aug. 19, 1920, TLS (Office of the Secretary of the Treasury, General Correspondence, 1917-1932, RG 56, DNA).

To Joseph Leland Kennedy

My dear Joe: [The White House] 16 August, 1920

Mrs. Wilson has shown me your letter of August eleventh,[1] and I take the liberty of answering it myself.

As you evidently anticipate, it is not wise, either in your own interest or in the interest of the service, that I should intervene in your case. Whatever was done, it would be considered an act of favoritism and you would not profit by it.

In haste   Affectionately yours,   [Woodrow Wilson]

P.S. I will of course take pleasure in looking up your record in the department.

CCL (WP, DLC).

[1] J. L. Kennedy to EBW, Aug. 11, 1920, TLS (WP, DLC). Kennedy asked Wilson to call his work to the attention of John Skelton Williams "and see if the services which I have done during my time as a National Bank Examiner . . . would not cause Mr. Wil-

liams to designate me as the Superviseing National Bank Examiner for the 10 and 11th Federal Reserve Districts."

To John Skelton Williams

My dear Mr. Comptroller: [The White House] 16 August, 1920

I have a nephew, J. L. Kennedy, serving in Iowa in some minor capacity, I believe, in connection with the bank examinations, and I write to ask if you will not be kind enough to send me a memorandum as to whether his services have been satisfactory or not.

Cordially and faithfully yours,   [Woodrow Wilson]

CCL (WP, DLC).

From the Diary of Josephus Daniels

August Tuesday 17 1920

Cabinet. Colby stated that the French Charge de Affairs had sent to his gov. as its official position a story in the Wash Post[1] by that "skunk Fox" (as WW called him) and the French foreign office had given it out as America's action.[2] WW told Colby to let the French gov. know that the French chg de Affairs was persona non grata & should be sent home.

Colby had intercepted telgm that England was in sympathy with Japan's position.[3] It had been talking otherwise. WW said "Take it up & let us know if such hypocrisy is going on." England sympathizes with any nation that follows its example—grabs everything it can. It hated Germany because that nation got into the grab game but got in too late.

Poland minister[4] had been told he must not make appeals to the people here & start propaganda. An Ambassador was sent home for doing so,[5] though we had sympathy for Poland and its plight.

WW read Oliver Herfords poem, "The Marionette" in N. Y. World of the 16th. with zest & appreciation

[1] See the news report printed at Aug. 7, 1920.

[2] Fox himself explained what happened to his article in "U. S. AND FRANCE STAND TO-GETHER . . . ," *Washington Post*, Aug. 13, 1920, as follows:

"The forecast of America's policy, as communicated to me by one in a position to know, was printed in The Post last Saturday and caused something of a sensation in diplomatic circles, especially as up to that time there had been no inkling of the fact that an important declaration was coming from the United States government. . . .

"No sooner had this forecast appeared in print than some member of the French embassy here took steps to verify its accuracy, after which he cabled it to the French foreign office, presumably with the statement that it represented the position which America was about to announce. But through some inexplicable mix-up in Paris some one at the French foreign office gave out part of the text of the article as an official announcement from the government of the United States."

The French Chargé at this time was Louis-Elie-Joseph-Henry, Prince de Béarn et de Chalais. He remained as Counselor of the French embassy through the end of the Wilson administration.

[3] The intercepted telegram was probably Lord Curzon to Sir A. Geddes, July 30, 1920, printed in Rohan Butler and J. P. T. Bury, eds., *Documents on British Foreign Policy, 1919-1939*, First Series, XIV (London, 1966), 77. After commenting briefly on another subject, Curzon concluded his telegram with the following statement: "We could not in any case have joined United States Government in representations to Japanese Government about their action in Siberia." This, of course, was a reference to Colby's note of July 16, 1920, printed as an Enclosure with BC to WW, July 16, 1920 (first letter of that date), Vol. 65. Norman Davis, in a conversation with Geddes on or before July 11, had urged that Great Britain join the United States in an emphatic demand that Japan evacuate its troops from northern Sakhalin. Geddes had replied that Great Britain would "cooperate wholeheartedly" in any well thought out plan of action, but that the note proposed by Davis seemed "incomplete in itself," and that the British government would have to consider its implications very carefully before committing itself to supporting it even in amended form. Sir A. Geddes to Lord Curzon, July 11, 1920, printed in *ibid.*, pp. 70-71.

[4] That is, Prince Kazimierz Lubomirski.

[5] Apparently a reference to the recall of Constantin Theodor Dumba, the Austro-Hungarian Ambassador to the United States, in September 1915, about which see the index references to his name in Vol. 34 of this series and Arthur S. Link, *Wilson: The Struggle for Neutrality, 1914-1915* (Princeton, N. J., 1960), pp. 645-50.

To Edward William Bok

My dear Mr. Bok: The White House 17 August, 1920

I need hardly say that I am very much gratified by the suggestion of your letter of August thirteenth, but you will hardly expect me to make a definite answer at present. My plans for the future are all conjectural, and I think it extremely doubtful whether I shall make public addresses on pending questions of the day, since I have no intention whatever of qualifying as a Mr. Butt-in-sky.

With sincere regard,

Very truly yours,   Woodrow Wilson

TLS (WP, DLC).

From John Skelton Williams

Dear Mr. President: Washington August 17, 1920.

In reply to your note of August 16th, 1920, making inquiry as to the character of services rendered by National Bank Examiner Kennedy, I take pleasure in stating that Mr. Kennedy is now rendering efficient and satisfactory service in the important work in which he is engaged.

Mr. Kennedy was commissioned as a National Bank Examiner on April 15, 1913. For a while his progress was slow and his promotions were proportionately so. In the past two or three years there has been a distinct improvement in his work, and I see no reason why he may not look forward to steady promotion.

After the passage of the Federal Reserve Act and establishment of regular salaries for National Bank Examiners instead of "fees," Mr. Kennedy received compensation of $2400 per annum—the usual initial salary.

On October 6, 1916, he was promoted to $3,000. He was not advanced again until February 1, 1918, when his salary was raised to $3,300 per annum.

On March 1, 1919, his salary was increased to $3,600; on August 1, 1919, to $3,900; and on January 1, 1920, his compensation was made $4,000. His last increase was on July 1, 1920, when his salary was raised to $4,200 per annum.

The number of men in the Field Examining force at present is 143. There are only 30 Field Examiners receiving $4,200 or more, while 113 National Bank Examiners receive salaries ranging from $2,400 to $4,000.

Mr. Kennedy's progress was retarded by an awkwardness in his correspondence and his omission to present his views and recommendations clearly and succinctly. This little impediment has caused some criticism of him on the part of the Banks with which he has been thrown in contact.

He has, however, to a large degree, overcome this disability; and at any rate his ability to make satisfactory examinations of National Banks and to see and correct with firmness the troubles and unsatisfactory conditions which he finds, quite over-balance the minor defect to which I have referred.

I am pleased to say that the awkwardness of expression which formerly appeared in his correspondence did not manifest itself in the same degree in conferences and discussions with the bankers, by whom I believe he is held in high esteem.

I have written you very frankly, for I am sure you would prefer that I should do so.

As it may be of interest to you in this connection, I beg leave to hand you with this a letter which I received from Mr. Kennedy on July 4, 1918; also a copy of my reply to him. I also hand you with this Mr. Kennedy's letter to me of July 21, 1918, informing me that he had decided to refuse the Vice Presidency of the National Bank in Sioux Falls, South Dakota, which had been offered to him and retain his position as a National Bank Examiner.

I will repeat in conclusion that I am confident that Mr. Kennedy will now continue to progress, and to merit further advancement.

I am gratified to be able to give you this favorable report.

Respectfully and Faithfully yours,   Jno. Skelton Williams

TLS (WP, DLC).

To John Skelton Williams

My dear Mr. Comptroller: [The White House] 18 August, 1920

It was extremely kind of you to write me your full letter of August seventeenth about my nephew, Mr. Kennedy, and I am very much gratified that you were able to make so good a report of his progress. I think he is doing his best to deserve approval.

Thank you for having let me see the enclosed letters, which I am returning.

Cordially and faithfully yours,   [Woodrow Wilson]

CCL (WP, DLC).

From Bainbridge Colby, with Enclosure

My dear Mr. President: Washington August 18, 1920.

I beg to hand you herewith a letter from Mr. Lloyd George, addressed to you, and marked personal and confidential. I have just received it through the British Embassy and I send it to you with unbroken seal.

It was not accompanied by the copy, which is usual, where the communication is addressed to the Chief of State.

Very respectfully yours,   Bainbridge Colby

TLS (WP, DLC).

E N C L O S U R E

From David Lloyd George

COPY[1]

PRIVATE AND PERSONAL   10 Downing Street, Whitehall, S.W. 1.
My dear Mr. President,   5th August 1920.

I want to send you for your personal and confidential information a letter about the present position in Europe with the object of eliciting for my own information your confidential advice as an old colleague on the Peace conference. I always look back with pleasure on the period during which we co-operated in Paris in endeavouring to lay the foundations of the post-war world on just and firm lines, and I should like you to know what I think about the present position and to get your opinions from the more detached standpoint which you at present occupy, in return. Before I proceed,

---

[1] The Editors have not found the original copy of this letter. As noted below, this copy is from the Davis Papers, DLC.

however, will you allow me to say how glad I have been to hear the good news about your steadily improving health, more particularly from our ambassador. I fear that your breakdown was caused by the super-human exertions you made both in Paris and afterwards, and I never realised the extent and the value of your exertions so clearly as I have since your personal co-operation has ceased and I have been left to wrestle with the problems of Europe without your valued guidance and help.

These problems are hardly less difficult than when you left Europe. France, which undoubtedly suffered far more seriously than any other nation on the Allied side, has not yet begun to forget the war. She is still living in the war atmosphere; she is still deeply hostile to Germany, and intensely suspicious of everything Germany does; perhaps naturally, she cannot forget that Germany is a nation of more than 60 million people, whereas her own population is only 40 million. This fact darkens and distorts her outlook on foreign affairs and makes the continuous process of readjustment which is now taking place, and which must continue to take place if we are to establish a real appeasement in Europe, extremely difficult.

The position is all the more difficult since Nitti fell,[2] and Italy has been represented, not by a politician, but by an official.[3] Nitti was always in favour of reconciliation and appeasement in Europe, and while the present Government seems to follow very much the same policy, the real power is Giolitti and he is too old to travel to our meetings. Moreover, he is too much absorbed in troubled domestic affairs to give much heed to the affairs of the outside world. Millerand himself is an absolutely honest, sincere and moderate man. Like all Frenchmen he is obsessed with distrust of all Germans, but his temper is essentially moderate. He has a very unreasonable majority behind him which is continually being goaded by a violent and vindictive Press, which plays upon the French passions and distorts the facts. The main burden, therefore, of insisting on moderation, the moderation which is just as essential in France's own interest as in that of other nations, falls upon British shoulders, and the fact that it is always Britain which has to place itself in opposition to French demands, and that this burden is not now shared either by the United States or Italy, tends to make Anglo-French relations very difficult. Still, we have managed to pull through the Spa Conference not unsuccessfully. It looked at one time as if the action of the German industrial magnates in attempting to force the German Government to refuse to France, Italy and

[2] About which, see NHD to JPT, June 23, 1920, n. 1, Vol. 65.
[3] The Italian Foreign Minister, Count Carlo Sforza, a career diplomat.

Belgium the coal to which they were entitled, would force us to agree to the occupation of the Ruhr. Fortunately, however, Simons,[4] the German Foreign Minister, was made to see that it would be disastrous to allow such a thing to happen, and the Germans finally came round, and we were able to get an agreement without resort to coercion. The disarmament question was the real crux of the meeting. We found that Germany still possessed three million rifles, many thousands of machine guns and trench mortars, and five or six times the number of big guns permitted under the Treaty. She further had nearly a million armed men in some sort of military or semi-military formations. This was clearly a real menace to the peace and liberty of Europe, especially in view of the Eastern situation, and we insisted on the surrender of the war material by the autumn and on the reduction of the personnel to the figure provided under the Treaty, by the end of the year. I think that considering that this was the first occasion on which we had met the Germans and had a real discussion with them face to face since the war, the result of the Spa Conference was satisfactory, especially now that both the German and the French Parliaments have confirmed the agreements entered into by their Governments.[5] Having got round this first corner on the road to a real European settlement, I hope that the next time we meet the Germans things will be easier to manage. It all depends, of course, upon the way in which the Germans carry out their undertakings to disarm and to deliver coal. If the present German Government were to fall, we should be up against a very difficult situation.

I only wish that America were authoritatively represented at these conferences. The presence of a detached and impartial representative of yourself and your great country at our deliberations, standing now, as you stood at Paris, for justice and moderation, would undoubtedly contribute enormously towards the speed and certainty with which Europe returned to normal conditions.

[4] Walter Simons, Foreign Minister since June 25, 1920.

[5] The German delegates at Spa had signed, on July 9, a protocol on disarmament by which they agreed to fulfill the terms of the Versailles Treaty on this subject by January 1, 1921. *New York Times*, July 9 and 10, 1920. The text of the protocol is in Butler and Bury, eds., *Documents on British Foreign Policy*, First Series, VIII (London, 1958), 480-81. The protocol on coal deliveries, accepted by the German delegates on July 16, the final day of the conference, stipulated that Germany was to deliver 2,000,000 tons of coal a month to France during the six months beginning August 1, 1920. In return, Germany would receive financial credits depending upon the actual amount of coal delivered. *New York Times*, July 17 and 18, 1920; text in Butler and Bury, pp. 643-44.

Millerand presented the Spa protocols on disarmament and coal shipments to the Chamber of Deputies on July 20. Although the agreements were vigorously attacked by André Tardieu and Louis Loucheur, Millerand won a vote of confidence by 420 to 152. *New York Times*, July 21, 1920. The Reichstag approved the Spa agreements by a vote of confidence in the government of Chancellor Konstantin Fehrenbach on July 29. London *Times*, July 30, 1920.

As regards the Adriatic question, since you left Paris we have had two very different people to deal with from Orlando and Sonnino. Tittoni thoroughly disapproved of his predecessor's policy, and Nitti was even more pacific than Tittoni. The Giolitti Government appears to be moderate in its policy on this question, but I have not yet seen this remarkable old statesman and am not therefore able to speak with the same knowledge. I understand, however, from Sforza, the Foreign Minister, that he is anxious to settle the Adriatic question in a reasonable way, though he wants to score a success in domestic policy before he can face further concessions in external affairs. The negotiations for a settlement between Italy and Yugo-Slavia almost came to a successful issue before Nitti fell, and I think if pressure is put upon both sides to settle, we might get a final solution to this problem before long.

I earnestly urge you, therefore, to press the Yugo-Slav Government to be moderate in its views, and to do its utmost to come to an agreement directly with Italy. I will certainly do the same by the Italian Government, though I do not think it requires any pressure from me to persuade them to moderation, as their action in Albania[6] already shows. I hope to see Giolitti shortly in Switzerland and I shall talk to him in this sense.

As regards Germany, the real danger there is that there is no effective government. The last election showed a movement towards the extremes, both right and left, and the present government, as Simons said to me himself, is a kind of trait d'union between parties. Simons is a very straight, honest fellow, but although he is putting up an excellent fight I do not think he has got the strength behind him to master the German situation. However, as long as he remains foreign minister we can rely upon Germany following a sensible and honourable policy.

As regards Russia, the outlook is as baffling as ever and we are by no means out of the wood. The Poles, as you know, advanced into Russia against the advice of all the Allies and especially of Great Britain, and are now reaping the inevitable reward of their folly. But the advance of the Soviet armies to the German and Czecho-Slovak borders would be a very serious thing for Europe

[6] Provoked by an Albanian nationalist uprising and his own domestic problems, Giolitti had announced in the Chamber of Deputies on June 29 his determination to recognize the full independence of Albania, which had been partially occupied by Italian troops during the war. *New York Times*, July 1, 1920. He let it be known in July that ultimately all Italian troops would be withdrawn from Albania. *Ibid.*, July 19 and 29, 1920. Negotiations were under way between the Albanian provisional government and Italy at this time; a preliminary protocol was signed on August 22; and the last Italian troops departed from their stronghold in Vlorë on September 3. See Stefanaq Pollo and Arben Puto, *The History of Albania, From its Origins to the Present Day*, trans. Carol Wiseman and Ginnie Hole (London and Boston, 1981), pp. 171-80.

and we have been doing our best to preserve the independence of Poland, and to make the Soviet armies stop outside its ethnographic boundaries. The issue is still in doubt, Armistice negotiations have been begun and proposals have been made for a general conference in London to draw up a final peace for Eastern Europe and to re-establish the relations between Russia and the Allies. At the same time we sent an Anglo-French Mission to Warsaw with General Weygand as the principal military adviser to try and reorganise the Polish army for purposes of defence. I append a report from Hankey[7] which shows you the deplorable state of affairs he found there. The Poles are an embodiment of perverse inefficiency. It is like trying to save a drowning man who does all the silly things he is wanted not to do and does nothing he is begged to do. It is evident that the threat we made at the same time to break off the trade negotiations unless Russia respected Polish independence is a more powerful weapon than Polish military resistance. The French Government has throughout taken the line that it would not enter into any relations with Soviet Russia unless the Soviet Government admitted responsibility for its predecessor's debts. They agreed, however, to attend the proposed London conference provided the Polish question was the first question to be settled. If Poland is safely preserved on fair terms they will go on to discuss the resumption of normal relations with Russia, which will turn principally on the manner in which Russia is willing to treat the debt of 21,000,000,000 francs lent to her before the war by the French investor.

As I have said the future is quite uncertain. On the one side, if Russia wishes for a fair armistice with Poland and consents to the

[7] Accompanying this copy of Lloyd George's letter is an undated Hw note from Davis to Colby, which reads as follows: "This report was sent to the President by Mr. Lloyd George—with his letter to the President. Sec'y Houston turned it over to me—I think you will be interested in it." The copy of Hankey's report is missing, but it is printed in Butler and Bury, eds., *Documents on British Foreign Policy*, First Series, XI (London, 1961), 429-34. The mission to Poland included Hankey; Edgar Vincent, 1st Baron D'Abernon, the British Ambassador at Berlin; Maj. Gen. Sir Percy Pollexfen de Blaquiere Radcliffe, Director of Military Operations at the War Office; Jean Jules Jusserand; and Gen. Maxime Weygand. It had been in Warsaw from July 25 to about August 5. For an account of its visit, see Piotr S. Wandycz, *France and Her Eastern Allies, 1919-1925: French-Czechoslovak-Polish Relations from the Paris Peace Conference to Locarno* (Minneapolis, Minn., 1962), pp. 165-68.

Hankey had left Warsaw on July 30 and wrote his report during his journey home. He was very pessimistic about the prospects for the Polish government and armies in their struggle against the Red Army. Although he suggested policy alternatives for the British government to cover all contingencies, he came close to predicting that the Soviet armies would overrun all Poland and put an end to the independent Polish state.

As it turned out, Hankey and Lloyd George's despair about Poland's fate was unfounded. By the time Colby sent Lloyd George's letter to Wilson, the Polish armies had defeated the Red Army in the battle of Warsaw and within two months would drive the remaining Soviet armies out of Poland. See Norman Davies, *White Eagle, Red Star: The Polish-Soviet War, 1919-1920* (London, 1972), pp. 188-238.

London conference there ought to be real peace, in a military sense, from one end of Europe to the other, by the end of the year. On the other hand, if the Soviet Government decides to break with the rest and overwhelm Poland, which the experts say she can do, then we are in for a new period of revolutionary unrest which will have consequences both on internal and external situation, which no one can foretell. If, however, the first alternative proves to be the right one, and a conference takes place this autumn, between Russia and the Allies, I should greatly like to know whether it will be possible for the United States to be represented at it. I should greatly welcome it if you could send some one of real authority to take part in its deliberations. It would make a great difference if you could.

The Turkish question is gradually settling down. We decided to leave the Turks in Constantinople partly because the three Allies themselves had not the unity or strength to take over the government of the town, partly out of deference to the strong pressure of Moslem Indians who had fought for us during the war, partly because it made it easier to put pressure on Turkey to behave properly to its minorities in the future. For the rest, we followed the ethnographic principle as closely as we could. But when it came to enforcing our terms, there was only one force available with which to do it, and that was the Greek army. The forces of the Allies in those parts are barely sufficient to defend the Straits, and, as a matter of fact, the divergences in policy in regard to Turkey were so wide that their ability to do even that was a little doubtful. So when Mustapha Kemal decided to challenge the Allies we authorised the Greeks to advance. There were many prophets of failure, but I always thought Venizelos would succeed, in fact I was the chief, if not the only advocate, of the policy, and I am very glad to say that he lived up to our highest hopes and defeated the Kemalists with the greatest ease.

The most difficult aspect of the problem is still Armenia. The Allies have not the strength with which to protect it, and the Greek forces are at the other end of Asia Minor. Since the refusal of the Senate to take any responsibility for Armenia I do not see what can be done, unless we can re-establish the authority of the Sultan, who has signed the Treaty, which provides for Armenian independence, over the whole of Anatolia.

Syria is still in a mess. I do not think either the French or Feisal have tackled the situation very well.[8] But the definite establishment of French authority ought to clear the air, and I hope, pave

[8] About this situation, see n. 1 to the Enclosure printed with WW to BC, March 29, 1920, Vol. 65.

the way for a lasting settlement. Palestine has got a fair start under Herbert Samuel.[9] Mesopotamia is more difficult. The Arabs cannot yet run a democratic government and there is no obvious person, like Feisal, to put on the throne. Sir Percy Cox,[10] however, is going out in a month or two and I hope that when he arrives things will begin to straighten out, and he will get an Arab state into being.

This, I think, almost covers the ground. I should very much like to hear your views as to the future, and especially as to what part you think we can expect America to play after the election is over. By that time, unless the attempt to make peace with Russia has failed, and we are in the midst of a new war with Bolshevism, I hope that things will have really quietened down. Then the League of Nations will have a real chance. Up to the present we have still been peace-making and the machinery of the League has been too slow-moving, and has in other ways not been well adapted to the urgent necessities of the aftermath of the great storm. But by next year we ought to have progressed a good way towards the normal, and political controversy ought to have taken the place of military operations. Then the machinery of the League will come into play, and I hope, the United States will come back again into the councils of the Powers. A tremendous lot depends upon that. We shall not be able to control the forces in Asia and Europe and elsewhere which have been liberated by the war and Bolshevism without active American co-operation, and I should much value your advice as to what we can expect in that respect.

I come now to the other question I wish to write to you about, and that is the knotty problem of Inter-Allied indebtedness. Indeed, I promised Mr. Rathbone long ago that I would write to you about it, but I have had to put it off for one reason and another till now. The British and French Governments have been discussing during the last four months, the question of giving fixity and definiteness to Germany's reparation obligations. The British Government has stood steadily by the view that it was vital that Germany's liabilities should be fixed at a figure which it was within the reasonable capacity of Germany to pay, and that this figure should be fixed without delay because the reconstruction of Central Europe could not begin nor could the Allies themselves raise money on the strength of Germany's obligation to pay them reparation until her liabilities had been exactly defined. After great difficulties with his own people, M. Millerand found himself able to accept this view,—but he pointed out that it was impossible for France to agree to accept anything less than it was entitled to under the Treaty unless

[9] Sir Herbert (Louis) Samuel, British High Commissioner to Palestine.
[10] Sir Percy (Zachariah) Cox, High Commissioner to Iraq.

its debts to its Allies and Associates in the war were treated in the same way.

This declaration appeared to the British Government eminently fair. But after careful consideration they came to the conclusion that it was impossible to remit any part of what was owed to them by France except as part and parcel of all round settlement of Inter-Allied indebtedness. I need not go into the reasons which led to this conclusion which must be clear to you. But the principal reason was that British public opinion would never support a one-sided arrangement at its sole expense, and that if such a one-sided arrangement were made it could not fail to estrange and eventually embitter the relations between the American and the British people with calamatous results to the future of the world. You will remember that Great Britain borrowed from the United States about half as much as its total loans to the Allies, and that after America's entry into the war, it lent to the Allies almost exactly the same amount as it borrowed from the U. S. A. Accordingly the British Government has informed the French Government that it will agree to any equitable arrangement for the reduction or cancellation of Inter-Allied indebtedness, but that such an arrangement must be one which applies all round. As you know, the representatives of the Allies and of Germany are meeting at Geneva in a week or two to commence discussion on the subject of reparation.

I recognise that in the midst of a presidential election and with Congress not in session it is impossible for the United States to deal with this question in a practical manner, but the question is one of such importance to the future of Europe, and indeed to the relations between the Allied and Associated Powers that I should very much welcome any advice which you might feel yourself able to give me as to the best method of securing that the whole problem could be considered and settled by the United States Government in concert with its Associates at the earliest possible moment that the political situation in America makes it possible.

There is one other point which I should like to add. When the British Government decided that it could not deal with the question of the debts owed to it by its Allies except as part and parcel of an all-round arrangement of Inter-Allied debts, the Chancellor of the Exchequer[11] told Mr. Rathbone that he could not proceed any further with the negotiations which they had been conducting together with regard to the postponement of the payment of interest on the funding of Great Britain's debts to America.[12] I should like to make it plain that this is due to no reluctance on the part of

[11] That is, (Joseph) Austen Chamberlain.
[12] See NHD to WW, May 26, 1920, n. 1, Vol. 65.

Great Britain to fund its debt, but solely to the fact that it cannot bind itself by any arrangement which would prejudice the working of any Inter-Allied arrangement which may be reached in the future. If some method can be found for funding the British debt which does not prejudice the larger question, the British Government would be glad to fall in with it.

I entirely agree with you about making Geneva and not Brussels the meeting place of the Assembly of the League. Brussels is still too much under the influence of the feelings engendered by the war to be a good scene for the first general meeting of the League.

I trust that I have not inflicted too long a letter upon you, and I earnestly trust that your impending release from the responsibilities of your great office will enable you to regain your normal health.

With best wishes to yourself and Mrs. Wilson,

Ever sincerely yours,   D. Lloyd George.

TCL (N. H. Davis Papers, DLC).

From Bainbridge Colby, with Enclosure

My dear Mr. President: Washington August 18, 1920.

I beg to enclose herewith

(1) Translation of the French Note[1] responding to the statement contained in our recent Note to the Italian Ambassador that we would regard with satisfaction a declaration by the Allied Powers that the territorial integrity and true boundaries of Russia should be respected.

This Note was published by the French Foreign Office before we received it. I have today given copies of it to the Press.

(2) Memorandum from the Japanese Government in reply to our Note of July 16th,[2] addressed to the Japanese Ambassador, on the subject of Japan's occupation of the northern half of the island of Sakhalien.

I wish to place this in your hands without delay, although I hope to complete within a day or two a memorandum which I trust you may find of some assistance in considering the Japanese position.

Very respectfully yours,   Bainbridge Colby

TLS (WP, DLC).
    [1] Prince de Béarn to BC, Aug. 14, 1920, T MS (WP, DLC), printed in *FR 1920*, III, 469-70. Béarn informed Colby that the French government was in "entire agreement" with the principles formulated in Colby's note to Baron Avezzana of August 10, printed as an Enclosure with BC to WW, Aug. 9, 1920. Béarn's letter contained a lengthy denunciation of the Soviet government and declared that France would never recognize that regime.
    [2] Printed as an Enclosure with BC to WW, July 16, 1920, Vol. 65.

ENCLOSURE

August 13, 1920.

IMPERIAL JAPANESE EMBASSY
WASHINGTON.
MEMORANDUM.

The Japanese Government are happy to note that the United States Government, through the note of the Secretary of State dated July 10th, giving frank expression to its views upon the declaration made by the Japanese Government on July 3rd respecting (1) occupation of certain points in the Province of Sakhalin (2) withdrawal of Japanese forces from Trans-Baikalia region and (3) maintenance of the Japanese troops around Vladivostok and at Khabarovsk, has expressed much gratification on the decision of the Japanese Government to withdraw their troops from the Trans-Baikalia region. At the same time, the Japanese Government regret that the United States Government fails to see the reasons which compelled the Japanese Government to take the first and third of the above-mentioned decisions.

Passing for the moment the first point, and referring to the third point, the political situation in Vladivostok and its neighborhood is far from being secure, nor is public order there restored as yet owing to the fact that the authority of the Provincial Government in Vladivostok is not yet fully established. The Japanese Government therefore are unable to leave to the Provisional Government there the protection of Japanese subjects in that district numbering about 7,000. Moreover, the lawless Koreans living in the vicinity, evidently under the influence of Russian bolshevism, are not only constantly creating disturbances on the borderland of Korea, but, armed and banded, they often penetrate into the interior of the country and make raid upon the civilian population taking toll of many lives and causing immeasurable damage to their property, a situation which is almost tantamount to a state of war. Confronted with so serious and pressing a danger to the peace and safety of Korea,—danger, moreover, behind which lies the formidable menace of bolshevism,—the Japanese Government, not unnaturally, look upon the situation with grave concern. The maintenance of the Japanese forces in the neighborhood of Vladivostok is thus a measure of self defense absolutely necessary for the protection of the Japanese residents there, as well as for the preservation of order and security in Korea.

As regards Khabarovsk, which is a point of special importance on the line of communication with Nikolaievsk, capital of the Province of Sakhalin, it is also indispensable that a certain number of troops should be left there in order to maintain communication with the Nikolaievsk garrison. In this connection it may well be pointed out that the maintenance of the Japanese troops in Vladivostok and Khabarovsk, which is thus necessary for safeguarding the interests of Japan and of the Japanese people in these regions, will also be conducive to the promotion of the general welfare of the Russian population.

To revert now to the first point: the United States Government appears to conclude that the occupation of certain points in the Province of Sakhalin has no relevance to the Nikolaievsk affair, on the assumption that Nikolaievsk is located in Primorskaya or the Maritime Province on the mainland of Siberia, whereas the Sakhalin Province includes only the northern portion of the island of that name. The information in the hands of the Japanese Government indicates that by virtue of the Russian Imperial decree of the 26th of February, 1914, the town of Nikolaievsk and its neighborhood was separated from the Maritime Province and incorporated in the province of Sakahlin together with the northern portion of Sakhalin Island, and Nikolaievsk has since then been the capital of the Province. Thus there being no shadow of doubt as to Nikolaievsk being within the administrative boundary of the Province of Sakhalin, the observation of the United States Government in this respect seems to be not well founded.

The note of the United States Government adds that from the Memorandum transmitted to it by the Japanese Ambassador in Washington, it does not appear that Japanese subjects in the northern portion of Sakhalin Island have sustained any injuries, nor does it appear that the Russian authorities in that Island were in any way involved in the atrocities at Nikolaievsk or chargeable with any responsibility therefor; nor does the Memorandum appear to suggest any reason for assuming that the occupation of the said Island would operate as a protection to the lives and property of the Japanese residents on the Siberian Mainland. The occupation of the northern portion of the Sakhalin Island has been found necessary, at the same time as the occupation of Nikolaievsk, because of the geographic situation in which that port is placed, and is calculated to further a sentlement of the present affair.

The occupation of certain points in the Province of Sakhalin is a measure which,—in the absence of any responsible government in Russia to whom representation could usefully be made, with a view to obtaining redress for the wrongs so wantonly committed against the Japanese subjects by an inhumane and lawless band such as the so-called "partisans,"—the Japanese Government were compelled to adopt, pending the establishment of a legitimate government and the satisfactory adjustment of the Nikolaievsk incident. Cases of this kind are not wanting in international law, nor does such a step constitute any violation of the mutual understanding which has been maintained by the Governments of Washington and Tokio since 1918.

It is pointed out in the note under review that despite injuries very similar to those sustained by Japan, other nations have refrained from the adoption of any course which involved encroachment upon Russian territory in the time of Russia's helplessness. The Japanese Government do not know whether other nations have sustained any such calamity as has now befallen Japan. Apart from that question, however, the occupation of certain points in the Sakhalin Province is a measure, as explained above, unavoidable in the present circumstances where there is no other means for securing redress for the injuries so painfully received, and it would be entirely beside the mark if it were construed as an act of territorial aggression.

The United States Government is believed to be well aware of the enormous sacrifices made by Japan in the past, from a feeling of deep sympathy in the present agony of Russia, and the Japanese Government have not the slightest intention of making any departure from this policy. Yet a disaster such as that which Japan met with at Nikolaievsk being one which has no precedent in the national experience of the country, it cannot be difficult to perceive that the entire nation would on no account have tolerated any measure short of that which has been adopted by the Japanese Government.

The Japanese Government feel persuaded that in full appreciation of the circumstances above set forth the United States Government will not be unwilling to take a sympathetic view of the decision of the Japanese Government as announced in the declaration above referred to.

T MS (WP, DLC).

From Bainbridge Colby

My Dear Mr. President: Washington August 18, 1920.

On examining the carbon copy of the letter I sent you accompanying the memorandum of the conference between Ambassador Morris and the Japanese Ambassador on the California situation,[1] I don't think I indicated clearly that we hoped to obtain some guiding comment from you on the subject.

We think the policy outlined in the memorandum is sound and

workable, but we would not think of proceeding on the lines indicated without your approval.

It is a very delicate and pressing matter and I would be much aided by your advice on it.

Very respectfully yours,   Bainbridge Colby

TLS (WP, DLC).
    [1] Printed as an Enclosure with BC to WW, Aug. 5, 1920.

To David Franklin Houston

My dear Houston: [The White House] 19 August, 1920

It would afford me a great deal of assistance if you would tell me what you think of the enclosed papers, one a letter from Mr. Lloyd George and the other an extract from the report made by Sir Maurice Hankey.

Cordially and faithfully yours,   [Woodrow Wilson]

CCL (WP, DLC).

From Albert Houston Roberts

Nashville, Tenn., August 19, 1920.

A congratulatory message from you to Tennessee legislature this morning might be of great assistance to suffrage forces in fight to prevent reconsideration of vote of ratification nineteenth amendment.[1]   Gov. A. H. Roberts.

T telegram (WP, DLC).
    [1] After several days of delay and amidst intense lobbying and charges of bribery and corruption, the Tennessee House of Representatives voted, on August 18, fifty to forty-six in favor of ratification of the woman-suffrage amendment. Tennessee thus became the thirty-sixth state necessary to complete the process of ratification. *New York Times*, Aug. 19, 1920. By August 19, forty-seven members of the House had signed a pledge to vote to reconsider ratification. However, as it turned out, House Speaker Seth M. Walker was unable to muster enough votes for a motion to reconsider, and it was voted down on August 21. *Ibid.*, Aug. 20-22, 1920. Governor Roberts was temporarily prevented from certifying the ratification by a court order obtained by the antisuffragists. He did certify the ratification on August 24, after Dick Latta Lansden, the Chief Justice of the Tennessee Supreme Court, issued a writ vacating the lower court order. Bainbridge Colby issued a proclamation on August 26 which announced that the amendment was part of the Constitution. *Ibid.*, Aug. 21, 23, 25, and 27, 1920. See also Eleanor Flexner, *Century of Struggle: The Woman's Rights Movement in the United States* (Cambridge, Mass., 1959), pp. 321-24.

To Albert Houston Roberts

[The White House] 19 August, 1920

If you deem it proper will you not be kind enough to convey to the Legislature of Tennessee my sincere congratulations on their

concurrence in the Nineteenth Amendment. I believe that in sending this message I am in fact speaking the voice of the country at
large.   Woodrow Wilson.

T telegram (Letterpress Books, WP, DLC).

From Josephus Daniels

Dear Mr. President: Washington. Aug. 19. 1920.

Upon reflection and full consideration I have decided to recommend as Assistant Secretary Mr. Gordon Woodbury, of New Hampshire. He is a graduate of Harvard, trained in the law, a prosperous
business man, a life-long Democrat, and is warmly endorsed by all
our friends in New Hampshire. I have had a long talk with him
and feel sure his appointment would be approved. He has been a
consistent and loyal advocate of your policies, is a gentleman of
character and courtesy. Enclosed is a brief statement which I
asked him to prepare which gives you his record.[1] His ancestor,
Levi Woodbury, was Secretary of the Navy, under Jackson, I
think.[2]

I do not believe you could name a better man and if his fitness
appeals to you I hope you will let me know soon because there is
work for the Assistant Secretary which ought not to be long delayed—a delay which is due, of course, to me.

Mr. Woodbury is now in the city. I believe we have excellent
chance of defeating Moses[3] in New Hampshire this year and all
our friends in that State are back of Mr. Woodbury.

                     Sincerely yours,   Josephus Daniels

ALS (WP, DLC).
   [1] T MS (WP, DLC).
   [2] From 1831 to 1834.
   [3] That is, Senator George Higgins Moses, Republican, one of Wilson's bitterest opponents.

Sterling Ruffin to Edith Bolling Galt Wilson

Dear Mrs. Wilson—   Cape Vincent, New York August 19. 1920.

It was a very great pleasure to have your letter, forwarded to me
here and received last evening. I am enclosing, with pleasure, prescription for the eruption on the President's chest. I am afraid to
promise that it will do much good, because a good deal of pigment
has been deposited in the skin and such deposits are apt to be permanent; but it may do some good and is certainly worth trying.
The prescription is for a lotion and it should be applied on a pledget
of cotton freely as many times a day as convenient, say three or
four times, but certainly twice.

I do hope the President is encouraged and that he is able to realize some improvement as the weeks go by. Such a tedious long drawn out illness tries the bravest souls and that it should have come to him at such a time with literally the weight of the world on his shoulders was the world's misfortune. If things only go right this fall—if our ticket can only pull through—the great and noble things for which he has fought will be in sight. If they go wrong, God help us.

This is a little fishing town on the St Lawrence River just as it is leaving Lake Ontario. The bass fishing is very fine when the weather is good and the weather has been very fine since I came a week ago. Good motor boats, good guides and a fairly comfortable hotel make fishing very luxurious.

Please give my kind regards to the President.

Faithfully yours,   Sterling Ruffin

ALS (EBW Papers, DLC).

To Bainbridge Colby

My dear Mr. Secretary: The White House 20 August, 1920

I think that what Morris said to the Japanese Ambassador here is sound to the point of obviousness, and I will be very glad indeed to receive any outline from you of the policy which you think it would be best to base upon it.

Cordially and faithfully yours,   Woodrow Wilson

TLS (SDR, RG 59, 811.5294/92, DNA).

To Josephus Daniels

My dear Daniels: The White House 20 August, 1920

I am perfectly willing to accept your judgment about Mr. Gordon Woodbury and hope that he will justify your confidence in every way.   Cordially and faithfully yours,   Woodrow Wilson

TLS (J. Daniels Papers, DLC).

From Josephus Daniels

My dear Mr. President: Washington. August 20, 1920.

You have named the Postmaster General, Admiral Benson, Mr. Rogers and the Under Secretary of State to represent this country at the Preliminary Conference on World Wide Communications to be held in Washington September 15, 1920.

The British have appointed nine delegates and the Japanese Delegation is composed of nine. In the personnel of each of these delegations there are representatives of the various departments, and in every case the navy is represented. The Naval Communication Service is the largest and most important communication service under the direct control of our Government, and it is working diligently to preserve interest in communication service. The Director of Naval Communications is Admiral W. H. G. Bullard,[1] who has made a reputation at home and abroad, and he is the ablest man in the Navy on radio and communication matters. I think he ought to be a representative of the United States in this conference on September 15th, and would be very happy if you could designate him and increase the United States representation by one.

Sincerely yours,   Josephus Daniels

TLS (WP, DLC).
  [1] Rear Adm. William Hannum Grubb Bullard.

To George A. Foster

My dear Mr. Foster: [The White House] 21 August, 1920

Your letter to me about Harlakenden[1] lays me under a great temptation, because I admire the house very much and became very fond of it while I was occupying it, but I am afraid there are too many obstacles in the way of my purchasing it to permit me to consider it.

I wonder if it would be asking too much to ask Mr. Churchill[2] if he could kindly give me an idea of the average annual cost of keeping the place up. And perhaps you can tell me whether the furnaces in the house are adequate to keep it heated throughout the winter.

With thanks for your letter,

Sincerely yours,   [Woodrow Wilson]

CCL (WP, DLC).
  [1] G. A. Foster, real estate and insurance broker of Concord, N. H., to WW, Aug. 17, 1920, TLS (WP, DLC). Foster informed Wilson that he had recently listed for sale Harlakenden, in Cornish, New Hampshire, in which Wilson and his family had vacationed in the summers of 1913, 1914, and 1915. (See the index references to Harlakenden in Vol. 39). The property, including 150 acres of timber and pasture land, was being offered for $75,000. "It occurs to me," Foster wrote, "that you or someone you know might be interested in the purchase of this property."
  [2] Winston Churchill, the American novelist, who owned Harlakenden.

From Josephus Daniels

My dear Mr. President: Washington. August 21, 1920.

With reference to your communication concerning the MAY-
FLOWER,[1] I have directed Commander Holmes that the MAY-
FLOWER may go out on Monday for a practice trip to get her personnel in shape. The MAYFLOWER will leave Monday, but will be
back in Washington on Thursday or Friday so that it will be ready
for any service at that time which you may desire.

Faithfully yours,   Josephus Daniels

TLS (WP, DLC).
  [1] WW to JD, Aug. 13, 1920.

From the Diary of Josephus Daniels

August Saturday 21 1920

Dinner at Army and Navy club. Gen. Crowder talked of Selective
Draft.

WW called on Secy. Baker & said he wished an act drawn by 10
next day to call every young man into military service.[1] The War
College had worked out a plan for Registration by P. O. Dept. mail
carriers. In Civil War there had been a system which required
months to get into action. Crowder said he did not think either
would serve the purpose and was trying to devise a plan when a
member of Congress called. He told him at some length of the
problem, and as the Congressman was leaving he said to Gen C "If
we can arrange for every man to vote on one day why can't it be
managed for every man to register on one day" Having said this in
passing, without thinking he had contributed to what later developed in the act, the Congressman went out. With that as the germ
Gen C— says he presented the draft of the act to Baker next morning, it was approved & passed with little change, & Baker assigned
him to carry it out. Gen C— is now engaged in a plan for like draft
in war for men to register for all kinds of labor. Thinks it should
include all men and women under 65

  [1] Crowder later said that this visit by Wilson to Baker occurred on February 4, 1917,
the day after Wilson severed diplomatic relations with Germany. Crowder's account of
the origin of the Selective Service Act of May 18, 1917, was corroborated by his former
aides and accepted by his biographer. It subsequently became the standard historical
account. See Hugh S. Johnson, *The Blue Eagle: From Egg to Earth* (Garden City,
N. Y., 1935), p. 73; David A. Lockmiller, *Enoch H. Crowder: Soldier, Lawyer, and
Statesman* (Columbia, Mo., 1955), pp. 152-54; and, most recently, Robert H. Ferrell,
Woodrow Wilson and World War I, 1917-1921 (New York, 1985), p. 16, and Frederick
S. Calhoun, *Power and Principle: Armed Intervention in Wilsonian Foreign Policy*
(Kent, Ohio, 1986), p. 163.
  However, Crowder's memory was very defective. Wilson's visit to Baker was on Feb-

ruary 15, not February 4, 1917, and there is no evidence that Wilson asked Baker for a selective service bill at that time. Rather, he apparently asked Baker to have Crowder prepare a joint resolution authorizing him to increase the naval and military forces if Germany committed an overt act of war while Congress was in adjournment. This would authorize him to enlarge the Regular Army and National Guard up to their war-time strength of approximately 500,000 men and to raise a temporary force of 500,000 volunteers under the Volunteer Act of 1914. Crowder and his aides wrote a joint reso-lution to this effect. However, Crowder, like the other members of the General Staff, was an advocate of conscription as opposed to voluntary enlistment. He included in his draft resolution a clause giving the President discretion to recruit these forces by con-scription if necessary, using Section 79 of the National Defense Act of June 3, 1916. This section authorized drafting men into reserve battalions of the National Guard.

Crowder submitted his joint resolution to Baker on February 23, 1917. Wilson's re-action to Crowder's proposal, if Baker ever showed it to him, is not known. Wilson cer-tainly did not use Crowder's draft. Instead, he went before Congress on February 26, 1917, and asked for authority to arm American merchant ships in the hope of deterring submarine attacks against them.

Actually, Crowder's draft resolution did not provide the basis for the Selective Service Act of 1917. Rather, this measure was prepared by Crowder and his staff in conjunction with Baker and a council of generals in the War Department between March 27 and March 30, 1917. See John Whiteclay Chambers II, *To Raise an Army: The Draft Comes to Modern America* (New York, 1987), pp. 125-51.

Two Letters to Josephus Daniels

My dear Mr. Secretary: The White House 23 August, 1920

I have your letter of August twentieth. I must say I think the criticism which you have been hearing of the Postmaster General in connection with the work of the delegation on international communications is unjust and unjustified, and I do not see that there is any convincing argument for an increase of our delegation in the fact that other delegations are larger, but I am, nevertheless, willing to add Admiral Bullard to the delegation in view of his spe-cial knowledge of a particular kind of international communica-tions and would be obliged if you would talk the matter over with the Secretary of State and, if he is of the same mind, ask him to advise me what method of appointment I should follow.

Faithfully yours,   Woodrow Wilson

My dear Mr. Secretary: The White House 23 August, 1920

Allow me to acknowledge the receipt of your letter of August twenty-first,[1] enclosing an extract from a letter written by Admiral Andrews,[2] now commanding our forces in the Adriatic, to Admiral Coontz.[3] I would be obliged if you would send a copy of this letter to the Secretary of State.

Sincerely yours,   Woodrow Wilson

TLS (J. Daniels Papers, DLC).
[1] JD to WW, Aug. 21, 1920, TLS (WP, DLC).
[2] Not found.
[3] Adm. Robert Edward Coontz, Chief of Naval Operations.

From the Diary of Josephus Daniels

1920 Tuesday 24 August

Cabinet. The Jones Shipping bill undertakes to denounce certain parts of 28 treaties giving equal rights in shipping with our own people, "the favored nation" clause.[1] It would enable Interstate Com. to give lower rates to goods brought in American ships & give other privileges amounting to a subsidy. The other nations protest that a treaty is not a scrap of paper & cannot be abrogated except by mutual consent & Congress undertakes to exercise executive functions when it impairs terms of treaty. Under act notice must be given in 30 days Colby must act or defy Congress. WW was for declaring Congress could not change a treaty, but Alexander & WBW said he had signed the bill and therefore approved it. Best thought seemed that Colby should notify countries of the law & ask them to consent. If they refused then to take matter up with Congress which would shortly thereafter be in session. But troublesome question.

[1] About this provision of the Jones Act, see J. W. Alexander to WW, June 25, 1920, n. 2, Vol. 65.

To Edward William Pou

My dear Mr. Pou: The White House 24 August, 1920

I know of no one whose judgment I would rather take in the matter of a judicial appointment than your own,[1] and I know of no one more worthy of the praise that you bestow upon him than Finis Garrett,[2] but I have this scruple: Just at this critical stage in our history I should feel it unwise to take out of the House of Representatives the best men our party contains.[3] This is fighting time and our fighting forces ought to be undiminished.

Cordially and faithfully yours,   Woodrow Wilson

TLS (E.W. Pou Papers, NcU).
[1] Wilson was replying to E. W. Pou to WW, Aug. 17, 1920, TLS (WP, DLC).
[2] Finis James Garrett, Democratic congressman from Tennessee, whose appointment as judge for the Western District of Tennessee Pou had recommended.
[3] However, see WW to AMP, Nov. 18, 1920.

From David Franklin Houston

Dear Mr. President: Washington August 24, 1920.

I have given very careful consideration to the letter of the 16th of August, addressed to you by Senators Dial, Simmons, and

Fletcher, a copy of which was transmitted to me by Mr. Tumulty under date of the 19th instant. The Senators express the opinion that the War Finance Corporation should resume operations in assisting the financing of exports, at least so far as agricultural products are concerned.

On May 10, 1920, I publicly announced that at my request the War Finance Corporation had suspended the making of further advances in aid of exports, except pursuant to commitments theretofore made. The War Finance Corporation was a war agency and its general powers expire six months after the termination of the war and the special powers conferred upon it under the Victory Loan Act, authorizing assistance in the financing of exports, expire one year after the termination of the war. These special powers were granted after the Armistice when business had suffered a recession in consequence of the cancellation of war orders, and when there was a fear that exports might decline and unemployment exist. The Corporation continued to exercise its special powers in a relatively small way until there was a certainty that there would be no sudden upsetting of the business situation of the country by suspended or diminishing exports. The situation that was feared did not materialize. On the contrary, the export business not only did not decline, but actually increased. Private interests did not fail to finance exports and there seemed no reason why the Government should continue to interpose in the situation with a view to stimulating exports, particularly when the Treasury was compelled to resort from time to time to temporary borrowing in part to meet its present obligations.

There has been no change in the general situation since I issued my statement on the 10th of May. This power was granted to the War Finance Corporation to serve a certain purpose and to be exercised during the period of readjustment immediately following the Armistice. It is true that a technical state of war exists, but it is also true that nearly a year and a half has elapsed since the power was granted to the War Finance Corporation to aid in financing exports. When Congress authorized such loans by the Corporation, it was presumed that peace long ago would have been established and the power terminated.

The Senators state that they would not make the request if it required a bond issue to accomplish the purpose. They may be technically correct in stating that it would not require a bond issue to make the loans which they suggest, but it would require issues of certificates of indebtedness for the purpose. It would be necessary to obtain by the sale of certificates of indebtedness to the public, at rates of interest ranging as high as 6%, every dollar lent to render such assistance. In the existing circumstances, it seems clear that the Government should enter the borrowing field as seldom as possible and then for the lowest possible sums. It would be a question, as I stated on the 10th of May, whether the Government should continue to aid and stimulate exports, considering their present volume privately financed, even if the Treasury had surplus funds. It seems clear to me that it should not continue to do so when the Treasury has to resort to borrowing from time to time.

I am sure that if Senators Dial, Simmons, and Fletcher will analyze the situation in the light of what I have said above, they will agree with me that the War Finance Corporation should not resume active business.　　Faithfully yours,　D. F. Houston.

File W.W.

TLS (WP, DLC).

From Josephus Daniels

My dear Mr. President:　　　　　Washington. August 24, 1920.

Referring to your letter of August 23rd in reply to one in which I suggested that Admiral Bullard be added to our delegation for the Conference on International Communications, you state: "I must say I think the criticism you have been hearing of the Postmaster General in connection with the work of the delegates on International Communications is unjustified." I wish to state that I have heard no criticism whatever of the Postmaster General in connection with the work of this delegation, and my suggestion of Admiral Bullard was prompted solely by his knowledge and the large part the Navy plays in international communication. The criticism to which you refer has never reached my ears, and if it had, it would have received no consideration from me.

Regarding your suggestion, I will see the Secretary of State.
　　　　　　　　　　Sincerely yours,　Josephus Daniels

TLS (WP, DLC).

Joseph Patrick Tumulty to William Edward Dodd

My dear Professor Dodd:　　　The White House 24 August 1920.

I have laid before the President the contents of your letter of the 22d of August.[1] He deems the suggestion it contains thoroughly worth while and would make time and opportunity for it if he felt his physical condition justified him; but just at present it is particularly necessary that he should conserve his strength in every possible way. He feels for the present unequal to such a conversation as you so kindly propose.

With best wishes,   Sincerely yours,   J P Tumulty

TLS (W. E. Dodd Papers, DLC).
¹ It is missing.

To Bainbridge Colby, with Enclosure

My dear Mr. Secretary: The White House 25 August, 1920

I have read the enclosed, but do not know how to reply to it. I would be very much obliged if you would have the proper reply made, because, of course, the department knows the rights and wrongs of the matter and I do not.

I did not know that we were represented by Bailly-Blanchard.¹ We have been unfortunate in our representation there, and I hope that matters are in better shape than they used to be.

Cordially and faithfully yours,   Woodrow Wilson

TLS (B. Colby Papers, DLC).
¹ Arthur Bailly-Blanchard, career diplomat, Minister to Haiti since May 22, 1914. It is a sign of the degree to which Wilson had lost touch with Haitian affairs and policy toward Haiti that he had forgotten that Bailly-Blanchard, whom he had always disliked, was still in Port-au-Prince.

ENCLOSURE

Port-au-Prince, August 6, 1920.

Le President de la Republique d'Haiti a l'honneur de porter a la connaissance de votre Excellence le fait grave suivant d'apres lettre officielle du conseiller financier au Secretaire d'Etat des finances les indemnites dues pour le mois de juillet au President de la Republique aux Secretaires d'Etat et aux Conseillers d'Etat sont retenues d'ordre de Monsieur Bailly-Blanchard, Ministre des Etats Unis, au nom de la nation je proteste aupres de votre Excellence contre cette mesure de violence qui est une atteinte faite a la dignite du gouvernement et du peuple Haitien.

[Philippe Sudre] Dartiguenave,   President d'Hayti.

T telegram (SDR, RG 59, 838.51/943, DNA).

From William Oxley Thompson

My dear Mr. President: Washington August 25, 1920.

The Anthracite Coal Commission appointed by you to hear and decide the questions in dispute between the Anthracite coal operators and miners, has completed the work assigned and transmits herewith the report of the findings and awards.

There is a majority report and a minority report.[1]

The Commission is now ready to adjourn unless it shall be your pleasure to call upon us for further service.

Very respectfully,   W. O. Thompson, Chairman.

TLS (WP, DLC).
[1] There is a digest of this report (T MS) in WP, DLC; the report was printed as RE-PORT, FINDINGS, AWARD OF THE *United States Anthracite Coal Commission* . . . (Washington, 1920).

The majority report reviewed labor-management relations in the anthracite coal industry since the establishment of the Anthracite Coal Strike Commission in 1902 and had high praise for the success of its Board of Conciliation in promoting labor-management cooperation in the anthracite region.

The majority members of the Anthracite Coal Commission then explained and justified their award: they had attempted to make the position of "the men performing common ordinary labor more tolerable and of preserving the differentials between the several classes of labor," but without doing anything that might justify an increase in the price of anthracite coal.

The majority report sustained the workers' demand for a new two-year contract and ordered increases in wages of 20 per cent for contract miners, of 22 per cent for "company men," of 17 per cent for "consideration miners," of 17 per cent for "contract miners' laborers and consideration miners' laborers," and of 17 per cent for "monthly men." Some demands of the miners were referred to the Board of Conciliation. The majority report denied the demand for time-and-a-half pay for overtime and double pay for Sundays and holidays; the demand for recognition by the operators of the United Mine Workers as "a party to the contract" was granted; and the demand for the "closed shop" and "check-off" was denied. The award granted and denied other demands. The majority report estimated that its award would result in the payment of about $18,000,000 in back pay and that the total increase in wages would aggregate at least $85,000,000.

The minority report was issued by Neal J. Ferry, an official of the United Mine Workers of America, who said at the beginning of his report that the U. M. W. would of course carry out the award of the majority "with the most scrupulous care and with the utmost good faith." All the energies of the U. M. W. would be "devoted to this end." However, Ferry recommended wage increases beyond those granted by the majority's award, recognition of the right of collective bargaining by the miners through representatives of their own choosing, and the eight-hour work day.

To George Creel, with Enclosure

My dear Creel: The White House 26 August, 1920

The Harpers recently asked me what my views were with regard to a proposition for the translation of the volume of my speeches which they published,[1] and I have just taken the liberty of sending them the enclosed letter.

Always   Faithfully yours,   Woodrow Wilson

TLS (G. Creel Papers, DLC).
[1] As the Enclosure reveals, Wilson returned the letter from Harper & Brothers to the publisher.

E N C L O S U R E

To Harper & Brothers

My dear Sirs: The White House, 26 August, 1920

My Secretary, of course, referred the enclosed to me and in reply I have to request that you will confer concerning the whole matter with Mr. George Creel, 505 Fifth Avenue, New York City, whom I have asked to represent me in all matters of this sort.

Very truly yours,   Woodrow Wilson

TCL (G. Creel Papers, DLC).

From Bainbridge Colby

My dear Mr. President: Washington August 26, 1920.

I venture to lay before you the following appeal addressed to you by Mr. Avetis Aharonian, President of the Delegation of the Armenian Republic, and transmitted through our Embassy in Paris:

"Treaty with Turkey recognizing independent Armenian State[1] and providing for your supreme arbitration for its frontiers being signed the Armenian nation respectfully awaits your high decision with full confidence in your equity and proved sympathy for their sufferings. Hundreds of thousands of refugees whose lives have been saved by generous American relief are eager to return to their devastated homes to make early accom[m]odations for winter and are waiting for your decision which will warrant occupation of those regions."

In this connection I beg to state that Professor W. L. Westermann, who was expert adviser upon the Near East with the American Peace Commission at Paris, is now here working on a special report upon the southern and western boundaries of Armenia in accordance with your acceptance of the invitation of the Supreme Council to arbitrate these boundaries. Associated with him in this work are Major Lawrence Martin of the General Staff, who was a member of General Harbord's Mission, and Mr. H. G. Dwight[2] of the Near Eastern Division of this Department. Professor Westermann's report will be submitted to you before the end of September.   Faithfully yours,   Bainbridge Colby

Ackn & file W.W.

TLS (WP, DLC).

[1] That is, the Treaty of Sèvres, signed at that French town on August 10, 1920. For Articles 88 to 93 of this treaty, dealing with Armenia, see Fred L. Israel, ed., *Major Peace Treaties of Modern History, 1648-1967* (4 vols., New York, 1967), III, 2084-88.

[2] Harry Griswold Dwight.

To Joseph Patrick Tumulty, with Enclosures

[The White House, c. Aug. 27, 1920]

I fully concur in the Secretary's conclusions & w'd be deeply obliged to him if he w'd prepare for my signature the proper letters & documents to carry out his recommendations   W.W.

ALI (WP, DLC).

ENCLOSURE   I

From William Bauchop Wilson

Memorandum for the President.

My dear Mr. President: Washington August 27, 1920.

Referring to the Anthracite Coal Commission's report which you transmitted for my consideration, I am of the opinion that the report should be accepted and printed, with the modifications which I am suggesting hereafter.

In addition to the minority report, there has been protest entered on behalf of the miners by Thomas Kennedy, Chairman of their Scale Committee, against the majority award, and the suggestion made that "you use the powers of your high office to have the majority report set aside and that the Commission be reconvened to modify their proposals or the minority report be accepted as the basis of the award by the President." By the terms of the submission it was not intended that the President should make any award. It was proposed by the President that he would appoint "a commission to hear and decide the questions in dispute between the anthracite coal operators and miners." Both the operators and miners accepted the proposition and agreed to abide by the award of the Commission. The Commission has now reached a conclusion by the decision of a majority of the members. There is also a minority report. The conclusion of the Commission as expressed by its majority should be accepted by both sides insofar as it is within the terms of the submission.

There is, however, one provision in the award and one statement in the minority report that I particularly desire to call to your attention. Mr. Kennedy in the protest I have referred to says, concerning the majority report of the Commission: It "contains provisions that will make for trouble and turmoil in the anthracite region and its denial of justice in its wage provisions will intensify matters. Its proposed provision for the payment of back money due in several payments is an insult to the anthracite mine workers and sets aside the common accepted principle of payment of back money in one full payment." Mr. Kennedy's protest against any of the provisions of the award that are within the terms of the submission should not be acceded to, but his communication raises the question of whether or not the manner of payment of back pay was within the jurisdiction of the Commission.

In a communication to the operators and miners of the Anthracite Wage Scale Committee under date of May 21, 1920,[1] you said: "I shall insist that the matters in dispute be submitted to the determination of a commission to be appointed by me, the award of the commission to be retroactive to the first of April in accordance with the arrangement you have already entered into." That was one of the bases of submission, and in my judgment excludes from the jurisdiction of the Commission the entire question of back pay and its manner of payment. A disposition is being shown in some quarters to discredit the report of the Commission in advance of its publication. If it can be shown that the Commission, even in a minor matter, exceeded its jurisdiction, it will give opportunity of accentuating discontent. No stronger means could be used to tide them over the period when discontent can be fomented than the knowledge that their back pay would be paid to them in a lump sum and can not be received at all unless they accept the award of the Commission. For this reason the last paragraph in Section G of the award on Demand No. 2 should be stricken out from the award as beyond the jurisdiction of the Commission, and the balance of the award accepted, printed, and put into effect.

In the minority report Mr. Ferry says: "In order that you may have our point of view in brief form, however, and may have quickly accessible the facts and principles on which we have based our case before the Commission, we are submitting herewith and making an integral part of this report the following documents." Then follows a list of documents, including the opening and closing statements of Mr. Philip Murray, representing the mine workers, the report to the Chairman by his economic expert and adviser and correspondence resulting therefrom, and a series of monographs prepared for the mine workers for submission and rejected by the Commission as not being relevant to the case. These documents represent in part the miners' side of the controversy. So far as I am aware there is only one reason that can justify the publication of them, and that is, to inform the public of the reasons that have guided the minority in making its report. I look upon the suggestion as being unfair to the minority, unfair to the majority, unfair to the public, and not at all within the terms of the submission. It would certainly be unfair to the minority member of the Commission to give to the public the impression that he had arrived at his conclusions solely upon the evidence presented by the United Mine Workers and without giving consideration to the evidence presented by the other side. It would be unfair to the other members of the Commission because the evidence upon which they acted was not given to the public. It would be unfair to the public because it would give them only a one sided story. If any of the argument and evidence is to be printed at public expense, it should all be printed. As near as I can estimate the amount of material submitted to the Commission, it would make upwards of two thousand pages of solid printed matter and a number of pages of tabulations. The cost of printing would be many thousands of dollars for which no appropriation is available. There is sufficient appropriation to print the report if these documents are not added. No one ever thinks of asking a court to print the evidence and argument upon which it arrives at its conclusions, but each side is at liberty to print any or all of the evidence and argument that it believes to be to its interest to publish. I can see no reason why that course should not be pursued in the case of a wage commission which is a judicial body. If either side desires the publication of the matter presented to the Commission, it should appeal to Congress for an appropriation for that purpose.

For these reasons a letter should be sent by you thanking the members of the Commission, the majority and minority, for their work and the integrity of their action, advising them that the decision relative to back pay is beyond their jurisdiction and not effective, and that the evidence and argument can not be printed unless and until Congress has made an appropriation for that purpose. The report should then be printed, with your letter to the Commission giving your reasons for the action taken.

Under the terms of the submission it was provided that "when the award of the Commission is made it will be written into an agreement between the anthracite operators and miners in such manner as the Commission may determine." The Commission has made no finding concerning the manner in which the award should be written into an agreement between the operators and miners, further than to say that "the Commission approves the request for recognition of the United Mine Workers of America as party to the agreement in adjusting the differences between the operators and miners in all their contractual relations between the parties, and directs that the form of contract entered into as provided in this award shall be between Districts 1, 7 and 9 of the United Mine Workers of America, as represented by the Presidents of the three Districts, and the anthracite operators." The representatives of Districts 1, 7 and 9 of the United Mine Workers and the representatives of the operators of those Districts should be immediately called into conference for the purpose of writing into a mutual agreement the award of the Commission.

If you so desire I shall be glad to undertake the arrangements for that purpose, and will also look after the matter of printing the report.   Faithfully yours,   W B Wilson

TLS (WP, DLC).
  ¹ Printed at that date in Vol. 65.

ENCLOSURE II

(Proposed letter to the Members of the Anthracite Coal Commission.)

Messrs. W. O. Thompson, Chairman,
  W. L. Connell,
  Neal J. Ferry,
           Members, Anthracite Coal Commission.

Gentlemen: August 27, 1920.

I am in receipt of the report, findings, and award of the United States Anthracite Coal Commission, and the minority report thereon, and take this opportunity of thanking each of you for your painstaking and intelligent application to a just solution of the difficult and delicate problems you had to deal with and the conscientious manner in which you have arrived at your conclusions. While the adjudication of any dispute necessarily results in some disappointments, I am sure that the spirit with which you have acted will receive the commendation of the great bulk of the American people. I accept the conclusions of the majority, within the limits of its jurisdiction under the terms of the submission, as being the award of the Commission.

Protest has been entered on behalf of the miners by Mr. Thomas Kennedy, Chairman of the Scale Committee of the miners, against that portion of the award which provides for the payment of back money due in several payments. That raises the question of whether or not the decision on that point exceeds the terms of the submission. In a communication to the operators and miners of the Anthracite Wage Scale Committee under date of May 21, 1920, I said: "I shall insist that the matters in dispute be submitted to the determination of a commission to be appointed by me, the award of the commission to be retroactive to the first of April in accordance with the arrangement you have already entered into." That was one of the bases of submission and excludes from the jurisdiction of the Commission the entire question of back pay and its manner of payment. For this reason the last paragraph of Section G of the award on Demand No. 2 should be stricken out, and the balance of the award accepted, printed, and put into effect.

In the minority report Mr. Ferry states that he is submitting certain documents and making them an integral part of his report. If it is the intent to have these documents printed as an integral part of the minority report, it would seem to me to be manifestly beyond the purview of the work of the Commission. These documents represent in part the miners' side of the controversy. So far as I am aware there is only one reason for the publication of them, and that is, to inform the public of the evidence that has guided the minority in making its report. I am sure that the minority member of the Commission does not desire to give to the public the impression that he had arrived at his conclusions solely upon the evidence presented by the United Mine Workers and without giving consideration to the evidence presented by the other side. The publication of the documents referred to without at the same time publishing the balance of the evidence and arguments would undoubtedly create that impression. If any of the argument and evidence is to be printed at public expense, it should all be printed. That would require several thousand pages of solid printed matter and a great number of pages of tabulations. The cost of printing would be many thousands of dollars for which no appropriation is available. No one ever thinks of asking a court to print the evidence and argument on which it arrives at its conclusions, but each side is at liberty to print any or all of the evidence and argument that it believes to be to its interest to publish. I can see no reason why that course should not be pursued in the case of a wage commission which is a judicial body. If either side desires the publication by the Government of the matter presented to the Commission, it should appeal to Congress for an appropriation for that purpose.

In directing these changes, which, after all, are but minor matters, I want to be understood as having a high appreciation of the great task you have performed and the splendid services you have rendered to the country.   Sincerely yours,[1]

T MS (WP, DLC).
[1] This was sent verbatim as WW to W. O. Thompson and others, Aug. 30, 1920, TLS (Letterpress Books, WP, DLC).

To Bainbridge Colby

My dear Mr. Secretary: The White House 27 August, 1920

Thank you for your kindness in sending me the parcel received from the Foreign Office in London on behalf of Lord Robert Cecil.[1] I hope that you will ask Mr. Davis to convey to Lord Robert an expression of my warm appreciation, and particularly of my deep pleasure with the inscription in the volume, together with my warm personal regards.

Cordially and faithfully yours,   Woodrow Wilson

TLS (SDR, RG 59, 811.001W69/906, DNA).
   [1] About which, see R. Cecil to WW, July 1, 1920, Vol. 65.

From George A. Foster

Sir: Concord, N. H. August 27, 1920.

In reply to your inquiry of August 26, relative to "Harlakenden House," I am inclosing herewith copy of letter just received from Mrs. Churchill.[1]

I think this answers your inquiries but if it does not please call upon me again for any further information as I should be very glad to furnish same.   Yours very truly,   G A Foster

TLS (WP, DLC).
   [1] Mabel Harlakenden Hall (Mrs. Winston) Churchill to G. A. Foster, Aug. 27, 1920, TCL (WP, DLC). Mrs. Churchill gave details about the heating of the house and concluded that all but the west wing, which could be closed off, could be kept "very comfortable" in winter. She did not give any cost estimate for the annual upkeep of the house but said only that "a small family would be very comfortable there with four servants or even three."

To Josephus Daniels

My dear Mr. Secretary: The White House 28 August, 1920

Just a word in your ear:

I received recently a number of messages about departmental business through third persons (Doctor Grayson and others) and I write to beg that you will communicate with me directly whenever there is anything that it is necessary for me to decide. Communicating through third persons leads to all sorts of delays not only, but all sorts of vagueness in the statement of the business.

I am sure you will understand and acquiesce.

Cordially and faithfully yours,   Woodrow Wilson

TLS (J. Daniels Papers, DLC).

From Bainbridge Colby

My dear Mr. President: Washington August 28, 1920.

I have received your letter of August 25, and I have read the enclosure transmitted therewith with much concern. The telegram addressed to you on August 6, by the President of Haiti, and referred to in his communication, was sent from the White House to this Department for acknowledgment. It seemed proper that the Department's reply should be conveyed through the American Minister at Port-au-Prince, and he was accordingly instructed by telegraph on August 12, to leave with the President of Haiti a note verbale, of which I beg to transmit a copy herewith.[1] Acknowledgment also will be made of this further communication from President Dartiguenave in accordance with your instruction.

The situation in Haiti has been a difficult one for some months past. The Haitian Government has adopted an attitude of frank antagonism to our Legation and to the American officials whose appointment was provided for by the Treaty between the United States and Haiti of September 16, 1915.[2] This attitude of antagonism has rendered impracticable the necessary cooperation between the two Governments in carrying out the objects of the Treaty, which as you may recall, provided for the maintenance of the tranquility of Haiti, for the taking of steps to remedy the condition of the Republic's revenues and finances and in general for the carrying out of plans for the economic development and prosperity of the country.

The chief source of difficulty has been the refusal of the Haitian Government to abide by the agreement which it entered into with this Government on August 24 of 1918, to submit all legislation to the American Legation for approval before passage and promulgation. The result of this refusal on the part of the Haitian Government has been the passage recently of many laws reported by our Legation to be unsound and uneconomic, which rendered impossible the achievement of the aims of the Treaty of 1915.[3] The Haitian Government likewise has been unwilling to accept the recommendations of our Treaty officials looking towards the adoption of measures believed to be necessary for the wellbeing of the country and in the best interests of the Haitian people themselves.[4]

During the past two years, in order to make the financial situation of the Government easier, this Government has not insisted upon a strict interpretation of Article 5 of the Treaty, which provides that all sums collected by the General Receiver of Customs shall be first applied to the payment of the salaries and allowances of the General Receiver and the Financial Adviser; secondly, to the interest and sinking fund of the public debt; thirdly, to the maintenance of the constabulary; and lastly, to the payment of the current expenses of the Haitian Government. Upon definite refusal of the Haitian Government, however, to cooperate with this Government in carrying out the objects of the Treaty, the American Minister notified the Haitian Government that until cooperation between the two governments was once more made possible by a change in the attitude of the Haitian Government, the Government of the United States would insist upon strict observance of the provisions of Article 5 of the Treaty. It is this action, resulting in the temporary suspension of the salaries of the Haitian officials, which is alluded to by President Dartiguenave in his telegram of August 6. I believe the present crisis would probably have been prevented by the exercise of more tact and discretion on the part of our officials in Haiti.

In view of the situation which now exists, it has appeared advisable to Secretary Daniels and myself that the Military Representative of the United States in Haiti should be at Port-au-Prince. Admiral Snowden,[5] who at present holds that position, is likewise Military Governor of Santo Domingo, and is too much occupied with his duties in the latter Republic to devote the attention now necessary to his duties in Haiti. It seems, therefore, advisable that Admiral Snowden be relieved of these additional duties and that Admiral Knapp[6] be appointed Military Representative of the United States in Haiti. I have great confidence in Admiral Knapp's judgment and discretion and in his ability to cope with the situation because of his past experience.

While I have received information which leads me to believe that the Haitian Government is already willing to adopt a more conciliatory attitude, a personal element has entered into the situation, and the members of the Haitian Government seem reluctant to make any concessions at the present time to our officials in Port-au-Prince. I beg to suggest to you, therefore, the desirability of appointing Admiral Knapp your personal representative in Haiti, as well as Military Representative, in order that he may be enabled, during the period of his stay in Haiti, to deal directly with the members of the Haitian Government, either alone or jointly with our Minister, and be thus enabled to adjust more easily the difficult and unfortunate situation which has arisen.

Faithfully yours,   Bainbridge Colby

TLS (WP, DLC).
¹ The *note verbale* was included in BC to A. Bailly-Blanchard, Aug. 12, 1920, printed in *FR 1920*, II, 774-76. It stated that the action of the American Minister in cutting off the salaries of Dartiguenave and other Haitian officials had been taken because of the

recent disinclination of the Haitian government to cooperate with American officials in carrying out the terms of the treaty of 1915. However, the American Minister had been instructed that he might suspend the cut-off of the salaries if, in his opinion, this might lead to a better understanding and greater inclination to cooperate on the part of the Haitian government.

² About this treaty, see the index references under "Haiti, and treaty" in Vol. 34.

³ For a list and summary of these laws, see the Haitian Department of State for Foreign Affairs to the State Department, c. Sept. 8, 1920, printed in *FR 1920*, II, 789-93.

⁴ For a summary, see *ibid.*, pp. 794-96.

⁵ Rear Adm. Thomas Snowden.

⁶ That is, Harry Shepard Knapp.

From Edward Nash Hurley

Dear Mr. President: Chicago August Twenty Eighth 1920

The business interests of Great Britain are buying the control, at exceptionally low prices, of many industrial corporations in Germany and Austria, with the understanding that they are to furnish working capital.

Other British firms are furnishing raw materials to manufacturers in Germany and Austria and these raw materials are manufactured into finished products, and, on order of the British the goods are shipped to England or for export to other countries in British ships.

The British are also working on a similar plan for Italy. France is putting forth every effort to cooperate with Poland on the same basis, and a bitter commercial rivalry now exists between England and France owing to Great Britain's aggressive methods.

On account of the unfortunate fact that we are not at peace with Germany and Austria there is a feeling of fear on the part of many that we should not publicly express a desire to trade, or to be helpful to these two countries.

My thought is that the Government should urge our business interests to work out a plan that would enable France, Belgium, Italy, Poland, Germany and Austria to purchase our raw materials, farm and manufactured products without the financial aid of our Government, but one in which our Treasury Department could acquiesce.

I have discussed this vital matter with the Secretary of Commerce' Office, but, as it is so much a matter of general administration policy, I thought it wise to briefly discuss it with you in this way. If you are interested in a plan I will be very glad to work it out and place it in the hands of the Government Agency that you designate.

I am delighted that you are recovering so rapidly. With kind personal regards, I am,   Cordially yours,   Edward N. Hurley

TLS (WP, DLC).

From Francis Bowes Sayre, Jr.

Dear Grandfather: [Vineyard Haven, Mass., c. Aug. 28, 1920]

How are you? We are well. This is a nice beach. I can swim. I like to row. Will you come and see us? Please write me a letter.

With love from all   X X X   Francis

ALS (WP, DLC).

From Enoch Williams and Others

Wilkes-Barre, Penna., August 29, 1920.

WHEREAS, we the representatives of the United Mine Workers of America, of District Number One, at a meeting held August 28, 1920, urge the acceptance of the minority report of the commission appointed by you to make the awards in the anthracite region as we believe that the acceptance of said report is the only means to promote peace in the anthracite region and

WHEREAS, It was also decided at this meeting in the city of Wilkes-Barre that we wish an answer on or before September first, 1920, otherwise all men will refrain from work. Signed

Enoch Williams, Chairman,
305 West Taylor St., Taylor, Pa.;
Martin McDonough, 123 North Cameron
Avenue, Scranton, Pa.;
Lewis Davis, 447 East South St., Wilkes-Barre, Pa.;
Garfield Lewis, 305 Milwaukee Ave., Old Forge, Pa.;
Rinaldo Capellini, 17 Champerline St., Plainesville, Pa.

T telegram (WP, DLC).

From William Bauchop Wilson, with Enclosure

Memorandum for the President.

My dear Mr. President: Washington August 30, 1920.

Referring to the telegram from Enoch Williams, and others, representatives of the United Mine Workers of America of District No. 1, which you were kind enough to refer to me for my advice, I am of the opinion that a telegram similar to the draft which I herewith inclose should be sent to this committee and a copy of it given to the public.

I am returning the telegram herewith.

Faithfully yours,   W B Wilson

TLS (WP, DLC).

E N C L O S U R E

THE WHITE HOUSE August 30, 1920.

Replying to your telegram of August twenty-ninth, your attention is particularly directed to the following language contained in the minority report of Mr. Ferry of the Anthracite Coal Commission,

"In conclusion, Mr. President, we wish to say as we did in the beginning that the Majority Report shall have the full practical acceptance of the officers of the United Mine Workers of America, and we shall devote ourselves to its application, as we obligated ourselves to do when we submitted our cause to this Commission."

That was the manly and honest thing for Mr. Ferry to do. He courageously sets forth his views in the minority report and then just as courageously declares he will abide by the decision of the majority, as the miners had obligated themselves to do. It should be understood that there was no agreement between the operators and miners to have me decide the questions at issue. With the many other important duties devolving upon me I could not have devoted the time necessary to hear and digest all of the evidence presented. I therefore proposed the creation of a commission whose findings would be binding upon both parties. The representatives of the miners on the Scale Committee declined to accept the suggestion until it had been submitted to a convention of the United Mine Workers of Districts One, Seven and Nine. In that convention by a vote of the men direct from the mines a resolution was adopted accepting the proposition and solemnly obligating the mine workers to abide by the award. By all the laws of honor upon which civilization rests, that pledge should be fulfilled. Any intimation that the anthracite mine workers will refuse to work under the award because it does not grant them all that they expected is a reflection upon the sincerity of the men who constitute the backbone of the community in which they live. Collective bargaining would soon cease to exist in industrial affairs if contracts solemnly entered into can be set aside by either party whenever it wills to do so. I am sure that the miners themselves would vigorously protest against the injustice of the act if the President attempted to set aside the award of the Commission because the operators had protested it.

May I add that I am personally and officially interested in promoting the welfare of every man who has to work for a living. Every influence my Administration has been able to exert has been exercised to improve the standards of living of the nation's working men and women without doing any injustice to other portions of our people. A large part of the domestic fuel supply of the eastern States is dependent upon the continued operation of the anthracite coal mines. Any prolonged stoppage of production will mean hardship and suffering to many people, including millions of wage workers and their families. Yet if your communication, declaring your intention to refrain from working unless I set aside the award of the Anthracite Coal Commission on or before September 1, 1920, is intended as a threat, you can rest assured that your challenge will be accepted and that the people of the United States will find some substitute fuel to tide them over until the real sentiment of the anthracite mine workers can find expression and they are ready to abide by the obligations they have entered into.

You are therefore advised that I can not and will not set aside the judgment of the Commission, and I shall expect the anthracite mine workers to accept the award and carry it into effect in good faith.   Woodrow Wilson.[1]

T MS (Letterpress Books, WP, DLC).
    [1] Tumulty, in JPT to EBW, Aug. 30, 1920, TLS (WP, DLC), strongly urged that Wilson approve this telegram. Wilson did so and it was sent, as well as given to the press, on the evening of August 30. See, for example, the *New York Times*, Aug. 31, 1920. The T MS of the proposed telegram was pasted in the Letterpress Books.

To Franklin Delano Roosevelt

Dear Mr. Roosevelt: The White House 30 August, 1920.

Acknowledging receipt of your letter, tendering your resignation as Assistant Secretary of the Navy, I take occasion upon the acceptance of the same, to express appreciation of the able, efficient, and patriotic service you rendered your country in that responsible position during the seven and a half years of your incumbency embracing the period of the World War when the navy's contribution won world appreciation.

With congratulations upon the distinguished honor that has come to you and with cordial greetings and sincere good wishes, I am   Faithfully yours,   Woodrow Wilson[1]

TLS (F. D. Roosevelt Papers, NHpR).
    [1] Wilson repeated verbatim a draft of this letter (T MS, WP, DLC) sent to him in JD to WW, Aug. 27, 1920, TLS (WP, DLC).

To Bainbridge Colby

My dear Mr. Secretary: The White House 30 August, 1920

Thank you for your letter of August twenty-eighth about the trouble in Haiti.

I am quite ready to concur in your suggestion that Admiral Knapp be assigned to the post of Attache there, but my mind stumbles a little at your suggestion that he be designated as my personal representative. Will not that introduce an element of confusion? As I understand it, every Minister and every Ambassador is, in the view of international law, my personal representative, and I should suppose that designating Admiral Knapp as my personal representative will put him upon an equal footing with the Minister to Haiti and confuse their functions and authorities. Is it not so? But perhaps I do not understand as clearly as I should what you had in mind.

I will be very much obliged if you would show this letter to the Secretary of the Navy and confer with him in any way that is convenient in the circumstances.

I take it for granted that the newspapers were not correct in stating that a warship had been sent to Danzig, because the matter had never been mentioned to me and is a very serious step in the circumstances.

Cordially and faithfully yours,   Woodrow Wilson

TLS (B. Colby Papers, DLC).

From the Diary of Josephus Daniels

August Tuesday 31 1920

WW at cabinet meeting asked if I had ordered ship to Dantzig— as the papers printed. Yes, at the request of the State Department for the protection of American citizens

"Rats" he said. That is the excuse always given for sending ships that ought not to go, French & British wish them to help out We have no right there & State Dept ought not to have asked ship.

To Bainbridge Colby, with Enclosure

My dear Mr. Secretary: The White House 31 August, 1920

Referring to the enclosed telegram from Minister Crane, I would be very much obliged if you would instruct him to express to Counselor Tenney[1] my warm personal appreciation of the services he has rendered this Government and the Chinese people and my earnest hope and request that he will not retire but will remain with the Legation and continue to perform services which have become invaluable.

Cordially and faithfully yours,   Woodrow Wilson

TLS (B. Colby Papers, DLC).
  [1] Charles Daniel Tenney.

E N C L O S U R E

Peking, August 30, 1920.

Our valued counsellor Tenney plans to retire soon and return to America. His many years fine service to China in various capacities as educator and legation secretary; his unfailing sympathy, wisdom and devotion have so established him in the minds and hearts of both government and people that there is great dismay. No one has been held in such esteem with them since our other famous secretary, Dr. S. Wells Williams.[1] President Hsu[2] has sent him an appeal and our colleagues at the legation have expressed themselves in the same sense, as there is no one among them so competent and influential to advise just now. I shall miss him very much and feel that his going will be serious loss. He is in excellent condition and I believe a word of appreciation from you would hold him during our administration.

Mrs. Crane[3] is well and happy here. We send you and Mrs. Wilson affectionate messages and are happy to learn that you are prospering.   Crane.

T telegram (B. Colby Papers, DLC).
  [1] Samuel Wells Williams, missionary, Sinologist, diplomat; Secretary of the American legation in Peking, 1856-1876.
  [2] That is, Hsü Shih-ch'ang.
  [3] That is, Cornelia Workman Smith Crane.

To Francis Bowes Sayre, Jr.

My dear Francis: [The White House] 31 August, 1920

It was a real pleasure to get your letter, and I was delighted to see that you had written it yourself. You may be sure that I am very anxious to come and see you all. The only question is whether I shall be well enough to get that far away or not.

I am glad to hear that you can swim and to learn from your letter that you are all well. Please give my love to all, and keep plenty for yourself.

    Your affectionate grandfather,   [Woodrow Wilson]

CCL (WP, DLC).

From Jessie Kennedy Dyer[1]

My dear Uncle Woodrow: Memphis, Tenn. Aug. 31—'20.
    Please do not ignore this letter, but let me have a reply, of some kind, at your earliest convenience. You have always been mighty good about answering my letters and I hope you will find it convenient to answer this one at an early date. I am going to open my heart to you and appeal to you for help. We are strictly "up against it," to use a common expression. Our rent has been raised twice in less than a month and we were paying *all* we could afford to pay at first. Mr. Dyer's salary is only $150.00 a month and he is getting as good salary as is paid any one in his profession here (undertaker & embalmer). With rent raised, price of coal almost twice what we had to pay last year, water rates, gas rates, light rates, street car fare and almost everything else higher than it has ever been and no more money coming in than before these things went up, what can we do? We can't possibly meet these increased rates feed & clothe & school our three children and keep our heads above water to save our lives. The house we are in is an *old* place with no bath, no hot water connections and no way of heating except grates. We could rent out a room and get back part of rent but no one wants a room in a house like this. Here is what I want to do but can't because I haven't the necessary money to make even the initial cash payment. I want to buy a moderately priced place, pay 6 or 7 thousand for it and pay for it by the month. If we could borrow the purchase price from some one and pay cash for the place we could get a better place for less money. We can't afford to borrow just the first cash payment for this reason—we could not possibly make monthly payments on house, on loan and keep up taxes, insurance and so forth. Our *only* chance would be to borrow entire amount from one person and give them a mortgage on house: monthly notes could be made and deed on place be held by lender until place would be paid for. Can you help us out in this? No one knows how I hate to appeal to you or *any one* for this kind of help but I am getting desperate. We are having to live now in a neighborhood where our children have to be thrown with children that we don't want them to be with at all and I'm sorry to say they are not the children we brought to Mp. at all, as hard as I try to keep them

good & pure. I can't stand to think that we will be compelled to put up with this, and maybe worse, indefinitely. Mr. Dyer is doing the very best he can and works day & night, sick or well. He does not know that I am making this appeal to you and I wont tell him of it unless you see fit to make us the loan. I will see to it that you get your monthly payments and I assure you that you will not lose by your kindness but will gain the gratitude of a desperate mother who is anxious for her children to have a better home and better surroundings. I will work my finger nails off but what you are re-paid every cent you lend us. I will anxiously await a reply to this letter and will, of course, hope for a *favorable* reply but rest assured I will bear you no ill will if you feel that you cannot comply with my request. I will expect you to keep this to yourself *please*, as I do not intend to mention to any one that I have written to you. Love from all.   Lovingly—Your niece Jessie K. Dyer

Marion broke her right arm a few weeks ago—getting along O.K. Was compound fracture just above wrist. Another extra expense.

ALS (WP, DLC).
    [1] Mrs. Harvey H. Dyer, Wilson's niece, daughter of Anderson Ross Kennedy and Marion Williamson Wilson Kennedy.

George Creel to Edith Bolling Galt Wilson

Dear Mrs. Wilson: New York City August 31, 1920.

I must confess that it took me off my feet to receive the President's almost casual letter that carried in it an agreement to my proposition.[1]

I will see Harpers at once, and will come to Washington some time in September for a talk with you, if you will let me. Any number of things are coming up, and each one is bigger than the other.

I enclose a letter that is only one of hundreds that I receive.[2]

I am at the present moment making up my mind whether to give the next two months to the campaign. To satisfy my conscience, I made offer of my services at once, and felt myself fortunate to be snubbed, and even ignored. However, a tremendous change has come over them, and I am now considered indispensable.

With devoted regards to you and the President, I am as always
                        Sincerely,   George Creel

TLS (EBW Papers, DLC).
    [1] See the Enclosure printed with WW to G. Creel, Aug. 26, 1920.
    [2] It is missing

From the Diary of Josephus Daniels

1920 Wednesday 1 September

Colby showed me letter from the President saying he was surprised to see in the papers that a ship had been ordered to Danzig. I had ordered it at C's request. C— wrote President the reasons, he had information that American refugees had been coming into D & thought it wise for their protection, & had not thought it necessy to confer with Prdt & he regretted it, & said I hoped to detain Huse before he reached D—. WW wants to be consulted & keep in touch with all things growing out of treaty Colby told me that he had since had information that an Am. ship going into D— might be misunderstood

W.W. had objected to Knapp's going as his personal representative, as suggested by Colby at K's request. I told him I agreed with WW & thought all Knapp needed was a letter from him & his mission was to compose differences and that I would regard a military govt as a tragedy.

Lejeune & Butler[1] left for Haiti to study conditions and to make reports as to marine occupation. They do not like possibility of Knapp's being in charge of marines on the island.

[1] That is, Maj. Gen. John Archer Lejeune and Brig. Gen. Smedley Darlington Butler, about whose earlier experiences in Haiti, see Anne Cipriano Venzon, "The Papers of Smedley Darlington Butler, USMC, 1915-1918," Ph.D. dissertation, Princeton University, 1982.

To David Franklin Houston

My dear Mr. Secretary: [The White House] 1 September, 1920

I would be very much obliged if you would read the enclosed copy of a letter from Mr. Edward N. Hurley[1] and let me have your comments and views upon it.

Cordially and faithfully yours,   [Woodrow Wilson]

CCL (WP, DLC).
[1] E. N. Hurley to WW, Aug. 28, 1920. Wilson also sent Hurley's letter to Joshua W. Alexander in WW to J. W. Alexander, Sept. 1, 1920, CCL (WP, DLC).

To Bainbridge Colby, with Enclosure

My dear Mr. Secretary: The White House 1 September, 1920

The enclosed letter from the Undersecretary of State raises a question similar to the one I wrote you about recently in connection with Haiti, that is to say, the question of the status of the functions of the "personal representatives." I am inclined to acquiesce in the course suggested by Mr. Davis but would like first to have your own opinion with regard to the complications that might arise if we in effect had two Ministers in Cuba at the same time.

Cordially and faithfully yours,   Woodrow Wilson

ENCLOSURE

From Norman Hezekiah Davis

My dear Mr. President: Washington [Aug. 31, 1920]

On July 28, last, Secretary Colby sent to you a letter[1] regarding the developments which had arisen in connection with the Presidential elections to be held in Cuba next November, recommending, in view of our special responsibilities in Cuba, the publication by our Legation in Habana of a statement which should make plain the policy of our Government concerning these elections, and suggesting the desirability of sending to Cuba after the coming elections your personal representative to confer with the President-elect and inform him that this Government expected the coming administration to undertake a definite program of reform. The recommendations made in this letter received your approval.[2]

Because of recent disquieting changes in the political situation in Cuba, it is feared that the publication of the statement recommended in Secretary Colby's letter will not alone suffice to insure the holding of fair elections next November or to prevent all possibility of an armed revolt by the members of one of the political parties. I beg therefore to suggest that the visit of your personal representative to Cuba be made immediately instead of after the elections.

You will recall that General Crowder in 1919, upon the invitation of President Menocal, went to Habana and collaborated with the leading members of both political parties in Cuba in effecting a revision of the Electoral Law. In November of the same year the Department of State urged President Menocal to extend to General Crowder an invitation to return to Cuba to witness the manner in which the Electoral Law he had taken such a large part in drafting was put into effect. This President Menocal refused to do, on the ground that his political opponents would herald General Crowder's visit as supervision of the coming elections by the United States, and would consider General Crowder's presence there a rebuke to his administration. President Menocal, however, gave positive assurances at that time that he himself would answer for the strict fulfillment of the Electoral Code, insofar as its fulfillment might depend upon his Government, and promised that the elections in November 1920 would be held with all possible guarantees and with the utmost impartiality. The Department thereupon instructed the American Minister at Habana[3] to accept the assurances given by President Menocal that the new Electoral Code would be carried out by the Cuban Government to the letter and in the spirit in which it was drafted, and to state that supervision of the elections would therefor[e] not be undertaken by the United States.

One of the promises most explicitly made by President Menocal was that his Government would guarantee that no fraud or intimidation would be permitted in the conduct of the elections, and that if any instances of this kind occurred they would be most vigorously prosecuted by the means provided for in the Electoral Code. Notwithstanding these definite assurances, the Department's attention has repeatedly been drawn to acts of fraud and violence which it is alleged the Conservative authorities have permitted or condoned.

While the Department has been able to secure accurate information concerning only a few of the many charges brought, it has reason to believe that numerous acts of fraud and violence have occurred during the electoral period which have not been prosecuted, and that in many instances the provisions of the Election Law have not been complied with. It would thus appear that notwithstanding President Menocal's assurances of last November, assassinations and acts of intimidation and fraud have taken place as they have in the past and the extreme measures which have been employed mostly by Conservatives in this early stage of the electoral period presage more radical means of coercion as the campaign develops.

On August 25, the Department of State was advised that the various Conservative factions, organized originally as separate parties as provided in the original draft of the Electoral Code, had arranged a coalition which was only made possible by the amendments to the Crowder Law, which amendments you will remember were approved by President Menocal notwithstanding the protest of the Department of State. As a result of this coalition Alfredo Zayas has been nominated as the candidate of the Conservative Party for the Presidency.

Upon the announcement of the formation of the Conservative coalition, the leaders of the Liberal Party, which is supporting the candidacy of José Miguel Gomez for the Presidency, threatened to abstain from the elections altogether and announced their intention of requesting this Government either to supervise the elections or to refrain from intervening in case a revolution took place.

The Legation has been instructed to publish at the earliest opportunity the statement of the policy of this Government which has been transmitted to it by the Department of State. Party animosity, however, is now so bitter and conditions have become so tense that it is now doubtful whether the statement to be published by our Legation will suffice to control the situation.

I believe that this Government must make every endeavor to avoid being called upon once more to intervene by force in Cuba in order to check a revolt brought about by one of the political parties which alleges that it is being defrauded because of the method in which the elections are being conducted by the party opposed to it.

In view of the reasons briefly set forth, I have therefore recommended that the visit of your personal representative to Cuba should be made immediately instead of after the elections, in order that he may now represent directly to the Cuban Government that because of its special obligations in Cuba this Government desires that steps be taken to have full investigation made of all charges brought regarding the conduct of the elections and to enforce strict compliance with the Electoral Code. If this suggestion meets with your approval, I beg to submit for your consideration the desirability of instructing your representative also to confer with the candidates of both parties and to state most forcibly to them that this Government desires that the elections shall be conducted in such a way as to secure a free expression of the will of the Cuban people. I beg to suggest that General Crowder be appointed to undertake this duty. There is no individual in whom so much confidence is justly placed by the members of both political parties in Cuba. It is thought that his presence there alone may do much to quiet the agitation now existing, and that his recommendations to the Cuban Government and to the candidates of the two political parties may bring about a return of popular confidence in the electoral machinery, and will likewise tend to have the salutary effect of restraining the Liberal Party from abstaining from the elections or from fomenting any active revolt on the ground that they are being prevented from freely exercising the right of suffrage. I feel constrained to make this suggestion to you because of my belief that this is one step, short of actual supervision, which may prevent this Government from being obliged to intervene once more in Cuba.

Faithfully yours,   Norman H. Davis

TLS (B. Colby Papers, DLC).
    [1] Printed at that date in Vol. 65.
    [2] Wilson wrote "Approved" on this letter.
    [3] That is, Boaz Walton Long.

To Bainbridge Colby

My dear Mr. Secretary: The White House 1 September, 1920

I would be very much obliged if you would refer the enclosed letter[1] to the experts who are preparing to advise me with regard to the boundaries of Armenia, in order to obtain their judgment about the particular case submitted.

Cordially and faithfully yours,   Woodrow Wilson

P.S. I would be obliged if you would have the gentlemen who wrote this letter apprised of the fact that it is receiving our careful consideration.

TLS (B. Colby Papers, DLC).
    [1] It was almost certainly H. C. Wallace to BC, Aug. 20, 1920, which was a digest of A. Aharonian and Boghos Nubar Pasha to WW, July 22, 1920, with numerous enclosures, reproduced in Appendix V, No. 9, W. L. Westermann, L. Martin, and H. G. Dwight, "Full Report of the Committee upon the Arbitration of the Boundary between Turkey and Armenia," T MS (WP, DLC). The communication from Aharonian and Boghos Nubar presented Armenian claims concerning the boundaries of the Armenian Republic.

Three Letters from Bainbridge Colby

My dear Mr. President: Washington September 1st, 1920.

I am just back from Provincetown this morning and I take up immediately your letters of August 30th and 31st, received in my absence. Of the several matters to which your letters relate, the matter that seems most to require instant attention is the dispatch of a warship to Danzig. I fear I have committed an error in this matter, and whether or not that be your judgment after reading the enclosed record, I deeply regret that it did not occur to me to submit the matter to you before acting.

The history of the matter is contained in the enclosed dispatch of August 24th from Ambassador Wallace,[1] the Department's letter bearing my signature, dated August 27th, addressed to the Secretary of the Navy, and his reply of August 28th.

The letter which I signed was prepared in the Department. It had been carefully considered and as my thought rested on it briefly in the rush of departmental business it seemed a proper and a consistent thing to do, in view of our information that a large number of refugees has been crowding into Danzig where conditions are unsettled and somewhat menacing. In fact, the Department has been strongly urged to make arrangements for granting visas en bloc in order to relieve the distress and pressure at that port.

The single end in view, i.e., the protection of American lives, was explained by cable to our Commissioner at Danzig.[2] This morning we are in receipt of a cable from him, that he believes the projected visit of a warship unnecessary for the purpose stated and that it may be given a political interpretation. I think therefore I should not hesitate to request that the vessel's orders be countermanded.

Let me repeat, my dear Mr. President, my sincere regret that I did not give the matter sufficient reflection to perceive the propriety and importance of submitting this matter for your approval.

Very respectfully yours,   Bainbridge Colby

[1] H. C. Wallace to SecState, Aug. 24, 1920, printed in *FR 1920*, III, 393-94. Colby's reply was BC to H. C. Wallace, Aug. 25, 1920, printed in *ibid.*, pp. 394-95.
[2] William Dawson.

My dear Mr. President: Washington September 1st, 1920.

The direction imposed upon you by Section 34 of the Merchant Marine Act, to give notice of the termination of certain treaty provisions, which are in conflict with the right of this government to impose discriminating duties and tonnage charges, has received our earnest and time-consuming examination and study. We have called into conference Secretary Alexander and Secretary Payne, and today we have had the advantage of a conference with Ambassador Davis, who was Solicitor General at the time a similar question was presented in connection with the Seamen's Act. The result of our study and conference is a notice in the form herewith enclosed.[1] It goes as far, I think, as possible in the direction of a literal compliance with the mandate of Congress, and stops short of a definitive breach of any treaty.

I think in view of the full discussion of the subject at last week's Cabinet meeting I need not go more fully by letter into the questions involved. If, however, there is any point upon which you desire a fuller discussion, I shall be glad to do my utmost to meet your wishes.   Very respectfully yours,   Bainbridge Colby

TLS (WP, DLC).
[1] The enclosure was a draft letter to Robert Underwood Johnson, T MS (WP, DLC). It instructed Johnson to present a copy of the Merchant Marine Act of 1920 to the Italian Minister for Foreign Affairs, calling his attention particularly to Section 34 (about which, see J. W. Alexander to WW, June 25, 1920, n. 2, Vol. 65), and to arrange with that official for the abrogation of those provisions of the Italian-American Treaty of Commerce and Navigation of 1871 which were nullified by Section 34.

My dear Mr. President: Washington September 1st, 1920.

Do you think it is inadvisable for any reason to give out the enclosed correspondence with the Polish Government?[1] Mr. Davis thinks it would be well to make it public. The Department has collected the notes in the form enclosed and before handing them out I would like your judgment.

The reasons for publishing it are as follows:

1. The fact that communications were being exchanged with the Polish Government has already been widely mentioned in the press.

2. The note of Premier Witos addressed to you has already found its way to publication through Polish channels.

3. The contents of the Polish communications have already been published in fragmentary form.

4. By not publishing the correspondence we are throwing around the subject an air of mystery which is reflected in the inquiries from the press, which are increasingly pointed and suggest that there is a divergence of view between this country and Poland, when quite the reverse is the fact.

Very respectfully yours,   Bainbridge Colby

TLS (WP, DLC).
¹ Offset copy of press release, dated September 1, 1920, reprinting the following documents:

K. Lubomirski to BC, Aug. 28, 1920, printed in *FR 1920*, III, 396-97. The Polish government, Lubomirski said, wished to thank Colby for the "essential principles" on the Polish situation expressed in BC to C. R. Avezzana, Aug. 10, 1920, printed as an Enclosure with BC to WW, Aug. 9, 1920. Colby's expression of support for Polish independence and territorial integrity, as well as his "open condemnation" of the Bolshevik government of Russia, had had a profound moral effect in turning the tide of the Polish-Soviet war during the battle of Warsaw. This war, the letter concluded, was a defensive war forced upon the Poles by the Bolshevik invasion and was not a war against the Russian people.

The second item was W. Witos to WW, July 31, 1920, printed as an Enclosure with BC to WW, Aug. 4, 1920.

The third item was BC to John Campbell White, Aug. 21, 1920, about which see WW to BC, Aug. 5, 1920, n. 1.

The fourth item was K. Lubomirski to BC, Aug. 30, 1920, printed in *FR 1920*, III, 397-98. This letter embodied the response of Prince Eustachy Kajetan Władysław Sapieha, the Polish Minister of Foreign Affairs, to Colby's note of August 21. Sapieha expressed appreciation for Colby's "friendly advice" but pointed out that Poland's provisional eastern frontier laid down by the Paris Peace Conference had not been respected by the Bolsheviks. "In spite of the diplomatic intervention of our allies," he wrote, "the red army has for a whole month advanced and ravaged territory which is admitted by all as being ethnografically Polish. Notwithstanding the sympathetic attitude of our allies, the Polish nation had to face the danger alone, and political events proved that it must in the first place rely upon its own military strength. If military operations necessitated the measures to prevent a renewed invasion of Poland, it could hardly be considered fair that artificial boundaries that do not bind our opponent should interfere with the military operations of the other."

From Francis Patrick Walsh

Dear Mr. President: Washington, D. C. September 1, 1920

Honorable Terence McSwiney, the democratically elected Mayor of one of Ireland's largest and most important municipalities, is confined in the Brixton jail in England, for the commission of acts which are held by the free peoples of the world to be not only in-nocent, but praiseworthy.[1]

He is dying of starvation, and his attending physicians assert that, unless immediately released, his death will ensue within the next twelve hours.

I have been requested by the organizations of American citizens of Irish blood, numbering millions in membership and sympathetic affiliation, to appeal to you to use your good offices to save his life.

If you could see your way clear to make direct official or personal appeal to Mr. Lloyd George, we feel sure that this tragedy would be averted.

We therefore beg of you to make this direct appeal, either offi-cially, or in the name of our common humanity.

With assurances of my deep despect [respect] and esteem, as always,   Sincerely yours,   Frank P. Walsh

Ackn & file   WW

TLS (WP, DLC).
[1] Terence Joseph MacSwiney, the Lord Mayor of Cork, was arrested and charged with sedition by British authorities in that city on August 12. He and others arrested with him promptly began a hunger strike. He was pronounced guilty of sedition by a court martial on August 16, was deported to England on a British destroyer a day later, and was lodged in Brixton Prison in London on August 18. *New York Times*, Aug. 13, 16-19, and 31, 1920. By August 31, he was reported to be in critical condition because of his refusal to take food, and a Roman Catholic chaplain and members of his family were allowed to be at the prison at all times. *Ibid.*, Sept. 1 and 5, 1920. MacSwiney's case had by this time become an international cause célèbre. As it turned out, he died in Brixton Prison on October 25 after seventy-four days of fasting. *Ibid.*, Oct. 26, 1920.

Two Letters to Bainbridge Colby

My dear Mr. Secretary: Washington 2 September, 1920

I think the instructions you drafted to be sent to Ambassador Johnson at Rome are certainly the proper instructions if we are going to act under the direction of Congress in this matter, but I have a strong feeling that inasmuch as it is clearly not the Consti-tutional right of Congress to direct the President to do anything whatever, particularly in regard to foreign affairs, I ought to stand stiff upon the prerogatives of the Presidential office. It is my own judgment, therefore, that it is best to take no action whatever in these matters. The binding force of treaties and the reciprocal ob-ligation which treaties imply are involved, and I think the matter altogether too sacred to be handled as Congress wishes it to be handled.[1]

Cordially and faithfully yours,   Woodrow Wilson

[1] The proposed instructions were never sent.

My dear Mr. Secretary: The White House 2 September, 1920

I think there is not only no objection to the publication of these papers, but that it is highly desirable that they should be published, and I hope that you will exercise your own judgment in the matter.[1]   Cordially and faithfully yours,   Woodrow Wilson

TLS (B. Colby Papers, DLC).
   [1] The press release summarized in BC to WW, Sept. 1, 1920 (third letter of that date), n. 1, was published in, e.g., the *New York Times*, Sept. 3, 1920.

To Joseph Patrick Tumulty, with Enclosures

Dear Tumulty: The White House [Sept. 2, 1920].

This is more than futile: it is grossly impertinent. I wish I knew some way to rebuke it. It is a piece of confounded impudence.
                                                The President.

TL (WP, DLC).

E N C L O S U R E   I

From Joseph Patrick Tumulty

Dear Governor: The White House, 2 September 1920.

I hate to pass this telegram on to you, but it is from a very good Irish friend of ours. I know how impossible it is to do anything, but I thought you would like to see this expression of opinion.
                                                Tumulty

TLS (WP, DLC).

E N C L O S U R E   I I

                          Chicago, Ills., September 2, 1920.

The League of Nations will be ratified in November if the President will make friendly representations to the Premier or King for Terrence McSwiney. He will also rehabilitate himself with the Irish people by this act.   George E. Brennan.[1]

T telegram (WP, DLC).
   [1] Brennan had emerged as the leader of the Democractic party in Chicago and in Illinois following the death of Roger C. Sullivan. *New York Times*, July 7, 1920.

From Bainbridge Colby

My dear Mr. President: Washington September 2nd, 1920.

There has been a crescendo pressure on the State Department for the last few days, in the shape of letters, telegrams (nearly a hundred), personal calls from "picketers," and Mr. Frank P. Walsh,—all asking some intercession in behalf of the Mayor of Cork, now in Brixton jail, and who seems to have brought himself to death's door by voluntary starvation.

It is needless for me to even mention to you the entire absence of legal justification for any representations or action on our part. McSwiney is a British subject, in jail as the result of the infraction of a British law, and the judgment of a presumably competent tribunal. Even on "humanitarian grounds,"—the basis of most of the appeals to which I have referred,—there seems to be a lack of support for any intervention, as the man is the victim of himself and no one else.

And yet—his death would be deplorable, and it's [its] effects not easy to estimate in advance.

The thought occurred to me that I might take advantage of my acquaintance with the officials of the British Embassy to express, in the most informal and friendly way, our concern for the effect on public opinion of a successful martyrdom, and the hope that the British government might find a way to avert the man's death, without too great a sacrifice of consistency.

Or—is the subject one which I had best let alone?

I enclose a letter received from Mr. Frank P. Walsh,[1] which I am told is identical with one which he addressed to you on this subject.   Very respectfully yours,   Bainbridge Colby

TLS (B. Colby Papers, DLC).
[1] F. P. Walsh to BC, Sept. 1, 1920, TLS (WP, DLC).

To Gordon Woodbury

My dear Mr. Woodbury: [The White House] 3 September, 1920

I very much appreciate your letter of the first of September.[1] You may be sure that it gave me real pleasure to designate you for your present post. I was, among other things, not unmindful of the fine family tradition which you represent.[2] I shall look forward with pleasure to our association.

Cordially and sincerely yours,   [Woodrow Wilson]

CCL (WP, DLC).
[1] G. Woodbury to WW, Sept. 1, 1920, TLS (WP, DLC).
[2] See JD to WW, Aug. 19, 1920.

To Joe Cowperthwaite[1]

                                      The White House
My dear Mr. Cowperthwaite: 3 September, 1920

It is my confident hope that I may again have the pleasure of visiting the Lake region in April of next year. I am writing to ask if it will be possible for you to accommodate my little party at that time. The party will consist of Mrs. Wilson and myself and Mrs. Wilson's brother.[2] I should like very much to have two connecting rooms for Mrs. Wilson and myself and, if possible, an adjoining bathroom; and for Mrs. Wilson's brother a bedroom convenient to a bath. I retain the most delightful memories of my former stay with you, and have only to beg that you will regard the information contained in this letter as private, inasmuch as it is my desire to travel next year *incognito*.

With the best wishes,

                        Sincerely yours,   Woodrow Wilson

TLS (received from the Willowsmere Hotel, Grasmere, England).
  [1] At this time, proprietor of the Prince of Wales Lake Hotel, Grasmere, England.
  [2] John Randolph Bolling.

From Albert Sidney Burleson, with Enclosure

My dear Mr. President: Washington, D. C. September 3, 1920.

I endeavor at all times to spare you the troubles and worries of the Postal establishment, and it is with sincere regret that I feel it necessary to impose on your time and attention by bringing before you a matter that has for months been the source of much worriment to me and about which I am in doubt as to the action that should be taken. During the war as you know the Congress passed the Espionage Act, copy of which I attach.[1] Under this act, as Postmaster General chargeable under the law with its enforcement, a number of magazines and newspapers were excluded from the mails, and the second class mail privilege of some of them withdrawn. The action of the Postmaster General in every instance without exception where it was challenged has been upheld by the Courts. After the Armistice certain newspapers and magazines, of the same character, against which action had been taken, made application for a renewal or the granting of the second class mailing privilege. An examination of a number of the issues of these publications discloses that the general tenor of the matter published therein has undergone no change, but on the contrary has in some instances become more extreme. In nearly every case there is an insidious attempt to keep within the letter of the law, but in effect to inculcate in the minds of their readers a belief that this Government should be overthrown by force, to encourage a belief in modern communism, to hold up as an ideal Government the Soviet System in vogue in Russia, to consolidate a class which, encouraged to accept as true that Capitalism is dominant in our Country, may be induced by direct action (as this term was used by the Third Internationale of Moscow) to aid in wresting the control of Government from this so-called capitalistic class. The ultimate effect of all this propaganda is an encouragement to violence and those crimes described in Section 211 of the Penal Code which declares matter tending to incite arson, murder, or assassination to be nonmailable.

The question troubling me is what action shall I take in cases of such publications where application is made on their behalf for the second class mailing privilege, and also what action shall I take in renewing this privilege to papers and magazines which during the war had this privilege withdrawn. If the Treaty of Peace had been ratified, it had been my purpose, as I informed you, to take up all applications of publications which were held in abeyance on account of violations of the wartime provisions of the Espionage Act and promptly dispose of them, but we are still technically at war and there is doubt in my mind as to whether any action should be taken on these cases until peace is accomplished.

I enclose a memorandum of the Solicitor for the Post Office Department with reference to cases arising under both the wartime legislation and our permanent laws, also a number of issues of "The Liberator,"[2] and the answer filed in my behalf in the New York Call case.[3] These show typical matter of the class in question. I invite your particular attention to paragraph forty-five, page twenty-nine, of the answer in the Call case.

Being desirous to conform to your wishes would appreciate it if you would examine these papers and drop me a line or advise me at the next Cabinet meeting what course you think I should take with reference to giving such publications the second class mailing privilege.   Faithfully,   A. S. Burleson

[1] This and the other enclosures mentioned in this letter (except for the memorandum by W. H. Lamar printed as the Enclosure) are missing. For discussions of the issue of the First-Amendment right of free speech and expression, including the question of mailability of obscene and incendiary materials, wartime legislation, etc., see David M. Rabban, "The First Amendment in Its Forgotten Years," *Yale Law Journal*, XC (Jan. 1981), 514-95; D. M. Rabban, "The Emergence of Modern First Amendment Doctrine," *University of Chicago Law Review*, L (Fall 1983), 1205-1355; James C. N. Paul and Murray L. Schwartz, *Federal Censorship: Obscenity in the Mail* (Glencoe, Ill., 1961); Dorothy G. Fowler, *Unmailable: Congress and the Post Office* (Athens, Ga., 1977); and Zechariah Chafee, Jr., *Free Speech in the United States* (Cambridge, Mass., 1941).

[2] About which, see W. Kent to WW, May 20, 1918, Vol. 48.

[3] That is, the case of the *New York Call*, which Lamar discusses in the Enclosure; see also Chafee, *Free Speech in the United States*, pp. 104, 184, n. 64, 304-305.

E N C L O S U R E
William Harmong Lamar to Albert Sidney Burleson

Washington September 3, 1920.

MEMORANDUM for the Postmaster General.

During the period of active hostilities the second-class mailing privilege was withdrawn from a number of radical papers for habitually carrying matter nonmailable under the Espionage Act. The second-class mailing privilege was also denied to a number of new publications carrying similar matter.

Since the armistice these publications have been clamoring for the second-class mailing privilege while continuing to carry this revolutionary matter. Acting under your general instructions, no action has been taken on these applications for the second-class mailing privilege, the Espionage Act being still in force.

Recently a mandamus proceeding was instituted by the New York Call in the Supreme Court of the District of Columbia to compel the Postmaster General to grant the second-class mailing privilege to that publication. The answer of the Postmaster General sets out numerous violations of the Espionage Act by the Call as his reason for revoking the second-class mailing privilege and declining to grant its application for a renewal of the second-class mailing privilege.

Paragraph forty-four of the answer avers that Section 211 of the Criminal Code makes nonmailable "matter of a character tending to incite arson, murder, or assassination," and that Section 2 of Title XII of the Espionage Act provides that "every letter, writing, circular, postal card, picture, print, engraving, photograph, newspaper, pamphlet, book, or other publication, matter or thing of any kind containing matter advocating or urging treason, insurrection, or forcible resistance to any law of the United States is hereby declared to be nonmailable," and that under these sections of the law the second-class mailing privilege should not be given to the Call in view of the matter quoted from its columns in the answer.

Judge Hitz[1] has just rendered a decision in favor of the Call in which he does not consider the merits of the case, but disposes of it upon the technical proposition that while the acts mentioned do make individual issues of a publication nonmailable, they do not authorize the withdrawal of the second-class mailing privilege or the refusal to grant the second-class mailing privilege in case of a violation of those laws by a publication. This decision is in direct

[1] William Hitz, judge of the Supreme Court of the District of Columbia, rendered his decision on August 25. There is a brief discussion of it in the *New York Times*, Aug. 26, 1920.

conflict with the decision of Justice Augustus Hand in the Federal Court at New York in the Masses case,[2] and in my opinion cannot be sustained. Directions have already been given to have an appeal taken from Judge Hitz's decision.

The effect of Judge Hitz's opinion, however, has been to renew the efforts of other publications which have had the second-class mailing privilege denied, and we may at an early date expect great activity in the class of publications affected. Already the Liberator, successor to the Masses, and published by Max Eastman, one of the most extreme radical publishers, is now pressing an application for the second-class mailing privilege.

A copy of the answer in the Call case and six issues of the Liberator are attached.

Under the conditions now presented, I think we should determine upon some definite policy in handling this class of cases. Allow me to review briefly the legislation under which we are operating:

Section 3893 of the Revised Statutes of the United States (now Section 211 of the Criminal Code) was amended by the Act of May 27, 1908, reading as follows:

"Every obscene, lewd, or lascivious book, pamphlet, picture, paper, letter, writing, print, or other publication of an indecent character, and every article or thing designed or intended for the prevention of conception or procuring of abortion, and every article or thing intended or adapted for any indecent or immoral use, and every written or printed card, letter, circular, book, pamphlet, advertisement, or notice of any kind giving information, directly or indirectly, where or how, or of whom, or by what means, any of the hereinbefore mentioned matters, articles, or things, may be obtained or made, whether sealed as first-class matter or not, are hereby declared to be non-mailable matter, and shall not be conveyed in the mails nor delivered from any post office nor by any letter carrier; and any person who shall knowingly deposit, or cause to be deposited, for mailing or delivery, anything declared by this section to be non-mailable matter, and any person who shall knowingly take the same, or cause the same to be taken, from the mails for the purpose of circulating or disposing of, or of aiding in the circulation or disposition of the same, shall, for each and every

[2] Augustus Noble Hand had ruled in the federal district court in New York on September 14, 1917, that the issue of *The Masses* for September 1917 had been properly excluded from the mails by the Post Office Department, thus directly contradicting the earlier opinion of his cousin, Judge Learned Hand, in regard to the August 1917 issue of the same periodical. About Learned Hand's decision, see n. 2 to the Enclosure printed with WW to ASB, July 13, 1917, Vol. 43. There is a brief discussion of A. N. Hand's opinion in the *New York Times*, Sept. 15, 1917.

offence, be fined upon conviction thereof not more than five thousand dollars, or imprisoned at hard labor not more than five years, or both, at the discretion of the court. And all offences committed under the section of which this is amendatory, prior to the approval of this act, may be prosecuted and punished under the same in the same manner and with the same effect as if this act had not been passed; Provided, That nothing in this act shall authorize any person to open any letter or sealed matter of the first class not addressed to himself." "And the term 'indecent' within the intendment of this section shall include matter of a character tending to incite arson, murder or assassination."

This action of Congress was immediately preceded by a letter of President Roosevelt, of which the following is a copy:

"The White House,
"To the Department of Justice: March 20, 1908.

"By my direction the Postmaster General is to exclude La Questione Sociale, of Paterson, N. J. from the mails, and it will not be admitted to the mails, unless by order of the court, or unless you advise me further that it must be admitted. Please see if it is not possible to prosecute criminally, under section of the law that is advisable, the men that are interested in sending out this anarchistic and murderous publication. They are, of course, the enemies of mankind, and every effort should be strained to hold them accountable for an offense far more infamous than that of our ordinary murderer.

"This matter has been brought to my attention by the mayor of the city of Paterson. I wish every effort made to get at the criminals under the Federal law. It may be found impossible to do this. I shall also through the Secretary of State, direct the attention of the governor of New Jersey to the circumstances, so that he may proceed under the State law, his attention being further drawn to the fact that the newspaper is circulated in other States.

"After you have concluded your investigation I wish a report to you to serve as a basis for recommendations by me for action by Congress. Under section 3893 of the Revised Statutes, lewd, lascivious and obscene books and letters, publications for indecent and immoral uses, or for an indecent and immoral nature, and postal cards upon which indecent and scurrilous epithets are written or printed, are all excluded from the mail, and provision is made for the fine and imprisonment of those guilty.

"The newspaper article in question advocates murder by dynamite. It specifically advocates the murder of enlisted men of the United States Army and the officers of the police force, and the burning of the houses of private citizens. The preaching of murder and arson is certainly as immoral as the circulation of obscene and lascivious literature, and if the practice is not already forbidden by the law it should be forbidden. The immigration law now prohibits the entry into the United States of any person who entertains or advocates the views expressed in this newspaper article.

"It is, of course, inexcusable to permit those already here to promulgate such views. Those who write, publish and circulate those articles stand on the level with those who use the mails for distributing poisons for the purpose of murder, and convictions have been obtained when the mails have been thus used for the distribution of poisons. No law should require the Postmaster General to become an accessory to murder by circulating literature of this kind.   Theodore Roosevelt."

The Department of Justice found that there was no law authorizing the Postmaster General to exclude such anarchistic matter, from the mails, nor any criminal statute warranting prosecution, and the matter was brought to the attention of Congress which promptly passed the Act of May 27, 1908, above quoted.

Prior to the passage of the Espionage Act, this was the only general legislation affecting anarchists or anarchistic publications except the immigration law which excluded alien anarchists from this country. The present immigration act of February 5, 1917, provides for the exclusion of "anarchists, or persons who believe in or advocate the overthrow by force or violence of the Government of the United States, or of all forms of law, or who believe in [the overthrow] or are opposed to organized Government, or who advocate the assassination of public officials, or who advocate or teach the unlawful destruction of property; persons who are members of or affiliated with any organization entertaining or teaching disbelief in or opposition to organized government, or who advocate or teach the duty, necessity, or propriety of the unlawful assaulting or killing of any officer or officers, either by specific individuals or officers generally, of the Government of the United States or any other organized Government, because of his or their official character, or who advocate or teach the unlawful destruction of property."

The Espionage Act contains some legislation which is in force only in time of war and also contains much permanent legislation effective in time of peace as well as in time of war. Among its permanent provisions is Section 2 of Title 12 (Act of June 15, 1917) which is as follows:

"Every letter, writing, circular, postal card, picture, printing, engraving, photograph, newspaper, pamphlet, book, or other publication, matter or thing, of any kind, containing any matter advocating or urging treason, insurrection, or forcibly [forcible] resistance to any law of the United States is hereby declared to be nonmailable."

Since the signing of the armistice, the anarchists, I.W.W's, radical socialists and kindred organizations all espouse the Bolsheviki cause of Russia, and advocate a similar form of government for this country as a part of a world socialistic system, to be accomplished through revolutionary methods, including force and bloodshed.

It seems clear that the provisions of the Espionage Act, making nonmailable matter which tends to cause interference with enlistment in the army, the operation of the draft law, and the sale of bonds to raise money for the prosecution of the war, do not apply to the revolutionary matter referred to and now being published. But it would seem that the duty rests upon the Post Office Department to exclude such matter under the permanent legislation quoted unless and until the courts determine that this permanent legislation does not warrant the exclusion from the mails of this class of matter. If I am correct in this position, it would seem that the only course left open for the Post Office Department is to reject all applications for second class mailing privileges presented by publications which habitually publish the class of matter indicated, and declare nonmailable every individual issue of such publication in which such unlawful matter appears.

It will then be for the courts to pass upon the facts in every particular case presented to them.

The Post Office Department is being criticised by some newspapers for its course in handling seditious publications as thought [though] it was acting arbitrarily and had no duty to perform under the law; on the other hand, the public is often criticising the Post Office Department for permitting revolutionary matter to pass through the mails.

In my judgment, prompt action should be taken in every case and we should facilitate in every way a judicial determination of the questions presented by each publication as rapidly as possible.

W H Lamar Solicitor

TLS (WP, DLC).

To Albert Sidney Burleson

My dear Burleson: The White House 4 September, 1920

I realize the importance of the matter you call my attention to in your letter of September third and think that it would be wise if we discussed it in Cabinet. Will you not bring it up at the next meeting for consideration?

Cordially and faithfully yours,   Woodrow Wilson

TLS (A. S. Burleson Papers, DLC).

To Jessie Kennedy Dyer

My dear Jessie: [The White House] 4 September, 1920

You may be sure that it would be a pleasure for me to do what you ask in your letter of August thirty-first if it were possible for me to do so in justice to those whom I must serve and provide for, but it is not possible and it is my duty to say so. I sincerely hope that you will find some way out of your difficulties.

Affectionately yours,   [Woodrow Wilson]

CCL (WP, DLC).

Two Letters from Bainbridge Colby

My dear Mr. President: Washington September 6, 1920.

Referring to the trouble in Haiti, I think we need not face the embarrassment, which may flow from an attempt to define Admiral Knapp's duties and status, too rigidly.

Since the receipt of your letter,[1] I have conferred with Secretary Daniels and also with Admiral Knapp, and we are agreed that a letter from me to the Admiral can be written that will informally indicate to him his duties, without any suggestion of reflection upon our Minister.

We hope the situation will be helped by the injection of a new personality—a dignified and gracious one—into the discussion, and the necessary degree of accommodation between the Haitian officials and our Legation thus be reached, which will avert actual trouble.

If you approve this plan, I will write such a letter, and Admiral Knapp will leave promptly. The situation calls for some such expedient, I think.

I am, my dear Mr. President,

Yours faithfully,   Bainbridge Colby

[1] WW to BC, Aug. 30, 1920.

My dear Mr. President: Washington September 6, 1920.

A letter such as the enclosed[1] is what I have in mind for Admiral Knapp, and it may assist you to have it before you, in deciding as to our program regarding the Haitian situation—the subject of an earlier letter today.

Very respectfully yours,   Bainbridge Colby

TLS (WP, DLC).
    [1] It is missing, but it is printed as BC to H. S. Knapp, Sept. 8, 1920, *FR 1920*, II, 797-99. Colby's letter related in some detail the recent difficulties between the United States and Haiti and listed the recent laws which the President of Haiti would have to suspend in order to secure improved relations with the United States. About these laws, see B. Colby to WW, Aug. 28, 1920, n. 3.

To Bainbridge Colby

My dear Mr. Secretary: The White House 7 September, 1920

Thank you for your letter about Haiti and the mission of Admiral Knapp. I think it will be entirely satisfactory to send him such a letter as you suggest.

Cordially and faithfully yours,   Woodrow Wilson

TLS (B. Colby Papers, DLC).

From David Franklin Houston

Dear Mr. President: Washington September 7, 1920.

I received your note of September 1st a few days ago, together with the enclosure from Mr. Edward N. Hurley. I have been giving the matter presented by Mr. Hurley very careful consideration and am glad to submit the following comment:

Through private business channels large exports of commodities to Europe and other parts of the world are being financed. The scale is colossal. It is amazing to me that in existing circumstances it is possible for the business men of this country to finance exports on such a scale. It is difficult to see how Europe is able or will be able to meet the liabilities she is incurring. The total exports from this country in 1918 were $6,000,000,000; in 1919, $8,000,000,000; and this year they are running at the rate of $8,400,000,000. In 1918 the exports to Europe alone had an aggregate value of $3,800,000,000; in 1919, of over $5,000,000,000; and this year are running at the rate of nearly $5,000,000,000. The total balance against Europe for the three years indicated exceeds $12,000,000,000. It is noticable that the exports to the countries mentioned, namely, Belgium, France, Italy and even Germany and

Austria, are very large and that a great balance is piling up against them. In 1918 the exports to Belgium were 150 millions, to France 931 millions and to Italy 492 millions. In 1919 to Belgium 378 millions, to France 893 millions, to Italy 443 millions, to Germany 92 millions and to Austria 42 millions. The indications are that the exports this year will be, to Belgium about 325 millions, to France 720 millions, to Italy 400 millions and to Germany 240 millions.

Obviously it is not a question of the European countries securing imports from this country. They are undoubtedly importing in such volumes that inevitably the exchange situation must continue to be awry and that grave questions are raised as to the liquidation of the balances. The only question that can arise is as to whether or not the European countries are importing the sort of things, such as raw materials and manufacturing and farming equipment, which are necessary for industrial reconstruction purposes, or whether they are in part importing a considerable volume of things of the nature of luxuries which they had better do without. Of course it would be difficult to control the purchases of European countries and by any sort of machinery have them limit their purchases to strict necessaries. It would also be difficult to control the sale of things by American business men. I know of no feasible method of doing this. It would be undesirable for the Government to intervene through governmental machinery, and I imagine authority would not be granted for such intervention. If anyone can work out a private plan which will lead to a higher degree of satisfactory discrimination it would be well worth doing, but I seriously question whether Mr. Hurley or anyone else can do so. This problem, I understand, will be one of the things discussed at the forthcoming Brussels Conference.[1] I am not optimistic that a satisfactory scheme can be developed there, but if it cannot be developed there I do not believe it can be developed anywhere else.

Faithfully yours,   D. F. Houston

TLS (WP, DLC).
[1] The International Financial Conference, called by the League of Nations, was to meet in Brussels from September 24 to October 8. In addition to the former Allied nations, many countries neutral during the war, as well as Germany, Austria, Hungary, and Bulgaria, were represented at the conference. Russia and Turkey were not represented. Roland William Boyden attended the conference as an unofficial observer for the United States. For the proceedings, see International Financial Conference, Brussels, 1920, *Proceedings of the Conference* (5 vols., London, 1920).

From Simon Wolf

My dear Mr President.   South Poland, Me. Sep 7. 20.

For several months there have been malicious and untruthful attacks on the Jews, in Mr Henry Fords newspaper, the Dearborn.[1] Can you not use your good office and secure from Ford a promise to stop it? The attack is uncalled for, unjust and immoral, it leads to class hatred, and intensifies racial and religious prejudice. No one knows better than yourself, how nobly and patriotically the Jews have discharged every duty as American citizens. Wishing you health and cheer.   I am sincerely,   Simon Wolf.

P.S. When will your new book be ready?

ALS (WP, DLC).
[1] On May 22, 1920, Ford and several of his associates had begun publishing a series of strongly anti-Semitic articles in his weekly newspaper, *The Dearborn Independent.* The series ran in ninety-one consecutive issues of the publication, which was distributed nationwide, in part through Ford automobile dealers. The articles were later collected and published in book form as the Dearborn Independent, *The International Jew, The World's Foremost Problem* (4 vols., Dearborn, Mich., 1920-1922). These volumes were widely distributed both in the United States and abroad. They were translated into German and unquestionably influenced Adolf Hitler and other anti-Semitic thinkers of Germany and Austria. See Albert Lee, *Henry Ford and the Jews* (New York, 1980), pp. 13-66, and Allan Nevins and Frank Ernest Hill, *Ford: Expansion and Challenge, 1915-1933* (New York, 1957), pp. 311-23.

From the Diary of Dr. Grayson

Sept. 8, 1920

Morning exercise. Treatment. good humor. Mr & Mrs Sayre visitors.

Dr Axson reading, moving pictures, motor ride in afternoon.

Dinner Guests. Secy's. Colby, Payne.

Mr. Alvey Adee served in State Dept. 50 yrs. Comment on conversation between Secy Hay and Woo Ting Fang.[1]

"Hay was a little woozy—&
Woo was a little hazy."

Hw loose-leaf diary (received from James Gordon Grayson and Cary T. Grayson, Jr.).
[1] Wu T'ing-fang, Chinese Minister to the United States, 1897-1901 and 1907-1909.

Joseph Patrick Tumulty to Edith Bolling Galt Wilson

Dear Mrs. Wilson: The White House, 8 September 1920.

I hate to seem to press the case of the unfortunate colored girl[1] upon you, but if you could in a diplomatic way bring about its reconsideration, you would do a real service to humanity.

As you will see from the file, she seems to be utterly alone. It is usual in cases of this kind for the White House to be inundated with petitions and appeals; but in this case no one seems to be interested or care anything about her. District Attorney Laskey[2] is not a man with sentiment, by any means, but yet he with the Attorney General's office recommend "commutation to imprisonment for life."

TL (J. P. Tumulty Papers, DLC).
  [1] Josephine Berry of Washington, who had been convicted of murder and sentenced to be hanged. There will be more correspondence about this case in this volume.
  [2] John Ellsworth Laskey, United States District Attorney for the District of Columbia.

From the Shorthand Diary of Charles Lee Swem

9 September, 1920

The President today wrote to the Attorney General and asked if the President didn't have the powers of a magistrate. He said he would "like to hold up some scoffing automobilist and sit by the roadside and fine him about a thousand dollars."[1]

JRT transcript (WC, NjP) of CLSsh (C. L. Swem Coll., NjP).
  [1] Edmund William Starling of the Secret Service staff of the White House later described this episode as follows:
  "Frequently he was irascible, and we had trouble evading his unreasonable orders without embarrassment. He got the idea that no automobiles should pass us while we were driving, despite the fact that we proceeded at a very moderate rate of speed, frequently going at fifteen or twenty miles an hour so he could enjoy the scenery. Whenever a car passed us he would order the Secret Service car to pursue it and bring back the driver for questioning. . . .
  "We always told him that the car was going too fast to be overhauled. Then he decided that he wanted to be a justice of the peace so that he could arrest these drivers and try their cases." E. W. Starling, *Starling of the White House* (New York, 1946), p. 157.

To Alexander Mitchell Palmer

The White House

My dear Mr. Attorney General: 9 September, 1920

It is the popular impression, and it was my own impression when I came to Washington, that the President *ex officio* possesses the powers of a magistrate. I would be very much obliged if you would tell me whether this is true or not.

Sincerely yours,   Woodrow Wilson

TLS (A. M. Palmer Papers, DLC).

To Alvey Augustus Adee

My dear Mr. Adee: [The White House] 9 September, 1920

I understand that today rounds out for you fifty years of service in the State Department, and I must give myself the pleasure of congratulating you on your record and the Government on having possessed so faithful and devoted a servant.

With the best wishes,
              Cordially and sincerely yours,   [Woodrow Wilson]

CCL (WP, DLC).

To Sylvester Woodbridge Beach[1]

My dear Friend: [The White House] 9 September, 1920

It is always a pleasure to hear from you, and I thank you for your letter of September sixth.[2] I wish I could give myself the pleasure of seeing you in person, for it would be a real pleasure, but I find myself obliged to deny myself to everybody else and, of course, you will appreciate the embarrassment of exceptions.

With the best wishes,
              Sincerely yours,   [Woodrow Wilson]

CCL (WP, DLC).
    [1] Wilson's old friend, pastor of the First Presbyterian Church of Princeton, New Jersey, since 1906.
    [2] S. W. Beach to WW, Sept. 6, 1920, ALS (WP, DLC).

From William Bauchop Wilson, with Enclosure

Memorandum for the President.

My dear Mr. President: Washington September 9, 1920.

Referring to the telegram from Philip Murray and others, requesting you to direct that a meeting of the operators and miners joint scale committee of the anthracite coal field be held for the purpose of adjusting certain inequalities set forth in their telegram,[1] I would like to call your attention to some very important differences existing between the anthracite and bituminous coal fields.

It may be true, as stated in the telegram, that "the custom has been that whenever voluntary increases have been granted during the life of agreements in the bituminous districts, similar action has always been taken in the anthracite region," but the reverse has not been the case. For instance, on November 15, 1918, a voluntary increase in wages was granted to the anthracite coal miners during the life of an agreement. The increase was given by the operators because manufacturing concerns in nearby towns were paying higher wage rates and it was necessary to increase the wages at the mines for the purpose of retaining a sufficient number of workmen to produce an adequate supply of coal. The daily wage rate in the bituminous regions was sufficient to maintain the supply of workmen. The same justification did not exist for reopening the bituminous case, and although they were very insistent upon receiving an increase of wages at that time, the Fuel Administrator declined to permit any readjustment. Immediately a nation-wide agitation was inaugurated for a wage increase, which culminated in the strike of last November and the appointment by you of a Commission[2] to adjust the dispute.

In presenting their case to the Commission the bituminous miners placed no stress upon the daily earnings but contended that people had to live during the entire year whether they had opportunity for work or not, and the annual earnings was therefore the basis that should be taken into consideration. They were able to show that the opportunity to work in bituminous coal mines was a maximum of only two hundred days per year, and that fact had great weight with the Commission in rendering its award. The anthracite coal field is differently situated. The maximum opportunity of employment of the contract miners in the anthracite coal field is shown to be two hundred seventy-five days per year, while the opportunity for daymen is considerably higher. The daily earnings of the bituminous mine workers are larger than the daily earnings of the anthracite, but the annual earnings of the anthracite miners are larger than the annual earnings of the bituminous. These facts were taken into consideration by the Commission.

In the bituminous regions one-third of all the men employed are daymen, most of whom are key men in mining operations. In anthracite operations two-third of all the employees are daymen, less than half of whom are key men. The award of the Bituminous Coal Commission gave the lowest per cent. increase to the daymen. The award of the Anthracite Commission gives the highest per cent. increase to the daymen. The bituminous miners accepted the award and continued to work. The anthracite miners in large numbers, following the lead of so-called insurgents, have refused to accept the award.

The Bituminous Coal Commission had to deal with the problems arising out of varying physical conditions and local surroundings in every coal producing state in the union. The Anthracite Commission dealt only with the problems arising in five or six small counties of a single state. It was apparent to any man conversant with coal mining operations that the Bituminous Coal Commission could not in the brief time it could devote to the question avoid creating some inequalities within the territory under its jurisdiction. There was not the same likelihood of the Anthracite Commission producing such inequalities in the anthracite field. As a consequence the daymen in certain parts of the bituminous field protested, even to the extent of striking, against the inequalities existing in the mines in which they were engaged. No such basis is laid for the anthracite protest, but instead a claim of insufficiency of the award and inequalities as compared with bituminous mining. The award of the Commission makes a minimum rate for common labor of fifty-two and one-half cents per hour, while the maximum rate paid for common labor in manufacturing establishments in the anthracite region is fifty-one cents per hour, and, as I have already pointed out, the Commission had before it the facts showing that the daily earnings of bituminous miners were greater than the anthracite, and the yearly earnings of the anthracite miners greater than the bituminous.

In addition it should be understood that the award of the Commission gives to the anthracite mine workers an increase in wage rates since 1914 greater than the increase in the cost of living in the same period. In the case of the lower paid men the increase of the daily rate has been one hundred seventy per cent. as against ninety-five per cent. increase in the cost of living. The increase in the annual wage rate is still a larger percentage because of the greater opportunity for employment.

On August 30th, when the award of the Commission was about to be handed down, Enoch Williams and others, the leaders of the insurgents, wired you stating that the anthracite mine workers would refrain from working unless you set aside the award of the Anthracite Coal Commission on or before September 1, 1920.[3] In reply to that telegram you said in part:

"If your communication, declaring your intention to refrain from working unless I set aside the award of the Anthracite Coal Commission on or before September 1, 1920, is intended as a threat, you can rest assured that your challenge will be accepted and that the people of the United States will find some substitute fuel to tide them over until the real sentiment of the anthracite mine workers can find expression and they are ready to abide by the obligations they have entered into."[4]

These men have for a brief time at least made good their threat and succeeded in keeping a majority of the anthracite mines in idleness for more than a week under the guise of "taking a vaca-

tion." Of course, they are not deceiving anybody, not even themselves. Any action by which a body of men collectively refrain from
working, either through written agreement or oral understanding,
is a strike no matter what name you give it. Many of the men are
now going back to work, and I feel certain the situation will rapidly
clarify from now on. Any intimation on your part at this time that
you would even consider calling the joint scale committee together
for any purpose would be playing into the hands of those who have
defied you and lead to still further unsettled conditions. I therefore
recommend that you send a reply to them, such as the copy inclosed, and give the reply to the press.

Faithfully yours,   W B Wilson

TLS (WP, DLC).
   ¹ P. Murray *et al.* to WW, Sept. 3, 1920, T telegram (WP, DLC), which W. B. Wilson
summarizes in his letter to Woodrow Wilson.
   ² The Bituminous Coal Commission, about which see the index references to it in
Vol. 64.
   ³ E. Williams *et al.* to WW, Aug. 29, 1920.
   ⁴ See the Enclosure printed with WBW to WW, Aug. 30, 1920.

E N C L O S U R E

Gentlemen: September 9, 1920.

    I am in receipt of your telegram of September 3d, informing me
that you have written the award of the Anthracite Coal Commission into an agreement with the anthracite operators despite the
fact that you are convinced that the award in itself does not provide
that measure of justice to which you believe your people are entitled. I sincerely thank you for the promptness with which you have
acted notwithstanding your disappointment. It is a policy of that
kind, carried into effect by the rank and file of the workers, that
has made for the steady improvement of the conditions of the anthracite miners in recent years and which lays the foundation for
still further progress.

    You ask me to convene the joint scale committee of anthracite
operators and miners for the purpose of adjusting certain inequalities which you assert exist in the award of the Anthracite Coal
Commission. In that connection your attention is called to a telegram which I sent to Enoch Williams and others in reply to a telegram I received from them stating that the anthracite miners
would refrain from working unless I set aside the award of the Anthracite Coal Commission on or before September 1st. In that telegram I said:

    "If your communication, declaring your intention to refrain
from working unless I set aside the award of the Anthracite Coal

Commission on or before September 1, 1920, is intended as a threat, you can rest assured that your challenge will be accepted and that the people of the United States will find some substitute fuel to tide them over until the real sentiment of the anthracite mine workers can find expression and they are ready to abide by the obligations they have entered into."

Notwithstanding the plain warning contained in that telegram, which was given wide publicity, the majority of the anthracite coal miners, following the leadership of these men, have refrained from work under the guise of taking a vacation. In doing so they have not deceived any one, not even themselves. When a body of men collectively refrain from working by mutual understanding, however arrived at, it is a strike, no matter what name may be given to it. Our people have fought a great war and made untold sacrifices to insure among other things that a solemn agreement shall not be considered as a mere scrap of paper. We have declined to enter into friendly relations with governments that boast of their readiness to violate treaties whenever it suits their own convenience, and under these circumstances we could not look the world in the face or justify our action to our own people and our own conscience if we yielded one iota to the men in the anthracite coal fields who are violating the contract so recently entered into between themselves, the coal operators, and the Government of the United States.

I appreciate the earnestness of your efforts to get the men to return to work and commend your stand in support of the obligations of your contracts which all men must honor, but for the reasons stated above I regret that I can not grant your request to reconvene the joint scale committee of operators and miners.

Sincerely yours,[1]

T MS (WP, DLC).
[1] This was typed up, signed by Woodrow Wilson, and sent to P. Murray *et al.* on September 10, 1920 (TLS, Letterpress Books, WP, DLC). It was given to the press on that same day.

Stephen Samuel Wise to Joseph Patrick Tumulty, with Enclosure

My dear Tumulty: New York Sept. 9, 1920

Let me take up with you as briefly as I can a matter which I believe to be one of importance,—a matter which I am sure will command your deep and instant interest. Let me put it this way: During the war, we thought that the Jewish people in Europe had plumbed the very depths of sorrow and tragedy. Is it not unspeakable that, though the war be ended, the sorrows and sufferings of my people in Eastern Europe are more tragic than ever before in Jewish history,—and we are a people who have known suffering and tragedy.

I have today received a cable under date of September 8th from Morris Rothenberg of the New York Bar in which he states:

"Most reliable information treatment Jews Poland shocking. Soldiers rob, beat, tear beards worse before. Impossible walk streets ride trains. Numerous innocents shot pretexts Bolsheviks. Jews volunteered readily everywhere defence Poland but degraded army given dirtiest work. Jews driven out small towns approach enemy. Poles permitted stay. Jablono thousands Jewish soldiers concentrated without reason treated like offenders. Jewish deputies appealed several times. Ministry promised remedy conditions. Nothing done. Situation growing worse daily. Offenders unpunished encouraged."

It has occurred to me that it would be of the very greatest moral value if the President might see fit, as I think he ought, to send some message which would of course have instant currency throughout the world, especially wherever Jews dwell, giving expression to his own hope that the terrible sufferings of the Jews may and ought to cease without delay.

If I had a chance to see the President, I would venture to suggest that a brief word to the enclosed effect would not only be morally sustaining to suffering Jews the world over but have a very great value vís a vís those governments and peoples, which are doing them wrong.

In order to be of the greatest service, the thing must be done at once. The Jewish New Year's Day begins Sunday evening. If I could have a letter by Saturday or Sunday morning, it could be given out in such a way as to serve the ends that we have in mind.

With cordial regard and awaiting your early reply,

Faithfully yours,   Stephen S. Wise

In the event of the President being unwilling or unable,—and he ought to be neither,—to write to me in these terms, it would be of importance if the same kind of communication might come to me from Secretary Colby.

TLS (WP, DLC).

E N C L O S U R E

I am deeply moved by the reports which you send me of the trials and sufferings endured by your fellow-Jews throughout Eastern Europe. No American, whatever his racial origin or religious creed, can fail to feel the deepest sympathy with the Jews of Eastern Europe, who continue to bear not only the burden of war but also the sufferings incident to unenlightened and unjust treatment at the hands of governments and peoples.

I am of the hope that those nations with which our own land holds political commerce may do everything in their power not only to end the legal disabilities of their Jewish populations as provided for by the Minority Peoples clauses of the Peace Treaty, but all the injustices and wrongs which are laid upon them.

We know in this country wherein Jews of right enjoy entire equality how loyally they serve and how faithfully they support the purposes and ideals of our own nation.

I should greatly rejoice to learn through you that there has come about an amelioration of the status of the Jews in Eastern European lands. This government most earnestly desires that Jewish persecution be ended in all lands and for all time.[1]

T MS (WP, DLC).
[1] This was typed up and sent, with one emendation, as WW to S. S. Wise, Sept. 10, 1920, CCL (WP, DLC). It was published, e.g., in the *New York Times*, Sept. 12, 1920.

To Bainbridge Colby

My dear Mr. Secretary: The White House 10 September, 1920

Thank you sincerely for the enclosed.[1] It prompts me to ask that you request Professor Westermann and the advisers associated with him to make up for my signature formal report of an arbitral decision with regard to the boundaries I have undertaken to determine. It is impossible for me to form an independent judgment in this matter and I shall be quite willing to be guided by their conclusions, for I am confident of their impartiality and sense of justice.   Cordially and faithfully yours,   Woodrow Wilson

TLS (B. Colby Papers, DLC).
[1] Not found.

From Joshua Willis Alexander

My dear Mr. President: Washington September 10, 1920.

I am transmitting herewith memoranda[1] concerning the chief points mentioned in the letter of Mr. Hurley,[2] regarding the financing of raw materials for Central Europe, and investments there by Great Britain and France. These memoranda, with their more detailed inclosures, discuss briefly, (1) direct aid to exporters by the British Government, (2) financing of raw materials for Central Europe, and (3) investments in Continental Europe.

While it is often difficult to verify specific instances of economic penetration in Central and Near Eastern Europe by the chief European nations, there can be no doubt that such efforts are being made so far as the financial situation in Entente countries will permit. It is probably true that Great Britain, Holland, and possibly one or two other European countries, have taken up the question of trading with Central Europe more vigorously than our own commercial interests. At the same time, in my opinion and that of officials of the Bureau of Foreign and Domestic Commerce, who have been following the matter very closely, the matter of financing of raw materials for Central Europe and general participation in the reconstruction of France, Belgium, Italy, etc., has been very carefully considered by American bankers, manufacturers, and traders. The difficulty of finding free capital for our own domestic enterprises and the failure of the United States to make formal peace with the Central Powers are, of course, the important factors in this situation.

I believe that the Government should cooperate in every possible way, short of direct financial participation, in working out a plan for European reconstruction. Apart from the political possibilities of continued industrial stagnation in parts of Continental Europe, it is hopeless to expect a restoration of commercial equilibrium here or elsewhere until a greater measure of economic stability is attained in Europe. I should be very glad to discuss Mr. Hurley's plan with him in detail and to have the experts of the Department give immediate attention to his proposals.

Respectfully,   J. W. Alexander

Ackn & file   W.W.

TLS (WP, DLC).
    [1] The two enclosures still with this letter are "BRIEF SUMMARY OF PREVIOUS PROPOSALS FOR ASSISTANCE TO EUROPE" and "ACQUISITION OF INDUSTRIAL AND OTHER PROPERTIES IN EUROPE," T MSS (WP, DLC). The latter document detailed what was then known about British, French, Italian, and United States investments in Germany and Central European countries.
    [2] That is, E. N. Hurley to WW, Aug. 28, 1920.

Two Letters from Joseph Patrick Tumulty to Edith Bolling Galt Wilson

Dear Mrs. Wilson: The White House, 10 September 1920.

The criticisms of the Federal Reserve Board found in the attached letters[1] are characteristic of many that I hear on all sides.

Sincerely yours,   Tumulty

[1] Clyde Roark Hoey, Democratic representative from North Carolina, to A. W. McLean, Sept. 2, 1920; and Julian Shakespeare Carr, Democratic politician and industrialist of Durham, N. C., to A. W. McLean, Aug. 31, 1920, both TLS (WP, DLC). Hoey and Carr, like many other southern and western spokesmen at the time, accused the Federal Reserve Board of adopting a deflationary monetary policy which, they claimed, was one of the prime causes of the recent sharp decline in tobacco and cotton prices. For extensive discussion of this criticism of the Federal Reserve Board, see Link, "The Federal Reserve Policy and the Agricultural Depression of 1920-1921," pp. 334-48.

Dear Mrs. Wilson: The White House, 10 September 1920.

Mr. Morgenthau telephoned me to say that he has some important information about Mexico which he thinks the President ought to have. He wants to know if he can present it to him personally.   Sincerely yours,   Tumulty

I hope he will seek an interview with the Sec'y of State   W.W.

TLS (WP, DLC).

From Henri Gressitt[1]

Washington, D. C.,
My dear Mr. President: September Tenth, Nineteen Twenty.

Prompted by the suggestion in a newspaper article recently by Mr. Seibold of the New York World,[2] in which you were quoted as saying you would like to see John Drinkwater's "ABRAHAM LINCOLN" I am taking the liberty, at the request of Wm. Harris, Jr.[3] of offering a special performance here in Washington for you.

It is Mr. Harris' desire, if it should meet with your approval, to bring the entire original company down from New York for a performance at one of the local theatres, probably the National, the performance to be given exclusively for you and such guests as you care to invite, the entire house being at your disposal. As you probably know this company, with Frank McGlynn in the title role, has been playing in New York for the past year.

In making this suggestion may I be permitted to say personally that Mr. Harris is prompted to make this offer by his warm admiration for you and by his pride in what he considers one of the most wonderful theatrical productions of modern times. It is probably unnecessary to state that we will not give the matter any advance publicity and have no desire to exploit it commercially.

Owing to the ever present possibility of a change in bookings Mr. Harris suggests that any day next week or the week following, with the exception of the matinee days at the local theatre, be selected.

Respectfully,   Henri Gressitt

TLS (WP, DLC).
    [1] His letterhead identified him as the "personal representative" of William Harris, Jr.
    [2] That is, the news report by Seibold printed at June 17, 1920, Vol. 65.
    [3] William Harris, Jr., a theatrical producer of New York.

To Henri Gressitt

My dear Sir: [The White House] 11 September, 1920

I hope you will express to Mr. Harris my deep appreciation of the kind purpose expressed in your letter of September tenth. I am sorry to say that the state of my health makes it impossible for me to avail myself of this kindness, and I hope that he will feel that it is none the less deeply appreciated. I am sincerely disappointed that I cannot see the play.

Very truly yours,   [Woodrow Wilson]

CCL (WP, DLC).

From Bainbridge Colby

My dear Mr. President: [Washington] September 13th, 1920.

May I ask your brief attention to a suggestion I have to make regarding the acute paper shortage in this country which is largely attributed by paper manufacturers to the embargo upon the exportation of pulpwood from Canadian Crown lands.

You will recall that the Underwood Bill[1] which passed both Houses at the last session of Congress but did not receive your approval contemplated the appointment of a commission for the purpose of direct negotiation with the Canadian authorities, looking to the modification or lifting of the embargo. I think there is but one opinion that your action was correct in withholding approval of this measure. It had been accompanied during its legislative journey through the House and the Senate by a great deal of mischievous talk about retaliatory embargoes upon coal and other commodities which Canada obtains in great quantities from this country. A very surly popular opinion was developed in Canada which was reflected in the Canadian press and the feeling became very outspoken and wide-spread in Canada that we proposed some coercive interference with Canada in a matter of purely internal and domestic regulation.

The fact remains, however, that the Canadian paper manufacturers, and particularly the interests which control the supply of pulpwood, are laying a very heavy burden upon paper manufacture in this country and everyone who uses paper, the periodical as well as the daily press, seem to be a unit in feeling that some measures must be taken to relieve the present situation.

It has been suggested to me by prominent manufacturers of paper and some important newspaper proprietors (among them the New York World) that an informal committee of five or six prominent men in the paper trade might be requested by me to visit not the Dominion authorities but the Provincial authorities who are primarily responsible for the embargo policy, and by frank discussion it is hoped that better conditions will be brought about in the trade. I understand that some explicit encouragement has been received from pulp paper manufacturers in Canada to approach the subject in this way.

I took it up informally with the British Ambassador,[2] explaining to him that I did not wish to pursue any course that would be distasteful to the Dominion authorities, and the Ambassador in a recent visit to Ottawa discussed the question with the Dominion authorities. He reported to me the other day that the Canadian Government was entirely willing that the matter should be taken up in this manner and would offer no criticism or objection should we see fit to appoint such a commission. The latter would have no diplomatic character, ad lib. I would simply write a letter to certain men whose names have been suggested to me as commanding the confidence of the paper trade in general in this country and request them to act upon such an informal commission.

Does the procedure outlined meet with your approval? I may merely add that the pressure from the newspaper and publication trade for some such action is very great. The plan I have outlined may not hasten the relief but it will at least keep them busy.

Very respectfully yours,   Bainbridge Colby

CCL (B. Colby Papers, DLC).
  [1] S.J. Res. 152, introduced in the Senate by Oscar W. Underwood on February 2, 1920. Both houses approved a slightly amended version of the resolution on June 3. *Cong. Record*, 66th Cong., 2d sess., pp. 2341, 8364, 8438-40. Wilson killed the bill by a pocket veto.
  [2] That is, Sir Auckland Geddes.

To John Appleton Stewart[1]

My dear Mr. Stewart: [The White House] 14 September, 1920

I have your letter of September eleventh[2] but am a little vague about the object of it. You speak of celebrating the Tercentenary of the meeting of the First American Legislative Assembly and the Mayflower Compact. Of course, the first American Legislative Assembly and the Mayflower Compact did not fall in the same year, and I would be very much obliged if you would inform me a little further as to exactly what it is that you are preparing to celebrate. By the first American Legislative Assembly I assume that you mean the first Virginia Assembly, which, as I remember it, met in 1619.

Awaiting further particulars,

Very sincerely yours,   [Woodrow Wilson]

CCL (WP, DLC).
  [1] President of the Carbonating Co. of New York; chairman of the board of governors of the Sulgrave Institution, an organization devoted to the preservation of George Washington's ancestral home, Sulgrave Manor, in Northamptonshire, England, and to the promotion of Anglo-American friendship.
  [2] J. A. Stewart to WW, Sept. 11, 1920, TLS (WP, DLC). Writing on behalf of the Sulgrave Institution, Stewart described the elaborate plans of the organization for the celebration of "the Tercentenary of the meeting of the First American Legislative Assembly and the Mayflower Compact." He hoped that the Wilsons could be their guests at events in New York and in Norfolk, Virginia, or, if that was not possible, that Wilson could make some public statement on the occasion of the celebration. He also expressed the hope that Wilson might be able to receive some of the dignitaries from abroad who would be attending the celebration. For a detailed description of the organization's plans, see J. A. Stewart to WW, Sept. 16, 1920.

From Alexander Mitchell Palmer

Dear Mr. President: Washington, D. C. September 14, 1920.

In answer to your inquiry of September 9, 1920, as to whether the President *ex officio* possesses the powers of a magistrate, I have the honor to advise you that the word "magistrate" has been defined as follows:

"The word magistrate is not confined to Justices of the Peace and other persons *ejusdem generis*, who exercise general judicial powers but includes others whose duties are strictly executive" (12 Encyc. of U. S. Supreme Court Reports, 837).

"In a general sense a magistrate is a public civil officer, possessing such power, legislative, executive or judicial, as the government appointing him may *ordain*. In a narrow sense, a magistrate is regarded—perhaps, commonly regarded—as an inferior judicial officer, such as a justice of the peace." (2 Bouvier Law Dic. 92).

"A magistrate is a public civil officer, invested with some part
of the legislative, executive or judicial power given by the Constitution or the law; a generic term importing a public officer
exercising a public authority, * * * a judicial officer having jurisdiction in matters of a criminal or quasi criminal nature." (25
Cyc. 1662).

In Compton v. Alabama, 214 U.S. 1, 7, Mr. Justice Story said:

"I know of no other definition of the term magistrate than that
he is a person clothed with power as a public officer." (Citing 1
Black. Com. 146).

In the Federalist, the expression "Chief Magistrate" as applied
to the President is continually used, but only in the broad sense as
applied by Justice Story, ante. It is true, of course, that certain of
the executive departments working under the control of the President exercise *quasi* judicial functions; for example, the matters
coming within the powers of the Secretary of the Interior affecting
the public lands statutes. However, the powers which clothe the
President are solely those which are conferred upon him by the
Constitution, or which have been conferred by act of Congress
within the limits of the Constitution. These do not include the exercise of the judicial function carrying with it the power to commit
or punish offenders against the law. The distinction of authority is
preserved by Article III, Section 1, of the Constitution, which reads
as follows:

"The judicial Power of the United States shall be vested in one
supreme Court, and in such inferior Courts as the Congress
may, from time to time, ordain and establish. * * *"

The power of commitment and taking bail in cases involving offenses against the laws of the United States is lodged with certain
classes of officials by Section 1014, Revised Statutes; such being
Justices and Judges of the United States, Commissioners of the
United States Circuit (now District) Courts, Chancellors, Judges
of Supreme and Superior Courts, Chief or First Judges of Common
Pleas, Mayor of a City, Justice of the Peace or other magistrate of
any State, etc. It is obvious that such officials in acting under said
section, act in the narrow sense of the word "magistrate," as set
forth in the definitions I have quoted.

The precise question seems to have been ruled upon by Attorney
General Wirt, (June 23, 1818, 1 Op. A.G. 213). In that case the
President desired to be informed if he possessed power to direct
that an offender against the laws of the United States be bailed or
discharged without bail, on his own bond, to take his trial at the
next term. Attorney General Wirt said:

"The power which the President is thus called upon to exercise does not, in my opinion, belong to him by the Constitution and laws of the United States. The question of bail is a judicial, not an executive one * * * the President does not possess the power which he is called upon to exercise."

While the President is a "magistrate" in the broad sense that he is a "person clothed with power as a public officer," I am clear that he does not possess the powers of a magistrate in the usual and narrow significance of the word. He cannot exercise the judicial powers or perform the duties of an ordinary committing magistrate.   Faithfully yours,   A Mitchell Palmer[1]

TLS (WP, DLC).
[1] The Acting Attorney General, William L. Frierson, also replied to Wilson's inquiry in W. L. Frierson to WW, Sept. 18, 1920, TLS (WP, DLC). Frierson did not know that Palmer had already written his letter.

From Frank Park[1]

Dear Mr. President: Sylvester, Ga., September 15, 1920.

A letter from Mr. Tumulty, containing a note from you to me, just received.[2] I had no object other than making you a personal visit, and trying in my feeble way to interest you and make you pass the time more easily, but I readily understand that you can not see me personally, and I withdraw my statement, that unless you would permit me to present you the walking cane in person, that I was not going to present it. I have worked on it personally a good deal. I have it now in soak in a tank of crude linseed oil, which toughens and supples the fiber. As soon as it is finished and I return to Washington, I am going to carry it around and send it in to you.

I hope this finds you well, and that you are not suffering physically, and that you will soon be yourself.

With the kindest personal regards, I am most respectfully and obediently yours,   Frank Park

TLS (WP, DLC).
[1] Democratic congressman from Georgia.
[2] Both are missing in WP, DLC.

To Alexander Mitchell Palmer

[The White House]
My dear Mr. Attorney General: 16 September, 1920

I write to ask whether it is within my legal power in making appointments to designate a delayed date, as for example the fifth of March, when the appointee is to take office. I ask this question because in making some appointments I do not wish to disturb existing arrangements before the end of the administration.

Very sincerely yours,   [Woodrow Wilson]

CCL (WP, DLC).

From Joseph Patrick Tumulty

My dear Governor: [The White House] September 16, 1920.

The campaign for Governor Cox has now reached a critical stage, where his friends and yours feel that your laboring oar is needed to put the League and other issues before the public in the strongest possible way. Of course, they leave to your discretion the means that you will take to make your influence felt.

Edmund Moore, Governor Cox's closest friend, has been here in Washington and has been in conference with me with reference to this matter.

While Governor Cox is doing admirably, we feel that if the battle is to be won that it is up to you to lay the whole cause of the Democratic Party, with all of its aspects, before the public. The idea is to have you, beginning early in October, issue a weekly address to the American people, until the termination of the campaign.

If you have a few minutes I should like to talk to you about this.

Sincerely yours,   [Tumulty]

CCL (J. P. Tumulty Papers, DLC).

From John Appleton Stewart

Dear Mr. President: New York Sept. 16, 1920.

In reply to your kind note of September 14th, may I say that what we are celebrating are the beginnings of American institutions as expressed in the Virginia Assembly and the Mayflower Compact.

It is true that the Assembly met in July, 1619, and that the Mayflower Compact was not entered into until November 11, 1620. We began this celebration at a time which approximated six months after the anniversary date of the adjournment of the Assembly and six months before the date of the Mayflower Compact. Our purposes may be found in the address to the people of America which was issued on the 3rd of May of this year and which is published in the enclosed pamphlet on page 10.[1]

Our first work was in distributing to the public schools of America, through a Committee of which Dr. John H. Finley[2] is Chairman, a sheet for use in special instruction in respect of the Virginia Assembly and the Mayflower Compact; and subsequently in the general distribution to schools and societies of data which might be of use in the preparation of programs of celebration. We began our public celebrations in New York on Washington's birthday anniversary, the Vice President being present, with a service in St. Paul's, a convocation at three o'clock and in the evening a dinner.

Under the leadership of the sixty-six organizations associated with the Sulgrave Institution in giving direction to the celebration, hundreds of cities and villages have celebrated, with pageants, public addresses, etc., among these San Francisco, Detroit and Provincetown: the Dutch and British celebrations were also carried on in association with us and were attended by representatives of our organizations. Except in a meeting here and in London we did not formally celebrate the Virginia anniversary because of its coming in misdummer [midsummer], a reason which is of a species with that which is causing the Massachusetts people to defer celebrating the 1920 anniversary until 1921.

Our celebration will also include the focal dates of November 11th (Armistice Day and Compact Day) and November 25th, Thanksgiving Day, which this year will be observed throughout the English-speaking world.

Under an arrangement entered into in June, 1915, by all of the Sulgrave Institution branches throughout the world, we have been preparing for this celebration for over five years.

Following the celebration in New York City, September 27-30—which will conclude with a reception and luncheon at Princeton University—our guests and American delegates will proceed to Norfolk and afterwards to Virginia, there all too inadequately to celebrate Virginia's contributions to the upbuilding of our free institutions.

We should be gratified beyond measure to receive assurances of your sympathetic interest and some expression of sentiment which we can give to the world.

Believe me,

Respectfully and sincerely yours,   John A. Stewart.

TLS (WP, DLC).
[1] The Sulgrave Institution and other institutions, *International Celebration Meeting First American Legislative Assembly, the Mayflower Compact, the Pilgrim Fathers, which Mark the Beginning of Free Institutions in America* (New York, 1920).
[2] John Huston Finley, Wilson's old friend, at this time Commissioner of Education and President of the University of the State of New York (the Board of Regents).

Alexander Mitchell Palmer to Joseph Patrick Tumulty

Dear Joe: Washington, D. C. September 16, 1920.

Enclosed is a stenographic report[1] of the statement made by Samuel Gompers and of my reply at the hearing on the 14th instant, when the committee of the American Federation of Labor presented an appeal for general amnesty for political prisoners, so-called. You may show this to the President if you think proper.

Yours truly,   A Mitchell Palmer

File for reference, thanking Atty Gen'l for me   W.W.

TLS (WP, DLC).
    [1] "Minutes of Conference between the Attorney General and Representatives of the American Federation of Labor, September 14, 1920," T MS (WP, DLC). During this conference, Gompers asked that Wilson issue a proclamation of general amnesty for all political prisoners. Gompers and Palmer agreed that "political prisoners" should be defined as those convicted under the terms of the Espionage Act of 1917. In response, Palmer stressed the practical difficulties of making any such proclamation effective and said that, even if such a proclamation was issued, it would still be necessary for the Department of Justice to decide the case of each individual convicted under the Espionage Act on its own merits. This, he asserted, was exactly what the department was presently doing, and many persons had already been released or had had their sentences drastically reduced.

To Newton Diehl Baker, with Enclosure

My dear Mr. Secretary: The White House 17 September, 1920

I would be very much obliged for a suggestion from you as to the reply it would be wise and proper for me to make to the enclosed.

Cordially and sincerely yours,   Woodrow Wilson

TLS (N. D. Baker Papers, DLC).

E N C L O S U R E

From Emory Olin Watson[1]

My dear Mr. President: Washington D. C. September 15 1920.

As you are aware, the General War-Time Commission of the Churches represented twenty-seven Protestant denominations united in war work. After the Armistice, this General War-Time Commission dissolved and charged the General Committee on Army and Navy Chaplains of the Federal Council of Churches with the duty of carrying foward its unfinished business relating to chaplaincy matters. The suggestion was made that a commemorative medal conveying in tangible form a message of grateful appreciation of the splendid service rendered our men in the Army and Navy be presented to each of the Chaplains of these Churches. This medal is now ready for presentation.

At a meeting of the General Committee on Army and Navy Chaplains, held in Washington, D. C., September 13th, it was voted that prior to presenting the medal to the Chaplains, we ask the privilege of presenting one to you as an expression of appreciation by the Churches of your distinguished service to the Church and to the World through your leadership in winning the World War and bringing to the World the ideals of the Word embodied in the League of Nations.

The following Committee was appointed to ascertain your wishes and arrange for the presentation as may be agreeable to you at any time after September 23rd: Mr. William Knowles Cooper, Rev. Andrew R. Bird, Rev. Charles F. Steck, with Bishop William F. McDowell[2] and Rev. E. O. Watson, ex officio.

With highest esteem, I am

Sincerely yours,   E. O. Watson, For the Committee.

TLS (WP, DLC).
    [1] The Rev. E. O. Watson, Secretary of the General Committee on Army and Navy Chaplains of the Federal Council of the Churches of Christ in America.
    [2] Cooper, of Washington, D. C., was General Secretary of the Y. M. C. A.; the Rev. Andrew Reid Bird was pastor of the Church of the Pilgrims (Presbyterian) of Georgetown; and the Rev. Dr. William Fraser McDowell, Methodist Bishop in Washington, was chairman of the General Committee on Army and Navy Chaplains. The Rev. Mr. Steck lived at 1620 Riggs Place in Washington.

To Curtis Brown[1]

My dear Sir: [The White House] 17 September, 1920

I have and appreciate your letter of the sixth of September,[2] but am obliged to make the same reply to it that I made to your former letter.[3] I do not think this is the time to consider a biography of myself, and as for my personal memoirs, "there ain't going to be none," if I may use the vernacular. At least, if there are to be any, they are not yet visible on the horizon!

With appreciation,   Very truly yours   [Woodrow Wilson]

P.S. I am interested in what you say of the kind of services you undertake, and perhaps I owe it to frankness to say that I expect to put such matters in the hands of my friend, Mr. George Creel of New York.

CCL (WP, DLC).
    [1] Head of Curtis Brown, Ltd., an "International Publishing Bureau," with offices in London and New York.
    [2] C. Brown to WW, Sept. 6, 1920, TLS (WP, DLC).
    [3] See C. Brown to WW, March 9, 1918, Vol. 46, and WW to C. Brown, March 25, 1918, Vol. 47.

To Wilbur W. Marsh

My dear Mr. Marsh: [The White House] 17 September, 1920

May I not as a private in the ranks give myself the pleasure of contributing the enclosed to the expenses of the Democratic campaign? I feel very deeply that the very honor and destiny of the nation is involved in this campaign and that I and all citizens who love its honor and covet for it a high influence in the world should contribute to the success of the candidate who stands for the re-establishment of our position among the nations.[1]

Cordially and sincerely yours,   Woodrow Wilson

TLS (Letterpress Books, WP, DLC).
[1] There is in WP, DLC, a receipt from the Democratic National Committee, dated Sept. 18, 1920, showing that Wilson contributed $500. He had contributed $2,500 to the committee in 1916. See W. W. Marsh to WW, July 31, 1916, Vol. 37.

George Creel to Edith Bolling Galt Wilson

New York City
September Seventeenth,
My dear Mrs. Wilson: Nineteen Twenty.

I will be in Washington next Tuesday with James W. Gerard, the Former Ambassador, on business connected with the Democratic National Committee. He has some original documents of remarkable importance and has had them set in gold, frankincense and myrrh, or something like that, and he wants to give them to the President. As you know, the President has never seen him since his return from Germany. If a five minute interview can be arranged, I think it will be tremendously helpful. Since coming to know Gerard I have grown to a very real liking for him and his devotion to the President is really very beautiful.

If the President does not concur with this suggestion will *you* receive him with me?

As for myself it is of the utmost importance that I see the President for a few moments. Mr. Tumulty, over the telephone today, suggested the preparation of certain campaign statements. I want to get the President's exact idea with respect to these: but there is a matter of even greater importance that I want to take up with him. Frankly and confidentially, the new Mexican Government has insisted upon my acting as its political guide and spiritual mentor, and General Obregon is making any speech that I suggest.[1]

In my opinion, the President's Mexican policy has been one of his finest exhibitions of democratic belief and events today prove his wisdom and justice. I *know* that we can bring this policy to complete success. This is what I want to talk to him about. All he has to do is to tell me what he wants Obregon to do and it will be done instantly. Needless to say, I have no connection with the Mexican Government other than their belief in me and I am under no obligations to it. My one interest is my devotion to the President and my ardent desire to see him triumphant over the evil forces that hate him.

Will you be kind enough to telegraph me upon receipt of this?

Believe me,   Always sincerely,   George Creel

TLS (WP, DLC).

¹ This is the first intimation of Creel's involvement in Mexican-American relations at this time. Subsequent documents will relate his special mission to Mexico City and its outcome.

To John Appleton Stewart

My dear Mr. Stewart: [The White House] 18 September, 1920

Thank you for your letter of the sixteenth. I certainly hope that all your plans will be matured. I shall follow the progress of the celebration with the greatest interest, and regret only that the condition of my health prevents my taking a personal part on so notable an occasion. I should be happy, if it were possible, to attempt to put into words the unique significance of the things we are commemorating.   Sincerely yours,   [Woodrow Wilson]

CCL (WP, DLC).

Two Letters from Bainbridge Colby

My dear Mr. President: Washington September 18, 1920.

I beg to refer to the question, already much discussed, of sending General Crowder to Cuba, to impress upon the government the importance of conducting the approaching Presidential election fairly, and with honest observance of the new electoral code.

Since the receipt of your letter of September first, I have re-examined the question from every angle, and have had numerous conferences with General Crowder and with Mr. Davis whose recommendation that General Crowder should be sent was the subject of your letter.

The question presents many difficulties and decision is not easy.

It can be assumed in the first place that the outlook for a peaceful and fairly conducted election in November is not good. The preliminaries of the election (registration etc.) have been marked by frauds, intimidation and violence. Representations have been made to President Menocal on the importance of punishing offenders and upholding the law. He professes to be exerting all his powers to this end. Furthermore our legation has made a public announcement of the concern felt by this government that the election should be untainted by irregularities and its result accepted by the people.

The idea of sending General Crowder to Cuba at this time was to promote these objects. He is the author of the election law, and enjoys a wide favor, and a considerable influence with some of the political leaders of the island. The Liberal party, whose candidate is General Gomez, is apparently desirous that he should come.

On the other hand, President Menocal has evinced a strong opposition to his visit, professing to see in it a reflection upon his administration, his assurances, the self-capacity of his people, and an undeserved political lift to his adversaries. Menocal is not himself a candidate for re-election. His party, the Conservative, has effected a coalition with certain opposition groups, and is ranged behind Mr. Alfredo Zayas as its candidate.

General Crowder thinks he should not go unless invited, or at least assured of a friendly reception. We accordingly instructed our Minister to Cuba who was in Washington a few days ago and has just returned to his post, to sound the Cuban government on the question, and we have received a cable from him that President Menocal intimates that he may feel obliged to resign his office if General Crowder is sent.

There the matter stands. The Liberal leaders are talking of advising their followers to remain away from the polls, and there is believed by competent observers to be a chance of revolutionary outbreak if matters continue as they have been going.

I am not clear as to the wisdom however of trying to jam General Crowder down their throats. We might aggravate the very conditions we are anxious to compose. If we insist on his going, we may be rebuffed, and I am not certain that we are ready to take the decisions that would then be instantly devolved upon us.

I might add that the Cuban Minister,[1] with whom I talked on Thursday, thinks it would be a mistake to send General Crowder. He thinks his government is proceeding in good faith and doing the best it can. He thinks it would impair the moral influence of this government, so valuable to Cuba, if we were to intervene inconclusively at this stage of a bitter political contest, and that for Cuba's sake we should reserve our strength for the most critical situations, and then act only in the most decisive way, if we act at all.   Very respectfully yours,   Bainbridge Colby

[1] Carlos Manuel de Céspedes y Quesada.

My dear Mr. President: Washington September 18, 1920.

May I have the benefit of your judgment as to the advisability of a statement relative to your decision to observe the obligations of our treaties of commerce, notwithstanding the provisions of the Merchant Shipping Act, calling for their termination?

Ordinarily your decision would be communicated, I suppose, to Congress upon its re-assembling in December, and I am not aware of any duty to state it earlier. The Act, however, foreshadowed so startling a departure from the traditional policy of the United States, that your course thereunder has been the subject of much speculation and of the widest interest. The latter can hardly be appeased by silence, and already articles are appearing in the press, made up of guess-work and invention.

If you approve of a statement, it might take the form of an instruction to me or to the Department of State. I would be very glad to draft something for submission to you, if you will indicate your wishes.

I assume you would hardly wish to go into the legal argument about the distinction between partial abrogation and denunciation in toto, but would prefer to place your action upon the grounds already stated to me, i.e. the binding reciprocal force of treaties, and the absence of constitutional right on the part of Congress to impose a direction upon you in regard to foreign affairs.

These are the big reasons and therefore I think the best ones.
Very respectfully yours,   Bainbridge Colby

TLS (WP, DLC).

From William Bauchop Wilson

My dear Mr. President: Washington September 18, 1920.

I am compelled to trouble you about a matter which involves the good faith of your Commission appointed in October, 1917,[1] to secure the adjustment of labor disturbances and restore proper production for war purposes.

When the Commission arrived in Arizona, the Clifton-Morenci-Metcalf District was closed by a strike for a wage increase. The wage rates we found were much lower than the rates paid at Globe on the one side and Bisbee on the other. It became apparent that an increase was necessary to proper living conditions, and it was represented to us that one or more of the companies could not operate without loss at the then fixed price for copper if an increased wage rate was granted. That was particularly true with regard to the Shannon Copper Company. To have attempted to secure the operation of the other mines with the Shannon mines shut down would have been futile. Such a move would have been looked upon by the mine workers as an attempt to defeat them by sections.

We therefore advised a resumption of work at all the mines, including the Shannon, with provision for an increase in wage rates later after an expert engineer selected by us had gone over the accounts of the companies and determined what increase, if any, should be paid. We further agreed that if it was shown that any of the companies were operating at a loss, we would recommend to the President an increase in the selling price which would enable the company to operate at a reasonable profit and would not put the new wage scale into effect until the increased selling price was obtained. The agreement with your Commission was promptly and loyally obeyed. It was found upon full investigation that a wage increase was necessary, and the Shannon Copper Company alone of the operating companies could not operate without a loss.

In the meantime the War Industries Board had been created, and in order to avoid troubling you with what we considered a matter of detail we made an attempt to secure relief from that Board. During the time that the War Industries Board was considering the proposition the labor situation became so critical that it threatened seriously to curtail the production of copper, and acting upon the belief that relief would finally be secured from the Board, the Commission directed that the new wage rate be put into effect. Several months were lost in presenting the matter to the War Industries Board, and when it finally reached an adverse decision, you were making preparations to go to Versailles, and we did not feel we were justified in presenting a matter of such relatively minor importance when your every energy was devoted to international affairs.

The Shannon Copper Company's operation was essential to industrial peace, and at the request of the Commission and upon the assurance that the matter would be presented to you, it continued its production. When the Armistice was signed and the emergency was over, the Shannon shut down. A claim of the Shannon Company was then filed under the Dent Act[2] for $388,582.54, of which $116,829.82 was stated to be for actual losses in operation. The Board allowed the excess wages paid but denied further relief. Upon appeal to the Secretary of War, all relief was denied upon memorandum holding that your Commission was not a contract making body, and even if such contract existed there was no proof that you would have acted favorably upon your Commission's recommendation of an increased selling price.

The Commission may not have been a contract making body in the sense that the War Department or the Navy Department was a contract making body, but it was directed by you to look into the causes of unrest in these fields and to devise and apply a remedy if possible. We found the wage rates in the Clifton-Morenci-Metcalf region so low as compared with other districts that they were a disturbing factor in the whole copper producing section. We therefore made a trade agreement between the operators and miners and included in it a proviso that we would recommend to you an increase in the selling price of copper for any mine that could not operate without operating at a loss. We feel that if we had brought the matter directly to you at the time, the allowance would have been made and the present embarrassment avoided. I am firmly convinced that the remarkable record made by Arizona after the settlement of the labor troubles by your Commission, showing a production of more than 100,000,000 pounds of copper in excess of the normal 800,000,000 pounds, was due in a very large measure to the means provided by your Commission and the resultant cooperation of all concerned, particularly the Shannon Copper Company. The suspension of this mine would have had a psychological effect upon the balance of the state, as it would have been attributed to the failure of your Commission to make good its promise made on your authority.

The amount claimed by the Shannon Copper Company is $388,582.54, of which $116,829.82 is stated to be actual losses in operation, and the balance, $271,752.72, would represent profits. The Shannon Company was operating at a loss before the strike took place and contemplated shutting down. I am not satisfied in my own mind, therefore, that it is entitled to the amount of profit it is claiming. I am quite clear, however, that it should be reimbursed for all its losses. There is not included in the $116,829.82 the full amount of the losses of the company. The Commission found when it decided that in the interests of peace in the copper regions the wage award should be put into effect, that the Shannon Company had not the means to make back payment of the award. The War Industries Board had not decided the question pending before it, and funds were not available from the Government to help out in the situation. It consequently made arrangements with private interests to advance $16,000.00 to meet the back pay-roll. If that $16,000.00 was added to the $116,829.82 actual losses and a reasonable amount allowed for attorney's fees, I would feel that the Government had faithfully fulfilled its part of the agreement.

I therefore recommend that the claim of the Shannon Copper

Company to the amount of $150,000.00 be allowed, and if the amount can not be settled by the War Department, that you direct its payment out of the unexpended balance of your fund[3] now in the hands of the Shipping Board.

Faithfully yours,   W B Wilson

TLS (WP, DLC).

[1] That is, the President's Mediation Commission, actually appointed on September 19, 1917. About its activities, see the index references to it in Vols. 44-47.

[2] "An Act to Provide Relief in Cases of Contracts Connected with the Prosecution of the War, and for Other Purposes," introduced by Stanley Hubert Dent, Jr., Democratic congressman from Alabama, on December 7, 1918, and signed by Wilson on March 2, 1919. It authorized the Secretary of War to "adjust, pay, or discharge any agreement, express or implied," that had been entered into during the war by any agent acting under his authority, or under that of the President, with any person or company for purposes connected with the prosecution of the war. 40 *Statutes at Large* 1272. See also *Cong. Record*, 65th Cong., 3d sess., *passim.*

[3] That is, Wilson's $100,000,000 War Emergency Fund.

Two Letters to Bainbridge Colby

My dear Mr. Secretary: The White House 20 September, 1920

Replying to your letter of September eighteenth, I think that it is hardly necessary to volunteer a public statement about my decision to observe the obligations of our treaties of commerce without regard to the provisions of the Merchant Shipping Act, but I think I read between the lines of your letter that you think it might be well to check speculation and stop the guessing that is going on. I would, therefore, be very much obliged indeed if you would act upon your suggestion that you draft something for my examination in connection with this.

Cordially and faithfully yours,   Woodrow Wilson

My dear Mr. Secretary: The White House 20 September, 1920

I find myself very much in accord with your judgment about the matter of sending General Crowder to Cuba, and hope that you will pursue the course that you yourself have suggested.

Cordially and sincerely yours,   Woodrow Wilson

TLS (B. Colby Papers, DLC).

To Frank Park

My dear Friend: [The White House] 20 September, 1920

I warmly appreciate what you have told me about the walking cane, and you may be sure that when I get it I shall prize it as of peculiar value, because of the friendship which it reminds me of.

          Cordially and sincerely yours,   [Woodrow Wilson]

P.S. It is evident that in your generosity you realize why I cannot give myself the pleasure of personal interviews.

CCL (WP, DLC).

From Newton Diehl Baker, with Enclosure

Dear Mr. President: Washington. September 20, 1920.

I return herewith the letter of the Reverend E. O. Watson, secretary of the General Committee on Army and Navy Chaplains. I do not know whether you would care to receive personally the committee, but the medal which they desire to present does represent a splendid service to the Army and the country performed by the chaplains of the Protestant churches, and the action of the General Committee in presenting one to you is most appropriate, and the basis of presentation suggested in the next paragraph to the last of their letter seems to me just and important.

Of course, if you are willing to receive Bishop McDowell and his associates and accept the medal from their hands, a note from Mr. Tumulty to Mr. Watson to that effect, and fixing the day, would be all that is necessary. If, however, you prefer not to do that, you might ask the committee to present the medal to you through me, and with that thought in mind I venture to submit a suggested letter for you to send Mr. Watson.

          Respectfully yours,   Newton D. Baker

TLS (WP, DLC).

E N C L O S U R E

My dear Mr. Watson: 21 September, 1920

I have received your letter of September 15 and deeply appreciate the action of the General Committee on Army and Navy Chaplains voting me one of the medals designed for presentation to the chaplains who, under the auspices of the Federal Council of Churches of Christ in America, served through the great war with the Army and Navy.

I have known, of course, from the Secretary of War and the Secretary of the Navy, of the fine cooperation which the Federal Council gave to their departments in the selection of chaplains for our great military forces, and I have known from them, too, of the devotion and sacrificial spirit with which the chaplains ministered to the troops, bearing their hardships with them and carrying the comfort and consolation of their ministry to the front-line trenches under conditions where only the brave could survive. I shall feel myself honored to have a medal which commemorates such service and such valor, and deeply appreciate the thought of your Committee which associates me in the fellowship of these splendid men.

I am especially sensible of the action taken by your Committee which associates the gift of this medal to me with the ideals of our Christian faith embodied in the Covenant for a League of Nations. Our soldiers surely fought a good fight for the Master's cause, and I devoutly pray that their sacrifice may be sanctified by the acceptance of the principles embodied in the Covenant, establishing a new order of peace based on justice among the nations of the earth, so that the conclusion of this great and terrible war may be in fact a peace which will pass the understanding of the old order and be in verity and fact a Christian peace.

I regret that I am not able to receive in person the Committee appointed to convey the medal to me, but I have asked the Secretary of War to receive it for me and to express again my appreciation at the time of its presentation.

Cordially and sincerely yours,[1]

T MS (N. D. Baker Papers, DLC).
[1] This was sent verbatim as WW to E. O. Watson, Sept. 21, 1920, TLS (Letterpress Books, WP, DLC).

Isaac Landman[1] to Joseph Patrick Tumulty

Dear Mr. Tumulty: New York September 20, 1920.

As you are probably aware, there is at present being conducted in this country a campaign against the Jews. You know, of course, that most anti-semitism is due to the fact that non-Jews are filled with false ideas regarding their (the Jews') ideals.

I have attempted in the current issue of The American Hebrew, to present certain facts about the Jews which I am very desirous to have you, as a man in a position to mould public opinion in America, take note of.

I am taking the liberty, therefore, to send you a copy of this issue under separate cover, hoping that you may take the time to look through it and if you will be so good, to send me a comment upon the idea expressed in my editorial.

Cordially yours,   Isaac Landman.

TLS (WP, DLC).

¹ Editor of *The American Hebrew*. Following receipt of this letter, the one from Simon Wolf printed at September 7, 1920, and undoubtedly others that were not saved, Tumulty and Wilson embarked upon an initiative, the object and details of which can only be inferred from the few documents concerning it which have survived.

We think that the initiative was to send Edward N. Hurley on a secret mission to Henry Ford to attempt to persuade him to call off his anti-Semitic campaign described in n. 1 to the letter from Wolf.

Tumulty sent a telegram to Hurley on September 30 asking Hurley to telephone him at the White House as soon as possible. JPT to ENH, Sept. 30, 1920, T telegram (E. N. Hurley Papers, InND). We assume that Hurley did call and agreed to undertake the mission to Ford, because Tumulty sent the following telegram to Ford on October 4: "The President is requesting his warm friend Edward N Hurley of Chicago to see you at once and lay before you a matter which is very near his heart." JPT to H. Ford, Oct. 4, 1920, T telegram (MiDbF). Ford's assistant secretary replied on the same day saying that Ford would see Hurley and asking when to expect him. Fred R. Dolsen to JPT, Oct. 4, 1920, T telegram, *ibid*. A few minutes after receiving Dolsen's telegram, Tumulty sent the following to Hurley: "The President sincerely trusts that you will go to Detroit at once and lay before Mr. Ford urgency of matter we discussed over telephone. Suggest you get in touch with Alfred Lucking when you reach Detroit before you see Mr. Ford." JPT to ENH, Oct. 4, 1920, T telegram (E. N. Hurley Papers, InND). Lucking, a former Democratic congressman from Michigan, was the general counsel of the Ford Motor Company.

It is not altogether clear whether Hurley did indeed see Ford and Lucking. Tumulty informed Hurley at 3:27 p.m. on October 4 that Ford's secretary had told him that Ford would see Hurley at Dearborn and wanted to know when he would arrive. JPT to ENH, Oct. 4, 1920, T telegram, *ibid*. Tumulty sent another message to Hurley on the following day: "Important for you to telephone me tonight." JPT to ENH, Oct. 5, 1920, *ibid*. The next evidence we have concerning this matter is a telegram from Hurley to Tumulty on October 12: "Expect to be in Washington Thursday. Will you be there. Please answer." ENH to JPT, Oct. 12, 1920, *ibid*. To this, Tumulty replied that he would be in Washington all week and would be glad to see Hurley. JPT to ENH, Oct. 12, 1920, *ibid*.

This is all the evidence we have found about this episode. Whatever documents concerning it that were once in the Tumulty and Wilson Papers were destroyed. To be more specific, the file in the Wilson Papers on Henry Ford seems to have been completely destroyed. Lee's *Henry Ford and the Jews* does not mention these negotiations, nor does Nevins and Hill, *Ford: Expansion and Challenge, 1915-1933*.

Whether our surmise that Hurley saw Ford and presented a message to him from Wilson is correct or not, that message did nothing to deter Ford in his anti-Semitic campaign which, as we have said, continued unabated until 1922 and even longer in the *Dearborn Independent*, apparently contrary to Ford's instructions.

From Edward William Bok¹

This copy is NUMBER *18*
of a special edition of fifty copies
made for personal presentation

My dear Mr. President: [Philadelphia] September 20 1920

I remember the interest you showed in my work when many years back I was waging my patent-medicine fight. You heartened me then: you have heartened me often since. All through the years which have brought so much to you, I have had the fullest confidence in your ideals and purposes, just as I have to-day. And as a slight token of that confidence, I venture to lay this in your hands, asking you to be lenient and to read it for what it is: the simple story of a struggle made, against terrific odds, by

Your admiring friend   Edward W. Bok

[1] The following is printed and handwritten in the flyleaf of Edward W. Bok, *The Americanization of Edward Bok: The Autobiography of a Dutch Boy Fifty Years After* (New York, 1920), in the Wilson Library, DLC.

To William Bauchop Wilson

My dear Mr. Secretary: The White House 21 September, 1920

I have your letter of September eighteenth about the copper matter and note your suggestion that claim of the Shannon Copper Company "should be paid out of my fund." Unhappily, I regard that fund as absolutely exhausted so far as my power to draw upon it is concerned under the law which appropriated it, and suggest that the best and most legitimate method of meeting this claim is to submit the claim to the Congress. You will no doubt be able to suggest the right channel for doing this.

Thank you very much for your full account of the difficulties involved. It seems to me that the matter was handled as well as it could be in the circumstances.

Cordially and faithfully yours,   Woodrow Wilson

TLS (received from Mary A. Strohecker).

From John Roberts[1]

Mr. President: [Washington] September 21, 1920.

For over forty years I have been spiritual adviser to prisoners in the District Jail, both white and colored, and have been spiritual adviser of every person who has been hung in the District within that time.

I am writing this letter asking for a stay of 30 days for Frank Bowman, who is under sentence to be hanged tomorrow. I do not ask for a pardon, but only that he be given 30 days more as he is not prepared to meet his Maker.[2]

I also plead for a commutation of the sentence of Josephine Berry, who is under sentence to be hanged next month, to life imprisonment. I do not do this on the ground that she is a woman but because of the very low degree of her intelligence. She is a little woman weighing hardly over 70 pounds and very ignorant. Under

the circumstances I hope you can see your way clear to commute
her sentence to life imprisonment.

Respectfully yours,   John Roberts

TLS (WP, DLC).
  ¹ His address was 35 Pierce St., N.W., and he worked in the Bureau of Printing and
Engraving. He does not seem to have been a minister.
  ² Wilson drew a brace around this paragraph and a marginal line connecting it with
the following WWhw: "Send this to the Att'y Gen'l with my OKeh W.W." W. L. Frierson
to JPT, Sept. 21, 1920, TLS (WP, DLC), says that the stay was granted.

Robert Henry Murray¹ to Henry Morgenthau

Washington DC Sept 21 [1920]

C[reel] had hour with chief today and dined there tonight His
condition most distressing At first while measurably receptive was
not especially interested subject but interest grew as conversation
proceeded Is strongly inclined to do nothing but leave problem as
legacy to successors Fears that southerners [Mexicans] will not
play fair Asked quote Are you sure they will deal honestly with me
and keep pledges if I do this unquote Seems saddened disillusioned suspicious result his experience with former elements in
government Finally expressed willingness to leave decision to C It
reasonable assume will do as he advises C naturally reluctant to
accept this great responsibility which manifestly be embarassing
to him if things go wrong Chief wants him go south interview leaders there and report fully on situation Chief also has idea Republicans anxious to have him take responsibility of recognizing and
consequent blame if it does not work out² John D Ryan³ sent em-
issary today to Colby urge him to recommend recognition Did not
find C responsive to suggestion contact with you so did not press
matter Full details when I see you here Thursday

Robert H Murray.

T telegram (H. Morgenthau Papers, DLC).
  ¹ Robert Henry Murray, distinguished investigative reporter with a longtime interest
in Mexican affairs.
  ² Creel later wrote about this meeting (he slightly misremembered the date) in his
Rebel at Large: Recollections of Fifty Crowded Years (New York, 1947), p. 228, as follows:
  "In October, 1920, for example, I went to him with a suggestion for the settlement of
the Mexican question. Roberto Pesqueira, Mexico's special envoy and a dear friend of
mine, had come to me with President Adolfo de la Huerta's hope of recognition by the
United States, and carrying full assurance of Mexico's desire for an early resumption of
fraternal relations. It looked like a good opportunity to crown the President's Mexican
policy with success, and in Washington I explained the offer and expressed a willingness to go to Mexico unofficially and at my own expense.
  "The President approved without a single dissent, and I then asked for a categorical
statement of the terms on which recognition would be granted. In reply he spoke for a
full thirty minutes, covering every detail of our controversies with Mexico, quoting the
substance of this speech and that speech, and never hesitating for a name, a date, or a

fact. Not even when he was at the peak of his power was he more the master of his mental processes."

The reader will take this account for whatever it is worth.

[3] John Dennis Ryan, chairman of the board of the Anaconda Copper Mining Co., prominent in wartime mobilization, now vice-chairman of the central committee of the American Red Cross.

From Stephenson Waters McGill[1]

My dear Mr. President: Memphis, Tenn. Sept. 22, 1920.

The Southern Presbyterian Church is seeking to establish a great university in the City of Memphis. With this university there will be combined Southwestern Presbyterian University at Clarksville.

All proper Presbyterian authorities[2] have approved the move. A campaign is being planned to raise $1,500,000 as a preliminary fund. The campaign will open on Friday October 8th at a dinner meeting of business men with Commissioner P. P. Claxton[3] as principal speaker.

We understand that your Father was at one time a professor in the University of Clarksville.[4] For this reason as well as for the additional reasons of the high esteem in which you are held by Southern Presbyterians and the exalted position which you occupy, we would like very much to have a letter or statement from you commendatory of the project.

We would like to have this statement from you so that it may be read at an early meeting of the Executive Committee & interested citizens.

With highest esteem, I am,

Cordially yours,   S. W. McGill

TLS (WP, DLC).

[1] Field Secretary for the southern Presbyterian Church; "manager" of the executive committee of "A College for Memphis Campaign."

[2] The Synods of Alabama, Louisiana, Mississippi, and Tennessee.

[3] Philander Priestly Claxton.

[4] He was Professor of Didactic, Polemic, and Historical Theology at Southwestern Presbyterian University at Clarksville, Tenn., 1885-1893. Southwestern University was merged into Southwestern at Memphis in 1925. The college changed its name to Rhodes College in 1984.

From Joe Cowperthwaite

Dear Sir,   Grasmere. Sept 22. 1920.

I was indeed pleased to receive your letter of the 3rd inst, and you may rest assured that everything will be done to carry out your wishes in every particular.

We will look forward to the month of April and sincerely hope that nothing will occur to prevent your visit.

Yours ever faithfully   Joe Cowperthwaite

ALS (WP, DLC).

From Bainbridge Colby

My Dear Mr. President;   Washington September 23, 1920.

The recognition of the *de facto* government of Bolivia presents itself as a matter of deserving consideration at the moment in view of recognition by Great Britain, Peru and Paraguay.

The present government is a junta of three persons who have been performing the functions of the President since the recent coup d'état.[1] The overturn of the former government was accompanied by but slight disturbance and the country appears to be tranquil. The junta has announced a general election in November, at which a Congress will be selected, to first act as a constitutional convention. It is the program that there shall be a popular election of a President after the Congress is chosen. Until these steps are taken it can hardly be asserted that the present government has the formal support of the people of Bolivia, and we incline to the view that recognition at any stage of this transition period may turn out to be premature. We are informed that this is the opinion of both Argentina and Brazil. Chile has withheld recognition for the additional reason that it regards the present government as inimical in feeling, if not in purpose, to Chile.

Argentina has expressed a desire to act in conjunction with this country in the matter of recognition. I think it might have salutary results in the future if we should act with Argentina and Brazil and postpone recognition until the three governments are agreed that the moment has arrived for it and, in any event, until after the elections announced for November.

If this course commends itself to you, I will see that our embassies in Argentina and Brazil are instructed accordingly.

Very respectfully yours,   Bainbridge Colby

I concur   W.W.

TLS (SDR, RG 59, 824.00/154a, DNA).
[1] About this coup, which occurred on July 12, 1920, see *FR 1920*, I, 372-74. The junta, which called itself the Provisional Council of Government, was composed of José Maria Escalier, Bautista Saavedra, and José Manuel Ramirez. They overthrew the government of José Gutiérrez Guerra

From Bainbridge Colby, with Enclosure

My Dear Mr. President: Washington September 23, 1920.

I have drafted the enclosed statement of your decision not to disturb our commercial treaties, despite the direction sought to be imposed upon you by the Merchant Shipping Act, and submit it for your consideration.

I have endeavored to express your decision briefly and simply, and have employed the expedient of following it with a comment of my own in order to carry some explanatory matter which I think is helpful, but which you would hardly volunteer in announcing a decision.   Very respectfully yours,   Bainbridge Colby

Approved   W.W.

TLS (B. Colby Papers, DLC).

E N C L O S U R E

September 23, 1920.

The Department of State has been informed by The President that he does not deem the direction, contained in Section 34 of the so-called Merchant Marine Act, an exercise of any constitutional power possessed by the Congress.

Under the provisions of the section referred to, the President was directed within ninety days after the Act became law, to notify the several Governments, with whom the United States had entered into commercial treaties, that this country elected to terminate so much of said treaties, as restricted the right of the United States to impose discriminating customs duties on imports and discriminatory tonnage dues, according as the carrier vessels were domestic or foreign, quite regardless of the fact that these restrictions are mutual, operating equally upon the other Governments which are parties to the treaties, and quite regardless also of the further fact that the treaties contain no provisions for their termination in the manner contemplated by Congress.

The President, therefore, considers it misleading to speak of the "termination" of the restrictive clauses of such treaties. The action sought to be imposed upon the Executive would amount to nothing less than the breach or violation of said treaties, which are thirty-two in number and cover every point of contact and mutual dependence which constitute the modern relations between friendly States. Such a course would be wholly irreconcilable with the historical respect which the United States has shown for its international engagements, and would falsify every profession on our belief in the binding force and the reciprocal obligation of treaties in general.

Secretary Colby, commenting on the point made by The President, that Congress had exceeded its powers, called attention to the veto by President Hayes of an Act passed by congress in 1879, which required the President to give notice to China of the abrogation of Articles V and VI of the Burlingame Treaty. President Hayes declared that "the power of making new treaties or of modifying existing treaties is not lodged by the Constitution in Congress, but in the President, by and with the advice and consent of the Senate, as shown by the concurrence of two-thirds of that body." On this subject, as well as the effect of an attempted partial abrogation of a treaty, as contemplated by the recent Act, the words of President Hayes are significant. Said he:

"As the power of modifying an existing treaty, whether by adding or striking out provisions, is a part of the treaty-making power under the Constitution, its exercise is not competent for Congress, nor would the assent of China to this partial abrogation of the treaty make the action of Congress in thus procuring an amendment of a treaty, a competent exercise of authority under the Constitution. The importance, however, of this special consideration seems superseded by the principle that a denunciation of a part of a treaty, not made by the terms of the treaty itself separable from the rest, is a denunciation of the whole treaty. As the other high contracting party has entered into no treaty obligations except such as include the part denounced, the denunciation by one party of the part necessarily liberates the other party from the whole treaty."

The Merchant Shipping Act was approved June 5th, in the final rush of the session's close, with no opportunity to suggest, much less secure its revision in any particular. To have vetoed the Act would have sacrificed the great number of sound and enlightened provisions, which it undoubtedly contains. Furthermore, the fact that one section of the law involves elements of illegality rendering the section inoperative need not affect the validity and operation of the Act as a whole.

T MS (B. Colby Papers, DLC).

From William Little Frierson

My dear Mr. President: Washington, D. C. September 23, 1920.

I beg to acknowledge receipt of your letter of September 16, 1920, asking me whether it is within your legal power to make appointments to take effect March 5, 1921. In reply, I beg to advise you that it is well established at common law that an officer clothed with authority to appoint to public office can not make a valid appointment thereto for a term which is not to begin until after the expiration of his own term of office unless the power to do so is expressly conferred upon him by statute. The authorities to this effect are reviewed in the late case of State v. Sullivan, 81 Ohio State Reports, 79, 92. Speaking generally, the statutes providing for Presidential appointments do not confer such power and you can not make appointments for terms beginning after March 4th, next. I am not now aware of any exception to this rule, though I would not say there are none. If you desire to be advised on this subject, with respect to any particular office, I can, of course, advise with certainty.   Respectfully,   Wm. L. Frierson

TLS (WP, DLC).

To Bainbridge Colby, with Enclosure

My dear Mr. Secretary: The White House 24 September, 1920

The suggestion made by Mr. Tumulty in the note attached to the enclosed article seems to me to have a good deal of merit. I submit it to your judgment, so that my own may be corrected if I am in error. If you agree with me that it is a good suggestion, will you not be kind enough to draft and forward the messages suggested?
        Cordially and faithfully yours,   Woodrow Wilson

TLS (B. Colby Papers, DLC).

E N C L O S U R E

From Joseph Patrick Tumulty

Dear Governor: The White House, 23 September 1920.

I beg to call your attention to this remarkable editorial from the Philadelphia PUBLIC LEDGER.[1] The Republicans are greatly worried about the effect on public opinion of this settlement and I am wondering if we are taking full advantage of it. Don't you think it would be well to send messages to Paderewski and the Lithuanian representative congratulating them on their efforts in stopping the war through the League of Nations, saying that the Peace Treaty and the League are now the law for all the countries of the world, excepting the United States, and expressing the hope that the United States will soon join the other nations of the world in preventing other wars.   Sincerely yours,   Tumulty

TLS (WP, DLC).
[1] "LEAGUE STOPS TWO WARS," undated clipping from the Philadelphia *Public Ledger* (WP, DLC). It had high praise for the success of the League Council in persuading Poland and Lithuania to cease fighting and submit their border dispute to its mediation and for the Council's successful mediation of the dispute between Sweden and Finland over possession of the Åland Islands.

To Henry Morgenthau

My dear Morgenthau: The White House 24 September, 1920

Thank you for your letter of September twenty-third. I have sent it, because of its importance, to the Secretary of State, and I think he will communicate with you with regard to the subject matter of it.   Cordially and faithfully yours,   Woodrow Wilson

TLS (WP, DLC).

To Bainbridge Colby, with Enclosure

My dear Mr. Secretary: The White House 24 September, 1920

I send for your perusal the enclosed interesting letter from Mr. Morgenthau, whose nomination as Ambassador to Mexico the Senate has never confirmed. I suggest, in view of Mr. Davis's recent conversations with the representative of Mexico and your and his recent conversation with Mr. Creel,[1] that you send for Mr. Morgenthau and have a conversation with him on this important and perplexing subject.

          Cordially and faithfully yours,   Woodrow Wilson

TLS (B. Colby Papers, DLC).
[1] Creel saw Colby and Davis on September 21. Creel also saw Wilson on the same day.

E N C L O S U R E

From Henry Morgenthau

My dear Mr. President!   Washington Sept 23/20

Believing that it is very important that prompt action be taken in the Mexican matter, I have come over here to seek the privilege of bringing the matter directly to your attention and will greatly and deeply appreciate a brief interview in which I could state the case and answer questions.

Carranza who spurned our friendship and was unappreciative of the help you rendered him has been displaced. The transition to the new Government and the suppression of the banditry was accomplished without any murdering by the Obregonistas.

Peace prevails—there has been a bloodless election and the present authorities are evincing every desire to obtain the necessary strength to maintain a fair Government. This they can only do by your recognition. They claim to be ready & willing to anticipate any proper requirements that *You* & not the oil interests may make of them. The sincerity of their intentions is shown by their open avowal at home, of their seeking the friendship of the US.—notwithstanding that Car[r]anza had made such an attitude unpopular. They wish to secure our co-operation, no doubt partly because owing to the present economic conditions of the world, they are totally dependent upon it.

They will have to continue to remain so for many years, & this self-interest is a great guarantee for their good behavior.

They are also influenced by their fear of republican success on November 2nd. They well know the outrageously false & misleading character of the testimony taken by the Fall Committee[1] & the danger of General Wood being put in charge of military affairs as Sec'y of War and that he will use this opportunity for personal glory—& depend upon the Fall testimony as a justification of intervention.

No recognition will prevent the development of a strong Government & may lead to war. Recognition will give the strongest set that has come to the surface an opportunity to utilize the present combination of propitious circumstances and establish a firm government—& give you the chance to prevent the success of the mischief makers & Jingoes in our midst who want war.

                    Yours Very Sincerely,   H. Morgenthau

ALS (B. Colby Papers, DLC).
    [1] Again, see n. 1 to the news report printed at Dec. 4, 1919, Vol. 64.

From Joseph Patrick Tumulty

Dear Governor: The White House 24 September 1920.

Last night I dictated the attached reply to Senator Harding's attack on Panama Canal tolls, which I think is conclusive.[1] Frankly, I do not want to seem to be suggesting a thing because of any personal vanity, but if we could give out every few days official replies of this kind, it would help a lot.

I received many letters from various parts of the country congratulating us on the statement which the TIMES printed the other day, showing the inconsistencies of the Republican party on the League of Nations.[2] The attached letter from Mr. Campbell[3] is a fair sample. This man is one of the prominent Republicans of New Jersey.

If the National Committee were functioning, I would not make this suggestion. I am also enclosing another statement[4] which is a sample of the kind which would be issued, not under my name but as official statements from The White House. I am sure the whole country would read them and it would be an excellent way of getting our case before the people; they would also pave the way for your statement.   Sincerely yours,   Tumulty

TLS (J. P. Tumulty Papers, DLC).
  [1] It is missing. However, it was printed, under the heading "Cites Republicans to Refute Harding," in the *New York Times*, Sept. 26, 1920. In a speech in Marion, Ohio, on September 20, Harding had strongly attacked Wilson for advocating the repeal, in 1914, of the law which had exempted American coastwise shipping from the payment of tolls for use of the Panama Canal (about which, see the index references to "Panama Canal tolls controversy" in Vol. 39). Tumulty, in his refutation of Harding's charges, pointed out that many prominent Republicans, such as Lodge, Root, Brandegee, Colt, Gronna, and McCumber, had voted for repeal of the tolls exemption, and he quoted at length from a statement by Root in support of Wilson's position.
  [2] "White House Reply Made to Harding on the League. Tumulty, after a Talk with Wilson, Disputes Conflict with the Constitution. Quotes Republican Chiefs. Taft, Wickersham, Straus and Hoover Cited in Opposition to Nominee's Stand," *New York Times*, Sept. 22, 1920.
  [3] It is missing.
  [4] This enclosure is also missing.

To Joseph Patrick Tumulty

Dear Tumulty: The White House [c. Sept. 24, 1920].

I think it would be a fundamental and vital mistake for the White House, directly or indirectly, to engage in a debate of any kind with Harding, and I cannot be a party to it, either directly or indirectly. The thing to do is to prepare the answers you have in mind and send them to the National Committee to serve as briefs for their speakers. If they do not use them, I know of no remedy.
                    The President.

TL (J. P. Tumulty Papers, DLC).

From Bainbridge Colby, with Enclosures

My dear Mr. President: Washington September 25, 1920.

I beg to acknowledge the receipt of your letter of the 24th enclosing Mr. Morgenthau's letter to you, dated the 23d, on the Mexican situation. As suggested by you, I have had a conference with Mr. Morgenthau, who feels that the time is near, if not at hand, for the recognition of Mexico, on terms that will satisfy every reasonable condition that we would be likely to attach to such action on our part.

Mr. Morgenthau brings us no new facts, but there is value in getting the reaction of his candid and well-meaning mind on this subject, which you very adequately describe as important and perplexing.

We have, as I think you know, received some rather skittish overtures from the Mexican Government during the last few weeks. The most direct approach has been through Mr. Calderon Iglesias, whose credentials indicate that he is an Ambassador in all respects save our recognition and acceptance. In addition to Mr. Iglesias, there are also in this country in some form of representative relation to the Mexican Government, Mr. Pesquiera and Mr. Alvarado.[1]

Mr. Davis has talked with both Iglesias and Pesquiera.[2] I have refrained from a meeting with either, on the theory that I could thus signify a little reserve on our part, so long as the discussions were informal, and I might even say experimental. Both profess a desire for early recognition, freely admit the dependence of Mexico for rehabilitation on the support of this country, and protest their willingness to meet all reasonable conditions.

On our side we have emphasized the policy of this country to respect the right of Mexico to direct its administration without interference from us, but have indicated the importance from the standpoint of recognition that Mexico should give convincing proof of her ability as well as disposition to sustain her international obligations, such as the protection of life, and property acquired in good faith, and in conformity with Mexican law. To these suggestions, the most ready assent has been given.

The discussion, however, does not get beyond talk. Either the Mexican spokesmen are not sure of their government, or the latter is not sure of itself.

There is a good deal of veiled strategy in the situation—propagandists, press agents, informal emissaries, oil men, attorneys and various like bedevilments. I hope we can have a talk with you soon about the whole situation. It would be the most helpful thing possible, and I think the time has arrived when it is needed.

I received a call from Mr. Creel, after his interview with you on Tuesday. He outlined his plan, which seemed to me very promising. Yesterday I received the enclosed letter from him, which indicates a change of program not fully explained. I enclose a copy of my reply to his letter.

Very respectfully yours,   Bainbridge Colby

TLS (WP, DLC).

¹ Roberto V. Pesqueira (not Pesquiera) Morales, Mexican businessman and financial agent of the De la Huerta government; and Gen. Salvador Alvarado, who had come to the United States to negotiate a loan for the Mexican government with American bankers. See Robert Freeman Smith, *The United States and Revolutionary Nationalism in Mexico, 1916-1932* (Chicago and London, 1972), pp. 186-87.
² Memoranda of these conversations are printed as Enclosures with NHD to WW, Sept. 28, 1920.

E N C L O S U R E   I

George Creel to Bainbridge Colby

New York City
September Twenty-Second,

Dear Mr. Secretary: Nineteen Twenty.

With respect to the matter we talked of yesterday, I will not be able to make up my mind for several days as yet. A personal matter of rather embarrassing nature has arisen and until it is cleared up to my complete satisfaction I cannot go to Mexico or take any further interest in the hoped for settlement.

The more I think about the matter, however, the more I am impressed with your view as to the possibilities of a trap. It is not alone that the matter would have to be staged carefully in order to prepare the country for action, but it is also the case that the representations of the other people should be so generous and so binding as to minimize the possibility of ill-faith or future failure.

Please do not let anyone, not even your associates, know of my interest in this matter. If I decide to go into it again I will come to Washington to see you.

Believe me,   Always sincerely,   George Creel

TLS (B. Colby Papers, DLC).

E N C L O S U R E   I I

Bainbridge Colby to George Creel

My dear Mr. Creel: [Washington] September 24, 1920.

I have your letter of the 22nd. It is a little cryptic and of course I am much interested to learn what has happened to so quickly turn you away from the plan you outlined to me and which seemed so interesting. However, I shall abide your own good time and pleasure in going more fully into the matter and only write to assure you of my unabated interest in your suggestion.

Yours faithfully,   Bainbridge Colby

CCL (WP, DLC).

Three Letters from Bainbridge Colby

My dear Mr. President: Washington September 25, 1920.

Ambassador Davis proposes to return to London in about ten days, with a view to relinquishing his post not later than January first.

He and I have had an intimate talk about his situation, and the causes that prompt him to anticipate by a few months the expiration of his appointed term. The drain upon his purse has been heavy and he confides to me that he is at the end of his tether. I think also he has either accepted or has under advisement some attractive professional offers in New York, which contemplate his return before January. This would leave the Embassy in charge of Mr. Butler Wright,[1] who has the rank of Counsellor, and a very fine reputation in the service for efficiency. When I remarked to Mr. Davis that you might, however, feel, in view of the international situation, that you could not allow so important an Ambassadorship to be vacant, he said he would be glad to resign at once if that would simplify the situation. He thinks, however, he should in any event return to his post and spend a brief time there for purposes of leave-taking. I urged him to serve out his term, but he is quite resolved as to what he must do.

If you wish to make a new appointment, I suppose the earlier the position is available, the easier it will be for you to get the man you want.

I am led to believe that Mr. Davis may place his resignation in your hands before he sails on October sixth.

Very respectfully yours,   Bainbridge Colby

[1] Joshua Butler Wright.

My Dear Mr. President: Washington September 25, 1920.

May I pause in the rush of business just long enough to say to you how truly admirable I consider your action on the commercial treaties. I am not unmindful of the fact also that you reached your decision with no help from your advisers. On the contrary we plied you with plausibilities which only you could have brushed aside so completely.

You are right—beyond question, and I think, when the real significance of your stand for the inviolability of treaties is appreciated, as well as the scale upon which Congress had proposed to commit us to an opposite and indefensible course, you will have abundant cause for satisfaction.

Faithfully always,   Bainbridge Colby

My dear Mr. President: Washington September 25, 1920.

Referring to the enclosed memorandum from Mr. Tumulty and the editorial from the "Public Ledger"[1] on the reported agreement of Lithuania and Poland to submit their disputed boundaries to the League of Nations and pending the latter's decision, to desist from hostilities, I beg to say that our latest advices are that hostilities between the two countries have been resumed and therefore there is no background at the moment for a congratulatory message. The information received by the Department is to the effect that the Poles demanded the withdrawal of the Lithuanian troops to the line of demarcation fixed by the Supreme Council on December 8, 1919. To this Lithuania agreed, provided Poland would withdraw from contact with this line, and establish a neutral zone which would embrace the towns of Seiny and Punsk. This proposal was rejected by the Poles, who apparently feared that some military use would be made of the neutral zone by the Bolshevik forces.

The hopeful factor in the situation is the apparent willingness of both countries to entertain the idea of a submission of the issue between them to the League of Nations, although the point of actual submission has not been reached.

You will be interested to know that a telegram from Riga, dated yesterday, states that there is a general feeling in that city that negotiations for a preliminary peace between Poland and Soviet Russia are viewed as presenting distinct prospect of success.

Very respectfully yours,   Bainbridge Colby

TLS (WP, DLC).
   [1] See the Enclosure printed with WW to BC, Sept. 24, 1920 (first letter of that date), and n. 1 thereto.

From Newton Diehl Baker

Dear Mr. President: Washington September 25, 1920.

For sometime Prince Lubomirski, the Polish Minister, has been seeking to buy from the War Department large quantities of materials declared surplus out of our war accumulations. Some months ago I established three principles to control the disposition of such surplus supplies:

1. No materials would be sold for export which could be used in this country by our own citizens.

2. No surplus would be sold either to a foreign government or for export to a foreign country without the approval of the Secretary of State as to the propriety of such export from the point of view of our international relations.

3. No sale would be made on credit to any foreign government without the approval of the Secretary of the Treasury to such addition to credits already extended by our Government to foreign nations.

Large sales have heretofore been made to Poland, aggregating about $140,000,000, for which we hold the unsecured obligations of the Polish Government. I, therefore, told Prince Lubomirski that the War Department could not increase the credit already extended without the concurrence of the Secretary of State and the Secretary of the Treasury.

The original requests of Poland for purchases of surplus supplies have now been very much reduced and are restricted to reclaimed uniforms and articles of clothing which have been worn by our soldiers and have now been sterilized, repaired, and cleansed, and are not available for reissue to our soldiers and not saleable to our own people. The Secretary of State believes that it would be proper to sell such surpluses to Poland. I have discussed the matter with the Secretary of the Treasury, and he feels that if the sales are limited to materials of the kind I have described there would be no embarrassment from the Treasury standpoint in the sales being made.

I submit the question to you because sales made by the War Department to Poland are instantly seized upon by the group of newspapers which criticise assistance rendered by us to Poland as being an intervention against Russia. As I understand the situation, the Secretary of State has notified Poland of our sympathy with its independence and its effort to establish securely its present government. These sales would be in harmony with that assurance. My personal judgment is that the sales could properly be made, and I so recommend. If, however, there are considerations which ought to be weighed and have not here been properly considered, I would be grateful for an indication of your view in the matter.

Respectfully yours,   Newton D. Baker

I concur   W.W.

TLS (N. D. Baker Papers, DLC).

From Joseph Patrick Tumulty

Dear Governor: The White House September 25, 1920.

I do not know whether you want to pay any attention to this letter.[1] If you do, it is an excellent opportunity. Of course, you practically answered these questions on your Western Trip. I am sending you, herewith, memorandum of questions which you answered covering this subject.[2]   Sincerely,   J P Tumulty

Irish Question Pres. OK's

TLS (WP, DLC).
    [1] Edwin M. Swartz to WW, Sept. 20, 1920, TLS (WP, DLC). The writer, a lawyer of Los Angeles, pointed out that the Republicans claimed that, in ratifying the Versailles Treaty (and Article X of the Covenant) the United States "would be bound to support England in holding Ireland under subjugation." "Is it not a fact," he asked, "and so understood by the high contracting parties at the time the Covenant was drawn and approved, that Article X was to prohibit one Nation from grabbing any territory of another Nation? And, also, is it not true that when you said Article X was the heart of the Covenant, that you meant by that the European wars had nearly all been caused by National landgrabbers, and that this Article would cure that evil?"
    [2] This enclosure is missing. However, JPT to E. M. Swartz, Sept. 27, 1920, CCL (WP, DLC), repeated the memorandum embodying questions about Ireland and Wilson's replies thereto printed at September 16, 1919, Vol. 63. Tumulty's letter was given to the press and was published, e.g., in the *New York Times*, Sept. 29, 1920.

From John Sharp Williams

At Home

My dear Mr President: [Yazoo City, Miss.] Sept 25 1920

I see things in the newspapers to the effect that some about headquarters are desirous that you should take part in the campaign. If they mean that you shall go out and make speeches, don't do it as your health is of more importance now to the party, the nation, and the world than it is important that you should do *that*. Everybody knows that you want our success, and the most effective way of impressing that fact on your friends—if indeed it needs impressing—is *not* the exploitation of your energies as a "stump" speaker. One great speech, perhaps, delivered in a hall—not too large—would carry the message that I doubt not is in you, to the

American people & to the friends of Peace & the Prince of Peace throughout the intellectual & civilized world. *Conserve yourself* as our mainstay—not *for* yourself, of course, but for things vastly higher than any of us as individuals. You know I would not advise any course with the view merely of self-protection. The people are not fools—though some of them, now as always, are. Those of them worth while know where your heart is. The voice can go with it to them in a better way.

I remain as always: your good, though thank God, not even your best friend,   John Sharp Williams

ALS (WP, DLC).

From Joseph Patrick Tumulty, with Enclosure

My dear Governor: The White House 26 September 1920.

I think I have found a suitable way to begin our attack if you care to take part in this campaign. The whole country is filled with the poison spread by Lodge and his group and it has to do principally with the attacks made upon you for failing to consult anyone about possible changes in the Treaty and your reluctance toward suggesting to your associates on the other side changes of any kind.

George Creel and I have examined the cables that passed between you and Mr. Taft[1] and we have prepared a statement which is attached to this letter.[2] This statement, with the Taft cables will be a knockout, (I know that Mr. Taft is already preparing a book on the Treaty which will carry these cables)[3] and will clear the air and show how contemptible our enemies have been in circulating stories. We have carefully gone over the Covenant and find that nearly every change suggested by Mr. Taft was made and in some cases you went further than he asked.

George Creel is of the opinion that the statement should come from the White House.   Sincerely,   Tumulty

TLS (J. P. Tumulty Papers, DLC).
   [1] W. H. Taft and A. L. Lowell to WW, Feb. 10, 1919; WW to W. H. Taft, Feb. 14, 26, and 28, 1919; and W. H. Taft to WW, March 1, 1919, all in Vol. 55; W. H. Taft to WW, March 18, 21, and 28, 1919, all in Vol. 56; W. H. Taft and A. L. Lowell to WW, April 10 and 12, 1919, both in Vol. 57; W. H. Taft to JPT, May 5, 1919, Vol. 58; and W. H. Taft to WW, June 28, 1919, Vol. 61.
   [2] There is a copy of this press release in WC, NjP.
   [3] It was published as Theodore Marburg and Horace E. Flack, eds., *Taft Papers on League of Nations* (New York, 1920). It included, for the most part, speeches and articles by Taft from 1915 to 1919. In the last ten pages of the book, the editors, "with the consent of President Wilson," published some of the correspondence cited in n. 1, as well as a few letters between Taft and Tumulty.

ENCLOSURE

In view of the statements that have frequently been made, that the President was unwilling to confer with the Senate with reference to the League of Nations, public attention ought to be called to the fact that when the President returned from France in February 1919, with the first draft of the covenant of the League of Nations, he invited all the members of the Senate Committee on Foreign Relations and all the members of the House Committee on Foreign Affairs to the White House to dinner for a formal consultation. Republicans and Democrats alike were there, and the President discussed the proposed covenant then.

A few days later Senator Lodge produced his famous round-robin, signed by thirty-seven Republican Senators, who declared that the League was not acceptable in the form presented, but made no suggestions of any kind for its improvement as a means of preserving peace. In this connection it may be stated that not one single suggested amendment, received from any responsible source, went unheeded, the majority being incorporated in the revised draft virtually verbatim.

After the President returned in July, 1919, with the treaty and the final draft of the covenant, he again conferred with all the members of the Senate Committee on Foreign Relations. The conference was public in the sense that official stenographers were present and the questions and answers were given to the newspapers as rapidly as the transcripts could be made. This meeting betrayed on the part of the Republican Senators no desire to understand the covenant. Their attitude was one of implacable hostility. Previous to that the President had appeared before the Senate in person and discussed the treaty in submitting it, something that no other President has done in more than a hundred years.

Ex-President Taft was one of the men whose views were asked and whose criticism was invited. The cable correspondence, initiated by him as a result of his study of the draft agreement, is herewith submitted as a proper and necessary contribution to the present discussion.

CC MS (J. P. Tumulty Papers, DLC).

To Joseph Patrick Tumulty

Dear Tumulty: [The White House, c. Sept. 26, 1920]

I have read your letter of September twenty-sixth with a sincere effort to keep an open mind about the suggestions you make, but I must say that it has not changed my mind at all. No answers to Harding of any kind will proceed from the White House with my consent.

It pleases me very much that you and Creel are in collaboration on material out of which smashing answers can be made, and I beg that you will press those materials on the attention of the Speakers' Bureau of the National Committee. It is their clear duty to supply those materials in turn to the speakers of the campaign. If they will not, I am sorry to say I know of no other course that we can pursue.   The President.

TL (J. P. Tumulty Papers, DLC).

Two Letters to Bainbridge Colby

My dear Mr. Secretary: The White House 27 September, 1920

I think it is most unfortunate that Mr. Davis should retire from his Ambassadorship at this time, and I think that he ought to be induced to reconsider his decision if it is possible for him to do so.

I judge from your letter that you think it would be best, if he does resign, to have him resign at once and proceed to the choice of a successor. I agree with you in this and am anxious to know whether anyone has occurred to you as a suitable successor. Will you not consider the matter and let me know? My own thought has centered upon Mr. Baruch.

Cordially and faithfully yours,   Woodrow Wilson

My dear Mr. Secretary: The White House 27 September, 1920

Replying to your letter of September twenty-fifth about the Mexican situation and your conversation with Mr. Morgenthau, let me say that I greatly deplore the necessity Creel has been under to postpone his trip, for I think it will pave the way for definite action. Until the Mexican Government has acted upon the intimations given it through Mr. Davis's conversation with Pesquiera, I do not think that it will be wise to extend formal recognition to it, but this judgment I hold subject to correction if you should find conclusive reasons to the contrary.

Cordially and faithfully yours,   Woodrow Wilson

TLS (B. Colby Papers, DLC).

To Stephenson Waters McGill

My dear Mr. McGill: [The White House] 27 September, 1920

I have your letter of September twenty-second, in which you ask me to endorse the plan for a college to be established by the Presbyterian Church in Memphis. I must frankly say that I do not believe in denominational colleges and I think that their multiplication would be a very serious mistake. I know that you will understand this very frank expression of my judgment. It is based upon long observation and experience.

Very sincerely yours,   [Woodrow Wilson]

CCL (WP, DLC).

To Royal Meeker

My dear Meeker: [The White House] 27 September, 1920

I have your letter of the eleventh of September[1] but do not feel that I can send you the sort of letter which you ask for in it, because you ask for a statement from me of the services which the Labor Office can perform. That is a large order. My own judgment is that the Labor Office should show what functions it ought to perform by performing them, and feeling its way from experience to experience.

Hoping that you are enjoying your new work and finding it what you expected.   Sincerely yours,   [Woodrow Wilson]

CCL (WP, DLC).
   [1] R. Meeker to WW, Sept. 11, 1920, TLS (WP, DLC). Meeker had recently become the Chief of the Scientific Division of the League of Nation's International Labour Office at Geneva, charged with gathering, compiling, and publishing statistical and other information relating to labor and industry. Meeker told Wilson that the office had decided to establish a "popular-scientific monthly review," entitled *International Labour Review*. He asked Wilson for a brief statement, to be published in the first issue of the review in October, on his "views of the International Labour Office in its relations to the industrial and labour problems of the world; the important problems which it can and must deal with; and the service it can perform in bringing into more harmonious relations Governments of the world, as well as employers and employees in industry."

To Joseph Patrick Tumulty

Dear Tumulty: The White House [c. Sept. 27, 1920].

I entirely agree with the judgment of the Secretary of War in this matter[1] and would be very much obliged if you would have prepared for me a proclamation along the lines he suggests.[2]

The President.

TL (WP, DLC).

¹ It concerned a request by the executive board of the League for the Protection of American Prisoners in Germany that Wilson designate Sunday, November 14, as Armistice Sunday. Marie B. Snook and Harriet B. Calkins to WW, Sept. 15, 1920, TLS, enclosed in John Arthur Elston, Republican congressman from California, to WW, Sept. 16, 1920, ALS (WP, DLC). Tumulty had forwarded this correspondence to Baker and had asked for his advice on the matter in JPT to NDB, Sept. 22, 1920, TLS (WP, DLC). In his reply, Baker pointed out that, of course, Wilson had no right under existing law to establish Armistice Day as a legal holiday. "Under all the circumstances," Baker concluded, "I am rather inclined to think that the President might permit himself to express in some public way the hope that on Sunday, November 14, this year, our participation in the great war will be solemnly remembered and our heroic dead tendered a thought of in connection with the religious exercises ordinarily conducted on that day. Beyond this, I think it would not be wise for him to go at this time." NDB to JPT, Sept. 23, 1920, TLS (WP, DLC).

² JPT to NDB, Sept. 27, 1920, TLS (WP, DLC), informed Baker of Wilson's request. Baker then prepared for Wilson's signature a letter to Representative Elston saying that Wilson strongly approved the observance of Armistice Day and that "November 14 this year, being the Sunday immediately following the anniversary of the armistice, should be observed in all churches by suitable memorial services for the heroic American soldiers and sailors who gave their lives to their country in the World War." The letter also said that Wilson would direct that the American flag should be displayed at half mast at all public buildings, military posts, etc. This letter was typed up, and Wilson signed it, but it was not sent: WW to J. A. Elston, Oct. 1, 1920, TLS (WP, DLC). Wilson then apparently asked Baker to draft a new statement in the form of a proclamation. Baker sent this to the White House in NDB to R. Forster, Oct. 5, 1920, TLS (WP, DLC). The proclamation as issued is printed as an Enclosure with JPT to WW, Oct. 6, 1920 (first letter of that date).

From Hamilton Foley¹

Dear Mr President,   Pittsburgh, Pa. September 27, 1920.

I want to match your $500. I cannot do it directly but, with your approval, I can give the *League of Nations* much more than $500. worth of publicity.

May I write to Editors and offer to send them paragraphs from your Addresses during your last western trip, to be printed in what newspapermen call "boxes"—in each issue from now until Election Day? Of course these Addresses have been placed before the newspapers, but it seems to me everyone has forgotten how much of detail and of instructive explanation you have given in your Addresses during your last western tour,—how you said more in single paragraphs than most speakers tell in columns of words.²

Surely you will believe there will be no personal advantage to me in this; and, I hope, you will believe, I am now, more than ever,

Most sincerely and respectfully yours,   Hamilton Foley³

ALS (WP, DLC).

¹ Former editor of the *Panama News Letter*, a weekly paper published in the Panama Canal Zone, at this time associated with the Radium Chemical Co. of Pittsburgh.

² The Editors do not know to what extent Foley succeeded in this project in the autumn of 1920. However, he later compiled "President Wilson's official and detailed explanation of the League of Nations Covenant and the Treaty of Versailles" in a widely distributed book entitled *Woodrow Wilson's Case for the League of Nations* (Princeton, N. J., 1923).

³ A note (T MS, WP, DLC) by Swem attached to this letter states that Wilson had "no objection to this."

A Report of an Interview by William Waller Hawkins[1]

[Sept. 27, 1920]

There was a timidity, almost an apologetic effect in President Wilson's manner as he sat in his arm-chair and smiled a cordial welcome—a smile that slipped rather to the right side of his face in a curiously pathetic way. The eyes were clear and direct. There was no doubt that the mind was working normally. But physically, he was only the shattered remnant of the man who less than two years ago set out for Paris. The ravages of his long illness were visible in his face. His left arm lay helpless at his side, the fingers of the hand half clenched as if drawn permanently in that position. It was clear at first glance that he had suffered not only physical torment but that the constant attacks and abuse to which he has been subjected had cut deeply.

Here was the shell of a man literally burned out by the fire of his own ideal.

But the mind and the ideal were still there, even if the body had broken down at the time when they most needed it.

"I am pleased to see you," he said, "I have a great interest in The United Press and respect for it.

"You will please pardon my not rising."

It was the manner in which he made this latter statement which gave me the impression of timidity—the sensitive apologetic attitude of a person suffering from nervousness. As I approached, he had taken off a wide-brimmed Panama hat with his right hand and laid it on the table beside him as he extended his hand to me in a very friendly greeting. He was seated on the south portico of the White House where he spends most of the day if the weather permits. This portico overlooks the south lawn, toward the monument, and is concealed from the distant street by the thick trees so that he has complete privacy.

[1] Veteran newspaperman; affiliated with various papers in Missouri and Kentucky and, since 1907, with the United Press Association, whose president he had recently become. The interview was arranged by Robert Jacob Bender of the United Press, for whom Wilson had the highest regard and who was one of the three reporters who had accompanied him on the *George Washington* to the peace conference. Bender, in a letter to Tumulty, said that Hawkins was "seeking information and help, not a story." "He doesn't desire to write anything," Bender continued. "He desires to get the help that one seeks from one who knows better than anyone else about a given subject. . . . It is an honest desire on his part to get the president's ideas on world conditions and to help Hawkins in his work—and nothing else—that prompts him to seek an audience." R. J. Bender to JPT, c. Sept. 21, 1920, TL (WP, DLC). Tumulty, in conveying Bender's request to Mrs. Wilson, emphasized that Hawkins was one of Wilson's "devoted admirers." JPT to EBW, Sept. 21, 1920, TL (WP, DLC).
Hawkins saw Wilson at the White House at 10:45 a.m. on September 27, 1920. In a note accompanying his report, Hawkins stated that Wilson had agreed to talk to him on condition that nothing about their conversation would be printed and that even the fact of his visit to the White House would be kept confidential. The interview was never published.

Mrs. Wilson sat near him. She greeted me very cordially and continued her sewing. From time to time, she joined in the conversation and seemed very cheerful altho there could be no doubt of her constant solicitous watching of the President. The apologetic manner appeared again as he took up his hat and said:

"You will pardon me, if I put on my hat. I like to keep my hat on. I'm really interested in your new responsibilities and wish you every success. Where is Mr. Howard[2] now?"

I told him about Howard's new work and mentioned the fact that Howard had asked me to express our appreciation of his assistance at the time we first entered South America.[3] I explained briefly the manner in which our South American service had grown.

"I am glad to hear it," he said, "I was greatly interested in Mr. Howard's work in South America and I can feel that the situation there has been relieved. If you can, I wish you would give him my kindest regards and best wishes for a great measure of success in his new work."

I mentioned the fact that our chief trouble in South America is that of communication and that we were working with Walter S. Rogers in connection with the forthcoming Communications Congress whereupon he said:

"Mr. Rogers is the best posted man we have on cables. He knows about them and they can't fool him. They can't put anything over on him. You know I appointed him on the Communications Commission."

I then explained that I chiefly desired to know his confidential opinion regarding Bolshevism or in a broader sense, the general economic situation in the world.

"I am very glad to talk with you on this topic with the understanding, of course, that our conversation is confidential.

"I do not fear Bolshevism but it must be resisted. Bolshevism is a mistake and it must be resisted as all mistakes must be resisted. If left alone, it will destroy itself. It cannot survive because it is wrong.

"The Poles are too impetuous. My natural sympathy is all with the Poles but by invading Russian territory, the Poles give Lenine and Trotsky their greatest possible strength. They make it possible for Lenine and Trotsky to stir up the spirit of national defense.

"I have had an intimation that the Italian Government is taking

[2] That is, Roy Wilson Howard, former president of the United Press Association (1912-1920); at this time, chairman of its board of directors and chairman and business director of the Newspaper Enterprise Association and the Scripps-McRae newspapers.
[3] About this matter, see R. W. Howard to WW, Jan. 12, 1918, printed as Enclosure II with G. Creel to WW, Jan. 15, 1918, Vol. 45; WW to R. W. Howard, Jan. 16, 1918, Vol. 46; and WW to Whom It May Concern, Jan. 29, 1918, *ibid.*

an enlightened view of Bolshevism and is inclined to let it work itself out."

(In analyzing the above statements, there seems to be a conflict between the assertion that Bolshevism must be resisted and the statement that if left alone it will destroy itself. If I had pointed this out, I feel sure the President would have explained he meant that it was necessary for the Poles to resist the attempt at invasion by the Soviet armies, but that once driven back into Russia, the Bolsheviki should be left alone.)

"In this connection, I can tell you that for the first time, I have a man who can write a note for me," continued the President. "You know, heretofore, I have always had to write them myself. But the note on the Polish situation[4] was written by Colby. It was his note not mine. He is a great man. He is the first one I have ever had who could do it."

"But, of course, it was your note just the same," said Mrs. Wilson with a smile.

"Of course," he replied, "we talked it over and discussed it and I gave him my ideas, but it was his verbiage, he actually wrote it. He is the first man I have had who could do it."

I mentioned that he had had rather a rare line of assistants. This seemed to amuse him and he continued:

"Bryan has the strangest mind of any man I have ever known. Facts mean nothing to him except the opportunity for argument. He thinks only of argument. Why, at the beginning of the war he argued that the nations had gone into the war against their will and all we had to do was to ask them and they would withdraw. But, I said we had asked them and they refused. But that fact was of no avail to Bryan. He continued his argument just the same." Later referring to Bryan he said:

"Bryan has a very high forehead but he is not a high-brow."

"What of Lansing?" I asked.

"Oh, Lansing, he wasn't even true."

Here Mrs. Wilson interjected:

"Speaking of Bolshevism, we have had some of it right here." (Obviously referring to Lansing.)

I asked him for his opinion as to the broader aspect of the labor situation, not confining it to actual Sovietism but to the conditions as we now face them in this country. In response, he said:

"Labor has not had its fair share. There can be no doubt about that. There must be some adjustment looking toward a partnership. A system where one party arbitrarily says to the other that it can have so much and no more, cannot survive.

---

[4] For which, see the Enclosure printed with BC to WW, Aug. 9, 1920.

"Profit-sharing will not do. Profit-sharing will always be looked upon as a sort of charity. There must be representation on boards of directors and in the management of business so that Labor will actually know what is going on.

"As it is, when management says to Labor: 'We can't raise your wages,' Labor does not know whether it is true or not. If Labor had representation in the management it would know the facts and not demand the impossible. I believe that Labor is entitled to know the truth.

"If the truth could be known on both sides, there would be no trouble."

The President said the situation of the Democrats in the forth-coming election might seem a little bit unfavorable just now but that it is "only for a few days."

"A Republican victory, with a period of great reaction," he said, "would bring on the most terrible industrial situation in this country. Such reaction would be the greatest possible means of developing Bolshevism here."

I asked him as to his opinion of the candidates.

"Governor Cox is a man of very high ideals who will do his utmost," said the President, "I have great confidence in him."

"Harding is nothing. At my conference with the Senate Foreign Relations Committee, Harding at one point said:

" 'But what if the United States did not live up to its obligations?'

"To this I replied:

" 'Senator, that is a supposition which no real American would entertain.'

"He apologized and spent the rest of the evening trying to explain."[5]

I asked the President if it were true that he intended to take a more active part in the campaign in behalf of Cox. He replied:

"I haven't decided yet," and then added, "I will do anything I can to help."

With this he smiled and it was hard to tell whether it was a sadly rueful smile at the realization of his inability to do much on account of his physical condition or a smile at the prospect of something he proposed to do. It is my impression that it was a smile of bitter regret.

Here Mrs. Wilson said that she had just received a letter from a woman in Los Angeles stating that Mr. Wilson had been so badly treated by the Democrats, that he should organize a fourth party to be called the "Wilson Party" and head it himself. The reference to

[5] For this exchange, which Wilson here paraphrased in a very abbreviated form, see the notes of a conversation with members of the Senate Foreign Relations Committee printed at August 19, 1919, Vol. 62.

his having been badly treated by the Democrats did not provoke any remonstrance on the part of the President but he and Mrs. Wilson seemed to accept it as a matter of recognized fact. However, the President showed that he had no illusions as to his condition when he said to me with a spark of the old humor in his eye:

"I suppose at that distance, I look like a damn fool."

I asked the President if he contemplated making public the income tax returns anytime before election. He looked surprised as if he had never thought of it and said he had no such idea. Whereupon Mrs. Wilson said:

"Why? Aren't they confidential?"

It was explained that the President could make the returns public if he chose. If was clear that this suggestion did not appeal to Mrs. Wilson as she said:

"I'm always against fighting with any tools that the other fellow hasn't got."

It was suggested that that would be a good rule if both sides observed it, whereupon the President said:

"The other fellows don't even stick to the truth."

He added, however, that he had no idea of making the returns public.

I asked him if there was anything serious in the Japanese situation.

"No. No, I think not. I haven't talked to the Secretary of State about if [it] for several days, but I don't think so."

It was obvious that he hadn't given much thought to the Japanese situation, or, if he had, considered it wise to avoid the appearance of having done so.

In reverting to the political situation I asked him why the Democrats had not made better use of the obvious material which they have at hand, such as the Federal Banking system.

"The Federal Bank system has been used effectively by Governor Cox," said the President. "It is a particularly strong argument in the campaign because it is in that sort of thing that the Republicans have always claimed to excell [excel]. I always had a high regard for Senator Root until he made a speech which referred to the currency, issued under the Federal Bank system as 'fiat currency.'[6] That was either a deliberate falsehood or ignorance and I lost my regard for him from that time. No currency could be better secured."

[6] During the debate on the Federal Reserve bill in the Senate on December 19, 1913, Root had delivered a long and impassioned speech against certain features of the proposed measure, which he had claimed, would lead to inflation, a stock market crash, and eventual national ruin. *Cong. Record*, 63d Cong., 2d sess., pp. 828-36. See also Arthur S. Link, *Wilson: The New Freedom* (Princeton, N. J., 1956), pp. 236-37.

The reference to Senator Root brought up the situation in the Republican camp regarding the efforts of Harding to consolidate the opinions on the League of Nations, held by his various supporters. While the President made no direct comment, it was clear that he thought it very likely that Senator Root would cause Harding great embarrassment.

"It cannot be denied that Senator Root has been working on a proposition[7] which can have its being only thru the functioning of the League of Nations," he said.

Toward the latter part of the interview, the President gave evidence of increasing nervousness and it was obvious that it was time for me to go altho he was cordial to the last. I thanked him and said:

"It's a great pleasure to find you looking so well."

In response to this, he smiled again in that embarrassed, apologetic sort of manner and said:

"When a man is suffering from nervous prostration, he doesn't always show it."

In thinking over the interview, I am impressed most with the pathetic picture of this man who during the last two years has played such a gigantic part in the history of the world.

I have on the wall of my office a photograph of the House of Representative[s] taken on the night in April, 1917, when he read his declaration of war. Refreshed by this picture, my memory of him as he was then is very clear and keen.

When I think of him as I saw him yesterday I experience the mixed emotions of pathos and anger.

I feel that something ought to be done about it; that if, as he believes, Cox in truth has taken up his torch to carry it forward, the Democratic organization has failed lamentably in presenting its case to the public.

I am reminded with great force of the last lines of the greatest poem the war produced:

"Take up our quarrel with the foe:
To you, from failing hands, we throw
    The Torch; be yours to hold it high!
    If ye break faith with us who die,
We shall not sleep, though poppies grow in Flanders Fields."[8]

T MS (B. Colby Papers, DLC).
  [7] That is, the establishment of a Permanent Court of International Justice.
  [8] From John McCrae, "In Flanders Fields," first published in *Punch*, CXLIX (December 8, 1915), 468.

From James Middleton Cox

Omaha, Neb., Sept. 27, 1920.

It would be helpful if I might have your permission to use cable messages passing between yourself and Judge Taft showing your acceptance of his proposals.[1] Will you not please forward to me en-route? Cause of the League of Nations is winning as the clouds set up by a partisan opposition are being driven away.

James M. Cox.

T telegram (J. P. Tumulty Papers, DLC).
[1] Wilson's, or Tumulty's, reply to this telegram is missing. However, future documents will reveal that the material Cox requested was sent to him and that he did make use of it.

From the Diary of Josephus Daniels

September Tuesday 28 1920

Cabinet—Houston spoke at length against the misunderstanding in the South about the Federal Reserve Board & said they wanted money to hold cotton. "The people of the South ought to depend on themselves" said WW

Much politics talked

From Norman Hezekiah Davis, with Enclosures

My dear Mr. President: Washington September 28, 1920.

Secretary Colby has written you of my recent conversation with Mr. Pesqueira, but in case you care for a full report, I enclose herewith a memorandum of that conversation.

I am also enclosing a memorandum of my conversation with Mr. Iglesias some days ago. I should have sent this to you sooner, but in some way it was overlooked. The latter I should like to have you read, at your convenience.

Yours faithfully,   Norman H. Davis

TLS (WP, DLC).

E N C L O S U R E   I

September 23, 1920

MEMORANDUM OF CONVERSATION WITH MR. PESQUEIRA,
FINANCIAL REPRESENTATIVE OF MEXICO.

Mr. Pesqueira first outlined the efforts which General Obregon, President de la Huerta, Mr. Calles[1] and himself (all of Sonora and old friends) had made and are making to get Mexico on her feet and to establish and maintain the closest friendly cooperation with the United States, which they all deem essential. He then said they were willing and prepared to settle fairly and justly all controversies between the two countries and that there were no outstanding questions which would offer any difficulty of immediate settlement except possibly that with the oil interests, but even in this respect the Mexican Government was willing to go to practically any extreme of concession which would be fair to all interests concerned to dispose of this problem which has caused so much feeling and misunderstanding. In an endeavor to reach a settlement with the oil interests he had held several conferences with the International Committee in New York.[2] His first object was to find out just what their contentions are, but so far this has been a difficult task. They have confined themselves principally to berating the Mexican Government and have asserted that unless and until the Mexican Government protects their interests and meets their demands there will be no recognition by the United States Government.

I told Mr. Pesqueira that, while this Government will insist upon fair and equitable treatment to Americans and their properties in Mexico, it will not press any unreasonable claims; that if and when the time arrives when this Government considers it opportune and advisable to extend recognition to the Mexican Government it will not be based upon some one isolated question such as that of the settlement of the oil controversy; that it would be well to bear in mind that no interests or groups will be able to deliver the United States Government, and that I would not care to have the Mexican Government misled into believing that a settlement of this one question would automatically result in recognition. I told him this Government is not attempting to pass upon the validity of titles, leases, etc. in Mexico and that it must necessarily take an impartial position in respect to conflicting claims of American oil interests in Mexico. I further told him that the United States Government does not contemplate dictating conditions on which recognition will be extended, but that when recognition is extended it will be based on the general principles heretofore followed and laid down by this Government in such cases and after Mexico has taken such measures as will in the opinion of this Government justify recognition. I also said nothing would be gained for Mexico or the United States by the renewal of official relations until the removal of the obstacles which have heretofore prevented the normal, satisfactory, official relations which should exist between two friendly peoples.

Mr. Pesqueira then said they were most anxious to have an impartial study made of the oil controversy and that the Mexican Government would be prepared to adhere to the recommendations so made. He then told me that a treaty or some definite arrangement could be made between the two Governments, providing for the automatic disposal of all questions in controversy, and that, if they could not come to a satisfactory understanding in the very near future with the oil interests, they could probably be disposed of by an agreement between the two Governments, providing for an arbitration commission to be named by the two Governments whose decision would be binding on Mexico. He urged that such arrangement should be effected with the de la Huerta regime and that the present Government be recognized, because as Mr. de la Huerta goes out of office in December he would not have to take into consideration the political aspects to the extent that Obregon would have to do, and that, if all of these questions could be settled and recognition extended now, Obregon could then take office with a clean slate. He said that of course Obregon would approve of any arrangements that de la Huerta makes.

Mr. Pesqueira said that the Mexican people were now beginning to realize that President Wilson has been the greatest friend Mexico has had, and that it would have a wonderful effect and would be a complete vindication of his policy to have the Mexican Government recognized by his administration.

I again repeated to Mr. Pesqueira that no one was more desirous of being helpful to Mexico than President Wilson, but that in my judgment the last thing he would consider doing would be to dictate to Mexico the conditions upon which he would extend recognition; that it was entirely within the control of Mexico to bring about conditions and a situation which would justify, in the opinion of this Government, the extension of recognition; that the time in which such a situation can be brought about is entirely within the control of the Mexican Government and people, but that it would be impossible now to state just what would remove all of the obstacles to recognition; that nothing would be gained by renewing official relations until Mexico can show that the Mexican Government not only desires to protect life and property and respect valid rights, but that it has taken definite and effective measures to repair the damages which have been committed and to give proper assurances against a repetition of past inability or reluctance to comply with the ordinary international obligations incumbent upon a member of the Society of Nations.   NHD

P.S. In the course of the conversation Mr. Pesqueira stated that he was satisfied he had found a solution to the Chemizal [Chamizal] case[3] which would be satisfactory to the United States and which Mexico would agree to, namely, that Mexico would release in favor of the United States all claim on the Chemizal property, containing some 60,000 acres, in consideration of an agreement that Mexico should have for irrigation purposes the surplus water from the river which may not be required for use in the United States. He also said that there would be no difficulty in arriving at a satisfactory settlement of the Colorado river controversy.

NHD

[1] Plutarco Elías Calles, military and political leader who had been active in the overthrow of the Huerta regime; former Governor of Sonora (1917) and Secretary of Industry, Commerce, and Labor from May 1919 to February 1920; one of the authors of the Plan de Agua Prieta, which had led to the overthrow of Carranza; at this time, Secretary of War and of the Navy and a member, together with Obregón and de la Huerta, of the ruling Sonora triumvirate; President of Mexico from 1924 to 1928.
[2] The International Committee of Bankers on Mexico, established in the autumn of 1918 by the leading American, British, and French financial institutions with the unofficial endorsement of the State Department and headed by Thomas W. Lamont of J. P. Morgan & Company. The purpose of the committee was to integrate and coordinate all questions involving loans, bonds, and the reorganization of Mexican finances. See Smith, *The United States and Revolutionary Nationalism in Mexico*, pp. 128-32.
[3] About this case, see Sheldon B. Liss, *A Century of Disagreement: The Chamizal Conflict, 1864-1964* (Washington, 1965).

E N C L O S U R E   I I

September 14, 1920.

MEMORANDUM OF CONVERSATION WITH SENOR IGLESIAS CALDERON
MEXICAN REPRESENTATIVE.

Semor [Señor] Iglesias Calderon informed me that he had asked for an interview to make the following statements:

First. That he had not sent the communication to Mexico published in some of the papers which stated that he had had an interview with Secretary Colby; that this must be some mistake of the Foreign Office in Mexico; and that he would give out an announcement to the press rectifying the error. He regretted this incident very much, and asked me to tell the Secretary how much he regretted the mistake.

Second: Although the President had just asked him if he would accept the post of Minister of Foreign Affairs, he had declined this, thinking it his duty to return to Mexico to represent his constituents who had recently elected him as Senator from the Federal District. He regretted leaving the United States but as he came here primarily to deliver to President Wilson a personal letter from President de la Huerta, and for a general interchange of views for the purpose of bringing about a better understanding, he felt that he should return to Mexico within a short time to fulfill his duties as Senator-elect. He stated he regretted very much to return to Mexico without being able to present to President Wilson this letter. I informed him that I feared the presentation of the letter might create an erroneous impression and be construed as a resumption of official relations between the two governments, and I inquired the purport of the letter. He said it was merely a letter from President de la Huerta informing President Wilson of his election as President of Mexico by the Mexican Congress, and of his desire to cooperate in a most friendly way with the United States. He offered to show me the letter informally, and expressed the hope that if the President could not receive him in order to accept the letter, he would like very much to present the letter to me as the President's representative. I agreed to let him know later if either could be done.

   Third: He then informed me that he had received a personal telegram from President de la Huerta, requesting him to inform me that the Mexican Government is most desirous of clearing up every misunderstanding with the Government of the United States, and of making every possible effort to take such steps as would remove the obstacles in the way of a resumption of official relations between the two Governments; and that in order that we might obtain a clearer understanding of the problems with which Mexico is confronted and of the various questions involved, he hoped very much that President Wilson would send a personal representative to Mexico to take up such questions directly with the Mexican Government. I told him that I could not give him any answer regarding this, but would inform the President.   NHD

TI MSS (WP, DLC).

From Thomas William Lamont, with Enclosure

Dear Mr. President: New York September 28th, 1920.
   The enclosed letter from Buckley Wells,[1] Vice-President of Harper & Bros. explains itself. Wells is a fine fellow with good clear practical ideas. Some time, if you feel like permitting him to meet you for a moment, I should be very grateful, and in any event I

know that you will give his letter the consideration that it deserves; for we are all hoping, as time goes on, to hear from you more and more frequently. I wonder, by the way, whether you have seen ex-President Eliot's article in the last Atlantic Monthly[2] in regard to how the independent voter should cast his ballot. Mr. Eliot has made a wonderfully fine size-up, I think, of your two administrations.

With cordial personal regards to both yourself and Mrs. Wilson, in which my wife[3] joins me most sympathetically, I am,

Most sincerely yours,   Thomas W. Lamont

[1] Thomas Bucklin Wells.
[2] Charles W. Eliot, "The Voter's Choice in the Coming Election," *The Atlantic Monthly*, CXXVI (Oct. 1920), 527-40.
[3] That is, Florence Haskell Corliss Lamont.

E N C L O S U R E

Thomas Bucklin Wells to Thomas William Lamont

Dear Mr. Lamont: New York, N. Y. September 27th, 1920.

You have shown your friendly interest in the affairs of this House so often that I hesitate to call upon you again and am only venturing to do so because at this time a matter of really great importance is involved.

As you know, we have had for many years the distinguished honor of being the President's publishers. In addition to those titles which we originally published, we have been able to bring together with the President's consent, many of his books which appeared originally under other imprints. We have also published the President's speeches from time to time and those little volumes have had a wide distribution.

Naturally, we are most desirous of continuing the connection that has added such distinction to our list, and this desire brings me to the point of my letter.

I have never had the honor of meeting the President, and since Mr. Duneka's[1] death, our uniformly pleasant relations with Mr. Wilson have been almost entirely a matter of correspondence. But now, when the publishing world is wondering what the President's future literary plans may be, I would very greatly appreciate the privilege of talking these matters over with him, but I would like to go to the White House as something other than a totally unknown representative of Harper and Brothers.

If, at this time, when we are all rejoicing over the President's recovery, you think it fitting to write him briefly on our behalf suggesting our interest and your own in whatever writing plans he may have in mind, and our wish to put ourselves at his service in the future as we have in the past, you will be doing us a great kindness and I shall then have less hesitation in asking for a brief interview.

No other matter now engaging our attention is of comparable importance and I hope you will think it not improper to comply with my suggestion.

Trusting that I am not asking too much of you, I am

Very sincerely yours,   Thomas B. Wells

TLS (WP, DLC).
[1] Frederick A. Duneka, genergal manager and secretary of the board of directors of Harper & Brothers from 1900 to 1915; vice-president from 1915 until his death on January 24, 1919.

From William Edward Dodd

Dear Mr. President: Washington, D. C. Sept 28, 1920

I have been asked by Dean Evarts B. Greene of the University of Illinois,[1] formerly a Progressive, whether I can give him any statement about your relations with Colonel Roosevelt which he or I might give out. From my book[2] Greene supposes that some of your friends, perhaps with your approval, tried to bring the Colonel into a more reasonable attitude toward you and the administration.

I have no copy of the book at hand or I would cite the passages. But Mr. Tumulty has Dean Greene's letter to me.[3] In view of the *very grave risks* the country is under of making one of the tragic blunders of history, I am constrained to ask you if you could give me any statement that I could use in Illinois. I saw Mr Tumulty today and he suggested that I write you.

I have several appointments to speak in Illinois during October. The subject is the League of Nations and the present situation. As there are so many Progressives in the region about Chicago who greatly admire you and wish to carry all their fellows to Cox and the League idea—Mrs. Kellogg Fairbank, Mrs. Virginia Le Roy[4] and several men like Merriam,[5] as I think—it would seem that you could frame a statement that would give them aid.

My address will be Round Hill, Va. till Sunday when we return to Chicago.

Pardon this break into your time. You must know how I am enlisted in the cause you have proclaimed so ably.

Yours Sincerely   William E. Dodd

ALS (WP, DLC).

[1] Evarts Boutell Greene, historian of the colonial period of American history; Professor of History at the University of Illinois.
[2] That is, *Woodrow Wilson and His Work* (Garden City, N. Y., 1920).
[3] E. B. Greene to W. E. Dodd, Sept. 21, 1920, ALS (WP, DLC).
[4] Janet Dyer (Mrs. Kellogg) Fairbank and Mrs. Virginia Leroy, whose husband's name cannot be found. She was an ardent Wilson supporter and a vice-president of the League to Enforce Peace.
[5] Charles Edward Merriam, Professor of Political Science at the University of Chicago; prominent civic reformer.

To Bainbridge Colby

My dear Mr. Secretary: The White House 29 September, 1920

I have the greatest respect for Mr. Davis's judgment, but I cannot concur in the conclusion that he suggests in the enclosed letter.[1] It is my conscientious conviction that it would be just as serious a mistake to agree to the English and French proposal in its new form as it would have been to agree to it in its original form. There is a nigger in this woodpile and it is better to burn the whole pile, for I think it would be unconscientious for one of the trustees to agree to the use of this money by anyone of its co-trustees in any way.   Cordially and faithfully yours,   Woodrow Wilson

TLS (B. Colby Papers, DLC).
[1] NHD to WW, Sept. 28, 1920, TLS (B. Colby Papers, DLC). Davis informed Wilson that the British and French governments had requested the United States to approve a plan for the disposal of the gold delivered by Russia to Germany pursuant to the Treaty of Brest-Litovsk and subsequently taken in trust for Russia by the Principal Allied and Associated Powers under the terms of the Armistice and the Versailles Treaty. The governments had originally proposed to apply this gold to the payment of a portion of advances made by them to Russia from the proceeds of the Anglo-French loan of 1915 (about which, see the entries under "Great Britain and the United States," Vol. 39) which was due to mature on October 15, 1920. However, the State Department, with Wilson's concurrence, had rejected this scheme on the ground that it was unwise to single out any particular nation as a preferred creditor, especially if this nation was one of the trustees of the Russian gold. Moreover, Colby and Davis had suggested that, if this gold was to be put to productive use, a portion of it should be applied to the protection of vital Russian interests, such as the maintenance and improvement of the Chinese Eastern Railroad. Davis pointed out that the British and French governments seemed to agree to this proposition, but only on the condition that the balance of the Russian funds, too, be employed productively and that either government be designated as custodian and as agent of the Principal Allied and Associated Powers. In particular, the two governments now desired to use the Russian gold temporarily to assist France in repaying its share of $250 million of the Anglo-French loan which it might otherwise not be able to repay on time. Davis stated that both he and Colby felt that the United States should accommodate the British and French governments and acquiesce in their latest proposal.

To John Sharp Williams

My dear Friend: The White House 29 September, 1920

Your letter of September twenty-fifth has pleased me very much and I am again your debtor for material encouragement. You are most thoughtful and I am glad your judgment concurs with mine, because I feel very much fortified thereby.

 With the warmest regard,
     Cordially and faithfully yours, Woodrow Wilson

TLS (J. S. Williams Papers, DLC).

To Alexander Mitchell Palmer, with Enclosure

              The White House
My dear Mr. Attorney General: 29 September, 1920

 I have the most implicit confidence in the sensible, practical judgment of Senator Glass and I am not at all willing that Mr. Flood[1] should have anything to do with naming appointees in Virginia. I, therefore, send you the enclosed letter from Senator Glass in order to accompany it with the request that you prepare the appointment of Mr. Chitwood[2] for my signature.
     Cordially and faithfully yours, Woodrow Wilson

TLS (A. M. Palmer Papers, DLC).
 [1] Henry De La Warr Flood, Democratic congressman from Virginia and ranking minority member of the House Foreign Affairs Committee.
 [2] Joseph Howard Chitwood.

E N C L O S U R E

From Carter Glass

Personal and Confidential

Dear Mr. President: Washington, D. C. September 27th, 1920.

 On May 28th, last, I suggested the name of Mr. Joseph H. Chitwood for appointment to the vacancy in the United States District Attorneyship for the Western District of Virginia caused by the resignation of Mr. R. E. Byrd.[1] Senator Swanson authorized me to say that the appointment of Mr. Chitwood would be most acceptable to him also. Six of the nine Democratic representatives in Congress from Virginia endorsed Mr. Chitwood, as did many other persons of professional repute and likewise most of the Bar Associations of the territory embraced in the Western District of Virginia.

 Mr. Chitwood has been the Deputy United States Attorney during the entire incumbency of Mr. Byrd and was recently designated by the Court as Acting United States District Attorney. I thought his advancement would be a merited reward of his exceedingly efficient performance of his duties in the minor position.

My letter to you on the subject was, in the usual course, referred to the Attorney-General, who has not, however, acted. Meanwhile, as I am reliably told, certain politicians in Virginia, as a prelude to the San Francisco Convention, undertook to arrange the Federal patronage of the State, and this particular position was assigned to Representative Flood, who has presented a man of his own selection for the place. The person selected by Mr. Flood is a highly reputable gentleman, but has no merit, professional or otherwise, not possessed by Mr. Chitwood. Furthermore, I should very much regret to see the Federal patronage of Virginia dispensed in the fashion proposed, and I would be personally obliged if you will find it agreeable to designate Mr. Chitwood for the position of District Attorney.

With cordial regards and best wishes for your health, believe me
Sincerely yours,   Carter Glass.

TLS (A. M. Palmer Papers, DLC).
  [1] Richard Evelyn Byrd.

To Carter Glass

My dear Senator: [The White House] 29 September, 1920

I have your letter of the twenty-seventh backing up your letter of May twenty-eighth about Mr. Chitwood and have just written to the Attorney General expressing my desire to appoint Mr. Chitwood. I have the utmost confidence in your practical good judgment.   Cordially and faithfully yours,   [Woodrow Wilson]

CCL (WP, DLC).

To Edward William Bok

My dear Bok: [The White House] 29 September, 1920

It is fine to have your book and to have you send it to me with such a message. I am grateful and encouraged.

With the most cordial good wishes,
Faithfully yours,   [Woodrow Wilson]

CCL (WP, DLC).

From Walter Stowell Rogers

Dear Mr. President: Washington, September 29, 1920.

In justice both to Mr. Charles R. Crane and myself, I want you to know certain facts regarding the Washington Herald.

Upon Mr. Hoover's return from Paris, he told me that he wanted to devote himself to public service and to ally himself with the progressive forces of the country. I gathered at the time that he was favorable to the League of Nations and recognized the value of the achiev[e]ments of the administration.

He asked me to buy the Herald for him. I did so. Believing in Mr. Hoover's progressivism, Mr. Crane took a small interest.

Mr. Hoover then asked me to look after the paper until he could make Washington his home. At that time he was busy with the Industrial Conference. Later he went to New York and, as you know, became a candidate for the republican nomination and steadily got farther away from the policies we believed he would support.

After the republican convention he went to California for the summer. Upon his return he told me of his decision to support Harding. He also told me that he intended to take a subordinate place in the Herald to Julius Barnes. I expressed myself somewhat vigorously regarding Mr. Barnes. Making it clear, of course, that I would not work with Mr. Barnes. Naturally enough the latter wanted someone in charge of the paper who would look to him and carry out his instructions.

Mr. Barnes wanted me out of the paper and I wanted to get out. Consequently I have severed my connection with the Herald, except I remain a member of the Board of Directors, temporarily.

Mr. Crane is no longer under obligation to contribute, and his present interest is being transferred to another company.

I am sorry about the Herald. There is an opportunity here and a need for a liberal fighting paper. I am disappointed in Mr. Hoover. I, like many other people, am disillusioned. I had hoped he might turn out to be a force furthering progressive movements.

Mr. Suter,[1] one of your Princeton students and one of my associates during the war, is also leaving the paper.

With warmest possible personal assurances, I am

Yours sincerely,   Walter S Rogers

TLS (WP, DLC).
[1] Herman Milton Suter, a special student at Princeton University, 1895-1898; publisher and editor of the *Nashville Tennesseean* from 1907 to 1912 and general manager of the *Philadelphia Evening Times* from 1912 to 1913; served with the Foreign Press Cable Service Bureau of the Committee on Public Information in Paris in 1918, editing American home-town news for the troops of the A.E.F.; at this time, publisher and editor of the *Washington Herald*.

George Creel to Edith Bolling Galt Wilson

Dear Mrs. Wilson—   New York City Wednesday [Sept. 29, 1920]

I think it is a certainty that I will leave for Mexico Sunday afternoon. I have a commission from Collier's to do a series of articles, which will not only take care of my expenses but also somewhat compensate me for my time.

I am going to be in Washington Friday to see Mr. Tumulty on some political matters, and will take advantage of the visit to see Mr. Colby. I will call up the White House Friday morning, and if it is at all convenient, would like to see you and the President.

I should have written before to tell you how much I was heartened by my visit. Save for a certain effect of depression, the President looked almost better than when I saw him last. It brought a lump in my throat to see him less than able to fight in the old driving way, but it was a tremendous relief to feel that his complete recovery now seems certain.

I feel very strongly about this Mexico business. As does every one else I want to see the question answered, but I want to see it answered *right*. Not only must there be a complete and generous recognition of the wisdom and courage of the President's policy— because of its effect on the public opinion of the whole world—but there must be the certainty that the new government is honest in this recognition, and has faith at its heart.

It is not only that I have a program of things that ought to be *done*—I have a program of speeches that must be *made*.

Sincerely   George Creel

TLS (WP, DLC).

To Thomas William Lamont

My dear Lamont: [The White House] 30 September, 1920

I have your letter of September twenty-eighth about Mr. Wells, Vice-President of Harper & Brothers, and have read also Mr. Wells's letter with the greatest interest and appreciation.

I could no doubt arrange to see Mr. Wells, and it would be a pleasure to meet him, but I am writing Mr. Wells today requesting him to see a man into whose hands I have placed the management of the very matters Mr. Wells wants to talk to me about in order to relieve myself as much as possible of business cares in the months to come.

The Evening Post[1] is certainly doing splendid work for the League and the great cause which we have at heart.

With most cordial regards and best wishes from both Mrs. Wilson and myself to Mrs. Lamont and yourself,

Cordially and faithfully yours,   [Woodrow Wilson]

CCL (WP, DLC).

¹ Lamont had bought the New York *Evening Post* from Oswald Garrison Villard in 1918 and installed Edwin Francis Gay as editor in January 1920.

To Thomas Bucklin Wells

My dear Mr. Wells: [The White House] 30 September, 1920

Mr. Lamont has given me the pleasure of seeing your letter of September twenty-seventh to him. It would be a pleasure to me to meet you, and I shall be glad to arrange it some time.

I appreciate the whole tone of your letter and its references to me very much, but I am going to suggest that you have a talk about the matter you wish to discuss with me with Mr. George Creel, 505 Fifth Avenue, New York. Mr. Creel has generously consented to act as my agent and spokesman in matters of publication in the months to come, and I would be very much pleased indeed if you and he would have a talk about any question concerning my future publications that you may desire to develop at the present time.

With the best wishes,

Sincerely yours,   [Woodrow Wilson]

CCL (WP, DLC).

To Walter Stowell Rogers

My dear Rogers: [The White House] 30 September, 1920

Your letter of September twenty-ninth has warmed my heart. It proves you just the open-minded, loyal friend of progress that I deemed you to be, and I want to thank you sincerely for it.

With the most cordial good wishes,

Faithfully yours,   [Woodrow Wilson]

CCL (WP, DLC).

From Joseph Patrick Tumulty

Dear Governor: [The White House] 30 September 1920.

This man Spencer is going around making all sorts of outrageous statements. We could destroy him by denying this.[1]

The Secretary

TL (J. P. Tumulty Papers, DLC).
[1] "This man Spencer" was Senator Selden Palmer Spencer, Republican of Missouri. In a speech in St. Louis on about September 27, he had quoted Wilson as saying to the Rumanians and Serbs at the Paris Peace Conference that, "if any nation ever invaded their territory, he would send the American Army across the seas to defend their boundary lines." In reply to a request from the *St. Louis Post-Dispatch*, he said that Wilson made this statement at the Eighth Plenary Session of the conference. Spencer then quoted Wilson as saying: "You must not forget that it is force which is the final guarantee of peace. If the world is again troubled, this guarantee given you means that the United States will send to this side of the ocean their armies and fleet."
What Wilson actually said at the Plenary Session on May 31, 1919, is printed in Vol. 59 at that date. Actually, Spencer's attribution was not a bad paraphrase of what Wilson had said. Wilson did not say in so many words that American troops would be sent to protect Rumanian and Serbian boundaries, but he certainly implied that such would be the case.
Tumulty's letter to Wilson was prompted by the *St. Louis Post-Dispatch* to Charles Griffith Ross, Sept. 29, 1920, T telegram (J. P. Tumulty Papers, DLC). Ross was the *Post-Dispatch's* Washington correspondent.
Tumulty issued a press release on October 2 saying that Wilson's attention had been called to Spencer's statement and that Wilson had authorized him, Tumulty, to say that Spencer's statement was "absolutely and unqualifiedly false." *New York Times*, Oct. 3, 1920.

From Alexander Mitchell Palmer[1]

Dear Mr. President: Washington, D. C. September 30, 1920.

I have your letter, enclosing a communication from Senator Glass in reference to the appointment of Joseph H. Chitwood as United States Attorney for the Western District of Virginia to succeed R. E. Byrd, resigned, and requesting me to prepare the appointment of Mr. Chitwood for your signature.

I am sending the commission to you herewith, but I feel bound to say that no good purpose would be achieved by the appointment of Mr. Chitwood at this time because he is now serving as United States Attorney under appointment by the court. As Byrd's resignation became effective on June 3rd, two days before the Congress adjourned, the only effect of a recess appointment would be to deprive Chitwood of his salary until he is confirmed by the Senate. Section 1761 of the Revised Statutes provides:

"No money shall be paid from the Treasury as salary to any person appointed during a recess of the Senate to fill a vacancy in any existing office, if the vacancy existed while the Senate was in session and was by law required to be filled by and with the advice and consent of the Senate, until such appointee has been confirmed by the Senate."

It has been my thought, therefore, that since Mr. Chitwood, whom Senator Glass indorses, is now serving, he should be nominated for the place when the Senate reconvenes.

When the vacancy occurred, I was asked by Mr. Tumulty to make no recommendation until I had talked with you about it, which you will remember I did at the first opportunity. You then indicated that you desired to follow the recommendation of Senator Glass. In the meantime, however, the Congress had adjourned and Chitwood had been appointed to the place by the court and I decided that it would be best to leave the matter in that shape and send the nomination to the Senate the first Monday in December.[2]

I note Senator Glass' statement that "certain politicians in Virginia, as a prelude to the San Francisco convention, undertook to arrange the federal patronage of the State and this particular position was assigned to Representative Flood, who has presented a man of his own selection for the place." I trust it is unnecessary for me to say that if any politicians in Virginia did undertake any such arrangement, it was a matter concerning which I knew nothing and about which I was neither consulted nor advised. Mr. Glass' letter is the first intimation that I have ever received of any such arrangement.   Faithfully yours,   A Mitchell Palmer

TLS (WP, DLC).
[1] Underlining below by Wilson. He also drew a vertical line and a question mark in the left-hand margin of this paragraph.
[2] A notation on this letter says that Chitwood was given a recess appointment on October 1, 1920, as of September 1, 1920.

Robert Wickliffe Woolley to Joseph Patrick Tumulty[1]

Dear Joe: Washington September 30, 1920.

Within the past two weeks I have made a trip to Chicago and one to Detroit on official business and regret to report that I find conditions anything but encouraging. All seem to agree that Cox is a wonderful candidate, but that behind him is 100 per cent inertia if not actual paralysis. The wretched incapacity and total lack of vision that seem to characterize Chairman White's entire organization are heart-rending. Hope of getting any support worth while from that source has been practically abandoned by the rank and file of our workers and well-wishers. Indeed, it is now too late to expect real results from the Campaign Committee, no matter how many Ouija boards and Aladdin's lamps get on the job.

The President himself is now our one hope. I assure you that the Democrats with whom I talked enthused tremendously over the news that a series of statements on the issues of this campaign are to be forthcoming from the White House. Your authoritative letter of Tuesday on the Irish question was fine.[2] I overheard a group of men in the station at Buffalo applauding it.

You doubtless saw the wonderful editorial on Wilsonism published in the Philadelphia Record of September 14th.[3] How effective it would be if we could circulate ten million copies of it? Enclosed is an editorial from the Pittsburgh Post of September 22nd, entitled "Harding and the soul of America." It seems to me to furnish the text and a skeleton suggestion for a marvelous broadside by the President. The kind of statement that only he can make along these lines would electrify the country. And let me emphasize the fact Joe, that if the League of Nations is to be saved—this is the supreme consideration—only the President can save it.

I also enclose a clipping from the Detroit Journal of September 27th which is a fair sample of the mendacity that characterizes the fight being made by the Republicans. Having gained control, by purchase or otherwise, of the principal daily papers of the country outside of New York and one or two other cities of less importance, and having noted the inability of the Democrats to raise funds with which to defray the cost of advertising space in which to reply, the Republicans are lying without stint with the knowledge that it will be impossible for the Democrats to nail even feebly 20 per cent of their lies before election day. This makes it all the more important that the President take the situation directly in hand. I am delighted that he proposes to do so.

The unvarnished truth is that at the present moment we are licked to a frazzle, and in the next ten days we have got to turn the tide absolutely or it will be too late. For God's sake, don't listen to rosy reports that some fair weather Democrats may bring in. I think you will agree I have never been considered a pessimist. Don't think me one now. I am giving you hard facts gathered first hand. The urgency of the situation cannot be over-emphasized.

I do wish the President were well enough for me to lay the case before him as I see it.

In the name of humanity, let's save the League! It is now headed for the rocks.

With warm regards, I am

Cordially and earnestly yours,   R. W. Woolley

TLS (WP, DLC).
[1] Tumulty sent this letter to Mrs. Wilson with the following comment: "I think the President would like to read this letter from Bob Woolley." JPT to EBW, Sept. 30, 1920, TL (WP, DLC).
[2] See JPT to WW, Sept. 25, 1920, and the notes thereto.
[3] This clipping is missing; the clippings mentioned below accompany this letter.

To William Edward Dodd

My dear Professor Dodd: The White House 1 October, 1920

I have your letter of September twenty-eighth and very sincerely appreciate the motive which led you to write it, but I must tell you frankly that my opinion of Mr. Roosevelt, if publicly expressed, would not commend me to his followers. I have studiously refrained in the past from making any public reference to Mr. Roosevelt.   Cordially and sincerely yours,   Woodrow Wilson

TLS (W. E. Dodd Papers, DLC).

To Joshua Willis Alexander

My dear Judge Alexander: [The White House] 1 October, 1920

I have your letter of September thirtieth[1] about John S. Willis[2] of San Francisco and note what you say about Senator McKellar's support of Mr. Willis as a candidate for membership in the Shipping Board. Personally, I do not regard Mr. Willis's antecedents as a desirable preparation for such an appointment, and I must candidly and confidentially say to you that any recommendation of Senator McKellar would only prejudice me against the person recommended. He has been thoroughly false in all his relations to the Administration.
        Cordially and faithfully yours,   [Woodrow Wilson]

CCL (WP, DLC).
    [1] J. W. Alexander to WW, Sept. 30, 1920, enclosing K. D. McKellar to J. W. Alexander, Sept. 29, 1920, both TLS (WP, DLC). McKellar's letter introduced Willis to Alexander and strongly endorsed his candidacy for membership on the Shipping Board.
    [2] Traffic Manager of the Foreign Commerce Association of the Pacific Coast.

From Joseph Patrick Tumulty

My dear Governor: The White House 1 October, 1920.

George Creel and I have just gone over your statement[1] again with the utmost care. We are more than ever impressed with its strength and value. There are certain sentences, however, which, in our opinion, ought to be left out, as follows:

"Everyone who believes in government by the people must rejoice at the turn affairs have taken in regard to this campaign. This election is to be a genuine national referendum. The determination of a great policy upon which the influence and authority of the United States in the world must depend is not to be left to groups of politicians of either party, but is to be referred to the people themselves for a sovereign mandate to their representatives. They are to instruct their own government what they wish done."

However much we want this to be the truth, the fact remains that it is not true in any degree. There is not a single national magazine in the United States that is presenting our side of the case, not ten per cent of the daily press is presenting the case of the League, and there is the added fact that lack of money and lack of proper organization has deprived us entirely of any machinery that might enable us to make a proper presentation of our own.

Because of this, we are of the belief that it is not a genuine referendum. For you to make such a statement at this time would stop us, in the event of defeat, from pointing out the utter unfairness of this imperfect referendum.[2]

Sincerely yours,   J P Tumulty

TLS (J. P. Tumulty Papers, DLC).
  [1] It is printed at Oct. 3, 1920.
  [2] Wilson returned this letter with the following Hw note: "I am sorry, but I cannot agree W.W."

From Alexander Mitchell Palmer

Dear Mr. President: Washington, D. C. October 1, 1920.

In the case of the United States v. Rose Pastor Stokes,[1] a situation has developed which I deem of sufficient importance to call to your attention.

Mrs. Stokes was tried, convicted and sentenced for a violation of the Espionage Act. Upon writ of error to the Circuit Court of Appeals for the Eighth Circuit, the judgment was reversed (264 Federal, 18). The ground of reversal was that the instructions to the jury by the court below were somewhat inflammatory and, consequently, prejudicial to defendant's rights. The question now is, Shall we try Mrs. Stokes again? The case must either be set for trial or dismissed at the November term of the District Court for the Western District of Missouri, and the United States Attorney is asking me for instructions.

Mrs. Stokes is a conspicuous member of the ultra-radical element and her offense was quite as clear as that of many others who were convicted and punished under the Espionage Act during the war. Many of these have served either the sentences imposed by the court or smaller terms of imprisonment to which you have commuted their sentences. In view of the great pressure on behalf of so-called political prisoners and because this defendant is a woman and the war is over for all practical purposes, I am very strongly inclined to think that we ought to drop the case; but as it involves a question of policy which will affect the disposition of indictments pending against other persons not yet tried, I would appreciate it if I could have your view as to what ought to be done.

Yours faithfully,   A Mitchell Palmer

TLS (WP, DLC).
¹ About which, see W. Kent to WW, June 3, 1918, n. 1, Vol. 48, and TWG to WW, Aug. 21, 1918, Vol. 49.

From Thomas William Lamont

Personal

Dear Mr. President: 23 Wall Street October 1st, 1920.

I have understood that you plan from time to time, in the course of the campaign, to give out certain statements designed to assist the Democratic candidate.

If you will allow me to say so, you could make most effective use of Senator Harding's recent statement on the Panama Tolls question. Mr. Tumulty's statement, excellent as it is, was, I think, more or less lost in the public press.¹ If you will read just what Senator Harding said in his statement, I think you will agree with me that in all probability Harding never wrote that paragraph. It sounds to me as if it were written for him by one of Hearst's men, because the attitude of the Hearst papers at the time was almost word for word similar to this paragraph from Harding's speech.

This statement of Harding's is one of the most amazing that could possibly come from a Republican. He speaks of your "own partisans" in the Panama Tolls controversy, which is the same phrase that is constantly used against you in the League of Nations. He speaks of our constitutional right to rule our own destiny and to do as we choose with our own ships in our own canal, apparently regardless of our treaty obligations. This has a sound much like the opposition to the League of Nations.

Finally, and what is perhaps most important, he invites comparison with your action in the Panama Tolls controversy and your action in connection with the League of Nations. It is "the same President" who has in both cases tried to betray the interests of his country. Does this not afford you an excellent opportunity? The country needs a ringing statement on the importance of America maintaining its international relations with honor and with dignity. America is the strongest nation in the world. It is grown up. It should keep its international relations free from its domestic prejudices. It should handle and talk about its international relations with dignity and with restraint.

In any statement to the foregoing effect, you could set out clearly your whole position in the Panama Tolls question and show how indisputably it was in accord with the position of the accredited Republican leaders, like Root, Choate, and even Lodge. You could then take this statement of Harding's and show how false it is in its statement of fact and in its reasoning, and what a low appeal it makes to the passions of his countrymen. You could then *accept* the comparison which Harding makes between your Panama Canal stand and your League of Nations stand. Can Senator Root, or Senator Root's supporters, possibly defend Harding's Panama Tolls statement? Can Senator Lodge, or Senator Lodge's supporters, possibly stand for such a statement? Can the many admirers of John Hay, or of Joseph H. Choate, permit such a distortion of History?

You will probably consider that the whole point has been sufficiently made in Mr. Tumulty's statement, but, as I say, admirable as it is, I believe that the topic deserves a wider utterance, such as only you would have, and I don't believe the campaign will afford any possible opportunity that is better.

I spoke to Norman Davis about this over the telephone only the day before yesterday.

With great respect,

Sincerely yours,   Thomas W. Lamont

TLS (WP, DLC).
¹ About Harding's speech and Tumulty's reply, see JPT to WW, Sept. 24, 1920, and n. 1 thereto.

Two Letters from Bainbridge Colby

My dear Mr. President: Washington October 2, 1920.

General Pershing's proposed visit to South America is not turning out to be quite so simple a matter as we thought it would. You will recall that the idea was first suggested by the Secretary of War, moved, I think, by a desire to keep the General suitably and agreeably occupied. He had wound up the affairs of the A.E.F. and was something of a problem to the Secretary.

It now develops that despite the assurances we have received from the countries on his projected itinerary, that his visit will be most welcome (The Argentine Republic yet to be heard from), there is a feeling of reserve in some quarters, to which I at first did not attach the importance it seems really to merit.

Both Dr. Rowe,¹ the Director of the Pan American Union, and

Mr. Welles,[2] the Chief of our Latin-American Division, have stated their belief from the time the General's visit was first suggested that it did not quite fit the situation, and have expressed the hope that I could make the trip,—an idea that I at once dismissed as not to be thought of.

A few days ago I received a call from the Brazilian Ambassador,[3] who with much delicacy, but evident earnestness, put the question to me directly. I have given the matter some reflection, and it seems of sufficient importance to submit for your opinion, as we hardly wish to adopt a course which we are assured before we start will not have the effect we desire to create.

Let me state briefly the points that have been urged upon my consideration.

1. The visits of the President of Brazil, and the President of Uruguay,[4] while formally visits to the United States, were in a very large sense inspired by the respect and admiration which the peoples of South America felt for you personally and which they desired to manifest in the most impressive way they could.

2. A soldier, even the most distinguished, does not appeal to the thoughts which are uppermost in the mind of South America. It is interested in the peaceful ordering of the world, reconstruction, Pan-American co-operation in latter day tasks, in your philosophy of justice to all nations. A soldier hardly carries these connotations, and a uniform is not the garb in which South America finds the United States most ingratiating.

3. If you could not return the visits, which is what they desired above all things, it was hoped that you would designate someone who stood in a very close representative relation to you, and who might be assumed to speak for the government and people of the United States, in a way that a soldier ordinarily does not. Furthermore it is felt that the return of these important visits is a matter for this Administration. If left to its successor, the significance of the whole incident, both their visits and our reciprocation, would be distinctly sacrificed.

On the other hand, it seems unthinkable for me to leave your side at this time. In almost every direction I turn, there is some delicate and pressing matter, requiring the most careful study and watchful attention, and I should hate to think that a moment might come when you needed me, or only wanted me, and I should not be here.

The trip with a stop of two days in Rio, two in Montevideo, and two in Buenos Aires, using the fastest available ship, would consume five weeks.

Very respectfully yours,   Bainbridge Colby

TLS (WP, DLC).
   [1] That is, Leo Stanton Rowe.
   [2] (Benjamin) Sumner Welles, about whom, see n. 1 to BC to WW, Nov. 13, 1920 (third letter of that date).
   [3] Augusto Cochrane de Alençar.
   [4] Epitacio da Silva Pessôa and Baltasar Brum.

My dear Mr. President: Washington October 2 1920.

Ambassador Wallace has informed the Department that his Colleagues desire to proceed immediately to the signature of a Treaty recognizing Roumanian sovereignty over Bessarabia, and have expressed the hope that the United States would join them in this action.[1]

In view of our consistent refusal to approve a policy which tended toward the dismemberment of Russia, as so recently emphasized in the note to the Italian Ambassador,[2] I should be inclined to instruct Ambassador Wallace that we would not sign a Treaty disposing of Bessarabia and further that, in our opinion, hasty action in this matter would only tend to give the Bolsheviki another pretense for arousing national spirit on the ground that the Allies were disposing of Russian territory.

I await your views as to the propriety of such a course and should be glad to know whether you consider it sufficient to state our position to the Conference of Ambassadors or desire me to make a definite protest against the contemplated action of the Allies.

Faithfully yours,   Bainbridge Colby

I entirely share your view and hope you will send the instructions you suggest   W.W.[3]

TLS (SDR, RG 59, 871.014 Bessarabia/4, DNA).
   [1] H. C. Wallace to SecState, No. 1765, Sept. 29, 1920, T telegram (SDR, RG 59, 871.014 Bessarabia/3, DNA).
   [2] Printed as an Enclosure with BC to WW, Aug. 9, 1920.
   [3] Colby sent the following note to Wallace on October 5: "In view of the consistent refusal of this Government to approve a policy which tended toward the dismemberment of Russia, as so recently emphasized in the note to the Italian Ambassador, you should inform your colleagues that you have been instructed not to sign at this time any treaty disposing of Bessarabia. You should add that it is the Department's opinion that hasty action in this matter would only tend to give the Bolsheviki another pretense for arousing national spirit on the ground that the Allies were disposing of Russian territory at a time when a representative Russian Government could not be heard." BC to H. C. Wallace, Oct. 5, 1920, T telegram (SDR, RG 59, 871.014 Bessarabia/3, DNA).

From William Gibbs McAdoo

Dear Governor: New York Oct. 2, 1920.

I have promised to start October 12th on a speaking trip for Governor Cox which will take me to the Pacific Coast and back. It will be a strenuous affair, but I am glad to undertake it for the sake of the cause. I intend to feature the League of Nations strongly in my speeches, and am wondering if there is not a great deal of ammunition in Washington which can be used with great effect. I have in mind, for instance, the cable interchanges between Mr. Taft, President of the League to Enforce Peace, and yourself, and perhaps between other prominent Republicans and yourself, concerning the League Covenant. If these Republican leaders made specific suggestions which were incorporated in the League Covenant, the facts could be brought out with great effect, but the authenticity of these suggestions must be clearly shown.

I wonder if you would not put me in possession of all the available information of this character which you think could be used with propriety. I have also sent a line to Colby today, asking him to give me such information as he can, but he will, of course, hesitate to do so unless he has your sanction. The time is very short and I am very busy as well, so that, if you can expedite the sending of any available material to me, it will be most helpful.

Nell is going with me on the trip. I think we have a hard fight on our hands, and that it is going to take heroic effort to win the battle, but I am by no means hopeless.

Nell joins me in dearest love for you and Edith.

Affectionately yours,   W G McAdoo

TLS (WP, DLC).

A Statement[1]

[*Oct. 3, 1920*]

My Fellow-Countrymen:

The issues of the present campaign are of such tremendous importance, of such far-reaching significance for the influence of the country and the development of its future relations, and I have necessarily had so much to do with their development, that I am sure you will think it natural and proper that I should address to you a few words concerning them.

Every one who sincerely believes in government by the people must rejoice at the turn affairs have taken in regard to this campaign. This election is to be a genuine national referendum. The determination of a great policy upon which the influence and authority of the United States in the world must depend is not to be left to groups of politicians of either party, but is to be referred to the people themselves for a sovereign mandate to their representatives. They are to instruct their own Government what they wish done.

The chief question that is put to you is, of course: Do you want your country's honor vindicated and the Treaty of Versailles ratified? Do you in particular approve of the League of Nations as organized and empowered in that treaty? And do you wish to see the United States play its responsible part in it?

You have been grossly misled with regard to the treaty, and particularly with regard to the proposed character of the League of Nations, by those who have assumed the serious responsibility of opposing it. They have gone so far that those who have spent their lives, as I have spent my life, in familiarizing themselves with the history and traditions and policies of the nation, must stand amazed at the gross ignorance and impudent audacity which have led them to attempt to invent an "Americanism" of their own, which has no foundation whatever in any of the authentic traditions of the Government.

Americanism, as they conceive it, reverses the whole process of the last few tragical years. It would substitute America for Prussia in the policy of isolation and defiant segregation. Their conception of the dignity of the nation and its interest is that we should stand apart and watch for opportunities to advance our own interests, involve ourselves in no responsibility for the maintenance of the right in the world or for the continued vindication of any of the things for which we entered the war to fight.

The conception of the great creators of the Government was absolutely opposite to this. They thought of America as the light of the world, as created to lead the world in the assertion of the rights of peoples and the rights of free nations; as destined to set a responsible example to all the world of what free Government is and can do for the maintenance of right standards, both national and international.

This light the opponents of the League would quench. They would relegate the United States to a subordinate role in the affairs of the world.

Why should we be afraid of responsibilities which we are qualified to sustain and which the whole of our history has constituted a promise to the world we would sustain?

This is the most momentous issue that has ever been presented to the people of the United States, and I do not doubt that the hope of the whole world will be verified by an absolute assertion by the voters of the country of the determination of the United States to live up to all the great expectations which they created by entering the war and enabling the other great nations of the world to bring it to a victorious conclusion, to the confusion of Prussianism and everything that arises out of Prussianism. Surely we shall not fail to keep the promise sealed in the death and sacrifice of our incomparable soldiers, sailors and marines who await our verdict beneath the sod of France.

Those who do not care to tell you the truth about the League of Nations tell you that Article X. of the Covenant of the League would make it possible for other nations to lead us into war, whether we will it by our own independent judgment or not. This is absolutely false. There is nothing in the Covenant which in the least interferes with or impairs the right of Congress to declare war or not declare war, according to its own independent judgment, as our Constitution provides.

Those who drew the Covenant of the League were careful that it should contain nothing which interfered with or impaired the constitutional arrangements of any of the great nations which are to constitute its members. They would have been amazed and indignant at the things that are now being ignorantly said about this great and sincere document.

The whole world will wait for your verdict in November as it would wait for an intimation of what its future is to be.

WOODROW WILSON.

Printed in the *New York Times*, Oct. 4, 1920.
    [1] There is a WWsh draft of one sentence of this statement; a WWT draft of one paragraph; an EBWhw draft of one sentence; and a T draft, with WWhw and EBWhw emendations, in WP, DLC. The penultimate draft, signed by Wilson and with one WWhw emendation, is in the C. L. Swem Coll., NjP. The WWT is the first that we have seen since Wilson suffered his stroke on October 2, 1919.

To Bainbridge Colby

My dear Mr. Secretary: The White House 4 October, 1920

I have read with great interest your letter of October second about the visit to the Latin-American States.

I hate to see you go away more than you can possibly hate it yourself, but the ideal thing would be for you to make the trip. It would make an impression that no other visit could make, and you would have in your mind circumstances and conditions which no other visitor could be so well acquainted with. I hope that you will consider the matter and that you will, if possible, arrange to go. I believe the union in action and thought of this hemisphere will be of the greatest consequence to the world in the future and that we ought not to omit anything that may possibly bring it about. It is the only available offset to the follies of Europe.

I know you will consider this matter generously, as you do everything.

With warmest regard,

                    Cordially and faithfully yours,   Woodrow Wilson

P.S. Of course, I am assuming that you and Baker will confer
about this matter, and that we shall all pull together.

                                        Woodrow Wilson

TLS (B. Colby Papers, DLC).

To Alexander Mitchell Palmer

                                        The White House
My dear Mr. Attorney General: 4 October, 1920

I have your letter of October first about the case of Rose Pastor
Stokes and hasten to reply. I believe that Mrs. Stokes is one of the
dangerous influences of the country and I hesitate to advise that
the suit against her be dropped, but I feel the embarrassment of
pressing the suits now which began under the authority of the Espionage Act, because I think the country feels that the time for that
is past. I hope, therefore, that you will not make an exception of
Mrs. Stokes's case, but rather put it on the same footing that you
are putting all others that have arisen in the same way. I think this
is the fair and wise thing to do.[1]

                    Very sincerely yours,   Woodrow Wilson

TLS (A. M. Palmer Papers, DLC).
   [1] Samuel O. Hargus, Assistant United States District Attorney for the District of Western Missouri, announced on October 28, 1920, that Mrs. Stokes' case would not be
brought up for trial at the November term of the District Court, as originally scheduled.
No reason was given for this decision. *New York Times*, Oct. 29, 1920. As it turned out,
Mrs. Stokes was never retried.

To William Gibbs McAdoo

My dear Mac: The White House 4 October, 1920

I was glad to get your letter of the second, and you may be sure
I would be glad to comply with its request if I had material that I
thought would be serviceable to you. The particular material to
which you refer—the cablegrams of Mr. Taft and others—has been
put at Cox's disposal and it would be awkward now to place it elsewhere, as you will see. I am not particularly keen about having it
exploited anyway, because I am ashamed to have taken the advice
of those insincere men who are not trying to help but trying to
embarrass and hinder. Tumulty has got together some excellent

material which I am going to ask him to send you. It contains the germs of many fine campaign speeches.

   With love from us both to you all,
                    Affectionately yours,   Woodrow Wilson

TLS (W. G. McAdoo Papers, DLC).

To Thomas William Lamont

My dear Friend: [The White House] 4 October, 1920
   I am very much obliged to you for your letter of October first. Your advice is interesting, not only, and most welcome, but always sets my thoughts going, and I am particularly gratified because I know the motives which prompted it. For the present I am awaiting developments, to make sure when and how I ought to take part. It is not easy to determine offhand.
   With warm regard,
                    Cordially and sincerely yours,   [Woodrow Wilson]

CCL (WP, DLC).

To William Woodward[1]

My dear Mr. Woodward: [The White House] 4 October, 1920
   Now that the sheep are returning to you, I want to send with them, as it were, a word of deep appreciation from Mrs. Wilson and myself of your kindness in supplying us with so fine and interesting a flock. We have enjoyed them and shall miss them very much; and while they were here, they always reminded us of your generosity.   Cordially and sincerely yours,   [Woodrow Wilson]

CCL (WP, DLC).
   [1] Of Bel Air Farm, Collington, Md. About the White House sheep, see Evangeline C. Booth to WW, May 22, 1920, n. 1, Vol. 65.

From Bainbridge Colby

My dear Mr. President: [Washington] October 4, 1920.
   Referring to the California-Japanese question,[1] we are being urged by the Japanese Ambassador among others to issue a statement (it might take the form of a letter to the Governor of California) for the purpose of allaying popular excitement in Japan.
   The policy of any statement at all at the present time seems to me questionable.

The proposed State law, initiated by popular petition, denying the Japanese the right to lease land, is assured of passage at the November election, I am convinced. Its opponents admit this. Governor Stephens, of California, Senators Phelan and Hiram Johnson, and the press of the State, backed by an overwhelming sentiment are in favor of the law. Both candidates for President have declared themselves in accord with California's attitude toward the Japanese, and the platform of both National parties contain planks of almost identical meaning in favor of the exclusion of Asiatics or non-assimilable races, and laws subsidiary to that purpose, which may be passed.

The proposed law, when passed, cannot be modified except at another election, which is a year off, and in the meantime there is no method by which it can be modified, or its operation suspended or postponed.

It is this measure, which is the immediate cause of Japan's uneasiness and growing resentment. Its effect will be to bar agriculture to the Japanese as an occupation, except as farm laborers. Much of the richest land in the State is now in their control, which in some counties amounts to fifty and even seventy-five per cent. The solution of this very perplexing problem will, I think, be worked out in the courts. The proposed law is open to weighty attack as violative of our treaty stipulations, and also on constitutional grounds, which seem to me strong.

Pending the actual adoption of the measure, as yet speaking strictly, only indicated, my idea would be to say and do nothing, despite the natural desire in some quarters to reassure public opinion in Japan. We can *do* nothing effectual, and whatever we *say* may have the reverse effect to what we intend. Nothing could satisfy Japan except some statement that this Department views the measure as one of doubtful legality, and will take means to block its enforcement. If we were to take refuge in amiable generalities it would seem weak, and might embolden the extremists in Japan, without satisfying the more reasonable sections of her people.

In either event, just at this moment when opinion in California is inflamed by the wind-up of a campaign in which this question is in the forefront of local interest, we would be criticised at home as lukewarm in support of the American position. Undoubtedly comment would ensue which might still further exacerbate Japanese opinion, and leave us worse off than if we said nothing.

My reason for writing you at this length, is that the program prepared by Ambassador Morris and approved by you, contemplates in his opinion, some such statement, as I have discussed, and we would not of course take a new tack, which involved any departure from your instructions, without your concurrence.

Very respectfully yours,   Bainbridge Colby

CCL (B. Colby Papers, DLC).

¹ See the Enclosure, a memorandum by R. S. Morris, printed with BC to WW, Aug. 5, 1920, and the notes thereto.

From Joseph Patrick Tumulty, with Enclosure

My dear Governor: [The White House] 4 October 1920.

I am calling your attention to the attached telegram. You will notice that Senator Spencer says that my denial originated entirely in my own mind and that I falsely made the announcement, and that it did not have your knowledge and sanction. I am also attaching the statements I sent you the other day.

Senator Spencer is making so many outrageous statements in Missouri that I think there is justification for your personally telegraphing him. This is a chance to squelch this gentleman, and end the matter.   Sincerely yours,   [Tumulty]

CCL (J. P. Tumulty Papers, DLC).

E N C L O S U R E

Senator Selden Palmer Spencer,   The White House,
St. Louis, Missouri.   4 October, 1920.

Newspaper representatives have called my attention to a statement given by you to the St. Louis papers, containing the following quotation:

"I do not for a moment believe that the President made any such denial, or that the matter was ever called to his attention, as J. P. Tumulty indicated in his letter. Anyone who knows the situation at Washington knows that Mr. Tumulty is himself conducting the administration of government far more than the President of the United States, and has become accustomed to issue orders and make statements originating entirely in his own mind, but falsely announced as having back of them the knowledge and sanction of the President."

I shall not attempt to characterize the reflection upon the President himself which is found in this statement. I shall leave to your own conscience to say whether you consider this statement as worthy of a Senator of the United States. The statement you make charging that I have falsely issued a denial at the White House that the President had promised American military aid to the Roumanians and Serbs is one that I cannot allow to pass without comment. It is a fact that the President, in his own handwriting, authorized me to say that the alleged quotation from you contained in the St. Louis Post Dispatch was false. If you doubt the authenticity of the President's authority, his written direction to me is on file in the White House,[1] where either you or any representative you may appoint may examine it.   J. P. Tumulty.[2]

T telegram (J. P. Tumulty Papers, DLC).
    [1] We have not found this note in either the Wilson or Tumulty Papers.
    [2] This telegram was printed in the *New York Times*, Oct. 5, 1920.

From Louis Wiley[1]

Dear Mr. President: [New York] October 4, 1920.

    Permit me to offer you my congratulations on your message to the American people issued today. Your appeal for the ratification of the League of Nations by the vote of the people is a clarion call for the vindication of the country's honor. You have challenged the opposition to add to the burdens of the world by holding the United States aloof in a policy of isolation. Your statement throws the responsibility for the rejection or acceptance of the League of Nations on the American people. May their voice in November be the victory of a free land taking its responsibility in the maintenance of right international standards!
    With regards,   Always sincerely yours,   Louis Wiley

TLS (WP, DLC).
    [1] Wilson's old friend, business manager of the *New York Times* since 1906.

From Newton Diehl Baker

My dear Mr President   Washington October 4, 1920

    I am deeply ashamed at the disloyalty of Mr Crowell.[1] His course seems to me essentially dishonest and, I am sorry to have to say, dictated by the low motive of ambition to secure place under Senator Harding, should he be elected. My chief distress is that you should be annoyed by such conduct from one for whose selection I am responsible. The Secretary of War has made some mistakes, even if they are not the ones with which his critics charge him!
                         Respectfully yours,   Newton D. Baker

ALS (WP, DLC).
    [1] In a statement issued by the Republican National Committee on October 3, Benedict Crowell, former Assistant Secretary of War, declared that he had always favored

American membership in the League of Nations. However, he said, the Wilson administration had failed to get the United States into the League in spite of the fact that "75 per cent of the Senate were in favor of it." "It seems evident," he continued, "that Governor Cox is making many promises regarding the League which he may not be able to fulfill. Senator Harding is wisely noncommittal on the subject. . . . I have every confidence in Senator Harding's judgment and believe he will do the right thing when the proper time comes. I therefore favor the election of Harding and Coolidge and a Republican Congress. With an administration and Congress of the same political faith earnestly working together, I am confident the problem will be settled right." *New York Times*, Oct. 4, 1920.

Charles Lee Swem to Edith Bolling Galt Wilson

Mrs. Wilson: The White House [c. Oct. 4, 1920].

I do not know exactly to what the President referred when he asked for the Santo Domingo papers. I send the attached as all I have on the subject.[1]   C. L. Swem.

TL (WP, DLC).
[1] Actually, it was J. A. Lejeune to JD, Oct. 4, 1920, TCL (WP, DLC). This lengthy memorandum about Haiti, not the Dominican Republic, combined a "diary" of Lejeune's tour of inspection to Haiti, September 4-13, 1920, with an estimate of the military situation in that country, especially in regard to the First Brigade, U. S. Marines, stationed there. He presented a highly favorable account of the work of the marines in Haiti and of the regard in which they were held by the general population.

A Memorandum by Homer Stillé Cummings

Monday, October 4th 1920.

In Washington, telephoned to the White House to secure interview with Mrs. Wilson. Later through Mr. Hoover, received invitation to take supper at the White House that evening at 7:30 P.M. Went to the White House at 7:30 P.M. and dined with Mrs. Wilson and her brother, Mr. Bolling.[1] I returned to her the code book which I used in San Francisco. It had been my purpose when telephoning for an interview simply to have an opportunity to return the book to her own hands. I had not expected to be invited to supper. Evidently she had thought something of special importance had come up for she had spoken to the President about my having called and he asked her to confer with me. When I told her I had nothing special to say, she said that she knew the President would like to see me anyway, if it were only to say good-bye before I went on my Western trip and she arranged for an interview with the President for the following day. At the table that night there were only three people, Mrs. Wilson, Mr. Bolling and myself. It was a very quite [quiet] and simple affair and entirely informal. I thought Mrs. Wilson seemed a little tired and worn but she was very cheerful and as always, very amiable. Naturally we talked over the political situation. She seemed deeply interested and was hopeful of success in November. I asked her how she thought the President would feel if Cox were defeated and she said that she feared that it would have a very depressing effect upon him. We talked of the manner in which the campaign had been mismanaged and maltreated by those in charge and she seemed quite familiar with the existing situation. I began to tell her about what happened at Columbus at the time George White was appointed Chairman, and [she] seemed very anxious for me to continue the story so I told her the whole story of the matter as I understood it.[2] She seemed to be favorably impressed by the kind of campaign that Governor Cox was now making and thought it a distinct improvement over the manner in which it had been commenced.

I told her in addition to returning the code book that I really did want to say something to her, something that I did not quite feel like saying to the President himself. I told her that in my judgment the prospects of success were not very promising and that if Gov. Cox were defeated, there would be varying views as to the reasons for it and that I hoped that the President would not take any position during the campaign which would justify the claim that he had taken the campaign out of the hands of Governor Cox and made himself responsible for the result. She said that she had no doubt but that they would blame the President in any event. I told her that I quite realized that but that I didn't want anyone to have the opportunity to be able to make such a claim with any plausible reasons to support it. I said that the whole cause had been so imperilled by the manner of its treatment that if unfortunate results followed, those who had produced them ought to be chargeable with the result. I also added that I knew that great pressure would be brought to bear upon the President to get him to issue statements and that in desperation, the pressure would be constantly increased as time went on and that I hoped that he would not speak too frequently, or become involved in any controversial matters and I said that his record had been so clear up to-date that it would be unfortunate if in the pressure of the campaign, things were said by him which would not be fully justified when we came to review the situation, not only after the election but five or ten years hence. She said that it would be pretty hard to persuade the President to take himself into account in the matter and that he seemed curiously unconcerned about his own place in history. I said, however, that I thought that whatever he wrote, should be written as if it were to be read ten years from now. She said she didn't know whether she would get a chance to express these views to the President but from what she knew about his attitude, that she felt sure that he did not intend to be very active in the campaign.

There was much more that was discussed and then amiable social things were talked of. She told some amusing anecdotes, one in particular with reference to the manner in which Chief Justice White conducted himself while attending a concert. It appears that the old man is very fond of music and for some unknown reason, likes to sit in the front row and more or less under his breath but still audibly sing as the artists sing, much to their distress and annoyance and it doesn't make any difference whatever whether the songs are in French or Italian or English, the old man keeps up his persistent humming and despite the efforts of his wife to stop him. I don't know how the matter came up but I told Mrs. Wilson of the efforts to obtain a Bible while at the Murray Hill Hotel. The story seemed to amuse her very much and she said she would tell the President about it.

After dinner, I remained a little while and then left.

T MS (H. S. Cummings Papers, ViU).
¹ That is, John Randolph Bolling.
² See the memorandum by H. S. Cummings printed at July 26, 1920, and n. 1 thereto, Vol. 65.

To Selden Palmer Spencer

[The White House] 5 October 1920.

I have just been shown your statement, that my Secretary's denial of the previous statement by you that I had promised American military aid to Roumanians and Serbs was issued by him without my knowledge and sanction, and that you did not for a moment believe that I had made any such denial, or that the matter was ever called to my attention. I wish to say that your statement was called to my attention by Mr. Tumulty, and that I requested him to issue the denial to which you refer. I reiterate the denial. The statement you made was false.   Woodrow Wilson.

T telegram (Letterpress Books, WP, DLC).

From Selden Palmer Spencer

[St. Louis, Oct. 5, 1920]

I beg to acknowledge receipt of your telegram of Oct. 5, in which you deny that you promised American military aid to Rumanians and Serbs and that previous denial which Mr. J. P. Tumulty had made was at your request. The statement of yours to which I have often referred in my address was the statement in the stenographic notes of the eighth plenary session of the Peace Conference, in which you are reported to have said to Premier Bratiano of Rumania, as follows:

"You must not forget that it is force that is the final guaranty of the public peace. If the world is again troubled, the United States will send to this side of the ocean their army and their fleet."

The statement was made upon the floor of the Senate on Feb. 2, 1920, by Senator Reed, and so far as I have learned has never been denied until now. It has been widely circulated over the United States. If you did not make that statement to Premier Bratiano, I should be much indebted if you will be good enough to inform me.

Printed in the *New York Times*, Oct. 6, 1920.

To Newton Diehl Baker

My dear Mr. Secretary: [The White House] 5 October, 1920

I knew that you would feel just as I did about Crowell's statement, and I hope you won't worry about the fact that you recommended him for appointment. Black sheep sometimes slip into the fold in spite of us. Of course, I have found out now that I never did like Crowell!

                    Cordially and faithfully yours,   [Woodrow Wilson]

CCL (WP, DLC).

To Joe Cowperthwaite

My dear Mr. Cowperthwaite: The White House 5 October, 1920

Your very kind letter of September twenty-second is very much appreciated, but I am sorry and embarrassed to say that my letter found the wrong destination. It was intended for the Rothay Hotel in Grasmere Village.

I hope that I shall have an opportunity next year to express my appreciation of your courtesy in person.

    With the best wishes,
                    Sincerely yours,   Woodrow Wilson

TLS (received from the Willowsmere Hotel, Grasmere).

From Norman Hezekiah Davis

My dear Mr. President: Washington October 5, 1920.

The Preliminary Conference on Communications convenes here next Friday, October eighth. One of the first questions to be taken up will be the allocation of the German cables. As you will recall, it was not originally contemplated that this question would be handled in this Conference.

I should like very much to discuss this matter briefly with you in order to get your views and instructions, and also information as to some of your conversations in Paris on this subject. I shall be absent tomorrow, but if it is agreeable and convenient for you to see me a few minutes on Thursday, please let me know.[1]

Cordially and faithfully yours,   Norman H. Davis

TLS (WP, DLC).
[1] A shorthand note on top of this letter reads: "The President will see him tomorrow morning at 10:45."

Edith Bolling Galt Wilson to Cleveland Hoadley Dodge

My dear Mr Dodge: The White House Oct. 5/1920

We both loved your letter,[1] and it was so like your big generous self it made us home sick for a sight of you.

When are you coming for that much delayed visit? We hope the time on the "Corona" did you worlds of good, and that you and Mrs Dodge[2] are both strong and well, and all the daughters[3] sons[4] & *grand-babies*[5] the same.

My dear patient is much stronger and fighting with all his splendid courage against all the odds that have surrounded him, not only physical, but those deeper scars that were meant for the heart! He asks me to give you his warm love and say that your friendship is one of the props that no matter how hard he leans on, never fails, never disappoints.

Thank you for letting us see a copy of your letter to Mr Gerard— it was very stimulating, and like you to always say the loyal generous thing.

We both send you love, and the same to dear Mrs. Dodge.

from yours Faithfully   Edith Bolling Wilson

ALS (WC, NjP).
[1] It is missing.
[2] That is, Grace Parish Dodge.
[3] Elizabeth Wainright Dodge (Mrs. George Herbert) Huntington (1884-1976) and Julia Parish Dodge (Mrs. James Childs) Rea (1886-1965). G. H. Huntington died in 1953; Elizabeth married Dumont Clarke (1883-1960) in 1955.
[4] Cleveland Earl Dodge (1888-1982) and Bayard Dodge (1888-1972).

⁵ Elizabeth and George Huntington had no children. At this time, Julia and James Rea had five children: William Holdship (born 1912), Cleveland Dodge (1913), Grace (1915), Ruth (1916), and James C., Jr. (1917). Cleveland Earl and Pauline Morgan Dodge had a daughter, Elizabeth, born in 1920. Bayard and Mary Bliss Dodge had two daughters: Grace (born 1915) and Margaret (1917).

Our thanks to Phyllis Boushall (Mrs. Cleveland Earl Dodge, Jr.) Dodge for this information.

A Memorandum by Homer Stillé Cummings

Tuesday, October 5th 1920.

At 10:45 A.M. I went to see the President, the appointment having been arranged by Mrs. Wilson. The President was sitting on the back portico and waved his hand cheerfully to me as I approached. We didn't talk very much politics. It seemed to me that he rather wanted to avoid the discussion of serious matters, and of course, I said nothing to depress him. In the course of the conversation, I suggested to him that there was one fortunate thing about so great a cause and that was that it could not be defeated, and that any reversal must of necessity only be temporary in character. The President said of course that is so but if Harding is elected, and gives the country the kind of government that we have every reason to expect we shall come very close to having a revolution in this country and the prospects that we shall have war with Mexico is very great.

He said that this would be very embarrassing to all of us because if the Republican administration got the country into war, they would expect everybody to support the President in his prosecution of it. The President spoke of the labor conditions and the impossibility of forcing labor back into the position that it occupied prior to the war. He said that forces of this kind were like great rivers and that they could be damned [dammed], but that ultimately these restraints would be broken and that there would be a great flood and then he added, rather quizzically, and there isn't apt to be any Noah to rescue us. He mentioned the political campaign and the manner in which it had been handled and expressed great distress over that aspect of the situation. I suggested that it would have been a simple matter under proper auspices to have invoked the assistance of a fine body of men and women who regarded the League of Nations as a sort of religion and that if the campaign had been properly managed and the candidate and his associates had been of the character which would have justified the confidence of these people, many of whom were Republicans, by instinct, that we would have had a great movement in this country for the redemption of American honor which might easily have proved irresistible. He said "Yes, that is the pity of it. You and men like you," he said, "are Crusaders. These other people are politicians."

I then told him something of my plans and outlined the trip which I expected to take, and quite anxiously I thought, he turned to me and said "Don't try to do too much" and added "If I had it to do over again, I would have had longer intervals of rest between my speeches." I said that my wife felt the same way about it, had urged me not to undertake too much and had said to me "the President has almost killed himself with his cause and there is no reason why you should do the same thing." I told him, however, that I felt entirely equal to the program which had been outlined and called his attention to the fact that it made a great deal of difference whether one was being quoted accurately from stenographic notes every day as he had been or whether one could use matter more or less repititious in character. I told him that I always found it a very distinct added strain if I had to make three or four speeches in the same city to audiences which contained many people who heard all of the speeches and that the task that he had undertaken on his western tour was almost beyond the power of any human being, and that I worried about it from the beginning.

He then turned to lighter subjects, some anecdotes were told and then Mrs. Wilson said I told the President what you said last night and I didn't get my head taken off either. I told her that I was happy that she had survived and that I had not had the courage to say it to him and that I was glad that it had been said. All the while he smiled amiably and then pushed over to me the inevitable saucer of cake which appears to be part of his diet. I asked him if he was giving this to me out of consideration for me or as part of the program—to rid himself of the cake and he said "I am afraid anxious most of all to get rid of the cake." I took a small nibble of it and asked Mrs. Wilson if she told the President the Bible story and she said that she had, that she had wanted him to wait and have me tell it to him but he insisted that she should tell it, so I found that the Bible story had already been told. I had only intended to stay a few moments but I found afterwards when I left that I had been there about forty minutes.

On the way out, I saw Mr. Tumulty and had quite a little talk with him. He said there was nothing new about the Cabinet matter. I said I had never really heard how the President feels about it and Tumulty said that the President had offered Alexander a place on the Shipping Board and had intimated that Alexander might resign from the Cabinet but Tumulty said that Alexander did not seem to want to resign from the Cabinet, and that the matter had not reached any very definite state. Well, I said, if Alexander goes on the Shipping Board ultimately, what will the President do about his successor? And Tumulty said: "Why, of course, he will appoint you. He told me that he would." I told Tumulty that I would really like the appointment if it came about naturally even if it meant only two or three months in the Cabinet, because I could see that if we were defeated in this election, the work of rehabilitating the party would have to be taken up and that it was important as I viewed it that the friends of the President and those who sympathized with his policies and purposes should be the dominating force in the reorganized party and that the prestige of having been in the President's Cabinet would aid me very materially in any work that fell to my lot and thay [that] really this was the only reason that I cared anything about the appointment. He said that he understood this perfectly, that he was going to have a talk with old man Alexander and see if he could not pry him loose.

T MS (H. S. Cummings Papers, ViU).

Fred A. Carlson[1] to Charles Lee Swem

Dear Mr. Swem: Chicago October 6, 1920.

I noticed in the Chicago papers of today, Wednesday, October 6, 1920 (The Chicago Tribune and the Chicago Herald-Examiner) Washington and St. Louis dispatches in regard to Senator Spencer's statement that President Wilson "had promised American military aid to Roumania and Serbia in the event of the invasion of those countries," and the President's letter in regard thereto.

In a St. Louis dispatch dated October 5, Senator Spencer is quoted as follows:

"The statement of yours to which I have often referred in my addresses was the statement in the stenographic notes of the eighth plenary session of the peace conference, in which you are reported to have said to Premier Bratianu of Roumania as follows:

" 'You must not forget that it is force that is the final guaranty of the public peace. If the world is again troubled the United States will send to this side of the ocean their army and their fleet.'

"The statement was made upon the floor of the senate on Feb. 2, 1920, by Senator Reed, and so far as I have learned has never been denied until now. It has been widely circulated over the United States. If you did not make that statement to Premier Bratianu, I should be much indebted if you will inform me."

The Eighth Plenary Session was a secret session and my impression is that you were not there. I may be wrong about that. However, I reported the proceedings, and wrote up the statement which President Wilson made. The report of the proceedings was mimeographed, and I suppose there are copies in Washington.

I have just gone over my notes (my shorthand notes), and I can find no such statement as is alleged in the St. Louis dispatch which I quoted, and which it is therein alleged "was made upon the floor of the Senate on February 2, 1920 by Senator Reed." Therefore I will quote in full the President's statement in the secret plenary session of May 31, 1919. Will you please call it to the attention of some responsible person in Washington, if you find that there is not a copy of the transcription of the English shorthand notes. It is just barely possible that the quotation by Senators Reed and Spencer was from a translation into English of M. Mantoux'[2] translation into French of the President's remarks, and as you know, the translations sometimes mixed things up a bit.

Following is a transcript of my shorthand notes of President Wilson's statement at the Eighth Plenary Session (Secret) of the Peace Conference, held at the Quai d'Orsay, Saturday, May 31, 1919:
. . .[3]

I wish I were in a position to make public what the President said, for I feel that the President is sadly misquoted, but of course, as the meeting was a secret one, I can say nothing. If it is thought that this letter is an indiscreet one, destroy it. But, if necessary, I will be glad to swear to the accuracy of the above transcript, and I hope a complete refutation of the charge will be made.

Yours sincerely,   Fred A. Carlson

P.S. Will you please ascertain whether it would be improper for me to write a letter to Senator Spencer saying that I reported President Wilson's address in which he is alleged to have made the statement charged by Senator Reed, and that the quotation made by Senator Reed is incorrect? And that I say nothing further?

F.A.C.

TLS (J. P. Tumulty Papers, DLC).
[1] Shorthand reporter of Chicago.
[2] That is, Paul-Joseph Mantoux, interpreter for the French delegation at the Paris Peace Conference.
[3] Here follows the text of Wilson's speech printed at May 31, 1919, Vol. 59. Swem handed Carlson's letter to Tumulty.

To Selden Palmer Spencer

[The White House] 6 October, 1920

I am perfectly content to leave it to the voters of Missouri to determine which of us is telling the truth.[1]

Woodrow Wilson.

T telegram (Letterpress Books, WP, DLC).
[1] This telegram set off a political firestorm. The Republican National Committee, Spencer, Reed, and others all claimed that stenographic reports of Wilson's speech at the Eighth Plenary Session proved the accuracy of Spencer's allegation. Senator Hiram W. Johnson furnished to Spencer a copy of Wilson's remarks as he had had them printed in the *Congressional Record* of December 4, 1919. *New York Times*, Oct. 7, 1920.
    The following day, October 7, Tumulty tried his hand at damage control by issuing a statement to the effect that there was no stenographic record of the proceedings of the Eighth Plenary Session in his possession and that, insofar as Wilson knew, there was "none in this country." Tumulty added that it was up to Spencer and others to "produce the proof." This evoked a telegram to Spencer from the distinguished American journalist in Paris, Herbert Adams Gibbons, that he had a copy of the stenographic report and a statement from the Secretariat of the Peace Conference that it could not give out a report of the proceedings of that meeting without the consent of all nations which had had representatives there. This in turn prompted the *New York Times* to say editorially that Wilson should at once publish a correct report of what he had actually said at the Eighth Plenary Session. The *Times* added that it might have been more courteous for Wilson to reply to Spencer by giving out a correct report of what he had said. *Ibid.*, Oct. 8, 1920.
    A report in the *Times* from Washington on October 9 said that the White House had received a stenographic report of Wilson's remarks from Fred A. Carlson, who had been the chief stenographer of the American delegation at Paris. The story also said that White House officials were elated to receive this report and were preparing a statement to the country. *Ibid.*, Oct. 10, 1920.
    Tumulty issued a press release on October 11 (T MS, WP, DLC), which was published in the afternoon papers of that day and the morning papers of the following day. It reproduced in full Carlson's letter to Swem of October 6. It also printed the text of Wilson's remarks in parallel columns from the transcript printed in the *Congressional Record* of December 4, 1919, and the "official version" from Carlson's letter. The *New York Times* noted that the version printed in the *Congressional Record* was a reprint of a syndicated article by the renowned correspondent, Frank H. Simonds, who had stated that it was "a translation from the French of an alleged official report of the session." Publication of Tumulty's press release drew from Spencer the retort that he could see no radical difference between the two versions, and that the official version clearly proved that "nothing can conceal the pledge which the President attempted to make for this country by which American soldiers are to be sent overseas whenever the world is again troubled." In another report, the distinguished corporation lawyer of New York, Paul D. Cravath, said that publication of the "official version" had vindicated Senator Spencer. Cravath added that Mantoux was "a most accurate interpreter." Reed chimed in: "For the life of me I cannot see how the stenographic report in any manner helps the President's case. It is, in fact, a complete verification of the body of the charges heretofore made." *Ibid.*, Oct. 12, 1920.
    Tumulty's press release provided the *New York Times* with an opportunity to come to Wilson's and Tumulty's rescue by saying editorially that undoubtedly Spencer had proceeded in good faith and that he ought now to acknowledge his mistake "frankly and courteously." *Ibid.* The *Times*, on October 13, quoted from the Westminster Confession of Faith in counseling Spencer to resort to prayer for his salvation.
    This was not quite the end of the controversy. Gibbons, who was then in Washington, said that he had talked to representatives of the small powers after the Eighth Plenary Session, and that they had the clear understanding that they had been given definite military assurances by Wilson. Wilson's successor in the McCormick Chair of Jurisprudence and Politics at Princeton University, Edward S. Corwin, opined that the Carlson and French versions of Wilson's speech were "substantially the same." Senator Borah said that the official version sustained "every charge we have ever made against this gigantic autocracy based on force." *Ibid.*, Oct. 14, 1920.
    Most of these reports were front-page, lead stories in the *New York Times*, often accompanied by large headlines. We have not surveyed other newspapers but assume that

they gave equal prominence to the controversy, to which far greater coverage was given than to Cox and Harding's speeches during the period covered by this note. In our opinion, it was one of the most important incidents of the presidential campaign of 1920.

To Bainbridge Colby

My dear Mr. Secretary: The White House 6 October, 1920

The other day you asked me what my feeling was about Ambassador Davis making political speeches and I think I conveyed to you the impression that I did not think it altogether proper. I wish now to correct that impression, because if Ambassador Davis can confine himself to the great issue of the League of Nations he may be of very material service to us, and I hope that he will do all that it is possible for him to do.

Cordially and faithfully yours,   Woodrow Wilson

TLS (B. Colby Papers, DLC).

To Louis Wiley

My dear Mr. Wiley: The White House 6 October, 1920

Thank you for your letter of October fourth. It cheers and encourages me. I am mightily pleased that you think what you do of the statement I issued on Monday.

May I not say how much I admire the splendid course the Times is pursuing editorially? Please convey my warmest regards to the editorial staff.

Cordially and sincerely yours,   Woodrow Wilson

TLS (L. Wiley Papers, NRU).

To Joseph Patrick Tumulty, with Enclosure

Dear Tumulty: [The White House, c. Oct. 6, 1920]

Can we get a copy of the letter referred to that Mr. Schurman[1] would be willing for me to use?[2]   The President.

TL (WP, DLC).

[1] Wilson referred to W. G. Harding to Jacob Gould Schurman, former President of Cornell University, printed in the *New York Tribune*, Sept. 18, 1920, a portion of which Tumulty reproduced in the Enclosure.

[2] Tumulty wrote to Schurman on October 7, saying that Wilson would like to have copies of Schurman's letter to Harding and Harding's reply. Schurman replied to Tumulty on October 11, 1920 (TLS, WP, DLC), saying that his letter to Harding was private and that he could not send it, and enclosing a clipping from the *New York Tribune* with Harding's letter referred to above. Tumulty attached a note to this letter and clipping with the following comment: "Returned from house without comment."

E N C L O S U R E

From Joseph Patrick Tumulty

Dear Governor: The White House 6 October, 1920.

I think the letter of Senator Harding to Jacob Sherman containg [contains] the statement we discussed this morning. The following paragraphs are germane:

"I recognize that the world's peace is now to a great extent intertwined with the settlement of Versailles. From that settlement I would save all that is good and useful. An association of nations for purposes of conference and a world court with jurisdiction of justiciable questions would, I am confident, now be accepted by all nations.

"This plan, we have been repeatedly assured by European statesmen, would meet their approval. Mr. Lloyd George has frankly expressed opinion that the League of Nations covenant might well be changed for the better. Certainly it is our thought to improve, to save and build upon whatever is good rather than to abandon the good there is and repudiate the world's aspirations for peace.

"Viscount Grey has generously proposed that the Americans be instrusted with drafting a reconstruction scheme. It is apparent that the enlightened leadership of Europe wishes us to do this, and I should feel that to refuse would be a dereliction. As I view it, we have an opportunity to do a great service to the world if we will but undertake this effort which the world wishes us to undertake."

Sincerely,   Tumulty

TLS (WP, DLC).

From Joseph Patrick Tumulty, with Enclosure

Dear Governor: The White House, 6 October, 1920.

I prepared some weeks ago a review of the attitude of the churches of America toward the League of Nations. It would be a wonderful thing if you could make a great appeal to the churches, based upon this memorandum.

Sincerely yours,   J P Tumulty[1]

TLS (WP, DLC).
[1] A CLSsh note at the top of this letter reads: "Hold on file."

ENCLOSURE

Have the churches of America any influence over the destiny of the nation? This question occurs to the minds of thoughtful people when contemplating efforts in progress to permanently establish peace in the world.

By an inexorable decree of public will church and state are disassociated in the scheme of our government. The mingling of religious creeds with politics is intolerable to the spirit of America. A strong, moral sentiment, however, lies at the foundation of the republic and in this sentiment the churchman, as well as the statesman, has concern. Churches have no concern in politics, but they have in the well being of mankind. They have no place in government, but they have in civilization.

Church statistics show that there are in America about forty-two million souls making profession of church membership, in one denomination or the other. The moral force of this great body of citizens to sustain the integrity of American character for truth and justice should be overwhelming.

In the church membership of America all forms of occupation and all shades of political opinion are represented. The churches are not interested in and do not concern themselves with the occupation or party affiliation of their members, except that they condemn immorality in either private life or political action.

The significance of the designation "Christian Civilization" is comprehensive enough to include the Old as well as the New Testament. It includes even those who do not profess the creed of any church but accept the philosophy of human brotherhood, equal rights and honesty of action.

The attainment of peace is the aim of all Christian civilization and a special mission of all churches of all creeds, in common.

Is[a]iah in his prophesies, before the coming of Christ, says that out of Zion shall go forth the law and the word of the Lord from Jerusalem:

"And he shall judge among the nations and shall rebuke many people: and they shall beat their swords into ploughshares and their spears into pruning hooks: *nation shall not life up sword against nation, neither shall they learn war any more.*"

The angel of the Lord, heralding the birth of Christ to the shepherds, "keeping watch over their flock by night" proclaimed:

"Glory to God in the highest, and on earth peace, good-will toward men."

In his sermon upon the mountain, portraying the blessings which flow from virtue obedient to God, Christ said:

"Blessed are the peacemakers: for they shall be called the children of God."

The highest blessing of all was this of the peacemakers.

If the profession of faith by any member of any church is regarded by him as more than a mere form, his sympathies, his prayers, and his actions must be directed toward the attainment of peace on earth. The churches of America have recognized this; many have earnestly and devoutly endorsed the League of Nations to maintain peace and no church organization has taken a position in opposition.

The annual conference of the Methodist church held at Des Moines, Iowa; the Presbyterian General Assembly held in Philadelphia and the Baptist National Association assembled at Washington, D. C., endorsed the League of Nations unanimously. These great assemblies of Christian churches gave their earnest and unqualified sanction to the efforts of the peacemakers at Versailles to form a league among the nations of the world to promote a better understanding, to restore and maintain peace throughout the world.

At the Triennial General Convention of the Protestant Episcopal Church held at Detroit, a resolution was adopted pledging the support of the church to "all movements which aim to draw closer the nations of the earth." This resolution was adopted unanimously and expressses the conscience of that church.

The National Council of the Congregational Church, in convention in Grand Rapids, Mich., adopted resolutions urging ratification of the League of Nations covenant, "without amendments and with only such reservations as shall strengthen the moral influence of the United States."

Resolutions favoring the League of Nations were adopted by the Baptist missionary convention of the State of New York held at Gloversville, N. Y.

The Unitarian General Conference held in Baltimore, over which former President Taft presided, unanimously adopted a resolution amending [commending] the League of Nations and expressing hope for the "ratification of the peace treaty now before the Senate of the United States, with such reservations and interpretations only as shall not endanger or unduly delay its passage."

The New York section of the Council of Jewish Women, held in New York October 24, at which 1,500 women were assembled, the following resolutions were adopted:

WHEREAS, the League of Nations presents the only hope of lasting peace and of ultimate disarmament, and

WHEREAS, the League of Nations would establish peace on the

high moral plains of justice and freedom, to weak nations as well as to strong, and

WHEREAS, The safety and liberty of our own country is in every way protected by the covenant, be it

RESOLVED, That the New York section of the Council of Jewish women, consisting of 3,600 citizens in meeting assembled, endorses the covenant of the League of Nations.

The Federal Council of the Churches of Christ in America, at their meeting in Baltimore adopted resolutions endorsing the League of Nations, and calling upon the ministers of the churches of the nation to exert every possible influence upon the President and the Senate to secure the immediate ratification of the covenant with such reservations only as are necessary to safeguard the Constitution of the United States.

The following is an excerpt from an authorized copy of the Pope's Reconciliation Encyclical under the heading "Society of Nations Desirable," dated Rome, May 23d, 1920:

"Things being thus restored in the order desired by justice and charity, and the peoples reconciled among themselves, it would be truly desirable, Honorable Brethren, that all States should put aside mutual suspicion and unite in one sole society or rather family of peoples, both to guarantee their own independence and safeguard order in the civil concert of the peoples. A special reason, not to mention others, for forming this society among the nations, is the need generally recognized of reducing, if it is not possible to abolish it entirely, the enormous military expenditure which can no longer be borne by the States, in order that in this way murderous and disastrous wars may be prevented and to each people may be assured, in the just confines, the independence and integrity of its own territory."

If the moral influence of church organizations is as widely extended as church membership would indicate; if the moral teachings accepted by all churches are observed by all who profess to adopt them, then the sentiment of the American people is overwhelmingly in favor of the movement put into concrete form by the covenant of the League of Nations to bring together the nations of the world in an agreement to avoid war.

The Church membership of America being for the League of Nations, to preserve peace and prevent future wars, this question presents itself: if the candidate who favors America "Going In" is defeated and the candidate who declares "I am not" is elected, does it mean that the Church has lost its influence? Can this be true?

The League of Nations issue is of more vital concern to the Church people of America than any question presented since the burning moral issue involved in the great crisis of our country which resulted in the bloody civil war.

T MS (WP, DLC).

From Joseph Patrick Tumulty, with Enclosure

Dear Governor: The White House, October 6, 1920.

The Secretary of War has now prepared in the form of a statement to be given to the press the substance of the draft proclamation and letter heretofore prepared concerning the observance of Sunday, November 14th, as Armistice Sunday.[1] If you approve, I will have copies of the statement made and given out.

I have had drafted, for your signature, an Executive Order carrying out the direction referred to in the last paragraph of the statement prepared by Secretary Baker, and attach it hereto.[2]

Faithfully yours,   Tumulty

TLS (WP, DLC).
    [1] NDB to R. Forster, Oct. 5, 1920, TLS (WP, DLC), enclosing the T MS printed as the Enclosure.
    [2] T MS (WP, DLC).

E N C L O S U R E[1]

The President authorizes the following statement to be made:

There has been transmitted to me a suggestion that I name Sunday, November 14, as Armistice Sunday, in order that the religious services held throughout the country on that day may be given an especial note of remembrance for the heroic service and sacrifice of those who died for America in the World War. The selection of a formal day which shall annually be set aside to commemorate our participation in the World War will some day doubtless be effected through legislation, and already Memorial Day, rich in heroic memories, has acquired additional significance as being appropriate also to the commemoration of the heroes of the World War. I am, however, so heartily in favor of the suggestion that has been made that I take this occasion to express publicly my approval of the idea.

November 11, 1918, will always be memorable as the beginning of the end of the most terrible and destructive of all wars. Our beloved country took a noble part in hastening the arrival of the day hailed by the whole world as the dawn of peace; but close upon the day of victory followed the realization of loss, and the anniversary will bring with it solemn thoughts to the mind of every American,

memories of brave men who fell, sympathy for their living rela-
tives, and those religious reflections in which nations, like individuals, must seek hope and consolation. That November 14 this year,
being the Sunday immediately following the anniversary, ⟨should⟩
will, I hope, be observed in all our churches by suitable memorial
services for the heroic American soldiers, sailors, and marines who
gave their lives to their country in the World War, seems to me
eminently fitting and proper, and I commend the suggestion to
those who conduct such services.

I shall direct that the flag of the United States at all military
posts, naval stations, on vessels and on buildings of the United
States be displayed at half-mast on that day as a token of the Nation's participation in the exercises elsewhere held.[2]

T MS (WP, DLC).
[1] Word in angle brackets deleted by Wilson; words in italics added by him.
[2] This proclamation was published in the newspapers on October 9, 1920.

From Joseph Patrick Tumulty

Dear Governor: The White House October 6, 1920.

There is a very distressing situation throughout the country with
reference to the coal situation and it hourly grows more acute, as
shown by the telegrams arriving at the office from different parts
of the country. There has been a conference held in Washington
which has been participated in by public utilities representatives
from Ohio, Indiana and Illinois, representatives of the National
Coal Operators Association, transportation officers of the railroads
involved and representatives of commerce. The purpose of the conference was to devise means to increase the coal movement from
the so-called Appalachian Region and Lake Erie Ports by water to
the northwest and also to increase the supply of coal available for
the requirements of Ohio, Indiana and Michigan.

Mr. Alvord,[1] upon whom we have been relying to keep us in
touch with this acute situation during the past few months was
also present. The situation is made more difficult at this time by
the unusual requirements for coal, owing to the fact that the stocks
were largely reduced last winter and by the further fact that the
car equipment of the railroads is not adequate to meet the situation, and take care of the shipment of other commodities which
ought to be shipped in open door cars.

Another phase of the situation has reference to the coal requirements of New England. New England requires annually approximately 25,000,000 tons of soft coal. In the past 60% of the New
England coal requirements moved from tide-water ports to New

England by water. At the present time 60% of the coal going into
New England is moving by rail. The result is that efforts are being
made to force through by all-rail routes a much larger volume than
the railroads were designed to carry and this results in congestion
at Hudson River crossings and also an accumulated and unnecessary delay of cars in New England and restricts the movement of
other freight to and from New England. This phase of the situation
would be relieved and the whole situation improved if an arrangement could be made to induce the movement of a larger volume of
coal from tide-water ports to New England by water. At the present
time about 800,000 tons a month are moving to New England by
water. This might be increased to the extent of 500,000 tons per
month if people could be induced to ship that way. If the movement of coal to New England could be increased to the extent of
500,000 tons per month it would in effect release from 10,000 to
15,000 coal cars for coal carrying service in other parts of the country and this could be accomplished if additional boats were put into
service between upper Atlantic points, at Chesapeake Bay, at Philadelphia and New York and would carry coal at a rate not exceed-
ing slightly less than existing all-rail rates.

The matter of the utilization of these ships has been presented
to Admiral Benson and an effort made to induce the Shipping
Board to look upon the emergency features of this business, but it
was said that the boats could not carry coal with profit at a rate less
than the existing rate, which is not prohibitive.

The recommendation is made that a sufficient number of shipping boats be allocated to this service and that they carry coal at
an aggregate rate not greater than the present all-rail rate, or on
such terms as to induce a maximum movement of coal to New
England by water transportation. This, regardless of whether it is
profitable or not.

Admiral Benson did not feel free to do this, because it might result in a deficit to the Shipping Board, for which he would be open
to criticism.

My own opinion is that the country would commend and not
criticise.

P.S. Mr. Alvord, upon whom we have relied in all these matters,
agrees with me in the opinion that I express.

TL (WP, DLC).
¹ That is, E. M. Alvord, Assistant to the Director General of Railroads.

Two Letters to Bainbridge Colby

My dear Mr. Secretary: The White House 7 October, 1920

There seem to me in the matter referred to by the Acting Secretary of the Navy in the enclosed letter[1] the seeds of what might grow to be serious trouble, and I am sending you what he sent to me in order that you may keep in touch with the Navy Department in an endeavor to prevent any foolish thing from happening.

Cordially and faithfully yours,   Woodrow Wilson

[1] G. Woodbury to WW, Oct. 6, 1920, TLS, enclosing paraphrases of Vice Adm. Henry Pickney Huse, Commander, United States Naval Forces in Europe, to Chief of Naval Operations, Oct. 5, 1920 (two telegrams of the same date) and JD to H. P. Huse, Oct. 5, 1920, T MSS, all in the B. Colby Papers, DLC. Huse in his first telegram stated that the British Admiralty had reported two "Bolshevik" submarines to be in the Baltic Sea, headed for Danzig. The British intended to treat the submarines as hostile. Huse asked if American destroyers in the area should also consider them hostile and if they should attack them. His second cable urged that they be so treated and attacked. Woodbury, who actually sent the cable in reply which went out over Daniels' name, reminded Huse that the United States was not at war with Russia and ordered that the submarines were not to be treated as hostile "unless they commit some overt act or you have evidence of their hostile intent." Woodbury stated in his covering letter that no further action in the premises was contemplated at present.

My dear Mr. Secretary: The White House 7 October, 1920

I am an old correspondent of Robert Underwood Johnson's and have always found his letters a little difficult to comprehend. I generally lay them down without being certain just what he is driving at. Perhaps there may be some scrap in this letter[1] which will be useful to you with regard to the Italian situation.

Cordially and faithfully yours,   Woodrow Wilson

TLS (B. Colby Papers, DLC).

[1] R. U. Johnson to WW, Sept. 20, 1920, ALS (B. Colby Papers, DLC). Johnson's letter was indeed a rambling effusion. His brief discussion of Italian politics was typical. "The salient feature of the Italian situation," he wrote, "is the policy of the Government toward the lawlessness of the extreme Socialists. One now sees that Nitti's *laissez faire* policy has gone far to undermine the respect of the unthinking classes for law. Giolitti has disappointed expectations by following in the train of Nitti in this respect, though in his announcement of policy he laid stress on the execution of the law. Of course a firm policy is more difficult after a weak one. One can wink a little here and there at small violations of order but to permit wholesale confiscation of factories is to confess as Sforza did to me that to enforce private rights would be to bring on a revolution. He feels sure he understands the psychology of his people and that a mild treatment of the disease will cure it. The Catholics brought about Nitti's fall because he was too lax. I shall be surprised if they do not turn against Giolitti for the same reason. But, perhaps, his concession to the Socialists in the withdrawal from Valona and in the metal-workers' strike, have made him feel more secure in the saddle."

From Joseph Patrick Tumulty

Dear Governor: The White House, 7 October, 1920.

In every way the speech of Senator Harding at Des Moines today[1] is the most significant of all his utterances with reference to the League. It is the first speech he has made where he definitely urges rejection. I think this gives us the opportunity to lift the campaign out of the squabbling and centralize public attention on the great issue involved. Even a short statement from you for tomorrow's papers will be most appropriate at this time. If you take advantage of it, the Republicans will be in a panic within a week.

Sincerely yours,   J. P. Tumulty

No.   W.W.

TLS (J. P. Tumulty Papers, DLC).
  [1] In this speech, Harding declared that he did not want to clarify the obligations of the United States as a potential member of the League of Nations by means of reservations. "It is not interpretation," he said, "but rejection that I am seeking. My position is that the proposed league strikes a deadly blow at our constitutional integrity and surrenders to a dangerous extent our independence of action." The difference between Cox's position on the League and his own was a matter of "simple words": "He favors going into the Paris League and I favor staying out." Harding did, however, indicate in vague terms that he would work to create a new association of nations which would properly safeguard American rights. *New York Times*, Oct. 8, 1920. Extensive extracts from the *New York Times* report are printed in Arthur M. Schlesinger, Jr., and Fred L. Israel, eds., *History of American Presidential Elections, 1789-1968* (4 vols., New York, etc., 1971), III, 2443-49. For discussions of the background of Harding's Des Moines speech and its significance in winning over irreconcilable Republicans and alienating pro-League Republicans, see *ibid.*, pp. 2381-83, and Wesley M. Bagby, *The Road to Normalcy: The Presidential Campaign and Election of 1920* (Baltimore, Md., 1962), pp. 137-39.

From Solomon Bulkley Griffin[1]

My Dear Mr President: Springfield, Mass. Oct 7, 1920.

I am moved to send you a word of sympathy & of cheer. Time, the great adjuster, will cherish your name in highest honor among those who served their day and generation with full devotion to ideals that will be seen to be the realities in human service and progress.

The day of this illumination is on the way. May it arrive so that you may see and know the healing it is to bring!

I wish that you might realize now how many of the people I know & esteem hold you in tender regard at this time.

With all good wishes, I am, as ever

Very Sincerely Yours   Solomon B. Griffin

ALS (WP, DLC).
  [1] Retired editor of the *Springfield*, Mass., *Republican*.

To Bainbridge Colby, with Enclosure

My dear Mr. Secretary: The White House 8 October, 1920

I am sure you will read with as much interest as I did this letter from Minister Gonzales.[1] Do you think that it would be wise and profitable at this time to approach Chile and Peru with regard to arbitration? I am quite willing to do so if you think the time not inopportune and the prospect of success reasonably good.

Cordially and faithfully yours,   Woodrow Wilson

TLS (B. Colby Papers, DLC).
[1] Actually, he was the first United States Ambassador to Peru.

ENCLOSURE

From William Elliott Gonzales

Dear Mr. President: Lima, September 22, 1920

It was with great regret I left Washington on my way to Lima without seeing you, but it is with keen gratification, both as a personal friend and as having public interests at heart, that I hear of your continued betterment in health.

This is the first mail from here since my return from Cuzco, where I had the honor and pleasure of representing you in the reception of a degree from that old University. I have written the Department a formal and the usual wooden report of my trip, a copy of which will, of course, be furnished to you, but there were some side lights that I wish to present in this personal letter.

How little the most thoughtful of us know or can even imagine of the future! This thought came to me in the Hall of the University at Cuzco, when I recalled that just a little more than nine years before I had introduced you to an audience in the "Secession Church" on the occasion of laying the corner stone of the Y.M.C.A. building, and to my introductory remarks you quoted something containing "Lord save me from my friends."[1] Then, in 1911, that I would be representing you in the old Inca Capital in 1920, would have seemed as strange a prediction as could be imagined.

But while we cannot foretell happenings, we can forecast results, and I have taken considerable credit to myself for my forecast of results made in Columbia that day. And you, my dear Mr. President, despite many disappointments, despite the misjudgements and misrepresentations and all the other evils to which even the most single-hearted patriot in public life is heir to, would have had a thrill of satisfaction and your heart would have warmed, could you have passed for five hundred miles through southern

Perú, from the port of Mollendo on the Pacific across the back-bone of the Andes to Cuzco and realized that these poor people, far away from us geographically and far away from us in degree of progress and civilization, yet worship at the shrine of Right and Justice, and love the man who has done so much to give those words a new meaning in international conversations; and that they honor and look with hope and faith toward the country that has come to feel something of his spirit! The untutored Indian of these vast mountain regions, knowing nothing of government, or its forms, and receiving little benefit through government, know your name. No railway station, away up in the ice-bound altitudes, is so insignificant but someone there knows that "Woodrow Wilson is the Apostle of Justice," and in his language shouts his belief as you pass.

The Peruvians' admiration for the spirit of Right and Justice in international affairs is unquestionably made more keen because of their territorial losses as the result of the war with Chile,[2] and the constant menace of Chile on their southern frontier. Only in July, a short while before my visit to Cuzco, there was grave danger because of the massing by Chile of many thousands of troops within the retained provinces of Tacna and Arica. This danger will remain and continue a serious detriment to the development and well-being of both countries, and must inevitably, soon or late, break into a war in which Perú will be overwhelmed, unless the "Question of the Pacific" is settled; and I see no hope of settlement except through definite steps by the United States to secure an agreement to arbitration.

Minister Maginnis,[3] at La Paz, is convinced the time is ripe for a move in that direction; I am of the same opinion and believe conditions in Chile are such that she would be more disposed to listen to a proposal for arbitration than she has been at any time in forty years. Both my view and that of Mr. Maginnis have been expressed in despatches to the Department of State. But I do not know who is now in charge of the Latin-American Division or what the opinion of that Division may be; and I do know that the Secretary is very busy. To be frank, the Department, in times past, has had no definite policy regarding this question. Back in the Eighties, Mr. Blaine sent Mr. Trescot, of South Carolina, as Special Ambassador to Chile and then resigned and Trescot's powers were emasculated by Mr. Blaine's successor.[4] About the same time we objected to the intervention of France in the matter, holding it was a question for America. Yet the reading of memoranda filed by officials in the Department in the past ten years will show that the Department has been much divided as to whether the United States would consent to arbitrate the question if opportunity offered. We have, in fact, moved in circles.

It would seem that the indecision as to whether it would be politic for the United States to act on a board of arbitration has operated against a definite sustained move for a settlement of a question that is worrying every country in South America. Or the inability to know in advance which avenue of approach to Chile would insure success has operated for inaction. And we never get anywhere by being afraid to move in a good cause because uncertain of success.

It would be a blessing to this continent and of great material advantage to the United States if this issue were now brought to a final determination; but if a settlement is not accomplished during your administration long, indefinite delays may occur. And, personally, I have little hope of a positive move unless you, Mr. President, inspire it.

In the first decade or two after the Peruvian-Chilean War, the correspondence shows that our diplomatic representatives in those countries were, each one, a pretty strong partisan of the country to which he was accredited, and as the disposition to take sides is more or less natural, partisanship may yet have sway. However, while I have very firm beliefs as to the injustice suffered by Perú, with a strong sympathy for a proud people who were overpowered and are frequently menaced, and while feeling that when the Chileans were designated as the "Yankees of South America" a grave injustice was done the Yankees because the spirit of the Chileans to a degree that is truly remarkably is that of the Germans in the days of their arrogance of power, the question of the rights or the wrongs of either country is not the issue and has no influence over me—that is for arbitration. Whether Peru gets all or nothing of what she considers her rights, is not now at issue. The great thing is the removal of the menace of conflict so that each country may be able to turn once more to the full work of development. Either country could lose all at issue and be benefited by a final settlement, if the decree were through a tribunal which would save the self-respect of the people.

The need of Bolivia for an outlet to the sea makes the issue a triangular one, but with provision made for the settlement of the main issue between Chile and Perú, it would be relatively easy to secure something substantial for Bolivia's benefit.

The sentiment in South America is strongly for a settlement and an early settlement of the "Question of the Pacific." The Brazilian Minister, the Colombian Minister and the Cuban Minister[5] in private conversations within the past week have not only so expressed themselves, but spoken as if the only power to bring about a settlement was the United States. Brazil, I believe, would gladly cooperate. None of them pretends to know how it should be done. In my opinion, Santiago is the place where the work should be begun, with great friendliness, with great earnestness and, of course, with understanding and tact.

Forgive me for imposing this lengthy letter upon you, my dear and always greatly esteemed friend, but the spirit has moved me, and I am always confident of your understanding of the motive.

Most sincerely yours,   William E. Gonzales

TLS (B. Colby Papers, DLC).
[1] About the ceremony in the First Baptist Church of Columbia, S. C. (the building in which the South Carolina Convention voted for secession on December 17, 1860), see the news report printed at June 2, 1911, Vol. 23.
[2] That is, in the War of the Pacific, 1879-1883, between Chile, Bolivia, and Peru. About the Peruvian-Chilean dispute over the provinces of Tacna and Arica, one long-standing legacy of that war, see WW to J. L. Sanfuentes Andonaegui, Dec. 4, 1918, Vol. 53.
[3] Samuel Abbot Maginnis.
[4] William Henry Trescot, South Carolina lawyer, historian, and diplomat. James Gillespie Blaine was succeeded as Secretary of State by Frederick Theodore Frelinghuysen on December 19, 1881. On Trescot's aborted mission, see William Jefferson Dennis, *Tacna and Arica: An Account of the Chile-Peru Boundary Dispute and of the Arbitrations by the United States* (New Haven, Conn., 1931), pp. 157-72.
[5] Silvino Gurgél do Amaral, Fabio Lozano, and Luis A. Baralt.

To Bainbridge Colby

My dear Mr. Secretary: The White House 8 October, 1920

With regard to the enclosed,[1] I am inclined to agree with Mr. Davis that it will be well for us to name an American representative (in which case my choice would be Professor Charles H. Haskins of Harvard, who did notable work in connection with the Peace Conference in Paris, particularly with regard to the Saar district), but I want your judgment in the matter, please.[2]

Cordially and faithfully yours,   Woodrow Wilson

TLS (B. Colby Papers, DLC).
[1] H. C. Wallace to SecState, Oct. 5, 1920, printed in *FR 1920*, I, 34, saying that Paul-Joseph Mantoux, head of the Political Secretariat of the League of Nations, had told Wallace that Léon Bourgeois and A. J. Balfour were still eager to have an American representative on the League's commission to arbitrate the dispute between Sweden and Finland over the Åland Islands.
[2] Norman Davis informed Mantoux on October 9 that Wilson would consider favorably his request. *Ibid.*, p. 35.

From Elmer Talmage Clark[1]

Dear Mr. President: Nashville, Tenn. Oct. 8th, 1920.

The Methodist Episcopal Church, South, is in the midst of a Christian Education Movement, the purpose of which is to thoroughly indoctrinate our two million members in the south with the supreme importance of education, to impress the young people with its importance, to make the educational method central in all our work, and to raise at least $33,000,000 for our ninety schools and colleges and for the education of young ministers.

In this enterprise a word of endorsement from you would be much appreciated by our people, and if you can consistently give it you will thereby be rendering a most valuable service to a high cause, the importance of which at the present time you fully appreciate. Any commendatory statement you care to make in regard to the necessity of education, the value of Christian Education, or the fundamental nature of our present movement can be used to good advantage. I venture, however, to express the hope that your statement will be framed with reference to the Christian Education Movement which we have now in progress.

I enclose herewith a booklet which will explain our campaign in greater detail, and express to you my sincere gratitude for the kindness which I am sure you will be glad to render to a great cause.

Sincerely yours,   Elmer T Clark

TLS (WP, DLC).
  [1] Secretary of the Department of Publicity of the Educational Campaign Commission of the Methodist Episcopal Church, South.

To Josephus Daniels

My dear Mr. Secretary: The White House 9 October, 1920

The only reason I send you the enclosed is that Mr. Gatewood[1] claims that he has not had a hearing. I am sure that if he has not, you will wish to remedy the oversight. I have no personal judgment about the case.   Faithfully yours,   Woodrow Wilson

TLS (J. Daniels Papers, DLC).
  [1] Lt. Comdr. Robert Gatewood, U.S.N., of the navy recruiting station at Raleigh, N. C. For details of his case, see JD to WW, Oct. 11, 1920.

From Joseph Patrick Tumulty, with Enclosure

Dear Governor: The White House 10 October 1920.

I prepared the enclosed as a basis for a tentative statement if you care to look it over.   Sincerely,   J P Tumulty

TLS (WP, DLC).

ENCLOSURE

The election of Senator Harding as President, and the election of a Republican Senate and House of Representatives, would certainly signalize the triumph of the reactionary forces in the United States.

It would mean that America is to violate its sacred national honor by turning its back upon the Allies with whom we fought and won the war and by declining to keep the faith of agreements upon which the war was ended.

It would mean the death of the League of Nations, the last and best hope of despairing mankind.

It would mean a shameful, separate peace with Germany, and her escape from the payment of indemnities for the wreck she brutally wrought in the world.

It would mean a speedy return to the age-old system of secret diplomacy, of balance of power, of enlarging competitive national armaments, of the arming of each nation in constant preparation for war, and the certainty that unending wars will result to deluge the earth again in human blood.

The history of the Republican Party in Congress, during the past year or more, the platform of that Party, and the utterances of its candidate for the presidency, are all against the Peace Treaty with the League of Nations, and inevitably lead to these conclusions.

It would mean—at the very dawn of America's great day of better life for all of our people, of greater degree of economic freedom, of the more equal distribution of wealth, and of the larger participation in their government—a return to the power of the forces of reaction and their destruction of the progressive achievements of the past eight years: the repeal or radical change of the tariff commission act, and the throwing of the tariff question again into partisan controversy, and the restoration of special privilege to the favored few who have always been heavy contributors to the Republican campaign funds; the trade commission law, by which unfair competition has been prevented and fair business secured in its future; the farm loan law, by which that vast body of citizens, the farmers, are freed from the burden of usury and have come into their day of prosperity and happiness; and the many acts for the securing of justice and equality of opportunity for the laboring people—the eight-hour law, the minimum wage law, the workmen's compensation act, the act declaring that labor is not a commodity, and many other laws of similar beneficent character.

It would mean that the control of the finances, the money and the credit, of the nation would again be centered in Wall Street in the hands of the few, to be used for their benefit rather than for the benefit of those who have produced that wealth, as at present.

It would mean the emasculation of the Federal Reserve Act, conceived and enacted by a Democratic Congress, or else the organization of its Federal Reserve Board in the interest of Wall Street instead of its organization and administration as at present, in the interest of all legitimate business throughout the country, whether large or small. Since that law was enacted the money earned by each section of the country has been allowed to remain in, and be used for the benefit of, that section where earned, rather than taken to Wall Street to be manipulated for the oppression of the masses and for the benefit of the favored few who, under all former Republican administrations, have been allowed to control it. The Federal Reserve Act enabled the United States to finance the war and to aid, to the extent of nearly ten billion dollars, the Allies to carry their great burden: and it has enabled the American people to keep business in all lines going without wreck or panic, to secure and enrich our whole people, and to preserve trade, credit and prosperity for all of our people; and, surely, they will not surrender this instrumentality of their prosperity and happiness to the Republican Party which will turn it into an instrument for their financial oppression.

It would mean that American Labor, which we have emancipated from intolerable conditions until today it stands free, unfettered, with its face hopeful to the dawn, is again to be put in the category of commodity and denied its share of the wealth and civilization it helps to create.

It would mean an immediate return to the burden of competitive great armaments, on land and at sea—with no benefits to any in all the world except the manufacturers of arms and munitions of war.

It would mean the speedy repeal of Federal taxation laws enacted by a Democratic Congress under which a portion of the current profits of business is taken each year to sustain the nation's obligations and credit, and the substitution of bonds for practically the whole amount of our great national war debt to bear a high rate of interest and to be paid off by those who toil—in order that the very rich may escape their proper burden of current taxation.

The present contest, as between Senator Harding and Governor Cox, involves special class privileges as against the general common good; the administration of the finances and credit of the nation for the benefit of a favored few in Wall Street as against their present administration, impartially as to locality and industry, in each corner of the whole country; a protective tariff so high as to add billions to a special and pampered class at the expense of all others in the land; a nebulous, undefined phantom promise of international understanding as against the League of Nations in concrete and definite form made in keeping with the fundamental needs and the agonized prayers of a despairing world; an orgie of class wealth, class exemption from government burdens, class domination of Republican party counsels and government as against the correct rule and practice of Democratic legislation and administration—of equal and exact justice to all men and special privileges to none, of the greatest good to the greatest number, and of equality in sharing the burdens and likewise the benefits of these free institutions.

This is the final turning point in the life of this nation. It stands on the mountain top and looks out on the smiling valleys of guaranteed peace, assured prosperity, and established equality of opportunity if it will but go forward and finish the work before it. Will the people now choose rather to pause, to turn back, and again to enter the hideous death's valley through which they have passed in order to reach their present status—equality denied, great riches and great poverty, unending international controversies, class domination, the catastrophe of recurrent panics and consequent social disorders, and lastly the horrors of devastating war—to which Senator Harding and the Republican Party will bid them go and will, if elected, surely lead them?

God forbid!

T MS (WP, DLC).

From the Diary of John William Davis

Oct. 10, 1920

Luncheon at White House. Mrs. Wilson, Sec. & Mrs. Bainbridge Colby, John Randolph Bolling & Dr. Stockton Axson, & ourselves. Mrs. W. referred to President's nervous dread of seeing people, apologizing for fact that he was not in evidence & had not seen me. A curious inaccessibility for the leader of a great party & Chief

Magistrate of a nation. What could better justify Grayson's advice to him last January to resign.[1]

Hw bound diary (J. W. Davis Papers, CtY.).
[1] See n. 1 to the extract from the Diary of Ray Stannard Baker printed at Feb. 4, 1920, Vol. 64.

To John Collins and Others[1]

[The White House]
October 11, 1920.

I am in receipt of your telegram advising me that the Anthracite miners have returned to work in accordance with the terms of their agreement, and asking that I call the representatives of the Anthracite operators and miners into joint conference for the purpose of adjusting inequalities in the present agreement.

I congratulate you and the miners you represent upon the prompt manner in which you have complied with the award of the Anthracite Coal Commission. I am convinced that the future of collective bargaining depends upon the fidelity with which each side adheres to the terms of their contracts. If any inequalities exist in an agreement I can see no objection to their being corrected if both sides can agree upon a remedy.

In compliance with your request, therefore, I will request the representatives of the Anthracite operators and miners, and do hereby request them to meet in joint conference in the City of Scranton, Pa., on Monday, October 18th, 1920, at 11 A.M., for the purpose of adjusting any inequalities in their present agreement as they may mutually agree should be adjusted. I am sending a copy of this telegram to the Secretary of the Joint Scale Committee of the Anthracite coal fields, with a request that it be communicated to both operators and miners.   Woodrow Wilson.

T telegram (Letterpress Books, WP, DLC).
[1] This telegram was a reply to J. Collins et al. to WW, Oct. 5, 1920, T telegram (WP, DLC). William B. Wilson drafted Woodrow Wilson's reply and embodied it in WBW to H. L. Kerwin, Oct. 7, 1920, TCL (WP, DLC). Woodrow Wilson approved this text verbatim. John Collins was president of the Scranton local of the United Mine Workers of America.

To Frank Miles Day[1]

My dear Mr. Day: [The White House] 11 October, 1920

I wonder if you could make it convenient sometime soon to come over and spend two or three days as my guest here. I am thinking of building a house if I can, and I very much want your advice and guidance. There are a good many "if's" in the case, the chief "if" being if I have money enough.

It will be a great pleasure to renew our old association and I hope that your work has continued at Princeton along the same fine lines as before.

With sincere regard,

Very truly yours,   [Woodrow Wilson]

CCL (WP, DLC).
¹ (1861-1918), architect of Philadelphia, who had drawn the plans for, and supervised the construction of, Holder Hall and Tower at Princeton University in 1908-1909.

From William Gibbs McAdoo

Personal and *Confidential*.

Dear Governor: New York October 11th, 1920

I feel that I ought to write you about a matter where I think a grave injustice is being done, and with very serious hurt to the commercial interests of the country. I do so with great reluctance because I never like to burden you with cares of any kind but I think you ought to know the real truth of the situation I shall describe. I had hoped to get this off my mind before I leave here tomorrow night on a speaking trip which will keep me on the road until Election Day, but I have been unable to get it settled in the State Department.

In the Pan-American Financial Conference, in 1915, the subject of improved cable connections with the East coast of South America was strongly stressed by the delegates from Brazil, Uruguay and Argentina. At the meeting of the International High Commission (at Buenos Aires, 1916,) this same subject was again discussed and it was the consensus of opinion that the two things most needed to improve our commercial, and other relations with South America, were shipping facilities and improved cable communications.

I took a great interest in this subject, in connection with the general Pan-American work in which the Treasury engaged, and I was a member of the Committee on Cable Communications, at Buenos Aires. I was a participant also in the discussions which resulted in the adoption of resolutions calling for an International Cable Conference. Out of this, I think, sprang the conference now being held at Washington.

I was so impressed with what the East Coast of South America's people said of the necessity for improved cable communications that I assured them I would use every effort in my power to secure it. On my return to the United States I took the subject up with Mr. Carlton,[1] President of the Western Union Telegraph Company, (the only one which I felt had either the money or the enterprise to undertake it), and asked him to investigate the situation and to lay this cable as an important national enterprise. He agreed to consider the matter.

As a result of Mr. Carlton's investigations it was found that the only feasible means of accomplishing the result was for the Western Union Telegraph Company to lay a cable from Miami to Barbados and to get the Western Telegraph Company, of Great Britian, to lay a cable from Barbados to Manranham, Brazil where connections would be effected with the Western Telegraph Company's old established cable system reaching all important points in Brazil, Uruguay and Argentina.

The Western Company has merely a preferential right in Brazil, which right, by the way, expires in 1930. It has no monopoly. This preferential right consists in preventing any other cable company from laying a cable between any two points in Brazil already served by the Western Company lines but the new company may touch as many points in Brazil unserved by the Western Company lines as the Brazilian Government may permit.

If the Western Union had undertaken to build a competitive line all the way from Brazil to Uruguay and Argentina, with this handicap of the Western Company's preferential rights, the investment would have been prohibitive and the service it would have been able to render would have been far less satisfactory than by making a connection with the Western Company and giving to all of our merchants and people the benefits of an immensely improved facility.

Under the contract between the Western Union and the Western Company, the new service will be furnished at rates reduced 30% below the existing rates and much more expeditious service can be given and in much greater volume.

More than a year ago the Western Union Company contracted with a British concern, (deep sea cables are only made in Great Britian) for 1600 miles of cable, required to connect Miami and Barbados. There are only a few cable ships in the world and it is very difficult to get them. Contracts must be made far in advance. The Western Union contracted for one of these cable ships to lay the cable in August 1920. It proceeded on the assumption that, having been encouraged by a former Secretary of the Treasury,

---

[1] Newcomb Carlton.

and the International High Commission, consisting of all the South American delegates, to undertake this work, there would be no difficulty in getting a landing permit in our own country.

In March 1920, application was made for the permit in usual course. All efforts to secure the permit proved of no avail, notwithstanding the fact that the War Department had recommended it. Meanwhile, the cable ship appeared off Miami with the cable. The Western Union had no control over the contractor. If the cable were not laid at that time, not only would there be serious deterioration in the cable itself (which, like a fish, lives only in water) but the opportunity to use the cable ship would be lost and could not be secured again for, perhaps, another year.

Thereupon, the Navy Department was summoned to prevent what the Government supposed—and very unjustly—to be an attempt on the part of the cable ship to lay the shore end of this cable.[2] There was never any intention to do this. This cable ship is deep draft and could not come into shallow water. The shore end of the cable was transferred to a light draft Western Union vessel which was in the Harbor of New York, with instructions not to go to Miami until the permit could be secured from the Government.

The Western Union Company naturally turned to me in the circumstances since I had interested them originally in the enterprise and asked me to act as their counsel in the matter. I agreed not only for professional reasons but because of my interest in the matter from the standpoint of our Pan-American relations.

I assured Mr. Colby that he could call off the Navy and that the Western Union would not undertake to lay the shore end of the cable until the Government gives its consent, that the Western Union could not prevent the laying of the deep-sea portion of the cable from the point outside of the three mile limit to Barbados. This cable had been laid and the Western Company's cable has been laid from Barbados to Brazil, so that 3200 miles of deep sea cable are lying idle awaiting permission from our Government to lay the three mile shore end to Miami.

I have had numerous conferences with the State Department. I think Mr. Davis is fully convinced that the permit to the Western Union should be granted. I have suggested that a permit revocable at the will of the Government be granted the Western Union Company, pending a final adjustment of the matter, so that the cable may be put into operation and our people and those of South Amer-

---

[2] For the correspondence which led to the navy's intervention, see BC to WW, July 17, 1920 (third letter of that date), and WW to BC, July 20, 1920 (third letter of that date), both in Vol. 65.

ica be given the opportunity to get the improved service at reduced rates. I have felt, from what Mr. Davis has told me, that such a solution of the matter would be entirely satisfactory.

Mr. Davis said, however, that you were inclined to the view that nothing should be done until the conclusion of the International Cable Conference. I hope that you will not take this position because the International Cable Conference may not, in any case, be able to affect this situation, and if it reaches any conclusion that would affect it, negotiations with the various Governments concerned would undoubtedly have to follow and this might take years. If action on the Western Union permit is deferred until that time, a very great loss would be brought upon it and very great injury, it seems to me, would be done to our own interests.

By granting a revocable permit, as I have suggested, under any reasonable conditions the Government may deem fit to impose, it seems to me, that every interest of our Government is fully protected and no injustice or injury is done to those, who in good faith, are seeking to improve our cable facilities.

The chief objection, as far as I have been able to discover it, has been raised by the Central and South American Cable Company, (now called the All-American), with which the Western Union line creates a very active competition at greatly reduced rates. This Company is represented by Mr. Root's law firm and has been especially active in representing to the Department that the Western Union's competitive lines will be creating a monopoly—a most extraordinary position and an entirely unsupportable one.

The All American Company, as things stand today, has the chief monopoly in South America. It has monopoly in Peru, Mexico and Ecuador and has been resisting any effort on the part of the Western Union to establish a competitive system on the West Coast of South America. I am frank to say I am unable to see the virtue of the All-American Company's position, or why it should be given any consideration in the matter.

The situation is quite urgent because of the great loss which the Western Union Company now sustains because of its idle investment in 1600 miles of cable laid to Barbados. Our own business men and the business men of Brazil, Uruguay and Argentina are urging that they be not deprived of this cheaper and improved facility.

Of course, neither Mr. Davis, nor Secretary Colby know that I am writing to you about this matter. I do not wish to seem to be going over their heads and I assure that I am not since I have found Mr. Davis very sympathetic with our position in this matter.

I felt, however, that I ought to explain this to you, particularly since I think you must be laboring under a misapprehension of the real conditions.

I hope very much that you will sanction the granting of the revocable permit I have suggested in order that the cable may be put into use without unnecessary delay. I am sure that the interests of the Government can be protected by granting this permit.

It is difficult for me to leave New York with this matter undetermined because I feel an obligation to my clients in the circumstances but I am going anyway with the hope that something can be done even in my absence.

Please forgive me for having to burden you with this subject. I would not have done so but for the necessity of my being away so long on this political trip.

All join me in dearest love for you and Edith.

Affectionately yours,   W G McAdoo

P.S. Of course the fact that I would like to go away with my mind relieved is no reason for consideration of the matter. I mean only that if it could be disposed of on its merits promptly it would ease my mind. Incidentally we are not strong with business generally and I think it is always helpful when such things are promptly settled.   WGM

TLS (WP, DLC).

From Josephus Daniels

My dear Mr. President: Washington. October 11, 1920.

I have your letter of October 9th, with the enclosure from Mr. Gatewood. You state that Mr. Gatewood claims that he has not had a hearing. On the contrary, I had Mr. Gatewood ordered to Washington when the letter came from the young lady in Raleigh, who is one of the finest young women of the State and granddaughter of the late Governor Holt,[1] who charged that he, Gatewood, who had been drinking, entered her berth on the sleeping car in his night clothes and said he wanted to have a talk with her. She screamed and was so undone that she was almost a nervous wreck.

When Gatewood came to Washington, I asked him to give an account of himself. He admitted that he had been drinking in Raleigh but was not intoxicated, and I told him to make a statement in writing of his whole movements and all about it. He said that his going into the berth of Miss Wright was because while the car was dark he mistook her berth for his own and he had no intention of insulting her. In his statement, which he furnished by direction, he attributed as the motive for this young lady's charging him with this conduct that he boarded in the same boarding house with her in Raleigh and she and her mother were resentful because he paid attention to other young ladies in the boarding house and never paid her any attention. This marks him as a cad, and I took the matter up with the Chief of the Bureau of Navigation[2] who agreed with me that he ought to be put out of the Navy; but the young lady, hating the notoriety did not wish officially to prefer the charges, and so the reprimand was put on his record. He gets off very lightly, and if he had not done anything else but make the statement that the young lady was trying to destroy him because he had not paid her social attention that would be such ungentlemanly conduct as to demand that he be severely reprimanded as the very least of punishment. At least this is my judgment.

Sincerely yours,   Josephus Daniels

P.S. I am enclosing you a copy of his statement to me and a copy of the statement of the young lady.[3]

TLS (WP, DLC).
  [1] Thomas Michael Holt, Governor of North Carolina, 1891-1893.
  [2] Rear Adm. Thomas Washington.
  [3] [Louise Wright] to Addie Worth Bagley Daniels, Sept. 14, 1920, TCL (WP, DLC), and R. Gatewood, "Statement of Trip to Wilmington, N. C., from Raleigh, N. C.," n.d., T MS (WP, DLC).

To Joseph Patrick Tumulty

Dear Tumulty: [The White House c. Oct. 12, 1920]

Please answer all requests of this sort[1] to the effect that they are so numerous that it is impossible for me in my present state of health to respond, much as I should like to do so.

The President.

TL (WP, DLC).
  [1] Wilson was replying to JPT to WW, Oct. 11, 1920, TL (WP, DLC): "What is your wish in the matter of the attached request?" It was James McClintic, chairman of the speakers' bureau in the Democratic campaign headquarters in Chicago, to JPT, Oct. 9, 1920, T telegram (WP, DLC): "I have several hundred ministers who have agreed to preach sermon favor League of Nations Sunday October twenty fourth. I want to get from President Wilson two hundred word statement on League of Nations to be furnished each minister, send same to me. Advise if satisfactory to President."

To William Gibbs McAdoo

My dear Mac: The White House 12 October, 1920

You are mistaken in thinking that I am acting under the influence of misrepresentations in regard to the landing of the cable at Miami, and nothing in your letter seems to me to justify a change of my judgment that matters of this sort should not be acted upon until the Conference on International Communications has reached and reported its conclusions.

Affectionately yours, Woodrow Wilson

TLS (W. G. McAdoo Papers, DLC).

From Lee Slater Overman and William Julius Harris

My dear Mr. President: Washington, D. C., October 12, 1920.

There is now sitting in the City of Washington a convention composed of thirty odd farmers' organizations of the United States, and they have invited a number of Senators and members of Congress to come here and meet with them. We have been appointed by this convention a committee to request that you will give them a hearing, together with your Cabinet, the Federal Reserve Board, and the [War] Finance Corporation, and discuss the low price of farm products from a financial standpoint.

If you cannot hear them yourself and be present, they are specially desirous that you have such members of your Cabinet as are in the City, the Federal Reserve Board and the Finance Corporation to meet and give them a hearing.

We think it highly important that this request be not turned down. The psychological situation is such that it would be highly injurious to the Democratic cause in this country to refuse this request, and we think that we are entitled to a hearing, and earnestly urge that if you cannot meet with them that you have this meeting called at some hour tomorrow when a committee representing this convention can be here.

Several members of both Houses of Congress appointed with us on this committee to lay this matter before you are here, and they will be in session only today and tomorrow, and will thank you to give us an immediate answer.[1]

Very sincerely yours, Lee S. Overman
Wm J. Harris

TLS (WP, DLC).

[1] "Please explain to these gentlemen that it was impossible for me to comply with this request within the period of the meeting of the gentlemen referred to." WW to JPT, c. Oct. 13, 1920, TL (WP, DLC).

From Ignace Jan Paderewski

Paris, October 12, 1920.

1802. Paderewski has requested me to transmit the following message to the President.

"Mr. President. Your illness has been a misfortune for mankind and a disaster for Poland. Since the will of God made you temporarily abandon the leadership in world's affairs, everything turned against my country. Her eastern frontiers, the Galician question, remain unsettled, and war is raging in the east inflicting upon the exhausted country appalling losses. In East and west Prussia oppression, terror and fraud have decided the plebiscite in favor of our enemy.[1] Poland rights and duties of protecting the Vistula have become empty words for she will never be able to exercise the control as granted by the peace treaty having obtained along the river a strip of land in many places only fifty yards wide. Two months ago notwithstanding the generous support of your most distinguished ambassador Mr. Wallace, we lost the greatest part of Teschen, Silesia, Spisz and Orawa.[2] Undisputeably Polish territories, communes, with hundred per cent of Polish population have been without plebiscite assigned to the Tchecs. The entire railway line running through our territory, all the coal mines without exception, factories, forests, practically all the objects of real economic, even prospective value, have been attributed to them. My proposal to divide between the two countries the output of coal in all the existing mines under the supervision of the League of Nations has been disregarded, rejected, the city of Teschen has been mercifully given to us but without the railway station, without gas and waterworks which all have been given to the Tchecs. Out of 234,000 Polish inhabitants of Teschen Silesia we lose 139,687, out of 70,000 Poles living in Spisz and Orawa we lose 45,057 besides 35,000 in the district of Czacza. All these brothers of ours including those picturesque mountaineers some of whom had the honor of laying personally before you their righteous claims[3] have been condemned to pass over like property to another owner and the new owner proves to be worse of all oppressors. Our people there are chiefly Protestant and our Protestant clergy have been insulted and beaten in public places, teachers and renowned professors have been murdered, Polish schools are being closed by military force and now thousands of Poles are being expelled from that Polish land, the minority rights having even been denied to us.

The Polish Government having been forced to bow before the verdict which was imposed on them at the very moment when the Bolshevist armies were at the gates of Warsaw, the wronged inhabitants there protested against iniquity, against this wilful transgression of your noble and lofty principles. Today it is my sacred duty to bring to your attention the fact that your principles may be violated anew.

During the peace conference you told me Mr. President that even if Danzig does not legally belong to us we shall practically have the very essence of it. You also assured me that every care will be taken that the plebiscite in Upper Silesia should be conducted in a correct and legitmate way. Poland regarded these assurances as equally solemn as the peace treaty. Efforts, however, are being made to render them ineffective void.

There is a plan to establish in Danube [Danzig] a joint harbor board consisting of Polish members and Danzigers in equal numbers. This body is to become the owner of all properties which according to the treaty of Versailles was to be divided in an equitable way between Poland and the free city and also it is to assume all the rights and duties attributed to Poland by the treaty. The President of the board will be a foreigner and the recent experience with Sir Reginald Tower[4] has taught us what it would mean. If the plan is carried out the Polish members will be always out voted and Poland will receive none of the privileges guaranteed her by the peace conference. The establishment of a harbor board as a substitute for Poland's authority in Danzig would be a positive violation of the treaty of Versailles.

Owing to the absence of American troops and of American members of international commission the situation in Upper Silesia becomes increasingly critical. The French part of the commission is doing its utmost to preserve order and uphold justice but the armed force is not strong enough for the heavy task. German military organization still exists. German military spirit still prevails. We are in possession of facsimiles plans and documents fully demonstrating that it is the intention of the German military caste which is in this part of the former empire more powerful than in any other, even East Prussia, to involve the province in a civil war during the plebiscite. Serious riots already have taken place, murders have been committed, properties even belonging to the Germans have been looted and destroyed by agents imported for that purpose from distant parts of the Empire. Persons born in Upper Silesia who never lived and never will live in this province are being organized into battalions, regiments, and divisions. The function of these bands will be not only to vote but to terrorize the whole population for there is very considerable German element in Upper Silesia which will gladly vote for Poland if it is permitted to do so freely. On the other hand orders have been issued by German authorities, and we have facsimiles of some of them, to prevent the

Poles, natives of Upper Silesia who live in the interior of Germany, from coming home at the time of plebiscite. We have appealed to the conference of Ambassadors and brought to their knowledge the above facts. It is, however, our firm belief Mr. President that only through your mighty support, our rights in Danzig will be protected, that only by your intervention will a miscarriage of justice in Upper Silesia be averted and measures be adopted to prevent abuses, frauds, and crimes which must lead to civil war. 1,300,000 Poles in Upper Silesia expect justice from you Mr. President in the hope that you will generously forgive my appealing again in behalf of a country which is already so greatly indebted to you. I beg to remain Mr. President with deepest reverence and infinite gratitude, your most obedient servant."   Wallace.

T telegram (SDR, RG 59, 860c.01/332, DNA).
[1] Plebiscites in Allenstein and Marienwerder on July 11, 1920, had gone heavily in favor of Germany.
[2] About the settlement of this complicated and bitter dispute between Czechoslovakia and Poland, which was largely in the former's favor, see Dagmar Perman, *The Shaping of the Czechoslovak State: Diplomatic History of the Boundaries of Czechoslovakia, 1914-1920* (Leiden, 1962), pp. 228-75, and Wandycz, *France and Her Eastern Allies*, pp. 75-103, 148-60.
[3] About this visit, see the extract from the Grayson Diary printed at April 11, 1919, Vol. 57.
[4] Sir Reginald (Thomas) Tower, High Commissioner of the League of Nations in Danzig.

From James Henry Taylor[1]

My dear Mr President: Washington, D. C. October 12, 1920.

There is in our local jail a young negro girl, Josephine Berry, who has been convicted of murder and sentenced to be hung on Friday of this week, so I am informed.

This girl is said to be about fifteen years of age, though claiming to be about nineteen or twenty, has had no advantages or education, and can neither read nor write. She is reported to be a pitiable object, who has no idea of the wrong she may have committed.

It is stated that her trial did not bring out all the evidence that might have been submitted to the court and that she had a colored lawyer who did not handle the case to the best advantage of the accused. The impression abroad is that the evidence submitted was incomplete.

A number of disinterested parties, who are concerned largely about the justice of the case, feel that it would be a great disaster and a blot upon the District of Columbia, should the sentence of execution be carried into effect.

I am writing therefore to add my word of appeal that your executive clemency may be extended and that a stay of sentence may be secured until the accused may have the opportunity of further hearing. I understand that the execution is set for Friday, October 15.

Rev. Dr Harry Mitchell, pastor of the Metropolitan Methodist Church at Third and C sts N.W. this city, has the facts in the case which he is prepared to submit.

I beg to remain;   Very sincerely,   James H. Taylor

TLS (WP, DLC).
  [1] Wilson's pastor, minister of the Central Presbyterian Church of Washington.

To James Henry Taylor

My dear Friend: [The White House] 13 October, 1920

I appreciate the high motive which led you to write your letter of October twelfth about Josephine Berry, but it is really not a plea for executive clemency so much as a plea for a re-hearing of the case on evidence not yet submitted or submitted in the wrong light and in the wrong way. As you will see, this would put me in the position of a reviewing court, a position which I have always felt it unwise for me to assume. I am sorry to say that I cannot substitute myself for a court and jury, sorry as I am that it is thought that the case was not handled properly when it was before the court.

With the warmest regard,
          Cordially and faithfully yours,   [Woodrow Wilson]

CCL (WP, DLC).

To William Bauchop Wilson

My dear Colleague: The White House 13 October, 1920

My heart goes out to you in profoundest sympathy in your tragic loss.[1] I hope that my affectionate regard may be of some service to you in a time like this.

          Cordially and faithfully yours,   Woodrow Wilson

TLS (received from Mary A. Strohecker)
  [1] Agnes Williamson (Mrs. W. B.) Wilson, the Secretary's wife of thirty-seven years and mother of their eleven children, had just died.

To Alexander Mitchell Palmer

The White House

My dear Mr. Attorney General: 14 October, 1920

The death sentence of Josephine Berry is hereby commuted to imprisonment for life.   Very truly yours,   Woodrow Wilson

TLS (A. M. Palmer Papers, DLC).

To Elmer Talmage Clark

My dear Mr. Clark: [The White House] 13 October, 1920

I of course have heard with the most complete sympathy of the Christian Education Movement which has been inaugurated by the Methodist Episcopal Church, South.[1] I hope that it will meet with the greatest success. Every man who understands and loves the country must wish education brought to the highest point of development and efficiency and to be shot through at every point with Christian principle.

Very sincerely yours,   [Woodrow Wilson]

CCL (WP, DLC).
[1] Wilson was replying to E. T. Clark to WW, Oct. 8, 1920.

From Norman Hezekiah Davis

My dear Mr. President: Washington October 14, 1920

With reference to your letter to Secretary Colby[1] regarding the nomination by you of an American to be appointed on the Aaland Island Commission by the Council of the League of Nations, the attached despatch has just been received transmitting an official request that you make such an appointment.[2] May I ask if it is your wish that the Department communicate to Professor Haskins your desire that he act on this Commission, or will you communicate with him direct?   Faithfully yours,   Norman H. Davis

TLS (WP, DLC).
[1] WW to BC, Oct. 8, 1920 (second letter of that date).
[2] H. C. Wallace to SecState, No. 1808, Oct. 13, 1920, T telegram (WP, DLC).

Joseph Patrick Tumulty to Edith Bolling Galt Wilson

Dear Mrs. Wilson: The White House 14 October 1920.

I worked all last night on the Root matter, with Carter Glass, in preparing the attached.[1] I deeply regret that the President has seen fit to turn it down. You can see for yourself how wonderful a story it would make. It is a deadly attack on the whole campaign of poisonous propaganda that is being pursued by the Republicans.

I wish you could help me in this matter.

You will remember some weeks ago that I had up with the President the matter of releasing to the public the Taft correspondence.[2] He finally said he had no objection to Governor Cox's using this material.   Sincerely yours,   Tumulty

TLS (J. P. Tumulty Papers, DLC).

[1] It is a CC MS in the J. P. Tumulty Papers, DLC, and addressed the question of whether Wilson was willing to confer with the Senate during the drafting of the Covenant. Tumulty reproduced the following documents, along with his own connecting commentary: WW to JPT, Feb. 14, 1919, printed at that date in Vol. 55; and WW to EMH, March 31, 1919, enclosing FLP to RL, March 27, 1919, listing Root's proposed amendments to the Covenant, printed at March 31, 1919, in Vol. 56. Tumulty then went on to assert that "every material amendment proposed by Mr. Root having any essential bearing on the business in hand, was embodied in the covenant of the League of Nations as brought back by President Wilson." Tumulty devoted four pages to proving that this was true and concluded: "It will thus be observed that so far from repelling Mr. Root, and men of his type, the President promptly brought to the attention of his associates every suggestion that Mr. Root made and substantially embodied nearly every one of them in the draft of the covenant."

[2] See JPT to WW, with Enclosure, Sept. 26, 1920, and WW to JPT, Sept. 26, 1920.

Edith Bolling Galt Wilson to Joseph Patrick Tumulty

My dear Mr. Tumlty   [The White House] Oct. 15, 1920

I took this up this morning, as you asked—but the decision seems so positive, I have to return it.

I am sorry and I know the President appreciates all your work and the fine reason that prompted it.   Faithfully   E.B.W.

ALI (J. P. Tumulty Papers, DLC).

To Norman Hezekiah Davis

My dear Davis: The White House 15 October, 1920

I have your letter of October thirteenth about the appointment of an American on the Aaland Island Commission. I write to request that the Department communicate to Professor Haskins my desire to name him and secure his consent. If he consents, I request that the proper papers be made out.

Faithfully yours,   Woodrow Wilson

TLS (SDR, RG 59, 758.6114A1/129, DNA).

To John Joseph Pershing

My dear General Pershing: The White House 15 October, 1920

I warmly appreciate your thoughtful kindness in sending me a special copy of your final report, and the inscription pleased me very much indeed.[1] This affords me an opportunity to congratulate you on the notable services you have rendered your country, and to wish for you every good thing in the future.

Cordially and sincerely yours,   Woodrow Wilson

TLS (J. J. Pershing Papers, DLC).
[1] "To the President,—
The Hon. Woodrow Wilson:
"With deep appreciation of his support and confidence during the trying days of the World War, and much great admiration, respect and esteem,
"John J. Pershing"
Hw inscription in J. J. Pershing, *Final Report of Gen. John J. Pershing Commander-in-Chief American Expeditionary Forces* (Washington, 1919), Wilson Library, DLC.

From Samuel Gompers

Sir: Washington, D. C. October 15, 1920

The last annual convention of the American Federation of Labor, June 1920, adopted resolutions that the President of the United States, the Attorney General and the Secretary of War should be urged to grant amnesty to the political prisoners of the war with Germany and Austria.

No doubt the Attorney General has advised you of the conference which I, together with a number of representatives of organized labor recently had with him regarding the matter.

The object of my addressing this communication to you now is to convey to you the earnest belief entertained by my associates and myself that if you should issue a proclamation granting amnesty to the political prisoners it would have a most beneficial effect upon a large part of our people, help to allay feelings that have been aroused, and indeed, have a general tranquilizing effect. And this, despite the fact that, as stated by the Attorney General, that in the event of the issuance of such a proclamation by you it would devolve upon the Department of Justice to scrutinize each case before the freedom of the political prisoner could be effected.

May I express the hope that the matter as above submitted may commend itself to your favorable consideration and action?

Yours respectfully,   Saml. Gompers

Ackn & file   W.W.

TLS (WP, DLC).

From Harry Kent Day

My dear Mr. Wilson: Philadelphia, Pa. October 15th, 1920.

Your letter of October 11th to my brother, the late Frank Miles Day, has been handed to me as one of his Executors. I regret to have to tell you that my brother's death occurred very suddenly about two years ago.

Under the circumstances and desiring if possible to be of assistance to you, I mention the following facts:

You will recall that while you were at Princeton, the firm was Frank Miles Day & Brother. Later Mr. Charles Z. Klauder,[1] who had been with us many years, was admitted to the firm and two years later I retired, the name becoming Day and Klauder and so continues. Since the death of my brother, the practice has been carried on by Mr. Klauder who is a Fellow of the American Institute of Architects. You may recall having met him at Princeton.

His success in maintaining the high artistic and other standards of the old firm has been remarkable. I am sure you would get a very high estimate of his ability from Mr. Henry B. Thompson.[2] All former clients have continued their relations with Mr. Klauder and many new ones have been added. In all the work at Princeton he has contributed an important, though before his inclusion in the firm, an unrecognized part, and especially is this true in the sphere of design.

He is now occupied with important projects for nearly all the Universities and many of the larger colleges in the East, as well as with other classes of work.

May I, therefore, suggest that Mr. Klauder would be eminently suited to advise you. If you desire it, I am sure he will be willing to come to Washington to assist you in any way.

That you so happily revert to the work at Princeton is very gratifying. I can assure you it is still being "continued along the same fine lines" as you so kindly put it.

As I reread the above, I feel it savors too much of business and fails to convey any idea of the great loss of my brother's death and the appreciation of and the many references to his high character and worth.

With sincere regards,   Very truly yours,   H. Kent Day

TLS (WP, DLC).
¹ Charles Zeller Klauder.
² Henry Burling Thompson, Wilson's old friend on the Board of Trustees of Princeton University, chairman of its Committee on Buildings and Grounds.

From Norman Hezekiah Davis

My dear Mr. President: Washington October 16, 1920.

The Department has received a telegram from the American Minister at Havana, stating that some 50,000 laborers in Havana are now out of work. We are advised that widespread alarm exists lest the attempt be made by party leaders to use the dissatisfaction of this element in order to promote serious disturbances in connection with the political meetings which are now being held. It is probable that a general strike will be called on October 18th and if this should occur, the already tense situation would undoubtedly be further aggravated. The Minister has suggested the advisability of sending an American warship to Havana to remain there until more normal conditions are restored.

It is possible that trouble may also arise, because of unsettled conditions, at various points throughout the Island, and I am inclined to believe that the visits at this time of warships to Havana and to the ports of Santiago and Cienfuegos, would create a most salutary impression and would tend to prevent serious trouble. Similar visits of American warships in the past have always had a most quieting effect. It seems to me that we would be justified in using our influence in this way to prevent disturbances which would make it difficult, if not impossible, for the Government to hold fair and orderly elections.

I should be glad if you would let me know whether the sending of these vessels as a precautionary measure, in the hope that their presence in Cuban waters may prevent, if possible, serious disturbances during the next few weeks, meets with your approval.

Faithfully yours,   Norman H. Davis

TLS (WP, DLC).

From Edwin Anderson Alderman

My dear Mr. President: Charlottesville Oct. 16, 1920.

The University of Virginia is preparing to celebrate the centennial of its foundation next June. As a culmination of that function, we are endeavoring to secure a birthday gift to the University of three million dollars, and the executive management of this campaign is forming an Honorary National Committee composed of citizens of the country representing the widest and most diverse interests. It is their very earnest hope and my very earnest desire that you, as the most distinguished son of this University now living, will consent to the use of your name upon the Honorary National Committee. You will not, of course, be asked to render any service, save the invaluable influence of your name in endorsing this effort to place on a sure basis a great American University, which you know and understand, and which cherishes you with a deep and abiding affection.

Faithfully yours,   Edwin A. Alderman.

TLS (WP, DLC).

Edith Bolling Galt Wilson to Norman Hezekiah Davis

My dear Mr. Davis: The White House Sunday Oct. 17/1920

Your letter of the 16th in regard to sending war ships to Havana, etc. has just reached the President, and he wishes me to tell you he deems such an order unwise at this time.

He says he will have a talk with you about it later.

With warm regards

Faithfully yours,   Edith Bolling Wilson

ALS (N. H. Davis Papers, DLC).

From William Gibbs McAdoo

Dear Governor: Enroute Missouri. October 17th, 1920.

I have now made all told nineteen speeches in Pennsylvania, Ohio and Indiana. I have been greatly impressed by the interest of the people everywhere in the League. But for the appalling misrepresentations of the true meaning and effect of this great enterprise, I am sure the people would overwhelmingly endorse it. Our one hope is to get the truth to them in the brief time remaining before the election.

I have had wonderfully enthusiastic audiences everywhere, cul-
minating in a most extraordinary meeting at four o'clock in the
afternoon yesterday at Indianapolis. I never saw greater enthusiasm nor more intelligent attention to a discussion. I feel sure that
we shall carry Indiana. In Ohio conditions are not so good and of
course little is to be expected from Pennsylvania. My observations,
however,—necessarily casual as I am moving so rapidly,—are that
there is a drift to Cox and that if it continues to grow until election
day, he ought to win. I hope sincerely that he does. I am doing
everything in my power for him.

I wish you could hear the really beautiful things which people
are telling Nell and me about you. The deep affection in which you
are held by thousands of your countrymen is, of itself, a great reward, no matter how vilely you have been misrepresented and
abused by the enemy. I have almost lost my voice again but I have
24 hours rest today and hope to be in shape for two big meetings
in Colorado tomorrow.

Please forgive me for troubling you about the Western Union
matter[1] but I feel very keenly about this situation since, as I wrote
you, I was instrumental in trying to secure this improved facility
for South American trade and commerce. Having done so in my
official capacity as Secretary of the Treasury, and President of the
International High Commission of all Latin-American countries
and in furtherance of their expressed desire, it seems as if this Administration was repudiating me if it refuses to grant the permit to
land this cable at Miami.

In view of the fact that every right of our Government can be
preserved and that it will not be prejudiced in any action it may
wish to take at any time by granting the revocable permit I have
suggested, I earnestly hope that you will be able to give this your
personal consideration. Unless you see tangible or practical reasons for not granting the permit (and I am frank to say I have not
discovered them, in my frequent talks with Colby and Davis) I
wish sincerely that you could see your way to grant at least the
revocable or temporary permit.

I feel keenly my responsibility in this matter, especially the
professional one, under which I am now laboring, and which I
have been forced to ignore by entering upon this campaign.

Nell was delighted to receive your and Edith's telegram on her
birthday and will write you herself. I shall drop you a line from time
to time as we go through the country.

Would it be possible for you to have Hoover or Grayson telegraph
me care Private Car Philadelphia, Ogden, Utah, that you received

my letter and that you will, or will not, give the matter consideration.

   With love for all,   Affectionately yours,   W G McAdoo

TLS (WP, DLC).
   ¹ WGM to WW, Oct. 11, 1920, and WW to WGM, Oct. 12, 1920.

To Norman Hezekiah Davis

My dear Davis: The White House 18 October, 1920
   I did not think it wise to order warships to Cuba because I feel
that we are authorized to intervene there only in case of revolution
and not when we may fancy that revolution is impending. To do
that would, in my opinion, be to induce further disorders and perhaps bring about the very thing we want to prevent, because we
should certainly be charged with being there in the interest of one
or the other of the contesting parties, and thereby passions would
be greatly inflamed.
                     Cordially and faithfully yours,   Woodrow Wilson

TLS (SDR, RG 59, 837.00/2117, DNA).

To Bainbridge Colby, with Enclosure

My dear Mr. Secretary: The White House 18 October, 1920
   The enclosed letter from the Secretary of War is so important
and I so entirely concur in its conclusions that I think it my duty
to send it to you for your perusal and consideration. You will no
doubt sooner or later be in conference with the Secretary of War
about the Cuban business.
                     Cordially and faithfully yours,   Woodrow Wilson

E N C L O S U R E

From Newton Diehl Baker

-:Personal and Confidential:-

My dear Mr. President: Washington. October 16, 1920.
   There is one situation about which I feel it necessary to write
you quite definitely before I leave for the West.
   For some time, as you know, there has been grave apprehension
of trouble in Cuba growing out of the approaching election. Our
military observer in the Island is reporting confidentially that the

prospects are not good and goes so far as to recommend that one regiment of infantry, at war strength, be ordered to Cuba for station and distribution at such points as may develop critical situations in the course of the election. With this recommendation I am not in sympathy, as it seems to me it would be impolitic for the Government of the United States to assume that difficulty is likely to arise in the election, and the sending of such a force by way of anticipation would undoubtedly be construed as evidence of a desire on the part of the United States to control the election in the interest of one or the other of the candidates. I understand there are some Marines on the Island already, though I do not know for what purpose. Nevertheless, I think it must be conceded that, while not probable, revolutionary outbreaks in Cuba are possible within the next few weeks.

The whole situation is complicated by the recent and profound economic disturbance in Cuba due to the fall in the price of sugar. Many of the great sugar producing enterprises there have changed hands comparatively recently on the basis of the current high prices, and the banks of the Island are undoubtedly heavily involved in financing these transfers. The fall in the price of sugar has occasioned something approaching economic collapse and the conjunction of this with the presidential election in the Island may increase the possibility of trouble and, indeed, bring the trouble even before the election takes place.

I have in the most highly confidential way, taking nobody into my confidence but General March, prepared a full division of the army and placed it under the command of General Harbord, so that it is ready at once for any expeditionary movement which may turn out to be necessary in your judgment. The division in question would be an adequate force for any intervention, it is fully manned, fully armed, and made up of as seasoned soldiers as we have. General Harbord, as you know, was in command of the Marines in the Chateau Thierry fight, and later was in command of the entire Services of Supply in France, having about five hundred thousand men under his direction. He later, by your direction, headed a commission to study conditions in Armenia and Turkey. He is an officer of the highest quality, sound discretion and large experience.

The transports operated by the War Department are adequate to convey any such expedition should one be necessary and if any emergency arises in my absence, General March, and he alone, knows of these precautionary measures. I venture to suggest, therefore, that if any action becomes necessary, you request the Secretary of State to deal with General March directly in the matter rather than through Mr. Williams,[1] the new Assistant Secretary, whose attention is being given to other matters in the Department and who has not as yet caught up with any of the military business.

Should any such expedition be necessary, it would not seem to me wise to send General Pershing as his recent operations have been upon a very much larger scale and such a task would be more appropriate to a Major General than to the General of the Armies.

I hope you will understand that I am far from advising or even expecting any intervention in Cuba; indeed, I should regard the necessity for such intervention as a very great misfortune, but I do feel that you ought to know that, in the event action becomes necessary, the War Department is prepared to the last detail to act at once.

The creation of a division ready for such expeditionary service has been entirely easy to bring about without causing the slightest comment. As you know, under the army reorganization bill the tactical organization of troops into divisions in [is] contemplated, and General Harbord's force has come together quite naturally as the first and sample divisional organization into which the peace-time army will be divided as the scattered elements are brought more and more together.

Respectfully yours,   Newton D. Baker

TLS (B. Colby Papers, DLC).
    [1] That is, William Reid Williams, about whom see NDB to WW, July 28, 1920, Vol. 65.

To Bainbridge Colby, with Enclosure

My dear Mr. Secretary: The White House 18 October, 1920

Perhaps you have not noticed in this morning's Washington Post an article by that skunk, Albert Fox, who always writes what is either false or malicious, to the effect that the French Government has approached Senator Lodge with regard to certain important international matters.[1] I thought I would ask you to read the article and if you deem it of sufficient importance to inquire of the French Embassy whether there is any foundation whatever for the statement.

I take the liberty of enclosing a copy of a letter I have just written to Mr. Harding.

Always
Cordially and faithfully yours,   Woodrow Wilson

TLS (B. Colby Papers, DLC).
    [1] Albert W. Fox, "POWERS DOUBT PACT," *Washington Post*, Oct. 18, 1920. Fox reported that Harding's announcement that the French government had sent a spokesman to him to ask him unofficially to lead the way in forming a new association of nations did

not surprise the diplomats who had abandoned hope of ever seeing ratification of the Versailles Treaty by the United States. France had not only communicated unofficially with Harding, but Ambassador Jusserand had also consulted Lodge and other senators with "a view to establishing order out of the International chaos threatened by the failures of the present league to either prevent war or promote harmony." The truth was, the report concluded, that several European governments had completely lost faith in the League and realized that some practical arrangement between the nations had to supplant it.

E N C L O S U R E

To Warren Gamaliel Harding

My dear Sir:　　　　　　　　　[The White House] 18 October 1920.

In the New York Times of yesterday, Sunday, October 17, 1920, I find a dispatch dated St. Louis, October sixteenth, which purports to report recent public utterances of yours. In it occurs the following:

> "Replying to criticisms of his proposal for an association of nations, he said in a rear platform speech at Green Castle, Indiana, that he already had been approached 'informally' by a representative of France, who asked that the United States lead the way to a world fraternity."

I write to ask if this is a correct quotation and if you really said what is there attributed to you. I need not point out to you the grave and extraordinary inferences to be drawn from such a statement, namely, that the Government of France, which is a member of the League of Nations, approached a private citizen of a nation which is not a member of the League with a request "that the United States lead the way to a world fraternity." The Department of State has always found the Government of France most honorably mindful of its international obligations and punctiliously careful to observe all the proprieties of international intercourse. I hesitate, therefore, to draw the inferences to which I have referred unless I am assured by you that you actually made the statement.

Very truly yours,　　Woodrow Wilson[1]

CCL (B. Colby Papers, DLC).
[1] Also TLS (Letterpress Books, WP, DLC).

From Warren Gamaliel Harding

Dear Mr. President: Marion, Ohio. Oct. 18, 1920.

I have before me a press copy of your letter to me of this date, though I am not in receipt of the original copy. I am glad to make a prompt reply.

It is very gratifying that you hesitate to draw inferences without my assurance that I am correctly quoted. The quotation as reported in your letter is not exact. The notes of the stenographer reporting my remarks quote me as saying, "France has sent her spokesmen to me informally, asking America in its new realization of the situation to lead the way for an association of nations." I am sure that my words could not be construed to say that the French Government has sent anybody to me. The thought I was trying to convey was that there had come to me those who spoke a sentiment which they represented to be very manifest among the French people, but nothing could suggest the French Government having violated the proprieties of international relations. Official France would never seek to go over your high office as our Chief Executive to appeal to the American people or any portion thereof.

I can see no impropriety in private citizens of France, or in Americans deeply friendly to France, expressing to me their understanding of sentiment in that friendly Republic.

It is not important enough to discuss, perhaps, but I very respectfully urge that an informal expression to me is rather more than that to a private citizen. I hold a place as a member of the Foreign Relations Committee of the United States Senate, which is charged with certain constitutional authority in dealing with foreign relations, and I am necessarily conscious that I am the nominee of the Republican Party for president of our Republic. In the combination of these two positions it ought not to be unseemly that some very devoted friends of a new and better relationship among nations, no matter whence they come, should wish to advise me relating to aspirations to cooperate with our own Republic in attaining that high purpose. Let me assure you again of the observance of all the proprieties and again assert that the French Government has maintained that great respect for your position to which I myself subscribe.

With great respect, I am,

                              Very truly,   Warren G. Harding

TLS (WP, DLC).

From Norman Hezekiah Davis

My dear Mr. President:　　　　　　Washington October 18, 1920.

You may be interested to know that the French Chargé[1] informed me this afternoon that he has no knowledge of and doubts that anyone representing France formally or informally has approached Senator Harding, or anyone else regarding the United States leading the way to a world fraternity. The Chargé also told me he had communicated to his Government the published statements on this subject and has requested that he be authorized to issue a statement denying that anyone has been authorized officially, unofficially or indirectly to make any such representations on behalf of France.　　Faithfully yours,　　Norman H. Davis

TLS (WP, DLC).
[1] That is, Prince de Béarn et de Chalais.

To William Byron Colver

My dear Colver:　　　　　　Washington 18 October, 1920

I wish with all my heart that I could persuade you to accept a reappointment to the Federal Trade Commission.[1] Ever since I put you on it I have felt a sense of security about the work of the Commission which I had not felt before, and it would seem to me to be a very great pity for you to divorce yourself from the public service in a work so highly important and delicate and which ought to be continued along the lines established during your membership in the Commission. Is it useless to hope that you will change your mind? I trust that it is not.

With warm regard,　　Faithfully yours,　　Woodrow Wilson

TLS (WC, NjP).
[1] Colver had written to Tumulty on August 20 that he did not desire to be reappointed to the Federal Trade Commission. This letter, which was meant for Wilson's eyes, expressed deep affection and high regard for Wilson and all that he stood for. Receiving no reply to this letter, Colver wrote again to Tumulty on September 11, saying that he could not close some business arrangements until he had been released by Wilson. He also suggested the appointment of a woman as his successor. On September 14, Tumulty informed Mrs. Wilson that Colver was asking whether Wilson had accepted his resignation. If so, Tumulty suggested, Wilson should write Colver a letter of appreciation of his services. Wilson wrote at the bottom of this letter: "I hope to dissuade him." A month later, Tumulty wrote to Wilson saying that Colver could not consider reappointment and that he, Tumulty, hoped that Wilson would write him "an acceptance of his decision." "He is a fine fellow," Tumulty added, "and I hope you will do this." Wilson wrote at the bottom of this letter: "I have received no letter of resignation or other communication from him." Tumulty sent Colver's letters to Wilson on October 16, and Wilson then wrote his letter of October 18 to Colver. W. B. Colver to JPT, Aug. 20, 1920, ALS; W. B. Colver to JPT, Sept. 11, 1920, ALS; JPT to EBW, Sept. 14, 1920, TL; JPT to WW, Oct. 14, 1920, TL; and JPT to WW, Oct. 16, 1920, TLS, all in WP, DLC.

To Harry Kent Day

My dear Mr. Day: [The White House] 18 October, 1920

It is with the keenest grief that I learned of the death of your brother, Mr. Frank Miles Day. I had not for some reason heard of it at all. I had learned to prize his friendship as well as to admire his gifts and professional capacity and feel a sense of personal loss in his departure.

I hope that you will be kind enough to transfer to Mr. Klauder the invitation which I wrote to your brother, and say to Mr. Klauder that if he will let me know when he can come down and the train by which to expect him, I will have him met at the station and brought immediately to the White House.

With best wishes,   Sincerely yours,   [Woodrow Wilson]

CCL (WP, DLC).

To Charles Edward Bacon[1]

My dear Mr. Bacon: [The White House] 18 October, 1920

I appreciate your letter of October fourteenth[2] very much. I have several times had it in mind to write an elementary history of the United States but have always been turned away from the design by one circumstance or another, until now it seems extremely improbable that I shall ever have the opportunity to undertake it.

May I not thank you, nevertheless, for the suggestion?
                        Very sincerely yours,   [Woodrow Wilson]

CCL (WP, DLC).
   [1] President of Allyn and Bacon, textbook publishers of Boston.
   [2] C. E. Bacon to WW, Oct. 14, 1920, TLS (WP, DLC).

From Joseph Patrick Tumulty

My dear Governor: The White House, 18 October 1920.

You will see from the enclosed clipping[1] that Governor Cox is making good use of the present depression in the prices of wheat, wool and cotton.

Governor Harding,[2] of the Federal Reserve Board, called upon me last Friday and said that the prices began to decline most rapidly after the Des Moines speech of Senator Harding,[3] and that the Democrats were not taking full advantage of the present depression as occasioned by the attitude of opposition on the part of the Republicans to the League of Nations.

Governor Harding said that the Federal Reserve Act was being blamed for the depression in prices, and, in fact, that it was caused by the delay in ratifying the treaty.

Senator Ransdell wrote a letter today, calling attention to a speech made by Mr. Taft, sometime ago, in which he put the responsibility on the Republicans for "numbing" prosperity.[4] Governor Harding thinks that it would have a wonderful effect on the country if you could embody the facts in his letter in reply to Senator Ransdell. I am passing the suggestion on to you.[5]

Tumulty

TLS (J. P. Tumulty Papers, DLC).
  [1] From the Baltimore *Evening Sun*, Oct. 18, 1920. It reported on a speech by Cox in Syracuse, N. Y., on that date. Cox predicted "dollar wheat" and an accentuation of the business recession just beginning if the United States did not join the League.
  [2] That is, William Procter Gould Harding.
  [3] About which, see JPT to WW, Oct. 7, 1920, n. 1.
  [4] J. E. Ransdell to WW, Oct. 18, 1920, TLS (J. P. Tumulty Papers, DLC). Taft, in a speech to the state convention of the League to Enforce Peace at Albany on June 7, 1919, said that businessmen should blame "short-sighted" Republicans, and not Wilson, for further delay in peace and "waiting prosperity" on account of their efforts to eliminate the Covenant from the treaty with Germany or "materially" to change its provisions.
  [5] Indeed, Tumulty prepared a draft of a long letter to Senator Ransdell for Wilson to sign. It is a T MS, dated Oct. 19, 1920, in the Tumulty Papers. The letter blamed the current agricultural depression in the United States on the refusal of Republican senators to permit ratification of the Versailles Treaty and American membership in the League.

From George P. Hampton[1]

Dear Mr. President: Washington, D. C. October 18, 1920.

The seriousness of the present condition of farmers' credit constrains us to make a direct appeal to you to exert the maximum power vested in you under existing legislation to secure adequate short time credit for farmers to save them from being forced to dump their crops upon the market at ruinously low prices, that will permit middlemen hoarders to secure control of these crops to the serious detriment of agriculture and without benefit to the consumers of farm products.

During several months the Farmers' National Council has tried to get the Federal Reserve Board and the Secretary of the Treasury to meet existing farmers' short-time credit needs. The Governor of the Federal Reserve Board and the Secretary of the Treasury assert that these needs are being met, but they have produced no figures which in our judgment justify their statements, and the testimony of farmers and livestock growers in many sections of the country is exactly to the contrary.

Information secured by the Federal Farm Loan Board in replies to an inquiry which it recently made of 3,978 Farm Loan Associations, created under the Federal Land Bank Act shows that farmers have to pay, except in a few eastern states, and one or two southern states, usually 8 to 10 per cent, and often 11, 12, and 15 per cent for short time loans,—in some instances they pay 20 to 24 per cent. Out of the 3,978 Farm Loan Associations, 2,501 reported to the Federal Farm Loan Board between August 5th, and September 30th. Only 1,418 reported that money was available, for short-time credit to farmers and the interest rate even in these localities was usually 8 to 12 per cent, with the exception of a very few states where the prevailing rate was 6 to 7 per cent. 292 associations reported that short-time credit for farmers was not available; 314 that there was a fair supply, and 477 reported a scarcity. A very large proportion of the associations stated that interest rates had gone up one to two per cent or more since last year. In a few cases bonuses and commissions were charged, while frequently notes were discounted, thereby materially increasing the actual interest rate reported.

In response to the nation-wide demand and in compliance with the expressed desire of government officials, farmers increased their acreage in staple crops very materially this year. They ask only cost of production plus a reasonable profit, which naturally must cover the losses from crop failures due to droughts and other conditions over which farmers have no control. The financial interests of America consider production the only legitimate field for farmers' activities. There cannot be a permanent agriculture in our country under such conditions. Farmers must have credit to enable them to market their crops in an orderly consecutive way to meet effective consumption demands. There is no danger that farmers can, nor do they desire to secure, exorbitant prices for their products, while the slump during the last three and a half months in prices which farmers received for their products at the farm, means a loss to farmers of around two and a half billion dollars, and that many farmers, probably hundreds of thousands, will not get cost of production, even.

The Department of Agriculture within a week announced the result of a survey of farm profits covering a period of seven years in two areas and five in a third area showing that comparatively few of the farmers, in the groups studied, have made any profit during the years of relatively high prices, and that most of them regardless of the number of workers on the farm in the family are making less than $500 in cash per year, above the things the farm furnishes for the family living. No other construction can be placed upon the reply of the Federal Reserve Board to the recent request

of farm organizations that the government enable farmers to secure short time credit at reasonable terms than that the Reserve
Board does not feel the need of such action. Its suggestion that
America's chief market for raw and manufactured products is at
home, comes unfortunately at this time in view of the fact that the
importation of farm products to this country last year was over two
and a half billion dollars, and about equals the total slump in prices
farmers receive for their products on eight farm staples since July
1st, this year.

In our judgment under the circumstances the government
should meet the present emergency with the general public welfare in view.

We respectfully ask that the Secretary of the Treasury issue
Treasury certificates of indebtedness to the extent of $250,000,000
and if necessary, $500,000,000, and deposit the proceeds in na-
tional banks to be loaned to farmers as short time loans at not to
exceed one per cent in excess of the prices the government has to
pay for the money, to enable farmers to market their crops in an
orderly way and save them from being forced to dump them. We
thoroughly appreciate the difficulty involved in the government's
going into the money market, but it is, in our judgment, no less to
the interest of consumers, than of farm producers that both consumers and producers be saved from the severe blow to agriculture
which will result if farmers are discouraged and in self-defense
forced to curtail their production next year.

Yours sincerely,   Geo. P. Hampton

Ackn   W.W.

TLS (WP, DLC).
[1] Managing Director of the Farmers' National Council.

From Tom Scott

Dear Sir   Grasmere, Oct. 18th, 1920

You will be sorry to hear my Uncle Mr Cowperthwaite passed
away on Thursday Oct 7th at St Annes on Sea after two years illness & it is my intention to carry on his business, without any alteration. As you know I have been with him all my life & remember
your visits in 1903 & 1908 & you may rest assured that when you
come to the Rothay, no effort will be spared to make your visit thoroughly comfortable & enjoyable.

With Best wishes I am   Yours, Sincerely   Tom Scott

ALS (WP, DLC).

To Norman Hezekiah Davis

My dear Davis: The White House 19 October, 1920

I have your letter of yesterday concerning what the French Charge has said with regard to Senator Harding's statements. You will notice that Harding does not say that anybody claiming to represent France had given him any assurances. You have no doubt read my letter to him and his letter to me, which have been printed in the papers, and you will see that he is now claiming merely that he has been listening to certain citizens of France or certain friends of France in this country. I suggest that you ask the French Charge to find out, if he can, what citizen or citizens of France, if any, have been trying to guide one of our party candidates and thus indirectly affect the result of the elections. It may be that the whole thing is of Mr. Harding's invention. I am quite ready to believe it. I have never for a moment thought that the French Government was doing anything irregular.

I am quite willing to comply with the French Charge's request "that he be authorized to issue a statement denying that anyone has been authorized officially, unofficially or indirectly to make any such representations on behalf of France," and appreciate the suggestion on his part.

Cordially and faithfully yours,   Woodrow Wilson

P.S. I am sending over to you some additional information obtained from a St. Louis Post Dispatch which I am sure will interest you.

TLS (N. H. Davis Papers, DLC).

Two Letters from Joseph Patrick Tumulty

Dear Governor: The White House 19 October, 1920.

A summary of Mr. Root's speech[1] has been telephone[d] me by the Democratic National Committee. It follows the lines laid down in the letter of the thirty-two Republicans to Mr. Harding[2] a week ago, but Root tries to give the impression in a most adroit way, that no suggestions from outside sources were considered. Those who have read the speech in New York consider it a very adroit affair and are asking us to let them have whatever material we have at this end.

My own opinion is that Bainbridge Colby is the man to handle this and that he ought to be invited by the National Committee to make a big speech in reply to Root, in New York on Friday night and use the data I forwarded to you some days ago.[3] Would you be willing to consider this matter?   Sincerely,   Tumulty

[1] Elihu Root, former Secretary of War, Secretary of State, and Senator from New York, was the elder statesman of the Republican party and in many respects the voice of American conservative traditions at this time. This speech, delivered at Carnegie Hall in New York under the auspices of the National Republican Club on October 19, was the only address that he gave during the presidential campaign of 1920.

Root said at the outset that he would concentrate his remarks on the League of Nations, and he declared that he personally desired, and he thought a large majority of the American people earnestly desired, "an organization among civilized nations through which the nations shall cooperate to prevent further wars, and that the United States shall do her full share in that organization."

Root went on to describe the peacekeeping machinery of the Covenant and objections that had been raised to it in the United States. He also commented on objections that had been raised on the ground that the Covenant impaired American sovereignty in regard to the Monroe Doctrine and certain domestic issues. The reservations to the treaty had been framed to meet these objections, he said, and Wilson had twice prevented the Democrats in the Senate from voting to give the Senate's consent to ratification with these reservations. Cox insisted upon ratification of the treaty as Wilson had negotiated it, while Harding had voted for ratification with the reservations and would do so again in the same circumstances. Root then quoted from the Republican platform plank calling for an international association of nations and from Harding's speech of August 28 saying that he strongly favored a league of free nations to maintain peace.

The objections to an unreserved Covenant, Root said, were not frivolous. Root then concentrated on objections to Article X, which, as he said, Wilson had declared was the "heart of the League." There could be no doubt, Root said, that Article X would oblige the United States to go to war, if necessary, to defend the boundaries of member states. Wilson had told the members of the Senate Foreign Relations Committee, in his meeting with them on August 19, 1919, that Article X would impose an absolutely compelling moral obligation upon the United States. Root then alluded to the controversy between Wilson and Senator Spencer, quoted from the "official" version of Wilson's remarks to the Eighth Plenary Session, and remarked that it was perfectly clear that Wilson had said that the sovereignty of the small powers would be guaranteed by the armed force of the great powers.

It was "most objectionable," Root continued, that the American people should give such a solemn and positive guarantee for all time to come. Wilson had made such a guarantee in his speech to the Eighth Plenary Session, and it would be a breach of the Covenant if Congress refused to back it up. No one could say whether the American people would in the future be willing to support Article X, and the worst thing that a nation could do was to make a treaty and then break it.

Thoughtful people everywhere realized that the world could not be made "good, moral, peaceable by compulsion." Real progress toward peace could come only from the moral forces that make for peace: "respect for law, a sentiment for justice, a knowledge of truth, a desire for conciliation." The covenant had to be revised. Article X was a throwback to the Holy Alliance. "What free nations need for their independence is not a guarantee of favor by the more powerful. It is a guarantee of justice under law, supported by civilized public opinion." The nations of Latin America had rejected Wilson's proposal for the Pan-American Pact based upon a provision similar to Article X. They had feared and rejected it on the ground that it would result in the domination of the weak by the strong, as had in fact happened in Haiti and the Dominican Republic.

"The conception which would make the alliance of Article X. the heart of a league to promote [the] peace of the world," Root concluded, "is a negation of the opinion held by the wisest, most experienced and most devoted men who have labored in all civilized countries for generations to advance the cause of peace. It is a negation of the opinions held without exception by the rulers and statesmen who have led the policies of the United States for generations. It is a mistaken conception, and it ought to be repudiated by the American people not merely for their own interest but in the interest of the peace of the world." From the complete text in the *New York Times*, October 20, 1920.

[2] This statement of thirty-one Republicans, printed in *ibid.*, Oct. 15, 1920, was probably drafted by Root no later than October 9 and was revised by Cravath and Schurman. As Leopold points out, Root and his friends all assumed that Harding would of course be elected, and their statement was designed to remind him and all Republicans of the

commitment that their party had made in its platform. Richard W. Leopold, *Elihu Root and the Conservative Tradition* (Boston, 1954), pp. 147-48. See also Philip C. Jessup, *Elihu Root* (2 vols., New York, 1948), II, 413-14.

The statement said that the signers, who wanted the United States to do her full part in association with other civilized nations to prevent war, had earnestly considered how they might contribute most effectively to that end by their own votes in the coming election. The question before the country was not whether the United States should join such an organization as the League; it was whether it should join under Wilson's exact terms or with changes of provisions objectionable to great numbers of Americans. The round robin of March 1919 (about which, see the extract from the Grayson Diary printed at March 3, 1919, and n. 1 thereto, Vol. 55) had warned Wilson that the senators who signed it could not approve the Covenant in its then present form, although they sincerely desired that the nations of the world should unite to promote peace and general disarmament. Wilson had refused to accept any modifications in the Covenant whatsoever, and enough Democratic senators had voted against the treaty with reservations to prevent its ratification. The statement of the thirty-one then quoted the Republican platform supporting an international association and Harding's speech of August 28 in favor of "a society of free nations, or an association of free nations, or a league of free nations." "The question accordingly," the statement continued, "is not between a league and no league, but is whether certain provisions in the proposed league agreement shall be accepted unchanged or shall be changed." The statement then went on to condemn Article X in the same terms that Root would use in his speech just summarized. The "true course" to bring the United States into an effective league to preserve peace was not to insist with Cox upon acceptance of Article X, or some such provision, but frankly to call on the other nations to agree to "changes in the proposed agreement which will obviate this vital objection and other objections less the subject of dispute." Then followed the most important sentence: "The Republican Party is bound by every consideration of good faith to pursue such a course until the declared object is attained." Conditions in the European countries made it essential that the stabilizing effect of the Versailles Treaty should not be lost by them, "and that the necessary changes be made by changing the terms of that treaty rather than by beginning entirely anew." The statement then said that Harding had approved this position in his speech of August 28, and that the signers therefore believed that they could most effectively advance the cause of international cooperation to promote peace by voting for him.

The statement was signed by Lyman Abbott, Nicholas Murray Butler, Robert S. Brookings, Paul D. Cravath, Charles W. Dabney, William H. P. Faunce, Frank J. Goodnow, Warren Gregory, John Grier Hibben, Herbert Hoover, Charles Evans Hughes, Alexander C. Humphries, Ernest M. Hopkins, Bishop William Lawrence, Samuel McCune Lindsay, A. Lawrence Lowell, John Henry MacCracken, Samuel Mather, George A. Plimpton, Henry S. Pritchett, Charles A. Richmond, Elihu Root, Jacob Gould Schurman, Henry L. Stimson, Oscar S. Straus, Henry W. Taft, Isaac M. Ullman, William Allen White, George W. Wickersham, W. W. Willoughby, and Ray Lyman Wilbur. Most of the signers were college or university presidents or professors, or members of the executive committee of the League to Enforce Peace. William Howard Taft did not sign the statement only because he was on a speaking tour and was unavailable.

[3] See JPT to EBW, Oct. 14, 1920, n. 1.

Dear Governor: The White House 19 October 1920.

I want to call your attention to certain excerpts from Viereck's[1] statement.

"We have decided that there must not be another Democratic President for a generation. We have fought and we have come back. We shall redeem our promise in full at the polls."

I wish we could call the public's attention to these monstrous statements and warn the country just what is afoot.

                                   Sincerely,   Tumulty

TLS (J. P. Tumulty Papers, DLC).

¹ During a speech at Cleveland on October 16, Cox had assailed George Sylvester Viereck, editor of *The American Monthly* (formerly *The Fatherland*), as a "professional German-American." In response, Viereck, on the following day, had sent a telegram to Cox, stating that the 6,000,000 German Americans were loyal citizens and, for that very reason, were opposed to Cox's candidacy. "You forget," Viereck declared, "that the Wilson reign of terror is at an end. No aspersion upon the loyalty of Americans of German descent can intimidate them into voting for the alter ego of T. Woodrow Wilson." *New York Times*, Oct. 17 and 18, 1920.

Two Letters to Joseph Patrick Tumulty

Dear Tumulty: The White House [c. Oct. 19, 1920].

This is something which it is the duty of the National Committee to make widely public, and I am sure that Governor Cox can do so with great efficacy, particularly when he has a text for indicating that he does not wish to be supported by pro-Germans of any kind, a statement which I personally hope he will make at an early date.¹

The President.

¹ In fact, Tumulty had already sent a telegram to Cox calling attention to Viereck's statement and adding: "Why not send him telegram such as the President sent O'Leary?" JPT to J. M. Cox, Oct. 18, 1920, T telegram (J. P. Tumulty Papers, DLC). Wilson's telegram to J. A. O'Leary is printed at Sept. 29, 1916, Vol. 38.

To our knowledge, Cox did not issue the kind of statement that Wilson suggested. In a speech at Akron on October 29, Cox did ask Harding the following question, among others: "Does your platform authorize you to make a pledge to George Viereck and to declare for a separate peace with Germany to secure, as he says, votes of the pro-German party in America?" *New York Times*, Oct. 30, 1920.

Dear Tumulty: The White House [Oct. 20, 1920].

There is absolutely nothing new in Root's speech and I do not see any necessity to answer it. Certainly I would not be willing to have so conspicuous a representative of the Administration as Mr. Colby take any notice of it. Let me say again that I am not willing that answers to Republican speakers or writers should emanate from the White House or the Administration.

The President.

TL (J. P. Tumulty Papers, DLC).

From Joseph Patrick Tumulty

My dear Governor: The White House, 20 October 1920.

Of course nothing will be done in the Root matter, according to your suggestion to me of this morning; but I feel it my duty to advise you that nearly all the reports from the men whose judgment and opinion are usually good are to the effect that unless you will intervene and take a more active interest in the campaign, the Administration will be repudiated at the election.

There is a slight drift towards Cox, but unless you take advantage of it and speed it up, there is very little hope.

Tumulty

TLS (J. P. Tumulty Papers, DLC).

To Joseph Patrick Tumulty

The White House [c. Oct. 20, 1920].

Of course I will help I was under the impression that I was helping. But I will do it at my own time and in my own way

W.W.

ALI (J. P. Tumulty Papers, DLC).

To William Gibbs McAdoo

[The White House] 20 October, 1920

Sorry I have not considered it wise to reconsider the Miami matter.[1]   Woodrow Wilson.

T telegram (Letterpress Books, WP, DLC).
    [1] Wilson was replying to WGM to WW, Oct. 17, 1920.

From Herbert Bayard Swope[1]

Personal

My dear Mr. President: New York October 20, 1920.

If any doubt existed on the subject of your health it would be removed immediately upon reading the virile and helpful statements that recently have come from you on the political situation. I congratulate you on your recovery, and I congratulate the country that you have been spared to it, so that it may profit by your counsel and guidance for, I hope, many years to come.

I think you know my own sentiments toward you well enough to realize how deep a source of pleasure it is to be of service in your behalf. I am bold enough to believe that in offering you the suggestion, which I am embodying in this letter and which is its principal excuse, you will agree that I am proving of assistance in calling to your mind what is probably an oversight. That oversight lies in the fact that, apart from your personal expressions of appreciation, there has been no recognition whatsoever of an official nature given Baruch for the work he did before, during and after the war. It would be supererogatory for me to attempt to characterize his efforts. You know best how singleminded, how devotional, how idealistic and how honest they were and, too, how finally effective were the results he achieved. When I see a man of the type of Cravath honored by a D.S.M., I am forced to the conclusion that the only reason Baruch has not been similarly distinguished is because, in the heavy pressure upon your time, you have had no opportunity to give the matter thought.

Baruch is not aware I am writing this letter, and we both know him well enough to be certain he would oppose it if he had such knowledge. I am moved to take this action, however, because I believe you would want me to and because I am convinced that some public expression of approval is the least to which he is entitled as compensation for his years of unselfish and sacrificing service. It is true that you yourself, perhaps the most deserving of all for such recognition, have received none, but your reward will be given by history, which will write your name down beside that of Lincoln, Jefferson and Washington.

From a personal standpoint I regret you were unable to see your way clear toward accepting the proposition Ralph Pulitzer laid before you a month or two ago,[2] for the idea was largely mine, but I realize that the method you have devised of utilizing your efforts after you leave the White House is possibly even more effective than the one The World offered you, and so I am content with your choice, as I know it has been made after a painstaking examination as to which plan offers you the greatest opportunity to be of aid to the country and to the world.

Pray remember me to Mrs. Wilson, and believe me to be always with admiration and respect,

Faithfully yours,   Herbert Bayard Swope

TLS (WP, DLC).
  [1] Wilson's old friend, at this time one of the editors of the New York *World*.
  [2] See WW to R. Pulitzer, July 7, 1920, n. 1, Vol. 65.

A Questionnaire[1]

[c. Oct. 21, 1920]

Please Answer These Questions
All replies absolutely confidential

(1)   Is your power of concentration strong or weak?
       Just about medium, I should say.
(2)   Is your memory good or poor?
       Rather good.
(3)   Do you lack confidence in yourself?
       No.

(4) If you lack power of concentration, have you reason to believe that you inherited this disability, or was it acquired at school, in consequence of the unattractiveness of your studies?
If I had inherited characteristics, I should have inherited the greatest power of concentration, for both my parents had it.

(5) Has there been a change for the worse in your memory? If so, can you indicate the cause? Has it been since a particular illness, a great trouble, excessive mental toil, or some physical injury? State the nature of the illness or shock.
Rather for the better than for the worse.

(6) Is "interest-power" necessary for persistent effort, or can you carry through an uninteresting task by "will-power" alone?
By will power alone.

(7) Can you attend to a conversation or read for any length of time without your mind wandering?
Yes

(8) Do you suffer much from self-consciousness or shyness?
A good deal from shyness.

(9) What is the general condition of your health at the present time?
I am suffering from nervious [nervous] exhaustion.

Printed form with T answers (WP, DLC).
   ¹ This questionnaire was enclosed in G. Creel to WW, Oct. 21, 1920, printed form letter (WP, DLC). Creel wrote as president of The Pelman Institute of America, Inc., New York, saying that Wilson had favored him with an inquiry about Pelmanism, and that Creel had asked the secretary to send Wilson a copy of a booklet, *Mind and Memory*. The letter urged Wilson to read the booklet, because it gave a "clear-cut presentation of Pelmanism—what it is, and what it will accomplish for you, if you will conscientiously apply its principles to your every-day life." Pelmanism, the letter went on, was "the science of success." Creel said that he had brought Pelmanism to the United States from England a year ago, and that thousands of Americans had already enrolled in "this world-famous course." Pelmanism came to the subscriber in twelve "Little Gray Books." Each student received "individual and personal attention." Its cost was low ($35, or $50 on the installment plan), and its benefits could not be measured in money alone: "Pelmanism builds to a richer, more interesting, more useful life. It is for the young and the old; it benefits all classes, all creeds. It acts on vision and imagination as a tonic. Pelmanism teaches you the POWER OF DECISION. You must either go forward or go back. It is for you to decide today that you are going to do what 500,000 others have done—study and apply the principles of Pelmanism."
   The questionnaire that Wilson filled in was on the left hand of a page, the right-hand side of which were printed the "Special Enrollment Terms." Wilson did not fill in this column except to give his age as sixty-four. We have printed Wilson's answers, which Swem typed, in italics.

To William Shepherd Benson¹

[The White House] 21 October, 1920

I am taking the liberty of appointing you as a member of the new Shipping Board and beg that you will indicate your acceptance.

Woodrow Wilson.

T telegram (Letterpress Books, WP, DLC).
    ¹ Other such telegrams were sent on October 21 or soon afterward to Martin J. Gillen, John A. Donald, Frederick I. Thompson, Isaac H. Lionberger, Gavin McNab, Theodore Marburg, and Joseph N. Teal. Of this group, Benson, Donald, Thompson, and Teal accepted. On November 13, Wilson announced the appointment of the full board (all members had accepted): Admiral Benson, Chairman; Frederick Ingate Thompson of Mobile, Ala.; Joseph Nathan Teal of Portland, Ore.; John A. Donald of New York; Chester Harvey Rowell of Fresno, Calif.; Guy Despard Goff of Wisconsin; and Charles Sutter of Missouri.

James Middleton Cox to Edith Bolling Galt Wilson

My dear Mrs. Wilson: En Route October 21 1920

    I would be tremendously pleased and honored if President Wilson and yourself could come to the New York meeting Saturday night.
    I feel that our fight is won; and I should like the President to have the opportunity before the campaign closes to attend a large assemblage and see there the evidence of affection that the people bear for him.
    With assurances of the highest esteem, I am
                        Most respectfully yours,   James M Cox.

TLS (WP, DLC).

From Bainbridge Colby

My dear Mr. President: Washington October 21, 1920.

    Professor Haskins is unable to accept appointment as a member of the Aland Island Commission, owing to "certain University and personal obligations which are imperative." He suggests *Professor A. C. Coolidge*, whose work on the Peace Commission in Austria, Professor Haskins speaks of highly, adding that he is familiar with the situation in the Baltic and has a knowledge of the languages in that region.
    I submit this name to you promptly, as we are informed that the Commission hopes to begin its labors at an early date and to complete them before the end of December.
                        Very respectfully yours,   Bainbridge Colby

    I agree   W.W.

TLS (B. Colby Papers, DLC).

From Joseph Patrick Tumulty, with Enclosure

Dear Governor: [The White House] 21 October 1920

In accordance with your instruction, I have referred the letter from Edward A. Gowen[1] to the Secretary of Labor, who states in the letter attached hereto that he thinks these so-called outlaw strikers have been punished enough, and that while he understands and appreciates the attitude of the Brotherhood Chiefs, he advises that they be called into conference and whatever influence is possible be used to induce them to withdraw their opposition to the reinstatement of these outlaw strikers, with all their seniority rights.   Faithfully yours,   Tumulty

TLS (WP, DLC).

[1] E. A. Gowen to JPT, Oct. 5, 1920, TLS (WP, DLC). Gowen wrote on behalf of a group of railroad workers from Pennsylvania who had been dismissed for participating in a wildcat strike against the Baltimore & Ohio Railroad in the spring of 1920. Gowen had approached Tumulty in early August and asked for Wilson's help in overcoming the opposition of both the railroad management and the brotherhoods to a reinstatement of the strikers with full seniority rights. E. A. Gowen to JPT, Aug. 6, 1920, TLS (WP, DLC), and E. A. Gowen to JPT, Aug. 31, 1920, ALS (WP, DLC). In his letter to Tumulty of October 5, cited above, Gowen said that he had "put our case in writing, for you to present to the President." This letter is missing in WP, DLC. Gowen's letter of October 5 complained that, despite Tumulty's earlier assurances, no action had been taken in the matter.

E N C L O S U R E

William Bauchop Wilson to Joseph Patrick Tumulty

My dear Mr. Secretary: Washington October 21, 1920.

Referring to the correspondence relative to the reinstatement of the so-called outlaw strikers in the railway service, which you transmitted to me under date of October 8th, my judgment is that these men have now been punished sufficiently for the inconvenience they caused the public to act as a preventative to a recurrence of similar activities in the future. If you can bring any influence to bear on the chiefs of the Railway Brotherhoods to induce them to withdraw their opposition to the reinstatement of these men with all their seniority rights, I think the matter can be straightened out satisfactorily.

I understand and appreciate the attitude of the brotherhood chiefs. The future of their organizations and of the trade union movement depends upon the fidelity with which they adhere to contract obligations and upon their being free from sporadic strikes that do not represent the combined judgment of the workers expressed through their regular organizations. To them, therefore, these unauthorized strikes meant not only a blow at their particular organizations but at the whole trade union movement. They naturally feel that strong disciplinary measures are necessary to maintain the reputation of their organizations and prevent future occurrence of similar incidents. In a general way I agree with them, but I feel that the purpose has been accomplished and that to continue the disciplinary methods would simply mean unnecessary hardship to those engaged in the outlaw strike without any corresponding benefits.

It should be bourne in mind that so far as most of these men, if not all of them, are concerned there were numerous extenuating circumstances. The brotherhood chiefs had themselves been pressing vigorously for changes in the wage rates to meet the changes in the cost of living. In that they had the support of the rank and file of the railway workers of the country. The patience displayed by the chiefs in dealing with the different delays that took place could not be expected to be universally indorsed by the rank and file. When, therefore, at the height of their impatience a surreptitious movement for one big union was inaugurated and a general strike to enforce their demands was declared it found sufficient dissatisfaction with the existing conditions to make a formidable showing. To that must be added the fear that every working man has of the stigma of "scab." To be a traitor to one's fellows in an industrial conflict is to incur the greatest social ostracism that can come into any working man's life. It applies not only to the man himself but to his family, even to the third and fourth generation.

For these reasons I would advise that you call the brotherhood chiefs into conference and use whatever influence you can to induce them to withdraw their opposition to the reinstatement of these outlaw strikers, with all their seniority rights.

Cordially yours,   W B Wilson

TLS (WP, DLC).

From William Edward Dodd

My dear Mr. President: University of Chicago October 21, 1920.

Your reply to my inquiry about the late Colonel Roosevelt[1] settled to [the] point. But I would like to say that I personally never entertained different opinion from that expressed by you. That will appear in more than one place in my book.

But I was so convinced that you had been fair and more than fair to him both in the canvass of 1912 and in the matter of the proposed appointment to France[2] that it seemed likely that you might say as much which was what I thought might do some good, although Professor Greene had in mind the idea that you had really sought to enlist the Colonel in some particular endeavor. But of this enough. I am proud of a President and a leader who will do right to his own cost and maintain his integrity against all comers.

If you will allow me to say a word: There is a great unexpressed feeling of admiration and devotion among the people of this region, in spite of a press hardly equalled in our history for misrepresentation. At Lansing, Michigan, where I spoke twice last Sunday to Republican audiences, there was expressed a sense of humiliation and shame at what has been permitted these last two years. For two hours I spoke of the methods, amounting to conspiracy, of the Senate leaders and never a man left the hall. When I had finished, Republicans arose and declared that they would never vote the ticket so long as the party remained under its present leadership. Others declared that they had voted for you and had never abandoned you and your cause at any time, nor would they do so now. I never had quite such an experience.

This is not to boast of any oratorical effects or any particularly telling arguments. It is in my opinion the expression of deep-seated feeling that underlies this wave of unjust and partisan attack that sometimes seems so distressing to those who have always tried to maintain their faith in democracy.

Nor is the tone different in Chicago. At the University several of your friends have discussed the work of those terrible days at Paris before large audiences. Although this is normally a Republican centre, the same spirit, described above, is evidenced. In Evanston and at Win[n]etka audiences, known to be Republican in general tendency, have expressed the deepest admiration for the great work you have done and shown the heartiest contempt for the men who have sought in a thousand ways to undo that work. The native stocks of this region seem to me to have seen clearly and to have broken party ties in order to support a man whom they admire and love.

I know many others must write you similar accounts. Yet I venture this one in the hope that it may not be unwelcome and that it may offer some compensation for all that you have suffered during the last two years.

If we could only make it clear that the league of nations, the only important, positive fruits of the great war that we may surely reap, is the one issue, that is, focus all eyes upon that, I believe the majority would be very great.

Yours sincerely,   William E. Dodd

TLS (WP, DLC).
¹ WW to W. E. Dodd, Oct. 1, 1920.
² That is, as head of a division or corps in the A.E.F. For documents and notes relating to this matter, see the entry, "Roosevelt, Theodore," in the Index in Vol. 42.

To James Middleton Cox

[The White House] 22 October, 1920

Mrs. Wilson and I regret more than I can say that we cannot get to New York for the meeting you refer to in your kind letter of October twenty-first. It would be delightful to come to sustain you by our presence and show our deep interest in the success of which I am glad to find you are confident. You may be sure we would come if it were physically possible.   Woodrow Wilson.

T telegram (Letterpress Books, WP, DLC).

To Herbert Bayard Swope

My dear Swope: [The White House] 22 October, 1920

I subscribe to all that you say about Baruch and am surprised to find that I cannot account for his not having received the same recognition of his services that others less deserving have received. You may be sure that I shall omit no opportunity to remedy the mistake.

In haste   Sincerely yours,   [Woodrow Wilson]

CCL (WP, DLC).

To Thomas L. Snow¹

My dear Mr. Snow: [The White House] 22 October, 1920

Some years ago, you may remember, I commissioned your brother-in-law,² who was then at Heimera, to make some furniture for me which he kindly offered to make. I am under the impression that he made a certain amount, and I assume that it is in storage somewhere near the lake. Can you tell me anything about it? I had the pleasure of paying him for it at the time I was notified of its completion. I would also appreciate any information you might give me as to the best way of having it shipped to me in case I should set up housekeeping and need it.

With the warmest regard and hoping that all is well with you,

Cordially and sincerely yours,   [Woodrow Wilson]

CCL (WP, DLC).
    [1] Wilson's old friend, proprietor of The Bluff at Judd Haven, Lake Rosseau, Muskoka, Ontario, where the Wilsons had vacationed in the summers of 1900 and 1904. In 1900, Wilson had purchased a small island in Lake Rosseau, together with some adjacent mainland, from Thomas L. Snow's brother, Cecil, and additional acreage from Thomas L. Snow in 1902. The property, consisting of approximately 100 acres, was in Wilson's estate at the time of his death. Wilson had earlier planned to build a house on this property.
    [2] H. J. Gregory-Allen.

To Edwin Anderson Alderman

                                                    [The White House]
My dear President Alderman: 22 October, 1920

Of course, you may use my name on the Honorary National committee which is to be appointed in connection with the attempt to celebrate the Centennial of the foundation of the University by raising an endowment fund of $3,000,000. I shall be glad to be associated with the effort.

    In haste, with warmest regard,
                            Sincerely yours,   [Woodrow Wilson]

CCL (WP, DLC).

From Joseph Patrick Tumulty

Dear Governor: The White House 22 October 1920.

Senator Pat Harrison who is in charge of the Speakers' Bureau at the New York headquarters, just had me on the telephone and asked me to say to you how much Governor Cox and the men at headquarters would appreciate a smashing blow from you by the middle of next week. They are all very enthusiastic.

The attached telegram from Doremus[1] speaks for itself.

You will be interested in the attached editorials from The Springfield REPUBLICAN[2] and the New York WORLD[3] showing the vacillating attitude of "our friend on the other side."

                            Sincerely,   J. P. Tumulty

TLS (WP, DLC).
    [1] Frank Ellsworth Doremus, Democratic congressman from Michigan, then in the Democratic campaign headquarters in Chicago, to JPT, Oct. 22, 1920, T telegram (WP, DLC): "We are coming from behind. Tremendous change in sentiment everywhere. Splendid reports coming in. Everybody feels it. It is in the air. Even Republicans admit it, but claim we haven't time to overtake them. Their only concern now is the calendar."
    [2] "After Election," Springfield, Mass., Republican, Oct. 21, 1920, clipping in WP, DLC. This editorial contrasted Harding's declarations on the League issue with those of Root and Taft and said that it was idle perhaps to continue "the farce of quoting him [Harding] either on one side or the other." It concluded, however, that Harding had every League opponent on his side and asked whether Root and Taft were "such imbeciles as not to know what they are doing."

³ "Government by Fraud," New York *World*, Oct. 22, 1920, clipping in WP, DLC, also contrasted Harding's utterances with those of Root and Taft and observed that the whole Republican campaign was based on the premise that the American people were fools. It concluded: "The same kind of fraud that is made a penal offense when practiced by an individual has been erected into a system of government by the Republican leaders of the United States."

From William Douglas Mackenzie,[1] with Enclosure

My dear Mr. President: Hartford, Conn. October 22, 1920.

You have encouraged me in the past to write to you on important matters. Here is one more such letter of daring.

I have been working hard and speaking in public for the election of Governor Cox. I have come to know the feeling of the people. Strange to say—thousands have not yet decided how to vote. We have won on the argument. *But* here is the greatest obstacle to our victory—the hearts of the people are filled with fear. They have been confused and made afraid that the League means war, and that the young men will be called to form large draft armies to keep the peace under the League. This fear is real and it is the chief factor in many minds against Governor Cox.

It cannot be remedied by argument. The Democratic Committee have not the money or the time to cover the Country with the counter-victory facts.

One man only can do it. It is yourself, Mr. President.

I do not mean that you should issue any appeal for a party vote, because this time parties are broken up.

But I do plead with you to issue next Tuesday a statement which will command the attention of the whole Country and instantly remove that deadly fear which is the one emotion now against the League.

In order to be clear, and having thought deeply over this vital point and the method of dealing with it, I have greatly dared. Here is a rough draft of such a statement, as in the name of our sacred cause, I beg from you. It puts the essential points before you as they are pressed to my mind, that you may see most clearly what I mean.

God bless and restore you!

Your affectionate friend, W. Douglas Mackenzie

TLS (WP, DLC).
¹ Wilson's friend of many years, President of the Hartford Seminary Foundation since 1904: distinguished clergyman and scholar.

E N C L O S U R E

As Election Day approaches, it is clear that one question out-tops all others in the minds of the citizens of the United States. All other questions, even the most important, have become secondary to that.

It is the question whether the United States shall or shall not take its rightful place in the League of Nations, which is now so firmly established with forty-three nation members, and which has already entered on its glorious work of securing the permanent peace of the world.

A large number of people are hesitating about their vote even though they do passionately desire peace and an association of nations authorized to make it secure forever. They have been made afraid of the League as already established, as one that is more likely to cause than to prevent war. This infamous suggestion, which forty-three nations have scorned, is based on the following arguments: First, that Article X pledges every Government in the League to make war whenever any changes of present national boundaries are made anywhere in the world.—This is false.

The Covenant provides in Article X that only those changes shall be resisted by the League of Nations which are produced by the "aggression" of one nation against another. Further, the Covenant in Article XVI provides that in case force needs to be used by the League to prevent an aggressive nation from crushing its neighbor, certain action will be taken. It will "recommend to the several Governments concerned" what effective force shall be used "to protect the covenants of the League." Article X must always be read with Article XV and XVI, as belonging together. Second, the cruel and false fear has been awakened especially in the hearts of the women of our land that the League of Nations will require the raising of large forces, even of draft armies, to keep the peace.

Let this fear die from all hearts! The exact opposite is the case. The Covenant of the League provides for the three steps, the first of which will be immediately taken, for reducing armaments through the world. Because the League is established, draft armies should never again be needed. The small regular armies which will be maintained by all the nation members of the League will be ample for all their purposes.

Enormous burdens of taxation will then be lifted from the shoulders of all industries and cruel fear from the hearts of all mothers of men.

The Monroe Doctrine has kept the Western Hemisphere free from external aggression for a hundred years. The Covenant of the

League of Nations will give the world for "a thousand years of peace."

Let all speakers of the League of Nations diligently present these facts to all our fellow citizens till election day, and free our land from the reproach of isolation and the hearts of our citizens from this false and cruel fear.

One chair in the Council of the League, three chairs in the Assembly of the League are vacant which belong to the United States.

Let them be filled to our great honor, and the joy of our fellow men over all the earth.

T MS (WP, DLC).

From Jacob David Schwarz[1]

Dear President: New York October 22nd, 1920.

On November 4th a group of one hundred prominent bankers, merchants, business men, educators and philanthropists, headed by Julius Rosenwald of Chicago, Congressman Julius Kahn of San Francisco, Mortimer L. Schiff and Manny Strauss[2] of New York will start on a forty day tour through principal cities of the country to bring the message of rejuvenated Judaism to the Jews of America.

The members of the "flying squadron" will address mass meetings, setting forth the spiritual needs of Israel and appeal for a stronger and more active Judaism. The tour is part of a national campaign to raise three and one half million dollars for a ten year extension program of the Hebrew Union College at Cincinnati (a college for the ordination of rabbis) for synagogue extension and Jewish education throughout the land by preventing the enactment of class legislation.

We are anxious to bring this matter prominently to the attention of the American people. Will you not, therefore, lend it your endorsement and send us a statement which we may give to the public during the tour of the "flying squadron?"

             Very sincerely yours,   Jacob D Schwarz

P.S. Marked copies of Union Bulletin, official organ of the Union of American Hebrew Congregations, explaining the forty day Tour are being forwarded to you, under separate cover.[3]

TLS (WP, DLC).
  [1] Rabbi Schwarz was Assistant Secretary of the Union of American Hebrew Congregations.

² Rosenwald and Kahn have appeared in this series many times. Mortimer Leo Schiff, a son of Jacob Henry Schiff, was a partner in the New York banking firm of Kuhn, Loeb & Co. Manny Strauss was president of Strauss System Service and lived at 1350 Madison Ave., New York.
³ They are missing in WP, DLC.

To Rolland Barr Bradley[1]

[The White House] 23 October, 1920

Please convey my warmest greetings to the meeting. The young men and women of the country should be even more deeply interested in this critical contest than other Americans, for the issues are the issues of the future. They will determine the future influence and greatness of the United States in the counsels of nations. They will determine our moral force in all the great pending contests of right with which the world is already quick. I believe that the young men and women of the country will see the vision of opportunity which now presents itself and will rally to the support of the perpetuation of the high ideals for which we fought in the great war.   Woodrow Wilson.

T telegram (Letterpress Books, WP, DLC).
¹ Bradley, a student at Columbia University of the Class of 1921, was president of the recently organized Young Americans' Democratic League, with headquarters at 617 Fifth Avenue. Henry Morgenthau, Jr., was a vice-president.

From James Middleton Cox

New York, October 23, 1920.

I regret more than I can say your absence, but I appreciate still more your expression of good will.   James M. Cox.

T telegram (WP, DLC).

From William Bauchop Wilson

My dear Mr. President: Washington October 23, 1920.

With further reference to the correspondence with Mr. Gowan [Gowen] and others relative to the reinstatement with seniority rights of men who engaged in the so-called outlaw railway strike of last spring, and my letter of October 21st to Secretary Tumulty on the subject, I have hesitated to take any definite action in the matter without specific authority from you because labor disputes on the railway systems of the country do not come under the jurisdiction of the Department of Labor. The policy of the Department, therefore, in the past has been simply to cooperate with those having jurisdiction whenever they felt that our cooperation would be helpful.

The situation complained of by Mr. Gowan is not exactly a labor dispute, but, more properly speaking, an aftermath of a labor dispute that has not been fully cleaned up. If you so desire, I will be glad to call a conference of the Railway Brotherhood Chiefs with a view to straightening out the difficulty.

Please advise me of your wishes in the matter.

Faithfully yours,   W B Wilson

TLS (WP, DLC).

From Bainbridge Colby

My dear Mr. President: Washington October 23, 1920.

A telegram received today from Professor A. C. Coolidge, of Harvard, states that he is not in a position to accept a place upon the Aland Island Commission.

Would you consider Ambassador Davis a good appointment for this work?

The name of Judge Abram I. Elkus also occurs to me. He is now a Judge of the Court of Appeals, the highest court in New York, and might be able to obtain a leave of absence. His experience as an Ambassador and his distinction as a Judge would make his appointment a suitable one.

Ambassador Davis, however, is leaving for England on November 2d, and would thus be able to undertake the work with more promptness, possibly, than anyone else. For the reasons I mentioned in my former letter this is an important aspect of the case.

Very respectfully yours,   Bainbridge Colby

TLS (WP, DLC).

From John Llewellyn Lewis

[Oct. 24, 1920]

Eleven thousand coal miners are on strike in Alabama for the right to deal with their employers through representatives of their own choosing—the right of collective bargaining, which was guaranteed them and all other workers by the Government for the period of the war in your proclamation of April 8, 1918,[1] which was recommended by the Bituminous Coal Commission in its award,[2] which has the sanction of an enlightened world opinion as evidenced by the labor provisions of the Peace Treaty, which was affirmed by your second industrial conference and which is pledged in the Democratic national platform adopted at San Francisco. These Alabama miners are being systematically blacklisted, a form of discrimination against which they were also guaranteed protection by their Government under its war powers.

These 11,000 mine workers have dependent upon them some 9,000 women and 22,000 children. This great number of people are being kept from starvation only by the pitifully meagre fare contributed by the Mine Workers' Union. Poverty in its most terrible form stalks through the mining camps of Alabama, accompanied by the twin spectres of malnutrition and disease. Every conceivable instrument of oppression is being used against these people by the powerful interests associated in the coal industry of Alabama. Thousands of eviction suits have occurred, and in a multiplicity of instances writs of attachments have been issued and the household furniture and personal possessions of the miners' families have been carted away from their humble domiciles. The mining villages are being policed by private policemen in the employ of the coal operators, and indignities and outrages have been inflicted upon the mine workers and their families. The officers of the Commonwealth of Alabama are seemingly co-operating with the coal operators. In token thereof the Governor is maintaining eleven companies of State militia on duty in the coal fields. This soldiery has invaded the constitutional rights of the citizens of the mining towns by suspending the right of public meetings and free assemblage and the enforcement of this decree by armed force.

Since the beginning of this strike every honorable attempt has been made by the representatives of the mine workers in Alabama to secure a settlement.

More recently the mine workers' representatives in Alabama in a further attempt to secure just consideration proposed that the President of the United States appoint a commission of his own choosing to decide all questions in controversy, the mine workers agreeing that the judgment of such a commission would be punctiliously observed. This offer also was rejected.

As the authorized representative of the half million mine workers who are members of the United Mine Workers of America and who ardently sympathize with the great struggle now being waged by the Alabama Mine Workers I most earnestly urge that you immediately direct the Department of Justice of the United States Government to institute such legal proceedings as may be necessary to compel observance of the principle of collective bargaining and the protection of the civil rights of the Mine Workers of Alabama.

Printed in the *New York Times*, Oct. 25, 1920.
¹ This proclamation established the National War Labor Board (William Howard Taft and Francis Patrick Walsh were named as the public members and became cochairmen of the board) for the mediation of all labor disputes affecting the conduct of the war. Wilson directed the board to follow the principles adopted by its organizing body, the War Labor Conference Board. One of them upheld labor's right to organize and guaranteed the right of workers to bargain "through chosen representatives," without interference from employers "in any manner whatsoever." See Valerie Jean Conner, *The National War Labor Board: Stability, Social Justice, and the Voluntary State in World War I* (Chapel Hill, N. C., 1983), pp. 27-30. Wilson's proclamation establishing the National War Labor Board is printed at April 8, 1918, Vol. 47.
² About which, see W. D. Hines to JPT, March 17, 1920, n. 1, Vol. 65.

To Bainbridge Colby

My dear Mr. Secretary: The White House 25 October, 1920

I have your letter of October twenty-third. I am sincerely sorry that Professor Coolidge is not in a position to accept a place upon the Aaland Island Commission.

I note your suggestion that Ambassador Davis should serve, but I must frankly say that I do not think that would be a suitable choice. Judge Elkus would make an excellent member and I hope that you will propose the appointment to him in my name.
                    Cordially and sincerely yours,   Woodrow Wilson

TLS (SDR, RG 59, 758.6114A1/130, DNA).

To William Bauchop Wilson

My dear Mr. Secretary: The White House 25 October, 1920

My own judgment is that it would not be wise for us at present to intervene in the situation complained of by Mr. Gowan [Gowen] and referred to in your letter of October twenty-third, but, as you know, I will always be inclined to yield to your judgment and follow out any plan that you might suggest.
                    Cordially and faithfully yours,   Woodrow Wilson

TLS (received from Mary A. Strohecker).

To Jacob David Schwarz

My dear Mr. Schwarz: [The White House] 25 October, 1920

Your letter of October twenty-second affords me a most welcome opportunity to express my very deep interest in the movement which is being pushed forward by the Union of American Hebrew Congregations to set forth the spiritual needs of Israel and to appeal for a stronger and more active Judaism, and also to raise money for a ten-year extension programme. I sincerely hope that the efforts the Union is making will be crowned with complete success.

Cordially and sincerely yours,   [Woodrow Wilson]

CCL (WP, DLC).

To William Edward Dodd

My dear Professor Dodd: The White House 25 October, 1920

Your letter of October twenty-first was very welcome, and I have read it with great interest and not a little reassurance. I thank you for it most sincerely.

I am very glad indeed that you understood my attitude towards your suggestion with regard to Mr. Roosevelt. I was sure that you would.

With warm regard,   Sincerely yours,   Woodrow Wilson

TLS (W. E. Dodd Papers, DLC).

To Jessie Woodrow Wilson Sayre

My dearest Jessie: [The White House] 25 October, 1920

I need not tell you how welcome your letter was.[1] I wait for your letters with the greatest interest and with the keenest desire to pick up every item I can about you and Frank and the children.

We are pegging along here in the usual way. I hobble from one part of the house to the other and go through the motions of working every morning, though I am afraid it is work that doesn't count very much. Margaret is settled in her apartment in New York and seems very jubilant over the whole change and the little home that it has brought her. Nell is in the West with Mac, as probably you know, and all I know of them is that the papers say that his voice has gone back and he has had to stop for treatment, temporarily at any rate. All our days follow the routine that you became familiar with when you were here, but no routine excludes constant thought of you and our other dear ones.

I do not like to disappoint Mrs. Brown,[2] but she has outlined for us such extravagant plans, I mean such extravagantly fanciful plans, for the wedding that I must in frankness say that I should not like to see the children included in the pageant. This is just a postponement of the pleasure of seeing them, a pleasure which I should be sorely disappointed if I did not have very soon.

With warmest love from us both,

Your affectionate   [Father]

P.S. I return the wonderful letter from Miss Pennington,[3] but have taken the liberty of keeping a copy of it rather than keep the letter.

CCL (WC, NjP).
    [1] It is missing.
    [2] Mary Celestine Mitchell (Mrs. Edward Thomas) Brown, wife of Ellen Axson Wilson's first cousin; mother of Marjorie Brown, who was to be married in Washington to Benjamin Mandeville King on December 28, 1920.
    [3] Mabel Vanderpool Pennington to an unknown person ("Most dear and sweet friend"), Sept. 8, 1920, TCL (WP, DLC), which reads in part:
    "I hope you had a lovely visit from Mr. and Mrs. Sayre. Great Heavens!—think of being His daughter, in these very solemn and terrible times!
    "I wonder if our Angel in the White House ever thinks of the anguish of those who watched his lofty courage through all his varied sufferings! I would throw my life away if I could so save him one heart-beat of his pain—and I don't mean physical pain, though I would do it for that, too.
    "Why, he is all that keeps us from despair! That such a life can occur among us—(dogs, I was going to say, but I like dogs)—stands as a star of hope for us—but what agony that our recognition and gratitude can't reach him and he be granted the homage and idolatry countless millions justly render him in their deepest hearts and souls!
    "Are you familiar with Browning's 'Paracelsus?' Do read in this connection the fifth and last section of it. He they stoned to death for his life's devotion to Humanity. The lines are very apt."

From Joseph Patrick Tumulty

My dear Governor: The White House 25 October 1920.

The concluding paragraphs of the accompanying letter contain a threat that unless you repudiate Governor Cox's utterances in Massachusetts interpreting Article XI, this organization, so-called "The Loyal Coalition," will "tour the doubtful states to apprise the voters, particularly those interested in the League of Nations, of the menace both to America and to the League of Nations, from Irish intrigue."[1]

The situation in Massachusetts is swinging our way. You will notice from the enclosed clipping that Dr. Eliot has given out a fine statement backing up your's and Governor Cox's interpretation of Article XI, as giving a forum to any distressed people who are asking for freedom and the right of self-determination.[2]

If you wish to say anything on this matter, this letter affords you a fine opportunity.

If I may suggest, it might be well to emphasize that the United States would be false to its history and its traditions if it were to enter into any agreement with other nations which would prevent a struggling people to achieve that which came to us from the Revolution of 1776.   Tumulty

I shall take no notice whatsoever of this and beg that you will take none whatever   W.W.

TLS (J. P. Tumulty Papers, DLC).
   [1] Demarest Lloyd to WW, Oct. 21, 1920, TLS (J. P. Tumulty Papers, DLC). Lloyd, the son of the late Henry Demarest Lloyd, was president of "The Loyal Coalition" of Boston. This group had earlier described itself as a nationwide organization for the preservation of American ideals and traditions. It had been formed specifically to combat "Sinn Fein propaganda." *New York Times*, May 8 and July 19, 1920.
   Cox, in a speech delivered on the Boston Common on the evening of October 19, 1920, had made the following statement: "For 700 years Ireland has sought to be free. In all that time they haven't been able to get their case into any fair court for consideration. But Article 11 of the covenant of the League of Nations provides for such a court. If I become your President I shall exercise the authority as President of a Nation which I am sure is going to become a member of the League of Nations and I shall myself present the matter of Ireland to the bar of the League. Some say that it is a domestic question and concerns England only. It has become a world question—more than that, a world tragedy. We have laws of Nations and laws of God, and to deny that a war of extermination is a question for the whole world to settle is to deny those laws. The war of extermination in Ireland ought to come to an end." *Boston Daily Globe*, Oct. 20, 1920. Cox had said much the same thing in a speech earlier that day in Worcester, Massachusetts. *Boston Evening Globe*, Oct. 19, 1920.
   [2] John J. Foley of Boston, president of the Central Council of the Irish County Association, had written to Charles W. Eliot, asking how the Irish question could be brought before the League of Nations for debate. Eliot replied as follows:
   "The veto which every nation possesses in the Assembly and the Council provided by the League of Nations relates to action by the Assembly or the Council, such as the passing of a resolution or order, or the making of an ordinance; but there is nothing to prevent the introduction of any international subject for consideration or discussion in either the Assembly or the Council. Indeed, it is a main object of the League to secure discussion of all difficulties arising or arisen between nations, in order, if possible, to prevent, by the force of international public opinion, the outbreak of war, or bring about an allayment of any international quarrel or strife which might cause war.
   "If the League of Nations were in unembarrassed operation, discussion of the Irish question in the Assembly or the Council would be absolutely appropriate and, indeed, a natural and desirable use of the representative bodies instituted by the League of Nations. I venture to suggest that the Central Council of Irish County Associations use all its influence forthwith—the time is short—in support of the Democratic Party and its candidate, Governor Cox, who has distinctly stated that if elected President he will bring the Irish problem to the attention of the League of Nations." *New York Times*, Oct. 24, 1920.

From Isabella Sheldon Owen Osgood[1]

                                        Princeton, New Jersey
My dear President Wilson: Monday October twenty-fifth [1920]

It has been in my heart many times to write to you to express my concern and sympathy in your illness, and my wishes for your speedy and complete recovery.

There is much else that I wish to say, without any real hope of being able to express it all.

Our warm admiration and affectionate regard for you have

grown and grown through all these years. We have seen you stand as the great prophet whom God has raised up for this crisis, as one of the two or three supreme men whom America has given to the world, and yet, through it all, we feel you the friend of your old Princeton friends.

Do you remember that in the mosaic above your head in Alexander Hall were the words Χιλίων ἐτέων ἀφικνέοται φωνή?[2] We little dreamed then that *your* voice[3] would indeed reach through the ages.

Each time that I re-read your great messages there is the same thrill, the same assurance that, founded on eternal truth, they are immortal, and a reawakened faith that somehow America will rise to the realization of her destiny.

In the group of the faculty here who are our intimate friends, you are always the beloved leader, and the inspiration for all that they are trying to do.

I need not tell you of our deep concern and anxiety when we saw you struck down like a soldier in battle, and our joy when the steady improvement in your health began.

With heartfelt wishes for your complete recovery, dear Mr. President, I have the honour to be

Always your devoted friend,   Bella Owen Osgood

ALS (WP, DLC).
    [1] Mrs. Charles Grosvenor Osgood.
    [2] "A voice reaches to a thousand years," adapted from Plutarch, *Moralia* 397A. (Courtesy of Bruce M. Metzger.)
    [3] Mrs. Osgood, who grew up in Princeton, probably heard Wilson deliver his address, "Princeton in the Nation's Service," in Alexander Hall on October 21, 1896, during the sesquicentennial celebration of Princeton University. The address is printed at that date in Vol. 10.

From Joseph Patrick Tumulty, with Enclosure

[The White House] 26 October 1920.

The Secretary begs to call the President's attention to this letter from George Creel, addressed to the Secretary of State.[1]

How did this come into our hands?   W.W.[2]

TL (WP, DLC).
    [1] Creel wrote about this letter to Tumulty as follows: "Please read & hand to President. Will come down tomorrow night, reaching there Wednesday a.m." G. Creel to JPT [c. Oct. 25, 1920], AL (WP, DLC). Creel had lunch with Wilson on October 28.
    [2] JPT to WW, Oct. 27, 1920, TLS (WP, DLC): "Dear Governor: Creel sent this to me, as his note attached shows."

E N C L O S U R E

George Creel to Bainbridge Colby

Dear Mr. Secretary: [New York] October 23rd 1920.

Mr. Pesqueira called me over long distance today and told me that he had not been able to see you and Mr. Davis together, but only Mr. Davis. Also that the interview was not conclusive and that the next engagement was for Tuesday.

As you know, my principal interest in the matter has been the vindication of the President. I have always felt that his Mexican policy was his finest expression of ideals in practice, and it is my hope to see this policy crowned with a success so complete as to leave no doubt of its wisdom in any mind.

I have the deep conviction that if anything is to be done it must be done before November 2. Recognition, if given after the election, would undoubtedly be attacked on the ground that another Chief Executive has already been indicated. The chief consideration, however, is the effect of positive action upon the election itself. There is not a doubt in my mind that the settlement of the Mexican question along big, fine lines will prove a tremendous factor in the campaign.

It is to this end that I have addressed every activity. As a private citizen, and at my own expense, I went to Mexico and secured agreement on every point in dispute. Publicly, bravely, President de la Huerta paid a great tribute to the courage and idealism of Woodrow Wilson and not only lauded the League of Nations, but made it plain that Mexico meant to enter if invited. Aside from these two things—that you felt sure he would not do—he stated that Mexico would pay every debt, agree to any fair border agreement, and that Mexico would pledge herself against the confiscation of private property.[1]

Mr. Pesqueira returned with me to the United States bearing the most complete power of attorney ever given to an agent. After talking with you and Mr. Davis I drew up an informal agreement to serve as the basis for a protocol. In this agreement there was provision for the formation of a claims commission, its findings to be final, provision for the formation of an arbitration commission, with first task to decide upon border control, and second task to settle every future dispute between the two nations, and a third provision that Mexico bound herself to give no retroactive effect to Article 27.[2]

I explained to Mr. Pesqueira that if he signed such a protocol that it bound his country absolutely, and that when the provisions were written into treaty stipulations after recognition, they would be superior to any law that might be passed. It was with this full knowledge that he gave his consent. I then showed the memorandum to you and your hearty approval made me feel that the whole matter was ready to go to the President.

As near as I could gather over the telephone, Mr. Davis is still of the opinion that Mexico should take action on Article 27 before we do anything. Is it not the case that Pesqueira's signature to the protocol, specifically authorized by de la Huerta, binds Mexico as surely as a nation can be bound?

There is no question that Mexico means to take such action with respect to Article 27, either in the form of a presidential decree, authorized by Congress, or by Supreme Court interpretation. There was clear understanding as to this, and we agreed upon fundamentals and form. I thought that it would have been done before this, but some very natural delays are developing owing to the fact that de la Huerta does not want to give the impression of "railroading." All of us, therefore, had the thought that an ironclad agreement against retroactive application of Article 27, included [in] a protocol, and signed by the duly authorized representative of the Mexican government, would meet every demand of the situation.

I want to assure you again of my faith in de la Huerta, Obregon and Calles. The Mexican people, however, are very bitter against the American oil men, however, and the Government, to retain confidence, must avoid the appearance of unconditional surrender.

I trust that you will take this letter up with Mr. Davis and see if some quick decision cannot be reached. Frankly, I see no reason why recognition should not come at once if Pesqueira signs the protocol. And recognition carries many big things in its train. It means that Mexico will be able to build strongly before March 4, and that the President's policy will have been brought to complete success, and that the interventionist attitude of Harding will be shown to the people in all of its ugly shamelessness.

De la Huerta and Obregon will follow with appreciations of what the President's policy has done for Mexico, also what his ideals have done for the world, and I am convinced that I can get him to embody an even stronger indorsement of the League of Nations. I am sending a copy of this letter to the President, more as a report than anything else.

Please convey my warm regards to Mr. Davis, and tell him how happy I was to know him.

Always sincerely,   George Creel.[3]

TCL (WP, DLC).

[1] De la Huerta spoke to a group of foreign correspondents on October 15 and gave them a statement expressing his hope for recognition by the United States. It was reported that the statement had been prepared in collaboration with President-elect Álvaro Obregón. De la Huerta asserted that the recent Mexican national elections had been held "in strict accordance with democratic procedure" and that Mexico had "already entered into a state of tranquility and reconstruction." On two of the most critical points of contention between the United States and Mexico, De la Huerta said the following:

"Our country opens its arms to foreigners in the same manner that it does to its own nationals, inviting them to come and share in our riches, to aid in the development of our national resources, and favors all enterprises willing to recognize the great truth that the national resources of a nation belong to the nation itself. Mexico will know how to comply with what on so many occasions she has said, and which I now desire to repeat. Our republic will pay all that it justly owes in conformity with all of the recognized principles of international law."

De la Huerta emphatically denied that the Mexican government had ever, or ever even intended, to confiscate the property of foreigners. "The Mexican government," he said, "will respect and cause to be respected all rights legitimately acquired under the protection of its own laws."

He declared that the present Mexican government would work with those of the United States and Guatemala to avoid "disturbances which might arise along the boundaries, in order to insure the stable peace and cordiality which at present prevail."

De la Huerta also paid a glowing tribute to Woodrow Wilson:

"President Wilson is a man of noblest ideals, proved in practice, and he has fought for them in his country against extraordinary forces of reaction in an exaggerated form. He has outlined the evolution of this people with unfailing certainty. He has been defending justice during these times when the peoples of the earth are shaken by stormy currents which disorganize the balance of society.

"He has striven nobly against the avalanche of interventionists who, not satisfied with the profits which they secure from their speculations upon our soil, desire to subjugate our people. He has endeavored in a thousand ways to bring about understanding between the laboring classes of his country and the laboring classes of our nation."

When asked his opinion of the League of Nations, De la Huerta replied: "It will be a beneficial institution to humanity. If its realization is not attained the responsibility will rest upon those who by means of political machinations are endeavoring to overthrow a noble idea which, if it became a fact, would bring with it peace between all nations and tranquility for the great human family." *New York Times*, Oct. 16, 1920.

[2] That is, Article XXVII of the Mexican Constitution of 1917, about which, see n. 2 to the extract from the Diary of C. P. Anderson printed at March 8, 1917, Vol. 41.

[3] The TLS is G. Creel to BC, Oct. 23, 1920 (SDR, RG 59, 812.00/24746½, DNA).

From Mary Fels Fels[1]

Dear Mr. President: Philadelphia Oct. 26, 1920.

A year, and more, before your first nomination I saw that you were the man who should and probably would, be our next President.

I worked for your second election with the fervor of one who felt the weal of the world was involved. I was right each time.

And now I am, and have all the time been, feeling and thinking that the people will not choose Harding, will not abet the Republican Senators. Instead, they will endorse—you.

And may I say that my own admiration for you increases and deepens constantly.

                    Very sincerely,   Mary Fels. (Mrs. Joseph Fels.)

ALS (WP, DLC).
  [1] Widow of Joseph Fels (about whom, see J. Fels to WW, Dec. 29, 1910, n. 1, Vol. 22). Mrs. Fels was active as a lecturer on, and advocate of, the single tax and Zionism.

A News Report

[*Oct. 27, 1920*]

WILSON URGES ARTICLE X. AS PLEDGE;
SHOWS ILLNESS IN PLEA FROM CHAIR

Washington, Oct. 27.—To a delegation of fifteen pro-League Republicans who were received by him in the White House this morning,[1] President Wilson, seated in a chair, read an address on the League of Nations. . . .

The occasion was impressive by reason of the fact that it marked the delivery of the first formal address that President Wilson had made since he was stricken more than a year ago. But it was additionally impressive on account of the perceptible effect of illness on the President and the emotion he showed while reading his address to the delegation.

His callers were shocked by the President's appearance, and as much was admitted in a guarded way in a formal statement given out in behalf of the delegates after their visit. The statement said that the members felt that this might be the President's final appeal to the conscience of his countrymen.

When the members of the delegation were ushered into the room at the White House where the ceremony took place they found President Wilson seated in a rolling chair. He did not at first seem to recognize any of the visitors, several of whom he had known. Then he spoke to Theodore Marburg of Baltimore, whom he called by name. The President announced last week the appointment of Mr. Marburg as a member of the Shipping Board, but Mr. Marburg has since declined the appointment.

Having reference to Mr. Marburg's declination, as it subsequently appeared, the President said to the latter: "I received a very unwelcome letter from you last week." He spoke so low that the members of the delegation gathered around him could not catch his words. Even Mr. Marburg misunderstood.

"I am glad you thought it a welcome letter, Mr. President," said Mr. Marburg.

"I did not say 'welcome,' I said 'unwelcome,'" responded the President, "It was a call to duty."

_____

  [1] At 11 a.m. in a small room off Wilson's study near the entrance to the White House.

Dr. Hamilton Holt of New York, who headed the delegation, read a brief address explaining the object of the visit. President Wilson then read his response. He apologized for not standing, and explained that he was sorry that he was obliged to read the address instead of delivering it without manuscript.

Although they were standing near him and there was silence in the room except for the sound of the President's voice, the delegates could scarcely hear what he said. Some of them described his voice as very thick and so low that it had no carrying force. It is doubtful if all that he said was heard or understood. The impression carried away from the President's room was that his progress toward recovery had been seriously retarded.

The formal statement in behalf of the delegation, given to the press by Dr. Holt after the call, read as follows:

"The members of the deputation were deeply touched by the physical appearance of the President, who received them sitting and plainly showed the effects of his long illness and the tremendous strain which he has been carrying. He read from a manuscript his reply to the address of the deputation, and was greatly moved as he did so.

"More than once his voice choked, especially when he referred to the soldier boys and the mothers of those who had fallen in battle. It was evident that he was voicing the profoundest emotions of his heart. The whole occasion was inexpressively solemn and tender.

"It was evident that the President's intellectual powers were in no way impaired, but the deputation felt that it was nothing less than tragic that the great President of the United States should have been brought to such a stricken physical condition as the result of his indefatigable labors for his country and for humanity.

"They felt that this might be the President's final appeal to the conscience of his countrymen in the supreme moral decision that they are called upon to make."

The members of the delegation were:

Dr. Hamilton Holt, editor of the Independent and head of the Committee of Pro-League Republicans of New York.

Theodore Marburg of Baltimore, former Minister to Belgium.

Edwin F. Gay, President of The Evening Post of New York.

John F. Moors,[2] Chairman of the League of Nations Club of Massachusetts.

Mrs. John F. Moors,[3] Treasurer of the Pro-League Republicans of Massachusetts.

---

[2] John Farwell Moors, senior member of the brokerage firm of Moors & Cabot of Boston.
[3] Ethel Lyman Paine Moors.

Mrs. Schuyler N. Warren,[4] New York, Director of the League for Political Education.

Schuyler N. Warren, Jr.,[5] New York.

Mrs. J. Malcolm Forbes,[6] Boston, President of the Women Voters Association of Massachusetts.

Joseph M. Price,[7] New York, Chairman of the Board of Trustees of the City Club.

John Bates Clark, Professor of Economics of Columbia University.

Dr. John Spencer Bassett, Professor of History, Smith College.

D. C. Rowse,[8] New York.

The Rev. Arthur J. Brown,[9] Honorary Vice President of the League to Enforce Peace.

George K. Hunton,[10] New York.

Colonel Samuel P. Wetherill, Jr.,[11] head of the Pro-League Republican movement of Philadelphia.

After Dr. Holt had presented the members of the delegation to the President he read this address:

"Mr. President, we are a group of men and women who, although we usually count ourselves Republicans, hold steadfastly to the conviction that the League of Nations transcends party politics and is the greatest moral issue that has confronted the American people in this generation.

"We have reason to know that we represent a vast number of other Republicans throughout the United States who are ready to put patriotism above party in the present critical hour.

"As your term of office is drawing to a close, and as the people are now about to express themselves on the League of Nations which your statesmanship has largely made possible, we feel it both a duty and a privilege to call upon you at this time in order to assure you that there are many Republicans who are proud to acknowledge your great services in the realm of international justice and who fully and deeply appreciate the personal sacrifices you have been forced to make for the cause nearest your heart.

[4] Alice Edith Binsse Warren.   [5] Schuyler Neilson Warren, Jr.
[6] Rose Dabney Forbes.
[7] Joseph Morris Price, president of the Improved Mailing Case Co. of New York and active in political reform in that city; chairman of the Fusion executive committee in the mayoral campaign of 1913; organizer and chairman of the Wilson Independent League in 1916.
[8] Unidentified.
[9] Arthur Judson Brown, distinguished clergyman and author; secretary of the Presbyterian Board of Foreign Missions and chairman of the committee on relations with France and Belgium of the Federal Council of Churches of Christ in America.
[10] Lawyer of New York, prominent in the movement for racial justice, later executive secretary of the Catholic Interracial Council and a director of the N.A.A.C.P.
[11] Samuel Price Wetherill, Jr., lieutenant colonel in the U.S.A. Reserve Corps; industrial engineer and manufacturer, active in social reform and philanthropic causes in Philadelphia.

"It was you who first focused the heterogeneous and often diverse aims of the war on the one ideal of pure Americanism, which is democracy. It was you who suggested the basis on which peace was negotiated. It was you, more than any man, who translated into practical statesmanship the age-old dreams of the poets, the prophets, and the philosophers by setting up a League of Nations to the end that cooperation could be substituted for competition in international affairs.

"These acts of statesmanship were undoubtedly the chief factors which brought about that victorious peace which has shorn Germany of her power to subdue her neighbors, has compelled her to make restitution for her crimes, has freed oppressed peoples, has restored ravaged territories, has created new democracies in the likeness of the United States, and above all has set up the League of Nations.

"When our forefathers met at Independence Hall, Philadelphia, over one hundred years ago, and signed the Declaration of Independence, they took no counsel of cowardice, but mutually pledged their lives, their fortunes, and their sacred honor to the principles enunciated in that immortal document. The United States of America resulted.

"If now, all the citizens of America who claim to be true friends of the Covenant, take no counsel of cowardice, but mutually pledge themselves to the great Declaration of Interdependence so nobly championed by you and the best of other good men in this and other lands, then the United States will enter the League, the United Nations of the World will result, and our boys whose blood hallows the fields of France will not have died in vain."

The Rev. Arthur J. Brown spoke as follows:

"Mr. President: Will you permit me as a Republican and as a clergyman to say that a far larger number of the Christian people of this country than you perhaps realize have you in their heart and pray that the blessing of Almighty God may rest upon you and give you faith and strength for your many burdens."

[To which Wilson replied: "Thank you all very much indeed. It has been a very special occasion to me."][12]

Printed in the *New York Times*, Oct. 28, 1920.
[12] JRT transcript (WC, NjP) of CLSsh (C. L. Swem Coll., NjP). A few minor corrections in the text above from this transcript.

A Statement[1]

My fellow-countrymen: 27 October, 1920

It is to be feared that the supreme issue presented for your consideration in the present campaign is growing more obscure rather than clearer by reason of the many arbitrary turns the discussion of it has taken. The editors and publishers of the country would render a great service if they would publish the full text of the Covenant of the League of Nations, because, having read that text, you would be able to judge for yourselves a great many things in which you are now in danger of being misled. I hope sincerely that it will be very widely and generally published entire. It is with a desire to reclarify the issue and to assist your judgment that I take the liberty of stating again the case submitted to you, in as simple terms as possible.

Three years ago it was my duty to summon you to the concert of war, to join the free nations of the world in meeting and ending the most sinister peril that had ever been developed in the irresponsible politics of the old world. Your response to that call really settled the fortunes of war. You will remember that the morale of the German people broke down long before the strength of the German armies was broken. That was obviously because they felt that a great moral force which they could not look in the face had come into the contest, and that thenceforth all their professions of right were discredited and they were unable to pretend that their continuation of the war was not the support of a government that had violated every principle of right and every consideration of humanity.

It is my privilege to summon you now to the concert of peace and the completion of the great moral achievement on your part which the war represented and in the presence of which the world found a reassurance and a recovery of force which it could have experienced in no other way. We entered the war, as you remember, not merely to beat Germany, but to end the possibility of the renewal of such iniquitous schemes as Germany entertained. The war will have been fought in vain and our immense sacrifices

[1] Wilson prefaced his reading of this statement with the following remarks: "Thank you, Sir. I have several things to apologize for. First is sitting, which I thank you for. And, second, for serving what my dear father called 'dried tongue' and reading instead of speaking without any script." JRT transcript (WC, NjP) of CLSsh (C. L. Swem Coll., NjP).

Wilson dictated a draft of this statement to Swem on October 24. Swem typed this draft, and Wilson made a number of literary changes in it. On October 25, Wilson dictated several additions for insertion, and Swem then typed up what became the penultimate draft. Swem's shorthand and typed drafts are in the Swem Collection.

Wilson's statement was printed on the first page, e.g., of the *New York Times* and New York *World*, Oct. 28, 1920.

thrown away unless we complete the work we then began, and I ask you to consider that there is only one way to assure the world of peace: that is by making it so dangerous to break the peace that no other nation will have the audacity to attempt it. We should not be deceived into supposing that imperialistic schemes ended with the defeat of Germany, or that Germany is the only nation that entertained such schemes or was moved by sinister ambitions and long-standing jealousies to attack the very structure of civilization. There are other nations which are likely to be powerfully moved or are already moved by commercial jealousy, by the desire to dominate and to have their own way in politics and in enterprise, and it is necessary to check them and to apprise them that the world will be united against them as it was against Germany if they attempt any similar thing.

The mothers and sisters and wives of the country know the sacrifice of war. They will feel that we have misled them and compelled them to make an entirely unnecessary sacrifice of their beloved ones if we do not make it as certain as it can be made that no similar sacrifice will be demanded of mothers and sisters and wives in the future. This duty is so plain that it seems to me to constitute a primary demand upon the conscience of every one of us. It is inconceivable to most of us that any men should have been so false or so heartless as to declare that the women of the country would again have to suffer the intolerable burden and privation of war if the League of Nations were adopted. The League of Nations is the well-considered effort of the whole group of nations who were opposed to Germany to secure themselves and the rest of mankind against a repetition of the war. It will have back of it the watchfulness and material force of all these nations, and is such a guarantee of a peaceful future as no well-informed man can question who does not doubt the whole spirit with which the war was conducted against Germany. The great moral influence of the United States will be absolutely thrown away if we do not complete the task which our soldiers and sailors so heroically undertook to execute.

One thing ought to be said, and said very clearly, about Article X of the Covenant of the League of Nations. It is the specific pledge of the members of the League that they will unite to resist exactly the things which Germany attempted, no matter who attempts them in the future. It is as exact a definition as could be given in general terms of the outrage which Germany would have committed if it could. Germany violated the territorial integrity of her neighbors and flouted their political independence in order to aggrandize herself, and almost every war of history has originated in such designs. It is significant that the nations of the world should have at last combined to define the general cause of war and to exercise such concert as may be necessary to prevent such methods. Article X, therefore, is the specific redemption of the pledge which the free governments of the world gave to their people when they entered the war. They promised their people not only that Germany would be prevented from carrying out her plot, but that the world would be safeguarded in the future from similar designs. We have now to choose whether we will make good or quit. We have joined issue, and the issue is between the spirit and purpose of the United States and the spirit and purpose of imperialism, no matter where it shows itself. The spirit of imperialism is absolutely opposed to free government, to the safe life of free nations, to the development of peaceful industry, and to the completion of the righteous processes of civilization. It seems to me, and I think it will seem to you, that it is our duty to show the indomitable will and irresistible majesty of the high purpose of the United States, so that the part we played in the war as soldiers and sailors may be crowned with the achievement of lasting peace. No one who opposes the ratification of the Treaty of Versailles and the adoption of the Covenant of the League of Nations has proposed any other adequate means of bringing about settled peace. There is no other available or possible means, and this means is ready to hand. They have, on the contrary, tried to persuade you that the very pledge contained in Article X, which is the essential pledge of the whole plan of security, is itself a threat of war. It is, on the contrary, an assurance of the concert of all the free peoples of the world in the future, as in the recent past, to see justice done and humanity protected and vindicated. This is the true, the real Americanism. This is the role of leadership and championship of the right which the leaders of the republic intended that it should play. The so-called Americanism which we hear so much prating about now is spurious and invented for party purposes only.

This choice is the supreme choice of the present campaign. It is regrettable that this choice should be associated with a party contest. As compared with the choice of a course of action that now underlies every other, the fate of parties is a matter of indifference. Parties are significant now in this contest only because the voters must make up their minds which of the two parties is most likely to secure the indispensable result. The nation was never called upon to make a more solemn determination than it must now make. The whole future moral force of right in the world depends upon the United States rather than upon any other nation, and it would be pitiful indeed if, after so many great free peoples had entered the great League, we should hold aloof. I suggest that the candidacy of every candidate for whatever office be tested by this question. Shall we or shall we not redeem the great moral obligations of the United States?

Mimeograph copy (A. S. Burleson Papers, DLC).

From George Foster Peabody

Saratoga Springs, N. Y., Oct. 27, 1920.

Thank you from my heart for the noble words you have addressed to us making so deeply impressive the solemn issue. I am sure it will make the people of all the world feel that they are in a real sense a part of your constant thought. I am confident that it will help greatly to assure the triumph of next Tuesday, of which I have felt sure all along. My heart goes out to you continually, and I rejoice greatly in this latest evidence of your power. The world has much in store for it from your future guidance.

George Foster Peabody.

T telegram (WP, DLC).

From Charles Grosvenor Osgood

Princeton, New Jersey

My dear President Wilson: October 27, 1920

May I express to you my deep concern for your safety and the sympathy which I have felt for you during these many months past, particularly during your illness. As a citizen I am but one of many thousands who are profoundly grateful to you, both for your heroic effort in the cause of justice and righteousness, and for what you have endured in this cause and for our sakes.

The great public measures of which you have been the inspired author, whatever their external history in this imperfect world—whatever momentary reactions they have provoked—have quickened in men's hearts instincts for justice that will, I am convinced, override all blind and selfish opposition.

You have, I know, made better citizens of us individually, and as surely as did Washington and Lincoln, you have, in act and utterance, liberated in this dear land of ours forces that will make for high and pure citizenship through untold generations.

But I must admit a deeper and more personal obligation to you. Dr. Johnson used to say that it was his purpose to teach men as long as he lived; and even in your high office as President, I cannot cease to think of you as a teacher of men.

I often look back to those happy days when you gathered us younger teachers to your leadership here at Princeton. Those were indeed happy days. Such release of energies, such vision and courage, I had never known before. And I can never forget the stirring comradeship, the happy labor for highest things, the intimations of a perfect world, of which we owed the promptings to you.

Since you were here, such courage and clearness of vision have not always been easy to keep. At times the spirit weakens and the vision fades. But if I recall the privilege I had as a teacher of association with you here, and consider your unwavering faithfulness to things of the spirit through these great but trying years, then weakness is rebuked and courage and vision restored. And I am profoundly sure that through the ages your words and acts must ever thus minister to the human spirit in its private and personal struggle.

I pray God that at all times His peace may be yours abundantly.

With warmest regard, I am

Faithfully yours,   Charles G. Osgood

ALS (WP, DLC).

Joseph Patrick Tumulty to John Llewellyn Lewis

My dear Mr. Lewis: The White House October 27, 1920.

I beg to acknowledge the receipt of your telegram of October 24th, and to say that the matter to which you refer is of such importance that the President wishes to confer with the Secretary of Labor concerning it. This will be done as soon as Secretary Wilson returns to the city.   Sincerely yours,   J P Tumulty

TLS (UMWA Archives).

To Charles William Eliot

My dear Doctor Eliot: The White House 28 October, 1920

I feel that I must give myself the pleasure of writing to say how much I admire the invaluable service you have been rendering to the cause of international justice and national honor. It must be an inspiration to the whole nation to read the statements that you have made, and I personally, as one of your fellow-citizens, want to express my sense of gratitude.

 With warmest regard,
   Cordially and sincerely yours, Woodrow Wilson

TLS (C. W. Eliot Papers, MH).

To Frank Lyon Polk

My dear Polk: [The White House] 28 October, 1920

 We have been greatly distressed by the news that you have had to undergo an operation, and I am sending you this line to express our affectionate sympathy and the hope that the operation was in all respects successful and will lead to an early and happy recovery of your full strength. We miss you very much.

 With warmest regard,
   Cordially and faithfully yours, [Woodrow Wilson]

CCL (WP, DLC).

To Joseph Patrick Tumulty

      The White House [c. Oct. 28, 1920].

Please get me out of this in some polite way.[1]

      The President.

TL (WP, DLC).
 [1] This letter was occasioned by James Edward West to WW, Oct. 25, 1920, TLS (WP, DLC). West, the "Chief Scout Executive" of the Boy Scouts of America, informed Wilson that his organization faced a serious financial crisis and was being forced to undertake a fund-raising drive. The first phase of this effort was to be a newspaper advertisement featuring a photograph of Wilson, who was Honorary President of the Boy Scouts of America. The same advertisement would also include photographs of James M. Cox, William G. McAdoo, Herbert Hoover, William H. Taft, and Warren G. Harding. Later advertisements would feature religious leaders and other groups of prominent men. A final large advertisement would include photographs and extracts from endorsements of the Boy Scouts by Wilson and others already on file at Scout headquarters in New York.
 Tumulty's letter to West of October 28, 1920, is missing. However, it is clear from J. E. West to JPT, Nov. 1, 1920, TLS (WP, DLC), that Tumulty requested that Wilson's photograph and endorsement be omitted from the advertisements. West explained that it had been too late to remove Wilson's photograph from the first advertisement, which appeared on November 1 (see, for example, the *New York Times* of that date), but that he had given instructions that the photograph and endorsement were to be removed from the final advertisement. This was in fact done. See *ibid.*, Nov. 6, 1920.

From Bainbridge Colby, with Enclosures

My dear Mr. President: Washington October 28th, 1920.

Referring to the question of the recognition of Mexico, I enclose the following papers, which in unrevised draft I understand Mr. Creel has read to you today,[1] viz:

1. A draft of a letter addressed to me, which Mr. Pesqueira, the Confidential Agent of Mexico, is prepared to write.
2. A proposed statement by me, for issuance to the press, simultaneously with the publication of Mr. Pesqueira's letter.[2]

The letter and statement it is proposed to release for immediate publication.[3]

On the question of recognition, it seems to both Mr. Davis and me, that the material conditions on which we have a right to insist, are satisfactorily set forth in Mr. Pesqueira's letter, and as I say in my proposed statement, it offers a basis on which the preliminaries of recognition can proceed.

I would not think of taking this important step without your explicit authorization, although Mr. Creel has reported his interviews with you and your general approval of this plan, in which I may say we fully concur.

Very respectfully yours,   Bainbridge Colby

I approve the plan as outlined here and over the 'phone
Woodrow Wilson

TLS (SDR, RG 59, 812.00/24757A, DNA).
[1] As has been noted, Creel had lunch with Wilson at the White House on October 28.
[2] That is, Pesqueira's letter to Colby of October 26, 1920, for which see n. 1 to the following document.
[3] Pesqueira's letter of October 26 and Colby's statement, printed below, were given to the press on October 29 and were printed, e.g., in the *New York Times*, Oct. 30, 1920.

E N C L O S U R E   I

My dear Mr. Pesqueira: Washington October 28 [27], 1920.

I have the honor to acknowledge the receipt of your letter of October 26th[1] and beg to express to you my sincere and deep gratification with your statement of the purposes and resolves of your Government. It cannot fail to be a source of satisfaction to the people of the United States that Mexico should signalize its emergence from the recent and lamentable disorders which have afflicted its people, and its return to a condition of internal tranquility by assurances so sweeping and so convincing of its disposition to meet the full measure of its international obligations. I am very desirous that your letter should meet with a response on behalf of this Government not less generous and trustful than your letter itself.

I, therefore, beg to assure you of the complete reciprocation of your cordial expressions, and in the prompt pursuit and further-ance of our joint aims, I take the liberty of suggesting that you submit to me a statement of the powers under which you are act-ing, and advise me whether, in the event of recognition, you are prepared, as I unhesitatingly assume to be the fact, to enter into a protocol which embodies the material proposals contained in your letter.

I am, sir,   Your obedient servant,

¹ This letter, not sent to Wilson, was R. V. Pesqueira to BC, Oct. 26, 1920, TLS (SDR, RG 59, 812.00/24701½, DNA). It is printed in *FR 1920*, III, 189-91. The text of the TLS follows:

"While the informal and frank conversations I have had with Mr. Norman Davis, the Under Secretary of State, have resulted in a cordial and thorough understanding, I beg the liberty of putting upon paper the exact position and the definite desires of my gov-ernment.

"As you know, and as the United States must see, it is a new Mexico that faces the world in pride and confidence. From border to border there is peace. Not a single rebel remains in arms against the federal government, and a whole nation thinks in terms of law and order and reconstruction. On September 5 our citizens cast their votes in due accord with democratic procedure, and Alvaro Obregon, the great soldier-statesman chosen to be president, is supported not only by a coalition of parties, but by a union of faith and patriotism.

"What you may not know, however, is the new spirit that animates my country. It is not only the case that our men and women have come to a deep and lasting appreciation of what Mexico owes to the idealism of President Wilson, so nobly and patiently exhib-ited in the unhappy years during which our oppressed millions fought against the in-justices that weighed them down for centuries. It is equally true that they have thrilled to the world vision of the President—his tremendous ideal of universal fraternity.

"Mexico today is not merely planning a future of happiness and justice for all within her borders. Out of our new strength we are willing and eager to play our proper part in the creation of a new and better order that will lift ancient burdens from the back of humanity.

"A first task, of course, is firm and enduring friendship between Mexico and the United States. Not only are we neighbors, but every other consideration points to the wisdom of an understanding that goes beyond mere treaties and sinks its roots into the heart of each nation. We have the same political institutions, the same aspirations, the same ideals, the same goals.

"Such a friendship is fast forming. The governors of Texas, New Mexico and Ari-zona—your border States—have already stretched out the hand of friendship, voluntar-ily telegraphing the President as to their faith in the stability, honesty and sincerity of my government.

"Our business is to set this friendship on foundations so firm that it cannot be shaken by the attack of reaction. Permit me, therefore, to deal in detail with certain slanders that have not only prejudiced the people of the United States, but which have aroused much bitterness in my own country.

"Mexico cannot but feel deeply grieved over the charge that she intends or has ever intended to disavow her obligations. President de la Huerta, as well as President elect Obregon, have on repeated occasions publicly declared that Mexico will respect all rightful claims duly proved as such, submitting herself to the recognized principles of international law.

"The Mexican Government is prepared to establish a joint arbitration Commission to pass upon and adjudicate the claims presented by foreigners on account of damages occasioned during the revolution. Any claim that cannot be adjusted by means of direct negotiations between the claimant and the Mexican Government will be submitted to the consideration of this Commission, whose decisions will be deemed final and bind-ing.

"Mexico has likewise upheld that, in order to place international relations on a solid foundation the existence of a permanent machinery or [of] arbitration is essential, for the purpose of deciding any difference. As regards the United States specifically, Mexico has already expressed her intentions in Article XXI of the Treaty of Guadalupe Hidalgo, and is prepared to enlarge and strengthen this machinery.

"Our plan is to establish a national program based on order and justice. It is our firm belief that the people of North America are just as faithful to their own high ideals. Hence, nothing could better shield the dignity of both republics, as nothing could be more efficacious for the continuance of peaceful relations, than the operation of a Commission of this nature, organized in accordance with recognized international practices.

"This policy should be made permanent, and the Mexican Government desires to cooperate in so far as may be needful towards this end.

"Another cause of deep national resentment for the Mexican Government, is the oft repeated assertion that our laws are of a retroactive and confiscatory nature, and that our national program is based on a policy of confiscation. This is entirely groundless. Not one square yard of land has been confiscated in Mexico, not a single legitimate right of property has been annulled. Nor do we intend to deviate from this fundamental policy. President de la Huerta, and President-elect Obregon have also made repeated public declarations to the effect that Article 27 of the Mexican Federal Constitution is not and must not be interpreted as retroactive or violative of valid property rights.

"We are a proud people, and the source of our pride is as high a conception of national honor as was ever erected by any nation. Therefore, Sir, when the Mexican government declares that it is willing and ready to assume full responsibility for all of its international obligations, it is a solemn pledge that will be kept to the letter.

"Present conditions in Mexico—the stability of the government, the spirit of the people—together with the plain statement of a sovereign people's purposes, all combine, it seems to me, to end misunderstanding, and I have the hope that your government will feel justified in recognizing the present government of Mexico, and in resuming official relations in order that [in] a spirit of true friendship and cooperation we may look forward to the necessary rehabilitation of Mexico.

"Please permit me to thank you for your many courtesies and never failing understanding. In the spirit of your great President you have not lacked in appreciation of our struggle for liberty, nor have you ever lost sight of the fact that the sovereignty of Mexico is the most sacred possession of our people. It is because of this attitude that I am able to write to you in such frankness and such sureness that you will understand this letter to be no mere political overture, but the honest expression of an honorable friendship."

ENCLOSURE II

My dear Mr. Secretary: October 28, 1920.

I am in receipt of your letter of the 27th inst., inquiring as to my specific authorities, and I am inclosing herewith my credentials as confidential agent of the Government and personal representative of President de la Huerta. I think that you will find them explicit and ample.

As for the statements contained in my letter to you of October 26, I beg you to rest assured that there was not one word that did not proceed from sincerity. In event of the resumption of official relations, I stand ready and willing, as the duly empowered representative of the Mexican government, to put each and every one of these statements in the form of a protocol between our two governments. In order that my position may remain clear, and that our discussion may continue without misunderstanding on either side, permit me to re-state the provisions which, in the opinion of my government, the protocol should contain.

The pending pecuniary claims arising from injuries to persons or property of American citizens, whether corporations, companies, or private individuals, against the United States of Mexico, and of Mexican citizens, whether corporations, companies, or private individuals, against the United States of America, shall be disposed of by the conclusion of a claims convention between the two governments which shall provide that all claims not settled by direct negotiations with the claimants within [blank] months after the date of the convention shall automatically go before a Mixed Claims Commission for its decision, which shall be final and binding on both parties with respect to all claims adjudicated by it. This Commission shall be composed of five members, two of whom shall be appointed by the Mexican Government, two by the President of the United States, and the fifth member shall be selected by these four. In the event of the failure to agree upon such fifth member of the Commission, the [blank] of [blank] shall be requested by the two governments to designate such member.

With regard to the provisions of Article 27 of the Mexican Constitution, the protocol shall provide that the Government of Mexico recognizes that such provisions are without retroactive effect and engages that they shall not be given such effect.

For the settlement of all other matters which are now or may be in controversy between our two governments, but which cannot be settled between them within six months, a convention shall be entered into to provide for the reference of such matters for final and binding decision to a Joint Commission to consist of one member to be appointed by the Mexican Government and one by the President of the United States, the two to select the third member. In the event of the failure to agree upon such third member, the two governments shall request the _____ of _____ to select such member.

I have the honor further to advise Your Excellency that, as has been abundantly evidenced, the government of which President de la Huerta is the head, is in a position to and will give adequate protection to the lives and properties of foreigners in Mexico, and is prepared to enter into claims conventions, similar to the one before mentioned, with the other interested powers of the world. Moreover, my government has not invalidated the legitimate rights of foreigners in private property, and, of course, will not engage in any such proceedings.

E N C L O S U R E   I I I

October 29th, 1920.

The Secretary of State, Bainbridge Colby, said:

"The discussions which have for some time been in progress with Mr. Pesqueira, representing the Mexican government, give promise of a speedy and happy outcome. The letter which he has addressed to me, and which I am today giving out for publication, is a very significant and, I may add, a very gratifying and reassuring statement of the attitude and purposes of the new government of Mexico. Mr. Pesqueira came to Washington bearing the fullest powers to speak and act on behalf of his government, and has exhibited throughout the course of the discussions a complete realization of Mexico's international obligations, just as his letter reflects clearly the firm resolve of his government to discharge them.

"I think I am warranted in saying that the Mexican question will soon cease to be a question at all, inasmuch as it is about to be answered, not only as it concerns the United States, but, indeed, the whole world as well.

"The new government of Mexico has given indication of stability, sincerity and a creditable sensitiveness to its duties and their just performance. While the full protection of valid American interests, which is clearly enjoined upon us as a duty, has at all times been a matter of primary concern to us, I may say that on the part of this country, there has been no attempt to prescribe rigid and definitive terms upon which a recognition of the Mexican government would be expressly conditioned. This we have deemed wholly unnecessary, and the disavowal by the Mexican representative of any policy of repudiation of obligations or confiscation of property or vested rights, either through retroactive legislation or future regulations, has the added value of being spontaneous and unprompted.

"There are certain pending matters in controversy between the two governments and our respective nationals, but these will be determined either by agreement or by the process of arbitration, to which Mexico is prepared to yield complete assent.

"The letter of Mr. Pesqueira offers a basis upon which the preliminaries to recognition can confidently proceed, and I am hopeful that within a short time the sympathetic friendship and the patient forbearance which President Wilson has manifested toward the Mexican people during the long period of their internal disorders will be fully vindicated. The desire reflected in Mr. Pesqueira's letter for the confidence and amicable regard of the United States is fully reciprocated, and I am happy to believe that the last cloud upon the ancient friendship of the two peoples is soon to disappear."

T MSS (SDR, RG 59, 812.00/24757A, DNA).

From Bainbridge Colby

My dear Mr. President: Washington October 28, 1920.

The Minister of Siam[1] has informed the Department that Prince Purachatr, the brother of the reigning King of Siam, is in this country and would greatly appreciate an opportunity to call upon you briefly.

If you find this suggestion, as I assume you will, a little irksome, I think <u>I can readily find an acceptable explanation</u>.[2] The Siamese Minister, however, was quite earnest in his desire that the matter should be brought to your personal attention.

May I say just a word in praise of your statement of yesterday. It was strong and persuasive and very lofty in tone,—an exceedingly valuable contribution to the campaign.

                         Very respectfully yours,   Bainbridge Colby

I would be very grateful if you would   W.W.

TLS (B. Colby Papers, DLC).
    [1] That is, Phya Prabha Karavongse.
    [2] Wilson underlined these words and then drew a line from "explanation" to his own reply at the bottom of the letter.

From Bernard Mannes Baruch

My dear Mr. President: New York October 28, 1920.

Mr. Swope has been good enough to show me the letter he addressed to you and the one you have sent him.[1]

I really don't think that a Distinguished Service Medal should be awarded to me, and I so expressed myself to Secretary Baker on one occasion when this matter came up. But I do believe that the men who were associated with me on the War Industries Board are undoubtedly as much entitled to the Distinguished Service Medal as any man who was awarded one because of civilian work. In fact, I would go so far as to say that there were certain men associated with me who are more entitled to the Medal than any one who received it for civilian work. I refer particularly to Leland L. Summers, who was more responsible than anyone else for the success of our explosives program and the breaking of the Du Pont grip in the erection of our powder plants; J. Leonard Replogle, who was

Director of Steel; Alex Legge, Vice-chairman of the Board, and in charge of organization work generally; Edwin B. Parker, Priority Commissioner; George N. Peek, in charge of Finished Products; and Chas. H. MacDowell, who was in charge of the Chemical Division.[2] In my opinion the work of these men should be recognized by the awarding to them of the Distinguished Service Medal. I have stated this to the Secretary of War, but he has refused on grounds that seem just and sufficient to him, but which do not in any way appeal to my sense of fairness or the facts in the case.

As for myself, the consciousness of having done the best I knew how for my country in its great hour of need is more than sufficient recognition. My pride in the possession of your friendship and the joy of service with you is greater reward than it seems possible can come to any man. So I would ask you, Mr. President, not to award this Medal to me; but if I deserve it, to award it to the men who really made it possible for me to serve as I did serve.

Very sincerely,   Bernard M Baruch

TLS (WP, DLC).
  [1] H. B. Swope to WW, Oct. 20, 1920, and WW to H. B. Swope, Oct. 22, 1920.
  [2] J(acob). Leonard Repogle, at this time president of the Vanadium Corp. of America; Alexander Legge, vice-president of the International Harvester Co.; Edwin Brewington Parker, general counsel of the Texas Co.; George Nelson Peek, president and general manager of the Moline Plow Co.; and Charles Henry MacDowell, president of the Armour Fertilizer Works.

From Joseph Patrick Tumulty

Dear Governor: The White House, 28 October, 1920

You and I discussed yesterday the advisability of writing a letter in which you would mention Governor Cox and speak of his acts as Governor of the State, and the fine character of the campaign he has carried on. If you are going to write the letter, now is the time.   Sincerely,   [Tumulty]

CCL (J. P. Tumulty Papers, DLC).

From Richard Heath Dabney

Dear Woodrow: Charlottesville 28 Oct., 1920.

It is a long time since I wrote to you—one reason being that I did not feel like bothering you during your illness when you were oppressed not only by countless cares but also by physical suffering. I break silence now merely to congratulate you upon your splendid address on the League of Nations which I read in today's paper, and to express my sincere hope that your health may soon improve. I have seized every opportunity to advocate the League, and shall make a speech on the subject tomorrow night at your birthplace, Staunton. The next night I shall speak about it in Richmond, and shall again urge it at Charlottesville the night before election day.

With heartfelt wishes for your recovery and for the triumph of this great cause to which you have sacrificed your health, I remain
Affectionately yours,   R. H. Dabney.

ALS (WP, DLC).

From Granville Stanley Hall[1]

Dear Mr. President: Worcester October 28, 1920

I am taking the great liberty of sending you my book, "Morale,"[2] because to my mind you best of all men in the world illustrate its highest, viz., international type. The admiration of President Eliot, as expressed in the last number of the Atlantic,[3] for the high ethical standards you have set the world does not surpass my own.

I do not, of course, expect you will now or ever have time to read my book or even read in it, not only because you have other things in mind but because the essence and a good part of the inspiration of it all you already have in your own soul.

Thus if you got anything from me as my pupil in the Johns Hopkins days, it is repaid manyfold by the fact that it is you more than anybody or any thing else who have prompted this product of my old age.

I am, with very great respect,
Faithfully yours,   G. Stanley Hall

TLS (WP, DLC).
   [1] The pioneering psychologist who had retired from the presidency of Clark University in June 1920. Wilson, during his graduate-student days at The Johns Hopkins University, had taken a course under Hall and thought highly of him.
   [2] G. Stanley Hall, *Morale, The Supreme Standard of Life and Conduct* (New York and London, 1920).
   [3] Charles W. Eliot, "The Voter's Choice in the Coming Election," *Atlantic Monthly*, CXXVI (Oct. 1920), 527-40.

To James Middleton Cox

My dear Governor Cox: [The White House] 29 October, 1920

As the campaign approaches its climax, I want to give myself the pleasure of writing to say with what admiration I have followed your course throughout the campaign. You have spoken truly and fearlessly about the great issues at stake, and I believe that you will receive the emphatic endorsement of the voters of the country. As one of those voters, and as one of your fellow-citizens, I want to express my entire confidence in you and my confident hope that under your leadership we may carry the policy of the national government forward along the path of liberal legislation and humane reform, until the whole world again sees an illustration of the wholesome strength of democracy and the happy fruit of what the founders of the republic purposed when they set this great government up.

Allow me to sign myself,

Your gratified and loyal supporter,   [Woodrow Wilson]

CCL (WP, DLC).

To Charles Zeller Klauder

My dear Mr. Klauder: [The White House] 29 October, 1920

Mrs. Wilson and I found your visit[1] very serviceable as well as pleasant and appreciate very much indeed the spirit in which you gave us your assistance and advice.

I write now to suggest that among the approximate estimates which you are now kindly undertaking to make you include one of the cost of carrying out what you have labeled the President's plan on the Q Street property,[2] on the assumption that the sixty-foot lot to the east is added to it. I am assuming that it is physically feasible to build according to that plan on that property, and think that I am safe in the assumption.

I also suggest that in this plan, and also in the others, you make the attempt of producing the scale of the building. In each case it is perhaps unnecessarily large, and no doubt a number of feet could be cut off without impairing the comfort or convenience of the building. I hope this will not entail much additional trouble, for you have certainly taken a great deal already.

Cordially and sincerely yours,   [Woodrow Wilson]

CCL (WP, DLC).

[1] Klauder visited the Wilsons at the White House on the morning of October 28.

[2] Mrs. Wilson writes in *My Memoir* (Indianapolis and New York, 1938), pp. 307-10, that, by this time, she and her husband had decided to buy or build a house in Washington because the Library of Congress was there, and the city was home to her. Wilson was enamored of a site on Conduit Road, with a beautiful view overlooking the Potomac River. At this point, that is, October 29, the Wilsons were also considering a site on Q Street, N.W.

From Edward Mandell House

Dear Governor: New York City, October 29, 1920.

During these last anxious days of the election, I would like you to know how often I think of you and wish for triumph of the great cause which you have sponsored and have advocated with such eloquence and force. I have an abiding faith in the aggregate wisdom of the people, and I feel that it will not now be long before America will join her sister nations in the League.

Faithfully yours,   E. M. House

TLS (WP, DLC).

Charles Moore[1] to Joseph Patrick Tumulty

My dear Sir: Washington October 29, 1920.

On reading the report of your talk in regard to the work of President Wilson during the past eight years,[2] I am impelled to write you now rather than to wait for perhaps a more convenient season.

The Library of Congress is the repository of the letters and papers of the Presidents of the United States. The papers of President Washington comprise some four hundred volumes; those of President Jefferson almost an equal number. A rough computation of the papers of President Taft places them at 250,000 individual pieces—copies of letters from him and the originals of letters to him. These have all been arranged and indexed, so that they can be readily examined, both by his biographer and, in after years, by the students of American history. Of course, the collection is not open to investigators during his lifetime, except by his express order. The letters and papers of President Roosevelt are also here in the Library; and they are used here by his biographer, and by such other persons as his literary executor permits to use them, but by no others.

In the course of a few months you will be arranging President Wilson's correspondence. Permit me to suggest that, with the President's approval, the papers be sent here directly from the White House, and be held subject to his and your order, and to be examined by no one—not even by the officials of the Library—without his permission. If you so desire, the boxes can be sealed. I am thinking to save inconvenience and storage by having these papers come directly to the Library, without going to the President's home and then being sent on from there. There are always dangers in transportation and dangers by fire.

I am not asking for a decision at this time, but am merely placing the matter before you, so that you can consider it while you are making your arrangements.[3]

I am,   Very respectfully yours,   Charles Moore

TLS (WP, DLC).

[1] Acting Chief, Manuscript Division, Library of Congress.

[2] Tumulty had spoken to a gathering of Democrats in Bethesda, Maryland, on October 28. Although he did urge the election of the Democratic ticket, his speech was primarily a moving tribute to Woodrow Wilson, both as political leader and human being. He briefly outlined his own long relationship with Wilson, noted the many achievements of the Wilson administration, and then devoted the bulk of his remarks to a discussion of Wilson's personality. Most of the anecdotes he told were later included in his book, *Woodrow Wilson As I Know Him* (Garden City, N. Y., 1921) and have become a part of Wilsonian lore. He stressed Wilson's warmer, more endearing, qualities, which he said were often obscured by his inability and unwillingness to publicize himself. He asserted that Wilson could and did accept advice before reaching decisions. He concluded with a touching contrast between the vibrantly healthy Wilson, who delivered the war message to Congress in 1917, and the broken old man in a wheelchair who reviewed a parade of war veterans in 1920. The full text of Tumulty's speech is printed in the *New York Times*, Oct. 29, 1920, and the speech was later printed in booklet form as Joseph P. Tumulty, *The Tribute of a Friend* . . . (New York, 1920).

[3] An Hw memorandum attached to this letter reads as follows: "Mr Forster. Answer, and say the President wants to keep his own papers."

To George Foster Peabody

My dear Mr. Peabody: The White House 30 October, 1920

You always know how to cheer me and your telegram of October twenty-seventh was peculiarly heartening. I thank you for it with all my heart.

Cordially and sincerely yours,   Woodrow Wilson

TLS (G. F. Peabody Papers, DLC).

To Mary Fels Fels

My dear Mrs. Fels: [The White House] 30 October, 1920

Thank you most sincerely for your letter of October twenty-sixth. It gave me a great deal of pleasure. It was thoughtful of you to write it.

Cordially and sincerely yours,   [Woodrow Wilson]

CCL (WP, DLC).

To Isabella Sheldon Owen Osgood

My dear Mrs. Osgood: [The White House] 30 October, 1920

You and Professor Osgood must have divined what cheer you would give me by the letters you have sent me. It is peculiarly

heartening and delightful to get such assurances from old and valued friends. I thank you with all my heart. Please accept my warm
regard.   Cordially and sincerely yours,   [Woodrow Wilson]

CCL (WP, DLC).

From Norman Hezekiah Davis, with Enclosure

My dear Mr. President: Washington October 30, 1920.

As you will no doubt recall, a meeting of the representatives of
the American, British, French and Japanese Banking Groups, acting upon the initiative of this Government, met at Paris in May,
1919, and drew up and initialed a tentative agreement for a Consortium for the making of loans to China for industrial and administrative purposes.[1] The agreement thus adopted was until recently
a matter of discussion and negotiation among the Governments
concerned with a view to their final approval.

During the past month, the representatives of the four national
Banking Groups met in New York and confirmed the Paris Agreement, with certain amendments and additions the advisability of
which had been developed by discussions during the intervening
period.

Now that the organization of the Consortium is thus definitely
agreed upon, it seems advisable that the four Governments should
make a statement as to the scope and purposes of the undertaking:
and to that end I venture to enclose, for your comment or approval,
a draft of the public statement which we would propose for that
purpose.

Should you desire to inform yourself more in detail of the terms
of the arrangement under which the Consortium has been constituted, I beg to refer you to the prints of the Agreement among the
Bankers under date of October 15th, and of the minutes of the
Bankers' meetings in connection therewith, which I am also enclosing herewith.   Faithfully yours,   Norman H. Davis

Approved   W.W.

TLS (SDR, RG 59, 893.51/3046, DNA).
[1] See B. Colby to WW, May 8, 1920 (first letter of that date), n. 1, Vol. 65.

E N C L O S U R E

The Government of the United States is gratified to learn that
the agreement tentatively adopted in May, 1919, at Paris by representatives of the investing public of America, Great Britain,

France, and Japan, covering the formation of the new Consortium for the assistance of China, has now been confirmed by the signature of the four banking groups. This international association thus coming into existence under the name of the Consortium has been organized with the full approval of the four Governments, and in the belief by them that the interests of the Chinese people can best be served by the cooperative action of their several banking communities to the end that the Chinese Government may be able to procure (through loan agreements involving the issue for subscription by the public of loans to the Chinese Government or other agencies involving a guarantee by the Chinese Government or Chinese Provincial Government) the capital required, particularly for the construction of improved means of communication and transportation. It is thus hoped to assist the Chinese people in their efforts toward a greater unity and stability, and offer to individual enterprise of all nationalities equal opportunity and a wider field of activity in the economic development of China. It is further believed that through such cooperative action a greater degree of understanding and harmony with reference to Far Eastern matters may be reached among all five of the nations involved.

T MS (SDR, RG 59, 893.51/3046, DNA).

From Norman Hezekiah Davis, with Enclosure

My dear Mr. President: Washington October 30, 1920.

The Japanese Ambassador states that as the Department has not publicly declared its position regarding the proposed legislation in California, the feeling is growing in Japan that the Federal Government is in sympathy with the California position. The negotiations with the Japanese Ambassador, conducted principally by Ambassador Morris, have proceeded most satisfactorily, and with minor exceptions have about resulted in an understanding in accordance with the policy outlined in Secretary Colby's letter to you and approved by you.[1]

The Japanese Ambassador now requests the Department to make some statement which would tend to quiet agitation in Japan. We also feel it might be well to do this and to let it be known that the two governments hope to have a satisfactory adjustment of the questions involved. I am therefore enclosing a statement, prepared by Secretary Colby, which it is proposed to release on Monday, if it meets with your approval.[2]

Faithfully yours,   Norman H. Davis

I consent   W.W.

TLS (photostat in N. H. Davis Papers, DLC).
  ¹ See BC to WW, Aug. 5, 1920, and its Enclosure, and BC to WW, Oct. 4, 1920.
  ² Davis' statement was published, e.g., in the *New York Times*, Nov. 2, 1920.

E N C L O S U R E

DEPARTMENT OF STATE

FOR THE PRESS
Japan.   November 1, 1920

In reply to inquiries, the Acting Secretary of State, Mr. Norman H. Davis, today made the following statement:

"The movement in California to recast the State laws affecting alien land tenure has been receiving since its inception, the close and interested attention of the Department of State. The relation of certain treaty provisions to the proposed measure is being discussed clearly and ably in California and will doubtless prove an element in the State's decision as to the adoption or rejection of the proposed measure. In the meantime the Department has had numerous discussions, of the most friendly and candid nature, with the Ambassador of Japan, and it is believed he thoroughly realizes, as we have sought to make clear, that no outcome of the California movement will be acceptable to the country at large that does not accord with existing and applicable provisions of law, and, what is equally important, with the national instinct of justice."

T MS (N. H. Davis Papers, DLC).

From William Joseph Martin

Dear Mr. President—   Davidson, N. C. October 30th 1920

I am too far from the center of things political to make any certain prophecy as to the outcome of next Tuesday's balloting. Before the result of the election is known, however, and without relation to its results I wish to say to you that my heart goes out to you in deep gratitude for your great service to our country and to the world. I make no effort to catalogue your eminent services and personal sacrifice in behalf of humanity; I would rather, in this simple way, voice the love and loyalty I have for you and my sense of gratitude to God for giving you to us.

The true issues *may* be clouded and the majority of our people *may* fail temporarily to support the measures which express the nobility of your soul, but thousands and tens of thousands love and will love you for your devotion to the needs of humanity. The time

WOODROW WILSON
1856 · 1924

The Wilson statue at the University of Texas at Austin

Bainbridge Colby and Norman Hezekiah Davis

Homer Stillé Cummings

The Democratic candidates in 1920: James Middleton Cox and Franklin Delano Roosevelt

Cox on the campaign trail

On the campaign trail

A young happy warrior

Harding on the campaign trail

The Hardings and the Coolidges

will come, later if not now, when the *united* hearts of your countrymen will ascribe to the feeling I have but can so imperfectly
express. May God, our Father, bless you and be very near to you in
the days of your trial and suffering, restoring you to bodily vigor
and, even amid the calumnies of your jealous foes, give to you the
"peace which passeth all understanding."

With the highest respect,

I am,   Very truly yours,   Wm. J. Martin

TLS (WP, DLC).

From Helen Hamilton Gardener

My dear Mr. President: Washington, D. C. October 30, 1920.

If you could know how many of us want to express to you our
affectionate admiration and realization of your splendid valor and
service to our country and to mankind, perhaps it would tend to
make you feel that while ingratitude and detraction are blatant
they are in no sense as universal as they seem.

One falls silent in the presence of great ability, great suffering,
great responsibility, great courage.

One can only hold out one's hands to you and say—God bless
and keep and comfort you. Our hearts are with you. Command us.
Having lived much abroad both in Europe and in the Orient, I believe I am in a position to know better than most of my countrymen
how great were your services to America. You exalted our Country
in the eyes of the world, as not any, not all, of our former chief
magistrates were able to do. You placed America upon a great and
noble plane before the eyes of the world. It had never approached
such a status before. Your offense was great in the eyes of the
small minded, the patriots for politics only, and so that bitter and
conscienceless fight upon you was launched and has swept the
ignorant into the furnace of fanatical hate.

But do not, I pray you, believe that the millions of silent but appreciative admirers of you and your work are indifferent because
they are silent. Some of us hesitate to lay upon you even the burden of reading one more letter, but we do not forget nor fail to appreciate your greatness and your value to your country and mankind.

I have the honor to remain, my dear Mr. President,

Yours very sincerely,   Helen H Gardener

TLS (WP, DLC).

To Edward Mandell House

My dear House: The White House 1 November, 1920

Thank you for your letter of October twenty-ninth. I appreciate your thought of me and your hopeful expectations of the ultimate result of the contests through which the world is now darkly struggling.   Sincerely yours,   Woodrow Wilson

TLS (E. M. House Papers, CtY).

To Richard Heath Dabney

My dear Heath: The White House 1 November, 1920

Thank you for your letter of October twenty-eighth. I need not assure you of the pleasure with which I receive any message from you or of my profound appreciation of your continued trust and friendship.   Affectionately yours,   Woodrow Wilson

TLS (Wilson-Dabney Corr., ViU).

To Helen Hamilton Gardener

My dear Mrs. Gardener: [The White House] 1 November, 1920

I am certainly your debtor for the delightful letter of October thirty-first which you were generous enough to write me. I appreciate not only it, but the many generous services which you have rendered my administration and the causes which we believe in. It is very delightful to have you connected with the Government in an official way.[1]

Cordially and sincerely yours,   [Woodrow Wilson]

CCL (WP, DLC).
[1] The reader will recall that she was now a member of the Civil Service Commission.

Joseph Patrick Tumulty to Edith Bolling Galt Wilson

Dear Mrs. Wilson: The White House 1 November, 1920.

Of course, I have no way of knowing what is going to happen tomorrow, but I have a faith and a confidence which are justified by everything I hear from all parts of the country that we are going to win. Surface indications are against us, but I am certain that beneath them there is a depth of conviction that will seek expression in the vindication of the President at the polls tomorrow.

I wish you could read and examine the letters that pour in here from all parts of the country. There is such a depth of love and appreciation of the President in them that I am amazed at its extent.

There is no doubt that the tide has turned. We can be certain of this and find great comfort in it. We are associated with the greatest force for good in the world. We know this in our very souls and no mere results of tomorrow can alter or change this in the least.

The attached letter[1] is a sample of the many that are reaching here from all parts of the country.   Sincerely,   Tumulty

TLS (J. P. Tumulty Papers, DLC).
  [1] It is missing.

From John Spargo

                                      Old Bennington Vermont
Dear Mr. President: November 1st, 1920.

On the eve of the election at which your successor is to be chosen, and which you will watch so anxiously for reasons far transcending any selfish considerations, I have felt that I wanted to send you a word of friendship and cheer. May I not, therefore, tell you of my profound conviction that the terrible campaign of misrepresentation of which you have been the victim during the past two years, amounting to such a spiritual crucifixion as few men have ever had to endure, has brought to every decent American a sense of humiliation and sadness? I trust that in the poignancy of your disappointment and suffering you will find comfort and cheer in the fact that millions of your fellow citizens hold you in affectionate esteem for the glory and honor you have added to the proud heritage of American citizenship.

May I add the conviction that the ideals to which you have given such generous service and matchless expression, and for which you have been called upon to suffer so much, will triumph, whatever the outcome of tomorrow's election, and that when the petty passions of the moment shall have been dispelled your countrymen will be united in a common pride and reverent joy that in the supreme crisis of history you stood, as America's spokesman, for the righteous and imperishable principles henceforth forever associated with your name?

I trust, dear Mr. President, that you will recover and live to witness these things. In the meantime, may the consciousness of your fellowship with the noblest and best of our human kind be a constant comfort and sustenance to you.

With assurances of continued confidence, admiration and high regard,

I am, Mr. President,

Very respectfully yours,   John Spargo.

TLS (WP, DLC).

From Thomas L. Snow

Juddhaven P O. Ontario. Canada.

Dear Mr President: November 1st/20

Owing to pressing duties out-doors for the last few days I have had to defer my reply to your letter of October 22. Impending winter was heralded a few days ago by several flocks of geese migrating south, and for the sake of our own and our animals' comfort for the next five months we have been busy hurrying forward certain precautions connected with stabling, as well as our own personal snugness and convenience.

What with the interval of sixteen years and a deplorably unretentative memory, I can not recall with clarity and precision certain of the details connected with the furniture which Gregory Allen was to have made for you. But at least I can make two statements in the matter which, I regret to think, will cause you disappointment—if not surprise.

It is certain that Gregory Allen made no furniture for you before he and his family left for British Columbia in 1906 (?): not, at all events, to the knowledge of either Mrs Snow or myself. We seem to recollect having understood in those far off days that the order to him for Mission furniture had been subsequently cancelled. But our memories in this respect are very foggy and unreliable. I have not written to my wife's brother-in-law these many years, but will ascertain his address and forward to him immediately a typed copy of your letter of October 22 so that he may personally explain the matter to you. Also I will endeavor to enclose his address herewith so that you, Mr President, may communicate with him if you wish.

As to what became of the oak lumber intended for your furniture (300 ft, possibly 400 ft) which we found here after the Gregory-Allens had left for B C, I myself can explain. It remained stored away from the weather in our stable loft for several (7 or 8) years. Will Miss Wilson recall, I wonder, that about seven or eight years ago (possibly nine) she wrote me enquiring as to the prospects of selling your landed property here, and asked if I would accept the agency of attending to same. In replying at length to Miss Wilson, I remember, among other things, reminding her of the oak lumber that we had stored and of the other small chattels belonging to her family, with a view of learning what disposal she desired should be made of these possessions. I received no reply from her, and a year later, wanting the space where the oak was stored; not requiring the wood for any special work of our own, and hard up—I well remember—for a little ready cash at the time, I sold the lumber to a party down the lake for the sum of twelve dollars—little enough, it may be thought, even in those days of low prices. I greatly regret having to make this melancholy report to you, Mr President, in respect to furniture which you are under the impression had been made—or partially made—for you. The fact that you will promptly receive from my Bank a draft on Washington to the amount of the proceeds ($12.00) which I received from the sale of your oak lumber, does not in the least minimize the regret which, in the past years, I have felt at parting with it. Your other few belongings left in my care in 1904, are intact:—6 cushions, 2 hammocks, 2 students lamps—. They hold for me a much more personal and intimate worth, and because of that, they have been stored away under my care all these years safe from use and appropriation by any one. To be sure, they must still be considered at your disposal whenever you shoud need them, but. * * *

Believe me to remain with the same warmth and admiration and solicitude as ever   Yours very faithfully   Thomas Snow

TLS (WP, DLC).

To Frank Lyon Polk

[The White House] 2 November, 1920

It is delightful to hear of your faring so well. Please accept our congratulations and most cordial good wishes for a steady and rapid convalescence.   Woodrow Wilson.

T telegram (Letterpress Books, WP, DLC).

To William Joseph Martin

My dear President Martin: The White House 2 November, 1920

Your letter of October thirtieth has given me the greatest pleasure. I value your friendship and approval most highly, and am glad, also, to get such a note of sympathy and support from the college to which I look back with so much pleasure and affection.

Cordially and sincerely yours,   Woodrow Wilson

TLS (NcDaD).

To Granville Stanley Hall

My dear Doctor Hall: The White House 2 November, 1920

In your kind letter of October twenty-eighth you have recalled in a way that gratifies me very much indeed my stimulating contact with you at the Johns Hopkins. I shall look forward with pleasure to an opportunity of reading your book, "Morale," and I am very much interested indeed to learn that you have written it and to get an intimation from you of its character and purpose.

With the warmest regard and best wishes,
          Cordially and sincerely yours,   Woodrow Wilson

TLS (G. S. Hall Papers, MWC).

To Eleanor Randolph Wilson McAdoo

My dear Nell: [The White House] 2 November, 1920

I know you will be interested in the enclosed letter from Katharine Duffield.[1] She seems to have developed in a most interesting way.

I am mighty glad to think of you and Mac as having finished the immense task of that trip and I hope with all my heart that Mac is really none the worse for the exertion. Your letter gave me real delight.

I am sorry that your birthday check should be so belated, but you know with how much love it is sent.

With warmest love from us both to you all,
                              Your loving   [Father]

CCL (WP, DLC).
[1] Daughter of the Rev. Dr. Howard and Katharine Nash Greenleaf Duffield of New York. Katharine Duffield was living at this time in Wilmette, Ill., as WW to Katharine Duffield, Nov. 2, 1920, TLS (WP, DLC), reveals. Dr. Duffield was pastor of the "Old First" Presbyterian Church of New York.

Three Letters from Norman Hezekiah Davis

My dear Mr. President: Washington November 2, 1920.

Some time ago an International Committee of Bankers on Mexico was formed by various banking groups in the United States, England, and France, to consolidate and protect the interests of various investors in Mexican securities. Subsequently, Dutch and Swiss bankers were included in the groups. J. P. Morgan is Chairman of the American group, but Lamont, who is alternate Chairman, has been taking the active lead in the matter and has kept me advised of developments. According to the record, the State Department informed the American group of bankers that there would be no objection to their joining the International Committee, provided the American group would have a predominating voice in the policy and activities of the Committee.

Some weeks ago, the British and French groups began to press the American group to send a joint committee to Mexico to investigate conditions and to take up at least preliminary discussions with the Mexicans. I discouraged this because we thought that a premature visit of such a committee might be construed as having political significance and deter the Mexicans from taking measures necessary to justify recognition. Lamont concurred in our views. Very recently, however, the British and French groups, being pressed by the investors they represent, have been more insistent upon sending someone to Mexico. To this end, Sir William Wiseman arrived last week. He comes primarily representing the French Committee, but also, I understand, carries in effect a proxy from the British Committee. Both Committees have recommended to Lamont that Wiseman go to Mexico to represent all of the groups. I have informed Lamont confidentially that this would be very unsatisfactory, and that when a committee does go to Mexico it should be headed by an American in whom we would have confidence. Lamont would, in my opinion, be the most satisfactory and dependable one to head a committee at the proper time, if he can possibly get away.

Lamont informs me that while the foreign committees are apparently desirous that no action should be taken which is not entirely agreeable to this Government, we ought, in his judgment, within a reasonable time, find a *modus vivendi*, or else it will be difficult, if not impossible, to hold the five-Power team in hand. Wiseman has informed him that he has, in any event, private business which will necessitate his going to Mexico and that if he were to discuss matters there on behalf of the British and French Committees he would do so on the theory that it would be necessary for the Government to commit itself to certain reconstructive attitudes as to foreign loans before any real discussions could be undertaken.

Lamont especially desires a hint as to the expediency of letting Wiseman go down there alone, and also calls our attention to the fact that the American bankers must show some disposition to our investors to "get busy."

Lamont is discreet and dependable and I think it would be wise to inform him that there would be no objection to a committee headed by an American, preferably himself, going to Mexico the

first part of December. This will give time to the Mexican Government, if it can and so desires, to take such action as would justify
your extension of recognition. I should be pleased to have your instructions and guidance in the matter.

Faithfully yours,   Norman H. Davis

My dear Mr. President: Washington November 2, 1920.

The High Commissioners of the Allied nations and the Allied
Generals in Budapest have formed themselves into a commission
to discuss questions of current interest and to pass on to each other
such information as they may have of conditions in Hungary. It is
understood that they do not, as a commission, approach the Hun-
garian Government.

Mr. Grant-Smith,[1] American Commissioner in Hungary, has
been invited by the Allied representatives to attend the meetings of
this commission and suggests that he be permitted to attend unofficially. He points out that for the protection and forwarding of
purely American interests, the knowledge gained at these meetings would be helpful.

I am inclined to believe that it might be helpful for our Commissioner to sit in unofficially with instructions to make it clear that
he cannot in any way bind the United States Government.

I should be grateful for an expression of your wishes in this matter.   Faithfully yours,   Norman H. Davis

[1] Ulysses Grant-Smith, a career diplomat.

My dear Mr. President: Washington November 2, 1920.

Judge Elkus has consented to accept the appointment from the
Council of the League of Nations on the Aland Island Commission.
We have, therefore, instructed our Ambassador at Paris to inform
the President of the Council of the League of your recommendation of Judge Elkus for the appointment. I presume the Council
will now make the appointment, after which an announcement
will be given out.   Faithfully yours,   Norman H. Davis

TLS (WP, DLC).

From Harry Augustus Garfield

Dear Mr. President: Williamstown, Mass. Nov. 2, 1920

The people have voted & in a few hours we shall know to what effect. While we await the count my thought turns to you. My heart goes out to yours as it has always done since first we met, but now with knowledge reinforcing affection for I know with how much steadfastness you have led us toward the high purpose which ought to be our chosen goal. Whatever the result of today's balloting we shall sooner or later take our part in the great enterprise of bringing the nations together, & our greatest debt will be to you. I hope otherwise, but am prepared to face a present disappointment—, keen only because I wish you to receive now the homage of a grateful people. Someday it will surely be expressed, but now would be both a happier experience for you & a better result for the world. In any event much may yet be accomplished before the 4th of March. Mrs. Garfield[1] joins me in warmest regard.   Affectionately yours,   H. A. Garfield

ALS (WP, DLC).
[1] Belle Hartford Mason Garfield.

From Charles Zeller Klauder

My dear Mr. President: Philadelphia November 2nd, 1920

Your letter of October 29th has been received.

I am endeavoring, as you suggest, to reduce the scale of the building and also to adapt the scheme labelled the President's plan to the Q Street property. I am verifying my ideas of probable cost by means of the cubic foot cost of residences recently built or estimated upon.

It does not seem possible to advance the problem as it now appears so that it may be presented on Thursday of this week as I had expected. I hope to present the results to you by Tuesday next, but I will write you later as to the earliest possible moment at which I shall be able to do so.

                    Sincerely yours,   Chas Z Klauder

TLS (WP, DLC).

Ray Stannard Baker to Edith Bolling Galt Wilson

My dear Mrs. Wilson: Amherst Massachusetts November 2 '20

I am writing this on election day. I have been deeply concerned over the recent unfavorable statements regarding the President's health. I hope they have been exaggerated.

I thought it might interest you and perhaps be cheering to the President to know with what enthusiasm his name has been greeted in recent meetings here even in rock-ribbed Republican New England. I have spoken at a number of large meetings during the last week in favor of the League of Nations and of Cox—especially two very fine ones at Springfield and Boston—in which every mention of the President's name was received with applause. This was particularly fine at the great meeting in Symphony Hall in Boston on Sunday night. The Boston *Herald* headed its account of this meeting: "Cheer Wilson as Hero of War."

I am certain that thousands of people in this country are coming to a clearer and juster view of what the President did in the War and at the Peace Conference: and this feeling is bound to spread— and spread. Nothing is more certain than the great place the President is to have in history.

I wish you would convey my deep and warm regard to the President. I know what he went through with at Paris: and it is going to be one of my occupations in the future to try to make that service clearer to the public.

I hope the President may speedily be stronger.

      With sincere regard, I am,   Ray Stannard Baker

ALS (WP, DLC).

From the Shorthand Diary of Charles Lee Swem

      3 of November Day after Election

The President said this morning that the Republicans had committed suicide.[1] It hadn't hurt the Democratic party any, but the country had been hurt in the eyes of the world.

The President spoke of a man who was married by a father,[2] the father being a reverend doctor. The father addressed the bride and groom before he married them and started off with: "Marriage is older than sin."

The President said that the lettered and numbered titles of the streets of Washington, D. C., bore him. It was silly, he said, to give such names to streets of a city that was bound to be historic. They should have been given names.

Speaking of "David Lawrence Incorporated," he said, "I wish he were disintegrated."[3]

JRT transcript (WC, NjP) of CLSsh (C. L. Swem Coll., NjP).

[1] Harding won the presidential election by the landslide total of 16,152,000 votes to 9,147,000 for Cox. The electoral vote was 404 for Harding to 127 for Cox. Cox carried only eleven states, all in the South. Harding carried Tennessee, thus breaking the "Solid South" for the first time since Reconstruction. The Republican party took ten Senate seats from the Democrats, which gave the Republicans a majority of twenty-two. Their majority in the House of Representatives was 303 to 131, the largest in the history of the Republican party.

[2] Wilson was undoubtedly speaking of his own father.

[3] David Lawrence, Princeton 1910, formerly A.P. White House correspondent, who had established his own news service in 1919 as "David Lawrence, Inc." Wilson had never been fond of him.

To David Lloyd George[1]

[The White House]

My dear Mr. Prime Minister: 3 November, 1920

I have read with interest your personal and private letter of August fifth[2] last and appreciate very much your frank account of the obstacles with which you are contending in an endeavor to bring about readjustment in Europe. When wounds of war and concurrent economic dislocation can be healed and righted only by justice, good will, sanity, and unselfishness, it is deplorable that militarism, selfishness, and vengeful desires should become predominant and prevent or retard orderly recovery. It is not easy to understand why wars, which arouse such high aspirations and require such willing and great sacrifices, should be followed by a lowering of ideals, prejudice, selfishness, and uncontrolled animosities, which so greatly increase the difficulties of establishing permanent conditions of peace. While you may at times have been fighting alone in the Supreme Allied Council for a liberal, just and constructive interpretation of the German Treaty, you have had, and, I am sure, can count upon having, the support of the United States in such a policy. We believe this is essential for the welfare of France herself. This Government has repeatedly urged such a course, and our position is undoubtedly known to France.

I shall be glad to cooperate to the extent of my ability in urging a fair and constructive settlement of the Adriatic question, including that of Albania. As to Albania, I am inclined to believe this

[1] Norman Davis drafted this letter through the sixth paragraph; David F. Houston drafted the balance of it. See the draft dated Nov. 3, 1920, T MS (N. H. Davis Papers, DLC), and D. F. Houston, *Eight Years with Wilson's Cabinet, 1913-1920* (2 vols., Garden City, N. Y., 1926), II, 133-37. There is only a TCL of Wilson's letter in the D. Lloyd George Papers, House of Lords Record Office. Its number is F|60|1|31.

[2] It is printed as an Enclosure with BC to WW, Aug. 18, 1920 (first letter of that date).

problem has been approached heretofore from the wrong direction, namely, that of settling the boundaries of Albania in accordance with the aspirations of Jugo-Slavia and Greece, without sufficient regard to the aspirations and rights of the Albanian people themselves. I now feel that if the prime objective is to accede to the just aspirations of the Albanian people a permanent solution of this perplexing problem may be had.

As to Russia, I cannot but feel that Bolshevism would have burned out long ago if let alone, and that no practicable and permanent settlement involving Russian territory and rights can be arrived at until the great Russian people can express themselves through a recognized government of their own choice.

As to the proposed conference between representatives of Bolshevik Russia and the Allies, for the purpose of reaching a trade agreement and, as I understand, subsequently extending recognition to the Soviet regime, I would not feel justified, under present conditions, in sending an American representative. I quite realize some of the difficulties with which you are contending, but as I am so firmly convinced that no useful purpose can be served through official relations with the Soviets, and that negotiations to that end merely tend to strengthen them and to prolong their power, I could not conscientiously enter into the proposed negotiations.

I believe we are in substantial accord as to the folly of the Poles. I have been fearful that their enthusiasm following temporary military successes may lead to insistence upon territorial arrangements which will be a source of future trouble.

May I now take this occasion to call to your attention an apparent misunderstanding which has arisen in regard to the Island of Yap? I have been surprised to learn that in the Preliminary Conference on Communications, now being held here, the Japanese Delegation has claimed that by decision of the Supreme Council on May 7, 1919, Japan was to hold under mandate all of the ex-German territory in the Pacific north of the Equator, including Yap. Ambassador Geddes also informs the Department of State that he has consulted your Foreign Office, which concurs in the Japanese view. I have looked up the records[3] and can understand how the minutes of May 7, 1919, read alone and without reference to previous discussions and understandings, may be interpreted as including Yap in the mandates to be allotted to Japan. In the meeting of May sixth, in the discussion regarding the allotment of man-

[3] For the discussions in the Council of Four referred to below, see the notes of the meetings on April 21, 1919, 4 p.m., Vol. 57; and May 1, 1919, 4 p.m.; May 6, 1919, 5:30 p.m.; and May 7, 1919, 11 a.m., Vol. 58.

dates in the Pacific, you expressed your understanding that the Japanese should receive a mandate for *certain* islands north of the Equator. I consented in principle to this, with the subsequent statement that in respect to all mandates the policy of the "open door" would have to be applied, and that there should be equal opportunities for trade and commerce of other members of the League. According to the minutes of May seventh, the wording which has caused the misunderstanding is as follows: "GERMAN ISLANDS NORTH OF THE EQUATOR. The mandate shall be held by Japan." I must admit that perhaps the wording is somewhat unfortunate. In order to avoid any misunderstanding, it would have been well and correct for my previous and unwithdrawn reservation as to Yap to have been reiterated. As the island of Yap had been previously excluded and placed in a specific category for future determination in connection with a consideration of the cable problem, I must have presumed, in reading the minutes, that it could not be included in this decision. On April twenty-first, at a meeting at my house with you and M. Clemenceau, in reporting my conversation of that morning with Baron Makino and Count Chinda, I stated, among other things, that I had reminded the Japanese delegates that it had been understood that Japan was to have a mandate for the islands in the North Pacific, although I had made a reservation in the case of the Island of Yap, which I considered should be international. At a meeting on May first, held in Mr. Pichon's room, in discussing cable communications, I stated that as all cable lines across the Pacific pass through the Island of Yap, which thus became a general distributing center for the lines of communication for the North Pacific, Yap should not pass into the hands of any one power. In substance, my understanding is that as the Island of Yap had previously been disposed of as above indicated it was *not* included in the decision of the Supreme Council of May seventh. I feel confident that your recollection and understanding will concur with mine, and I hope that you will so inform your Foreign Office in order that the present misunderstanding may be cleared up. The United States does not want the Island of Yap, but as it must form such an indispensable part in any constructive and proper agreement respecting international cable communications it is essential that it should not be controlled by any one power and that there should be complete freedom of action in dealing with it.

I turn now to the problem of inter-allied indebtedness which you raise. I must deal with this matter with great frankness, as I am sure you wish me to do. It is desirable that our position be clearly understood in order to avoid any further delay in a constructive settlement of reparations which may arise from the hope that the debts to this Government can form a part of such settlement. It will be helpful if first of all I indicate our legal situation.

The Secretary of the Treasury is authorized by United States law to arrange for the conversion of the demand obligations of the British Government into obligations having a fixed date of maturity, in accordance with the agreement of the British Government to make such exchange on demand contained in its existing obligations. In connection with such exchange, the Secretary of the Treasury has authority to arrange for the postponement of interest payments. No power has been given by the Congress to anyone to exchange, remit or cancel any part of the indebtedness of the Allied Governments to the United States represented by their respective demand obligations. It would require Congressional authority to authorize any such dealing with the demand obligations and the Congress has the same authority to authorize any disposition of obligations of the British Government held by the United States, whether represented by demand obligations or by obligations having a fixed date of maturity. It is highly improbable that either the Congress or popular opinion in this country will ever permit a cancellation of any part of the debt of the British Government to the United States in order to induce the British Government to remit, in whole or in part, the debt to Great Britain of France or any other of the Allied Governments, or that it would consent to a cancellation or reduction in the debts of any of the Allied Governments as an inducement towards a practical settlement of the reparation claims. As a matter of fact, such a settlement in our judgment would in itself increase the ultimate financial strength of the Allies.

You will recall that suggestions looking to the cancellation or exchange of the indebtedness of Great Britain to the United States were made to me when I was in Paris. Like suggestions were again made by the Chancellor of the Exchequer in the early part of the present year. The United States Government by its duly authorized representatives has promptly and clearly stated its unwillingness to accept such suggestions each time they have been made and has pointed out in detail the considerations which caused its decision. The views of the United States Government have not changed, and it is not prepared to consent to the remission of any part of the debt of Great Britain to the United States. Any arrangements the British Government may make with regard to the debt owed to it by France or by the other Allied Governments should be made in the light of the position now and heretofore taken by the United States, and the United States, in making any arrangements with other Allied Governments regarding their indebtedness to the

United States (and none are now contemplated beyond the funding of indebtedness and the postponement of payment of interest)
will do so with the understanding that any such arrangement
would not affect the payment in due course of the debt owed the
United States by Great Britain. It is felt that the funding of these
demand obligations of the British Government will do more to
strengthen the friendly relations between America and Great Britain than would any other course of dealing with the same.

The United States Government entirely agrees with the British
Government that the fixing of Germany's reparation obligation is a
cardinal necessity for the renewal of the economic life of Europe
and would prove to be most helpful in the interests of peace
throughout the world; however, it fails to perceive the logic in a
suggestion in effect either that the United States shall pay part of
Germany's reparation obligation or that it shall make a gratuity to
the Allied Governments to induce them to fix such obligation at an
amount within Germany's capacity to pay. This Government has
endeavored heretofore in a most friendly spirit to make it clear that
it cannot consent to connect the reparation question with that of
inter-governmental indebtedness.

The long delay which has occurred in the funding of the demand obligations is already embarrassing the Treasury, which will
find itself compelled to begin to collect back and current interest if
speedy progress is not made with the funding. Unless arrangements are completed for funding such loans and in that connection
for the deferring of interest, in the present state of opinion here,
there is likely to develop an unfortunate misunderstanding. I believe it to be highly important that a British representative with
proper authority proceed to Washington without delay to arrange
to carry out the obligation of the British Government to convert its
demand obligations held by our Treasury into long-time obligations.

The United States Government recognizes the importance, in
the interests of peace and prosperity, of securing the restoration of
financial and industrial stability throughout Europe. The war debts
of the Allied Governments, the treaty obligations of Germany under
the reparation clauses of the Treaty of Versailles and the annexes
thereto, and of other enemy and ex-enemy countries under the
treaties negotiated with them, the administration of countries under the mandates provided for by such treaties, and the existing
arrangements between the Governments of various countries have
or may have an important bearing in making plans to accomplish
such restoration.

It is very difficult for me at this time to state just what part

America can be expected to play after the election is over. I have great faith in the ultimate wisdom of the American people, and cannot but believe that once the prejudices and cross-currents which are beclouding the real issue have been dissipated America will cooperate unselfishly for the betterment of the world and dedicate itself to the service of mankind.

With assurances of high regard,

Sincerely yours,   [Woodrow Wilson]

CCL (WP, DLC).

To Norman Hezekiah Davis

My dear Davis: The White House 3 November, 1920

I have your letter of November second. I am not at all willing that Sir William Wiseman should go to Mexico representing directly or indirectly anybody in America, or in circumstances which would make the impression that he represented anybody except himself. I do not think that he ought to go at all to represent anybody. I entirely agree with you that whoever goes should be an American and that nobody but an American should speak for the American bankers. This is not the opportune time for the negotiation, anyway, and I think we should discourage the whole thing unless they will do it exactly as we suggest.

Cordially and faithfully yours,   Woodrow Wilson

TLS (N. H. Davis Papers, DLC).

From Newton Diehl Baker

My dear Mr President   Washington November 3, 1920

The advent of the conservative reaction shows that our people are terrified by the radicalism which hunger and misery have bred in Europe and have decided to keep away from contact with it. Of course we cannot keep away, but the republicans will try to build a wall about America and either fail because it cant be done, or succeed only to have it thrown down by the economic forces which are larger than the conscious efforts of men. The League of Nations is only one item in the reaction. Labor is at the threshold of the battle of its life—indeed I personally believe that the labor clauses in the Covenant of the League were the secret inspiration of the tremendous battle staged against the Covenant, though Article X was selected as the putative objection because it could be distorted most effectively to the shaken nerves and sick imagination of our people. But *Clio* cannot be fooled about all this and she is already writing down in her permanent record, great judgments which are just the opposite of the transient opinion of the day.

However all this may be, I personally have much to thank God for, for none of His gifts, however, am I or shall I be more grateful than that I have been privileged to follow your leadership and in some small way to be a part of your great work. I would not exchange my confident happiness in the righteousness of your work, for all the votes in the Electoral College, and I am only a few months ahead of the majority of my countrymen in my appreciation of its significance.

Affectionately and Gratefully   Newton D. Baker

ALS (WP, DLC).

From Bainbridge Colby

My dear Mr. President: Washington November 3, 1920.

I am bowed under the weight of disappointment and depression today, but my thoughts turn to you—solicitously and tenderly. I hope, my dear Mr. President, that your intrepid and dauntless spirit is not wearied or cast down.

The result is a complex of so many and such various ingredients. It will not dim (nothing ever can) the lustre of your leadership. When that was lost to us, we were lost. No one could bend the bow of Ulysses.

You have spoken the truth. You have battled for it. You have suffered for it. Your crown will be one of glory, and the heathen who have imagined vain things, will some day creep penitently to touch the hem of your garments.

I am so proud, Sir, to know you and to serve you, and so grateful that life gave me the opportunity to do both.

Sincerely always,   Bainbridge Colby

TLS (WP, DLC).

From Robert Wickliffe Woolley

Dear Mr. President: Washington November 3, 1920.

The pity of it all is that the people themselves have been grievously deceived. Their true feeling toward the League of Nations will yet find expression and may God help the leaders whose advice they followed yesterday.

Last evening I stood before a bulletin board and saw your picture
and that of the victorious candidate displayed. The applause accorded the President-to-be was tame and perfunctory compared
with that which greeted your picture. I then imagined myself in
1924 and looked backward. The acclaim I had just heard had become the mighty paean of a nation. The liars of yesterday were
silent, anathematized and deserted.

With great respect, I am always

Faithfully and sincerely   Robert W. Woolley

TLS (WP, DLC).

From Norman Hezekiah Davis

My dear Mr. President: Washington Nov. 3, 1920.

The people have just stopped to get their breath. They caught
the vision from you but havn't been able to hold it. You have given
America and the world more in seven years than they could digest.
Your unprecedented competent progressive and fruitful administration led the people to expect too much and they cannot properly
value what you have given and offered until they get the terrible
contrast and awakening that is coming. History gave us no reason
to expect anything else but somehow we did expect more because
you have carried the people in orderly progress further along than
any one else has ever done. I wish you could realize how very
much you have accomplished and that it will not be in vain.

Faithfully and affectionately yours   Norman H. Davis

ALS (WP, DLC).

From Kent Roberts Greenfield[1]

My dear Mr. Wilson: New Haven, Conn November third [1920]

This letter may seem an impertinence—it will probably never
reach you. But I cannot resist the impulse to write it, because I
think that some voice from the younger men, of my class and temper, ought to reach you directly.

We are sobered by what can only seem a huge backsliding of the
American people, but not too much discouraged. I do not think
that I stand alone in this point of view. It ought not to shock us to
find that we are of a generation that stoneth the prophets. Reflection upon the fact that it has been possible for a prophet to hold
political office for eight years enheartens me. For in that light we
have learned to regard you. You won me to personal allegiance in

a speech you made in Baltimore, in 1911, on "Municipal Government in the United States,"[2] when you made me to see, with a
thrill of delighted realization, that a pure idealism can be made
practicable in actual politics: and my personal faith in you, however tested by some features of the Democratic Administration, is
still firm this morning;—and my faith in the future, which would
be far less confident but for your record during these eight years.
In the face of such discouragements I often recall wise Emerson's
caution against expecting too much: "We think our civilization
near its meridian, but we are yet only at the cock-crowing and the
morning star!"

It might interest you to know that at our weekly History Department luncheon yesterday, fourteen of the sixteen present—including Allen Johnson, Professor Andrews,[3] and Charles Seymour,
whom you of course know—declared their intention to vote for Mr.
Cox, not, I am sure, from any devotion to him, or to the party, but
to the ideals that you represent.

Very sincerely yours   Kent Roberts Greenfield

ALS (WP, DLC).
[1] At this time Assistant Professor of History at Yale University; later Professor and
Chairman of the Department of History at The Johns Hopkins University and Chief
Historian of the Department of the Army.
[2] See the third news report printed at Dec. 6, 1911, Vol. 23.
[3] Allen Johnson, Larned Professor of American History and Chairman of the History
Department, and Charles McLean Andrews, Farnum Professor of American History,
both at Yale University.

From Eleanor Randolph Wilson McAdoo

Darling, darling Father,   [New York] Nov. 3rd 1920

I want just to send a line to tell you that I *know* that this is not
a repudiation of the League. Everywhere we went people told us
that it was the common belief that Harding would have to give us
the League, in spite of what he said—and that the election would
be settled on all sorts of entirely different issues. People are stupid,
beyond words, but they want the League—the majority—I know it
darling Father. And those that don't want it feel that way only because they have been lied to so constantly and so long.

Nothing can destroy what you have done—nothing in the whole
wide world.

I love you so much—and I want so much to see you—can I go
down soon darling?

With all my love to you both

Your adoring daughter   Nell.

ALS (WC, NjP).

A News Report

[*Nov. 4, 1920*]

PRESIDENT GREETS WHITE HOUSE CROWD

Hundreds of League Supporters Cheer Him on Lawn While He Watches.

Washington, Nov. 4.—President Wilson made his first public appearance in more than a year tonight when in his wheel chair he went to the east portico of the White House and greeted hundreds of Washington League of Nations adherents, gathered on the White House lawn to do him honor.

The crowd of men, women and children, bearing State banners and the national flag, under the leadership of John F. Costello, Democratic National Committeeman for the District of Columbia, assembled at Democratic national headquarters at 8 P.M. and marched to the White House, where the gates were open to the public for the first time since the beginning of the war.

As the President was lifted in his wheel chair up the steps from the interior of the White House leading to the east portico the crowd on the terrace below broke into applause and joined in singing "America."

Mrs. Wilson and members of the family stood about the President while the crowd sang. With an overcoat buttoned closely about him and a soft hat shading his face, the President sat silent, watching the throng below. There was more cheering as the song ended.

A soloist sang "Carry Me Back to Ole Virginny" and the crowd picked up the chorus. As the song ended amid renewed cheering a large bouquet of flowers was laid upon the balustrade before him.

Looking old and worn and showing plainly the ravages of his illness, the President made a pathetic figure. He lifted his hat and his lips parted as if to smile, but his face seemed tense with emotion. As an attendant wheeled the President back into the White House three cheers were given for "the first figure of the age," for "the first lady of the land," and for "the League of Nations." As Mrs. Wilson waved a final greeting from the doorway the crowd sang "The Star-Spangled Banner."

Printed in the *New York Times*, Nov. 5, 1920.

Joseph Patrick Tumulty to Edith Bolling Galt Wilson

Dear Mrs. Wilson: [The White House] 4 November 1920.

I thought you would like to see this editorial from today's New York TIMES.[1]   The Secretary

TL (WP, DLC).

[1] It was entitled "President Wilson." Its full text follows:

"Singularly felicitous at this time is Mr. Tumulty's quotation of an earlier saying of Mr. Wilson's:

" 'I would rather be defeated in a cause that some day will triumph than triumph in a cause that some day will be defeated.'

"All the essential Mr. Wilson is in that saying; the high, unselfish purpose, the tranquil courage, the long prevision that sees, beyond temporary discouragements, obstacles and disasters, the victory of justice, of right, the welfare of the country and the world. Popular thought may be slower than Mr. Wilson's, but that it will confirm his own on this cardinal policy of the League of Nations he can have no doubt. The people have not voted against the League. In a tangle of questions and complaints there has been no direct expression of popular opinion on that. American participation in the League must come because it is necessary to the peace and the prosperity of the United States. Meanwhile, Mr. Wilson suffers for a time the fate of Aristides.

"We Americans have our peculiar little ways with our great men. We make heroes of them. We worship them passionately. Then we depreciate them. We hate and damn them. Nothing is harsh enough to say against them when they are in office. When the best-hated of them leave office we begin to discover that they have again the vivid and noble qualities that we attributed to them once and then denied them utterly. The President who was lampooned, derided and denounced as a model of all imperfections and misdeeds is transformed imperceptibly into the ex-President in whom everybody takes a pride, who becomes a venerated public character. Especially is this true of strong and salient personages. Jackson, Cleveland, Roosevelt have been adored and burned, and then adored again. So will it be with Wilson. He, who has read so much history and written it so well, knows the process, the flow, the ebb, and finally the resurgent, unconquerable wave of popular favor.

"Of lasting posthumous fame, the late justice of history, Mr. Wilson is sure. The country owes and will pay him a more immediate obligation. His countrymen owe him much. They will not wait for posterity to clamor into deaf ears what should have been said by their living voices. If we are not mistaken, this hour of apparent petulance and ingratitude is the beginning of the reaction. Having vented all its griefs and irritations, as was its right, the country will think with a growing kindness of the man who has done so memorable a work for it, who has not spared, who has all but spent himself in its service. For long years yet may it be Mr. Wilson's fortune, when his retirement has softened the asperities of political opinion, to live in health and activity among his fellow-citizens and to receive from them, as his great predecessors have received, the honor, the regard and the affection that accompany the old age of illustrious American statesmen—after they are emeriti."

From Josephus Daniels

My dear Mr. President: Washington. 4 November, 1920.

I am enclosing you an editorial from today's New York Times.[1] Since that appeared, several newspaper men have asked me whether this government was offering to send Mr. Harding to Panama on a warship. I was very busy and did not make any answer. What do you wish done about the matter? I would be glad if you will let me know your opinion so that if the correspondents ask me this afternoon, I can tell them whether or not we will do it. Our program is to send the ships to navy yards for the next few weeks and, therefore, it could be done without interfering with any of the regular routine of maneuvers.

                    Faithfully,   Josephus Daniels

TLS (WP, DLC).
    ¹ "Mr. Harding's Visit to Panama," *New York Times*, Nov. 4, 1920, clipping (WP, DLC). The editorial suggested that the Navy Department make available a warship for Harding's proposed tour of inspection of the Panama Canal.

From Edwin Thomas Meredith

My dear Mr. President: Washington November 4, 1920.

I can not tell you how deeply disappointed I am in the result of the election. It is amazing to me that our voters should so little understand. That they will in time realize their mistake and the great obligation they owe you goes without saying. Nothing, however, can take from you the satisfaction of being right, nothing can take from you the glory of your position on the great issue of the campaign and, when our people come to a full realization of the situation, they will unquestionably go as far in the other direction. It has been a great privilege to follow you and it will be an even greater privilege in the future—a privilege which your supporters would not trade for anything in the world.

I feel confused. I feel of so little consequence. I feel so impotent, but I do have a consuming desire to be of service to you personally and to the cause. Will you, in your own good time, point the way?

With assurance of a devotion and loyalty I can not adequately express, and with constant wishes for your continued progress to complete health and strength, I beg to remain

                    Faithfully yours,   E. T. Meredith

TLS (WP, DLC).

From William Gibbs McAdoo

Dear Governor.   New York Nov 4, 1920.

I hope you wont construe the election as a verdict against the League. I am convinced, from my "speaking" experiences, that the people were simply determined on a change because of the prevailing discontent with taxes and everything else which had caused dissatisfaction during and since the war. The Republicans played upon this feeling most unscrupulously and skillfully. Racial distinctions were made and racial prejudices appealed to and the press was systematically debauc[h]ed. I am sure, however, that your great work for world peace will survive and that the Republicans will not dare attempt to destroy the League. Please therefore do not be discouraged however disheartening, at the moment, this victory for reaction may be.

I do hope that you continue to improve and that Nell and I may see you and Edith soon.

With love for you both,

Always affectionately   W G McAdoo

ALS (WP, DLC).

Charles Moore to Joseph Patrick Tumulty

My dear Mr. Tumulty: Washington November 4, 1920.

I have your note of yesterday, saying that, for the present at least, the President prefers to keep his papers in his own possession.

As I wrote you, I was not expecting an immediate decision in regard to sending the papers here; but I did wish you to have in mind the Library of Congress and its desire to be of service,—so often papers are lost because it is not considered that the Library desires such collections, and administers them with a view to serving both the depositor and the students of American history.

Whenever the President is ready to send his papers to the Library, they will be received and treated with the highest consideration.

I am,   Very respectfully yours,   Charles Moore

TLS (WP, DLC).

Stockton Axson to Jessie Woodrow Wilson Sayre

My dearest Jessie: Washington, D. C. November 4, 1920

I do not know that you are likely to receive an immediate report from Edith of your father's splendid condition after the landslide and whirlwind of Tuesday, and so I am sending you a line of reassurance.[1] He has never been finer than he is today, serene, steady, and his patriotism sublime.

Of course, the result of the election was never in doubt—even the magnitude of the result was to have been expected, and therefore some of us (including, I think, you and Frank) were anxious because your father seemed so confident of a Democratic victory—we feared the effect both on his physical health and that sustaining faith which he has always had in the people. Both fears were un-founded. Not since his illness began have I seen him look so much like his old self as he looked today—his color so good, his expression so calm. Once or twice this morning I noted a pathetic little pressure at the corner of his mouth, as if he were pressing back something—but for the most part his expression was both calm and strong, and this evening he was almost merry, laughed more than I have seen him laugh for a year, and told two or three characteristic anecdotes—not about politics. This morning he talked for some time about the election and the country—all the weight of his thought concerned the country, a deep and yearning desire that nothing unfortunate would befall it during these next four years—not a suggestion of bitterness, rather loving-kindness.

Dr. Grayson was over here last night talking about him, and said, what he has not said since last winter, that he believed that in another year your father will be on the golf course "playing chiefly with his right arm." The improvement during the last three or four weeks has been marked. You were here, my poor dear girl, in a period of morbid depression. As I look back now over the last three months I can see that there was a period in which he seemed at a standstill, and unfortunately your and Frank's visit fell in that interval.

I want you to remember this, dear,—it is *true*—not said merely for your comfort. I *know* that you can disabuse your mind of the thought that troubled you—that perhaps your visits are useless. It is *not* so. I shall never forget that last talk with you and Frank in the oval room—your distress, Frank silent, but none the less manifestly unhappy. I can understand it, and at the same time can see that the anxiety is unfounded.

There are things one knows, and yet can't explain. There are times when you may not unnaturally feel that you miss a demonstration of affection which is yours by right. But the affection is there, dear—never forget that. I know it. Genius is a mystery. Illness is another. But there come moments when your father says a little—never much—about your mother and you girls and old times which show how deep it all lies in his heart. I have said all this abominably, dear Jessie, and therefore, I fear unconvincingly—but the gist of it is quite simple. Your father loves you dearly—and is getting much better in health. With dear love for you and Frank and the children,   Your devoted Uncle,   S.A.

TCL (RSB Coll., DLC).
    [1] Axson had come to the White House on July 28 and had moved to the Benedick in Washington on September 3. He was there when he wrote this letter.

To James Middleton Cox

My dear Governor Cox: [The White House] 5 November, 1920

I hope that you know that no Democrat attributes the defeat of Tuesday to anything that you did or omitted to do. We have all admired the fight that you made with the greatest sincerity, and believe that the whole country honors you for the frank and courageous way in which you conducted the campaign.

With the most cordial good wishes and, of course, with unabated confidence,

Cordially and sincerely yours,   [Woodrow Wilson]

CCL (WP, DLC).

To Alexander Mitchell Palmer

The White House

My dear Mr. Attorney General: 5 November, 1920

Is it true, as I have heard,[1] that the Department of Justice trailed Mr. George Creel during his visit to Mexico? This is so outrageous a thing, and would constitute so direct an affront to myself, that I do not want to believe it unless I am told by you that it is true.

Very truly yours,   Woodrow Wilson

TLS (A. M. Palmer Papers, DLC).
[1] Creel was in Washington November 4 and undoubtedly talked with Wilson about this matter.

To Bainbridge Colby

My dear Mr. Secretary: The White House 5 November, 1920

After what we have put in the papers about Mexico, it seems to me certain that all sorts of interests and people interested in Mexican properties and in everything else Mexican will be seeking to get into the game. I writer [write], therefore, to beg (though I dare say it is not necessary) that the Department will receive and act upon no suggestions whatever from anybody connected with the oil interests down there. These are particularly dangerous interests and are certain to lead us astray if we follow their advice in any particular. I particularly distrust Mr. Doheny,[1] who has proved false in so many ways that it would be folly to trust him in any respect.

Pardon me if this warning is superfluous. Now that an administration is about to come in that will try to upset everything that we have done in Mexico, I feel particularly solicitous lest we should prepare the way for their mischief in any way.

With the warmest regard,

Cordially and faithfully yours,   Woodrow Wilson

P.S. I understand that Mr. Lansing is now paid attorney for Doheny. Beware of him, he is by nature and practice a snake in the grass.   W.W.

TLS (SDR, RG 59, 812.00/26464, DNA).
¹ Edward Laurence Doheny, petroleum producer of California and Mexico.

To Bainbridge Colby, with Enclosure

My dear Mr. Secretary: The White House 5 November, 1920

I send for your perusal, and for such items of information as may be valuable to you, the enclosed letter which I have just received from our Ambassador at Rome. If you are communicating with him soon, I would be obliged if you would make an appreciative acknowledgment of this letter for me.

Cordially and faithfully yours,   Woodrow Wilson

E N C L O S U R E

From Robert Underwood Johnson

Dear Mr. President: Rome, October 18, 1920.

As the resumption of negotiations on the Adriatic question slowly approaches—for I feel sure that, despite statements to the contrary, it is being held up, not only for the elections in Serbia but also for our own presidential elections—I am taking every means to keep *au courant* as I know you would wish me to do. Apparently official announcements in the press state that the Jugo-Slavs' basis of negotiation comprizes four points:

1. Fiume and the surrounding country to be under the direction of the League of Nations.

2. That the "Wilson Line" should be adopted in Istria.

3. Dalmatia and the islands to go to Jugo-Slavia.

4. Scutari to be assigned to Jugo-Slavia as compensation.

I understand that this is only a basis, not an ultimatum, and moreover is not definitely official. Apropos of the whole subject it may not be amiss to say that General Evan M. Johnson,¹ our military attaché, told me yesterday that after an extensive tour of inspection of Italian military hospitals in the north, he discovered, in talking with influential persons, that there has been a great moderation in Italy of the feeling against your position in the Fiume question, and in consequence against yourself personally. I think your telegram of sympathy in the matter of the earthquake disaster had a good effect.[2] It is astonishing how susceptible our Italian friends are to sympathy and consideration.

I think you will be interested to know the facts out of which grew the rumor that Orlando was coming to Italy [the United States] as your guest—a rumor which I see La Guardia utilised to make an attack upon you.[3] (By the way, I asked a friend of mine to tell him privately that he was doubtless mistaken in his premises.) Soon after my arrival I was informed by Sloane,[4] Chancellor of the Academy, that it was intended to have a special meeting in New York, in the nature of an international love-feast, with representatives from England, France and Italy and perhaps other countries. I was asked to arrange for an Italian representative, and after a careful inquiry I suggested Orlando as the most available man here, being out of politics, and being a scholar, an admirer of America and moreover a member of the Accademia dei Lincei. My overtures to him were favorably received, but as it proved impossible to get representatives of sufficient distinction from England and France, it was decided to abandon the scheme altogether. I was left in an embarrassing situation, but Orlando, whose heart was by that time really set upon going, accepted the situation like a gentleman, and that was the end of it.

He had previously told me that he had been invited by the President of Brazil[5] to visit that country, but did not think he should go. Some super-serviceable friend of his, putting two and two together and making five, stated in the press that through me you had invited Orlando to visit America. Orlando expressed his regret to me at this publication. He concluded to go to Brazil and sailed ten days ago.

There are evidences here that Giolitti will have to take a firmer stand for the law and order than heretofore. The papers today announce the arrest of Malatesta,[6] the noted anarchist and Deputy. Italy begins to see that her credit abroad is being greatly impaired by the situation here, which, however satisfactory it may seem to the Italian government as a temporary makeshift, is not likely to satisfy other countries. The need of Catholic support, if nothing else, will stiffen Giolitti's policy.

I shall await with great eagerness the result of the election. I cannot believe that it will be anything less than an indorsement of your high-minded and far-sighted action in Paris.

Respectfully and faithfully yours,   R. U. Johnson.

TLS (B. Colby Papers, DLC).

¹ Brig. Gen. Evan Malbone Johnson.

² A devastating earthquake, with aftershocks, had struck in Tuscany in early September. One hundred towns were badly damaged, hundreds of people were killed, and it was thought at the time that the Leaning Tower of Pisa was threatened. *New York Times*, Sept. 8, 9, 11, and 12, 1920. Wilson sent the following telegram to King Vittorio Emanuele III on September 11: "It is with heartfelt sorrow that I learned of the dreadful earthquake catastrophe which has befallen the people of Northern Italy, and I pray your Majesty to accept the deep sympathy of this Government and of myself in this time of suffering and sorrow." *Ibid.*, Sept. 12, 1920.

³ A news item in the *New York Times*, Aug. 21, 1920, reads as follows: "BUENOS AIRES, Aug. 20. President Wilson has offically invited ex-Premier Orlando of Italy to visit the United States, according to the Rome correspondent of La Nacion." A news report in *ibid.*, Aug. 22, 1920, revealed that Italian newspapers were commenting upon the rumor. It also reported that Fiorello Henry LaGuardia, then the Republican President of the Board of Aldermen of New York, had denounced Wilson's alleged invitation to Orlando as a political trick designed to attract Italian-American voters to the Democratic party in the coming election. Another report in the same issue said that the State Department had no knowledge of any such invitation to Orlando.

⁴ William Milligan Sloane, Wilson's former colleague at Princeton University; at this time, Seth Low Professor of History at Columbia University and Chancellor of the American Academy of Arts and Letters.

⁵ That is, Epitacio da Silva Pessôa.

⁶ Errico Malatesta, leader, journalist, and theorist of the world anarchist movement.

To Norman Hezekiah Davis

My dear Mr. Secretary: The White House 5 November, 1920

I do not think that it would be wise for us to take even an unofficial part in the conferences of which you speak that are going on at Budapest with regard to the conditions in Hungary.¹ Our unofficial part in conferences of this sort has not seemed to me to be of very happy result, and I think, therefore, we had better stand aloof, at any rate for the present.

> Cordially and faithfully yours,   Woodrow Wilson

TLS (SDR, RG 59, 864.00/403, DNA).
¹ Wilson was replying to NHD to WW, Nov. 2, 1920 (second letter of that date).

To Josephus Daniels

My dear Mr. Secretary: The White House 5 November, 1920

Will you not be kind enough to write to Senator Harding and say that, having heard that it was his wish to visit the Panama Canal Zone, I have requested you to put a warship at his disposal.

I suggest that the ship wait for him, if it is convenient for him, at Hampton Roads, and that you also offer him in my name the use of the Mayflower to go to Hampton Roads.

> Cordially and sincerely yours,   Woodrow Wilson

TLS (J. Daniels Papers, DLC).

To John Spargo

My dear Mr. Spargo: The White House 5 November, 1920

Your letter of November first has given me the greatest gratification, and I want to thank you very warmly for it. Such evidences of confidence are of the greatest value to me and soften many disappointments.

Cordially and sincerely yours,   Woodrow Wilson

TLS (J. Spargo Papers, VtU).

To William David Johnson, Jr.,[1] with Enclosure

My dear Mr. Johnson: [The White House] 5 November, 1920

I cheerfully comply with your request that I try my hand at a dedication for the LUCKY BAG[2] of the Class of 1921, and I hope that the enclosed will seem to you suitable and satisfactory.

Very sincerely yours,   [Woodrow Wilson]

CCL (WP, DLC).
 [1] Member of the Class of 1921 at the United States Naval Academy.
 [2] The yearbook published by the midshipmen.

E N C L O S U R E

To the men, our comrades, who gave their lives in the great World War for the vindication of the ideals of right, which are the ideals of America, and by whose example it is our hope to be prompted in the observation of every priniciple of honor, of service, and of patriotic devotion.

CC MS (WP, DLC).

To Robert Wickliffe Woolley

My dear Woolley: The White House 5 November, 1920

You are so constant in your friendship and confident support that it is delightful to think of you, and particularly gratifying to receive such a generous letter as yours of the third.

Cordially and faithfully yours,   Woodrow Wilson

TLS (R. W. Woolley Papers, DLC).

From Norman Hezekiah Davis, with Enclosure

My dear Mr. President: [Washington] November 5, 1920.

With reference to our conversation regarding the Island of Yap, I am submitting herewith for your consideration a proposed communication to be sent through to the ambassadors accredited to the principal Allied powers. The question is covered more fully in the draft of the proposed letter from you to Mr. Lloyd George, which was handed to you Tuesday with many apologies, but I am fearful that England, and especially France, will insist upon standing on the records of the minutes of May seventh as interpreted by them. The head of the French delegation to the Communications Conference,[1] who is also in the French Foreign Office, informed me that his government understands that Yap was alloted to Japan by the Supreme Council on May seventh. Strange to say, France is working very closely with Japan and we have much evidence to indicate that France and Japan have reached an understanding to work closely together in China and the Far East, but the British show increased indications of a desire to work in frank harmony with us.

I have given you this additional information, hoping that it may be of some assistance in enabling you to reach a decision as to what should be done under the circumstances.

Faithfully yours,   [Norman H. Davis]

CCL (N. H. Davis Papers, DLC); TCL (SDR, RG 59, 862i.01/124A, DNA).
  [1] Etienne-Marie-Louis Lanel.

E N C L O S U R E

During the recent sessions of the Communications Conference some question has arisen in regard to the disposition of the Island of Yap by the Supreme Council. It has been contended that this Island was included in the islands north of the Equator which were offered by action of the Supreme Council of May 7, 1919, under mandate to Japan. It was the clear understanding of this Government that for reasons vitally affecting international communications, the Supreme Council at the previous request of President Wilson, reserved for future consideration the final disposition of the Island of Yap in the hope that some agreement might be reached by the Allied and Associated Governments to place the Island under international control and thus render it available as an international cable station. For this reason it is the understanding of the Government that the Island of Yap was not included in the action of the Supreme Council on May 7, 1919.

In order to avoid misunderstanding on this point, you are instructed to read the foregoing to the Minister of Foreign Affairs and to leave a copy with him.[1]

CC MS (N. H. Davis Papers, DLC).
[1] This was sent, for example, as BC to Amembassy, Paris, No. 1625, Urgent, Nov. 9, 1920, T telegram (SDR, RG 59, 862i.01/49B, DNA). A note at the bottom of this telegram says that it was sent "Based on instructions from the President approving Mr. Davis' letter of November 5, 1920."

From Graham Patterson[1]

Dear Sir: New York November Fifth Nineteen-twenty.

In response to numerous cable and mail appeals from missionaries and laymen in North China, the Christian Herald has decided to issue a general appeal for funds for famine relief in the five provinces of Shantung, Chihli, Honan, Shansi and Shensi.[2] In doing this we are merely following a precedent which this magazine has set in other famine crises of China, to which we have sent on occasions more than one million dollars to relieve sufferers from flood and draught [drought].

Our most reliable information now indicates that more than 25,000,000 people are face to face with early death by starvation and cold.

In organizing relief measures in other years, we have had the very cordial support and encouragement of the government. Presidents McKinley, Roosevelt and Taft, during their terms of office, officially gave their approval to our efforts, and their words of commendation, in which they emphasized the current need of relief, had great weight with the great mass of people we are able to reach with our appeals.

If you can consistently follow these precedents I am sure it would mean many thousands of dollars would be made available to assuage in some measure the tremendous suffering that has grown out of this—the greatest famine in the history of China.

As in the past, this Fund which we are now undertaking to raise, will be administered by an interdenominational Committee in China, in cooperation with the American Minister and American Consular officials.

We will appreciate any word you can consistently send us in support of the undertaking.

Very sincerely,   Graham Patterson

TLS (WP, DLC).
[1] President and publisher of *The Christian Herald*, an ecumenical weekly magazine.
[2] Famine conditions in the provinces of Chihli, Honan, and Shantung were first reported in the *New York Times*, Sept. 13, 1920. A dispatch from Peking, dated Septem-

ber 12, indicated that critical conditions existed over an area of approximately 90,000 square miles, which contained a population of thirty to forty million. The report estimated that $200,000,000 would be needed to provide adequate relief and said that such a sum was far beyond the means of the existing Chinese government. The dispatch noted also that Charles R. Crane and the diplomats of other countries were organizing an international relief committee.

Later reports suggested that approximately 20,000,000 persons were affected by the famine which had been brought on by severe crop failures in the provinces named. *Ibid.*, Oct. 18 and Nov. 14, 1920.

From Louis Wiley

Dear Mr. President: [New York] November 5, 1920.

The outcome of the election is a keen disappointment, yet I believe the result does not express real opposition of the people to the great issue of the League of Nations. After a period of unusual stress, it is perhaps not surprising that the people appear to desire a change in the administration of their national affairs, without knowing what sort of a change they want or how it shall be brought about.

I recall a letter received from you in May, 1916, in which you said:

"I find that one has to detach oneself in large measure from the talk going on around one in order to see things steadily and see them whole, and sometimes that is very difficult indeed to do. Besides, one does not always know just how safe it is to do it and to trust one's own judgment; but I always try to think what the verdict would be after the event rather than in the midst of it."[1]

Time will soften the asperities of the campaign and in good time there will be ample manifestation of the public's appreciation of your unprecedented and statesmanlike service to the nation and to the world.

I rejoice that your health is permitting you once more to enjoy the open air. I read with pleasure this morning that you were able to see the great throng of your admirers who visited the White House grounds yesterday.

With the uncertainties and anxieties of the Presidential campaign past, I hope you will rapidly regain strength and vigor. After the strain of your eight years in the White House, I know you are looking forward to the end of your term with the consciousness of duty well performed and entitled to rest and recreation.

With regards,   Always sincerely yours,   Louis Wiley

TLS (WP, DLC).
    [1] WW to L. Wiley, May 11, 1916, Vol. 37.

From Frank William Taussig

My dear Wilson: Cambridge, Mass. November 5, 1920

You will not need to be told that if I address you in the familiar way of old times it is from no lack of respect for you or your office. I want to say from my heart that all who know you and sympathize with your ideals will feel toward you now exactly as they did before November 2. The back-swing was inevitable—it's a curious phase of human nature—and it was made the more violent by the iniquitous and too successful intrigue against the League. Heaven knows what the outcome will be. Our friends, the pro-Leaguers, who supported Harding, will have to make good somehow, and will have a pretty time doing so. But your place in history is secure, and will loom up higher as the world get[s] farther away from its present distracted state.

Remember me most kindly to Mrs. Wilson—don't trouble to acknowledge this—and believe me to be
                              always faithfully yours,   F. W. Taussig

TLS (WP, DLC).

From Jessie Woodrow Wilson Sayre

Darling, darling, Father,   Cambridge Mass. Nov. 5 1920

Four years ago today you were up in our little house in Williamstown.[1] Eleanor was christened and we sat beside a big fire and talked. Oh how blessed it was to have you there in our little house so that it could enshrine the memory of your having been there for ever and ever.

We want you in this little house too some day and we are already laying plans for the great event.

We think that after March fourth if you go right on to a ship the blare of publicity will follow you and you will hardly escape it, all the way across. And we were wondering if it wouldn't be a happy thought to have you come right up here where we could and would interpose between you and publicity until a few days had passed, when you could sail away on your little trip much more quietly.[2] We propose this plan so long ahead because we know you are making plans, most likely, already, and we want our idea included before they are entirely settled. Darling, darling Father, how we love you and how we long to have you back with us sitting here with us and seeing us as we are in the little nest we have made so that when you are away you can visualize us.

Several days ago I overheard Eleanor and Francis talking as they looked at a picture of George Washington hanging on the wall (Henry White gave it to us as a "mascot" by the way). Francis said "That is the first grandfather in the world" and Eleanor asked, "Is that the *greatest* grandfather in the world?" and Francis said "*No indeed* OUR grandfather is the greatest grandfather in the world." We, your daughters, dear father, who have known you so long know that you are the Greatest and that there are unknown and unguessed depths of greatness that only those who know and love you suspect. And we are so proud of you and of the great cause that will go marching on for all any one can do against it, for you and the belief of countless thousands whose belief you lifted up into faith *have created* it and it is a living thing. On election night when I couldn't sleep I picked up a life of Joan of Arc and read it through. It comforted me just a little because though they burned her, and her work seemed stultified and frittered away by intrigues and politicians it went on *inevitably* for she had made it alive.

We are very very sad up here except when we think of you and then we glow with such pride and faith and love that we are lifted up.

Later.

Your dear letter about Christmas[3] with its loving messages to us all was fully understood. We will have our Christmas here and then Frank and I will run down, if we may, for your birthday afterwards. That will give us a chance to see you again before the weeks stretch out too long, also we can attend the wedding without having to take part in the elaborateness of it. And we will count the days till we see you again.

The children are well. I told you, didn't I, about the little school we have here. Four other children, two boys and two girls, come in and Miss Larkin, our governess, teaches them from nine to eleven. They are making wonderful progress. Eleanor reads a page already and the mothers are delighted with the eagerness with which their children go to school. The whole idea is working out beautifully and I am quite proud of it.

The baby[4] is more winsome every day. He calls us all by name now except that he seems to merge his father and me sometimes into one calling us Fā-mā or Māfā occasionally. He is a sturdy youngster. His nurse stepped in doors for a *second* one day and came back to find him off the porch and tugging with all his might at a toy a little dog had seized and was trying to carry off. Eleanor is quite scared of this same dog but not so Woodjo!

We all send dearest love to you both and we are wishing that you and Edith might each tell on each other as to any hints of Christmas wishes you may have let fall. We would love to know what you both would *like*!

With a heart over flowing with love

Your adoring daughter   Jessie.

ALS (WC, NjP).
¹ About this visit, November 10-11, 1916, see the news report printed at Nov. 10, 1916, Vol. 38.
² Wilson had obviously talked to Jessie about his plans to go to the Lake District of England in 1921.
³ WW to Jessie W. W. Sayre, Oct. 25, 1920.
⁴ Woodrow Wilson Sayre, born February 23, 1919.

A Memorandum by Homer Stillé Cummings

Memorandum Washington Saturday [Nov. 6, 1920]

To-day I saw W.W. He is a mournful object and the whole household seemed tired. He used the very words Lloyd George reported and added "skunk" for full measure. As I dictate the foregoing memorandum, I have forgotten what the words were but they were the words of opprobrium referring to a French statesman, I think, Poincare.

T MS (H. S. Cummings Papers, ViU).

Two Letters to Bainbridge Colby

My dear Colby: The White House 6 November, 1920

I wonder if you will do me a very great favor. It is time for a Thanksgiving Proclamation and though I have no resentment in my heart I find myself very much put to it to frame a proper proclamation. I wonder if you would be generous enough to try your hand at it for me. I am enclosing a copy of a former proclamation¹ in order that you may see the form which is used. I hope you will not think I am imposing on you. I have the greatest confidence in your extraordinary power of felicitous expression.

Cordially and faithfully yours,   Woodrow Wilson

¹ This enclosure is missing.

My dear Colby: The White House 6 November, 1920

Thank you with all my heart for your personal letter of the third. What every thoughtful man most deeply and earnestly desires is loyal and generous friendship. This you have given me in extraordinary measure and quality, and I am greatly enriched. More complete satisfaction or reward I could not desire.

Your sincere and grateful friend,   Woodrow Wilson[1]

TLS (B. Colby Papers, DLC).
    [1] Wilson made a handwritten draft of this letter and asked Swem to type up copies of it for Colby and Baker. The WWhwL is in the C. L. Swem Coll., NjP. The copy to Baker is WW to NDB, Nov. 6, 1920, CCL (WP, DLC).

To Eleanor Randolph Wilson McAdoo

My darling Nellie: The White House 6 November, 1920

You may be sure that I treasure your letter of the third as I treasure very few others. No harm is done, so far as I can see, to me, or to anything essential. I am distressed only because the country is, I am afraid, in for a period of very great trial, for it is sure to be misguided and led into all sorts of difficulties and distresses.

We both join in love to you and Mac.

Your devoted   Father

TLS (W. G. McAdoo Papers, DLC).

From Josephus Daniels

My dear Mr. President: Washington. 6 November, 1920.

In pursuance of your letter of the 5th of November, I sent the following telegram to Hon. Warren G. Harding:

"The President desires me to say that, having heard you contemplated a visit to the Panama Canal Zone, he has directed me to place a warship at your disposal. I am also authorized to offer in his name the use of the MAYFLOWER to take you to Hampton Roads where the ship will wait for you if that suits your convenience. It will give me pleasure to make such arrangements as will be agreeable to you."

To this the Senator replied as follows:

"I most gratefully acknowledge your gracious telegram in which you convey the President's thoughtful courtesy in directing a warship to be placed at my disposal for a contemplated trip to Panama, along with the use of the MAYFLOWER for connection at Hampton Roads. Please assure the President of my grateful appreciation of his consideration, but I can not accept because I am traveling by railroad to a vacation point in Texas, and I have booked to embark from a gulf port for Panama. I thank you also for your courtesy." Faithfully yours, Josephus Daniels

Ackn & file W.W.

TLS (WP, DLC).

From James Middleton Cox

My dear Mr. President: Columbus November 6, 1920

I thank you most heartily for your very gracious letter of the fifth. Very frankly, the contest never was a personal matter with me because somehow I never quite realized I was running for the Presidency. The cause took possession of my very soul and I was fighting for it and it alone. It is infinitely better to have a shortage in votes than in principle. Human nature hasn't changed much since Shakespeare and the resentments growing out of the great convulsion of the war must be recognized as inevitable.

It doesn't seem just quite right that your international plans should not have been carried out while you were on duty. At the same time I am convinced that it ultimately will make for your added fame. The Almighty doesn't take us into His confidence.

The defeat did not bring the slightest sting to me. I went into the campaign without apology and came out of it the same way. I believe the history of the campaign will show that we held to the high idealism of our party. This thought is reassuring to me.

I trust that you are quite well.

With kind regards for yourself and Mrs. Wilson, I am

Very truly yours, James M Cox.

TLS (WP, DLC).

From Joseph Patrick Tumulty

Dear Governor: The White House, 6 November 1920.

Champ Clark has been defeated and I understand is broken hearted and in great financial distress. He has been a mighty good friend of ours in nearly everything and has made some very generous speeches in your behalf, especially his speech at the Jackson Banquet the night that Mr. Bryan sought to attack you.[1]

There is a vacancy on the Canadian Boundary Commission caused by the death of Governor Glenn of North Carolina. It would be a most gracious thing if you could appoint Speaker Clark on this Commission. The whole country would look upon it as an act of chivalry upon your part to one of your competitors at Baltimore.

I am just offering this suggestion to you off my own bat. He is one of the very few man [men] who could be confirmed by the public and the Senate.[2]   Tumulty

TLS (WP, DLC).
[1] About the Jackson Day Dinner and Bryan's "attack" on Wilson, see Wilson's message on that occasion printed at Jan. 8, 1920, and n. 1 to the memorandum by JPT printed at Jan. 9, 1920, both in Vol. 64. There are brief summaries of Clark's speech in the *New York Times* and the New York *World*, both of Jan. 9, 1920.
[2] Wilson did not make a written reply to this letter. Clark died in Washington on March 2, 1921.

From Bainbridge Colby

My dear Mr. President: Washington November 6, 1920.

No warning is superfluous, in dealing with the Mexican situation, and the note of caution contained in your letter of today[1] is much appreciated.

You are quite right that as a result of our recent announcement, "all sorts of people interested in Mexican properties, etc., will be seeking to get into the game." This has promptly taken place. Not a day passes without one or more calls from interested or *retained* parties, anxious to fathom our intentions, or to leave with us suggestions as to policy, usually very rigorous conditions of recognition, including remission of tax arrears, the validation of dubious land titles and the like, in all of which the personal interest is close to the surface and easily detected.

Yesterday I was asked by a representative of the Oil Producers Association, Mr. John Alvin Young of New York, if I had any objection to the Association retaining Ex-Attorney General Gregory to endeavor to see you and discuss the question of recognition with you directly. I told him the Association had retained so many people in connection with Mexico, that one more or less would hardly matter; but I further remarked that he would have some difficulty, I thought, in persuading Mr. Gregory to accept a retainer in this connection.

Other men, who have been conspicuous in your administration are said to be under retainer, and the number of persons whom I have reason to suspect of being employed to keep us under observation, is almost too large for me to enumerate here.

I have received numerous calls from the oil men and their attorneys. Some of these men are quite reasonable, but the dominant figures among them seem bent on keeping the situation in statu quo until they can try their hand with the new administration. Their purpose seems to be to dangle recognition and financial support in one hand, and with the other to threaten intervention. Thus by working on the needs and the fears of the Mexicans in general, and the cupidity and treachery of certain Mexicans in particular, they hope to bring about a condition whereby they can escape adequate taxation, appropriate the wealth of Mexico for themselves, fortify their monopolies, and exercise a controlling influence in the distribution of oil throughout the world.

I have sought to impress upon them that the recognition of Mexico was an affair between friendly nations, dependent upon certain assurances and proffers (and even guaranties) proceeding from Mexico; that we would not attempt to impose any precedent conditions, preferring to assume that Mexico understands the obligations resting upon a member of the family of nations, and that it was unnecessary for us to pursue a course, although strongly urged upon us, that might affront Mexico's national pride.

The letter of Pesqueira, which with my comment thereon, was published October 30th, was a very significant statement coming from a Mexican official. It went much further than anything I recall, as a statement of virtuous resolves, and I tried in my comment to be as gracious as possible without a premature commitment on the main question. You will remember that I spoke of the Pesqueira letter only as affording a "basis upon which the *preliminaries* of recognition could confidently proceed."

This is as far as we have got. A new crop of Doheny representatives has appeared upon the scene. There are reports of dissympathy between Obregon on the one hand, and the provisional President De la Huerta and his Minister, Calles, on the other. The oil men, apparently, hope for the postponement of recognition until Obregon's inauguration on December 1st. There are rumors of an impending conference near the Mexican border between Obregon and Senators Fall and Harding, in connection with the latter's visit to southern Texas. Also there are reports, which I have no means of confirming, that the oil men have undertaken to make a Diaz[2] of Obregon, and support him with money, and the shipment of arms in return for concessions which he stands ready to make.

We are marking time, and will report to you immediately any significant change in the situation, of course taking not the least action which has not your prior sanction.

Very respectfully yours,   Bainbridge Colby

TLS (WP, DLC).
[1] Actually, WW to BC, Nov. 5, 1920 (first letter of that date).
[2] That is, Porfirio Díaz, President and dictator of Mexico, 1876-1911.

From Bernard Mannes Baruch

My dear Mr President—   [New York] Saturday [Nov. 6, 1920]

There was no referendum upon the League of Nations.

All of those who voted for Gov. Cox voted for the League as it stands

The leaders of the Republican party so managed things that the vast majority of those who voted for that ticket believed they were voting for the League. Daily events since the election confirm me in that belief.

In addition to these misguided men and women there were massed with them all of the discontented and malcontents. The Germans, Irish, Italians Greeks Slavs voted the Republican ticket. Each one thought his country did not get all it was entitled to. Selfishness and misunderstanding combined with these evil forces to bring about the result.

It is true I am disappointed. But I am happy to know these hyphenates disagreed with me.

I am sure that right thinking people who were deceived will flock back to the banner of justice and help carry out our obligations.

You have today the greater respect love and admiration of the thinking and good men and women—greater I think than you have had at any time in the last few trying years through which we have passed

The poor misguided ones will yet rise up and call you blessed for your vision of a better world and the courage and will to hold out for it

The final result is certain. When it is all finished you will have the undying gratitude of those who have been true to the faith as well as that of those misguided ones who will live to curse those who have deceived them.

I would not be truthful if I did not say that at times bitterness and hatred came in to my heart nor would I be truthful nor even human if I did not admit that that bitterness and hatred were caused largely by my love and respect for you.

But I know your greatness and I am sure that each day that come[s] will bring to you the reward of a duty well done and a supreme satisfaction in having accomplished one of the greatest things for all mankind

Today your voice is the greatest in the world and each day will grow stronger and reach further

Devotedly and Affectionately   Bernard M Baruch

ALS (WP, DLC).

To Bainbridge Colby

My dear Mr. Secretary: The White House 8 November, 1920

The enclosed paper[1] came to me through my daughter, to whom someone sent it.

I have very little doubt that its statements are true, and it makes me very angry to think that they may be, but if they are they represent the most gross bad faith towards us and towards the other Allied and Associated Powers by the countries that have been assuming to manage European affairs since the adjournment of the Conference at Versailles. I send the paper to you in order that, if there are any inquiries or protests that you can properly make, I may have the benefit of your advice as to the course we should pursue. Poland not only deserves our friendship and such assistance as we can give her, but the injustice done her is certain to lead to international disturbances of the gravest character.

With warmest regard,

Cordially and sincerely yours, Woodrow Wilson

TLS (SDR, RG 59, 86oc.oo/332, DNA).
  [1] We have been unable to find this enclosure.

To George Creel, with Enclosure

My dear Creel: The White House 8 November, 1920

I send you the enclosed for what it is worth.

Faithfully yours, Woodrow Wilson

E N C L O S U R E

From Alexander Mitchell Palmer

Dear Mr. President: Washington November 8, 1920.

I have your letter of the 5th instant.

It is not true that the Department of Justice trailed Mr. George Creel during his visit to Mexico. We had no agent anywhere in Mexico while Mr. Creel was there.

An examination of our files, however, discloses a telegram from our agent at El Paso, under date of October 25th, in which he says that the Chairman of the Senate Committee (doubtless meaning Senator Fall) "stated had informant traveling with Creel." If Mr. Creel discovered any one trailing him, it was probably Senator Fall's man. Very cordially, A Mitchell Palmer

TLS (G. Creel Papers, DLC).

To Graham Patterson

My dear Mr. Patterson: [The White House] 8 November, 1920

May I not say that the attempts you are making to raise funds for the relief of the distress in China has my most hearty approval and applause? I hope with all my heart that it may be successful in every way.   Sincerely yours,   [Woodrow Wilson]

CCL (WP, DLC).

To Louis Wiley

My dear Wiley: The White House 8 November, 1920

Thank you warmly for your letter of November fifth. The whole staff of the Times must look back with gratification on the splendid and consistent work which the paper did for the right cause throughout the contest. It was fine to have at least one such paper in the country that can see straight and talk straight.

Cordially and sincerely yours,   Woodrow Wilson

TLS (L. Wiley Papers, NRU).

To Harry Augustus Garfield

My dear Garfield: The White House 8 November, 1920

You may be sure that your letter of November second gave me cheer and comfort, and I thank you for it very warmly.

I sincerely hope that all is going well with you and yours.

Cordially and sincerely yours,   Woodrow Wilson

TLS (H. A. Garfield Papers, DLC).

To Thomas L. Snow

My dear Mr. Snow: [The White House] 8 November, 1920

The information brought me by your letter of November first has caused me real distress, because I distinctly remember not only that Mr. Gregory Allen informed us that he had made certain furniture, but that we paid the bills he sent us for his work and the materials he had used. It distresses me to think that he should have misled us so.

It was a pleasure to hear from you and to know something of what is happening to you.

As always,   Your friend,   [Woodrow Wilson]

CCL (WP, DLC).

To H. J. Gregory-Allen

My dear Mr. Allen: [The White House] 8 November, 1920

Do you not remember several years ago making certain oak furniture, in the mission style, for Mrs. Wilson and me? I remember distinctly receiving information from you that you had made certain furniture and sending you payment for the work and material, according to your statement. I took occasion the other day to write to Mr. Snow of The Bluff to ask him if he knew anything of the whereabouts or disposition of the furniture you had made for us. He tells us in reply that he knows of no such furniture and states it is his recollection that you did not make any. I would be very much obliged if you would tell me what you know of the matter.

Very truly yours,   [Woodrow Wilson]

CCL (WP, DLC).

From Bainbridge Colby

My dear Mr. President: Washington November 8, 1920.

Ambassador Johnson has transmitted by cable the Italian Government's suggestion of Mr. Roland I. Ricci[1] as Ambassador to succeed Baron Romano Avezzana.

I beg to enclose a copy of Ambassador Johnson's cable,[2] also a second cable from him, in which he refers to Baron Aliotti,[3] whose name was previously suggested but shortly afterwards withdrawn upon the publication of some damaging reports.

You will observe the request that the Ricci nomination "be kept strictly secret" and that "the Italian Embassy in Washington is not to be informed or consulted." This curcumscribes [circumscribes] us in making the usual inquiries, particularly as Ambassador Johnson says "I know little as yet in regard to Ricci other than etc." and proceeds to mention a few general facts which I construe in connection with his assertion that he knows "little as yet." The Ambassador further says he is promised a biography of Mr. Ricci, which will be "sent on in due course." In his accompanying cablegram he says of Mr. Ricci, in comparison with Aliotti, that "though an altogether worthy man, Ricci cannot compare with him in fitness for this high office." In connection with Aliotti, I beg to transmit a letter I received from former Ambassador Thomas Nelson Page, dated October 5.[4]

The reason I am sending this mattor to you in this obviously incomplete state is because of the Ambassador's statement that "in view of the questions which arose both in Avezzana's case and regarding the agrément of Aliotti, I think the Italian Government would appreciate a very prompt reply to their suggestion of Ricci."

Is there sufficient appeal in Ambassador Johnson's request for prompt action to go ahead upon this meagre and somewhat conflicting report of Mr. Ricci's qualifications, or do you wish me to make the usual inquiries and obtain for you a more complete report upon Mr. Ricci?

Very respectfully yours,   Bainbridge Colby

TLS (WP, DLC).
    [1] Vittorio Rolandi Ricci, lawyer and faculty member of the University of Genoa; member of the Italian Senate.
    [2] R. U. Johnson to BC, Oct. 31, 1920, T telegram (WP, DLC).
    [3] R. U. Johnson to BC, Nov. 2, 1920, T telegram (WP, DLC). Baron Carlo Alberto Aliotti was a career diplomat who had served, among other places, in Russia, the United States, China, and Bulgaria. He was named the Italian Ambassador to Japan on November 9, 1920.
    [4] T. N. Page to BC, Oct. 5, 1920, TLS (WP, DLC). Page conveyed some information unfavorable to Baron Aliotti, most notably that he had opposed Wilson's policy of non-recognition of the regime of Victoriano Huerta in Mexico. Page characterized Aliotti as follows: "He is a very clever man and has held posts of some importance, but he has a reputation of being a great intriguer and with his past history he would certainly not be an element of accord between this Country and Mexico."

From Cleveland Hoadley Dodge

My dear President: New York November 8, 1920.

I have been hesitating for several days whether to do the part of Job's comforter, and I certainly do not want to bother you with any useless vaporings. I knew, without asking, that you would take the result of the election like a true sport, and not be absolutely prostrated, as some of your "dear friends" predicted, and I am glad to see by the morning papers that you have been out driving, and may be well enough to welcome some foreign Legations.

Now that there are five or six days prospective since the election, I do not feel as badly as I did last Wednesday morning. I come in contact almost every day with many prominent Republicans, and they all seem overwhelmed with the sense of responsibility, and the large number of prominent pro-League Republicans in this city feel very confident that their influence will be decisive in bringing about acceptance of the League, without too drastic reservations. They feel that the good working majority which the Republicans will have in the Senate will help their efforts, as the Johnson-Borah outfit will not be able to hold up the rest of the party.

I remember reading once a delightful history of the American people by a man named Wilson, who brings out very clearly the fact that the original Constitution of the United States was not perfect, and that after a few years, desirable amendments were made, so that it may be possible to even amend the Covenants of the

League so that the net result will be beneficial. In any event, I am sure of one thing, that the American people, by their big vote for the Republican ticket, did not thereby wish to repudiate your high ideals, and that the large majority of the American people want some sort of a League, whether it is exactly your League or not. One of my neighbors, who is a large employer of labor, says that the day after election he was talking to an Irishman who was working on his job who said "I do not know anything about the League but I am sure of one thing, that the people want the League, and the reason they voted against the Democrats was just like a man who was sick in bed, and he got tired of lying on one side and rolled over to the other side." Of course most unthinking people thought as soon as the war was over, everything would be serene and happy, not realizing the sick man had been very sick indeed and that it would take a long time for him to recover, and because things did not go as they expected, they blamed the party in power, and of course their unreasonable sentiments were energetically fostered by the Republican politicians. The Republicans of course are not going to have as easy a job as they have predicted and the thinking men amongst them realize that.

As a good Democrat, however, and a devoted friend of yours, I do not feel downcast, and still comfort myself with the two verses which carried me through the war, namely "God moves in a mysterious way, His wonders to perform," and "A thousand years in Thy sight are but as yesterday when it is past."

Now that the agony is over, I certainly trust you are going to regain some of your strength, and I am hoping that next month, if I am obliged to go to Washington, Mrs. Wilson will allow me to get a glimpse of you. Any way, I think of you continually, and pray that you may be spared and greatly blessed.

With warm regards from Mrs. Dodge and myself to both Mrs. Wilson and yourself,

Yours affectionately,   Cleveland H. Dodge

TLS (WP, DLC).

From the Diary of Josephus Daniels

November Tuesday 9 1920

Cabinet—Burleson said the Republicans had plenty of trouble— "But what I am thinking about" said W.W. "is the trouble that will come to the poor country."

What about Treaty? Should the President send it back to the Senate when it meets in December? B— said he should say in his

message that he would send it in later, & then hold till 4 or 5 days
before session & then send so it would be before the Senate when
that body convened March 4th. WW said that would look like a
trick & if he sent it in at all it should be in good faith. Long discussion as to whether he should send. Payne & I opposed or rather
expressed our feeling that no good could come. Reps would either
do nothing or would send it back with such amendments the President could not ratify & people would say he was stubborn. Baker
thought he could not accept without Section 10. Colby thought
much reason for sending. Has any President ever returned treaty
to Senate when it has been returned to him without assent? Colby
was asked to investigate & inform Senate

To Bainbridge Colby

My dear Mr. Secretary: The White House 9 November, 1920
    I have felt for some time, ever since the ugly disposition towards
the United States of the four Powers now attempting to run the
affairs of the world began to disclose itself, that our relationship
with Italy was becoming one of increasing rather than decreasing
difficulty. I, therefore, think that it would be very wise to make
careful inquiries concerning Mr. Ricci before we indicate that he
is *persona grata*.
    Thank you for your letter of November eighth with its enclo-
sures.   Cordially and faithfully yours,   Woodrow Wilson

TLS (B. Colby Papers, DLC).

From Bainbridge Colby

My dear Mr. President: Washington November 9, 1920.
    I respectfully, but none too confidently, submit the enclosed
draft of a Proclamation.[1] If it does not seem right, I would like very
much a chance to try it again.
                    Very respectfully yours,   Bainbridge Colby

TLS (WP, DLC).
    [1] This enclosure is missing.

From Norman Hapgood

Dear Mr. President: Washington, D. C. Nov. 9/20

I inclose part of a letter from the woman who handles Debs's correspondence.[1]

Would it not be a good way out of a bad mess to pardon him on the ground that news had reached you that his health was endangered?

Other countries are treating their consciencious objectors so much more liberally than we are: I don't know a case in Europe anywhere that compares with the Debs case in the intensity of war-psychology it indicates. It and other cases like it have separated some of my best and most influential friends from the administration.

Indeed, this campaign taught me, from repeated experience (what I guessed before) that the Department of Justice's seeing red, along with the State Department's Russian propaganda, is the greatest obstacle met by those of us who have been arguing that support of the Democratic party was the best way to encourage liberalism.

This is the third letter I have written you within a week[2] and I must let you alone in peace!

                    Yours sincerely   Norman Hapgood

ALS (J. P. Tumulty Papers, DLC).
[1] Mabel Dunlap (Mrs. Charles) Curry to N. Hapgood [c. Nov. 9, 1920], incomplete ALS (J. P. Tumulty Papers, DLC). She asked Hapgood's advice on publicity for the campaign to secure the release of Debs from prison. She stressed the need for prompt action in view of Debs' heart condition.
[2] The other two were N. Hapgood to WW, Nov. 4 and 8, 1920, both ALS (WP, DLC). The first enclosed Paul-Louis-Charles Claudel to N. Hapgood, Oct. 19, 1920, ALS (WP, DLC), containing an "appreciation" of Wilson by the French poet, dramatist, and career diplomat, who was at this time the French Minister to Denmark. Hapgood also criticized what he called the State Department's policy of "indirect intervention" and propagandizing against the Bolshevik regime in Russia. His letter of November 8 enclosed a clipping of H(erbert). G(eorge). Wells, "RUSSIA IN THE SHADOW," *New York Times*, Nov. 7, 1920, Sect. 8, p. 1, which, he said, supported his (Hapgood's) belief that the overthrow of the "Lenin government" in Russia would "merely assist in bringing in a cruel anarchy."

From Edward Wright Sheldon[1]

My dear Mr. President: [New York] November ninth, 1920.

During all these months that you have been bearing so bravely the physical and public burdens laid upon you, my profound sympathy has gone out to you increasingly. I should have written you before had I not been reluctant to touch a personal note in so momentous a crisis. It grieves me that the recent expression of the

popular will has not responded to the lofty purpose which has animated you. But I believe still that what you have so nobly advocated is one of the great human truths that wake to perish never,
and that it will triumph.

With warmest regards and most earnest wishes for your continued improvement in health.

Yours sincerely,   Edward W. Sheldon.

ALS (WP, DLC).
    [1] Wilson's classmate at Princeton; member of the Board of Trustees of the university.

From Sylvester Woodbridge Beach

Dear Friend: [Princeton, N. J.] Nov. 9, 1920

I must tell you how disappointed I was at the outcome of the
Election. I fear selfishness is dominating in the Republic as it does
in so many persons. But I do not despair. To lose a battle is not to
lose the war, and I believe that the next reaction will be as decisive
as was this last.

For yourself I have only deeper love and fuller confidence. Your
cause is mine, and I feel honored to suffer defeat, if it be only under your chivalric banner. You stand for all that is dearest and best
in the ideals of a free people, and this will be the verdict of all the
generations to come. My hope and prayer is that you may live to
know that the heart of America still beats responsively with yours.

With love to you all,   Sylvester W. Beach

TLS (WP, DLC).

From Charles Zeller Klauder

My dear Mr. President: Philadelphia November 9th, 1920.

My letter to you of November 2nd conveyed the thought that I
might be ready to present to you today some plans and a summary
of probable costs for the building in which you are interested. It
seemed necessary, however, in order to be certain that what you
assumed in your letter of October 29th in respect to the Q St. property might be verified, that I should have more definite information
as to that site. For that reason, I suggested by telephone to Mr.
Bolling[1] another careful inspection, for I did not wish again to walk
over these properties without permission. The visit was arranged,
but a subsequent telegram and letter from Mr. Bolling requested
that I defer it until you wished to confer with me.

However, I think you would be glad to know we have evolved

several schemes for the hill or Ridge Road property,[2] including one which proposes additions to the house at present on that site.[3] The latter, I am sure, you would find especially interesting.

In addition to this, we have made exhaustive inquiries to ascertain, as nearly as may be, the probable cost. The result would seem more favorable to you than the information I gave on my visit.

In view of your consideration of a house already built, I think an examination of our work would enable you the more readily to weigh the matter. The drawings could be either brought or sent to you. I naturally prefer always to present our drawings personally, in order that they may be fully explained.

Sincerely yours,   Chas Z Klauder

TLS (WP, DLC).
  [1] That is, John Randolph Bolling.
  [2] This was a tract of twenty-six acres, opposite the Bureau of Standards, at approximately Connecticut Avenue and Van Ness Street, N.W., which had a brick house on it. Mrs. Wilson writes in *My Memoir*, pp. 310-11, that Wilson ultimately rejected the purchase of this property on the ground that the government would probably need it for the expansion of the Bureau of Standards in the near future.
  [3] Klauder and his associates drew four sets of plans and elevations of the remodeled and, in one set, expanded brick house. They all portrayed a large but not grand two-story house with a "daughter's room," but without any real servants' quarters. A complete set of these drawings is at the Wilson House in Washington.

To Bainbridge Colby

My dear Colby: [The White House] 10 November, 1920

I thank you with all my heart for undertaking to prepare a Thanksgiving Proclamation for me, and I have read what you have prepared with real admiration, but I ask you to reread it and see if it does not make the impression on you that it has on me of containing between the lines the constant thought of the recent election. I think it would be misconstrued if the country got the impression that even in a Thanksgiving Proclamation we were thinking of our late defeat, and I have no doubt that you can pick out specific things to be thankful for in our recent national experience which can by no stretch of interpretation be considered as having any connection with political events.

Cordially and gratefully yours,   [Woodrow Wilson]

CCL (WP, DLC).

To Bernard Mannes Baruch

My dear Baruch: The White House 10 November, 1920

You always hold your helm true and therefore it is always steady-ing to get a message from you. I am greatly pleased by your mes-sage of Saturday and bless you for it.

Affectionately yours,   Woodrow Wilson

TLS (B. M. Baruch Papers, NjP).

To Richard Heath Dabney

My dear Heath: The White House 10 November, 1920

Thank you warmly for consulting me about the publication of the letters.[1] I hope you will understand my feeling when I beg that you will not allow their publication. There is nothing in them that I should wish to take back, but I have all my life had a passion for privacy which I hope may be indulged in this case.

Counting upon your invariable comprehension of my point of view.   Affectionately yours,   Woodrow Wilson

TLS (Wilson-Dabney Corr., ViU).
  [1] The letter to which Wilson is replying is missing. However, Dabney, in R. H. Dab-ney to J. R. Wilson, Jr., Sept. 13, 1921, ALS (received from Stuart I. McElroy), said that he had given a speech (presumably in Charlottesville, Virginia) about Woodrow Wilson in which he had quoted from letters from Wilson to himself. Before the press report of this speech was released, Dabney went on, he had sent it to Wilson asking whether he objected to the use of the quotations. Wilson then responded as he did on November 10, 1920.

From William Bauchop Wilson

My dear Mr. President: Washington November 10, 1920.

Referring to the discussion yesterday, I am inclosing you here-with copy of a speech delivered by me at Fairmont, West Virginia, on October 26, 1920.[1]

I have taken the ground that the real reason for the campaign of malicious misrepresentation which has been conducted against you and your Administration for the past four or five years was the constructive legislation you had secured, particularly labor legisla-tion, and the progressive policy you have pursued. I tried in all of my campaign speeches, including the one I am sending you, to impress that thought upon my audiences.

I would be very much gratified if you can find time to read it.

Faithfully yours,   W B Wilson

TLS (WP, DLC).

¹ "Speech of HON. WILLIAM B. WILSON, Secretary of Labor, Fairmont, West Virginia, October 26, 1920," mimeograph copy (WP, DLC). After adverting to his life in the trade-union movement, beginning with the Knights of Labor, and noting the Wilson administration's success in achieving nationwide woman suffrage, William B. Wilson went straight to his point of excoriating Republican leadership and apotheosizing President Wilson:

"Since the signing of the Armistice the little Senatorial clique at Washington that now controls the Republican Party and the reactionary portion of big business have conducted the most vicious campaign of misrepresentation that has ever occurred in the history of our country. There has been nothing equal to it, nothing even approaching it, since the small group of politicians undertook to discredit and destroy President Washington because he promulgated the Jay Treaty with England. They failed. The student of history has difficulty in locating the names of the men who made the attempt, while the name of Washington stands out as the bright and shining star in the firmament of our statesmen.

"There has been a definite reason for the campaign of misrepresentation that has been conducted. The present Administration, backed up by the Democratic organization, has enacted into law more social justice and social welfare legislation than any other Administration in our history. For that reason these groups have sought to discredit and destroy the greatest President we have ever had since Lincoln. They will fail. His reputation is made. His fame is established, and the name of Woodrow Wilson will be written on the pages of history as one of the great statesmen of all time. They know that they can not destroy him, but they hope that if they can bring him into temporary disrepute they will be able to defeat the Democratic candidates, secure control of the Federal and State Governments, introduce a reactionary policy, and go back to what Senator Harding calls 'normalcy.' "

William B. Wilson went on to review in detail every single piece of labor legislation enacted by Congress since the Democrats came into control of the House of Representatives in 1911, and he did not neglect the great general reform legislation of the Wilson administration.

Wilson devoted the last half of this long speech to a defense of the Covenant, interspersing his comments with sharp attacks on Harding and other Republican leaders as reactionaries, little Americans, and tools of Wall Street.

From Henry van Dyke

My dear President: Princeton, N. J. Nov. 10, 1920

Not comfort, for you have it: not consolation, for you do not need it: but congratulation, is what I want to send send [sic] you in my birthday letter.¹

You have fought a good fight, you have kept the faith, and thank God you have *not* yet finished your course. With your own eyes you will see the cause for which you risked all, triumphant! The Ark of the Covenant, despite the Flood of the last election, still floats, and the U. S. will scramble aboard at last, dripping but saved. Then you will be glad, because you built the ship.

If you had been in Alexander Hall the other day it would have done your heart good to hear the boys cheer when I brought out your name at the beginning of the Democratic meeting, as "Princeton's bravest and most famous son, who counted not his own life dear in the service of a great hope for the world."

You have carried yourself very nobly in these black storms of calumny, when your friends have been burning with indignation. You have earned the right to be serene and unmoved. That also will go into the portrait which History is painting of you:

integer vitae scelerisque purus.

Meantime we send you proud and affectionate wishes for health and strength to carry on and complete your high task.

Ever and as ever   Faithfully Yours   Henry van Dyke

ALS (WP, DLC).
[1] Van Dyke referred to his own birthday, November 10, not Wilson's.

To Josephus Daniels

My dear Daniels: The White House 11 November, 1920

Is there anything that can properly be done with regard to the enclosed case,[1] do you think? I am sending you the enclosed letter for such consideration and action as you may deem best.

Cordially and faithfully yours,   Woodrow Wilson

TLS (J. Daniels Papers, DLC).
[1] Wilson enclosed J. Franklin Bryan to WW, Nov. 9, 1920, TLS (J. Daniels Papers, DLC). The Rev. Mr. Bryan, pastor of the North Carolina Avenue Methodist Protestant Church in Washington, requested financial assistance for a member of his congregation, John Robertson. Robertson, then eighty years of age, had worked in the Washington Navy Yard for thirty-four years, until he had become medically unable to work some three years previously. Bryan asked that Wilson, by Executive Order or otherwise, provide a pension for Robertson.

To Henry Thomas Rainey[1]

My dear Rainey: The White House 11 November, 1920

I am sincerely grieved to learn that you failed to be elected to the next House. You have certainly been a kind of supporter and the kind of worker for right legislation which any President might be proud to be associated with, and you may be sure that I am sincerely grateful for all the disinterested service you have rendered since my administration began.

Cordially and faithfully yours,   Woodrow Wilson

TLS (H. T. Rainey Papers, DLC).
[1] Democratic congressman from Illinois since 1903. He was subsequently re-elected to Congress in 1922, was elected Speaker of the House of Representatives in 1933, and served in that office until his death in 1934.

To William Bauchop Wilson

My dear Friend: The White House 11 November, 1920
I am very much obliged to you for the copy of your speech delivered at Fairmont, Virginia, in October. I shall look forward to reading it when I can get the leisure of mind to do so. I have admired
throughout the earnest work you have done to clarify the issues
which the country have allowed to become so hopelessly obscured.
          Cordially and faithfully yours,   Woodrow Wilson

TLS (received from Mary A. Strohecker).

To Solomon Bulkley Griffin

My dear Mr. Griffin: [The White House] 11 November, 1920
It is particularly gratifying, in addition to the splendid support
given me and the things I believe in by the Springfield Republican,
to receive your personal letter of the seventh[1] with its delightful
assurances of confidence and approval. Thank you with all my
heart.   Cordially and sincerely yours,   [Woodrow Wilson]

CCL (WP, DLC).
  [1] That is, S. B. Griffin to WW, Oct. 7, 1920.

To Sylvester Woodbridge Beach

My dear Friend: [The White House] 11 November, 1920
Again I am your debtor for a cheering letter[1] which it was delightful to receive and read, and it enabled me to realize how true
and sincere your friendship is.
          Cordially and faithfully yours,   [Woodrow Wilson]

CCL (WP, DLC).
  [1] S. W. Beach to WW, Nov. 9, 1920.

From Bainbridge Colby, with Enclosure

My dear Mr. President: Washington November 11, 1920.
By way of postscript to the annexed letter, the thought occurs to
me that you may not care to refer in terms to the considerations of
a military nature which entered into the selection of certain boundary lines and positions. In the covering letter, addressed to the
President of the Supreme Council, there are three instances in

which such reference is made. I have marked one to illustrate on page 41.

I see no very definite objection to it, and yet as a matter of caution I call your attention to this relatively minor point.

Very respectfully yours,   Bainbridge Colby

ENCLOSURE

From Bainbridge Colby

My dear Mr. President: Washington November 11, 1920.

I beg to transmit herewith the full report of Professor Westermann and his associates, Major Lawrence Martin and Mr. H. G. Dwight, upon the question of the frontier to be fixed between Turkey and Armenia, with an appendix under separate cover containing the principal documents and technical studies upon which the report was based.[1]

In Section VII of the report the Committee has formulated a tentative draft of the covering letter to be addressed by you to the President of the Supreme Council and of your technical boundary decision, which are to be regarded as a single document.

I further beg to enclose a letter from Major-General James G. Harbord,[2] who has kindly given the Committee the benefit of his advice upon all phases of the report.

If you will let me know what changes you wish to make, either in the suggested decision or in the draft of your covering letter to the Supreme Council, I shall take pleasure in having them incorporated in the formal document, in duplicate, for your signature. The accompanying map will then be replaced by a more accurate one on the same scale, showing the boundary in greater detail.

Very respectfully yours,   Bainbridge Colby

TLS (WP, DLC).
[1] About which, see WW to BC, Sept. 1, 1920 (second letter of that date), n. 1. Wilson returned the enclosures with his letter to Colby of November 13, 1920. Davis later sent Wilson another copy of the report and its appendixes for his "personal records." NHD to WW, Dec. 31, 1920.
[2] J. G. Harbord to NHD, Sept. 17, 1920, TLS (WP, DLC). Harbord informed Davis of his full concurrence in the report of Westermann and his associates.

From Bainbridge Colby, with Enclosure

My dear Mr. President: Washington November 11, 1920.

I think my post-election feelings left their impress sub-consciously on the first draft. You are altogether right. It is a note that should not be revealed even to the most sensitive ear.

I have taken another "go" at it, trying to avoid a recital of our goods and fortune,—which might grate upon the nerves of some less happy peoples, but I trust sufficient to satisfy even "America first."   Very respectfully yours,   Bainbridge Colby

TLS (WP, DLC).

E N C L O S U R E[I]

THANKSGIVING—1920
BY THE PRESIDENT OF THE UNITED STATES OF AMERICA
A PROCLAMATION

The season again approaches, when it behooves us to turn from the distractions and pre-occupations of our daily life, that we may contemplate the mercies which have been vouchsafed to us, and render heartfelt and unfeigned thanks unto God for his manifold goodness.

This is an old observance of the American people, deeply imbedded in our thought and habit. The burdens and the stresses of life have their own insistence. ⟨To contemplate life's blessings, and to be grateful for them, appeals to the finer mood.⟩

We have abundant cause for thanksgiving. The lesions of the war are rapidly healing. The great army of freemen, which America sent to the defense of Liberty, returning to the grateful embrace of the nation, has resumed the useful pursuits of peace, as simply and as promptly as it rushed to arms in obedience to the Country's call. The equal justice of our laws has received steady vindication in the support of a law-abiding people, against various and sinister attacks, which have reflected only the baser agitations of war, now happily passing.

In plenty, security and peace, our virtuous and self-reliant people face the future, its duties and its opportunities. May we have vision to discern our duties; the strength, both of hand and resolve, to discharge them; and the soundness of heart to realize that the truest opportunities are those of service.

In a spirit, then, of devotion and stewardship, ⟨let us⟩ *we should* give thanks in our hearts, and dedicate ourselves anew to the service of God's merciful and loving purposes to his children.

Wherefore I, Woodrow Wilson, President of the United States of America, do hereby designate Thursday, the twenty-fifth day of November next as a day of thanksgiving and prayer, and I call upon my countrymen to cease from their ordinary tasks and avocations upon that day, giving it up to the remembrance of God and his blessings, and their dutiful and grateful acknowledgment.

IN WITNESS WHEREOF, I have hereunto set my hand and caused the seal of the United States to be affixed.

Done in the District of Columbia this ——— day of November, in the year of our Lord, one thousand nine hundred and twenty, and of the independence of the United States the one hundred and forty-fifth.

By the President:
  Secretary of State.

T MS (WP, DLC).
  ¹ Words in angle brackets deleted by Wilson; those in italics added by him. This proclamation was published, for example, in the *New York Times*, Nov. 13, 1920.

From Bainbridge Colby

My dear Mr. President: Washington November 11, 1920.

We have a cablegram from Mr. Gary, Minister to Switzerland, asking approval of his attendance as an observer at the forthcoming meeting of the Assembly of the League of Nations which convenes at Geneva on November 15.

There is something to be said for this suggestion, I think. The importance of the occasion is such that our resident Minister might be expected without instructions to follow the proceedings and report thereon to the Department. And if there is any embarrassment about specifically deputing someone to attend, the suggestion Mr. Gary makes might be a good compromise.

Mr. Gary, you may recall, was the Diplomatic Agent at Cairo before being appointed to his present post. He is regarded in the Department as a man of experience and discretion.

Will you kindly favor us with your instructions?
                    Very respectfully yours,   Bainbridge Colby

TLS (WP, DLC).

Edward William Bok to Joseph Patrick Tumulty

                              Philadelphia November eleventh,
My dear Mr. Tumulty: Nineteen hundred and twenty

Will you read this letter¹ and tell me if this is true with regard to the President's feeling for "If?" Should it be so, and you think he would like it, I would be delighted to have a special facsimile made of the original of the poem in Kipling's handwriting. I want to be sure before I go to the trouble, inasmuch as this might be nothing more than a rumor.

Will you let me know, and believe me

Very sincerely yours,   Edward W. Bok

TLS (WP, DLC).

[1] Henry Eckert Alexander to E. W. Bok, Nov. 10, 1920, TLS (WP, DLC). Alexander, formerly the editor and owner of the *Trenton True American* and an early supporter of Wilson's political career, was at this time on the staff of the Philadelphia *North American*. He offered to assist Bok in obtaining a high-quality facsimile of Rudyard Kipling's poem "If" to be presented to Wilson. Alexander explained that, during his period of contact with Wilson, he had learned that a newspaper clipping of the poem had "long been one of . . . Wilson's treasured possessions."

Three Letters to Bainbridge Colby

My dear Mr. Secretary: The White House 12 November, 1920

Thank you very warmly for your reconsidered draft of a proclamation for Thanksgiving. It is admirable and I shall adopt it with the greatest pleasure and with real gratitude to you.

Cordially and faithfully yours,   Woodrow Wilson

My dear Mr. Secretary: The White House 12 November, 1920

I do not feel that we have derived any particular advantage from having observers present at the various councils by means of which the other great Powers are now mismanaging the world, and therefore I do not feel that it would be wise for Mr. Gary to attend the Assembly of the League as an observer on our behalf. Indeed, I think that it would be open to misconstruction by those who are eagerly seeking the opportunity to put us in the wrong light with regard to everything that we do. On the whole, I should think it wise to advise Mr. Gary that he had better not attend.

Thank you for laying the matter before me.

Cordially and faithfully yours,   Woodrow Wilson

My dear Mr. Secretary: The White House 12 November, 1920

I can think of no form of acknowledgment of the enclosed telegram[1] which would not be either perfunctory or banal, and it occurs to me that you would think it good form to ask our Ambassador at London to express to the King my appreciation of the message.   Cordially and faithfully yours,   Woodrow Wilson

TLS (B. Colby Papers, DLC).

[1] George R I to WW, received Nov. 11, 1920, T telegram (WP, DLC). Its text is quoted in the Enclosure with BC to WW, Nov. 13, 1920 (fifth letter of that date).

To Edward Wright Sheldon

My dear Ed: The White House 12 November, 1920

Thank you with all my heart for your letter of the ninth. I hope you know what great store I set by your friendship and approval. If you do, you do not need to be told how much cheer and grateful appreciation your letter brought me.

                    Affectionately yours,   Woodrow Wilson

TLS (RSB Coll., DLC).

To Loring Ashley Schuler[1]

My dear Mr. Schuler: [The White House] 12 November, 1920

It would be a pleasure to see you and the editor of the Ladies' Home Journal on the errand you propose in your letter of November tenth,[2] but I am bound to say to you that it would be hardly worth your while to come. As you may suppose, many similar suggestions have been made to me and in considering them I have been forced to the conclusion that it is yet too early to form any definite plan with regard to literary work or with regard to the channels of publication. I must first settle my new life after the expiration of my term before I can know just what I can do and how I can do it. I am sure you will understand.

With much appreciation of your suggestion,
          Cordially and sincerely yours,   [Woodrow Wilson]

CCL (WP, DLC).
    [1] Managing Editor of the *Ladies' Home Journal.*
    [2] L. A. Schuler to WW, Nov. 10, 1920, TLS (WP, DLC).

To Charles Zeller Klauder

My dear Mr. Klauder: [The White House] 12 November, 1920

I find that I cannot remember whether among the estimates you generously undertook to make there was to be one of the cost of building on the river site.[1] You know how particularly interested I am in that site and in the plan I made for it.

As I understand it, the chief cost would be the wall which would sustain the rear part of the house as its foundation, the wall having its footing between the trolley tracks and the embankment on which the house would be built, and it occurs to me to ask whether by using some relatively cheap material (at least material that I assume to be relatively cheap, like fire brick or very ugly concrete blocks of which some people without taste are now building their houses) enough might not be saved to make it feasible to build there. You will know how to answer this question, of course, though I do not.

We think that we shall presently have concluded negotiations for a house already completed,[2] but if we do, we shall nevertheless need your services and advice with regard to certain improvements which it would be necessary to make, for example the putting in of an electric elevator.

Please do not feel that it would be an imposition on anybody for you to come and go over any one of the sites at any time that you think best in the prosecution of your studies. I am sure no owner that we have dealt with would have the least objection; and Mrs. Wilson and I will be very glad indeed to have you as our guest at any time that you feel you are in need of a restudy of a particular site on the spot.

Cordially and sincerely yours,   [Woodrow Wilson]

TLS (WP, DLC).
¹ The site on Conduit Road.
² This may have been the house at 2241 Wyoming Avenue, N.W., owned by Representative Alvan Tufts Fuller of Massachusetts, who had just been elected Lieutenant Governor of his state and would serve as Governor from 1925 to 1929. The Tafts occupied 2241 Wyoming Avenue when William Howard Taft became Chief Justice of the United States in 1921.

Two Letters from Bainbridge Colby

My dear Mr. President: Washington November 12, 1920.

We have received the enclosed cablegram from Admiral Bristol, dated Constantinople, November 10th.[1]

It states, as you will see, that the evacuation of Crimea is imminent, and the request is made that our High Commissioner at Constantinople be authorized to extend all possible aid to evacuate wounded and families of officers.

I assume that it would be proper to instruct Admiral Bristol to offer such asylum as the facilities at his command admit of, and, if you approve, I will do so at once upon receipt of your instructions.

Very respectfully yours,   Bainbridge Colby

Approved   W.W.

TLS (SDR, RG 59, 861.00/7678, DNA).
¹ N. A. McCully (via M. L. Bristol) to BC, Nov. 10, 1920, T telegram (SDR, RG 59, 861.00/7659, DNA). Rear Adm. McCully reported that Bolshevik forces were about to overrun the Crimea. Colby summarizes the rest of McCully's cablegram.

My dear Mr. President: Washington November 12, 1920.

We are in receipt of the enclosed cablegram from our Charge d'Affaires ad interim in Guatemala, which refers to the conference between the five Central American states which will take place at San Jose, Costa Rica, on December 1st, and communicates the expressed desire of the Guatemalan Government for a "statement of the views of the United States" on the subject.[1]

Do you think it desirable for us to make any expression on the subject?   Very respectfully yours,   Bainbridge Colby

TLS (WP, DLC).

[1] Herbert Stewart Goold to BC, Nov. 8, 1920, T telegram (WP, DLC).

From Josephus Daniels

My dear Mr. President: [Washington] November 12, 1920.

I have your letter of November 11, 1920, enclosing letter of the Rev. J. Franklin Bryan, Pastor of the North Carolina Avenue Methodist Protestant Church, in regard to the reemployment of John Robertson, 224 Twelfth Street, Southeast, City, in the Washington Navy Yard, in order that he may receive the benefits of the Retirement Act.

It appears that Mr. Robertson was discharged from the Washington Navy Yard on December 6, 1917, for missing six consecutive musters. As he has been separated from the service for a period of over three years he is not eligible for reinstatement as the limit of eligibility for reinstatement under civil service rules is one year.

In view of this fact I regret to inform you that there is no way in which Mr. Robertson can secure the benefits of the Retirement Act.   Faithfully yours,   Josephus Daniels.

CCL (J. Daniels Papers, DLC).

From Stephen Samuel Wise

Dear Mr. President: New York Nov. 12, 1920

You may recall that some months ago you addressed a letter to me on the sufferings of the Jewish people in Eastern Europe.[1] The enclosure, "The Jewish Tribune" of Paris, has just come to me and I beg to send it to you. What I like about the editorial statement is that, though written by a European, it reveals a clear understanding of what is happening in the world today, and of the place which is to be your own by the ultimate assent of mankind as the world's leader in its remaking.[2]

    With deep regard, believe me,

        Always faithfully yours,   Stephen S. Wise

TLS (WP, DLC).
  [1] It is printed as the Enclosure with S. S. Wise to JPT, Sept. 9, 1920.
  [2] S. Litovtzeff-Polyakoff, "President Wilson," *Jewish Tribune*, I (Oct. 15, 1920), 1-2. The author said that Wilson's letter, cited in n. 1 above, would probably have no immediate effect on the grim situation of Jews in eastern Europe, "whom the president defended with such sincerity and frankness." "But not withs[t]anding this," the editorial continued, "the letter of President Wilson will remain a document of immense value and gives satisfaction to the offended feelings of the Jewish people."
  The editorial concluded:
  "The speeches and messages of Wilson enraptured the best men of the world as well as the working masses, because, for the first time in History, one heard a representative of government speak the language of the conscience.
  "It seemed that the collective moral and the individual moral, hostile heretofore, were reconciled. For the first time one heard in the acts of states the heart beat and those beatings accompanied a human thought clear and pure as a crystal. Instead of using the un[n]atural strained style of the contemporary parliaments, Wilson had recourse to the simple sincere and sublime language, which reminds us of the divine language of the Bible.
  "It was a series of sermons, and, judging after the reception that was made to them, humanity was yearning for a spiritual chief. It seemed at one moment that Wilson became that chief of the civilized world. He called up all the nations to unite themselves and proclaimed that every people has an intrinsic value, as well as every individual in a whole nation. But inertia vanquished the good energies. Temporary and illusive interests will supplant the true and durable interests. Even, stones were thrown at the prophets of new ideas. * * * However, Wilson would not be Wilson if he were the hero of the sorry epoch we are living through. No, he is the hero of the future. People will come to his ideas."

Two Letters to Bainbridge Colby

My dear Mr. Secretary: The White House 13 November, 1920

    I have received the report of Professor Westermann and his associates which you were kind enough to send me, and understand from your letter that their conclusions are concurred in by Major General James G. Harbord. I feel that I am not qualified by any special knowledge whatever to review this report critically and that my wisest course, unless you suggest something to the contrary, is to accept it as it stands, begging you to make the changes you have yourself suggested in the covering letter.

        Cordially and faithfully yours, Woodrow Wilson

My dear Mr. Secretary: The White House 13 November, 1920

    I have your letter conveying to me the intimation received from our Chargé d'Affaires ad interim at Guatemala that the Central American states would appreciate a statement of the views of our Government on the subject of the conference they are about to hold in Costa Rica. If you have in mind any views which it would be serviceable to send by way of guidance to the conferees, I should be glad to concur, but I shall depend upon your judgment as to whether we should send any or not.

Cordially and faithfully yours,   Woodrow Wilson

TLS (B. Colby Papers, DLC).

Two Letters from Bainbridge Colby

My dear Mr. President: Washington November 13, 1920.

I beg to call your attention to information contained in a recent despatch from Mr. Charles S. Wilson,[1] American Chargé d'Affaires at Sofia to the effect that Mr. Georges-Picot,[2] formerly French High Commissioner in Bulgaria, has presented his letters of credence as Minister of Finance [France] to the King of Bulgaria;[3] France being the first of the former enemies of Bulgaria to enter into regular diplomatic relations with her.

The despatch further states that England, Italy, Belgium, Roumania and Greece have appointed Ministers to Bulgaria; that Spain and Holland already have Ministers there, and that it is expected that Germany, Austria and Turkey will soon appoint Ministers.

As of particular significance, it is added that both the King and the Prime Minister[4] have recently expressed the hope that the United States, which has never been at war with Bulgaria, will also appoint a Minister there and that this may be done before the appointment of Ministers from Germany, Austria and Turkey.

If the appointment of a Minister to Bulgaria should meet with your approval, the name of Mr. Charles S. Wilson, now Chargé d'Affaires at Sofia, may be worthy of your consideration. He has been in the Diplomatic Service since March, 1901, having been appointed at that time, Secretary of the Legation to Greece, Roumania and Serbia. He has subsequently occupied the posts of Secretary of Legation at Havana and Buenos Aires; Secretary of Embassy at Rome; Secretary of the Embassy at Petrograd, and Counselor at Madrid. Since October 23, 1918, he has held the post of Chargé d'Affaires at Sofia.

Mr. Wilson's record in the Diplomatic Service has been a good one. He has fulfilled his various duties conscientiously and with ability and at his present post, he has shown tact and good judgment. He is forty-five years of age.

Faithfully yours,   Bainbridge Colby

[1] Charles Stetson Wilson.
[2] François Marie Denis Georges-Picot.

³ King Boris III of Saxe-Coburg-Gotha.
⁴ Aleksandŭr Stamboliiski.

My dear Mr. President   Washington November 13, 1920.

I have an uncomfortable feeling about sending congratulatory telegrams on anniversary occasions in your name without first submitting them to you. The two messages which appeared in this morning's paper (enclosed herewith)¹ were, through the Department's fault, not brought to my attention until very late in the afternoon, and it was a case of sending them forward immediately or losing the effect of sending them at all. I have issued an instruction to the official in charge of these matters in the form enclosed.

Unless you wish not to be bothered with these matters, I will send all such messages on significant occasions to you for approval before their dispatch.

Very respectfully yours,   Bainbridge Colby

TLS (WP, DLC).
¹ Unidentified newspaper clipping (WP, DLC), datelined Washington, November 12. It quoted messages sent in Wilson's name on November 11 to President Alexandre Millerand of France, on the occasion of the anniversary of the founding of the French Republic, and to King Vittorio Emanuele III, on the occasion of his birthday.

From Bainbridge Colby, with Enclosure

My dear Mr. President: Washington November 13, 1920.

I beg to transmit herewith a memorandum upon our position in Santo Domingo which has been prepared by Mr. Sumner Welles,¹ the very efficient Chief of our Latin American Division.

It is a little long, but I have not attempted to condense it because it is thoughtful and I think you will be interested in its contents.

The suggestions set forth on page 5 relate to certain steps looking to our withdrawal, which may be taken immediately. Although they are only preliminary steps, and must of necessity be followed by many other measures, their adoption at this time would have an allaying effect on criticism which has been directed against our policy in Santo Domingo, and I think our position throughout Latin America would be strengthened through the evidence thus afforded of our mindfulness of the declarations of benevolent and disinterested purpose, made upon assuming control.

It is a little difficult to estimate the full measure of time which the process of withdrawal will take. It must be assumed that we would make our final withdrawal conditioned upon the substantial accomplishment of the main objects that we had in mind in undertaking the direction of Dominican affairs, and that we could hardly justify, even to the Dominicans, the abrupt and irresponsible cessation of our control, which in its larger aspects has undoubtedly been beneficial to the Dominican Republic.

Very respectfully yours,   Bainbridge Colby

TLS (WP, DLC).

¹ A junior career officer in the Foreign Service, he was graduated from Harvard College in 1914 and had served as Secretary of Embassy in Tokyo, 1915-1917, and Buenos Aires, 1917-1919, and as Assistant Chief of the Latin American Affairs Division, 1919-1920. Among his later accomplishments was *Naboth's Vineyard: The Dominican Republic, 1844-1924* (2 vols., New York, 1928), which provides the full background details of his account of Dominican affairs given in his memorandum printed below.

E N C L O S U R E

TO: The Secretary.   October 22, 1920.

There has been a very marked increase in the agitation among all classes of Dominicans during the last few months for an announcement by this Government as to the future policy to be pursued in the Dominican Republic. Particularly notable was the so-called Patriotic Week held during the month of June throughout the Republic for the purpose of collecting funds to be used in this country and in Latin America urging the restoration of the Government of the Republic to the Dominicans themselves. Our occupation of Santo Domingo has created an unfortunate impression throughout Latin America. A resolution was passed recently by the Colombian Congress expressing the hope of the Colombian people that the United States would not withhold longer from the Dominican people their right of self government. Agitation along these lines has existed also to a marked extent in Chile and in Argentina, and the Governments of Brazil and of Uruguay have expressed informally to the Department their solicitude as to our intentions in Santo Domingo.

The facts regarding our occupation of the Island are as follows:

During the forty years prior to 1907 sixteen revolutionary movements took place and the Republic was in a state of complete political and economic demoralization.

In 1907 the Governments of the United States and Santo Domingo concluded a convention by virtue of which, in order that the payment of the interest and amortization of the national debt of Santo Domingo, then amounting to twenty millions of dollars, might be guaranteed, the collection of customs was placed under the control of the United States, and the Government of Santo Domingo agreed not to increase its public debt without the previous approval of this Government.

At first financial conditions improved, but soon further revolutionary disturbances occurred and the Government of Santo Domingo, in order to raise additional funds, increased the public debt of the Republic without our approval consequently violating the terms of the Treaty of 1907. Thereupon, in 1915 this Government requested of the Dominican Government that a new Treaty be entered into providing for the continued collection of the customs under American control, the appointment of a Financial Adviser, and the control by the United States of the native constabulary. This the Dominican Government refused to agree to.

In the meantime the Dominican Minister for War, Desiderio Arias, under the then President, Doctor Jimenez,[1] started a revolutionary movement. Arias retained control of a considerable portion of the Dominican army and gained possession of the fortress of Santo Domingo City. Other forces loyal to the President controlled the country just outside the capital. Another civil war was therefore imminent and the United States, with the consent of President Jimenez, landed naval forces in Santo Domingo to prevent further bloodshed, and to protect foreign life. President Jimenez then resigned and instructions were given to our naval forces to land in the several ports of the country, in order that they might cooperate with the local authorities in restoring public order, and to watch over the election of a new President.

The Dominican Congress proceeded to elect Doctor Henriquez y Carvajal.[2] This Government refused to recognize the election unless it received satisfactory assurances that law and order would be maintained, and that the finances would be honestly administered, and to this end it required, before recognition of the new President, the execution of the Treaty requested in 1915.

The newly elected President refused to agree to our demands, and the American authorities declined to pay the Dominican revenues which it was collecting by virtue of the Treaty of 1907 to the members of a Government which it did not recognize. The deadlock continued for several months and finally this Government directed the naval forces in Dominican waters to assume the organization of affairs. Between May and November 1916 our naval forces occupied the whole of the Republic, putting down what little resistance they encountered.

On the ground that all endeavors to induce the Dominican authorities to conduct their Government in a manner satisfactory to the United States had proven fruitless, and with the declared

[1] Juan Isidro Jiménez.
[2] Francisco Henríquez y Carvajal.

intention of restoring order and prosperity to Santo Domingo a Military Government of the Republic was established on November 29, 1916 with Captain H. S. Knapp, U.S.N., as Military Governor.

In the Proclamation of Captain Knapp, dated November 29, 1916, establishing the Military Government, it was stated that the occupation was undertaken with no immediate or ulterior object of destroying the sovereignty of Santo Domingo, but was designed to assist the country to return to a condition of internal order which would enable it to observe the terms of the Treaty concluded with the United States in 1907, and the obligations resting upon it as one of the family of nations.

Provision can and should, of course, be made, before the Government of Santo Domingo is returned to the Dominicans, whereby the obligations assumed by the United States under the Convention of 1907 are safeguarded, and whereby this Government retains for a term of years the necessary measure of control over the Dominican finances, as well as over the native constabulary.

The question therefore arises whether the internal condition of the country is such that we would now be justified, in view of the promise made in the Proclamation establishing the Military Government, in announcing that we are now willing to take the first steps in returning to the Dominican people the right of self government.

Complete tranquillity has existed for some time throughout the Republic, and the people have been able to devote themselves to peaceful occupations without fear of disturbances.

Public order is maintained almost entirely by an efficient native constabulary officered by American Marines.

The finances of the country have been placed on a stable basis, and the Military Government has met all the expenses of the Government, has paid off all the indebtedness incurred in the year 1916, and had last year in the Treasury a total of nearly four millions of dollars.

The Internal Revenue Department has been re-organized; a settlement of the floating indebtedness has been brought about; a new customs tariff has been placed in operation, and an equitable system of property taxation has been established. Provision has been made for the registration of lands; laws have been reformed and modernized, and great improvements have been brought about in Public Works, in Sanitation, and in Education.

Commerce has reached a volume never before approached, and the gross revenues of the Republic, as the result of our administration, have increased from a total of some four millions of dollars in

1916 to an estimated total of over seven millions and a half in 1919.

Judging by the material prosperity of the country and by the internal order which now exists, it would appear that we were obligated by virtue of the promises made by the Military Government when first established to start turning back to the Dominican people the right of self government.

On the other hand American capital has been invested to a considerable extent in the Republic and American investors, in order that their investments may incur no danger, are exceedingly anxious that American control over the Dominican Government be retained for an indefinite period.

All the officers of the Military Government with whom the Department has spoken have expressed the opinion that the United States should continue to retain control of the Dominican Government for at least twenty or thirty years more, in order that all the improvements now being undertaken might be fully completed before the United States relinquished its control. They express the opinion that the present generation of Dominicans is not sufficiently educated to be enabled to undertake self government, and that a new generation must take their place before we would be justified in giving back to the Dominicans their government.

The educated Dominicans realize and appreciate the beneficial reforms which we have initiated, but it is freedom from the restraint which the Military Government imposes and the right of self government which they ask. I have spoken to several of them and they urge that this Government publicly announce that it is willing to begin the gradual return of the government to the Dominican people.

The consensus of their opinion is that they do not want an immediate return but a gradual return. They want the assistance of this Government in obtaining a complete reform of the present Election Law, and in a far-reaching revision of their Constitution. They are willing and even desirous that the United States retain control of their finances, and assume control of their native constabulary, but what they urge is that the United States at least begin to give back to them gradual control of their Government, and officially announce its intention of doing so to the people of the Republic.

I beg to suggest, therefore, that the following steps should be taken. They can be taken immediately and they would mark only the first of the many stages necessary in the re-establishment of local self government—a process which must necessarily extend over a period of several years:

a. The announcement by Proclamation by the Military Governor

that the Government of the United States intends now to begin to return to the Dominican people the government of their
country.

b. The appointment by the Military Governor of a Commission
of Dominicans to which shall be attached an American Technical Advisor. This Commission will be entrusted with the
general revision of the laws of the Republic, in particular the
drafting of a new Election Law and the formulation of such
amendments to the Constitution as may be deemed necessary. In order that the Dominican people may not feel that
this Commission is composed of Dominicans who do not represent public opinion, it is suggested that the Commission to
be appointed by the Military Governor be composed of the
eleven members of the Dominican Senate elected by popular
suffrage in 1914. Their term of office has not yet expired.

c. All suggested amendments to the Constitution and the initial
revision of the laws after acceptance by the Dominican Commission to be submitted to the approval of the Military Governor. After this fair start is achieved, it is hoped that there
will be no occasion to restrict further the free exercise by the
Dominican people of the Legislative power.

T MS (WP, DLC).

From Bainbridge Colby, with Enclosure

My dear Mr. President: Washington November 13, 1920.

I beg to inform you that I have received a letter from the Italian
Chargé d'Affaires[1] saying that in a telegram which he has received
from his Government, Count Sforza states that Mr. Trumbich, recognizing the moderation of the Italian terms in the settlement of
the Jugo-Slav boundary, accepted them on November 10 on behalf
of his Government.[2] These terms, he states, are summarized in the
telegram as follows:

"Frontier of Mount Nevoso, independence of Fiume, territorial
contiguity between Fiume and Italy, Italian sovereignty on (over?)
Zara, Lussin, Cherso, Lagosta and other minor islands."

Mr. Brambilla states in his letter that he has telegraphed for further and more precise details which he will communicate to me as
soon as they are received.

Mr. Johnson has also telegraphed that at the Foreign Office the
Secretary General confirmed the press announcement of the accord reached at Rapallo. From the information furnished him and
forwarded in his telegram, a copy of which is enclosed, I have had

a map prepared which indicates as closely as possible the new line of demarcation. This map also indicates the line proposed last April as well as that of the Treaty of London.

I am, my dear Mr. President,

Faithfully yours,   Bainbridge Colby

TLS (WP, DLC).
  ¹ Giuseppe Brambilla.
  ² For the negotiations leading to the treaty signed at Rapallo, Italy, on November 12, see Ivo J. Lederer, *Yugoslavia at the Paris Peace Conference: A Study in Frontiermaking* (New Haven, Conn., and London, 1963), pp. 276-308.

E N C L O S U R E

Roma. November 11, 1920.

Urgent. 424. At Foreign Office this morning I had personal interview with Secretary General.¹ He confirmed press announcement of accord at Rapallo with Jugo Slavia on line Sforza's announcement, see my 413 November 6, 5 pm. Some small details remain to be settled but following is officially stated by Contarini: to Italy is assigned Zara and Cherso, to Jugo Slavia the rest of Dalmatia including Sebenico. The frontier line gives to Italy Idria, Adelsburg and San Pietro and runs through Monte Nevoso reaching the Adriatic between Volosca and Castua which is given to Fiume. The Istrian line is to be contiguous with the independent state of Fiume. Italy to have the railway from Fiume to San Pietro. South of Monte Nevoso the higher altitudes go to Jugo Slavia and the lower altitudes to Fiume. Jugo Slavia also is to have Longatico and the adjacent valley. A commercial treaty also is being negotiated at Rapallo and Contarini stated that Italy would accord in both arrangements the most generous treatment to Jugo Slavs who he said care more for Dalmatia than for the new territory added to Italy's military frontier. The solution of this perplexing question is regarded as a personal triumph for Sforza. Map showing new arrangement promised me at earliest moment. Contarini feels confident that Italian public opinion will approve present arrangement.

Johnson.

T telegram (WP, DLC).
  ¹ Salvatore Contarini.

From Bainbridge Colby, with Enclosure

My dear Mr. President: Washington November 13, 1920.

I beg to acknowledge your letter of the 12th instant and to enclose a cablegram I have sent to our Ambassador in London, in pursuance of your request.

I beg to return a copy of the cablegram from King George, addressed to you on November 11th.

Very respectfully yours,   Bainbridge Colby

TLS (WP, DLC).

E N C L O S U R E

AMEMBASSY, LONDON (England)

For the Ambassador.   November 13, 1920.

The President is in receipt of the following cablegram from King George: QUOTE On the occasion of the second anniversary of the day on which the arms of the allied and associated powers in their struggle against the common enemy were crowned with success, I desire to offer you on behalf of the British people an expression of unalterable regard and esteem. END QUOTE.

I am instructed to request you to convey to the King with suitable impressiveness an expression of the President's appreciation of his message.   Colby

T MS (WP, DLC).

From George Crouse Cook[1]

My dear Mr. President: New York. 13th November, 1920.

This Company has recently taken over the SS. GEORGE WASHINGTON and is locating at various points certain items of the furniture and equipment which has been removed from the vessel.

It is understood that you are desirous of obtaining the desk used by you during your voyages upon this vessel and that you have been unable to do so. If this is the case, we shall be pleased to learn further particulars in order that we may make a special effort to obtain the desk in question.

Respectfully yours,   Geo. C. Cook

TLS (WP, DLC).
[1] Naval architect of the United States Mail Steamship Co., Inc., of New York.

Three Letters to Bainbridge Colby

My dear Mr. Secretary: The White House 15 November, 1920

I have been rendered very sad by what I have read in the papers about the alleged Jugo-Slav-Italian settlement. Italy has absolutely no bowels and is evidently planning a new Alsace-Lorraine on the other side of the Adriatic which is sure to contain the seeds of another European war. If it does, and the seeds develop, personally I shall hope that Italy will get the stuffing licked out of her. She has absolutely no conscience in these matters. Of course, however, if the Jugo-Slavs have entered into an agreement voluntarily with the Italian Government and wish it to stand as a settlement, I do not feel that we are obliged to defend them against themselves. I will be very much obliged if you would satisfy yourself entirely by a conference with the Jugo-Slavic representative here that the settlement is genuine, is voluntary, and that the Jugo-Slavs desire its confirmation, because nothing can stand without our acquiescence. The Treaty expressly reserves to the five principal allied and associated governments the final disposition of those portions of the former Austro-Hungarian Empire which are not definitively allotted in the Treaty itself.

Cordially and sincerely yours,   Woodrow Wilson

My dear Mr. Secretary: The White House 15 November, 1920

Personally, I feel disinclined to appoint a Minister to Bulgaria. I have found the Bulgarians the most avaricious and brutal of the smaller nations that had to be dealt with in the war and in the settlement of the terms of peace, though for a long time my vote was for Roumania in those respects. Being no longer committed to Roumania, I can perhaps transfer my suffrages to Bulgaria.

Cordially and faithfully yours,   Woodrow Wilson

TLS (B. Colby Papers, DLC).

My dear Mr. Secretary: The White House 15 November, 1920

Thank you for your letter of November thirteenth and the accompanying memorandum on our position in Santo Domingo which was prepared by Mr. Sumner Welles, the Chief of the Latin American Division. I am glad to agree with you that the steps he suggests should be taken looking towards a gradual withdrawal of our interference with the self-government of Santo Domingo, and I will be very glad if you would make the necessary announcements and prepare the necessary methods for the fulfillment of our assurances.

Cordially and sincerely yours,   Woodrow Wilson

TLS (SDR, RG 59, 839.00/2478, DNA).

To John Sharp Williams

My dear Friend: The White House 15 November, 1920

Your letter of November eighth[1] contained, as your letters always do, a great s[t]imulation for me. Your judgment I cannot but admire, because it is generally my own, and you put the same interpretation on the recent elections that I have myself put. You may be sure they shall have all the rope they want to hang themselves with, and that the hanging will be complete. They will know how to do it to the Queen's taste!

With warmest regard,

Cordially and faithfully yours,   Woodrow Wilson

TLS (J. S. Williams Papers, DLC).
    [1] It is missing in both the Wilson and Williams Papers in DLC.

To Stephen Samuel Wise

My dear Rabbi Wise: [The White House] 15 November, 1920

It was kind and thoughtful of you to send me your letter of November twelfth with its editorial from the Jewish Tribune which you were kind enough to enclose. I read it with real interest and gratification.

Cordially and sincerely yours,   [Woodrow Wilson]

CCL (WP, DLC).

To Samuel Hayward, Jr.

My dear Mr. Hayward: [The White House] 15 November, 1920

I of course very warmly appreciate the suggestion of your letter of November tenth[1] that you would be glad to assist us to find a quiet summer home in some part of New Hampshire or New England, but, unfortunately, it will not be possible for us to own more than one home and that one for all the year round, and therefore I have no choice but to let your kindness go with a mere Thank you, but the Thank you is said with the greatest sincerity and appreciation.   Cordially yours,   [Woodrow Wilson]

CCL (WP, DLC).
  [1] S. Hayward, Jr., to WW, Nov. 10, 1920, TLS (WP, DLC).

To Edward William Bok

My dear Mr. Bok: The White House 15 November, 1920
    Tumulty has handed me your letter of November eleventh about
Kipling's poem, "If." It is true that I have derived constant inspiration from that poem and have often consciously tried to live up
to its standards. I would greatly appreciate such a facsimile of the
poem in Mr. Kipling's handwriting as you generously suggest that
you may send me. Your friendship always gratifies me very deeply.
            Cordially and sincerely yours,   Woodrow Wilson

TLS (WP, DLC).

To Albert Sidney Burleson

My dear Burleson: The White House 15 November, 1920
    With regard to the enclosed,[1] I am sorry to say that I must ex-
press an entire unwillingness to have my effigy mounted as is suggested in association with the proposed memorial. Moreover, just
between you and me, I don't fancy the partner they offer me.[2]
            Faithfully yours,   Woodrow Wilson

TLS (A. S. Burleson Papers, DLC).
  [1] R. E. Vinson to ASB, Nov. 8, 1920, TLS (A. S. Burleson Papers, DLC). The Rev. Dr.
Robert Ernest Vinson, President of the University of Texas since 1916, informed Burleson that "Major" George Washington Littlefield, former captain in the Confederate
Army and a prominent rancher and banker of Austin, Texas, had donated $250,000 to
the university for the purpose of erecting a memorial gateway at the south main entrance to the campus. The plans for this memorial were being prepared by Chicago
architects with the assistance of Cass Gilbert. Pompeo Coppini, a sculptor of Chicago,
was making the bronze work for this memorial. The plans envisaged a joint memorial
of the Confederacy and of the World War in order to symbolize the reunion of the two
great sections of the nation. The prominent statues planned for the gateway were those
of Jefferson Davis and of President Wilson, who would be holding in his hands the
Covenant of the League of Nations.
    Vinson asked Burleson to bring this matter to Wilson's attention, to secure his con-
sent to the erection of the statue of himself, and to supply the sculptor photographs of
himself, "shoes, collar, gloves, hat, etc., so that the sculptor may be faithful in the manner of measurements, and might be able to discover a suitable model for the study."
Vinson added that he would be glad to come to Washington for a personal conference
with Wilson and others.
  [2] In spite of Wilson's reply, the committee of the university trustees in charge of the
project persevered. The entire project, which included a Littlefield Memorial Fountain
and numerous statues of Confederate generals and Texas worthies, in addition to those
of Wilson and Davis, was not completed until 1932. Meantime, Coppini's plans were
considerably altered, much to his displeasure. However, the main features of the arrangement were statues of the standing figures of Davis and Wilson, which were placed
on promontories in front of the main library building. To our knowledge, this is the only
standing statue of Wilson in existence.
    About Littlefield, see J. Evetts Haley, *George W. Littlefield: Texan* (Norman, Okla.,

1943). About Coppini, see his autobiography, *From Dawn to Sunset* (San Antonio, Texas, 1949). For good accounts of the project, see the articles by Bill Barnes and Jan Marston in the Austin *Daily Texan*, Oct. 14, 1961, and December 10, 1968, respectively.

To George Crouse Cook

My dear Mr. Cook: [The White House] 15 November, 1920

I warmly appreciate the courtesy of the Company in making the suggestion embodied in your kind letter of November thirteenth, but I am somewhat at a loss what reply to make.

So long as the GEORGE WASHINGTON and its contents were the property of the Government of the United States, I felt that it would be perfectly proper to put a portion of the furniture which she contained into use in the White House, and I did particularly desire to have the use of the desk which was in the stateroom I used as an office on the vessel during my voyages to and from Europe to attend the Peace Conference. But now that the ship and its contents have passed into other hands, I no longer feel that I am entitled to the use of anything that she contained at that time. If you can certainly identify the desk (I remember that it had little shelves at either end of its table space), I will be very glad to purchase it if you are willing to part with it and put a price on it.

I particularly appreciate your friendly thoughtfulness in taking the matter up with me.

Sincerely yours,   [Woodrow Wilson]

P.S. Will you please convey my thanks to the Directors of the Company?

CCL (WP, DLC).

To David Laurance Chambers[1]

My dear Mr. Chambers: [The White House] 15 November, 1920

I am of course gratified by the suggestion contained in your letter of November twelfth, written on behalf of the Company, but you have been misinformed as to my literary labors. Indeed, you will not be safe in assuming anything about me that you see in the newspapers to be true. They have no information whatever as to my personal plans, and will have none. My literary plans are all yet to make, and I am postponing the making of them until I shall be free.

I am none the less obliged to the Company for its expression of interest, and beg that you will convey to them my sincere thanks.
Very cordially yours,   Woodrow Wilson

CCL (WP, DLC).
¹ Princeton 1900, member of the firm of the Bobbs-Merrill Company of Indianapolis. Wilson was replying to D. L. Chambers to WW, Nov. 12, 1920, TLS (WP, DLC). Chambers said that newspapers had reported that Wilson had "already done some of the preliminary work of assembling and collating the data to be used as the basis for a diplomatic history of America's participation in the World War." He expressed the hope that his company might publish the completed work.

From Thomas Alva Edison

Sir: Orange, N. J. November 15, 1920.

I take pleasure in acknowledging the receipt of the Distinguished Service Medal and Citation forwarded by you to me through the Secretary of the Navy.¹
Respectfully yours,   Thos A Edison

TLS (WP, DLC).
¹ Daniels announced the award of the D.S.M. to Edison for his wartime services on November 12. *New York Times*, Nov. 13, 1920.

George Creel to Edith Bolling Galt Wilson, with Enclosure

Dear Mrs. Wilson;   New York City November 15, 1920

I inclose herewith copy of a letter to Secretary Colby. Unless you think that it will bother the President, please show it to him. I do not want him to be in any doubt as to my position. Believe me, with warmest regards,   Always sincerely   George Creel

TLS (WP, DLC).

E N C L O S U R E

George Creel to Bainbridge Colby

[New York] November Twelfth,
My dear Mr. Secretary: Nineteen Twenty.

In disassociating myself instantly and absolutely from the Mexican negotiations, I beg the privilege of summarizing in order to keep the record clear.

When I saw the President in late September,[1] I ventured an opinion that the Mexican question was commencing to look as if it might be answered. After eleven years of internal disorder, the Republic was finally at peace: no rebel remained in arms against the federal authority, business was being conducted on a gold basis, a national election had been held in peace and fairness, and, best of all, the men in power had the vision to see that the friendship of the United States was vital to Mexico's stability and prosperity.

These changes had been explained to me by representatives of Mexico with whom I was on friendly terms, and who were trying to induce me to visit their country for the purpose of writing on the new order. I did not wish to go, could not afford to go, and my mention of the matter to the President was entirely for his information. He seemed greatly impressed and urged me to make the trip, stating that such a visit, with its chance for informal and unofficial conversations, held every promise of helpfulness. I saw you, at his suggestion, and we reviewed the situation in detail. The whole discussion was so complete as to leave no room for misunderstanding. I consented to go, but insisted that it must be in my private capacity as a writer, paying every expense out of my own pocket, holding no authority, and under no obligations save to my conscience. The position of the United States was a matter of record. For seven years we had proved our friendship for Mexico by the exhibition of unexampled patience and forbearance. All that we had ever asked was merely Mexican compliance with international law, particularly in respect to the payment of debts, the adjustment of claims, and adequate protection to the lives and property of foreigners.

On my own money, then, and my own master in every respect, I went to Mexico and interviewed President-elect Obregon, Provisional President de la Huerta, Secretary of War Calles, and Secretary of the Treasury Alvarado.[2] Making it plain at every point that I spoke only as an American citizen and a writer, the issues in controversy were broached and discussed. On the part of the Mexican officials there was a very deep conviction that the natural resources of the country had been taken away from them, and that the people were not sharing in the profits of development. However, there was frank admission of the fact that Mexico could not develop her remaining resources, or launch her program of national reconstruction, without the support of the other nations of the world, a support conditional upon acceptance of obligation in the matter of

[1] About Creel's meeting with Wilson on September 21, see R. H. Murray to H. Morgenthau, Sept. 21, 1920.
[2] Salvador Alvarado.

claims and in freeing Mexican law of any hint of confiscation. I found a very distinct bitterness, bred by many unfortunate experiences with foreign investors, also the abnormal sensitiveness that invariably marks the attitude of a proud people in dealing with a stronger nation, but under all I saw a very real patriotism, a profound belief in the idealism of the United States and an intense desire for peace and friendship between the two republics.

I make bold to think that the simple straightforwardness of these talks was responsible for various speeches of General Obregon that carried amity and adjustment in every word, and for the remarkable statement of President de la Huerta[3] in which he declared the desire of Mexico to meet every international obligation and every international duty. In any event, Mr. Roberto Pesqueira was returned to the United States as confidential agent of the Mexican Government, empowered to take all action in the direction of friendship that did not surrender sovereignty or shame national pride.

Upon returning to the United States, I found that a very malicious speculation had been permitted to work unchecked. Interviews, credited to the State Department, "repudiated" me, painted me as a comic opera intruder in the sacred realm of diplomacy or else as a regrettably disturbing factor in delicate negotiations, while other statements denied that Mr. Pesqueira had been seen, would be seen, or that the question of Mexico was even under discussion. Fake interviews, cabled from the City of Mexico, had also been given free circulation, adding to confusion. I accepted your word, and that of Mr. Davis, that these various reports were without authorization, but I could not help feeling that the truth should have been declared. How much more simple and more just to have said that I had gone to Mexico on my own business as a writer, and that if I returned with information of value to the State Department, it would be received gladly, as the Mexican question was always open for settlement?

I reported to you in Washington on October 23, and described my visit in detail to you and Mr. Davis. It seemed to me that the way had been cleared for a resumption of the friendly relations that meant so much to both countries, and while the Latin pride of the Mexicans made them unalterably resolved not to be put in the position of accepting conditions, I gave it as my opinion that they were willing to make voluntary offer of all necessary adjustments.

Your enthusiasm was as generous as it was unstinted. You declared that I had broken the stupid deadlock of diplomacy, bringing

[3] See n. 1 to the Enclosure printed with JPT to WW, Oct. 26, 1920.

two peoples together in honesty and simplicity. Conversations were commenced with Mr. Pesquiera [*sic*] at once, and out of his enthusiasm he wrote you a letter on October 27[4] in which he threw diplomatic conventions aside, speaking to the American people in honor and sincerity. Frankly, nobly, he asked our friendship, meeting our declared positions by unequivocal statements that Mexico would settle every rightful claim: that the new order entertained no thought of confiscation, and that President-elect Obregon and President de la Huerta had made public and repeated declarations to the effect that Article 27 of the Mexican Constitution was not, and would not be interpreted, as retroactive or violative of valid property rights. This letter appealed to you as so fine and inspiring that you gave it to the press, together with a statement[5] in which you made these declarations:

"I think I am warranted in saying that the Mexican question will soon cease to be a question at all, inasmuch as it is about to be answered, not only as it concerns the United States but indeed the whole world as well.

"The letter of Mr. Pesquiera offers a basis upon which the preliminaries to recognition can confidently proceed."

The country's reception of the Pesquiera letter and your statement was remarkable in the unanamity of approval. Press and public men, regardless of party, hailed the two documents as the intelligent end of a bitter business. The governors of Texas, Arizona and New Mexico telegraphed the President, testifying to their belief in the stability and sincerity of the Mexican government, asserting satisfaction with border conditions, and urging speedy recognition.

All that remained to do, it se[e]med, was an exchange of informal notes, reducing general propositions to specific terms in order that there might be no misunderstanding as to what the treaty of the future would contain. I left Washington convinced that this procedure would be followed and happy in the thought that I had been privileged to be of some slight service to my country.

A week went by without action, however, and then the press began to fill with disquieting reports: the State Department was not engaged in discussions with Mr. Pesquiera, discussions were not contemplated, the two statements should not be taken too seriously, recognition was a vague uncertainty, etc., etc., together with ugly insinuations as to my own activities. I went to Washington on November fourth, this time for the purpose of protecting my repu-

[4] Actually, on October 26, 1920. Its full text is quoted in n. 1 to Enclosure 1 printed with BC to WW, Oct. 28, 1920 (first letter of that date).
[5] It is printed as Enclosure III with *ibid.*

tation. I had made myself responsible for the institution of an orderly process that the State Department had publicly approved:
why, then, was it interrupted? Why was Mr. Pesquiera's letter denied the courtesy of an answer? Why had enthusiasm died so suddenly, and why was I being subjected to guerilla attack?

I gathered that you were properly anxious that the interests of
the United States should be safeguarded, and that delay was
largely due to the summoning of Judge Parker,[6] representative of
the Petroleum Producers' Association. My anxiety was profound,
but I took comfort in the fact that the bases of settlement—claims
commission, arbitration commission and protection to life and
property of foreigners—had been fixed publicly, and could not be
departed from in honor.

On Friday, November 5, I was given a copy of the tentative draft
of the memorandum in which Judge Parker set forth the conditions which must be met by the Mexican Government as a precedent to recognition. In virtually every particular it departed from
the bases of agreement offered by Mr. Pesquiera in his letter, and
accepted by you in your statement. Instead of a claims commission, operating under the recognized practice of international law,
the Parker memorandum asked the United States to force the
Mexican government to accept unquestioned and unlimited liability in these terms:

"FIRST: The Mexican government recognizes its pecuniary responsibility for *all* damages arising from the death of, or injuries
to, persons, or damage to, or destruction of, property of foreigners, whether corporations, companies, associations or individuals, where such injuries, damages, or destruction were occas-
sioned [occasioned] by the acts of its own representatives, or by
*the acts of those engaged in insurrection or rebellion against the
then existing Mexican government, or in brigandage and beyond
the control of the then existing Mexican government.*"

Instead of simple insistence that Article 27 should not be given
retroactive effect, and that the private property rights of foreigners
should be protected against confiscatory legislation, the Parker
memorandum asked the United States to force the Mexican government into what was virtually an absolute and unconditional
surrender of sovereignty to the foreign oil interests in Mexico.

I saw you on Saturday, and made no effort to conceal my sense
of shock. I told you that such a memorandum would not only insult
Mexico, but that it would offend and anger the people of the
United States. You were explicit in your statement that the Parker

[6] That is, Edwin Brewington Parker.

memorandum would not be accepted but you were not explicit in stating your future course. Out of the doubts that seemed to possess you there came finally the admission that I was under grave suspicion of being in the employ of the Mexican government and in the pay of the oil companies.

As I explained to you, one lie answered the other, nor was it surprising that such lies should be told, for the average man finds it hard to believe that there are those so foolish as to give time and money without hope of other reward than the approval of conscience. All my adult career, devoted to what I conceived to be public service, has been subjected to this sort of attack, and my answer has always been a perfect willingness to submit my bank book to inspection. I stand ready to do this today. I paid every expense of the Mexican trip out of my own pocket, and not one cent has been or will be received by me from the Mexican government, the oil companies, the United States, or from any other source either directly or indirectly connected with the matter.

You were kind enough to say that you did not believe these rumors, but the fact of their circulation, together with the general hopelessness into which the whole affair had fallen, made me feel that an instant dissasociation from the negotiations was the one proper step.

At the risk of seeming to intrude again, may I give you my views on the situation as it stands today. The Pesqueira letter, written under date of September 27 [October 26], and made public on September [October] 29, together with your statement, has not yet been answered. Nor has Mr. Pesqueira been invited to the State Department for discussion. Aside from the feelings of the Mexican Government, already called upon to wait seventeen days for acknowledgment of a letter that you publicly acclaimed, what is more certain than that press and people will soon commence to demand an explanation?

I know, just as you know, that there are selfish interests in the United States—rich, powerful and unscrupulous—who do not want the Mexican question settled. They want a continuance of bitterness until the day when political conditions are ripe for the armed intervention that will guarantee their dividends with American bayonets. They are telling you that it is best to let matters rest until Obregon's inauguration on December 1, but when Obregon is President they will have other reasons to urge for further delay.

I have never ventured to press my course of action upon you. What I tried to do—what I did do, as you yourself admitted—was to break a diplomatic deadlock, secure an agreement on fundamentals, and bring the two republics face to face for frank discussions and honest settlement. All that I say now is that these discussions can not be broken off in honesty. If the Mexican government disrupts negotiations by refusing to deal concretely, then we are free from blame, but until such refusal, the responsibility rests squarely on our shoulders.

I have the deep feeling that the people of the United States are eager to see the Mexican question settled and I am just as firmly convinced that settlement is merely a matter of over-the-table discussions governed by law and justice without regard to the intrigues of privilege seekers or the pressure of purchased influence.

In conclusion, permit me to say that henceforth I reserve the fullest right to protect myself against attack, whether from the front or behind. There is no phase of this business of which I am ashamed—no detail that I am afraid to discuss in the open. Believe me, Very truly yours,[7]

CCL (WP, DLC).
[7] The TLS is G. Creel to BC, Nov. 12, 1920 (SDR, RG 59, 812.00/24774½, DNA).

From Norman Hezekiah Davis

My dear Mr. President: Washington November 15, 1920

I hasten to inform you that Ambassador Johnson, in two telegrams just received, reports that he is advised by the Italian Foreign Office that the text of the treaty between Italy and Jugo-Slavia on the Adriatic question is correct as published by the press. He states that he is promised a copy of it which he will forward as soon as possible and that he is mailing, by the next pouch, the Italian text as published in the press.

The Serbian Minister[1] has left with me a copy of a telegram received by him from Mr. Trumbich to the effect that the treaty has been signed whereby Italy obtains the frontier of the Sneznik and territorial continuity with Fiume, which is recognized as an independent state, and also the islands of Lussin, Cherso, Lagosta and Pelagosa, and Zara with restricted hinterland. The telegram from Mr. Trumbich adds that an accord has also been signed concerning the execution by Austria and Hungary of the treaties of St. Germain and Trianon.

I am, my dear Mr. President,
Faithfully yours, Norman H. Davis

Ackn & file W.W.

TLS (WP, DLC).
[1] Slavko Y. Grouitch (or Grujić).

From Charles Stedman Macfarland

My dear Mr. President: New York November 15th, 1920

In behalf of the Administrative Committee of the Federal Council of the Churches of Christ in America, it gives me pleasure to invite you to attend the Quadrennial Meeting of the Federal Council which will be held at Ford Hall, Boston, December 1 to 6.

The Administrative Committee recalls with pleasure and appreciation your presence and your messages at the original conference which initiated the Federal Council in 1905[1] and at the Annual Meeting of the Executive Committee in 1915.[2]

It is earnestly hoped that you may find it possible again to participate in the deliberations of the Council.[3]

Faithfully yours,   Charles S. Macfarland

TLS (WP, DLC).
   [1] See the notes for an address and the two news reports printed at Nov. 19 and 20, 1905, Vol. 16.
   [2] See F. M. North *et al.* to WW, Dec. 10, 1915, and Wilson's address printed at Dec. 10, 1915, Vol. 35.
   [3] "Dr. [Emory Olin] Watson left the attached letter at the office this morning and requested that the President be advised that the Federal Council of the Churches of Christ very earnestly hoped that the President would find it possible to send a message to the Council." [White House Staff] to WW, Nov. 17, 1920, TL (WP, DLC).

From Bliss Perry[1]

Dear Mr. President: Cambridge Nov 15. 1920

Ever since the election, I have wanted to say to you that your old friends are prouder of you than ever. I know that you are receiving many more such messages than you can possibly read, but when strangers are flooding you with expressions of devotion, Mrs. Perry[2] and I wish very much to be counted in. I should like to sit down with you once more and have one of our old talks about Burke and Bagehot and Lamb and Stevenson! Perhaps that will come yet, after you have unbuckled your Presidential armor and can turn again to "mere literature."

Do you remember how happy Mr. Cleveland[3] looked that night in the Nassau Club, just after leaving Washington behind him, when he put his gouty foot up into a chair, lighted a long cigar provided by "Bill" Libby,[4] and chuckled over the performance of some negro minstrels? I know you don't care for cigars—though you used to provide excellent ones for your colleagues—but the time is coming when you can put your feet up as high as you like, knowing that you have finished such a job as no American since Lincoln has accomplished. A temporary defeat in a noble cause is an essential ingredient of all true glory, and however the election may have gone in 1920, your magnificent record will endure. I think you have too much of the historian's training and philosophy not to be aware of this, and I hope that it comforts you daily.

I have imperilled my immortal soul by hating and despising all your enemies, and I propose to keep it up. Yet I trust that tranquil and happy days are coming for you, when you can forget the strain of the Presidency, read some of the old books over again, and, like John Wesley's father—or was it Hazlitt's?—"Keep on talking of glory and immortality until the end." You will never know how many friends you have won, but I beg you to remember that some of the oldest are not the least loyal, and among the old and loyal ones you must not forget to reckon the Perrys, now and always.

Affectionately yours,   Bliss Perry

ALS (WP, DLC).
¹ Wilson's old friend from Princeton days, at this time Professor of English Literature at Harvard University.
² Annie Louise Bliss Perry.
³ That is, former President Grover Cleveland.
⁴ William Libbey, Jr., longtime Professor of Physical Geography at Princeton University.

From H. J. Gregory-Allen

Dear Mr Wilson: Sechelt B C Nov 15/20

I received a letter from Mr Snow a day or so ago in which he sent me a coppy of a letter that you had written him on Oct 22 about the furniture that I was to make for you.

You left plans & and an order for some Mission furniture with me. The plans were burnt at the time Heimra was burnt & the lumber was delivered the following spring You sent me a postal note for the lumber which I turned over to the Mulchenbacker lumber co. but I did not receive any money for making furniture

You never sent me any fresh plans & I certainly understood that the order was cancelled

I stowed the oak lumber in Mr Snows barn before I left Muskoka some 16 years ago.   Sincerely Yours   H. J. Gregory-Allen

ALS (WP, DLC).

Edith Bolling Galt Wilson to Edward Mandell House

My dear Col. House: The White House [Nov. 15, 1920]

The faithful Wilkins¹ has just come to me to tell me he has two suits of clothes of yours which have been here two years. So I told him to pack and send them right on to you, as I was sure you had forgotten about them, and that in these "H. C. of L."[2] days it would be a refreshing and wonderful discovery.

So they will be following this very promptly.

I hope you are very well this Winter. My own dear One is slowly climbing the long hill which [he] seemed never to begin to ascend.

With remembrances to Mrs. House and all good wishes.

Faithfully yours   Edith Bolling Wilson

ALS (E. M. House Papers, CtY).
   [1] William J. Wilkins, White House head house cleaner, who served as Wilson's valet during Arthur Brooks' absence.
   [2] "High Cost of Living."

From the Diary of Josephus Daniels

1920 Tuesday 16 November

Cabinet—Palmer said proposition to Alien Prop. Cust.[1] by Americans to organize a 10 mil. co. & be given control of $170 mil. of money belonging to Germans—debentures to be issued—Germans in Germany to give their consent—& money to be used to open trade with Germany He said Sec. 9, conferred the power. Would help cotton. "Damn cotton" said W.W. Scheme a gigantic one for the favored company The President sat down on it hard as he did on Palmer's suggestion that the 500,000 cash belonging to the German Government be used to pay the holders of German bonds who live in the U. S. "Most of the holders of these bonds were German sympathizers" I said "and should wait until all other claims are met"

   [1] Francis Patrick Garvan.

From Paul Hymans[1]

Geneve (Nov. 16, 1920)

The Assembly of the League of Nations has by unanimous vote instructed me to send you its warmest greetings and to express its earnest wishes that you may speedily be restored to complete health. The Assembly recognizes that you have done perhaps more than any other man to lay the foundations of the League. It feels confident that the present meeting will greatly advance those principles of cooperation between all nations which you have done so much to promote.   Paul Hymans,

President of the Assembly.

T telegram (WP, DLC).

[1] Hymans had been elected President of the Assembly of the League of Nations by an overwhelming majority at its First Plenary Meeting on November 15, 1920, at 11 a.m. At the beginning of the Second Plenary Meeting in the afternoon of that day, George Nicoll Barnes moved that a tribute be sent to Wilson:

"Mr. G. H. Barnes (British Empire).—Before proceeding with the Rules of Procedure, might not this be a convenient time to pay also a tribute to President Wilson and to send a message to him expressing our hope that he may recover from his illness?

"We all know that President Wilson voiced the idea of a League of Nations in a magnificent way. We owe a great deal to him in the matter of this Conference having been convened, and I think it would be a timely thing if we sent a message to President Wilson. I move in that direction.

"The PRESIDENT. *Translation*: I am sure we shall all concur in the feelings expressed by Mr. Barnes. We shall fulfil a duty very dear to us in conveying our best wishes to the illustrious statesman, who, in Paris, spent so much time and devotion towards the realisation of the idea of a League of Nations, whose spiritual father he may be considered to be.

"(*The motion was carried.*)"

League of Nations. The Records of the First Assembly. Plenary Meetings. (Meetings Held from the 15th of November to the 18th of December 1920). (Geneva, 1920), pp. 42-43.

From Bainbridge Colby

My dear Mr. President: Washington November 16, 1920.

I beg to enclose a copy of a telegram[1] just received from Ambassador Johnson transmitting a biographical sketch of Senator Roland Ricci whom the Italian Government has proposed as Ambassador to the United States.

From this biographical report and from other information which I have obtained in regard to Senator Ricci, it appears that he is a very prominent lawyer of Genoa and a professor at the Law School of the University in that city; that he has a large and remunerative practice for important commercial and corporate interests, and is also interested in the newspaper TRIBUNA, which he is supposed to have materially aided when it was in financial straits, thereby gaining the gratitude of Giolitti during whose premiership in 1913 he was made a Senator. He has taken an active part in politics during the last ten years, in association with the Liberal Party. He was sent as the Italian delegate to the recent conference at Brussels. It is further understood that his relations with Mr. Giolitti are close and friendly and that his standing is high as a member of the Senate and of the Bar.

Before sending the telegram referred to above, Mr. Johnson cabled on the 9th instant in regard to this same matter, a copy of which message[2] I beg to enclose. This latter telegram reflects press comments on the recent transfers of Italian Ambassadors.

I am, my dear Mr. President,

Faithfully yours,   Bainbridge Colby

I have no objection to Ricci, though I expect to beard the Italian government about the time he gets here (*re* Adriatic)   W.W.

TLS (B. Colby Papers, DLC).
    ¹ R. U. Johnson to SecState, No. 430, Nov. 15, 1920, T telegram (SDR, RG 59, 701.6511/358, DNA).
    ² R. U. Johnson to SecState, No. 419, Nov. 9, 1920, T telegram (SDR, RG 59, 701.6511/355, DNA).

Edward Mandell House to Edith Bolling Galt Wilson

My dear Mrs. Wilson: New York City. November 16, 1920.

I had forgotten that the suits had been left in Washington. We have looked for them here but concluded that with so much moving they had been lost. Thank you for having them sent to me, and will you not please thank Wilkins for the care of them.

I am glad that the President is steadily improving. I am sure that when he is free from his heavy responsibilities he will soon become well again. My sympathy and affection have been with you both throughout the trying year that has passed.

I am enclosing copies of some letters which may be of interest to the President.¹

Mrs. House joins me in all good wishes for you both.

Sincerely yours,   [Edward M. House]

CCL (E. M. House Papers, CtY).
    ¹ EMH to B. M. Baruch, Nov. 10, 1920; EMH to S. Gompers, Nov. 10, 1920; EMH to W. S. Benson, Nov. 11, 1920, all CCL (E. M. House Papers, CtY). In his letter to Baruch and Gompers, House said that a group of Philadelphians were organizing a series of lectures to be given in the Academy of Music there by fifteen of the major American participants at the Paris Peace Conference. House invited Baruch and Gompers to participate. In his letter to Admiral Benson, to whom he had already written about this matter, House assured the Admiral that the lectures would be entirely nonpartisan and of a scholarly nature. There will be further correspondence about these lectures in the next volume.

To Paul Hymans

[The White House, Nov. 17, 1920]

The greeting so graciously sent me by the Assembly of the League of Nations through you has gratified me very deeply indeed. I am indeed proud to be considered to have played any part in promoting the concord of nations with the establishment of such an instrumentality as the League to whom increasing usefulness and success I look forward with perfect confidence. Permit me to extend my personal greetings to the Assembly, if they will be gracious enough to receive them, together with an expression of my hope and belief that their labors will be of immense value to the whole civilized world.   Woodrow Wilson.

T telegram (Letterpress Books, WP, DLC).

To Newton Diehl Baker

My dear Mr. Secretary: [The White House] 17 November, 1920

This is a very ill-natured telegram[1] and I am sorry on that account to send it to you, but since it concerns a matter over which you have jurisdiction I take the liberty of submitting it to you for any comment or advice you may be pleased to give it.

Cordially and faithfully yours,   [Woodrow Wilson]

CCL (WP, DLC).
[1] It is missing in both WP, DLC, and the N. D. Baker Papers, DLC. However, about this matter, see NDB to WW, Nov. 19, 1920, and subsequent correspondence.

William Gibbs McAdoo to Edith Bolling Galt Wilson

Dear Edith—   New York Nov. 17, 1920.

Please forgive me for using a pencil. Ever since I injured my right arm in an automobile accident some years ago it has been more difficult for me to write with a pen.

I am told again that the Republicans will appoint a Committee to investigate Santo Domingo shortly after Congress convenes in December. I should be sorry to see this done because I don't think we can defend our position in Santo Domingo. We can defeat the Republican plan by promptly doing justice ourselves and I am sure that we can do it effectively along lines that will protect every American interest while at the same time satisfying the people of San Domingo.

I enclose a brief I have had prepared in my office.[1] I wish you would read it. It isn't as long as it looks (only 24 pages) and I think you will find it very interesting.

Pages 18 to 24 outline the kind of action we could promptly take if the President would permit Counsel here for the San Domingans to act with the State Department instead of sending for a Committee of San Domingans as suggested in Sec. 2 p. 19.

I am their Counsel. I have not formally appeared before the State Department yet, but have had a member of my staff visit Mr. Davis informally. The time has arrived when I must either act or retire from the case and let some Republican lawyers be substituted for me. This would, I am sure be unfortunate. I know I can help more than any one else in the circumstances to get a satisfactory place for the San Domingans. If I retire now they (the Dominicans) will misunderstand and misconstrue it but if the President wants me out of the case, I'll retire immediately as I do not want to embarrass him. I wish you would ask him to indicate his wishes immediately as I do not want to be unduly embarrassed myself. I took the case in the first instance because I felt that it was better for the administration to have it in friendly hands. The San Domingans came to me because of my prominence in the Pan American Financial Conference and in the International High Commission work.

If the President promulgates a plan without the State Department giving consideration to the desires of the San Domingan people and without securing their cooperation, it will not meet the situation nor end the matter. We must do nothing which is or looks like the imposition of our will arbitrarily on San Domingo, as to the kind of government its people shall have.

I think it wise, therefore, to consult with the State Department and agree on a plan that will be acceptable to the people of San Domingo.

The simplest plan is to restore the deposed de facto officers of the Republic—those we put out in 1916—and to maintain a similar protectorate to that we exercise over Haiti until a new government is chosen by the people in a proper election. It is just this sort of question which ought to be settled by agreement between the State Department and Counsel for the Dominicans or a Commission representing them. The latter, however, involves needless delay and would give the Republicans their opportunity.

It is certain to my mind that the Censorship should be abolished immediately and the Military Courts as quickly as possible.

Dr. Castellanos[2] is President of the Patriotic League, for which we are acting and Dr. Henriquez is the deposed President of San Domingo. He is here in New York and in consultation with me.

I am sure that this situation will admit of no unnecessary delay.

My dearest love for you and the Governor. Nell and the babies are fine.   Devotedly Yours   W G McAdoo

ALS (WP, DLC).
 [1] "MEMORANDUM Re Intervention of United States in the Dominican Republic and Suggestions for Restoration of its Government," T MS (WP, DLC). This memorandum reviewed Dominican-United States relations between 1905 and 1920. It condemned the establishment of a United States military government by Admiral Knapp in 1916 and said that there had been many well-authenticated instances of brutality against Dominicans by the American forces. It recounted in some detail evidences of Dominican unrest over and protest against the acts of the military government since January 1920 and then went on in eloquent criticism of the alleged flagrant denial of all basic Dominican human and political rights. "Certainly the time has come," the memorandum said, "when some concerted action should be taken to establish a Government of the Dominicans by themselves. There is no wish to have the marines suddenly withdrawn. The

plan for restoration is discussed in more detail hereafter. They are perfectly willing to allow the customs to be administered by the United States as during the years following 1907."

The balance of the memorandum discussed the legal objections to President Roosevelt's intervention in 1905 and the validity in international law of the so-called Roosevelt Corollary to the Monroe Doctrine. Finally, the memorandum outlined a number of steps that might be taken by the State Department to restore self-government to the Dominican Republic.

It is interesting to note that the memorandum cited the article, Lewis S. Gannett, "The Conquest of Santo Domingo," in the New York *Nation*, CXI (July 17, 1920), 64-65, which presented the Dominican case to the American public for the first time.

² Furcy Castellanos.

From Thomas L. Snow

Dear Mr President: Juddhaven P O. Ontario. November 17th/20

I was surprised—anything but agreeably—to note from your letter of November 8th how clear and possitive is your recollection of the furniture transaction with Gregory Allen. There would seem to be frail hope that he will be able entirely to clear himself of the stigma of deceit, and just because this is so unpleasant a thing to contemplate I am nervously concerned that he will be frank and make honorable reparation to you as far as it lies in his power to do so. I can not think that he will do otherwise. At least he has the opportunity of explaining himself, since I immediately mailed him a copy of your letter to me of October 22nd.

It is not impossible that Gregory Allen may have made certain furniture to your instruction and removed the same to British Columbia when he and his family emigrated there, but if this was the case, I have not the least knowledge of it. I knew next to nothing of his affairs or possessions neither when he left Muskoka or later. It would greatly relieve me to learn later that Gregory Allen had reinstated himself in your estimation, and I shall not cease earnestly to hope that he will take every possible measure to that end.

With sincere good wishes for that physical comfort and that personal well-being concerning which the papers are so teazingly reticent,

Believe me, Mr President.
                        Very faithfully yours,   Thomas Snow.

TLS (WP, DLC).

From Edward William Bok

Philadelphia
November seventeenth,
My dear Mr. President: Nineteen hundred and twenty

I did not think for a moment that Tumulty would bother you personally about "If." But of course I am delighted to hear from you direct. I will at once have a facsimile of the poem in Mr. Kipling's handwriting made for you, and send it on when it is ready.

With always-continuing regard, believe me

Very sincerely yours,   Edward W. Bok

TLS (WP, DLC).

To Alexander Mitchell Palmer

The White House
My dear Mr. Attorney General: 18 November, 1920

I have read very carefully what you sent me about Mr. Evans and Mr. Hughes in connection with the appointment to the Judgeship of the Western District of Tennessee, and also your comment upon Mr. Finis J. Garrett,[1] but my own judgment is that Mr. Garrett is much the best appointment. I have had many personal dealings with him and believe that he is of just the quality we ought to prefer in appointments of this sort. I have therefore determined upon Mr. Garrett as the appointee for the Western District of Tennessee, and would be very much obliged if you would send me the commission for my signature.[2]

Cordially and sincerely yours,   Woodrow Wilson

TLS (A. M. Palmer Papers, DLC).

[1] A. M. Palmer, "MEMORANDUM TO THE PRESIDENT. *In re Judgeship, Western District of Tennessee, vice McCall, deceased,*" Oct. 4, 1920, TS MS (WP, DLC). Palmer stated that, among the many suggestions he had received for a successor to the late Judge John Etheridge McCall, the persons most worthy of Wilson's consideration were Marion Griffin Evans of Memphis, one of the leading lawyers of western Tennessee; Allen Hughes, former judge of the Circuit Court in eastern Arkansas; William Harris Swiggart, assistant attorney general of Tennessee; and Finis James Garrett, Democratic congressman from Tennessee since 1905 and one of Wilson's most loyal supporters. The appointment of either Evans or Hughes, Palmer pointed out, would be acceptable, and, between the two, Evans was "a shade the better." "While the appointment of Garrett would be a well merited recognition of a loyal and deserving Democrat," Palmer concluded, "his appointment would not be so well received in Tennessee as that of Evans and his experience would hardly justify the same confidence in his success as a Judge."

[2] As it turned out, Garrett's nomination did not reach the Senate floor until March 3, 1921, when due to Lodge's opposition, it was not confirmed. *Cong. Record*, 66th Cong., 3d sess., pp. 4399-4400. Garrett remained in the House of Representatives until 1929.

To Thomas Alva Edison

My dear Mr. Edison: [The White House] 18 November, 1920

Thank you for your letter of November fifteenth. You may be sure that such part as I played in the conferring of the Distinguished Service Medal and Citation was played with the greatest pleasure, because of my admiration for you and my entire confidence in you.

Cordially and sincerely yours,   [Woodrow Wilson]

CCL (WP, DLC).

To Charles Stedman Macfarland

[The White House]
My dear Doctor Macfarland: 18 November, 1920

I wish most unaffectedly that there was some likelihood of my being able to attend the Quadrennial Meeting of the Federal Council of the Churches of Christ in America, which is being planned to be held in Ford Hall, Boston, in December, and I am sure you will understand that it will not be. I hope that you will convey to the meeting in my name the most cordial greeting and an expression of the most confident hope that the work of the Council will result in the best things for the churches, for the nation, and for the world.   Cordially and sincerely yours,   [Woodrow Wilson]

CCL (WP, DLC).

To Joe Skidmore[1]

My dear Mr. Skidmore: [The White House] 18 November, 1920

Thank you for your letter of November ninth,[2] but I have no intention whatever of writing or publishing "memoirs." I have always acquiesced in the joke that there are three kinds of personal memoirs,—biographies, autobiographies, and ought-not-to-biographies. And whether mine ought to be or not, they will not be.

I am none the less obliged to you for your kind suggestion about the Laguna Life Publishing Company. As a matter of fact, I have made no plans with regard to my future literary work, except the negative conclusion above stated.

You will understand, of course, that this is only for your own and the company's information.

Sincerely yours,   [Woodrow Wilson]

CCL (WP, DLC).
[1] Business manager of the Laguna Life Publishing Co. of Laguna Beach, Calif.
[2] J. Skidmore to WW, Nov. 9, 1920, TLS (WP, DLC).

To Cleveland Hoadley Dodge

My dear Cleve: The White House 18 November, 1920

I am always grateful for your letters, but I am particularly grateful for yours of November eighth. This is inevitably a time of discouragement, and such messages from old and loved friends help mightily.

Mrs. Wilson asks me to thank you for sending the letters[1] of the little children who are your neighbors. We both read them with the greatest interest and pleasure.

Mrs. Wilson joins me in affectionate messages from us all.

Affectionately your friend,   Woodrow Wilson

TLS (WC, NjP).
  [1] They are missing.

To Bliss Perry

My dear Perry: The White House 18 November, 1920

Your letter of the fifteenth gave me the greatest pleasure and I thank you for it with all my heart. I need hardly tell you that the confidence of old friends is of special cheer and value to me just now.

Will you not thank Mrs. Perry for joining with you in the generous messages you sent, and believe me, as ever,

Your sincere friend,   Woodrow Wilson

TLS (B. Perry Papers, MH).

From Bainbridge Colby

My dear Mr. President: Washington November 18, 1920.

On receipt of your letter of the 15th I at once sought an interview with the Minister of the Jugo-Slavs to ascertain if he had further information concerning the details of the Jugo-Slav-Italian settlement beyond the meagre facts which I have already had the honor to transmit to you.

He has received nothing additional. I questioned him on the points mentioned in your letter, and requested him to ascertain the circumstances under which the settlement was reached, what pressure, if any, was applied to the Jugo-Slavic representatives, what were the motives and inducements operating to bring about the agreement, and also its effect upon public opinion in his country.

The Minister said that he had received information that the windows of the Foreign Office in Belgrade had been broken by demonstrants, and that there had been other displays of popular resentment.

I will forward to you promptly further information as it is received.

There was a newspaper report this week to the effect that our Ambassador at Rome had, in conjunction with the representatives of Great Britain and France, expressed satisfaction at the settlement. I cabled our Ambassador warning him to refrain from such expression on the merits of the settlement, and asking him if the report had any foundation.

Yours respectfully,   Bainbridge Colby

TLS (WP, DLC).

From Bainbridge Colby, with Enclosure

My dear Mr. President: Washington November 18, 1920.

I think I should forward to you the enclosed communication from M. Estrada Cabrera, who has been confined in prison in Guatemala since the recent overturn of his Government.[1]

The Department has on several occasions instructed the Legation in Guatemala City to make representations to the new Government as to the importance of treating the ex-President humanely. These representations have been received in good spirit, and we are informed that there is no undue hardship in Cabrera's present situation. I think that his successor, Herrera, would like to see Cabrera leave the country, but is apparently timid about braving a certain section of public opinion in Guatemala which is insistent that Cabrera should be punished for some of his alleged misdeeds. Our Minister[2] was in Washington not long ago and said that he thought an effort might be made after the first of the year to secure Cabrera's release, with a fair prospect of succeeding.

As you know, Cabrera has ruled Guatemala in a very despotic way, and yet he has been a consistent friend of the United States and loyal to its interests in the face of a good deal of hostile propaganda in Central America.

Very respectfully yours,   Bainbridge Colby

TLS (WP, DLC).

[1] The government of Manuel Estrada Cabrera, President of Guatemala since 1898, had been overthrown on April 15, 1920, by a coalition of conservative and liberal politicians under the leadership of Carlos Herrera y Luna. The United States had recognized the Herrera government on June 21, 1920. See the documents printed in FR 1920, II,

718-55, and Dana G. Munro, *Intervention and Dollar Diplomacy in the Caribbean, 1900-1921* (Princeton, N. J., 1964), pp. 457-65.
    [2] That is, Benton McMillin.

ENCLOSURE

(Translation)

To President Wilson: Guatemala, 24th September, 1920.

Owing to the imprisonment by which I am isolated and sacrificed, the most that I can say to you is that only in God and you rests my faith in obtaining justice and my liberty.

I beg you, Sir, to receive the bearer, Doctor Morales, who brings to you my appeal.

I am ever your sincere admirer, loyal ally of your country and yourself and affectionate servant,   M. Estrada Cabrera.[1]

T MS (WP, DLC).
    [1] The ALS, in Spanish, is in WP, DLC.

From Bainbridge Colby, with Enclosure

My dear Mr. President: Washington November 18, 1920.

I received this morning a letter from United States Judge George W. Anderson,[1] in Boston.

It is a letter, I think, you would be interested to read.
                        Very respectfully yours,   Bainbridge Colby

TLS (WP, DLC).
    [1] George Weston Anderson, United States district attorney for Massachusetts (1914-1917); member of the Interstate Commerce Commission (1917-1918); judge of the United States Circuit Court of Appeals in Boston since November 1918.

ENCLOSURE

George Weston Anderson to Bainbridge Colby

PERSONAL:

Dear Mr. Colby: Boston. 16th November, 1920.

That the leading Republicans are afraid that President Wilson will spoil their plans of a "Republican peace" by resubmitting the Treaty with a message to the effect that after "the solemn referendum" he will accept such reservations and modifications as the Senate think wise, comes to me from rather inside, but I think credible, sources. I hope he will do it,—briefly for the following reasons:

(1) *Probably* such re-submission would improve the prospects of a real League of Nations. I *think*, although it is not free from doubt, that he could get a better Treaty now than would come under the new administration. Panicky business conditions, among other things, will ground a considerable pressure for early action. Apparently, only restoration of order in Europe and an outlet for the tremendous mass of surplus products in this country, will prevent mighty serious financial and business conditions in this country.

(2) Such re-submission is a logical and consistent result of the solemn referendum and required to justify the position taken by the administration.

(3) It would tend to hearten and coordinate the now discouraged and disintegrated Democratic forces and to show how discordant and leaderless the Republican forces really are.

(4) It would tend to put President Wilson in the position to which he is entitled in history and in the minds and hearts of his countrymen: to bring into proper perspective his actual, great contribution to the cause of world organization,—to which cause he has sacrificed himself as gallantly as though he had been gassed on the Western front.

All of which I submit in deference.

Sincerely yours,   G. W. Anderson

TLS (B. Colby Papers, DLC).

From Oscar Ross Ewing[1]

My dear Mr. President: New York November [18] 1920

Although I know that numerous messages of loyalty come to you constantly, nevertheless, I want at this time to take the liberty of adding my own.

It seems to me that your leadership of the Democratic party is one of the great achievements of our history. You took a party largely dominated by the landed interests of the South and made it a genuine instrument of liberal progress, and, what is even greater, you took a party whose cardinal principle was states' rights and led it past mere nationalism on up to the magnificent vision of international cooperation and brotherhood.

Our party has been defeated, defeated by a combination of all the elements of discontent. The German who blamed the Democratic party for America going into the war joined hands with those bellicose individuals who blamed us for not going into it when Belgium was invaded. The capitalist who opposed our party because of your liberal labor policy voted with the laborer who thought we should have nationalized industries. The farmer who blamed the Democrats for the low prices of wheat and hogs united with those who felt we were responsible for the high price of bread and bacon.

These elements, as diverse as the poles, united to defeat us, but it is difficult to believe that they can work together to accomplish much that is constructive. Such a heterogeneous combination is ideal for the reactionary forces who are now in full control of the Republican party. The reactionaries alone know what they want and how to get it. They will keep the others from uniting, just as they did at the Chicago convention, and will work their own sweet way.

Out of the sorry confusion that is almost sure to come from such a situation will arise the opportunity of the Democratic party. It must take its stand on the foundations which you have given it and be the rallying point for the liberal forces of the country. It must cling to your idealism and justify your faith in it; and if it does, then this defeat is merely the travail for its birth into a new life of noble service for the uplift of mankind.

Of you, Mr. President, who have made all this possible, I cannot begin to express my admiration. You have had the vision splendid, and you have been true to it through every trial. Happily, you have given these ideals to the world in incomparable language and they will go down through the centuries as an inspiration to men every-where.

In addition to all that I have said, I want to add a special word of appreciation on your appointnent [appointment] of Mr. Justice Brandeis and Mr. Justice Clark[e] to the Supreme Court. There are far too few members of our profession who have any conception of the social and economic facts of life or see their vital connection with the administration of justice. Both of these gentlemen have social vision and it is indeed fortunate that you have given them the opportunity to make their views effective.

Again assuring you of my highest admiration and with the sincere wish that our country may have your wise counsel and our party your leadership for many years to come, believe me,

Most sincerely,   Oscar R. Ewing

TLS (WP, DLC).
    [1] At this time, a lawyer of New York; later assistant chairman and then vice-chairman of the Democratic National Committee; head of the Federal Security Agency, 1947-1952; one of the founders of the Research Triangle in North Carolina.

From Charles Zeller Klauder

My dear Mr. President,   Philadelphia Nov 18th, 1920.

I have noted carefully the contents of your letter of the 12th inst.

Since then, the study required to achieve a solution for the River site, such as will enable us to arrive at an approximate cost, has been proceeding.

The conformation of that site is clearly impressed on my mind, which warrants the preparation of careful sketches.

These I will bring to Washington on Monday, Nov 29th, to confirm my impression and I shall be prepared to remain and to confer with you at length should this meet with your convenience.

I am deeply appreciative of your very kind invitation to stop at the White House.

Most Sincerely yours,   Chas Z Klauder.

ALS (WP, DLC).

To Oscar Ross Ewing

My dear Mr. Ewing: [The White House] 19 November, 1920

Allow me to express my appreciation of your letter of recent date. It is very gratifying indeed to receive such assurances of friendship and approval.   Sincerely yours,   [Woodrow Wilson]

CCL (WP, DLC).

From Bainbridge Colby, with Enclosure

My dear Mr. President: Washington November 19, 1920.

I submit for your consideration a note to England on the Mesopotamia question, with particular reference to the true construction of a "mandate," and a side-long glance at the world's petroleum supply.

I also enclose a printed copy of the notes already exchanged between this Government and Great Britain, calling your particular attention to the final note of Earl Curzon, to which the enclosed draft is intended as a reply.

The importance of the prompt issuance of the proposed reply, or some reply, arises from the fact that the Assembly of the League of Nations is now in session, and it is feared that England may seek there some form of recognition or validation of its course in Mesopotamia, which seems in many respects to conflict with the plain implications of its position as a mandatory trustee.

Very respectfully yours,   Bainbridge Colby

Admirable note   I approve   Woodrow Wilson

TLS (B. Colby Papers, DLC).

E N C L O S U R E

Bainbridge Colby to Earl Curzon of Kedleston

My Lord: [Washington] November 20, 1920.

I have the honor to refer to your note of August 9[1] regarding the application of the principle of equality of treatment to the territories of the Near East to be placed under mandates, and specifically to the petroleum resources of those territories as affected by that principle.

Before considering the observations of His Majesty's Government on the general principles advocated by the United States, and agreed to by the Allied Powers, for application to the mandates over former Turkish territory, as outlined in the notes of May 12, and July 28, addressed to you on behalf of this Government, I think it will clarify the discussion to indicate certain of your statements and assurances which this Government has been pleased to receive. Thus, I note that the assignment to Great Britain of the mandate for Mesopotamia was made and accepted subject to no friendly arrangement whatever with any third Government regarding economic rights, which, of course, would have been wholly at variance with the purpose and contemplation of any mandate.

It is also gratifying to learn that His Majesty's Government is in full sympathy with the several propositions formulated in the note of May 12, above referred to, which embody or illustrate the principles which this Government believes should be applied in the mandated regions, and which are essential to the practical realization of equality of treatment.

[1] Lord Curzon to J. W. Davis, Aug. 9, 1920, transmitted in J. W. Davis to SecState, Aug. 11, 1920, T telegram (SDR, RG 59, 800.6363/163, DNA); printed in *FR 1920*, II, 663-67. Colby mentions and comments on its main points. Curzon's note was a reply to notes from the State Department of May 12 and July 28, 1920. They are printed in *ibid.*, pp. 651-55 and 658-59. The San Remo Agreement, referred to below, is printed in *ibid.*, pp. 655-58. This Anglo-French agreement, signed at the San Remo Conference on April 24, 1920, dealt with former German oil concessions in Rumania and the former Russian Empire but concerned Mesopotamia primarily. The agreement provided for a French share in the oil production of Mesopotamia, or French participation in private oil production and transportation facilities in that area, and for the granting of oil concessions to Franco-British companies in the French colonies of North Africa. See Laurence Evans, *United States Policy and the Partition of Turkey, 1914-1924* (Baltimore, 1965), pp. 292-97.

The statements of your note, to the effect that the British Government has refrained from exploiting the petroleum resources of the mandated territories in question; that the operations referred to have been conducted for purely military purposes under the immediate supervision of the army authorities and at army expense; and that no private interests whatever are in any way involved, are accepted with a full sense of the good faith of the British Government.

The Government of the United States notes that His Majesty's Government has found it necessary to suspend, during the period of occupation, the grant of facilities and opportunities to British as well as to other private interests to investigate the natural resources of the country, either for the purpose of acquiring new claims or strengthening old ones, and that there is no reason for assuming that the administration either of Mesopotamia or of Palestine has at any time failed to carry out the assurances of His Majesty's Government.

This Government welcomes your pledges to the effect that the natural resources of Mesopotamia are to be secured to the people of Mesopotamia and to the future Arab State, to be established in that region, and that it is the purpose of the British Government, fully alive to its obligation as a temporary occupant, not only to secure those resources to the Mesopotamian State, but also its absolute freedom of action in the control thereof, and in particular that it is far from the intention of the mandatory power to establish any kind of monopoly or preferred position in its own interest.

The Government of the United States appreciates, likewise, the concurrence with its view that the merits of all claims to rights alleged to have been acquired in the mandated territories before the outbreak of hostilities must be duly established before recognition of such claims will be accorded.

Adverting, at this point, to the views of His Majesty's Government regarding the nature of the responsibilities of mandatory powers under the League of Nations, I desire to call to the attention of His Majesty's Government, the fact that, while the draft mandate, Form A, was not adopted at Paris, it was the understanding of the American representatives, there present, that the British Government entertained and had expressed convictions favorable to said form, and that, presumably, its representatives would exercise their influence in conformity with those convictions.

I need hardly refer again to the fact that the Government of the United States has consistently urged that it is of the utmost importance to the future peace of the world that alien territory transferred as a result of the war with the Central Powers should be held and administered in such a way as to assure equal treatment to the commerce and to the citizens of all nations. Indeed it was in reliance upon an understanding to this effect, and expressly in contemplation thereof, that the United States was persuaded that the acquisition under mandate of certain enemy territory by the victorious powers would be consistent with the best interests of the world.

It is assumed, accordingly, that your statements with reference to Mandate A, together with the statement that the draft mandates for Mesopotamia and Palestine have been prepared with a view to secure equality of treatment for the commerce and citizens of all states which are members of the League of Nations, do not indicate a supposition on your part that the United States can be excluded from the benefits of the principle of equality of treatment.

This Government is pleased to find that His Majesty's Government is in full sympathy with the principles formulated in its communications of May 12, and July 28. But it is unable to concur in the view, contained in paragraph 15 of your note, that the terms of the mandates can properly be discussed only in the Council of the League of Nations and by the signatories of the Covenant. Such powers as the Allied and Associated nations may enjoy or wield, in the determination of the governmental status of the mandated areas, accrued to them as a direct result of the war against the Central Powers. The United States, as a participant in that conflict and as a contributer to its successful issue, cannot consider any of the associated powers, the smallest not less than itself, debarred from the discussion of any of its consequences, or from participation in the rights and privileges secured under the mandates provided for in the treaties of peace.

This Government notes with interest your statement that the draft mandates for Mesopotamia and for Palestine, which have been prepared, with a view to secure equality of treatment and opportunity for the commerce, citizens and subjects of all states, which are members of the League of Nations will, when approved by the interested Allied Powers, be communicated to the Council of the League of Nations. The United States is, undoubtedly, one of the powers directly interested in the terms of the mandates, and I therefore request that the draft mandate forms be communicated to this Government for its consideration before their submission to the Council of the League. It is believed that His Majesty's Government will be the more ready to acquiesce in this request, in view of your assurance that His Majesty's Government is in full sympathy with the various principles contained in the two previous notes of this Government upon this subject.

The establishment of the mandate principle, a new principle in international relations, and one in which the public opinion of the world is taking a special interest, would seem to require the frankest discussion from all pertinent points of view. It would seem essential that suitable publicity should be given to the drafts of mandates which it is the intention to submit to the Council, in order that the fullest opportunity may be afforded to consider their terms in relation to the obligations assumed by the mandatory power, and the respective interests of all governments, which are or deem themselves concerned or affected.

The fact cannot be ignored that the reported resources of Mesopotamia have interested public opinion of the United States, Great Britain, and other countries as a potential subject of economic strife. Because of that fact they become an outstanding illustration of the kind of economic question with reference to which, the mandate principle was especially designed, and indeed a peculiarly critical test of the good faith of the nations, which have given their adherence to the principle. This principle was accepted in the hope of obviating in the future those international differences that grow out of a desire for the exclusive control of the resources and markets of annexed territories. To cite a single example: because of the shortage of petroleum, its constantly increasing commercial importance, and the continuing necessity of replenishing the world's supply by drawing upon the latent resources of undeveloped regions, it is of the highest importance to apply to the petroleum industry the most enlightened principles recognized by nations as appropriate for the peaceful ordering of their economic relations.

This Government finds difficulty in reconciling the special arrangement referred to in paragraphs 18 and 19 of your note, and set forth in the so-called San Remo Petroleum Agreement, with your statement that the petroleum resources of Mesopotamia, and freedom of action in regard thereto, will be secured to the future Arab State, as yet unorganized. Furthermore, it is difficult to harmonize that special arrangement with your statement that concessionary claims relating to those resources still remain in their pre-war position, and have yet to receive, with the establishment of the Arab State, the equitable consideration promised by His Majesty's Government.

This Government has noted in this connection a public statement of His Majesty's Minister in Charge of Petroleum Affairs to the effect that the San Remo Agreement was based on the principle that the concessions granted by the former Turkish Government must be honored. It would be reluctant to assume that His Majesty's Government has already undertaken to pass judgment upon the validity of concessionary claims in the regions concerned, and to concede validity to certain of those claims which cover, apparently, the entire Mesopotamian area. Indeed this Government understands your note to deny having taken, and to deny the intention to take, any such ex parte and premature action. In this connection, I might observe that such information as this Government has received indicates that, prior to the war, the Turkish Petroleum Company, to make specific reference, possessed in Mesopotamia no rights to petroleum concessions or to the exploitation of oil; and in view of your assurance that it is not the intention of the mandatory power to establish on its own behalf any kind of monopoly, I am at some loss to understand how to construe the provision of the San Remo Agreement that any private petroleum company which may develop the Mesopotamian oil fields "shall be under permanent British control."

Your Lordship contrasts the present production of petroleum in the United States with that of Great Britain and some allusion is made to American supremacy in the petroleum industry. I should regret any assumption by His Majesty's Government or any other friendly power, that the views of this Government as to the true character of a mandate are dictated in any degree by considerations of the domestic need or production of petroleum, or any other commodity.

I may be permitted to say, however, for the purpose of correcting a misapprehension which your note reflects, that the United States possesses only one-twelfth approximately of the petroleum resources of the world. The oil resources of no other nation have been so largely drawn upon for foreign needs, and Your Lordship's statement that any prophecies as to the oil-bearing resources of unexplored and undeveloped countries must be accepted with reserve, hardly disposes of the scientific calculation upon which, despite their problematic elements, the policies of States and the anticipations of world-production are apparently proceeding. The Government of the United States assumes that there is a general recognition of the fact that the requirements for petroleum are in excess of production and it believes that opportunity to explore and develop the petroleum resources of the world wherever found should without discrimination be freely extended, as only by the unhampered development of such resources can the needs of the world be met.

But it is not these aspects of oil production and supply, in so far as they are of domestic interest to the United States, with which I am concerned in this discussion. I have alluded to them in order to correct confusing inferences, liable to arise from certain departures, which I believe I discern in Your Lordship's communication, from the underlying principles of a mandate, as evolved and sought to be applied by the Allied and Associated Powers to the territories, brought under their temporary dominion, by their joint struggle and common victory. This dominion will be wholly misconceived, not to say abused, if there is even the slightest deviation from the spirit and the exclusive purpose of a trusteeship as strict as it is comprehensive.

Accept, My Lord, the assurances of my most distinguished consideration. Secretary of State of the United States of America.

CCL (SDR, RG 59, 800.6363/196a, DNA).

From Bainbridge Colby

My dear Mr. President: Washington November 19, 1920.

We are drifting apparently into a sharp collision with the Western Union Telegraph Company.

The Company has resented the refusal of the Government to permit it to land a cable at Miami, Florida, to connect at Barbadoes with the cable of the British company which enjoys an exclusive monopoly of coastal communication in Brazil. You will recall your direction that this permit be withheld until the whole subject of international cable communication had been surveyed by the Communications Conference now in session.

The controversy has assumed two phases; first, with reference to cable connection with Brazil. And second, with reference to the transmission of the Department's messages by the Western Union Company.

(1) As to the Brazilian cable connection.

The Western Union Company has formally withdrawn its application for a landing at Miami and intimated that it will effect its connection with Brazil in Cuba, utilizing for that purpose its existing lines of communication between Cuba and Florida.

Its permit between Cuba and Florida is subject to revocation or modification. It does not, however, contain a clause which it is usual to insert in cable landing permits, that the Company shall not receive any exclusive privilege from any foreign government which excludes any person or company organized in the United States from a like privilege of landing. The Solicitor of the State Department,[1] therefore, suggests that the present permits, under which the Western Union Company maintains contact for its Cuban lines with the coast of Florida, be modified by the insertion of this customary provision. I therefore enclose a modification of the permit for your signature, provided you approve of the course herein outlined. With this modification of the permit, it is our hope that the Government will be in a position to prevent the Western Union Company from effectuating a connection with the English lines from Brazil in defiance of the Government's policy and in disregard of the Government's refusal to grant a permit for the Miami landing.

(2) With reference to the transmission of Department messages.

The Western Union Company gave us a notice, effective on November 10th, that from and after that date they would cease to transmit cable messages at half rates, as had been customary for years, and would in addition require payment in cash on the filing of messages, both domestic and foreign.

This is doubtless an expression by the Western Union Company of its irritation at the difficulties encountered at Miami, although it is explained as arising from the unadjusted accounts between the Company and the State Department.

For a long time it has been customary for the Western Union Company to collect full rates on foreign messages directed to the State Department and subsequently to rebate one-half thereof after the deduction of certain items of the cost of transmission, and after the actual receipt of the toll on the messages from other companies operating in the foreign field.

It is estimated by the Department that the Western Union Company owes the Government approximately $100,000. On the other hand, the Department owes the Company approximately $40,000. The Company has been very slow in its accountings and even slower in payment, and with the idea of expediting adjustment the Department has sought to withhold further payment until the amount due it on account of rebates was reduced substantially.

On this phase of the case I have requested the Army and Navy Intelligence Divisions to ascertain the points and avenues at which the Western Union Company's foreign business actually crosses our borders.

My thought is that the Government cannot permit the Western Union Company to protect itself against the discharge of its obligations by intentionally interfering with the transaction of public business or by subjecting this Government to a greater cost in the transmission of its cables than is exacted from other countries. There is also in the attitude of the Company an element of disrespect for the Government which, I submit, should not pass un-rebuked.

Therefore, as soon as I am able to submit to you a clear state-ment of the steps that we can take by way of effective retort and discipline, I will do so, but in the meantime I think it would be proper and expedient to sign the modified permit with regard to the Cuban lines, which is herewith enclosed.

Very respectfully yours,   Bainbridge Colby

I concur   W.W.

TLS (B. Colby Papers, DLC).
¹ Fred Kenelm Nielsen, a long-time career officer in the department.

From Newton Diehl Baker

My dear Mr. President: Washington. November 19, 1920.

I have your note of the 17th, inclosing the telegram from Theo-dore H. Lunde to Mrs. Wilson with regard to Benjamin Salmon. Lunde is a Chicago lawyer whose loyalty during the war was under investigation by the Department of Justice and he showed up so badly that he was kept under rather constant surveillance. Since the armistice he has been officious and impertinent with regard to the so-called conscientious objectors. I have long since ceased to reply to any communications from him although his requests for information are answered in the regular course by The Adjutant General.

The conscientious objector problems are at the disappearing point. There remain now in custody only thirteen of this class. They are entirely made up of men whose conscience was too active to permit them to fight but not active enough to keep them from radical and often disgusting and dangerous agitation. In accor-dance with a general rule, they are being rapidly released now, the rule being to release them after they have served that sentence which the courts are now imposing for similar offenses.

Salmon, about whom Lunde writes, has complicated the ques-tion of his own release by Habeas Corpus proceedings which have made it necessary to retain him in order to be able to respond to the Writ of Habeas Corpus he has had issued. He is insane al-though the doctors at Saint Elizabeths Hospital declare otherwise. He is now at Walter Reed Hospital and will be released in a day or two.   Respectfully yours,   Newton D. Baker

TLS (WP, DLC).

Three Letters to Bainbridge Colby

My dear Mr. Secretary: The White House 20 November, 1920

Thank you for your letter about your conference with the Minister of the Jugo-Slavs.[1] You are getting to the bottom of the matter, just as I hoped you would, and I shall look forward with interest to a subsequent conference with you about it.

Always

Cordially and faithfully yours,   Woodrow Wilson

[1] BC to WW, Nov. 18, 1920 (first letter of that date).

My dear Mr. Secretary: The White House 20 November, 1920

Thank you for your letter of the eighteenth about Cabrera of Guatemala.

Personally, I must admit that I have never been convinced that he was a sincere friend of the United States or of the governments united against Germany, but I am quite willing to receive your assurances in that matter, because you have been in contact with the evidence more intimately than I. I should be very glad to have you make any efforts you deem advisable and likely of success for his liberation from the incarceration to which he is now being so stupidly subjected.

Cordially and faithfully yours,   Woodrow Wilson

My dear Mr. Secretary: The White House 20 November, 1920

Thank you for letting me see Judge Anderson's letter.[1] I am sorry that you do not indicate whether you agree with him or not. So far as my own judgment is concerned, it is, ⟨for the present at any rate,⟩[2] entirely against the course he suggests. He does not know, as we do, that the so-called reservations proposed in the last Senate were not drawn in good faith and were not intended as what they purported to be, but really as nullifications of the Treaty itself. I would be very grateful indeed if you would ponder this matter and let me have the benefit of your thought with regard to it. It is, of course, of the most critical importance.

Cordially and faithfully yours,   Woodrow Wilson

TLS (B. Colby Papers, DLC).
[1] That is, the Enclosure printed with BC to WW, Nov. 18, 1920 (third letter of that date).
[2] Wilson's deletion.

To Bainbridge Colby, with Enclosure

My dear Mr. Secretary: The White House 20 November, 1920

I would be very much obliged if you would read the enclosed letter without prejudice. I have an entire confidence in Creel and a strong affection for him and think that much of his excitement is natural in the circumstances, because he has been so put upon and misrepresented by persons outside the administration as to madden him. What would you think of a three-cornered conference between yourself, Creel and myself before your departure? Creel, as I understand, is in town today and perhaps only for a brief time, but we could get hold of him even if we had to bring him back.   Cordially and faithfully yours,   Woodrow Wilson

E N C L O S U R E

From George Creel

My dear Mr. President: Washington, D. C., November 19, 1920.

I cannot, in conscience, permit the Mexican matter to go to smash without one last effort to save it. You know why I went to Mexico. It was to bring about a vindication of your policy. You know that I went at my own expense. And you must know that my visit was successful. The Mexicans met us on every point in controversy, and President de la Huerta paid you a very noble public tribute, virtually asking for admission to the League of Nations.[1] This took courage, for he had no doubt as to Republican victory.

Secretary Colby and Mr. Davis were enthusiastic. With their full approval, Mr. Pesqueira wrote a letter[2] that put the Mexican government on record as to a claims commission, an arbitration commission and non-retroactive guarantees with respect to Article 27. Again, with splendid disregard of Republican anger, you were praised as the savior of Mexico and the League of Nations was indorsed.

Mr. Colby gave the letter to the press together with a statement that assured the people of Mexican faith.[3] You saw both letter and statement prior to publication and were deeply touched. Nothing seemed more certain than that Mr. Pesqueira would be called to the State Department at once and asked as to his authorities and his concrete understandings in the matter of general pledges. Yet from that day to this, nothing has been done. The Pesqueira letter has never been answered. For twenty-five days he has been compelled to sit in painful and humiliating expectancy.

Why? As near as I can gather from the State Department's

mumbo jumbo, there is a question as to "Pesqueira's faith." Telegrams or letters have been intercepted, or something of that sort, or else an ear at a keyhole has made disturbing report.

I challenge the State Department to put these secret whisperings on the table. *But what if they were all true*? The man is on record with an open letter in which he gives specific pledges. Secretary Colby has assured the American people of his joy and faith in this letter. Is it all to go by the board because of some eavesdropper or cable opener? But what after all, has Mr. Pesqueira's personality got to do with it? He speaks for a government. It is certain specific pledges that we are asking of this government. If this government gives the pledges, what does it matter what Secretary Colby thinks of Pesqueira?

I believe that there is also much excitement over a public statement made by President de la Huerta on November 10.[4] I have read this statement. I know that it was inspired by the news that Judge Parker, attorney for the oil companies, was sitting in the State Department writing conditions for presentation to the Mexican government. Even so, the statement was not made until November 10, fifteen days after the Pesqueira letter. What tied the hands and tongue of the State Department during that period?

But this is water over the dam. On Tuesday, Mr. Pesqueira leaves for the City of Mexico. Before going, he will be compelled to make a statement. What can he say in this statement save that *he* believed in you and that the State department did *not* believe in you: that he wrote a letter; that Secretary Colby gave it to the press with glad acclaim: that he was assured of an instant answer and continuous conversations leading to an agreed settlement: that his letter has never been given the courtesy of an answer; that while he has cooled his heels, oil company attorneys have been permitted to work their will. Every attack has been made upon his faith and character; he has been called upon to watch purchased influence strike at him and his country and to sit silent while every effort has been made to shatter the political harmony of Mexico by creating division between de la Huerta and Obregon.

There is still time for action. The Pexqueira [Pesqueira] letter meets every American demand. Pesqueira himself is willing to agree that the subsequent treaty shall be framed to bind his government. Recognition is not a thing of the Medes and Persians. It can be taken away as quickly as it can be given.

After making solemn public pledges, is it possible to believe that the Mexicans will be mad enough to repudiate? They expect nothing from the Republicans. Already they have cut every bridge that Harding has built for them. He went to Point Isabel to meet Obregon and Obregon refused the meeting.[5] Senator Fall gave out a statement that Obregon had asked Mr. Harding to come to Mexico City. Today Obregon denies any such invitation.[6] Also today Mr. Pesqueira sent word to every Mexican consul to refuse to visé Senator Fall's passport, stating flatly that he wanted no open enemy of Woodrow Wilson in Mexico.[7]

At every point the Mexicans have stood foursquare with you. At every point we have bilked them.

Do you see the position in which they are left. We assured them that we wanted agreement only with respect to certain things. They gave this agreement. Then we turned our back.

Do you think that Obregon will open negotiations again? That even if he so desired, his people would permit him to overlook the insult to de la Huerta? While striking de la Huerta down, we have hamstrung Obregon with the same blow. If Pesqueira goes away, and makes his statement before he goes, you turn Mexico over to Harding and the oil people. You lose the opportunity to crown your Mexican policy with success, you alienate Central and South America and you give Japan an ally at our back. All because Mr. Pesqueira's "faith" has been made the object of secret assault.

You know my love for you and you know my passionate belief in your principles and policies. It is this love and the belief that must serve as an apology for a letter that is written out of my heart.

Devotedly,   George Creel

TLS (SDR, RG 59, 812.00/24782½, DNA).
   [1] See n. 1 to the Enclosure printed with JPT to WW, Oct. 26, 1920.
   [2] For the text of which, see n. 1 to Enclosure I printed with BC to WW, Oct. 28, 1920 (first letter of that date).
   [3] Colby's statement is printed as Enclosure III with *ibid.*
   [4] Creel was referring to a circular telegram from De la Huerta to all Mexican diplomatic representatives in foreign countries, dated November 5, 1920, and published in the Mexican papers on the next day. It read as follows:
   "Through telegraphic advices from abroad I am informed that the press of the United States as well as of Europe has published the rumor that certain governments in renewing their relations with ours have established or wish to establish specific conditions, it being stated that these will be included in protocols and special treaties.
   "You will deny these unfounded statements because as I have made public on more than one occasion the Government in Mexico will under no circumstances consent to relations with other countries being renewed upon the bases of conditions which affect the decorum of our fatherland.
   "It would not be just or acceptable that an attempt be made to impose upon us that which we are bringing to a realization voluntarily and through conviction. Our attitude based on morality and right shall be the only guarantee offered for considering our Republic to be in harmony with the other civilized peoples of the earth.
   "Negotiations of whatever nature they may be, entered by our representatives of whatsoever rank or standing, that do not conform to the policy announced by me on various occasions in public statements I have made and which is ratified by this circular shall not merit the approval of the Executive office at present in my charge." Printed in *FR 1920*, III, 193-94.
   As a result of De la Huerta's telegram and various statements by Mexican officials that seemed to contradict the assurances Pesqueira had given to Colby, Charles M. Johnston, the Chief of the Division of Mexican Affairs, had advised Colby to suspend

any further negotiations with Pesqueira. C. M. Johnston to BC, Nov. 9, 1920, TLI (SDR, RG 59, 812.00/27465½, DNA).

⁵ Harding went to Point Isabel, a village south of Brownsville, Texas, on November 8 for fishing and duck and deer hunting. There was some talk in the newspapers that he would meet Obregón there, but this prognostication proved to be incorrect. However, Harding, in company with Fall, did meet for an hour with Elias Torres, special envoy of the Mexican Foreign Secretary, Cutberto Hidalgo. Obregón may or may not have refused to meet with Harding, but he did deny that Elias Torres had gone to Brownsville as his personal envoy, as the newspapers had reported. New York Times, Nov. 4, 5, 8, 17, and 20, 1920.

⁶ Fall's statement to this effect is printed in ibid., Nov. 17, 1920.

⁷ R. V. Pesqueira, circular telegram dated Nov. 18, 1920, TC telegram (SDR, RG 59, 812.00/24782½, DNA).

From Bainbridge Colby, with Enclosure

My dear Mr. President: Washington November 20, 1920.

I did not know that Mr. Creel was in town last week until the receipt of your letter of today. I at once endeavored to locate him but learned that he had left Washington on Friday night. Your suggestion of a conference with Mr. Creel and myself appeals to me very strongly, and I will endeavor to arrange it at once. I think it might be well to have Mr. Davis present, as he has had so much to do with the discussions relating to Mexican recognition.

I received a letter from Mr. Creel this week, of which I understand he sent you a copy.[1]

You may be interested in the reply I made to Mr. Creel, of which I beg to enclose a copy.

I do not quite understand the heat which Creel shows in his correspondence. The Department has sought in every way to support his efforts, and until the receipt of his letter I thought we were in entire accord. He was a guest at my house at one stage of the matter and I sought in every way to help.

                    Very respectfully yours,   Bainbridge Colby

TLS (WP, DLC).
[1] G. Creel to BC, Nov. 12, 1920, printed as an Enclosure with G. Creel to EBW, Nov. 15, 1920.

ENCLOSURE

Bainbridge Colby to George Creel

My dear Mr. Creel: [Washington] November 17, 1920.

I received yesterday, November 16th, your letter bearing date November 12th, "disassociating yourself instantly and absolutely from Mexican negotiations."

I thought you had done that week before last when you expressed yourself to Mr. Davis and me in terms of such angry displeasure with Mr. Pesqueira for what you termed his inappreciation of our attitude and his insensibility to his duties to Mexico and to the opportunity that presented itself to him of contributing toward the result which all well-disposed persons in Mexico and this country desire, namely, the resumption, upon the right foundations, of friendly and free mutual intercourse.

You were so emphatic at that time in stating your belief that nothing should be attempted without the unmistakable, even the written, approval of the President-elect, General Obregon, that I am wholly at a loss to understand your letter of the 12th and the fact that you should have written it at all. I fully appreciate what you say as to the wholly voluntary character of your efforts in this matter. Although they were not in the least degree sought by the Department, their amiable purpose and the possibility of their being helpful were perceived and we were glad to avail ourselves of them.

On one point I must sharply challenge the statements of your letter, and that is that there was any attempt to belittle or disparage your efforts by the State Department. You say in your letter: "How much more simple and more just to have said that I had gone to Mexico on my own business as a writer, and that if I returned with information of value to the State Department, it would be received gladly, as the Mexican situation was always open for settlement." Indeed, I think I may have used almost those words on two or three occasions in replies to inquiries addressed to me by representatives of the press.

I note in your letter that "you reserve the fullest right to protect yourself from attack, whether from the front or from behind." You have no occasion to throw up any defences, even such as your letter of the 12th, so far as the State Department is concerned. As I have said above, and on more than one occasion have assured you, we appreciated the spirit in which you came upon the scene and the earnestness with which you pursued endeavors that you believed would lead to gratifying results.

Such communications, on the subject of Mexican recognition, as have been exchanged, have been suggested by you, and the discontinuance of communications—temporary, I hope—was also, as I have above stated, in compliance with your suggestion.

We shared your confusion arising from the purported message or circular of President De La Huerta in which, without referring by name to Mr. Pesqueira, he undoubtedly alluded to him and to the negotiations he was conducting in Washington. If the circular meant anything, it was a warning that Pesqueira had not the full support of his Government and that the latter reserved the right, despite the breadth of Pesqueira's authorizations, to form its own decisions.

With regard to the memorandum prepared by Mr. Parker, you had a copy of it before it was submitted to me, and when acquainted with its contents, I promptly stated to you that it was only Mr. Parker's suggestion, and that nothing of the kind would be acceptable to me as a basis, or even a feature, of any discussions with Mexico's representative.

The attitude of the State Department is one that has received such complete indorsement from you that it seems strange that I should now, in the light of your letter, be required to state it and defend it against the implications of your letter. As I conceive the position of this country, it is one of the friendliest expectation that Mexico will take her place among the nations with which enlightened intercourse is possible in conformity with modern standards of international conduct. We do not intend to define conditions of recognition, because we prefer to assume that the request for recognition will be accompanied by the assured performance of conditions which are essential to free intercourse between modern states. Protestations of good resolves are pleasant to receive and pleasant to acknowledge, but their significance arises entirely from the probability of their translation into acts, and is lost entirely if that prospect is either absent or not assured.

It is not permitted to me, my dear Mr. Creel, in discussing a matter of this nature, to write with quite such unrestraint as you indulge in. I have no desire to say or do anything that will not promote the result in view and which has been regrettably delayed, and therefore I propose to refrain from a discussion at the moment of other aspects of your letter.

The facts of the case, to an extent that possibly neither you nor the Mexican representatives appreciate, are at our command, and the course of the Department is necessarily governed by the facts.

Sincerely yours   [Bainbridge Colby]

CCL (WP, DLC).

To William Gibbs McAdoo

My dear Mac: The White House 20 November, 1920

Concerning Santo Domingto [Domingo],[1] I have of course had careful conferences with the State Department and I have, acting under its advice, done what I think is possible and best in the circumstances. I don't care a damn what the Republicans do. I have been part of this record from the first, and there is nothing in it to be ashamed of at any point.

I can't advise you, my dear fellow, whether to remain connected with the case or not. That is entirely a matter for your own judgment. Frankly, I don't think that your continuing to deal with it will have the least influence upon the effect which Republican mischief-making may have.

Please tell Nell that I have just had the pleasure of picking out one of the pictures she sent me and am rejoiced to have it. I did not get her express promise to keep the picture of herself, but I am going to keep it and hope she will forgive me.

With love from us all to you all, in haste

Affectionately yours,   Woodrow Wilson

TLS (W. G. McAdoo Papers, DLC).
[1] Wilson was replying to WGM to EBW, Nov. 17, 1920.

To John Franklin Jameson

My dear Jameson: The White House 20 November, 1920

I wish you would read the enclosed letter[1] and give me the benefit of any suggestions that may occur to you as to the best way in which the club referred to can busy itself in the excellent work which it has set before it. No doubt your work will have acquainted you with methods of which I know nothing.

With the best wishes,

Cordially and sincerely yours,   Woodrow Wilson

TLS (J. F. Jameson Papers, DLC).
[1] This letter is missing in both the Wilson and Jameson Papers, DLC; but see the following letter and J. F. Jameson to WW, Dec. 3, 1920.

To Robert Cummins Stuart, Jr.[1]

My dear Mr. Stuart: [The White House] 20 November, 1920

I shall be honored to have the Club referred to by you in your letter of November seventeenth bear my name, and I am grateful that it should be formed with such motives and with such generous appreciation of the services I have been able to render.

I shall, of course, keep the Club in mind and shall be glad to forward to it any suggestions that it is in my power to make with regard to the admirable work it is purposing to undertake.

Please express to the members of the Club my warm appreciation and believe me, with the best wishes,

Sincerely yours,   [Woodrow Wilson]

CCL (WP, DLC).
  [1] Of Houston, Texas, a student at Harvard University of the Class of 1921.

To Charles Zeller Klauder

My dear Mr. Klauder: [The White House] 20 November, 1920

I was very glad to get your letter[1] and to hear of the progress of your studies in the matter we are both interested in, and you will be most welcome on Monday. Pray let us know by telegram by what train to expect you.

Cordially and sincerely yours,   [Woodrow Wilson]

CCL (WP, DLC).
  [1] Wilson was replying to C. Z. Klauder to WW, Nov. 18, 1920.

From Josephus Daniels

My dear Mr. President: Washington. November 20, 1920.

The Secretary of State is planning to leave the latter part of next week for South America. The FLORIDA will meet him at Hampton Roads and take him down to South America and back. The Ambassadors from Brazil and Argentine and the Minister from Uruguay[1] will wish to accompany him to Old Point to give him bon voyage.

Secretary Colby would like to leave Washington on the MAYFLOWER and have these Ambassadors and the Minister as his guests, and I am writing to ask if you will authorize the use of the MAYFLOWER for this purpose. The MAYFLOWER will probably be away from Washington Friday, Saturday and Sunday.

Faithfully yours,   Josephus Daniels

TLS (WP, DLC).
  [1] That is, Augusto Cochrane de Alençar, Tomás Alberto Le Bretón, and Dr. Jacobo Varela.

Edgar Odell Lovett to Edith Bolling Galt Wilson

My dear Mrs Wilson   Houston, Texas. 21 November 1920

I am venturing to make of you a request that I have hesitated to address to the President in person. It is that you persuade him to give to the Rice Institute, in which he has had a very kindly interest from its first days, one of the many European diplomas or other academic testimonials he consented to receive, for a permanent place on the walls of the Faculty Chamber of this institution, where are hanging some of the formal expressions of goodwill received from foreign and American universities on the occasions of our early academic festivals.

And any dulness on my part either to any impertinence in the making of such a request or to any impropriety in the granting of it, will you not in the kindness of your heart attribute to my affection for the President and our desire to do him honour.

Very sincerely yours,   Edgar Odell Lovett

ALS (WP, DLC).

To Bainbridge Colby

My dear Mr. Secretary: The White House 22 November, 1920

Thank you for your letter of November twentieth and for your courtesy in letting me see your reply to Mr. Creel's letter of the twelfth. I admire both the spirit and the convincing character of that reply.

Cordially and faithfully yours,   Woodrow Wilson

TLS (B. Colby Papers, DLC).

To John R. Mott[1]

My dear Doctor Mott: The White House 22 November, 1920

I have learned with the most lively satisfaction of the plans for enlisting the cooperation of the students of America in behalf of their fellow-students in the war-stricken lands of Europe and the Near East. This effort commends itself to me not only because of its urgently needed humanitarian aspect, but also because of the influence it is certain to exert in promoting kindly and helpful relations between the leaders of tomorrow among the students of different lands and races. I bespeak for this most worthy cause the generous and self-sacrificing response of the student communities in all parts of the country.

Cordially and sincerely yours,   Woodrow Wilson

TLS (J. R. Mott Coll., CtY-D).

[1] Wilson received Mott at the White House at 10:45 a.m. on November 21. Mott, who had spent the spring and summer in Europe on a mission devoted to reconciliation, relief, and reconstruction, had come to see Wilson to report about his trip and to ask Wilson's support for European Student Relief, an organization founded in August 1920

by the World's Student Christian Federation. The following letter is a verbatim copy of
the draft (Hw MS, WP, DLC) which Mott had left with Wilson.

Mott kept the following notes of his interview:

"Asked abt France. 'France is now the head rep^{ve} of imperialism.' He approved JRM's
ref^{ce} to remark of Amb. Davis that 'France occilates bt fear & cupidity.'

"When JRM. said he cd not understand Lloyd George w ref^{ce} to Russia &c, he said: 'Don't
imperil your mind by trying to understand Lloyd George.' Later he said that L. George is not
moral. He illustrated it by ref^{ce} to agm^{ts} at Paris, also by ref^{ce} to claims made in pre-election
speeches.

"Agreed w JRM. that Venizelos is one of gtst men in Europe. 'I have an affectionate
regard for him.' 'See what Gardiner says abt him & you will see that he agrees w you.' "
Hw MS (J. R. Mott Coll., CtY-D).

Gardiner was Alfred George Gardiner, former editor of the London *Daily News*, publicist,
author, and one of Wilson's strongest spokesmen in the United Kingdom. Gardiner's
sketch of Vénisélos appeared in his *The War Lords* (London and New York, 1915), a
copy of which is in the Wilson Library, DLC.

From Norman Hezekiah Davis

My dear Mr. President: Washington November 22, 1920.

The present situation of the Mexican military and police organizations with respect to supplies of ammunition is very critical. Our embargo has closed both American and European markets, and as a result stocks of ammunition in Mexico are virtually exhausted. The police forces in some of the larger cities are reported as having, in many cases, only enough cartridges to fill the chambers of their revolvers, and army commanders are frequently obliged to share with one another their meagre supplies. Through intercepted radiograms, it has been learned that the Secretary of War has recently authorized the Commanding General at Nuevo Laredo to purchase all 30-30 cartridges obtainable in the vicinity of Laredo, paying at a rate of $110 per thousand.

It seems inconsistent that we should demand that the de facto regime afford protection to the thirteen thousand Americans in Mexico while denying it the privilege of replenishing its supply of ammunition from this country. It is a matter of record that the Mexican Government purchased in the United States in 1915 more than ten million rounds which, although paid for, have never been shipped owing to our embargo. Our present policy prevents the withdrawal of any part of this stock, and virtually compels the Mexican War Office to encourage violations of our neutrality laws. In other words, our embargo encourages Mexican officials to engage in an illicit traffic in ammunition, to obtain which they are obliged to pay profiteers' prices.

Recent occurrences in Mexico and along the border point to a possible recrudescence of disorders and internal strife. The labor situation is far from reassuring. Obregon's enemies are incubating a new revolution in Texas, which will probably be launched soon after his inauguration unless this Government takes energetic steps to prevent it. The demobilization of the Mexican army to one-half its present strength—a program to which Obregon is committed—will furnish many military malcontents as a nucleus for a new revolutionary movement.

In view of these circumstances, I recommend that the de facto authorities be permitted, under the Department's licensing system, to withdraw reasonable amounts of their own ammunition now held in bond in this country. To refuse this permission will encourage the enemies of the de facto authorities, and give the latter justifiable cause to suspect that our declarations of friendship are lacking in sincerity.   Faithfully yours,   Norman H. Davis

TLS (WP, DLC).

From the Diary of Josephus Daniels

November Tuesday 23 1920

Cabinet. Shall we permit the WU to lay cable at Miami? They have contract by which the British would control the cable to South America. The President denied them permission to land some weeks ago & Navy had given directions not to permit it. It turned out that the Secy of War had years ago given the permission to put cable over causeway. We have information that they will lay cable & connect it with cable to S. A. & thus defeat the President's determination that cable cannot be permitted to land in America. Pres. directed Baker to annul permit & let matters take their case in the courts.

To Norman Hezekiah Davis

My dear Davis: The White House 23 November, 1920

I have your letter of November twenty-second and realize the iniquity and occasional injustice of our embargo on the shipment of arms into Mexico, but there is one aspect of the case that I wish you would think of most carefully and advise me about. Men like Doheny and others who are deeply involved in the oil intrigues have shown more and more recently their somewhat desperate anxiety to have this embargo lifted. This fills me with suspicion and I would like very much to have a memorandum from you on that aspect of the subject. We cannot be too careful not to serve these predatory interests, because they intend the demoralization of our own politics and the control of Mexican politics.

Cordially and faithfully yours,   Woodrow Wilson

TLS (N. H. Davis Papers, DLC).

To Josephus Daniels

My dear Mr. Secretary: The White House 23 November, 1920

I have your letter of November twentieth and am glad to authorize the use of the MAYFLOWER to convey Secretary Colby and his party to the ship which will be waiting to carry him to South America.   Cordially and faithfully yours,   Woodrow Wilson

TLS (J. Daniels Papers, DLC).

To Thomas Foster Compton[1]

My dear Mr. Compton: [The White House] 23 November, 1920

Will you not convey my cordial greetings to the First Annual New York State Convention of the Young Americans' Democratic League which is to convene on November twenty-second [twenty-seventh]? It is the young men of the country who must correct the reaction and pessimism of some of the older men and push forward towards a realization of the genuine ideals of the republic, ideals which cannot be lived up to without courage and a constant renewal of fidelity to the purest conceptions of democracy and of international responsibility. My best wishes will follow the deliberations of the convention, and I shall hope for it the most entire success and the most widespread influence.

Cordially and sincerely yours,   [Woodrow Wilson]

CCL (WP, DLC).
   [1] A student at Columbia University of the Class of 1921 and national corresponding secretary of the Young Americans' Democratic League (about which, see WW to R. Bradley, Oct. 23, 1920, n. 1). Compton had asked Wilson to send "a message of inspiration and encouragement" to the first annual New York State convention of the league, to be held in White Plains on November 27, 1920. T. F. Compton to JPT, Nov. 22, 1920, TLS (WP, DLC).

To Newton Diehl Baker

My dear Mr. Secretary: [The White House] 23 November, 1920

The enclosed seems to refer to a very singular case and I am sure you will be willing to consider that case and determine whether there is any change of regimen that would be just and wise for Salmon.[1]

With the warmest regard,

Cordially and faithfully yours,   [Woodrow Wilson]

CCL (WP, DLC).
   [1] About Salmon, see NDB to WW, Nov. 19, 1920, and the next document. We have not found his letter to Wilson in the Wilson or Baker Papers, DLC.

From Newton Diehl Baker

My dear Mr. President: Washington November 24, 1920.

I have your note of November 23rd with regard to Benjamin J. Salmon (Conscientious Objector). You spoke to me yesterday at the cabinet meeting with regard to this note in view of statements I made about the Salmon case. I write this only to confirm my statement that in a few days he will be discharged. In the meantime, his letter, with its very fervent admiration of "more than one thousand heroic lads who bled on the battlefields of Europe, that democracy might live!", with whom he is now associated at Walter Reed Hospital, seems to me strangely at variance with the part he personally elected to take in that struggle. All the other things he complains of in his letter are, of course, the normal regulations affecting prisoners, which is his status and, of course, not affecting the patients at Walter Reed Hospital who comprise the major part of the population there.

Respectfully yours,   Newton D. Baker

TLS (WP, DLC).

From Albert Sidney Burleson, with Enclosure

My dear Mr. President: Washington November 24, 1920.

When we finished our preliminary labors on the Sub-Committee dealing with the drafting of the terms of the proposed Universal Electrical Communication Union, I requested Mr. Rogers to have the Secretariat prepare a copy of the draft of the Convention so far as it had developed,[1] in order that I might transmit it to you with a view to giving you an opportunity to look it over.

If you are willing to tax your strength to do so, Mr. Rogers and I would welcome any suggestions you might be kind enough to offer and would, of course, endeavor to have them embodied in the draft of the Convention, before the Sub-Committee submits its report.

Faithfully yours,   A. S. Burleson

[1] "UNIVERSAL ELECTRICAL COMMUNICATIONS UNION," T MS (WP, DLC); this draft convention is printed in FR 1920, I, 151-58.

Walter Stowell Rogers to Albert Sidney Burleson

To: The Postmaster General   Washington Nov. 24, 1920.
From: Walter S. Rogers
Subject: Communication Union

1. Enclosed is a draft of Convention of the new Communication Union, which is to replace the existing Telegraph Convention and the existing Radio-Telegraph Convention.
2. The new Convention is the result of our efforts to bring about a world-wide agreement dealing in a comprehensive manner with all forms of international communication.
3. The comprehensive character of the new Convention is due largely to American efforts thru many weeks of negotiation.
4. The new Convention covers not only telegraph, cable, and radio but other forms of signalling as well.
5. In the regulations to be annexed to the Convention are included for the first time provisions relating to radio-telephony, radio-direction finding ("radio compass"), radio beacon services (radio "lighthouses"), aircraft radio, and arrangements for radio dissemination of meteorological data. Consideration is also being given to broadcasting international time signals.
6. In the regulations also are provisions dealing with sound and visual signalling. These are new. Between now and the meeting of the general International Conference, regulations are to be prepared covering undersea signalling.
7. Consideration is being given to the gathering and dissemination of meteorological data for the benefit of aircraft.
8. The draft of the Convention attached hereto has been generally agreed upon. Certain minor modifications are still under consideration.   Walter S Rogers

TLS (WP, DLC).

Joseph Patrick Tumulty to Edith Bolling Galt Wilson, with Enclosure

Dear Mrs. Wilson: The White House, 24 November, 1920.

   The enclosed letter is from the Editor of one of the largest publishing houses[1] in the country.   Sincerely,   Tumulty

   [1] George H. Doran Company. Doran was actually the company's president and treasurer.

E N C L O S U R E

George Henry Doran to Joseph Patrick Tumulty

My dear Mr. Tumulty: [Washington] 23 November 1920.

Would you be willing, and being willing be so good as to present to the President my suggestion, which ultimately takes the form of a specific request, that he consider a proposal from me and my company for the world rights in any book which he might have in contemplation, dealing with the period of his Presidency, or particularly with the past five years and the great ethical and altruistic principles involved in this most dramatic period of the world's history.

While I would not want to feel that I was definitely committed to such a proposal, I would not think of asking the President to consider such a project unless I was prepared to pay $100,000, upon delivery of a manuscript which would contain not less than 150,000 words, and, of course, just as much more as the President might feel it necessary properly to overtake the subject.

So far as the serial rights throughout the world would be concerned, $100,000 would cover all such rights; but I would pay a royalty of twenty per cent on the selling price of all copies of the book sold in the United States; royalties in countries other than the United States to be a matter of adjustment.

This $100,000 would be an advance on account of serial and book rights.

On my return to New York I am going to take the liberty of sending to you for placing in the hands of the President some of our recent publications, together with catalogues and lists, which will give the President a fair estimate of our publishing endeavor.

At any and at all times I shall be very happy to come to Washington to wait upon you, or the President, in the event of the President being willing to pursue this matter further.

Sincerely yours,   George H. Doran

Memorandum from Mr. George H. Doran, on behalf of George H. Doran Company, to Mr. Joseph P. Tumulty, Secretary to the President.

TLS (WP, DLC).

From Bainbridge Colby, with Enclosure

My dear Mr. President: Washington November 25, 1920.

In the enclosed letter to Mr. Pesqueira, I have sought to embody your suggestions.

He expects to leave for Mexico late this afternoon. I am trying to hold him here, until I can deliver the letter to him. I had a few words with him this morning, and acquainted him with the purport of the letter, which seemed to please him.

I have inserted some pleasant references to him and the success of his mission, which he only partially deserves, but I think they will be helpful.

It is desirable, I think, that he should not depart without some response to his overtures.

Very respectfully yours,   Bainbridge Colby

TLS (WP, DLC).

E N C L O S U R E

Bainbridge Colby to Roberto V. Pesqueira Morales

My dear Mr. Pesqueira: [Washington] November 25, 1920.

The conversations which we have had since the receipt of your notable letter of October 26th,[1] I am very pleased to say, have been entirely in keeping with the spirit and tenor of the expressions it contained, and have quite confirmed the agreeable anticipations it aroused.

I think I may say, as one of the results of these discussions, that no doubt can reasonably be entertained of the high and enlightened purposes that actuate the present Government of Mexico, and I am fully persuaded that you realize the friendship and disinterestedness towards your country, which actuate this Government.

We have not required the assurances, so unqualifiedly given in your letter, of Mexico's regard for the discharge of her obligations, and of her respect for the principles of international law. Your suggestion of a joint arbitration commission to adjudicate the claims presented by citizens of other countries, for damages sustained as a result of disorders in your country, and the further proposal to enlarge and strengthen existing treaty provisions for the arbitration of all controversies, now pending or which may arise between our respective nationals, bring convincing support to your declarations, if that were needed.

You refer at length to the misunderstanding that has arisen, and which has widely prevailed, as to the true scope and effect of Article 27 of the Mexican Federal Constitution. That such misunderstanding has existed, and has exercised an unfortunate restraint upon the impulses of friendly Governments, in their desire to cooperate with the Mexican people in the recovery of the full measure of their material strength and prosperity, cannot be denied. But I can conceive of nothing better calculated to correct this misunderstanding and to allay the fears of those who have acquired valid titles, or who have made substantial investments in conformity with Mexican law, and in reliance upon its protection, than the statements of your letter referring to the declarations of President de la Huerta and President-elect Obregon to the effect that Article 27 "is not and must not be interpreted as retroactive or violative of valid property rights."

The interest of other nations in this subject should not, and I am convinced it is not, [be] attributed to any desire to influence or interfere with Mexico in the adoption and pursuit of any policy with regard to its lands and resources, which expresses its aspirations, and satisfies its people. Indeed, I may remark, that there is wide sympathy for the apparent desire of your country to inaugurate a policy which shall protect its great resources against waste, dispersal or other improvident treatment. The freedom to do this, which no one can dispute, nor even criticize, is in no sense compromised by the due respect for legally vested interests, which you so fully avow, with a convincing sincerity, which is beyond question.

It only remains to give these understandings, a form which is usual in dealings between friendly states, and I have the honor to suggest, as our fruitful discussions draw to a close, that commissioners be promptly designated by both Mexico and the United States to formulate a treaty, embodying the agreements, which have been reached as the result of your successful mission.

I am, my dear Mr. Pesqueira,
                    Sincerely yours,   Bainbridge Colby[2]

CCL (SDR, RG 59, 812.00/24701½, DNA).
    [1] For which, see, again, n. 1 to Enclosure I printed with BC to WW, Oct. 28, 1920 (first letter of that date).
    [2] This letter was given to the press on November 30 and published, *inter alia*, in the *New York Times*, Dec. 1, 1920.

To Bainbridge Colby

My dear Mr. Secretary: The White House 26 November, 1920

Mr. McAdoo has become, as perhaps you know, very much interested in the Dominican settlement, and in the letter which I enclose[1] makes a suggestion which he formally made to me that we call the representatives of the Dominicans themselves (I pass over his suggestion of calling in counsel, of which I do not approve) for the purpose of comparing views as to the best method of reestablishing civil government in the Island. I do not know what you will think of this suggestion, but I am sure, with your usual open-mindedness, you will be willing to turn it over in your mind and advise me concerning it.

With the warmest regard,
Cordially and faithfully yours,   Woodrow Wilson

TLS (B. Colby Papers, DLC).
    [1] WGM to EBW, Nov. 17, 1920.

To George Henry Doran

My dear Mr. Doran: [The White House] 26 November, 1920

Mr. Tumulty has handed me your letter to him of the twenty-third of November and I want to thank you very sincerely for the interest which that letter shows in my future writing.

Perhaps you will readily understand that it is not possible now for me to make definite literary plans for the future. I have felt obliged to postpone all plans until I have settled to a new method of life and found what it is possible for me to find time and opportunity to do.

Pray accept my thanks for your good wishes and your interest.
Sincerely yours,   [Woodrow Wilson]

CCL (WP, DLC).

To Edgar Odell Lovett

My dear Lovett: The White House 26 November, 1920

Mrs. Wilson has shown me your letter of the twenty-first of November to her. You may be sure I will think very seriously of complying with the complimentary suggestion it makes. I will confer with Axson about it and if I find a parchment that I think will be suitable for the use you suggest, I will ask him to take it down with him when he goes.[1]

With warmest regard,
Sincerely yours,   Woodrow Wilson

TLS (E. O. Lovett Papers, TxHR).
    [1] For a description of Wilson's gift to the Rice Institute, see E. O. Lovett to WW, March 20, 1921, n. 1.

To South Trimble[1]

My dear Mr. Trimble: [The White House] 26 November, 1920

The turkey arrived and was duly eaten, and we are certainly indebted to you for your kindness. We enjoyed it all the more because of the friendship of which its fine flavor reminded us.

Sincerely yours,   [Woodrow Wilson]

CCL (WP, DLC).
[1] Former Democratic congressman from Kentucky (1901-1907); clerk of the House of Representatives, 1911-1919 and 1931-1946.

To H. Adelman[1]

My dear Mr. Adleman: [The White House] 26 November, 1920

I am very much complimented by the suggestion contained in your letter of November twenty-second,[2] but venture to reply that perhaps you do not know that I am not a Mason. In such circumstances, I take it for granted that it would hardly be within the limits of custom to name a Masonic lodge after me, much as I should be complimented by such an evidence of confidence.

Very sincerely yours,   [Woodrow Wilson]

CCL (WP, DLC).
[1] Associated with the Columbia Trading Co. of New York. The Editors have not been able to identify him further.
[2] H. Adelman to WW, Nov. 22, 1920, TLS (WP, DLC).

From Bainbridge Colby

My dear Mr. President: Washington November 26, 1920.

The enclosed suggestion of a reply[1] to the telegram of today received by you from the President of the League Council[2] really expresses the action and the attitude of the last Congress, and yet I think it might be well to give a second thought to the subject before dispatching it.

The two significant actions of Congress on Armenia were: (1) The passage of the Senate resolutions authorizing you to send a warship and a force of marines to Batum;[3] and (2) the rejection of the invitation of the Supreme Council that this Government assume the duties of mandatory in Armenia.[4]

The preambles and resolutions of the Senate consist of five paragraphs in which the sufferings and dangers of the Armenians are recited, as well as our congratulations upon the recognition of the independence of Armenia; and then, without any sense of the incongruity, the Senate authorizes you to send a battleship to protect the lives and property of *citizens of the United States* at Batum. Batum is now a port of Georgia and is not the scene of the activities which so greatly menace the Armenians. The Turkish forces have occupied Kars and Alexandropol, both of which are interior points.

While the Senate has done nothing that meets the situation or offers authority even for practical measures of succor, it has expressed itself as deeply concerned for the safety of the Armenians, and it might take exception to that portion of the proposed reply which represents Congress as having "declared its unwillingness to assume any responsibility regarding Armenia." They have refused to assume responsibility in the past, but they have not actually declared an unwillingness to do so.

I have been considering the matter this afternoon, and have talked briefly with the British Ambassador as to what Great Britain could do, and have also had the good fortune to receive a call from your friend Mr. Frederick Jones Bliss.[5]

The Ambassador said that he did not know that England could do anything, her troops being so fully employed in Ireland, at home, in Mesopotamia and other widely scattered regions. Mr. Bliss, on the other hand, thought that a proffer of mediation by you might be the only effective action that could be taken in the situation. What do you think of replying to the telegram of M. Hymans saying that you are willing to mediate, and then sending Mr. Henry Morgenthau as your representative to discuss the situation with the contending parties?[6]

The situation comes upon the Western nations at a time when they are distracted and almost helpless in the post-war reaction. The possibilities of organizing an effective force are almost nil, and unless you exercise your moral authority it would almost seem that there is no way to avert the fate that hangs over the Armenians.

You might be rebuffed, and your representative might fail, but I think that it would be an action on your part which the world would welcome and history approve.

I talked over with Mr. Bliss the names of possible representatives and he seemed clearly of the opinion that Mr. Morgenthau would wield more influence than any man that he could name.

Another course would be to make inquiries of the British, French and Italian Governments as to what program of joint action they propose or would consider, and submit the replies with a report on the facts to Congress when it convenes in the session soon to begin. A reply to the effect that you propose to do this would be a very adequate response to the Hymans message.

I am not at all certain but that the reply suggested by you, despite these considerations, should be sent. It seemed advisable, however, to bring these thoughts to your attention.

Very respectfully yours, Bainbridge Colby

This is the course to take. Thank you   <u>W.W.</u>[7]

TLS (B. Colby Papers, DLC).

[1] That is, Wilson's suggested reply. It is printed as Enclosure I with BC to WW, Nov. 27, 1920.

[2] P. Hymans to WW, Nov. 26, 1920, T telegram (B. Colby Papers, DLC). Hymans informed Wilson that the League Assembly had passed a resolution on November 22, asking the Council "to arrive at an understanding with the governments with a view to entrusting a power with the task of taking the necessary measures to stop the hostilities between Armenia and the Kemalits." The Council, Hymans continued, had decided to transmit this resolution to the governments of all member states and to the United States in order to find a power that would be willing to use its good offices to put an end to the hostilities as soon as possible. Hymans emphasized that this proposal did not involve another request for the acceptance of a mandate for Armenia, and he concluded: "While the Council does not wish to suggest the assumption of duties which might be unwelcome it felt bound to offer to the United States the opportunity of undertaking this humanitarian task seeing that the fate of Armenia has always been of special interest to the American people and that the President of the United States has already agreed to delimit the boundaries of that country."

[3] See J. W. Gerard to WW, May 14, 1920, n. 4, and WW to Congress, May 24, 1920, both in Vol. 65.

[4] See n. 2 to the extract from the Daniels Diary printed at June 1, 1920, *ibid*.

[5] About whom, see WW to BC, March 29, 1920, and n. 1 thereto, *ibid*.

[6] Wilson drew a brace in the margin of this letter around this sentence and wrote the postscript underneath the brace.

[7] For Colby's draft reply see Enclosure II printed with BC to WW, Nov. 27, 1920 (first letter of that date).

From Norman Hezekiah Davis

My dear Mr. President: [Washington] November 26, 1920.

While considerable progress has been made in the Preliminary Conference on Communications in agreeing upon principles regulating the construction and operation of cables, we have not been able to reach an agreement on the distribution of the ex-German cables. On Monday at twelve I am to have a meeting of the subcommittee dealing with the latter question. We seem to have reached the stage where no one is willing to make any further concessions, and unless there is some decided change of attitude the next meeting may probably be the last one. If it is convenient and agreeable to you, I should like very much to discuss the matter briefly with you some time before Monday noon.

Faithfully and cordially yours,   [Norman H. Davis]

CCL (N. H. Davis Papers, DLC).

From Thomas William Lamont

Dear Mr. President: [New York] November 26th, 1920.

I have seen a copy of your letter of November 8th to Graham Patterson, of The Christian Herald, approving his efforts to raise funds for the terrible famine in China. Knowing my deep interest in China and my friendliness for the Chinese people Mr. Patterson has been conferring with me on the whole matter. What I feel is this: Patriotic and influential as The Christian Herald is, its appeal will be greatly handicapped without some public expression and some tangible step on the part of the head of the government. If, for instance, you were able to consider asking a few men to act as a committee in the matter—men of more or less nation-wide repute—I believe that the amount of money collected would be greatly increased.

In any event, I believe that we must all recognize, to our regret, that probably no great sum will be contributed; just because we have already run into hard times and people are feeling poor. The days of great money drives are, for the moment, over. Still I think the country would make a fairly satisfactory response, and, in view of the fact that, as was demonstrated to me more than once during my recent stay in China, all China looks to America for counsel and aid, I feel it would be most appropriate if we were to try to make some tangible response. The other nations of the world, of course, are too burdened with their own troubles to make much of a demonstration of friendship towards China. America, however, has the opportunity and the resources. I am wondering whether you would not consider yourself justified, on purely humanitarian grounds, in getting the thing started.

I have had some thought of writing to all the banks and bankers composing the American Group of the Chinese Consortium, asking whether they would be willing to contribute, and I have suggested to my own firm that we put ourselves down for ten thousand dollars. Just how far this particular appeal would get I am unable to determine. Up to date, the attitude of the American Banking Group towards China has been purely one of public service—it is all outgo and no income—but I am anxious to do everything I can in any possible direction.

Sincerely yours,   Thomas W. Lamont

TLS (WP, DLC).

To Newton Diehl Baker, with Enclosure

My dear Baker:　　　　　[The White House] 27 November, 1920

I send you the enclosed because you and I have frequently conferred about the subject matter and have always agreed in our decision. I would, therefore, be very much obliged if you would suggest a reply to Admiral Benson's letter embodying the views in which you and I have concurred.

Always
　　　　Cordially and faithfully yours,　[Woodrow Wilson]

CCL (WP, DLC).

E N C L O S U R E

From William Shepherd Benson

My dear Mr. President:　　　　Washington November 22, 1920.

1. It is provided by the first paragraph of Section 17, of the Merchant Marine Act, 1920, that the Shipping Board shall take over on January 1, 1921, the so-called Hoboken piers, and other terminal facilities which were formerly the property of the North German Lloyd and Hamburg American Steamship Companies. The control and operation, by the Shipping Board, of these piers and facilities is of vital importance to the successful operation of our fleet out of the port of New York. We have made extensive plans for improving and fully utilizing these piers when they are turned over to us at the designated time.

2. The second paragraph of Section 17 further provides that, whenever the President deems it necessary, the Shipping Board may have transferred to it such other terminals as were acquired by the War Department or Navy Department during the war emergency. It is a matter of urgent necessity that the piers and terminal facilities so acquired by the War Department now be utilized in general commerce, and it is only reasonable to believe and expect that the Shipping Board can better supervise the use of these terminals than can any of the other governmental departments. In view of these facts, I am, therefore, of the opinion that the Shipping Board should at once secure control of the so-called Army Bases, Quartermaster Terminals, or Quartermaster Depots at New York, N. Y., New Orleans, La., and Boston, Mass. In the case of the first two mentioned, it is desired that the bases be turned over in their entirety, and that the Boston Base be turned over with the exception of the eight story warehouse. This warehouse is at pres-

ent filled with Army material and, besides, the immediate use of the warehouse is not required by commercial shipping.

It had been my intention to request that the so-called Army Bases, Quartermaster Terminals, or Quartermaster Depots, at Norfolk, Va., Philadelphia, Pa., and Charleston, S. C., be turned over to the Board at this time. However, since I am informed that the Army has already either leased these three so-called bases, or has instigated proceedings working towards leasing them, to the cities in which they are respectively located, and since the control of these three terminals by the Board is not of immediate moment, I feel that their control and operation by the Shipping Board should be deferred. By this arrangement we can satisfy ourselves as to whether or not the greatest good to the United States develops from the use of these bases under Army supervision. A further point which leads toward this same conclusion, is the fact that I realize that the municipalities have a distinct part to play in developing the utilization of their port, and this arrangement will afford them ample opportunity to assist in the growth of our commerce.

3. I would therefore request that Executive Order No. 3350, dated November 5, 1920, be canceled, in order that nothing shall interfere with the fullest utilization of the Hoboken piers, when they come into possession of the Board on January 1, 1921.

It is further requested that, for the immediate needs of the Board, there be turned over to it the following facilities:

(a) The Hoboken Manufacturers Railroad
(b) The Brooklyn Army Base, with all of its railroad yards, piers, warehouses and other facilities.
(c) The New Orleans Quartermaster Depot, with all of its railroad yards, wharf, warehouses and other terminal facilities.
(d) The Boston Army Base, with all of its railroad yards, wharves, pier, pier sheds, wharf sheds, and other terminal facilities, with the exception of the eight story warehouse.

By these transfers, I am of the opinion that the greatest good will result to the American Merchant Marine.

I inclose copy of a report,[1] upon which my requests are based.

Very sincerely yours,   W. S. Benson

TLS (WP, DLC).
[1] Not found.

From Bainbridge Colby, with Enclosures

My dear Mr. President: Washington November 27, 1920.

I have drafted the enclosed reply to M. Paul Hymans, President of the Council of the League of Nations, in which I have sought to express your decision as to the form of response to his telegram of November 26th, which I attach hereto thinking you may care to refer to it.

If this reply meets with your approval, will you kindly sign it, and I will see that it is promptly transmitted by cable.

Very respectfully yours,   Bainbridge Colby

TLS (B. Colby Papers, DLC).

E N C L O S U R E   I

Suggested for a reply[1]

Replying to the communication of the Council of the League of Nations the Government of the United States regrets to be obliged to say the Congress of the United States has declared its unwillingness to assume any responsibility regarding Armenia

WWT MS (B. Colby Papers, DLC).
   [1] EBWhw.

E N C L O S U R E   I I[1]

I have the honor to acknowledge the receipt of your cabled message, setting forth the resolution adopted by the Assembly of the League of Nations, requesting the Council of the League to arrive at an understanding with the governments with a view to entrusting a power with the task of taking necessary measures to stop the hostilities in Armenia.

You offer to the United States the opportunity of undertaking the humanitarian task of using its good offices to end the present tragedy, being enacted in Armenia, and you assure me that your proposal involves no repetition of the invitation to accept a mandate for Armenia.

While the invitation to accept a mandate for Armenia has been rejected by the Senate of the United States, this country has repeatedly declared its solicitude for the fate and welfare of the Armenian people, in a manner and to an extent that justifies you in saying that the fate of Armenia has always been of special interest to the American people.

⟨I, therefore, in a spirit of prompt and sympathetic response to the request of the Council of the League of Nations, assure you of my willingness to use my good offices and to proffer my mediation, through a personal representative, whom I will designate, to end the hostilities now being waged against the Armenian people, and to bring peace and accord to the contending parties, relying upon the Council of the League of Nations to suggest to me the avenues through which my proffer should be conveyed and the parties to whom it should be addressed.⟩

T MS (B. Colby Papers, DLC).
  ¹ The paragraph printed in angle brackets struck out by Wilson.

From Bainbridge Colby, with Enclosure

My dear Mr. President: Washington November 27, 1920.

Referring to the enclosed letter from Mr. McAdoo, and replying to your letter of the 26th, I beg to enclose a proposed proclamation which we have prepared for the Secretary of the Navy, hoping that he may approve it and sanction its issuance.

It marks the beginning of what I trust will be a steadily pursued and not protracted process of withdrawal from Santo Domingo.

We took these steps upon the receipt of your letter of November 15th, in which you approved the program of gradually withdrawing from Dominican affairs as outlined in the memorandum which was prepared by Mr. Welles,¹ Chief of our Latin American Division.

The fear expressed in Mr. McAdoo's letter that the decisions of this Government will be taken without giving the Dominicans an opportunity to be heard, and without securing in advance their co-operation, is, I think, met by the terms of the proposed proclamation, which contemplates the appointment of a Commission of representative Dominican citizens to which shall be entrusted the amendment of the constitution and the general revision of the laws of the Republic.

I think under your authorization we are started in the right direction, and that the proclamation enclosed will do a great deal to allay discontent and criticism in Santo Domingo. It is true that we are announcing a program of only gradual withdrawal, and yet we would be open to sound criticism if we were to withdraw too abruptly, with important elements in our task still uncompleted.

I beg to return Mr. McAdoo's letter.
                    Very respectfully yours,   Bainbridge Colby

Approved   W.W.

TLS (B. Colby Papers, DLC).
  ¹ See the Enclosure printed with BC to WW, Nov. 13, 1920 (third letter of that date).

E N C L O S U R E

P R O C L A M A T I O N

WHEREAS, the friendly purposes of the United States in the employment, pursuant to rights derived from the Treaty of 1907, of its military forces within the Dominican Republic for the restoration of public order and the protection of life and property have been substantially achieved, and,

WHEREAS, it has always been the desire and intention of the Government of the United States to withdraw its aid as soon as it could do so consistently with the said purposes and as soon as the improved conditions in Santo Domingo to which the United States has sought to contribute gave promise of permanence,

NOW, THEREFORE, I, Thomas Snowden, Rear-Admiral, U.S.N., Military Governor of the Dominican Republic, acting under the authority and by direction of the Government of the United States, declare and announce to all concerned that the Government of the United States believes the time has arrived when it may, with a due sense of its responsibility to the people of the Dominican Republic, inaugurate the simple processes of its rapid withdrawal from the responsibilities assumed in connection with Dominican affairs.

Announcement is, therefore, made that a Commission of representative Dominican citizens will be appointed, the personnel of which will shortly be announced, to which it is my purpose to attach a Technical Advisor. This Commission will be entrusted with the formulation of amendments to the Constitution and a general revision of the laws of the Republic, including the drafting of a new Election Law. Such amendments to the Constitution and such laws, or such revision of existing laws, as may be recommended by the Commission, upon approval by the Military Government in occupation, will be submitted to a Constitutional Convention and to the National Congress respectively.

CC MS (B. Colby Papers, DLC).

Two Letters from Bainbridge Colby

My dear Mr. President: Washington November 27, 1920.

Referring to the tripartite agreement between Great Britain, France and Italy, mutually assigning spheres of "special interest" in Anatolia, I think you will find the enclosed memorandum interesting.[1] It is a condensed but quite complete statement of the available facts bearing on the situation, and I have attached a map, indicating with fair accuracy the areas of the respective spheres of "special interest."

The position of this Government on the principle of equality of right and opportunity within mandated regions, is pretty fully (and I hope clearly) stated in the Department's recent note to Earl Curzon.[2] Would you think it well,[3] to transmit a copy of this note to France and Italy, calling attention to its statement of the position of this Government, relative to its rights within mandated areas, and requesting an interpretation by both France and Italy of the Anatolian agreement (more properly, the Sevres Agreement of August 10.) in the light of our declarations.

As to England, it occurred to me that a reply to our recent note might be awaited, as the reply can hardly fail to discuss this question, with unavoidable application to Anatolia, or any other region, where the situation may be similar.

Very respectfully yours,   Bainbridge Colby

By all means   <u>W.W.</u>

TLS (B. Colby Papers, DLC).
  [1] The enclosure is missing in all collections and files. However, it was about the so-called Tripartite Pact, signed at Sèvres, France, by representatives of Great Britain, France, and Italy on August 10, 1920, which was designed to permit the creation of spheres of interest in Turkey. For obvious reasons, the Tripartite Pact was not embodied in the Treaty of Sèvres, signed also on August 10, 1920. See Paul C. Helmreich, *From Paris to Sèvres: The Partition of the Ottoman Empire at the Paris Peace Conference of 1919-1920* (Columbus, Ohio, 1974), pp. 251-57, 320-21.
  [2] It is printed as an Enclosure with BC to WW, Nov. 19, 1920.
  [3] Wilson drew a brace around most of this sentence and wrote here the comment printed below.

My dear Mr. President: Washington November 27, 1920.

As I scan the horizon of my desk, it looks as if the present time is about as good as any that is likely to come, for me to turn southward, and proceed on the trip, which you have done me the honor to direct me to make.

The "Florida" is waiting for me at Norfolk; the department has arranged a suitable personnel to accompany me, and when you say the word, I will be off and hurry through and hurry back.[1] Since your announcement appeared in the press,[2] I have received a very cordial invitation to visit Chile. This, however, would entail a stop in Peru, and coming home through the Canal, it would be difficult to explain a failure to make at least a brief stop in Panama.

I am rather reluctant to extend my journey beyond the limits originally projected. I have a feeling that my trip would lose something of distinctness and justification if I ramble around paying calls. To be sure, it would not lengthen the period of my absence, so much as one would think, as the distance by way of the west coast is so much less than the east coast. But I go to Brazil and Uruguay, in such a definite and distinguished capacity, as your deputy to return the visits of their respective Chiefs of State,[3] that I think it would be a sort of stepping down to continue on as an itinerant Secretary of State.

On the other hand, our Latin-American Division and Dr. Rowe, profess to see important objects (improved relations, deepened sense of contact, etc.) that might be gained by enlarging the original plans.

I would be grateful for an indication of your judgment or wishes on this point.

Matters in the Department do not wear a particularly troublesome aspect at the moment, and the immediate outlook is reasonably serene. But one can never tell, from day to day, what may develop, and I feel that the conservative course is to not unduly prolong my absence.

Very respectfully yours,   Bainbridge Colby

TLS (WP, DLC).
[1] Colby left for Brazil, Uruguay, and Argentina on December 4, 1920, and returned in late January 1921. For a detailed description of his trip, see Smith, *Aftermath of War*, pp. 141-51.
[2] See, for example, the *New York Times*, Nov. 10, 1920.
[3] Epitacio da Silva Pessôa, then President-elect of Brazil, had made a state visit to the United States in late June 1919. Baltasar Brum, President of Uruguay since March 1919, had visited the United States as Foreign Minister in August 1918 and had had lunch with Wilson at the White House on August 26, 1918.

From William Graves Sharp

Dear Mr. President: Elyria, Ohio November 27, 1920

I am wondering if it is too late in the preparation of your forthcoming message for me to make a suggestion—if I may be permitted to do so—concerning a subject in which I know you were at one time interested. I refer to the need of the Government acquiring suitable residences for our diplomatic representatives abroad.

I recall that on one occasion in discussing the subject with you in Paris at the time of renewing my request for your acceptance of my resignation, you announced your intention of recommending at some future time such legislation to Congress. I recall your saying that you intended to put the question in substantially this form: "Are you or are you not in favor of only rich men filling these posts?" With salaries less than half of what they should be, or for that matter of what is paid by all other of the more important governments, the financial sacrifice becomes too great for any but rich men to aspire to such honors.

Within a little more than thirty years there have been eight or nine different American embassy residences in Paris varying in dignity from the plainest apartments to private homes or "hotels," according to the ability of the particular ambassador to pay the rent. The same conditions, of course, exist in other capitals. I would be very glad to see such a recommendation incorporated in your message; even though it is not acted upon during this coming short and final session of Congress, I believe it will serve a useful purpose in calling the public's attention to such a need.

It must have been very gratifying to you—as it was to all your friends—to receive from Geneva that fine testimonial to your distinguished service in behalf of the establishment of a world peace.[1] While those of us who were on the ground over there fully understood the great value of that service and its welcome by all the statesmen of foreign countries, yet it made me happy and proud to have that fact so widely made known in America. It was the Marquis de Chambrun[2] whom you doubtless knew as a member of the Committee on Foreign Affairs in the Chamber of Deputies, who told me, after your first return to America—February 14, 1919—that your temporary absence from the deliberations of the Peace Conference had demonstrated how vitally important was your leadership among your fellow confreres. He said that soon after your departure they had found themselves quite hopelessly at sea on the determination of important questions and without any program. Certainly the deliberations of the Assembly at Geneva not only point to the need of a strong leader in whose unselfishness all the others have an abiding confidence, but to the need of the presence of the United States in full membership to dispell the doubt and distrust with which each agreement is entered into. Truth has a way of revealing itself past finding out.

With my best wishes, in which Mrs. Sharp[3] asks to join, for your continued improvement in health and strength, I am, believe me, my dear Mr. President,

With sincere regard,   Wm. G. Sharp.

TLS (WP, DLC).
  [1] See P. Hymans to WW, Nov. 16, 1920.
  [2] Charles-Louis-Antoine-Pierre-Gilbert-Pineton, Marquis de Chambrun, deputy of Lozère.
  [3] Hallie Clough Sharp.

From Lawrence Crane Woods[1]

Dear Mr. President: Pittsburg, Penna. November 27, 1920.

I am delighted to see by the newspapers the statement that you are walking now without a cane and are much better. I should think that what is going on over at Geneva would be a wonderful tonic for you.

The great personal tribute being paid to you there enables us all to see clearly where history is going to place you in this great world movement; but even far more than that we see what is going on there, the greatest hope for peace that humanity has ever known. You wrought well. Your idealism is today a great reality.

With the passion, bitterness and personality of war and politics removed, [the] United States has nothing in the world to do except to go in. I wish they could have gone in head first instead of backing in, but after all, humiliating and mortifying as that is, it is of minor consequence compared with this unbelievable and stupendous world league.

But oh, how those who love you rejoice in the personal tribute paid to you at Geneva by the President, by the great British Labor Leader, by the whole Congress itself in repeated acclaim of your beloved name.

It may seem cowardly to you but in many respects I am very glad that the Democratic party is not to be held responsible for what happens in this country and the world during the next four years. I do not see how Senator Harding can raise wages, increase profits, decrease Income Tax or Inheritance Tax. In fact I see everyone of these things going the wrong way, and as unfortunately we are trained and the Republicans have trained the people, for the past eight years particularly, to hold not only the Administration but the President personally responsible for everything that the people do not like, I cannot envy Mr. Harding's position.

But I am selfishly interested in his success as is every American. I trust I have learned my lesson by the outrageous attacks made upon you and will be given the grace to refrain from indiscriminate criticism, let alone vilification and vituperation, but support the President of the United States in every way in my power.

I am wondering whether you would like to have a suggestion as to a possible official appointment. It would be my own and those effected are not people in whom I am interested directly or indirectly, except as a citizen. I presume you are suffering from too many suggestions.

I should be glad, when you are out of the White House and I can visit with you without feeling that I am talking to the President of the United States. You do everything in your power to prevent that feeling but it is always there, and I presume it ought to be there.

Mrs. Woods[2] joins with me in affectionate messages to you and Mrs. Wilson.

I hope Stockton Axson is improving.

Cordially yours,   Lawrence C Woods

TLS (WP, DLC).
[1] Wilson's old friend and frequent correspondent; Princeton 1891; vice-president and assistant manager of the Edward A. Woods Co., a life insurance company of Pittsburgh.
[2] Rebekah Wilson Campbell Woods.

Bainbridge Colby to Joseph Patrick Tumulty

My dear Mr. Tumulty: Washington November 27, 1920.

With reference to the telegram addressed to the President by Mr. Graham Patterson, of the CHRISTIAN HERALD,[1] which you sent to me on November twentieth and which I am returning herewith, I do not believe that it would be advisable for the President to name three or five men to form a nucleus of a national committee under the auspices of the HERALD. It seems to me that it would be far more appropriate for the HERALD itself to select these men. There are so many relief organizations at the present time that I think the President would be embarrassed should he undertake to participate in the selection of a Committee representing any one of these organizations.   Sincerely yours,   Bainbridge Colby

TLS (WP, DLC).
[1] "Our China Famine Fund starting splendidly but every day makes it more imperative that tremendous relief be made available at earliest possible moment Will you name three or five men to form nucleus of national committee to aid in organizing appeal Cite President McKinley's action on Cuban relief 1897-1898 as precedent." G. Patterson to WW, Nov. 19, 1920, T telegram (WP, DLC).

Hamilton Holt to Joseph Patrick Tumulty

My dear Mr. Tumulty   New York November 27 1920

The speech by the President which you read to us the other day when we called upon you on behalf of the Armenians very greatly impressed me. You said that the speech has never been printed. Would it be possible for The Independent to print it in whole or in part? I hope so.

Did you have time to take up with the President the matter that I spoke to you about in regard to his future work?[1]

Yours sincerely   Hamilton Holt

TLS (WP, DLC).

[1] We have been unable to find any information about this meeting of Holt and others with Tumulty. Nor have we been able to identify the alleged unpublished speech by Wilson that Tumulty read to the group. The only other document relating to this matter is J. P. Tumulty to Hamilton Holt, Nov. 29, 1920, TLS (H. Holt Papers, FWpR), which reads as follows:

"I have your note of the 27th instant before me, and regret to inform you that the President would not consent to the publication of the speech you mention. I have as yet had no word from him on the other matter you have in mind."

A Hw note attached to this letter reads: "No further word from Mr. Tumulty on this matter."

From the Diary of Ray Stannard Baker

Sunday, Nov. 28th [1920].[1]

Mrs. Wilson invited me to lunch at the White House at one o'clock, but called me later & asked me to come at 12 noon. I did not know what for. I found that there were "movies" at 12 & we had luncheon later at 1: & after that I had a long talk with Mrs. Wilson & later dinner with Grayson when the whole talk was still of the tragedy at the White House. I was quite on fire to write about it—giving a true picture & did so (which see). Showed the article to Tumulty & he was all for it: said it was true, but both Grayson & Mrs. Wilson read it & were afraid of its effect (see Mrs. Wilson's letter) And yet I did not begin to describe how the sight of the President affected me. It was dreadful. I cannot get over it yet. A broken, ruined old man, shuffling along, his left arm inert, the fingers drawn up like a claw, the left side of his face sagging frightfully. His voice is not human: it gurgles in his throat, sounds like that of an automaton. And yet his mind seems as alert as ever. The thought of it—that powerful brain grinding ceaselessly as it were in a vacuum. I described in the article the "movies" which followed: This broken old man watching the pictures of his triumphs in Europe. He was practically silent throughout except for remarks like this in a dead, hollow, weary voice:

"It was rainy that day.—I remember making that speech—That was Sir Charles Cust."[2]—all as though he were speaking of some one else.

Mrs. Wilson & Grayson kept up a steady fire of amusing comments, evidently to cheer up the invalid but he never once seemed to notice. He has movies every day at noon but this is the first time he has asked for the European pictures. Mrs. W's brother, Bolling, brings him in photo play magazines & he goes over & marks the pictures he wants to see

At luncheon, Mrs. W. cared for him as for a baby, pinned his napkin up to his chin.

"You see," he said to me. "I have to wear a bib. It does not imply bibulousness."

Mrs. W. fixed his medicine & gave him a drink of whiskey. We had a silent grace. The President talked over a little, lamenting the want of leadership in the nation: and asked:

"But how can they (referring to Harding &c) lead when they do not know where they are going."

The subject of his message having arisen I made some suggestions that had been in my mind for some time: that he should make this message a kind of farewell address with strong words of warning & prophecy. He seemed much interested & said his mind had been run[nin]g along some such lines. Afterwards I developed the idea still further with Mrs. W. & she asked me to write a letter to the President: which I did (see!) & sent over.[3] Afterwards I took the same subject up with Tumulty & he agreed with me & said he also would make a memorandum for the President.

Poor tragic figure: poor president! He was so late in heaven, now in hell.

He talked with Grayson about resigning last January.[4] Grayson advised it strongly, especially on health grounds. But Mrs W objected. It would have been far better if he had!

Hw bound diary (R. S. Baker Papers, DLC).
[1] This entry was written on December 1, 1920, and backdated to November 28 to cover events of that date. Actually, the entry for November 28 follows the one for December 1 in Baker's diary. Also, he certainly wrote the article mentioned below on November 29; and Mrs. Wilson's letter, also mentioned below, is dated November 30.
[2] Wilson referred to one of his speeches in England in late December 1918. Sir Charles Cust was personal equerry to King George V and had been detailed to serve as Wilson's aide during his stay in England.
[3] We have not found this letter.
[4] About this matter, see n. 1 to the extract from the Diary of Ray Stannard Baker printed at Feb. 4, 1920, Vol. 64.

From Bainbridge Colby, with Enclosure

My dear Mr. President: Washington November 28, 1920.

The situation in Armenia is very obscure and I can get no information that throws more light upon it than the press reports. It appears that the Armenians and the Turkish Nationalists have reached an armistice and that some negotiation is under way. It is also clearly indicated that the Russian Red Army is in possession of some portions of the Armenian state. The mediation suggested by President Hymans of the League of Nations might thus bring you into some embarrassing contacts. It was with this in mind that I drafted the concluding sentences of the proposed reply to M. Hymans' telegram in which I asked that he indicate the avenues by which your proffer of mediation should be conveyed and the persons to whom it should be addressed. This, it seemed to me, would enable you to make a sympathetic response to the Hymans invitation, and would still afford you some room for a further decision before actually committing yourself to any plan of mediation.

I made some inquiries as to the situation through Ambassador Davis in London. His reply, dated November 26th, I beg to enclose. It would indicate that there is nothing to be gained from compliance with the narrow authority given to you in the Senate resolutions with relation to the dispatch of a battleship and a force of Marines to Batum.

Very respectfully yours,   Bainbridge Colby

TLS (WP, DLC).

E N C L O S U R E

London. Nov. 26, 1920.

1650. Your 1180, November twenty-fourth. Have informed Foreign Office as directed. In re warship at Batum Foreign Office unable to see how safety of Armenians would be in any way promoted. Nationalists are now astride railroad from Batum and communication with Armenia effectively interrupted. Armenians and Nationalists have signed armistice and are supposed to be negotiating at Alexandropol, but British Government without information as to details. Answering questions in their order: first. Georgia now in possession of Batum so far as known. No Allied troops there. Georgia would probably be adverse to landing of marines. Second. No apparent benefit would be accorded to Armenia. Third. Military supplies and fuel oil have been furnished to Armenians; but British and Allied Governments are not contemplating any other form of aid. Certainly not the despatch of troops. Fourth. In so far as recent changes affect the situation they tend to make protection of Armenians increasingly difficult.

Am informed that Assembly at Geneva has asked Council to find mediator between Armenians and Nationalists hoping America will undertake the task. There seem to be no facts available here pointing to probable success of such an effort.   Davis.

T telegram (WP, DLC).

A Draft of an Article by Ray Stannard Baker

[November 29, 1920]

I went in yesterday at noon to the White House to see the President. I shall endeavor to set down everything exactly as it was, as I saw it—as long as I live I shall never forget any incident of that extraordinary experience.

Through the door of the parlor where I waited I saw them presently lifting up and laying aside the heavy red rug of the main hall. The President was coming, walking slowly, with a cane, upon the smooth marble flags of the floor. He swung along heavily and slowly, with his left side drooping. His left arm hung inert; his eyes were extraordinarily large and brilliant. He was faultlessly dressed. To one who remembered vividly, upon so many former occasions the singularly active step, the alert, listening poise of the head, it could not but be a shock to see him thus; a shock of intense compassion, pity, which instantly gave way to amazement at the indomitable spirit of the man. It was in every line of his face, sharpened and deepened with suffering, it shone in his eyes, it was in the strong pressure of his hand, and in the jest with which he greeted me. There he stood, a broken, stooped, gray-faced, white-haired man, and yet he gave such a sense of unconquerable will, untameable life as cannot be described. It came to me with a rush what this man had been and meant to the world so short a time ago, and what he had borne in suffering and obloquy during the last terrible months—such various boundless, human suffering as men less sensitive than he cannot imagine! I have never had quite such an impression of a flaming human spirit, stripped utterly bare of everything and yet unconquerably going on, a fighter to the last ditch, a president to the end.

We passed on down the hall into the great ballroom of the White House. I had no idea what was to happen. That grand room with its faded glories, its echoes of ancient gaieties, was wholly bare and empty except for half-a-dozen chairs placed in the middle of it. It was almost unlighted and resounded to our steps. The President took his seat in the first of the chairs, Mrs. Wilson next, then a niece of Mrs. Wilson, Admiral Grayson and myself.

Immediately the machine behind us began to click and sputter and a picture flashed upon a screen at the far end of the room. If I had known beforehand that we were to see moving pictures and had been asked to guess what they were to be, I should have ventured everything else in all filmdom—whether romance or comedy or tragedy—before I should have dreamed of this.

And yet there the pictures were, flickering upon the screen: the really wonderful photographic record of the President's trip to Europe, which a hundred years from now will be a classic of the schools.

Instantly we were in another world: a brave, brilliant world, full of wonderful and glorious events. There we were sailing grandly into the harbor at Brest, the ships beflagged, the soldiers marshalled upon the quay and flying machines skimming through the air. There was the President himself, smiling upon the bridge, very erect, very tall, lifting his hat to shouting crowds.

By magic we are transported to Paris. There he was again, this time with the President of France, driving down the most famous avenue in the world, bowing right and left.

"It was roses, roses all the way ∗ ∗ ∗
The church roofs seemed to heave and sway
The church spires flamed, such flags they had."[1]

There in the distance was the Arc de Triomphe, symbol also of this later triumph and there a glimpse of the tomb of the great Napoleon guarding its dimmed glory.

Was there ever anything in the world before like this? Had any other human being in history such an experience? Was there ever such an event in Paris, or ever such a triumph come to Rome, even in the most glorious days of the Caesars?

The man back in the darkness of the great room sat bowed forward, looking at all this, absolutely silent.

Woodrow Wilson today is not only a living factor in our life, but already a character in history; one of the great inexplicable characters. He is one of those men who from the very beginning, and in whatever scene, has been appointed, chosen, doomed, to occupy the center of the stage. A corrosive kind of man, the powerful reagent of fluid social conditions, and whether the President of a university, the governor of a state, the chief magistrate of a nation, or the supreme figure in a world conference, a kind of center of life and heat, causing the fiercest adulations, separating society into its elements, starting new combinations—and engendering everywhere the fiercest human passions—the whole gamut from sheer worship to deadly hatred.

He was never anywhere negligible; he could never be brushed aside or got around. The politicians tried their best to avoid him in the last campaign; and though he was a broken invalid, they could not escape him. It was he and his policies that people fought about; he was the supreme issue.

While 30,000,000 people were voting for two puppets, let me tell

[1] From Browning's *The Patriot*.

you what the real man in the center of the stage was doing. Dr. Grayson had built a series of little low steps in the White House; and the sick man there, his body stricken but his spirit still unyielding, was there with his cane in his hand, trying and failing, day after day, failing and trying, to climb those little steps. They thought they had him down at Princeton, they thought they had beaten him in New Jersey, they said he failed at Paris—I am watching him climb those little steps. What does it matter if they lead only into history? He'll climb them.

I had almost forgotten the pictures, but the faithful and impersonal machine—the imperishable record—behind us is still sputtering and clicking. We are now crossing the English channel, two nations dispute the glory of guarding our passage. The warships of France come half way with us and give over reluctantly to the warships of Britain. And once we are ashore, were there ever such marching regiments of men, such bowing dignitaries, so many lords and lord-mayors? And here he is again riding behind magnificent horses, with outriders flying pennants, and people shouting in the streets, coming down from Buckingham Palace with the King of England! Was there ever anything like it before or since?

I do not pretend to explain this man, but I wonder at him. The world would be poorer, less interesting, without him. He is the symbol of a time: a "representative man"—a "nature" as Goethe called certain men to distinguish them from geniuses. At one moment, to those who have been closest to him, he seems the simplest, most sincere, most direct of men: at other moments he seems utterly remote, aloof, unapproachable, at one moment he appears a pathetically and utterly friendless and lonely human soul, wanting human love (as he has told a friend) but never achieving it, getting at best wonderfully gilded husks of respect, the glorious outer accoutrements of admiration, the inverted recognition of the envious. At another time he appears one of those insular figures not needing sympathy, that Mathew Arnold compares with the stars:

"These demand not that the things
    without them
Yield them love, amusement, sympathy."[2]

No, the pattern is yet too large to see in its entirety: and indeed it is not yet finished. One can only prick in here and there a detail which will sometime take its place where it belongs in the picture. For example, how explain the strange vein of mysticism or superstition in his nature? Other supreme men in history, who have had

[2] From Arnold's *Self-Dependence.*

a sense of their destiny, have also had a kind of interest or curiosity one can scarcely say faith, in portents, numbers, fortunate days. I remember once coming out of the Quai d'Orsay with the President and as we stepped into the waiting car, he called my attention to the number upon the door. It was 1921. I thought at first he meant to refer to the number as a date—the year 1921—a fateful year from many aspects. But it was the figures 1921 *added together* in connection with the date, that struck him. They made his "lucky number"—13. His name—Woodrow Wilson—has 13 letters: and all his life long events have yielded up the same magic number. His friends could give many such instances. All of this is not explained, or even commented upon, but merely noted, a fact upon which future biographers may waste their controversial ink. For this is certain: there will be no one judgment of history regarding Woodrow Wilson. He is the kind of man who has provoked controversy in his life, divided men into bitter opponents, or worshipful admirers, and so it will be to the end of time. The court of last resort, which history is supposed to be, will send down at last a divided opinion.

The show is over and done: the film has run its course (it was only a film!) the symbols of that glory have faded away with a click and a sputter. It was literally, to us there, so tense we had grown, as though the thread of life itself had snapped: as though we had fallen from some vast height into the dim, cold, dreary reality of a less interesting world. We are again in the grand, dim, ballroom. We draw a long breath and turn to see sitting there, quite immobile, quite silent, the stooped figure of the President.

Out of the surrounding darkness come figures. One places a foot against his foot so that he will not slip in rising. He rises slowly and with his cane shuffles out of the room without looking aside and without speaking.

One would dare not to lift the veil, even if he could, to speculate upon what was going on in the powerful, active, intense mind of this man, imprisoned thus in a ruin with nothing now but itself to feed upon. A man's capacity for suffering is in exact ratio to his power to think and to feel. What then must be the suffering here?

Well, the only bright spot left in the vacant room, as we retire, is the screen where symbols of departed glory so recently flickered away. It is clean, and light and bare: it is ready now for a new film, new pictures, a new story, new heroes.

But I am following the figure of the man walking painfully out of the room. If anyone could have seen that sight without a tremor of emotion in every fibre of his being, without tears in his eyes, I say he has no heart. And if he could see it without a passion of anger at the personal attacks (I do not refer to political opposition) the personal and slanderous attacks of insect minded enemies and soured friends and envious rivals, upon this broken man, this strange fated character, cast in heroic lines and set upon a heroic stage, then I say he has no soul, nor any power of imagination.

I think it is Voltaire who says that the most interesting man is the one who has endured the greatest extremes of human fate. Consider this man as he was in Paris two years ago: and consider him today.

In this account of a strange day of symbols I have yet one more symbol to report—to me one of the most striking of all. While at luncheon there began outside of the White House the slow parade, single file, of a group of sympathizers with Irish freedom. They were demanding apparently of this broken man that he straightway free Ireland! The pathetic faith of it: the pathetic faith of men in heroes and supermen! The idea that someone who has spoken true words can magically do for them what they can only do for themselves! This also was the very core of the tragic events at Paris: the still persistent idea that the world can be made over by the word of one man of whom possibly they have made a god or a president! And when their prayer is not answered, how they turn upon him and rend him in pieces. The world could have had the tables that were brought down out of Sinai, there in 1919: but they had already turned to the worship of the calf. And the tables fell and were broken—and who now is there to return to the heights and brave the anger of the Lord!

I had intended, when I began this article, to tell a great deal more about the President's actual work, the actual course of his day, but I see I lost myself in the drama there in the ballroom, that I have no more space. The President is slowly but surely getting better: he has been better since the election. He works hard at his desk a good many hours every day, he has not missed a single cabinet meeting since he began holding them last summer: he sees, now, quite a number of officials of the Government: he follows the newspapers closely, and for diversion takes daily rides in the park, and at other times reads (or listens to) stories by Stanley Weyman, Stevenson and Kipling.

T MS (R. S. Baker Papers, DLC).

To Thomas William Lamont

My dear Lamont: [The White House] 29 November, 1920

Thank you for your letter of November twenty-sixth. I am, of course, willing to do anything that is within my power to assist the Chinese in relieving their distress, and I think your suggestion of the appointment of a committee an excellent one, but I feel that you are yourself much better situated to suggest the personnel of such a committee than I am, and if you will be so kind as to suggest a committee, I will be glad to appoint it in any way that you propose.

Cordially and sincerely yours,   [Woodrow Wilson]

CCL (WP, DLC).

From Bainbridge Colby, with Enclosures

My dear Mr. President: Washington November 29, 1920.

Mr. Davis has reported your suggested amendment[1] to the telegram to the President of the Council of the League of Nations on the subject of mediation in Armenia.

I beg to enclose the proposed telegram revised in accordance with your suggestion. If you approve it, will you kindly sign and return it, as we think it should be dispatched promptly, and I furthermore suggest that it be given to the press, in view of the publicity that was given to the invitation.

Very respectfully yours,   Bainbridge Colby

TLS (B. Colby Papers, DLC).
[1] That is, the document printed as Enclosure I.

E N C L O S U R E   I

I am without authorization to offer or employ military forces of the United States in any project for the relief of Armenia, and any material contributions would require the authorization of the Congress which is not now in session and whose action I could not forecast. I am willing, however, upon assurances of the moral and diplomatic support of the principal powers, and in a spirit of sympathetic response to the request of the Council of the League of Nations, to use my good offices and to proffer by personal mediation through a representative whom I may designate, to end the hostilities now being waged against the Armenian people and to bring peace and accord to the contending parties, relying upon the

Council of the League of Nations to suggest to me the avenues through which my proffer should be conveyed and the parties to whom it should be addressed.

T MS (B. Colby Papers, DLC).

E N C L O S U R E   I I

I have the honor to acknowledge the receipt of your cabled message, setting forth the resolution adopted by the Assembly of the League of Nations, requesting the Council of the League to arrive at an understanding with the governments with a view to entrusting a power with the task of taking necessary measures to stop the hostilities in Armenia.

You offer to the United States the opportunity of undertaking the humanitarian task of using its good offices to end the present tragedy, being enacted in Armenia, and you assure me that your proposal involves no repetition of the invitation to accept a mandate for Armenia.

While the invitation to accept a mandate for Armenia has been rejected by the Senate of the United States, this country has repeatedly declared its solicitude for the fate and welfare of the Armenian people, in a manner and to an extent that justifies you in saying that the fate of Armenia has always been of special interest to the American people.

I am without authorization to offer or employ military forces of the United States in any project for the relief of Armenia, and any material contributions would require the authorization of the Congress which is not now in session and whose action I could not forecast. I am willing, however, upon assurances of the moral and diplomatic support of the principal powers, and in a spirit of sympathetic response to the request of the Council of the League of Nations, to use my good offices and to proffer my personal mediation through a representative whom I may designate, to end the hostilities now being waged against the Armenian people and to bring peace and accord to the contending parties, relying upon the Council of the League of Nations to suggest to me the avenues through which my proffer should be conveyed and the parties to whom it should be addressed.   Woodrow Wilson[1]

TS MS (B. Colby Papers, DLC).
[1] This was sent as WW to P. Hymans, Nov. 30, 1920, T telegram (WP, DLC). It was given to the press on November 30 and published, *inter alia*, in the *New York Times*, Dec. 1, 1920; printed in *FR 1920*, III, 804-805.

From Bainbridge Colby

My dear Mr. President: Washington November 29, 1920.

The Department of Justice is in possession of trustworthy information from its agents along the Border that Mexican malcontents are hatching a revolutionary movement to overthrow the Obregon regime. General Lucio Blanco, an ex-Carranza leader, is at the head of this movement, the rendezvous being in the neighborhood of Allen, Texas, on the lower Rio Grande River. It is believed that the movement will be launched on December 1st by a military invasion of Mexico, organized on American soil.

The Attorney General, before apprehending the leaders, awaits an expression of the views of this Department on the question of policy. I assume, subject to your approval, that the Attorney General should be requested to use every available means to prevent a violation of our laws by the leaders of this movement.

Very respectfully yours,   Bainbridge Colby

TLS (WP, DLC).

From the Diary of Josephus Daniels

1920 Tuesday 30 November

CABINET. Discussed low prices for farmers and the demand for legislation to assist them. Houston said we were exporting larger volume of agricultural products than ever, more he believed than Europe could pay for. He said that Eugene Myers,[1] formerly member of War Finance Corporation, resigned and went to help Harding, was urging it, but was more interested in getting money for his copper mines than for farmers. He deplored the sudden drop in farm prices but saw nothing the Treasury could do. He feared panic if the Treasury went in for inflation. He criticized John Skelton Williams for saying banks were sending money to New York to lend to speculators at high rate of interest & said very little went and that New York New England banks were lending money to the South & West. He said merchants & manufacturers needed money as much as farmers did—indeed that the trouble with prices of farmers products was that other people lacked money to buy farm products.

President seemed better & said he had not yet written his message & would like suggestions

Again declined to sell destroyers to Peru

He disapproved sending troops to West Va & Baker is to withdraw them. The Gov. of W Va wants him to declare martial law instead of the State taking care of conditions as it should do.[2]

---

[1] Eugene Meyer, Jr., who had been managing director of the War Finance Corporation from January 1919 until his resignation in May 1920.

[2] About the bloody coal miners' strike in West Virginia, see J. L. Spivak to WW, May 28, 1920, and n. 1 thereto, Vol. 65. Since the draft of the West Virginia National Guard into the United States Army in 1917 had left the state without a military force to deal with domestic disturbances, the Governor of West Virginia, in August 1920, had called upon Wilson to send in federal troops. They were withdrawn on September 29. As soon as they left, violence broke out again, and Baker sent in a battalion of 500 men from Camp Sherman in Ohio in late November. In fact, they were not withdrawn until early February 1921. *New York Times, passim.*

To Bainbridge Colby

My dear Mr. Secretary: The White House 30 November, 1920

Replying to your letter of November twenty-ninth, I beg to say that you correctly assume that the Attorney General should be requested to use every available means to prevent a violation of our laws by the leaders of the contemplated Mexican revolutionary movement. I think the public opinion of the country would expect and support such a course.

Cordially and faithfully yours,   Woodrow Wilson

TLS (B. Colby Papers, DLC).

Edith Bolling Galt Wilson to Ray Stannard Baker

Dear Mr. Baker: The White House, November 30th, 1920.

I know you will forgive a typewritten note, but it is late and I am anxious to get it off tonight.

I have just read your article and it is really inspired in that it is a vivid picture and one I am sure drawn straight from your heart. Personally I value it deeply for that reason.

But from the standpoint of the impression it would make upon the public, I think it would come as a great shock, but to us who have been constantly in touch and seen the great improvement it would seem to strike the wrong note.

From what you said to me on Sunday my impression was that you thought an intimate picture, reflecting the improvement and not the ravages of disease, would be very helpful at this moment. Please don't think me insensible to your wish to inform the public at large of the suffering, both mental and physical, which every hour of the past fourteen months has registered; but in view of your statement as to a possible investigation of conditions, it seems to me unwise to lay so strong an accent on your impression which stands reflected from your last interview in Paris. There is very much in the article that I think could be worked into another one, which would attain the end I think you seek.

Sincerely,   Edith Bolling Wilson

P.S. Thank you for letting me see this, and also for your note with enclosure to the President.

He did have in mind just about what you did, but he said it was very reassuring to know of your impressions.

Faithfully   EBW

11 ock. P.M.

TLS with EBWhw postscript (R. S. Baker Papers, DLC).

To Lawrence Crane Woods

My dear Woods: [The White House] 1 December, 1920

I read your letter of February [November] twenty-seventh with great pleasure. The danger, as I conceive it, is that the party in power may take us into the League in such a niggardly fashion, with "if's" and "but's" which so clearly proceed from prejudice and self-interest and a desire to play a lone hand and think first and only of the United States, that we shall lose all dignity and influence in the world. But I agree with you that they will hardly dare stay out. They are going to make consummate fools of themselves, it is evident, but that affords me no comfort because before being a party man I am an American and shall deeply grieve to see blunders, even those made by my opponents, which constitute a disservice to our beloved country.

Cordially and faithfully yours,   [Woodrow Wilson]

CCL (WP, DLC).

From Norman Hezekiah Davis

My dear Mr. President: Washington December 1, 1920

I hasten to inform you that the Italian Chargé d'Affaires[1] has handed to the Department this afternoon a communication[2] stating that the Italian naval force of the Adriatic has instituted an effective blockade today of the Independent State of Fiume and of the Islands of Arbe and Veglia.[3] Mr. Brambilla's note further states that the blockade began at ten o'clock this morning, but time will be given to permit friendly mercantile vessels to leave the harbor.

I am, my dear Mr. President,

Faithfully yours,   Norman H. Davis

TLS (WP, DLC).
    [1] That is, Giuseppe Brambilla.
    [2] G. Brambilla to BC, Dec. 1, 1920, TLS (SDR, RG 59, 860q.00/2, DNA).
    [3] Gabriele D'Annunzio, who had occupied Fiume with his volunteers on September 12, 1919, had just declared war against Italy and the islands of Veglia and Arbe, and the Italian fleet sailed against him on December 2, 1920.

From Cleveland Hoadley Dodge, with Enclosure

My dear President: New York December 1, 1920.

The Rev. Dr. Barton, of Boston, Secretary of the American Board of Missions, and Chairman of the Near East Relief, was in town today, and told me of an interview he had yesterday in Washington with Senator Lodge regarding Armenia, which was so significant that I thought you ought to know about it. I asked Dr. Barton to write it down in the shape of a letter to me which he has done, and I am sending you the letter as I think it will interest you. The Mr. Montgomery,[1] who went with him to see Senator Lodge, was one of the Information Staff which you had at Versailles, and is rather an authority on the Near East.

Dr. Barton has considerable influence over Senator Lodge owing to the fact that so many of the Senator's prominent constituents are Congregationalists, and he says that the Senator seems really anxious to do something for Armenia. Dr. Barton is a statesman himself, and knows conditions in the Near East better, probably, than almost anyone else, as he gets so many reports from his missionaries there. I told him that it seemed to me, if our Congress appropriated a large sum for the help of Armenia, it ought to be guarded over carefully by some proper Commission; otherwise the Irredentists in Armenia would seize the money, and any treaty or settlement which might be made between Armenia and the Turks on one side, and the Bolsheviki on the other, might be jeopardized. I am delighted that you have consented to make the attempt of mediation between the conflicting forces in the Near East, and sincerely trust and pray that out of it all may grow some happy settlement of all their troubles. Whether it would be wise for you to say anything about this in your Message, of course you know better than I, but I really think, from what Dr. Barton told me, that Mr. Lodge is sincere, and it may be a satisfaction to you to know that he would support some such recommendation as Dr. Barton mentions.

I am obliged to go to Washington the end of next week to attend the annual meeting of the Trustees of the Carnegie Institution, and expected, in a day or two, to write to Mrs. Wilson and ask her if there was any way by which she could let me meet herself and you, as I am perfectly crazy to see you both. I know that out of the kindness of her hospitable heart she will ask me to come to the White House, but that will be out of the question, as I have to take my physician along with me and, moreover, I shall have meetings all of Thursday afternoon and evening, and all of Friday morning, including the lunch hours, but if Mrs. Wilson would let me come in to afternoon tea, or possibly, if you were well enough, let me dine with you on Friday night, the tenth, it would make me happy beyond measure. Of course it may be a little far ahead for you to know how you will be feeling by the end of next week, and of course if you were not up to seeing me, any arrangement which Mrs. Wilson might make now could be changed subsequently, by simply dropping a line to the New Willard Hotel.

As I was writing you about the Armenian question, I have taken the liberty of putting all this in, rather than writing another letter to Mrs. Wilson, and I hope she will forgive me if I do not seem to fully recognize her prerogatives.

With warm regards to Mrs. Wilson, believe me

Ever yours affectionately,   Cleveland H. Dodge

TLS (WP, DLC).
    [1] Stuart Montgomery, Chief of the Russian Division in the secretariat of the American Commission to Negotiate Peace.

ENCLOSURE

James Levi Barton to Cleveland Hoadley Dodge

My dear Mr. Dodge:—   New York Dec. 1—20

In Washington yesterday, Mr. Montgomery and I had a long conference with Senator Lodge over the Armenian situation. At his suggestion we went to the Treasury department and there learned that the remainder of the International Loan Fund is not available for a loan to the Armenians, according to the terms of the act of Congress creating the fund.

Senator Lodge expressed himself as in sympathy with any steps which might be taken by the President to restore order and establish peace in Armenia, provided it did not involve this country in war. He said he believed Congress would approve.

He also expressed the opinion that Congress would approve of an appropriation of twenty millions or even more, as a loan to Armenia, to enable it to organize a government and protect itself against its enemies. He said the ini[ti]ative should come from the President. The expenditure of this fund, if loaned, should be under the supervision of a representative or representatives of the U. S.

The President will send a message to Congress next Monday. I believe, if he will recommend a loan to Armenia for the purposes named, it will receive favorable consideration from Congress. You have his confidence as few others have. Will you not write him at once upon this subject urging that, if he has not already done so, he make such a recommendation?

The League of Nations is urging this and undoubtedly will co-operate.   Most cordially yours   James L. Barton

ALS (WP, DLC).

From Arthur Bernard Krock[1]

Dear Mr. President,   Louisville, Ky. December 1, 1920.

I am enclosing two clippings—the cartoon and an editorial—from THE LOUISVILLE TIMES of today[2] which may interest you. For over eight years your very sincere supporter and admirer, it is a great satisfaction to find myself as warmly devoted to the human purposes you represent in this hour as during the period when acclaim was most general. I have always felt that no other administrator could have made so few mistakes in the perilous times through which you have conducted the nation, the world in fact, and that no other could have brought such equipment to the task.
                              Yours faithfully,   Arthur Krock

TLS (WP, DLC).
    [1] At this time editor of the *Louisville Times.*
    [2] The cartoon, entitled "Still the First Citizen of the World," depicted a healthy Wilson at his desk, reading the League of Nations' plea to him "to mediate in behalf of Armenia." The editorial, entitled "A Noble Concluding Work," praised Wilson for offering to use his personal mediation on behalf of Armenia. "True Americans," the editorial concluded, "will be proud of the fact that the PRESIDENT has been called upon for this noble service and has, in such honest spirit of duty, accepted it."

Ray Stannard Baker to Edith Bolling Galt Wilson

My dear Mrs. Wilson: Washington, D. C. December 1 '20

I want to thank you heartily for reading my small inadequate article and expressing your opinion so frankly. Of course I shall do nothing further with it in its present form, though I do wish later to set down in some way my own feeling about how the President

has suffered and come through, so courageously, in the last terrible months. I wish I could also set forth his views about the present
responsibilities and opportunities of America. We are going into
heavy, hard times, and much darkness of counsel, when we shall
miss his clear leadership. Perhaps at some future time I can combine what I have to say in this article with the inspiration which
would come from an interpretation of his outlook upon a sadly dis-
organized world. The people simply do not understand—*yet*!—the
character and message of the President! and if I live I'm going to
help to give them a better understanding!

Cordially yours,   Ray Stannard Baker

I am going to North Carolina for a week or ten days.

ALS (EBW Papers, DLC).

From the Diary of Ray Stannard Baker

Washington December 1st, 1920 Wednesday

I arrived here last Saturday. I had luncheon with Admiral Grayson & Secy Tumulty. Grayson told me fully about the President's
health: says he seems much better since election, but that his trouble is more of his nerves than before. He takes it less easily, does
not make light of it or joke as he did. He more easily loses control
of himself & when he talks is likely to break down & weep. Tumulty also said he often did this, especially when the League of Nations is mentioned. He is also often impatient & once threatened to
"throw out" all the nurses and "you too" (referring to Grayson). He
worries about his condition more than ever, calls Grayson often in
the middle of the night whether anything is the trouble or not and
insists upon something being done. He is irritated with a kind of
asthma. Tumulty is a large, warm-hearted supporter. He has the
true Irish loyalty (as expressed in his speech in Baltimore the other
day)[1] I am afraid I have misjudged him in the past. It is a very
terrible situation.

[1] To our knowledge, the only such speech that Tumulty gave during these months
was one at Bethesda, Maryland, on October 28, 1920. About it, see C. Moore to JPT,
Oct. 29, 1920, n. 2.

To Cleveland Hoadley Dodge

My dear Cleve: The White House 2 December, 1920

Thank you for your letter of December first with the enclosed
letter from Doctor Barton to you. I have read both with the greatest

interest and sympathy and shall take pleasure in recommending to the Congress that a loan to Armenia be authorized.[1] I sincerely hope that they will respond to the recommendation. I am sure the country will wish them to do so.

In haste   Affectionately yours,   Woodrow Wilson

TLS (WC, NjP).
  [1] Wilson did so in his Annual Message printed at December 7, 1920.

From Bainbridge Colby

My dear Mr. President: Washington December 2, 1920.

Dr. Honorio Pueyrredon, Argentine Minister for Foreign Affairs, is at present in Geneva as Delegate of the Argentine Republic to the Assembly of the League of Nations. Dr. Pueyrredon is a distinguished figure in the present Argentine Government and it is very probable that he will be the next President of Argentina. He has long been noted for his cordial sentiments towards this country. Dr. Pueyrredon has done much to further the establishment of the particularly friendly relations which now exist between this country and Argentina, and it has been due, very largely, to his influence that the Argentine Government has not committed itself to a Latin-American policy as opposed to a Pan-American policy.

It is Dr. Pueyrredon's intention to return to Argentina within the next two months and it has occurred to me that it would be a courtesy which would be highly appreciated by the Argentine Government if an invitation were extended by this Government to Dr. Pueyrredon to make a brief visit to this country as the guest of the United States before he returns to Argentina. May I ask whether you desire this invitation extended to Dr. Pueyrredon?

Very respectfully yours,   Bainbridge Colby

TLS (WP, DLC).

Two Letters from Josephus Daniels

My dear Mr. President: Washington December 2, 1920.

Referring to the discussion at the meeting of the Cabinet on Tuesday, I am sending you an advance copy of the Report of the Secretary of the Navy and am also enclosing herewith the first ten pages in which I have outlined what seemed to me to be the right attitude of our Government in view of world conditions. The first four pages will give you the program outlined, and the others will give you data which you may wish to see in connection with your message to Congress.[1]

Sincerely yours,   Josephus Daniels

TLS (WP, DLC).
[1] *ANNUAL REPORT OF THE SECRETARY OF THE NAVY*, Dec. 1, 1920, pp. 1-10; tearsheets (WP, DLC). Daniels reviewed the Navy Department's progress in expanding the fleet under the Naval Appropriations Act of August 29, 1916. The department, which had laid aside plans for construction of capital ships during the war in favor of destroyers and other antisubmarine craft, had now begun work on the sixteen battle-ships and battle cruisers authorized in the three-year program of 1916. This program, when completed, would bring the navy to an adequate force should the United States join "an organization to prevent war and promote peace." If, however, the United States was not to enter into any agreement with the other powers, now bound together in the League, Daniels went on, he felt compelled to approve the recommendation of the General Board of the Navy that Congress authorize another three-year program to be begun as soon as the capital ships now under construction were launched.

Daniels then continued at length to argue that such expansion of the fleet would be necessary only if the United States was determined to go it alone in the world. The choice was clear: either isolation and a fortress state or cooperation with other nations in reduction of naval armaments. As Daniels put it: "We have passed from isolation to leadership. Shall we pass from leadership back again to isolation?" Daniels devoted the balance of this portion of his annual report to a detailed report on the progress of the construction program and to commentary on British and Japanese building plans.

My dear Mr. President: Washington. December 2, 1920.

I am enclosing herewith a copy of a telegram received from Hon. Warren G. Harding in reply to the one sent him tendering the use of the MAYFLOWER for his trip from Norfolk to Washington.[1]

Sincerely yours,   Josephus Daniels

TLS (J. Daniels Papers, DLC).
[1] "Please thank the President for Mayflower tender Am obliged to travel to Washington by rail My gratitude to you." W. G. Harding to JD, Dec. 2, 1920, T telegram (J. Daniels Papers, DLC).

From David Franklin Houston, with Enclosure

Dear Mr. President: Washington December 2, 1920.

I am sending you herewith a statement bearing on financial matters which I hope may be of use to you in connection with your message.

As I am dictating this it occurs to me that it would be well for you to say something in your message as to the need of making generous provision for the care of sick and wounded soldiers. I shall try to prepare a brief statement of this subject for your consideration, and send it to you if possible tomorrow. In my report I am reiterating the position I took last spring against the bonus proposals, but I imagine you will not care to touch on this subject in your message.   Faithfully yours,   D. F. Houston.

TLS (C. L. Swem Coll., NjP).

E N C L O S U R E[I]

The nation's finances have shown marked improvement during the past year. The total ordinary receipts of $6,694,000,000 for the fiscal year 1920 exceeded those for 1919 by $1,542,000,000, while the total net ordinary expenditures decreased from $18,514,000,000 to $6,403,000,000. The gross public debt, which reached its highest point on August 31, 1919, when it was $26,596,000,000 had dropped on November 30, 1920, to $24,175,000,000. There has also been a marked decrease in holdings of Government war securities by the banking institutions of the country, as well as in the amount of bills held by the Federal Reserve Banks secured by Government war obligations. This fortunate result has relieved the banks and left them freer to finance the needs of agriculture, industry and commerce. It has been due in large part to the reduction of the public debt, especially of the floating debt, but more particularly to the improved distribution of Government securities among permanent investors. The cessation of the Government's borrowings except through short-term certificates of indebtedness has been a matter of great consequence to the people of the country at large, as well as to the holders of Liberty bonds and Victory notes, and has had an important bearing on the matter of effective credit control. The year has been characterized by the progressive withdrawal of the Treasury from the domestic credit market and from a position of dominant influence. The future course will necessarily depend upon the extent to which economies are practiced and upon the burdens placed upon the Treasury, as well as upon industrial developments and the maintenance of tax receipts at a sufficiently high level.

The fundamental fact which, at present, dominates the Government's financial situation is that 7½ billions of its war indebtedness mature within the next 2½ years. Of this amount, 2⟨½⟩ *and a half* billions are floating debt and 5 billions Victory notes and War Savings certificates. The fiscal program of the Government must be determined with reference to these maturities. Sound policy demands that Government expenditures be reduced to the lowest amount which will permit the various services to operate efficiently and that Government receipts from taxes and salvage be maintained sufficiently high to provide for current requirements, including interest and sinking fund charges on the public debt, and at the same time retire the floating debt and part of the Victory Loan before maturity. With rigid economy, vigorous salvage operations and adequate revenues from taxation, a surplus of current receipts over current expenditures can be realized and should be applied to the floating debt. All branches of the Government should cooperate to see that this program is realized.

I cannot overemphasize the necessity of economy in Government appropriations and expenditures and the avoidance by the Congress of practices which take money from the Treasury by indefinite or revolving fund appropriations. The estimates for the present year show that over a billion dollars of expenditures were authorized by the last Congress in addition to the amounts shown in the usual compiled statements of appropriations. This strikingly illustrates the importance of making direct and specific appropriations. The relation between the current receipts and current expenditures of the Government during the present fiscal year, as well as during the last half of the past fiscal year, has been ⟨upset⟩ *disturbed* by the extraordinary burdens thrown upon the Treasury by the Transportation Act, in connection with the return of the railroads to private control. Over $600,000,000 has already been paid to the railroads under this Act—$350,000,000 during the present fiscal year; and it is estimated that further payments aggregating possibly $650,000,000 must still be made to the railroads during the current year. It is obvious that these large payments have already seriously limited the Government's progress in retiring the floating debt.

I pointed out in my last annual message the urgent need of action by Congress to revise the tax laws and to make them more equitable and less burdensome without reducing the aggregate revenues below the point indicated by sound fiscal considerations. I again call your attention to the necessity of prompt action. The aggregate tax receipts of the Government, after this fiscal year and for two or three years to come, cannot safely be reduced below 4 billions a year. They may have to be kept at a higher figure; and there is no certainty that even the existing law will continue to yield the needed revenues. Indeed, in view of the Government's maturing obligations and the heavy burdens resting upon the Treasury and of shrinkage in incomes or readjustments in business, the question arises whether due regard for the protection of the Treasury and the credit of the Government does not, at the present session, require consideration by Congress of the problem of finding new sources of revenue. The Secretary of the Treasury will place before you general recommendations as to amendments to the revenue law which I hope may have your early consideration.

I reluctantly vetoed the Budget Bill passed by the last session of the Congress because of a Constitutional objection. The House of

Representatives subsequently modified the Bill in order to meet this objection.[2] In the revised form I believe that the Bill, coupled with action by Congress to revise its rules and procedure, furnishes the foundations for an effective National budget system. I earnestly hope, therefore, that one of the first steps taken by the present session of Congress will be to pass the Budget Bill.

T MS (C. L. Swem Coll., NjP).
    [1] Words in angle brackets deleted by Wilson; words in italics WWhw. For the way Wilson used this memorandum for his Annual Message, see that document printed at Dec. 7, 1920.
    [2] See the veto message printed at June 4, 1920, and n. 1 thereto, Vol. 65.

From Edward William Bok

                                Philadelphia December second
My dear Mr. President: Nineteen hundred and twenty

Of course I need not tell you the degree of heart-felt pleasure it gives me to send you to-day by express a reproduction of Kipling's "If."[1] I had this done by a new process which is absolutely unfadeable the inventor claims. It looks as if it were done on paper but the basis is actually some sort of composition that looks like paper and yet is not. I am very glad indeed to share my treasured possession with you of all men.

Believe me   Very sincerely yours,   Edward W. Bok

TLS (WP, DLC).
    [1] This item is in the Wilson Library, DLC.

A Memorandum by Cary Travers Grayson

                                                Friday, December 3, 1920.

On Friday night, December 3rd, I had a talk with the President on the subject of whether he would deliver *in person* his address on the assembling of Congress on Tuesday, December 7th. He told me that he would like very much to do so. I persuaded him, however, not to go to the Capitol. I reminded him of the fact that, before making any speech, he was always nervous even when he was feeling perfectly well, and that to deliver his address on an occasion of this kind, when he would undoubtedly receive a great ovation, would probably work upon his emotions to such an extent that he might not be able to complete the reading of his address. I told him that if his voice should give out (his voice is quite feeble after reading aloud ten or fifteen minutes), his object in going to the Capitol might be misconstrued and prove embarrassing to him. I said:

"There is no question about your being able to walk while at the Capitol, but I have given this matter a great deal of thought, and I am strongly of the belief that you should not go. Please do not go. Let me be the judge this time." His reply was that he thought my advice was good and that he would not go.

T MS (received from James Gordon Grayson and Cary T. Grayson, Jr.).

To Bainbridge Colby

My dear Mr. Secretary: The White House 3 December, 1920

I have your letter suggesting an invitation to the Argentine Minister for Foreign Affairs to pay a visit to the United States.[1] In all cases of this sort, I hesitate because we have no ready means for entertaining such visitors and I am myself unable to pay them the courtesies which they would expect and which I would desire to pay them. In such circumstances, I think it, on the whole, desirable that we should not invite distinguished foreigners oftener than we can make special preparation for their entertainment and for paying them the sort of honors which would be a real compliment.

In haste

Cordially and faithfully yours,   Woodrow Wilson

TLS (SDR, RG 59, 033.3511/23, DNA).
[1] BC to WW, Dec. 2, 1920.

To Norman Hezekiah Davis

My dear Davis: [The White House] 3 December, 1920

I feel that the enclosed telegram[1] more properly belongs in your hands than in mine, though it is addressed to me.

I must admit a considerable degree of embarrassment about the offer of Spain and Brazil to join us in trying to straighten out affairs in Armenia, but I suppose that the best thing to do is to wait for them to communicate with us, as Mr. Hymans says they will, and then we can determine how we are to meet their advances and what portion of their suggestions we are to act on. Is not this the most practicable course for the present?

Faithfully yours,   [Woodrow Wilson]

CCL (WP, DLC).
[1] This telegram is missing in all collections and files, but for further explication, see NHD to WW, Dec. 6, 1920 (second letter of that date).

To Charles Zeller Klauder

[The White House] 3 December, 1920

We would appreciate it if you would come down tomorrow and spend Sunday. Our plans are moving forward.

Woodrow Wilson.

T telegram (Letterpress Books, WP, DLC).

To Helen Coughlin

[The White House] 3 December, 1920

Allow me to say with what sincere distress I have heard of the death of your brother, Doctor Coughlin,[1] who was a true and valued friend of mine and, I always believed, a conscientious and most serviceable public servant. We shall miss him sadly.

Woodrow Wilson.

T telegram (Letterpress Books, WP, DLC).
[1] John William Coughlin, M.D., of Fall River, Massachusetts, active in Democratic politics in that state for many years, member of the Democratic National Committee since 1908, had died on December 3, 1920; Wilson's telegram was published in the *New York Times*, Dec. 4, 1920.

From Norman Hezekiah Davis, with Enclosures

My dear Mr. President: Washington December 3, 1920.

The enclosed replies have been given by England and Japan to the memorandum submitted by us to the four principal powers relative to the status of the Island of Yap.[1] Replies have not been received from France and Italy.

We have endeavored in the Communications Conference to reach agreement that any islands not used as military reservations may be used for cable relay stations. England, Italy and the United States have agreed to this principle, but Japan and France have refused to do so. The adoption of such a principle would have avoided the necessity of determining the political status of Yap before reaching a settlement of the cables in the Pacific. So far, Japan has not agreed to this, alleging that Yap has been assigned to Japan, and that the south Pacific islands are included in the class of mandates which are to be administered under the laws of the mandatory as integral portions of its territory, and that the laws of Japan do not permit the operation of cables by foreign interests on Japanese territory. I have stated that this Government has never assented to the Japanese mandate over Yap and have contended that in no event should such a law apply because Yap would not be Japanese territory even if assigned under mandate to Japan.

I am, therefore, transmitting for your consideration a communication to be sent to England and, with appropriate changes, to the other powers, explaining more in detail the basis of our position. I think we may well hope to get agreement from England and Italy at least to the effect that any islands held under mandate which are necessary for cable communications may be so used by any of the powers for the landing of cables and operation of relay stations, free from special taxation and local interference, supervision, and censorship of through messages.

Faithfully and cordially yours,   Norman H. Davis

P.S. We have not yet blown up in the attempt to reach a settlement of the German cables but may do so at any time.

Approved   W.W.

TLS (SDR, RG 59, 862i.01/124, DNA).
[1] It is printed as an Enclosure with NHD to WW, Nov. 5, 1920.

ENCLOSURE I

London Nov. 17, 1920.

1629. Your 1136, November 9, 4 P.M. Just received from Foreign Office "With reference to the memorandum as to the Island of Yap which was left at the Foreign Office on the eleventh instant by a member of your staff, I have the honor to remind your Excellency that all the islands in the Pacific north of the equator formerly in the possession of Germany, including the Island of Yap, were by decision of the Council of Four included in the mandate to be given to Japan. This decision is dated May seventh 1919 and has been published. President Wilson was himself present on that occasion. An examination of the minutes of that meeting discloses no record of his having made any reservation when the decision was taken, although it is on record that, when the Japanese claim to Yap had been discussed on previous occasions, the President had declared in favor of internationalizing the island.

Two. In these circumstances I have the honor to inform Your Excellency that it does not appear to be open to his Majesty's Government to regard the decision of May 7, 1919 as other than definitive.

I have the honor to be etc (signed) Lancelot Oliphant"[1]

Davis.

[1] Assistant Clerk in the British Foreign Office.

E N C L O S U R E   I I

Tokio, November 19, 1920.

Your 417, November 9, 4 pm., My 585, November 12, 5 pm. I have just received the following memorandum marked "confidential" from Foreign Office, dated today;

"The Department of Foreign Affairs of Japan has the honor to acknowledge the receipt of a memorandum of the United States Embassy under date of the 12th instant relative to the status of the island of Yap.

According to the definite understanding of the Japanese Government the Supreme Council on May 7th, 1919, came to a final decision to place under the mandate of Japan the whole of the German islands north of the equator. The decision involves no reservation whatever in regard to the island of Yap.

For the above mentioned reasons the Department of Foreign Affairs begs to inform the United States Embassy that the Japanese Government would not be able to consent to any proposition which, reversing the decision of the Supreme Council, would exclude the island of Yap from the territory committed to their charge."   Bell.[1]

T telegrams (N. H. Davis Papers, DLC).
[1] Edward Bell, American Chargé in Tokyo.

E N C L O S U R E   I I I

Amembassy, London (England).   December ⟨3⟩ 4, 1920.

For the Ambassador, for transmission to the Foreign Office.

I have transmitted to my Government your note of November seventeenth in reply to the memorandum submitted by me on the eleventh of November regarding the island of Yap, to which my Government has directed me to reply as follows:

There would appear to be no difference of opinion with regard to the reservations made by President Wilson and Mr. Lansing with respect to the island of Yap during various discussions of the Supreme Council and the Council of Foreign Ministers at the Peace Conference. For clearer understanding of the issue as to whether, on the part of the United States, it was agreed that all the ex-German islands in the Pacific north of the equator should be allotted to Japan, your attention is drawn to the following facts:

On April twenty-first, at the meeting of President Wilson, Messrs. Lloyd George and Clemenceau, President Wilson, in reporting his conversation of that morning with Baron Makino and

Count Chinda, stated among other things that he had reminded the Japanese delegates that it had been understood that Japan was to have the mandate for the islands in the north Pacific, although he had made a reserve in the case of the island of Yap, which he considered should be international.[1]

At the meeting of Foreign Ministers held on April thirtieth, 1919, at three p.m., in a discussion relating to cables, Mr. Lansing stated that there was a relevant question which he would like on future occasion to discuss, namely, whether in the interests of cable communications it would not be desirable that the island of Yap be internationalized and administered by an international commission in control of cable lines, and that he merely raised the question, although not on the agenda, in order to give warning that the question was in his mind and that he would propose it for discussion at a later time. He suggested that it was not necessary to maintain that all the islands should have the same status but that the island of Yap should be held to constitute a special case. Baron Makino took the position that the status of the island of Yap should be decided before the question of cables, Mr. Balfour replying that while the status of the island was a matter of great importance he did not think that the question of cables could be deferred, as it must be settled in time for the treaty with Germany; Germany could be required to give up all title to the island, and its status thereafter could be discussed among the Allies.

At a meeting on May first, held in Mr. Pichon's room, President Wilson stated that as the cable lines across the Pacific passed through the island of Yap, which thus became a general distributing center for the lines of communication for the north Pacific, Yap should not pass into the hands of one power. In the meeting of May sixth, in the discussion regarding the allotment of mandates in the Pacific, Mr. Lloyd George expressed his understanding that the Japanese should receive a mandate for *certain* islands north of the equator. According to the record, President Wilson consented in principle to this, with an explanatory statement that with respect to mandates the policy of the "open door" would have to be applied, and that there must be equal opportunities for the trade and commerce of other members of the League. The island of Yap, having been previously cited as a special case for particular future consideration was not intended to be included among the "certain islands" designated as available to Japan under mandate. This seems

---

[1] The minutes of this meeting and other meetings of the Council of Four mentioned below are printed at their respective dates in Vols. 57 and 58, and the meeting of May 7, 1919, in *PPC*, V, 506-509. The minutes of the meeting of the Council of Foreign Ministers, are printed in *PPC*, IV, 653-54.

obvious as Yap appears to have been the only island north of the equator in regard to the disposition of which there had existed any difference of opinion. There is no indication in the minutes of any further discussion with regard to this island. There is attached, as an appendix to the minutes of the meeting of May seventh, four fifteen p.m., a memorandum which obviously purported to be a codification of the agreement reached in the meeting of May sixth with reference to the north Pacific islands. Upon this we understand is based the assertion that Yap was assigned under mandate to Japan. Even this, however, does not expressly include all the islands in this particular category, although the qualifying word "certain" is omitted. According to the minutes of this meeting there was no discussion whatever on May seventh in respect to mandates. The minutes quoted the memorandum with the statement, merely, that "the following decisions were reached." The erroneous publication of such a decision of which this Government was not aware would not validate it. The President recollects no proposal offered in this meeting to change the decision of May sixth and is certain he agreed to no variance of the original proposition. He understood it was generally agreed that the island of Yap had been previously excluded and reserved for future determination in connection with the consideration of cable communications. In view of the President's reiterated objections to the inclusion of Yap in the mandate territories to be assigned to Japan, it is rather striking that the minutes of May seventh do not include any discussion whatever regarding Yap which would have been most natural had the President been prevailed upon to recede from his previous firm position. It is most logical that the withdrawal of the previously recorded objections would have been noted or at least that the decision would have been drafted in more specific language. It would seem clear that the President acted on the assumption that the island of Yap was not intended to be included in the decisions of May sixth and seventh.

It should also be noted that President Wilson, on August nineteen, 1919, before the Senate Committee on Foreign Relations, made the following statement when questioned concerning the status of the island of Yap:[2]

Quote—It is one of the bases and centers of cable and radio communication on the Pacific, and I made the point that the disposition, or rather the control, of that island should be reserved for the general conference which is to be held in regard to the ownership and operation of the cables. That subject is mentioned and dis-

---

[2] A transcript of Wilson's conversation with the members of the Foreign Relations Committee is printed at that date in Vol. 62.

posed of in this Treaty and that general cable conference is to be held.—Unquote.

This statement evidences the understanding of the President, and it is interesting that though wide publicity was given to the President's declaration at the time no comments were received by this Government from any nation indicating a contrary opinion. Furthermore, attention is called to the fact that the draft mandate covering the ex-German islands north of the equator, submitted to the meeting of the Heads of Delegations on December twenty-four, 1919,[3] contemplates that there may be a question as to what islands north of the equator should be allocated under mandate to Japan. Article three reads as follows: Quote—If any dispute should arise as to whether any particular island is or [is] not covered by the above mandate the matter shall be submitted to the Council of the League of Nations whose decision shall be final.—Unquote. The draft was not accepted, primarily on account of objections raised by the Japanese, which, however, did not relate to this particular provision. The point is cited merely as indicating an understanding that definite agreement had not yet been reached as to the final disposition of *all* the islands north of the equator.

It might also be observed that, assuming for the sake of argument the conditional allocation to Japan, the terms of the mandate have not been accepted by Japan or even as yet approved by the principal interested powers or the League of Nations. In such case it would appear that until the island is accepted under mandate upon terms approved by the powers concerned the status of temporary occupation must exist, which, in the circumstances, does not signify a vested interest in the island, and which admits of present determination of the conditions or terms of authority control and administration.

I am directed by the President to inform you that the Government of the United States cannot agree that the island of Yap was included in the decision of May seventh or in any other agreement of the Supreme Council. And in addition that as the island of Yap must form an indispensable part of the international communications it is essential that its free and unhampered use should not be limited or controlled by any one power. Even on the assumption that the island of Yap should be included among the islands held under mandate by Japan, it is not conceivable that other powers should not have free and unhampered access to, and use of, the island for the landing and operation of cables. This is a right which the United States would be disposed to grant upon any of its unfortified islands which may be essential for such purposes.

[3] Printed in *PPC*, IX, 637-65.

The Government of the United States expresses the hope that the above statements of fact will convince the British Government of the correctness of the position of the United States with respect to the mandate over the island of Yap; and also that the British Government will concur in the view of the United States that even if Yap should be assigned under mandate to Japan all other powers should have free and unhampered access to the island for the landing and operation of cables.

CC MS (N. H. Davis Papers, DLC).

From Newton Diehl Baker, with Enclosure

My dear Mr. President: Washington. December 3, 1920.

I venture to submit the enclosed as a suggested letter to Admiral Benson. Attached hereto is a letter for your information with regard to the Army bases to which the Admiral refers in his letter.[1] They were of course constructed out of funds appropriated for the War Department. This letter shows as to each the quantity of space, the present use by the Government, and the extent to which private commercial interests are already being served. There simply is no other place to put these vast accumulations of emergency and other supplies than in the storage warehouses built for them; but in any case, it would in my judgment be unwise to take away from the Army this permanent asset which will always be needed in part for the storage of its peace time equipment and supplies, and in the event of emergency will be needed to the fullest extent. One of our very great difficulties throughout the war was to find storage space, and it was the impossibility of finding such space that necessitated the construction of these great undertakings.

Respectfully yours,   Newton D. Baker

TLS (WP, DLC).
   [1] The Enclosure printed with WW to NDB, Nov. 27, 1920.

E N C L O S U R E

My dear Admiral   4 December, 1920

I have received and carefully considered your letter of November 22 in which you ask that Executive Order No. 3350, dated November 5, 1920, be canceled in order that nothing shall interfere with the fullest utilization of the Hoboken piers by the Shipping Board in accordance with the provisions of section 17 of the merchant marine act of 1920, and in which you further request that the Ho-

boken Manufacturers Railroad and part or all of certain Army supply bases be turned over to the Shipping Board for its use under
the second paragraph of section 17 of that act.

Executive Order No. 3350 was issued after very full consideration and primarily was dictated by my desire that the bodies of the
American dead now being returned from France and Belgium
should continue to be received in the most fitting and proper way.
This activity of the War Department ought not to be interrupted,
but rather pressed to an early completion, and I am informed by
the Secretary of War that under the present program for the return
of our dead that portion of the Hoboken piers reserved by the order
for that use can be turned over to the Shipping Board at an earlier
date than that prescribed in the order. Another of the Hoboken
piers I felt and feel should be retained by the War Department for
the use of the Panama Railroad Steamship Line, which now for the
first time has an adequate terminal in New York harbor and is using with maximum efficiency and intensity the pier under lease to
it. Originally authorized as a mere feeder to the construction enterprises of the Panama Canal, this line has now become a substantial
link between the United States and the Canal Zone, and serves an
increasingly useful purpose in developing and furthering American interests in the Caribbean. By its retention of the pier leased
to it, the double advantage is secured of a maximum use of the
facilities of the pier and a suitable and adequate terminus for this
important governmental agency.

Such other parts of the Hoboken piers as are reserved for the
present to the War Department by the order have to do with marine
repair shops and storage facilities needed so long as the War Department is obliged to maintain an overseas transport for the supply of our Army at Coblenz. Upon the cessation of that need the
portions of the piers serving it can of course be released to the
Shipping Board, and it may be possible to make an early transfer
of these repair shop facilities to the South Brooklyn base, thus
bringing about an earlier transfer of the space now occupied by
them on the piers to the Shipping Board.

With regard to the Hoboken Manufacturers Railroad, I shall be
very glad to sign an order transferring it to the Shipping Board if
you will be good enough to have one prepared and presented for
my signature.

With regard to the Army supply bases, I have had each installa-
tion mentioned by you investigated, and find that the storage space
in each case is being fully and usefully employed by the War Department at the present time, and that to transfer it to the Shipping
Board would necessitate the rental of equivalent storage space

elsewhere by the War Department at large cost both for rental and transfer of the property. It would be difficult to secure leased space giving the same shelter and protection to the property of the Government and the Congress has made no provision for the payment of such rental; so that the present transfer of the storage facilities so occupied by the War Department would be impossible.

The Army supply bases constructed during the war are great storehouses in which the ordinary and emergency supplies of the Army must be kept available for ordinary use and for immediate dispatch in case of emergency. They are essentially a part of any preparation for swift action, and they ought therefore never to be taken away from the War Department, or at least removed beyond its power of immediate resumption of control; nor should the piers and wharves which have been acquired by the country during the late war be separated from the control of the War Department in the event of need. In the interest of the general commerce of the country such parts of these facilities as are not needed in peace times should be made available for such commercial uses as will not prevent their immediate resumption by the Army if needed, and the policy of the Secretary of War to which you refer as effective at Norfolk, Philadelphia and Charleston I understand to be the general policy of his department with regard to all of these facilities. This will insure the commercial use of the facilities not needed by the Army, and by bringing into cooperation the local harbor controlling agencies and public authorities will advance the development of the ports in question in an harmonious and effective way. To the extent that there are pier and wharf spaces which are not needed by the Army at these terminals their devotion to commercial uses under revocable licenses or terminable leases is plainly in the public interest, and as the Shipping Board is primarily charged with the responsibility for the general maritime commercial interests of the country it would seem that the War Department should accommodate its policy, as far as practicable, to the recommendations and views of the Shipping Board in such matters. I have discussed the matter with the Secretary of War, and he tells me that he will be very glad to direct the Transportation Service to confer with and be guided by the Shipping Board in the formulation of rules and regulations and in the consideration of applicants for the use of such spaces. This I trust will bring about as satisfactory a use of these great properties as it is now possible to establish and follows, I believe, what should be the correct permanent policy of leaving the title to them in the War Department, which will always be able to protect its right of immediate resumption in the event of an emergency by any leases it authorizes.   Cordially and faithfully yours,[1]

CC MS (WP, DLC).
[1] Wilson had this letter typed up and sent as WW to W. S. Benson, Dec. 4, 1920, TLS (Letterpress Books, WP, DLC).

From Thomas William Lamont

Dear Mr. President: [New York] December 3rd, 1920.

I am more pleased than I can say with your cordial and generous letter of November 29th in regard to the situation with respect to the famine in China, and on Monday I shall communicate with you fully in response to your suggestion that I outline a method whereby a public committee could be appointed and function in this matter.

With great respect and profound regard, I am,
                    Sincerely yours,   Thomas W. Lamont

TLS (WP, DLC).

From John Franklin Jameson

My dear Mr. President: [Washington] December 3, 1920.

I hope I shall not seem to have neglected the letter you were so kind as to address to me on November 20. It reached me on the 26th, at my mother's[1] house in Massachusetts, just as I was starting out on some journeys that made reply impossible until I should have reached Washington, where also I wished to make an inquiry or two before answering.

On the day when you wrote to me, you were in my mind to an exceptional degree, for, in pursuance of your proclamation respecting the observance of November 21,[2] I had been invited by President Faunce[3] to come over from Boston to Providence and speak at Brown University on the Mayflower Compact and the Pilgrims, and I was much reminded, and reminded the audience in a way that I thought they liked, of those old days at the Brown University Lecture Association, when you came over from Middletown and stayed with me and gave that brilliant series of lectures, which many of my audience remembered with pleasure.[4]

I am very glad these young men of Harvard have established this Woodrow Wilson Club, and should be particularly gratified if I could make any valuable suggestions for their purposes.

1. It is possible that, beyond such collecting of material as any-body can do with money, in the open market, they might make a distinctive addition to the materials possessed by the Harvard College Library respecting the negotiations at Versailles, if there were any series of manifolded daily reports or summaries of the trans-actions of committees or other subdivisions of the Conference, that by your permission and at their expense could be copied for the Harvard College Library. If such materials are not yet open to pub-lic use, such a transcript might be deposited under restrictions op-erating up to a given date in the future.

2. While I have been led to suppose that files of French news-papers of the period of the Conference would not be a very valuable source for the knowledge of its history, I have been told that what was in the Paris edition of the *London Daily Mail* was exception-ally good. Perhaps, if this seems to you to have been the case, the club could procure for the Harvard College Library a file of that newspaper during the period.

3. At the expense of the Carnegie Institution, the National Board for Historical Service (a group of the best historical men) main-tained for two years, ending in July, 1919, a service consisting in securing of files of eighteen or twenty of the most important Ger-man newspapers, sent from month to month, and in drawing off from them and translating such portions as supplied valuable in-telligence toward the conduct of the war, which were constantly supplied here in Washington to the government departments to which one or another portion might be helpful. One complete set of all the translations has since been turned over to the Library of Congress, and constitutes the cream of the historical material con-tained in the German newspapers during those two years. The Li-brary of Congress would furnish at a low rate photostat reproduc-tions of all those parts relating to the negotiations at Versailles, if the club desired it. This material would, I should imagine, form a valuable means of getting the German view of the negotiations as they progressed.

4. The club might reprint in a small pamphlet the Covenant of the League of Nations and place copies of it in the hands of all graduate students, law school students, and senior undergraduates at Harvard. But people in Cambridge would know, though I do not, whether this would or would not be a superfluous thing. It perhaps does not fall within the scope of operations proposed by the club, since Mr. Stuart's letter speaks primarily of fortifying the library.

5. They might have an annual dinner with a good speaker, who might bring home to the minds of the students the principles which your conduct at Versailles represents.

6. But after all, the best suggestions that I can make are, I feel sure, of quite secondary value to those which they could obtain in Cambridge by direct conference with Professor Haskins, who was at Versailles and knows far more than I do of what was done there and of the materials for its history, and who, as a warm supporter of your administration would be glad to help the admirable work which the club has in mind.—I return Mr. Stuart's letter.

Though this letter is already too long, I do not wish to close it without a personal word. When you were first taken ill, I wished that such a message could go from me to you, but I felt sure that you ought not to be burdened by the task of even reading the multitude of such letters that would come, and that those about you would rightly see to it that you were not thus burdened. But let me now say what has been in my heart and mind. I have followed your administration, and especially your course in international affairs, with great admiration, with much pride in our early friendship and in the occasional evidences of friendly regards still continuing on your part, and with the earnest hope and belief that the high ideals which you have entertained respecting the position of America in the world will ultimately be realized in what is essential. I have followed your illness with the profoundest sympathy, have never passed in sight of the White House without deep feeling, and have rejoiced at all the evidences that have come to me of improvement in your health. I hope that the release from public cares, three months from now, may greatly speed this process of recuperation, and that you may be able to do still other great work for the country, and much of it. I wish you to know of my warm and abiding friendship and deep solicitude. Of my wish to be helpful in any matter, whenever I can, I am glad to see that you are already fully aware.

Believe me to be, with old affection and with the highest regard,
Very sincerely yours, [J. F. Jameson]

CCL (J. F. Jameson Papers, DLC).
¹ Mariette Thompson Jameson.
² That is, the Thanksgiving Proclamation, printed as an Enclosure with BC to WW, Nov. 11, 1920 (second letter of that date).
³ William Herbert Perry Faunce, D.D.
⁴ About this series of lectures, see WW to JRW, Jan. 13, 1889, ns. 1 and 2; and the news reports printed at Jan. 19, 1889, and Nov. 12, 1889, all in Vol. 6.

Charles Doolittle Walcott¹ to Edith Bolling Galt Wilson

Dear Mrs. Wilson: Washington, U. S. A. December 3, 1920.

The portraits of the great men of the war and Peace Conference are now nearly all painted, and the opening exhibition of them will be made at the Metropolitan Museum, New York, January 15 to February 15, 1921. I saw fourteen of these portraits in New York in October, and they are not only wonderful artistically but of the greatest historical interest. The entire collection will in due time be deposited here in the National Gallery of Art and form the nucleus of the National Portrait Gallery.

We must have the painting of President Wilson, as it would be most unfortunate not to have the portrait of the President of the United States in the collection, particularly as he has approved of the plan since its earliest inception. Just now, as far as I can learn, there is only one seeming obstacle, which is the approval by the President or yourself of the photographs of him from which Mr. Tarbell[2] may proceed to paint the portrait. If he could receive them now, and possibly later see the President long enough to get the personal impression necessary to complete a first sketch, the portrait could be made in time, if approved by the President, to be included in the first exhibition.

The President has such a strong, intellectual face and head that Mr. Tarbell cannot fail to make a great portrait. I would write to the President, but do not wish to trouble him in a matter about which I feel you will be interested to be of assistance to him.

I wish to thank you for giving, through Mrs. Julian James,[3] the beautiful dress for the historical collection of costumes in the National Museum.

The photographs, if approved, might be sent directly to Mr. Tarbell at the Corcoran Gallery of Art.

Sincerely yours,   Charles D. Walcott

TLS (WP, DLC).
  [1] Secretary of the Smithsonian Institution.
  [2] Edmund Charles Tarbell, principal of the Corcoran School of Art.
  [3] Cassie Mason Myers James of Washington.

From Charles Zeller Klauder

My dear Mr. President: Philadlephia December 3rd, 1920.

I have been pleased to receive your telegram today and answered by wire as follows:

"Will be glad to come to Washington tomorrow reaching Union Station at 3.30."

I chose a train which would give me two hours of daylight in Washington tomorrow should it be desired.

Sincerely yours,   Chas Z Klauder

TLS (WP, DLC).

To Arthur Bernard Krock

My dear Krock: [The White House] 4 December, 1920
   Thank you for your letter of December first. It was very welcome
and very cheering, and you may be sure that I appreciate and value
your friendship very deeply.
   With the best wishes,
                    Cordially and sincerely yours,   [Woodrow Wilson]

CCL (WP, DLC).

To Charles Doolittle Walcott

My dear Doctor Walcott: [The White House] 4 December, 1920
   Mrs. Wilson has shown me your letter of December third to her.
I do not feel physically equal to giving Mr. Tarbell a sitting, but we
will of course supply him with a photograph.
                    Sincerely yours,   [Woodrow Wilson]

CCL (WP, DLC).

From Norman Hezekiah Davis

My dear Mr. President: Washington December 4, 1920.
   With the object of reaching a definite and reasonable settlement
of German reparations against French obstructions, the British,
Italians and Belgians have finally gotten the French to consent to
a slow round-about process of bringing matters to a head. The plan
is admittedly complicated but it seemed to be the only one which
all parties could accept. The provisions are as follows:
   One. A conference at Brussels is proposed for the near future. It
is understood that, with the exception of the French, each Government will designate its representative on the Reparation Commission to act as expert at the proposed conference at Brussels. The
conference will consider only technical questions, and Germany
will be represented. The findings of the experts at Brussels will be
reported to the respective governments and the proces verbal of
their meetings will be communicated to the Reparation Commission.
   Two. A conference of Allied Ministers will meet at Geneva subsequent to the plebiscite in Upper Silesia, but at the latest during
the first fortnight of February, to discuss the question of reparations in its entirety. Representatives of Germany will attend this
conference in a consultative capacity. The Geneva conference will

report to the respective governments and each of these governments will inform its delegates on the Reparation Commission of the conclusions which it has reached on the report of its representatives at the Geneva conference.

Three. The Reparation Commission will then proceed, in accordance with the provisions of the Treaty of Versailles, to declare the total and the means of payment of the sums due by Germany, and will report to the Powers on Germany's capacity to pay.

Four. The Supreme Council will then consider what further steps should be taken, including guarantees and penalties.

The economic rehabilitation of Europe is an impossibility until the question of reparations is constructively settled. This is of peculiar importance to this country and I believe Mr. Boyden,[1] the unofficial American delegate on the Reparation Commission, should be authorized to attend the proposed conference at Brussels, provided he is invited by the other powers. The other powers seem to recognize that American interests are involved, and that the conference is primarily economic rather than political in character. Mr. Boyden states that his colleagues expect him to be present, and thinks that he will lose contact if he does not attend.

It is hoped that the majority of the representatives at the Brussels conference will recommend such reasonable and constructive action that the French will be forced to abandon their obstructionist tactics and permit the reparation problem to be definitively solved. I think representation at meetings dealing with this problem is entirely justifiable, but shall be pleased to have your directions.   Faithfully yours,   Norman H. Davis

TLS (WP, DLC).
[1] That is, Roland William Boyden.

From Norman Hezekiah Davis, with Enclosure

My dear Mr. President: Washington December 4, 1920.

Due to the rush caused by his departure yesterday, I was unable to ascertain whether or not Secretary Colby consulted with you regarding the despatch received from the President of the Council of the League of Nations inviting this Government to name representatives to sit in a consultative capacity with the Permanent Military, Naval and Air Commission. I am, therefore, enclosing the despatch received and would be pleased to have your directions.

We have not been under the impression that there is a real desire on the part of the Allies to give serious consideration to disarmament. I am not convinced as yet by this despatch that there has been a real change of sentiment, but fear that the move is taken for political purposes.

I am not clear as to your powers under the circumstances. Every effort is being made to have the United States act as a de facto member of the League, and I doubt the expediency of accepting the invitation. On the other hand, if you refuse, efforts will be made to create a wrong impression of our attitude. I suggest, for your consideration, that we reply that while the Government of the United States is very muchly interested in the question to be considered, it is not deemed advisable to accept the invitation without the approval of Congress, to whom the matter will be referred.

Faithfully yours,   Norman H. Davis

TLS (WP, DLC).

ENCLOSURE

Geneva. Recd. Dec. 1, 1920.

The Council of the League of Nations, acting on a unanimous recommendation of the permanent military, naval and air commission of the League, passed at its meeting in Geneva on November 25th, invites the government of the United States to name representatives to sit on that commission in a consultative capacity during the study by the commission of the question of the reduction of armaments, a study which the council has requested the commission to undertake forthwith.

The permanent advisory commission was constituted by the council of the league at its meeting in Rome last May and held its first session at San Sebastian in August. The commission is at present composed of military, naval and aerial officers of states represented on the council of the League. Its decisions are purely advisory and not in any sense binding, but they represent the common technical judgment of the experts of many countries.

It would of course be perfectly understood that the presence of the representatives of the United States would in no way commit the American Government to whatever opinions may be finally put forward in the report of the commission. Nor indeed can that report itself be more than a basis for the consideration by the members of the league of the measures of reductions in armaments which united action may enable them to achieve. Nevertheless just as in the case of the financial conference at Brussels' the presence of an American representative, whose function was only that of giving and receiving information, was an important factor in the success of the work of the conference so it cannot be doubted that the general consideration of the subject of the reduction of armaments will be greatly facilitated if the government of the United States can see its way to be represented in a similar manner at the meetings of the permanent advisory commission.

The problem is one to which public opinion in all countries attaches the highest importance.

It is unnecessary to point out that the reduction of armaments is essential for the well being of the world and that unless some measures of relief can be found by international cooperation for the excessive taxation due to armaments the general economic situation must become increasingly worse.

The council in extending this invitation cannot but hope that the government of the United States, particularly in view of the attitude of America towards the question of the competition in armaments, will not refuse to associate itself with the Governments of the members of the league in beginning the preliminary work necessary for ultimate success and to lend to the present effort an assistance which can in no way encroach upon its own perfect liberty of action.   Signed Hymans,   President of the Council.

T telegram (WP, DLC).
   [1] About which, see DFH to WW, Sept. 7, 1920, n. 1.

From Jesse Holman Jones[1]

My dear Mr. President: Houston, Texas Dec. 4, 1920.

I have wanted for a long time to write you a personal letter, but particularly since the November election.

I do not believe that the overwhelming Republican vote meant in any sense a repudiation of the League of Nations. I am firmly of the opinion that the people in this country want the League of Nations, but the thing dearest to the great majority of people is their pocketbook, and they thought the Republicans would, in some way, manage to reduce taxes, and possibly bring about a return of the prosperity to which all had become accustomed, and liked. No man has ever held the supreme position in the world that you have held during the last several years, and hold at this time. The great masses in our country believe in you as they believe in no other man, and it is this that the politicians and money power attempted to destroy. They were not in fact successful, because the people still know that you stand for the best interest of mankind throughout the world, and unselfishly. The arts of propaganda and camouflage, so well developed during the war, were turned to account by the Republican organization in this campaign. Many lifelong Democrats voted the Republican ticket, and in every case the reason is easily traceable to the material. It is regrettable, but a fact. The public is fickle, and often fooled by unscrupulous politicians. I recall a few years ago a candidate for governor of Texas, although a flagrant Anti-Prohibitionist, went into the prohibition districts of North Texas and carried them overwhelmingly against a Pro candidate, simply by promising the farmers a high price for their cotton; and so it goes, that men in politics, and ofttimes good men, stoop to very low methods. What I hope most is that you are not permitting this apparent change of sentiment to depress you. I feel certain that you are sage enough to understand the reasons, and that it was inevitable when conditions and men are taken into account. I believe that if the people were permitted to vote for you as against any other man in this country, or in the world, as their choice for president, or as the principal guiding hand of the world, eliminating, of course, party lines in our own country, that you would be the overwhelming choice in such a contest. Your life has been a fight for democracy, and my greatest desire and ambition has been to be of some slight service to you, and I shall be proud of the privilege to respond to any suggestion or call from you in the years to come. You must necessarily be an onlooker after March 4th, but you will be thinking and observing as the representative of silent millions.

With all sincerity and good wishes,

Your friend,   Jesse H Jones

TLS (WP, DLC).
    [1] Banker and capitalist of Houston; soon to become a member of the intimate circle of Wilson's friends.

From William Bauchop Wilson

My dear Mr. President: Washington December 4, 1920.

On June 3, 1920, I wrote you[1] inclosing a letter from M. Albert Thomas, Director of the International Labor Office, inviting the United States to send a representative of employers and a representative of workers to participate in an International Commission to study the question of regulating emigration and immigration and that of protecting the interests of wage earners not residing in their own country. As I interpreted the communication to mean that each country should have a representative of the Government, a representative of employers, and a representative of employees on the Commission, I recommended that Section 29 of the Immigration Act of February 5, 1917, be accepted as specific authority for you to send such representation and advised that it be done.

Upon receipt of your approval, I communicated with M. Thomas and learned that I had misinterpreted the action of the Governing Body and that the Governing Body had allotted to each of the eighteen countries one representative on the Commission, six of these countries to appoint representatives of the Government, six of them to appoint representatives of employers, and six of them to appoint representatives of workers. The United States was one of the countries listed to select workers' representatives. I called this matter to your attention on July 31, 1920,[2] and advised that the Director of the International Labor Office be informed that this Government could not participate in the meetings of the International Commission to study the question of regulating emigration and immigration and that of protecting the interests of wage earners not residing in their own country on the terms specified by the Governing Body and could only take part in the work of the Commission if the action of the Governing Body was revised so as to permit the United States to send three representatives in accordance with our original understanding, or, if that was not possible, to send a representative of the Government without the necessity of agreement with either employers or employees. You approved that recommendation, and M. Thomas was notified accordingly.

I am in receipt of further communication from the International Labor Office under date of October 19, 1920, confirming a telegram dispatched on October 16th, as follows:

"Governing Body of International Labor Office offers seat to representative of United States Government on Emigration Commission.   (Signed) Albert Thomas."

This action on the part of the Govening Body places the United States in a position where it can select a representive on the Emigration Commission who will represent the policies of the Administration as the agent of all of the people rather than the ideas of any one or two groups.

I now renew my recommendation that Section 29 of the Immigration Law be utilized by you as specific authority to appoint a representative of the United States Government on the International Commission to study the question of regulating emigration and immigration and that of protecting the interests of wage earners not residing in their own country.

The attitude of emigrant countries is so widely divergent from that of immigrant countries that the direct expression of our views in the constructive period of any program on the subject matter would be extremely valuable, particularly in view of the fact that we would not be morally obligated to accept the result if it is not satisfactory to us. The expense of sending such a Commissioner, together with such advisory and clerical assistance as he might need, can be borne from the general immigration fund. I am attaching hereto a copy of Section 29 of the Immigration Act.[3]

Since the possibility of appointing a representative of this Government upon the Emigration Commission has been under consideration, I have been looking into the question of finding a man with an attitude of mind and sufficient training and experience properly to represent the United States. As a result of my survey, I have in mind Mr. Rowland B(lenerhassett). Mahany, at present Solicitor and Acting Secretary of the Department of Labor on immigration matters.

Mr. Mahany is a Harvard man, is a lawyer by profession, was a member of the Committee on Immigration of the Fifty-fourth and Fifty-fifth Congresses, was Secretary of the American Legation at Chile 1890 to 1892, and Minister to Ecuador 1892-1893, during which time he negotiated the Santos Treaty. For more than six years he was one of the most effective labor conciliators of this Department, and represented it on the Foreign Trade Relations Committee of the Department of State and on the Board of Directors of the United States Housing Corporation. His views relative to the question of immigration are identical with those expressed by you in your messages to Congress. His broad experience, together with a naturally brilliant mind, would make him an ideal Commissioner, and I therefore recommend his appointment in the event that you decide that we should be represented on the Commission.

Faithfully yours,   W B Wilson

TLS (WP, DLC).
 [1] His letter is printed at that date in Vol. 65.
 [2] Printed at that date in *ibid*.
 [3] T MS (WP, DLC).

From Albert George Schmedeman[1]

Christiania. December 4, 1920.

Urgent. 74. For the President.

Strictly Confidential. I have the honor and the great pleasure to inform you that on December tenth the Nobel Committee of the Norwegian Storthing will announce in the Storthing the award of the Nobel Peace prizes for last year and this year to you personally and to Leon Bourgeois respectively. The Committee requests that you authorize me to receive the award on your behalf and to reply to the speech made in announcing it; it considers that the most acceptable speech I could make would at least include the reading of a message of appreciation from you. Permit me and the staff of this Legation to be the first to congratulate you on this honor which everybody must admit is but your due for your efforts towards founding the League of Nations.

Please reply by telegraph immediately.[2]   Schmedeman.

T telegram (PPAmP).
    [1] United States Minister to Norway.
    [2] Wilson's letter of acceptance is printed at Dec. 8, 1920.

From Alexander Meiklejohn[1]

Dear President Wilson,   Firenze, Dec. 5, 1920

I cannot refrain from sending you the last sentence of a letter which came a few days ago from my old teacher of philosophy at Cornell, Professor J. E. Creighton.[2] He is perhaps the most influential philosophical thinker in America just now. He writes, "I am still a believer in President Wilson's policies, and feel sure that we shall sometime come to recognize not only his high purposes, but his practical wisdom."

I have often wanted to write you but at so great a distance, measured in terms of acquaintance with the situation, have hardly known what to say. You will however, I am sure, appreciate the words of this teacher of philosophy.

We are away for a year trying to recover from and forget the strenuous activities of the past few years. This is a good place for doing it.

I am daring to hope that the newspaper statements of your attitude are true when they tell us of your confidence in future happening and future judgments on your work. It was a great task magnificently done.

Mrs. Meiklejohn[3] joins me in sending kindest regards and in expressing the hope that your health steadily improves. There is still a great deal for you to do and to enjoy and we hope that you will feel fit for it.   Sincerely yours,   Alexander Meiklejohn

ALS (WP, DLC).
    [1] President of Amherst College since 1912.
    [2] James Edwin Creighton, Professor of Logic and Metaphysics and Dean of the Graduate School of Cornell University.
    [3] Nannine A. La Villa Meiklejohn.

A Memorandum by Cary Travers Grayson

Monday, December 6, 1920.

On Monday afternoon, December 6th, Senator Lodge, Senator Underwood, the Democratic Senate leader, Representative Mondell, the Republican House leader, Chairman Fordney of the House Ways and Means Committee, and former Speaker Champ Clark called at the White House to notify the President formally that Congress was in session. They were escorted into the Blue Room. The President shortly thereafter walked into the room with the use of his cane, and said: "Gentlemen, I hope you will excuse me from going through the formality of shaking hands with you individually, but, as you see, I cannot yet dispense with my third leg." Thereupon Senator Lodge went through the usual formality of notifying the President that Congress had met; and the President replied that he would communicate a message to the Congress on the following day.

The President was standing quite close to Senator Underwood and whispered to the Senator: "I used the excuse of this 'third leg,' as I did not want to shake hands with Lodge." And Underwood and the President both chuckled.

The President told me afterwards: "Can you imagine what kind of a hide Lodge has got, coming up here in these circumstances and wanting to appear familiar and talk with me. His hide has a different anatomical arrangement than any I have ever heard of."

T MS (received from James Gordon Grayson and Cary T. Grayson, Jr.).

To Edward William Bok

My dear Mr. Bok: The White House 6 December, 1920

The very tastefully-framed copy of Kipling's "If" in a facsimile of his handwriting has come, and I must thank you for what I am sure will always be one of my most treasured souvenirs, the more treasured because it will serve as a memento of your generous friendship which I value most highly.

With the warmest regards,

Gratefully yours,   Woodrow Wilson

TLS (WP, DLC).

Two Letters From Norman Hezekiah Davis

My dear Mr. President: Washington December 6, 1920.

I share your embarrassment about the offer of Spain and Brazil to join us in the Armenian mediation.[1] It is not clear to me from the despatch of Hymans whether Spain and Brazil have specifically offered to cooperate with the United States or whether their offer was a general reply to the invitation sent to all the powers. I agree, however, that it is best to wait for them to communicate with us, especially as we must wait until the Council furnishes the information requested by you as to the most effective method of getting into touch with the belligerents. If Spain and Brazil do offer to cooperate we should, I think, inform them that while we welcome their cooperation we do not see how it can be made effective unless the delays incident to communications with those governments can be avoided by their Ambassadors here having full power to act.

Apparently a more serious complication, however, has arisen. It would appear from the recent despatches that the Bolshevists have gotten control of Armenia and are also directing the Kemalists. If this is verified it will probably be necessary to take a much more comprehensive survey of the situation before taking any action. Would it not be well for you to determine whom you will designate as your representative in order that he might take part in the preliminary discussions and considerations of this subject?

Faithfully and cordially yours,   Norman H. Davis

TLS (WP, DLC).
[1] Davis was replying to WW to NHD, Dec. 3, 1920.

My dear Mr. President: Washington December 6, 1920.

You will recall that after the overthrow in July last, of the Government of President Gutierrez Guerra of Bolivia, this Government, pursuant to your instructions, determined in accordance with the Governments of Argentina and Brazil, to postpone recognition of the new Government until it was ascertained whether that Government had the formal support of the people of Bolivia.[1] It was thought that the first opportunity of ascertaining whether the revolutionary Government counted upon popular support would be provided by the general elections which it was announced would be held for the purpose of electing a National Congress. These elections were held toward the end of November and resulted in an overwhelming victory for the revolutionary Government. The American Minister in La Paz[2] reports that the elections were orderly and tranquil throughout the Republic except in one department. The Congress recently elected will meet in convention on December 20, to revise the Constitution and to elect a provisional President. It is probable that further elections will be held next May for the election of a President in accordance with the present Constitution.

Since there appears to be now no question that the Government is supported by a great majority of the Bolivian people, I beg to submit for your consideration the advisability of according recognition to the Bolivian Government, as soon as a provisional President is elected, as the *de facto* Government of Bolivia, postponing entering into formal relations with the Government until it is permanently established. If you see no objection to this procedure, the Department will notify the Governments of Brazil and Argentina that this Government is prepared to enter into informal relations with the Government of Bolivia immediately after the election of the provisional President.[3]

Faithfully yours,   Norman H. Davis

All right.   W.W.

TLS (SDR, RG 59, 824.00/154b, DNA).
  [1] See BC to WW, Sept. 23, 1920 (first letter of that date).
  [2] S. Abbot Maginnis.
  [3] Wilson's underlining.

From Robert Underwood Johnson

Dear Mr. President: Rome December 6, 1920.

In my volume of verse, "Complete Poems,"[1] there is a piece with the refrain

"Listen to yo' gyarden angel
And yo' nabber kin go wrong."

Apropos of which I hope you will tell Mrs. Wilson that your friends feel sure that she will continue to be your gyarden angel, through these last months of your present public service, when there must be many conflicts between what you owe your country and what you owe yourself. You have earned by the great sacrifices you have already made for the highest idealism the right to preserve for future public use your best abilities, and this can only be done by saving yourself both worry and overwork. As one who reads with solicitude every word to be found concerning your health, I send you my best wishes and my enduring and grateful regard.

When you honored me by designating me Ambassador to Italy— a man without experience in "the career" and of no political weight or prominence—I knew that you did it because of my apparent acceptability to Italians, and that my only hope of justifying the selection lay in the confirmation and extension of whatever personal prestige I might have—through which alone I might be of use to our country. I feel sure therefore, that I may say to you without egotism that I have unmistakable evidences that I am *persona grata* here. This comes form various sources. For the tribute to Italian valor implied in my trip to the battlefront, I have been thanked in person by the King, the Ministers for Foreign Affairs & for War and by Generals Caviglia & Grazioli[2] (who commanded the Arditi)[3] & by many others. My efforts to promote the facilities for getting coal for Italy—which would have had greater result had there been no coal strike at home—have been deeply appreciated by the Government. The newspapers have given great prominance to (1) the Department's timely publication through our press of my denial that Italy is a dangerous place for tourists, and (2) to my comments on Italian achievements in the war and pluck in reconstruction—made after my trip to the North. Today the Y.M.C.A director Mr. Wikel[4] told me that an Italian newspaper man had told him that the press-gallery at the Deputies had a favorable opinion of me; and, lastly, I had a reception at the Academy of the Lincei the other day that warmed the cockles of my heart—being presented to the Academy by the president as a well-known firm and ardent friend of Italy, who, it was hoped, would long occupy his present post, &c., &c. Nor are other more general evidences wanting that your choice has not failed to establish the good relation here essential to public usefulness. And now enough of his majesty Myself.

I find I have to brace myself against a certain haunting pessimism that reaches Rome from all the other quarters of Europe— the foundation of it being the conviction of which there are only too many evidences, that nearly every Government is closely and continuously on the lookout for No. 1—even when recommending to us an altruistic policy in Armenia. I doubt if there is another country in the world that would have withdrawn from Cuba as we did twice, and our motives in doing so, though incomprehensible to many peoples, are at least recognized by the intelligent Italians whom I am cultivating. Of course we are not called upon to renounce the legitimate trade interests of America, and if in any future conflict of nations we are to have friends and allies (Heaven forbid that we should ever need them!) they will be of those nations with whom we have had trade relations of the sort that reveal our fundamental sense of honest and generous dealing. I am very proud of the spirit in which our countrymen approach Italians in seeking to establish trade here, and while, of course taking no responsibilities in commercial matters I am doing all I can to give reputable Americans opportunities to present their cases.

But beyond all material things I do not hesitate to lay emphasis on our desire for the good of all other nations. We must continue to give examples of generous and unselfish conduct, even in the face of rumors of combinations that may be made against us. In spite of the pessimists, we can overcome evil by good. The reaction against reaction is bound to come and I hope and believe our country will soon lead a new movement. I remember what Channing[5] said of the phrase "mere morality"—that it was like saying,"Poor God! with nobody to help him." The Great Past calls to us by all its sacred and blessed achievements to be "forward-looking men." Nothing can blot out the great work you have done for the peace of the world: it will pass into History as a precious heritage of your country.

Mrs. Johnson[6] and I send to Mrs. Wilson and you our sincerest good wishes for the New Year and I am, dear Mr. President, respectfully and faithfully yours,   R. U. Johnson

ALS (WP, DLC).
[1] *Collected Poems, 1881-1919* (New Haven, Conn., 1920).
[2] Count Carlo Sforza, Ivanoe Bonomi, Enrico Caviglia, and Francesco Saverio Grazioli.
[3] An elite corps of the Italian army, formed in January 1917 and used as first assault troops and in particularly risky operations.
[4] Unidentified.
[5] William Ellery Channing.
[6] Katharine McMahon Johnson. She died on December 31, 1920.

From William Goodell Frost[1] and Eleanor Marsh Frost

My dear Mr. President: Berea, Kentucky December 6, 1920.

Mrs. Frost and I have wished you to know that our hearts were with you in the great anxieties and trials of the past weeks.

We gave our son to die[2] for the high purposes which you announced in our world war, and we deserted our traditional allegiance to the Republican party in order to do our bit towards supporting your ideals for a League of Nations. We feel with you that it is better to suffer defeat for a cause that will sometime win than to triumph in a cause which must ultimately be defeated.

With admiration and faithful regard,
          Sincerely yours,   Wm G. and Eleanor M. Frost.

TLS (WP, DLC).
[1] Wilson's old friend, the President of Berea College since 1892.
[2] Cleveland Cady Frost (1896-1918), a graduate of Yale in the Class of 1917; 1st lieutenant in the Yale Battery of Field Artillery; killed when *U.S.S. Ticonderoga* was sunk by a German submarine on September 30, 1918.

From the Diary of Josephus Daniels

December Tuesday 7 1920

Solicitor of State Department[1] brought over agreement between the lawyer in Miami cable case by which suit would be withdrawn to enjoin me, the WU Tel Co would agree not to connect with cable to Barbadoes unless Congress, the executive or the courts should grant permission. In it I promised to secure revocation of order from the President. I said I could not sign but would put it up to the President. At cabinet meeting the President declined to compromise, saying the paper by implication surrendered the right of the executive to deny permission to land cable in this country. Baker, Burleson & Davis thought WW was wrong but he would not compromise.

Went to Capitol to hear President's Message. It was well read, but it was a great contrast to the days when he delivered it in person. It was unlike any other

WW said he could not understand how Lodge could have the effrontory to come to the White House, said he stood all the while and did not shake hands with any because he would not shake hands with Lodge.

[1] That is, Fred Kenelm Nielsen.

An Annual Message on the State of the Union

The White House, 7 *December, 1920.*

Gentlemen of the Congress: When I addressed myself to performing the duty laid upon the President by the Constitution to present to you an annual report on the state of the Union, I found my thought dominated by an immortal sentence of Abraham Lincoln's,

"Let us have faith that right makes might, and in that faith let us dare to do our duty as we understand it,"—

a sentence immortal because it embodies in a form of utter simplicity and purity the essential faith of the nation, the faith in which it was conceived and the faith in which it has grown to glory and power. With that faith and the birth of a nation founded upon it came the hope into the world that a new order would prevail throughout the affairs of mankind, an order in which reason and right would take precedence of covetousness and force, and I believe that I express the wish and purpose of every thoughtful American when I say that this sentence marks for us in the plainest manner the part we should play alike in the arrangement of our domestic affairs and in our exercise of influence upon the affairs of the world. By this faith, and by this faith alone, can the world be lifted out of its present confusion and despair. It was this faith which prevailed over the wicked force of Germany. You will remember that the beginning of the end of the war came when the German people found themselves face to face with the conscience of the world and realized that right was everywhere arrayed against the wrong that their government was attempting to perpetrate. I think, therefore, that it is true to say that this was the faith which won the war. Certainly this is the faith with which our gallant men went into the field and out upon the seas to make sure of victory.

This is the mission upon which democracy came into the world. Democracy is an assertion of the right of the individual to live and to be treated justly as against any attempt on the part of any combination of individuals to make laws which will overburden him or which will destroy his equality among his fellows in the matter of right or privilege, and I think we all realize that the day has come when democracy is being put upon its final test. The old world is just now suffering from a wanton rejection of the principle of democracy and a substitution of the principle of autocracy as asserted in the name but without the authority and sanction of the multitude. This is the time of all others when democracy should prove its purity and its spiritual power to prevail. It is surely the manifest destiny of the United States to lead in the attempt to make this spirit prevail.

There are two ways in which the United States can assist to accomplish this great object: First, by offering the example within her own borders of the will and power of democracy to make and enforce laws which are unquestionably just and which are equal in their administration,—laws which secure its full right to labor and yet at the same time safeguard the integrity of property, and particularly of that property which is devoted to the development of industry and the increase of the necessary wealth of the world. Second, by standing for right and justice as towards individual nations. The law of democracy is for the protection of the weak, and the influence of every democracy in the world should be for the protection of the weak nation, the nation which is struggling towards its right and towards its proper recognition and privilege in the family of nations. The United States cannot refuse this rôle of champion without putting the stigma of rejection upon the great and devoted men who brought its government into existence and established it in the face of almost universal opposition and intrigue, even in the face of wanton force, as, for example, against the Orders in Council of Great Britain and the arbitrary Napoleonic

Decrees which involved us in what we know as the War of 1812. I urge you to consider that the display of an immediate disposition on the part of the Congress to remedy any injustices or evils that may have shown themselves in our own national life will afford the most effectual offset to the forces of chaos and tyranny which are playing so disastrous a part in the fortunes of the free peoples of more than one part of the world. The United States is of necessity the sample democracy of the world, and the triumph of democracy depends upon its success.

Recovery from the disturbing and sometimes disastrous effects of the late war has been exceedingly slow on the other side of the water and has given promise, I venture to say, of early completion only in our own fortunate country; but even with us the recovery halts and is impeded at times and there are immediately serviceable acts of legislation which it seems to me we ought to attempt, to assist that recovery and prove the indestructible recuperative force of a great government of the people. One of these is to prove that a great democracy can keep house as successfully and in as businesslike a fashion as any other government. It seems to me that the first step towards proving this is to supply ourselves with a systematic method of handling our estimates and expenditures and bringing them to the point where they will not be an unnecessary strain upon our income or necessitate unreasonable taxation, in other words, a workable budget system, and I respectfully suggest that two elements are essential to such a system; namely, not only that the proposal of appropriations should be in the hands of a single body, such as a single appropriations committee in each house of the Congress, but also that this body should be brought into such cooperation with the departments of the Government and with the Treasury of the United States as would enable it to act upon a complete conspectus of the needs of the Government and the resources from which it must draw its income. I reluctantly vetoed the Budget Bill passed by the last session of the Congress because of a Constitutional objection.[1] The House of Representatives subsequently modified the Bill in order to meet this objection. In the revised form I believe that the Bill, coupled with action already taken by the Congress to revise its rules and procedure, furnishes the foundations for an effective national budget system. I earnestly hope, therefore, that one of the first steps taken by the present session of the Congress will be to pass the Budget Bill.

The nation's finances have shown marked improvement during

---

[1] Wilson's veto message is printed at June 4, 1920, Vol. 65.

the past year. The total ordinary receipts of $6,694,000,000 for the fiscal year 1920 exceeded those for 1919 by $1,542,000,000, while the total net ordinary expenditures decreased from $18,514,000,000 to $6,403,000,000. The gross public debt, which reached its highest point on 31 August, 1919, when it was $26,596,000,000, had dropped on 30 November, 1920, to $24,175,000,000. There has also been a marked decrease in holdings of government war securities by the banking institutions of the country, as well as in the amount of bills held by the Federal Reserve Banks secured by government war obligations. This fortunate result has relieved the banks and left them freer to finance the needs of agriculture, industry and commerce. It has been due in large part to the reduction of the public debt, especially of the floating debt, but more particularly to the improved distribution of government securities among permanent investors. The cessation of the Government's borrowings except through short-term certificates of indebtedness has been a matter of great consequence to the people of the country at large, as well as to the holders of Liberty bonds and Victory notes, and has had an important bearing on the matter of effective credit control. The year has been characterized by the progressive withdrawal of the Treasury from the domestic credit market and from a position of dominant influence in that market. The future course will necessarily depend upon the extent to which economies are practiced and upon the burdens placed upon the Treasury, as well as upon industrial developments and the maintenance of tax receipts at a sufficiently high level.

The fundamental fact which at present dominates the Government's financial situation is that seven and a half billions of its war indebtedness mature within the next two and a half years. Of this amount, two and a half billions are floating debt and five billions Victory notes and War Savings certificates. The fiscal programme of the Government must be determined with reference to these maturities. Sound policy demands that government expeditures be reduced to the lowest amount which will permit the various services to operate efficiently and that government receipts from taxes and salvage be maintained sufficiently high to provide for current requirements, including interest and sinking fund charges on the public debt, and at the same time retire the floating debt and part of the Victory Loan before maturity. With rigid economy, vigorous salvage operations and adequate revenues from taxation, a surplus of current receipts over current expenditures can be realized and should be applied to the floating debt. All branches of the Government should cooperate to see that this programme is realized.

I cannot overemphasize the necessity of economy in government appropriations and expenditures and the avoidance by the Congress of practices which take money from the Treasury by indefinite or revolving fund appropriations. The estimates for the present year show that over a billion dollars of expenditures were authorized by the last Congress in addition to the amounts shown in the usual compiled statements of appropriations. This strikingly illustrates the importance of making direct and specific appropriations. The relation between the current receipts and current expenditures of the Government during the present fiscal year, as well as during the last half of the last fiscal year, has been disturbed by the extraordinary burdens thrown upon the Treasury by the Transportation Act, in connection with the return of the railroads to private control. Over $600,000,000 has already been paid to the railroads under this Act,—$350,000,000 during the present fiscal year; and it is estimated that further payments aggregating possibly $650,000,000 must still be made to the railroads during the current year. It is obvious that these large payments have already seriously limited the Government's progress in retiring the floating debt.

Closely connected with this, it seems to me, is the necessity for an immediate consideration of the revision of our tax laws. Simplification of the income and profits taxes has become an immediate necessity. These taxes performed an indispensable service during the war. The need for their simplification, however, is very great, in order to save the taxpayer inconvenience and expense and in order to make his liability more certain and definite. Other and more detailed recommendations with regard to taxes will no doubt be laid before you by the Secretary of the Treasury and the Commissioner of Internal Revenue.

It is my privilege to draw to the attention of Congress for very sympathetic consideration the problem of providing adequate facilities for the care and treatment of former members of the military and naval forces who are sick or disabled as the result of their participation in the war. These heroic men can never be paid in money for the service they patriotically rendered the nation. Their reward will lie rather in realization of the fact that they vindicated the rights of their country and aided in safeguarding civilization. The nation's gratitude must be effectively revealed to them by the most ample provision for their medical care and treatment as well as for their vocational training and placement. The time has come when a more complete programme can be formulated and more satisfactorily administered for their treatment and training, and I earnestly urge that the Congress give the matter its early consideration. The Secretary of the Treasury and the Board for Vocational Education will outline in their annual reports proposals covering medical care and rehabilitation which I am sure will engage your earnest study and command your most generous support.

Permit me to emphasize once more the need for action upon certain matters upon which I dwelt at some length in my message to the Second Session of the Sixty-sixth Congress:[2] the necessity, for example, of encouraging the manufacture of dyestuffs and related chemicals; the importance of doing everything possible to promote agricultural production along economic lines, to improve agricultural marketing and to make rural life more attractive and healthful; the need for a law regulating cold storage in such a way as to limit the time during which goods may be kept in storage, prescribing the method of disposing of them if kept beyond the permitted period, and requiring goods released from storage in all cases to bear the date of their receipt. It would also be most serviceable if it were provided that all goods released from cold storage for interstate shipment should have plainly marked upon each package the selling or market price at which they went into storage, in order that the purchaser might be able to learn what profits stood between him and the producer or the wholesale dealer. Indeed, it would be very serviceable to the public if all goods destined for interstate commerce were made to carry upon every packing case whose form made it possible a plain statement of the price at which they left the hands of the producer. I respectfully call your attention, also, to the recommendations of the message referred to with regard to a federal license for all corporations engaged in interstate commerce.

In brief, the immediate legislative need of the time is the removal of all obstacles to the realization of the best ambitions of our people in their several classes of employment and the strengthening of all instrumentalities by which difficulties are to be met and removed and justice dealt out, whether by law or by some form of mediation and conciliation. I do not feel it to be my privilege at present to suggest the detailed and particular methods by which these objects may be attained, but I have faith that the inquiries of your several committees will discover the way and the method.

In response to what I believe to be the impulse of sympathy and opinion throughout the United States, I earnestly suggest that the Congress authorize the Treasury of the United States to make to the struggling Government of Armenia such a loan as was made to several of the Allied Governments during the war; and I would also suggest that it would be desirable to provide in the legislation itself

[2] That is, Wilson's Annual Message, printed at Dec. 2, 1919, Vol. 64.

that the expenditure of the money thus loaned should be under the supervision of a commission, or at least a commissioner, from the United States, in order that revolutionary tendencies within Armenia itself might not be afforded by the loan a further tempting opportunity.

Allow me to call your attention to the fact that the people of the Philippine Islands have succeeded in maintaining a stable government since the last action of the Congress in their behalf, and have thus fulfilled the condition set by the Congress as precedent to a consideration of granting independence to the Islands. I respectfully submit that this condition precedent having been fulfilled, it is now our liberty and our duty to keep our promise to the people of those Islands by granting them the independence which they so honorably covet.

I have not so much laid before you a series of recommendations, gentlemen, as sought to utter a confession of faith, of the faith in which I was bred and which it is my solemn purpose to stand by until my last fighting day. I believe this to be the faith of America, the faith of the future, and all the victories which await national action in the days to come, whether in America or elsewhere.

Woodrow Wilson.[3]

Printed in *Message of the President of the United States . . . December 7, 1920* (Washington, 1920).

[3] The first draft of this message, which Swem typed up in sections and pasted together, and on which Wilson made one handwritten change, is a T MS in the C. L. Swem Coll., NjP, as is a portion of the final typed draft, with Wilson's handwritten emendations.

To Norman Hezekiah Davis

My dear Mr. Secretary: The White House 7 December, 1920

I agree with you[1] that I ought at once to name the person who is to act as my deputy in the Armenian matter, in order that he may take part in the preliminary discussions and considerations of the subject, and I write to say that my choice falls upon Mr. Henry Morgenthau, in whose skill and good sense in such matters I have the highest confidence.

Cordially and faithfully yours,   Woodrow Wilson

TLS (SDR, RG 59, 760j.67/84, DNA).

[1] Wilson was replying to NHD to WW, Dec. 6, 1920 (first letter of that date).

From Thomas William Lamont

Dear Mr. President: New York. December 7, 1920.

Referring now to your cordial note of November 29th, requesting that I suggest the names of a possible committee on famine relief for China, and the method of functioning, I venture to enclose my suggestions, herewith. These consist, first, of a list of proposed committeemen, made up, as you will see, of leading citizens from all parts of the country, many of them of course already deeply interested in the movement for Chinese relief, many of them connected with churches, others being journalists, men of affairs, publicists, etc. I have had the position of each individual described, except in the cases where the names are too well known to require this.[1]

Second, I attach rough suggestions for your own consideration, of such public statement as you may see fit to issue in connection with the appointment of this committee.[2] When I submit to you a draft of this kind, I always do it with apology for my temerity, and you always say in return that at any rate it sometimes sets your thoughts going.

Third, in the same way, I suggest possible form of telegram to be addressed by you to each committeeman, notifying him of his appointment.[3] My thought, you will see, is not to make this appointment so formidable as to give the idea to the committeeman that the burden on him is to be great.

It would be necessary, I think, for you to designate the chairman for the committee.[4] But of course he would make no attempt to get the committee together as a body, because that would be impossible. I feel that the country is so burdened just now that we must not impose upon it a drive like the war drive for Red Cross, etc. What my idea would be is to take the existing organization of the Christian Herald, which is very well under way, appoint one of the Christian Herald people as executive secretary to the committee and let him, under the personal direction of the Chairman, whoever he may be, run the affairs of this new nation-wide committee,—the Christian Herald of course falling into the background.

As to the treasurership, that is not an important matter, but I think it would give a good flavor if it were proper to have Norman Davis of the State Department act as secretary. This would not be unnatural, in view of the fact that the American Legation is the source of the greater part of our information. I have an intense interest in China and in the Chinese people, and I trust that you

will not fail to let me know any way in which I can further the
situation.   Sincerely yours,

TL (WP, DLC).
    [1] His list filled two legal-sized pages.
    [2] A T MS. Wilson used it virtually verbatim for the statement printed at December 9,
1920.
    [3] This enclosure is missing, but see WW to E. N. Hurley, Dec. 9, 1920.
    [4] Lamont left blank the name in that portion of the statement concerning the appoint-
ment of a national chairman. Swem wrote in "Thomas W. Lamont of New York City."

From Norman Hezekiah Davis, with Enclosure

Dear Mr. President: [Washington] Dec 8/20.

    In spite of your instructions I hesitate to send this message on
your behalf without your seeing it. As it must go forward today may
I ask that you let me know if it is satisfactory?

                    Cordially yours   Norman H. Davis
    Approved by President

ALS (SDR, RG 59, 093.57N66/122, DNA).

                E N C L O S U R E[1]

                        Washington, December 8, 1920.

    RUSH. Your December 4.[2]

    The President has directed me to authorize you to receive the
award of the Nobel Committee and in reply to the speech made in
announcing it you are instructed to convey the following message
from the President:

    QUOTE: In accepting the honor of your award, I am moved not
only by a profound gratitude for the recognition of my earnest efforts in the Cause of Peace, but also by a very poignant humility
before the vastness of the work still called for by this Cause.

    May I not take this occasion to express my respect for the far-
sighted wisdom of the Founder in arranging for a continuing system of awards? If there were but one such prize or if this were to
be the last, I could not of course accept it. For mankind has not yet
been rid of the unspeakable horror of war. I am convinced that
our generation has despite its wounds made notable progress. But
it is the better part of wisdom to consider our work as only begun.
It will be a continuing labor. In the indefinite course of years before
us, there will be *abundant* opportunity ⟨a plenty⟩ for others to distinguish themselves in the Crusade against hate and fear and war.

    There is indeed a peculiar fitness in the grouping of these Nobel rewards. The Cause of Peace and the Cause of Truth are of one family. Even as those who love Science and devote their lives to physics or chemisty, even as those who would create new and higher ideals for mankind in literature, even so with those who love Peace, there is no limit set. Whatever has been accomplished in the past is petty compared to the glory and promise of the future.

Davis   Acting

TS telegram (SDR, RG 59, 093.57N66/122, DNA).
    [1] Words in angle brackets deleted by Wilson; word in italics added by him.
    [2] A. G. Schmedeman to WW, Dec. 4, 1920.

Two Letters from Norman Hezekiah Davis

My dear Mr. President: Washington December 8, 1920.

For your information, I am enclosing a cable transmitting the reply of the French Foreign Office to our first communication regarding the disposition of the Island of Yap.[1]

Yours faithfully,   Norman H. Davis

    [1] It is printed as an Enclosure with WW to NHD, Dec. 9, 1920.

My dear Mr. President: Washington December 8, 1920.

I do not know better how to deal with the enclosed letter from our friend Hoover[1] than to send it to you. If you are willing to issue an appeal, I shall be glad to prepare and submit it to you, if you so desire.   Yours faithfully,   Norman H. Davis

TLS (WP, DLC).
    [1] This letter probably related to the European Children's Relief Fund and was probably a handwritten letter which Wilson did not save. In any event, it does not exist in WP, DLC, the Davis Papers, DLC, the Hoover Papers at Stanford, or in the Herbert Hoover Presidential Library.

From Newton Diehl Baker

My dear Mr. President: Washington. December 8, 1920.

I submit herewith for your approval an order[1] fixing maximum limits of punishment, to be incorporated as a part of the new manual for the guidance of courts martial, which is in course of preparation. This manual was made necessary by the revision of the Articles of War as a part of the Army reorganization act of June 4, 1920.[2] I have left attached to the body of the order a memorandum of the Judge Advocate General[3] descriptive of the general theory upon which these maximum limits are prescribed by the President. You will observe that the departures from similar orders previously signed by you are all in the direction of less severe maximum penalties, there being no case of an increased, and many cases of decreased, sentences authorized.

After the termination of hostilities and the demobilization of the emergency army, we found a tendency toward very youthful army enlistments. No doubt the educational opportunities offered in the Army now attract younger men who desire to secure advantages which are not otherwise available for academic education and manual training. These youths, it seems to me, ought not to have as a part of the penalty for any minor offense committed by them a dishonorable discharge from the Army, as that constitutes a very permanent stigma and disability against future military service. This order, therefore, especially draws the attention of courts and reviewing authorities to that thought, and generally, I think, will lead when promulgated to a more earnest effort to adapt penalties to correctional uses rather than to merely punitive ends.

If you are in doubt as to the wisdom of the limit with regard to any offense included in the schedule, I should be very glad to send you a separate memorandum upon it.

Respectfully yours,   Newton D. Baker

TLS (WP, DLC).
¹ Wilson signed the Executive Order and had it sent to the State Department on December 10, 1920. Typed note at top of Baker's letter.
² About which, see n. 1 to NDB to WW, June 3, 1920 (first letter of that date), Vol. 65.
³ The Judge Advocate General to the Adjutant General, Dec. 6, 1920, T MS (WP, DLC). Baker also enclosed Judge Advocate General [E. H. Crowder], "MEMORANDUM of Changes in Proposed New Executive Order fixing Maximum Limits of Punishment," Dec. 7, 1920, T MS (WP, DLC).

From Carter Glass

Dear Mr. President: Washington, D. C. December 8, 1920.

I am right much interested today to note in the papers that you were on Saturday denied the privilege of shaking hands with Mr. Lodge by reason of the necessity of "leaning on your third leg." The nature of the incident, as I interpret it, perplexes me to guess how soon one may hope to drop in at the White House to get a coveted greeting and to pass a few words in a friendly way, as newly elected Senators are accustomed to do.

It requires a degree of temerity to surmise, after Lodge's failure, that anyone else might produce a psychological effect which would enable you to dispense with the "third leg" for a moment and "shake"; but, as is set forth in the ritual of an ancient order, "such things have happened."

Hoping that you may preserve the caution—more exactly, perhaps, the temper—which caused you to lean on that cane, I am, with best wishes for your good health,

Faithfully yours,   Carter Glass.

TLS (WP, DLC).

A Statement on Chinese Famine Relief

The White House December 9, 1920.

A famine, alarming in its proportions, today holds in its grip several important provinces in China. The crop failure is complete and the present distress which is great is likely, before winter has run its course, to become appalling. In fact our diplomatic and consular agencies in China inform me that the loss resulting from death in distressing form may run into millions of souls. It is certain that the local government and established agencies of relief are unable to cope with the magnitude of the disaster which faces them.

Under the circumstances, relief to be effective should be granted quickly. Once more an opportunity is offered to the American people to show that prompt and generous response with which they have invariably met the call of their brother nations in distress. The case of China I regard as especially worthy of the earnest attention of our citizens. To an unusual degree the Chinese people look to us for counsel and for effective friendship. Our churches, through their religious and medical missionaries, their schools and colleges, and our philanthropic foundations have rendered China an incalculable benefit, which her people recognize with gratitude and devotion to the United States. Therefore, not only in the name of humanity, but in that of the friendliness which we feel for a great people in distress, I venture to ask that our citizens shall, even though the task of giving is not today a light one, respond as they can to this distant but appealing cry for help.

In order to be assured of the orderly collection of such donations, large or small, as may be offered, I have invited a nation-wide committee, whose names are attached hereto, to lend their aid to this matter. I have designated Mr. Thomas W. Lamont, of New York City, to act as Chairman of this Committee, and Mr. Norman Davis, Under Secretary of State, to act as Treasurer.

I realize that this call, added to those for the underfed children of Eastern Europe and the afflicted peoples of the Near East, and to the needs of our own country, makes heavy the demand upon the bounty of the nation. I am confident, however, that all these plans will be answered in generous spirit.

Multigraph copy (WP, DLC).

To Norman Hezekiah Davis, with Enclosure

My dear Davis: The White House 9 December, 1920

How typical this is of the character of French action and tergiversation! Faithfully yours, Woodrow Wilson

TLS (N. H. Davis Papers, DLC).

E N C L O S U R E

Paris December 6th, 1920

1982. Referring to the Department's number 1625, November 9th, 4 pm. and my 1917, November 13th, 8 pm, regarding disposition of island of Yap. Following is text of note received to-day from Foreign Office under date of 1st, instant: "By a note under date of the 12th, instant, the United States Embassy was good enough to inform the Ministry for Foreign Affairs of the views of the American Government in the question of the island of Yap, which gave rise to discussion during the Communications Conference at Washington. The American Government understands that at the request of President Wilson the Supreme Council intended reserving the final disposition of that island on account of its importance as regards international telegraphic communications, and that consequently the island of Yap is excluded from the mandate conferred upon Japan over the islands north of the equator.

It is indeed true that at the meeting of May 1st, President Wilson manifested the desire that the island of Yap should be placed under a special regime, but this desire was not reiterated during the subsequent meetings, in particular that of May 2nd, when it was decided that Germany would have to waive all claims to the three Tsingtao cables in favor of Japan. Moreover, there were no reservations to the decision of the Supreme Council of May 7th, relative to the colonial mandates attributing to Japan mandate over the islands north of the equator.

Under these conditions it seems that the mandate conferred upon Japan covers the island of Yap as well as the other islands north of the equator." Wallace

T telegram (N. H. Davis Papers, DLC).

Two Letters to Norman Hezekiah Davis

My dear Davis: Washington 9 December, 1920

I have yours of December fourth, but surely we did act with regard to the suggestion of the League Council that we send representatives to sit in a consultative capacity with the Permanent Military, Naval and Air Commission. I feel with regard to that suggestion exactly as I did concerning representation on the Commission on Disarmament.[1]

Allow me also to reply to your other letter of December fourth in the same sense. I do not think we ought to consent to be represented at the conference which is going to take up again the method of reparation.

Cordially and faithfully yours, Woodrow Wilson

TLS (SDR, RG 59, 500c117/4, DNA).
[1] Wilson referred to the Permanent Military, Naval and Air Commission, which the League Council had instructed to study the question of a reduction in armaments. See NHD to WW, Dec. 4, 1920 (second letter of the date), and its Enclosure.

My dear Davis: [The White House] 9 December, 1920

Replying to your letter of December eighth, if by "our friend Hoover" you mean Herbert C. Hoover, I have only to say that he is no friend of mine and I do not care to do anything to assist him in any way in any undertaking whatever.

Faithfully yours, [Woodrow Wilson]

CCL (WP, DLC).

To Edward Nash Hurley

The White House Dec 9 1920

The seriousness of the famine situation in China has led me today to make public a statement in regard to it and to point out that unless outside aid is speedily afforded comma the loss in human life will be appalling stop Believing that the suffering and plight of this friendly nation will appeal to the compassion and bounty of our countrymen I have nominated a famine relief committee to lend the weight of their names to the plan for securing popular subscriptions for relief stop I have taken the liberty of naming you as a member of the committee and comma feeling assured that its duties will not prove onerous comma I venture to trust you will find it possible to serve Woodrow Wilson[1]

T telegram (E. N. Hurley Papers, InNd).
[1] This is the telegram that Wilson sent to the 128 persons named in Lamont's list.

To Jesse Holman Jones

My dear Jones: The White House 9 December, 1920

I have read your letter of December fourth with the greatest interest and appreciation. I have no doubt that your diagnosis of the election results is substantially correct; at any rate, I assure you I have not been in the least discouraged by the results and, I think and hope, I have not been misled by them.

With the best wishes,

Cordially and sincerely yours,   Woodrow Wilson

TLS (J. H. Jones Papers, TxU).

From Edward A. Gowen

Mr. President: Washington, D. C., December 9, 1920.

In answer to brief submitted to you by the Honorable William B. Wilson, Secretary of Labor, seeking to have you intervene in the unfortunate predicament of our railroad men,[1] you replied, under date of October 29th:

"To my mind I hold it ill advised to intervene at this time."[2]

Mr. President, may I request your good offices now not in behalf of all of our men but solely in the interests of our old and crippled men. You surely know, Mr. President, that these men, who have given the richest years of their lives to the railways, these men who have been injured in the interests of the railways, are if the present condition is to be made permanent totally divested of their right to labor, can no longer function as members of society, but are doomed to spend their remaining active years in idleness. Even, Mr. President, if they have sinned, surely that sin has been expiated by now, and the willing sacrifice of our young men in behalf of their old and crippled brothers should serve to satisfy even the most exacting discipline.

Mr. President, in my living faith as an American I submit, this, my final appeal to you, submit it in the interests of men who have bowed before the chastening rod of American women and children who needs must be the innocent victims.

Respectfully submitted,   Edward A Gowen

TLS (WP, DLC).

[1] See JPT to WBW, Oct. 21, 1920, enclosing WBW to JPT, Oct. 21, 1920.

[2] Gowen was actually paraphrasing WW to WBW, Oct. 25, 1920, a copy of which was probably sent to him.

To William Goodell Frost

My dear Friend: The White House 10 December, 1920

Your letter of December sixth cheered me very much and I want to thank you for it out of a full heart. Please give my warmest regards to Mrs. Frost and believe me always

Your sincere friend,   Woodrow Wilson

TLS (W. G. Frost Papers, KyBB).

To Bernard Mannes Baruch

My dear Baruch: The White House 10 December, 1920

I wish I could be present at the reunion of the War Industries Board tonight. Under your leadership, the Board did such fine and indispensable work during the great conflict that I should like to render my meed of praise and gratitude. Please convey my heartiest greetings and say how much I personally as an American feel indebted to them.   Affectionately yours,   Woodrow Wilson

TLS (B. M. Baruch Papers, NjP).

Two Letters from Norman Hezekiah Davis

My dear Mr. President: Washington December 10, 1920

By the pouch just arrived from Rome, the Department has received an Italian map[1] indicating the frontier lines of the Treaty of Rapallo. I hasten to send you this map which has been marked here in the Department to show the difference between the frontier line of that Treaty and what it would have been by the Pact of London and by the line indicated by yourself.

I am, my dear Mr. President,

Faithfully yours,   Norman H. Davis

[1] The map accompanies Davis' letter in WP, DLC.

My dear Mr. President: Washington December 10, 1920.

I am submitting herewith the draft of Presidential permit authorizing the Cuban American Telephone and Telegraph Company to lay, land, maintain and operate three telephone-telegraph submarine cables at Key West, Florida, connecting Key West with Habana, Cuba. This is the permit which I discussed with you about two weeks ago, and which you decided to grant. The delay in submitting it to you has been caused by recasting the original draft to accord with the results of the deliberations of the Communications Conference. It now provides that the permit is subject to any general treaties or conventions relating to electrical communications to which the United States is now or may hereafter become a signatory party.

The proposed cable constitutes an extension of the long distance telephone service of the American telephone and telegraph companies, but in accordance with modern practice it permits simultaneous use of the telephone wires for telegraph purposes. The telephone companies do not do a general telegraph business over such telegraph circuits, but lease them to press associations, business houses, and other interests. This permit, therefore, authorizes a service quite distinct from that provided by the ordinary telegraph submarine cable.

In the permit the United States reserves full rights to supervise and control both services and rates and retains a priority right for government telephone messages and for leasing circuits.

Faithfully yours,   Norman H. Davis

P.S. If this meets with your approval, will you please sign the permits in triplicate and return them with the enclosed papers to the Department for delivery to the company.

TLS (WP, DLC).

To Norman Hezekiah Davis

My dear Davis: The White House 11 December, 1920

I am sending the enclosed with my signature in triplicate, as you request, because of course your recollection of our conference about the matter is correct; but do you feel sure that this is not inconsistent with the attitude we have so steadfastly taken towards the Western Union?

Cordially and faithfully yours,   Woodrow Wilson

TLS (SDR, RG 59, 811.73/456, DNA).

To Carter Glass

My dear Glass: The White House 11 December, 1920

It makes me very cross that you should in any way, even in fun, associate yourself with Senator Lodge in speaking of an interview with me. You know my affection for you and how glad I always am to see you, and I beg that you will let me know what days it would be convenient for you to come, so that I may have a chance of assuring you that my "third leg" doesn't always work.

With warmest regard,

Faithfully yours,   Woodrow Wilson

TLS (C. Glass Papers, ViU).

From Jørgen Gunnarsson Løvland and Ragnvald Moe

Kristiania Dec. 11, 1920.

We have the honor to inform you that Nobel Committee of the Norwegian parliament has awarded you the Nobel peace prize 1919 with one hundred and thirty three thousands crowns diplomat and medal transmitted by American minister. Letter sent.[1]

Respectfully, Loveland, President;

Moe, Secretary.

T telegram (WP, DLC).
    [1] J. G. Løvland and Ragnvald Moe to WW, Dec. 10, 1920, TLS (SDR, RG 59, 093.57N66/126, DNA).
    At Wilson's request, Tumulty sent this telegram to Norman Davis, with the request that Davis should let him know how he should acknowledge the telegram from Løvland and Moe. JPT to NHD, Dec. 11, 1920, TLS (SDR, RG 59, 093.57N66/124, DNA). The reply is printed at Dec. 14, 1920.

From Henrik Samuel Sederholm[1]

Dear Sir,   Stockholm Dec 13th, 1920

The Nobel Committee of the Norwegian Storting having decided to confer upon you the Peace prize for 1919

Swed. Crowns 134.100:27,

we have the great honour to place at your disposal this sum in a check payable on the Stockholms Enskilda Bank, Stockholm.

We are making arrangements that Messrs. Brown Brothers & Co. in New York through their agent in Washington may hand you the said check in exchange for the assignment you have received from the Nobel Committee and which should be receipted as follows:

"Received from the Nobel Foundation the sum of One hundred and thirty-four thousand one hundred Swed. Crowns and 27 öre (Swed. Crs. 134.100:27) Washington etc.["]

Messrs. Brown Brothers & Co. will be instructed to advise you as soon as the check will be in the possession of their agent in Washington.

We are

Yours respectfully,   för Nobelstiftelsen, H. Sederholm

ALS (WP, DLC).
    [1] President of the Nobel Foundation.

From Newton Diehl Baker

My dear Mr. President: Washington. December 13, 1920.

A cablegram received today from the Philippine Islands contains the following message from Governor-General Harrison:

"Please express to the President my deep appreciation of his recommendations to Congress for Philippine independence.[1] The Filipino people will always be grateful to him."

Very sincerely,   Newton D. Baker

TLS (WP, DLC).
[1] In his Annual Message printed at Dec. 7, 1920.

From Frederick Henry Lynch [1]

Dear Mr. President: New York December 13, 1920.

You will remember that six years ago Mr. Carnegie established an endowment of two million dollars for the Churches to use in promoting international goodwill. This endowment was called The Church Peace Union. Twenty-nine trustees were chosen, about twenty of them clergymen, the rest laymen who were outstanding leaders of the various communions and at the same time had been interested in the promotion of international goodwill. You know something of the history of The Church Peace Union, what it has done and how it established and stood behind the Committee on the Moral Aims of the War. It is at present devoting most of its energy and funds to bringing together the leaders of the Churches of Europe and America in visits and conferences and to establishing groups in the various Churches of the world who will work for these great purposes. It has consistently stood behind the movement for the League of Nations from the beginning.

We have been careful upon all occasions when a Trustee has been removed by death or has resigned for one reason or another to fill his place with the most outstanding man whom we could find; thus, last year Bishop Brent and Mr. Taft[2] were added to our Board of Trustees. At the Annual Meeting last week there was one vacancy to be filled and the meeting was unanimous in proposing your name.

I think you would find it a real opportunity for service in the years that lie ahead, and I am sure Mr. Carnegie would have been extremely pleased had he thought that you were sometime to be among those who are administering his gifts. Before answering this letter would you be willing to see two or three of us, say, the President, Dr. William Pierson Merrill,[3] the Secretary, Dr. Henry

A. Atkinson,[4] and perhaps Mr. Hamilton Holt or myself, and let us present the opportunity to you. Or in any case, if you cannot do this, do not make your decision until we have had opportunity for further correspondence.

Yours very sincerely,   Frederick Lynch

TLS (WP, DLC).
  [1] Educational Secretary of The Church Peace Union.
  [2] That is, the Rt. Rev. Charles Henry Brent, D.D., and William Howard Taft.
  [3] Pastor of the Brick Church, New York.
  [4] The Rev. Henry Avery Atkinson, D.D., general secretary of The Church Peace Union and the World Alliance for International Friendship.

From Marjorie Brown

Dere Mister and Missis President,   [Washington, Dec. 13, 1920]

I am goin to be married on the 28 of December and I seen in the paper that it was Mister President's birthday last year and we talked it over and thought if it was the same this year it would be so nice to have you at our wedding. Of course if you was totel strangers I wouldent never take such a liberty but you remember my father and mother, Mister and Mrs. Brown who was through the white house sevrul years ago. I am marrying a Mister King and he will be mighty pleezed if you can come too.

Hoping you will be with us on the 28. I am

Respectfully yours   Marjorie Brown.

P.S. The wedding will be at 8.30.
P.P.S. We are goin to have ice creem.

ALS (WP, DLC).

From Jessie Kennedy Dyer

My dear Uncle Woodrow: Memphis, Tenn. Dec. 13, '20.

Allow me to congratulate you on having been awarded the "*Nobel Peace Prize*." I am so glad for you that some appreciation has been shown of the much good that you have done and the many almost mortal sacrifices you have made. Perhaps no one realizes how near you came to giving your life for a cause. I *do* & I hope the day will come when what you have done will be fully appreciated by *all* as it has already by *many*, I rejoice with you because of the award of this prize. It may seem like a small amount to *you*, but to me it would look like a fortune. In reality it would be that when you consider my husbands income is only $1800.00 per year. It would enable me to make many of my life long wishes and dreams come true. I have been trying to persuade myself that we can go to L. R.¹ for X'mas this year, but know we can't go. The railroad fare alone would be $32.00 and I *can't* squeeze that much out of our monthly check and have enough to pay actual expenses, so we have about decided it will be folly to think of making a trip when we are financially as hard up as we are.

You can readily see how *big* your prize looks to me and know that I am sincere when I say I *rejoice* with you over it. We are all moderately well & getting along some how. I do hope you are feeling better and will soon be real strong and well again.

Is Jessie to be with you for Christmas? I want to send them cards and would be so glad if you would tell me where she is to be. All join me in love to you and yours.

Affectionately Your Niece,   Jessie K. Dyer.

ALS (WP, DLC).
¹ Little Rock.

From the Diary of Josephus Daniels

1920 Tuesday 14 December

Cabinet. Wilson (WB) read long opinion in case of Martens¹ closing with opinion that he should be deported. Suggested that his opinion wasn't conclusive though his finding was just. The President said he had learned that no gathering or company could frame a paper—that Secy of Labor knew the thought and he could make such change as might be necessary.

Davis reported that cable convention had reached agreement to agree as to disposition of ex German cables by March. France, Japan & England now have all the cables & seem to wish to keep them

I dont see I grow any better said the President when after cabinet I asked how he felt

¹ About this case, see n. 1 to Enclosure I printed with RL to WW, April 2, 1919, Vol. 56; and n. 3 to the extract from the Daniels Diary printed at April 14, 1920, Vol. 65.

To Jørgen Gunnarsson Løvland and Ragnvald Moe

Washington, December 14, 1920

Please communicate to President Loveland and Secretary Moe of the Nobel Committee following answer from President Wilson in reply to their telegram informing him of award of the Nobel peace prize for 1919:

QUOTE. Permit me to express to you and through you to the Nobel Committee of the Norwegian Parliament my deep appreciation of the Committee's action in awarding to me the Nobel Peace Prize 1919. I have already requested the American Minister at Christiania to convey to the Committee my acceptance of this high honor and the hope that I cherish that through continued efforts the world may achieve the blessings of a lasting peace. Woodrow Wilson. END QUOTE.   Davis   Acting.

T telegram (SDR, RG 59, 093.57N66/122, DNA).

To Robert Wickliffe Woolley

My dear Woolley: [The White House] 14 December, 1920

Thank you very warmly for your letter of the thirteenth.[1] It is a matter of the greatest regret and even grief to me that you are retiring from your post. It has been such a comfort to rely upon your wisdom and your loyalty, as I have absolutely relied, and I shall carry with me always the most delightful recollection of our association.

I do not know what you purpose undertaking now, but you may be sure that my most affectionate friendship will follow you wherever you go and whatever you do. Your record has been of a sort to enable you to carry away the proudest recollections.

With warmest regard,
                    Faithfully yours,   [Woodrow Wilson]

CCL (WP, DLC).
[1] R. W. Woolley to WW, Dec. 13, 1920, TLS (WP, DLC). Woolley asked Wilson not to renominate him as a member of the Interstate Commerce Commission when his term expired on December 31, 1920.

To Marjorie Brown

My dear Marjorie: [The White House] 14 December, 1920

I know you will pardon a busy man for sending you a dictated letter. I need hardly tell you how glad I am to think of the happiness that is coming to you. My warm affection for Ben makes me particularly happy to think of the great thing he is going to gain on the twenty-eighth in your love and companionship. You may be sure that we will think of you all that day with the utmost affection and with the greatest confidence in a happy future for you both.[1]

Affectionately yours,   [Woodrow Wilson]

CCL (WP, DLC).

[1] Marjorie Brown and Benjamin Mandeville King were married in the ballroom of her parents' Washington home at 1712 I Street, N.W. at 8:30 p.m. on December 28. Family members and their friends constituted most of the more than 100 guests. The Rt. Rev. Troy Beatty, Bishop Coadjutor of Tennessee, officiated, and Margaret Wilson was the maid of honor and Stockton Axson the best man. Mrs. Wilson and the Sayres and McAdoos were also present.

The Wilsons had given a family dinner for the prospective bride and groom at the White House on Sunday, December 26. Since Wilson could not attend the wedding, Marjorie Brown and King were also invited to the White House to a luncheon on December 28 in honor of Wilson's sixty-fourth birthday. *Washington Post*, December 29, 1920; Head Usher's White House Diary, Dec. 26, 1920.

From Norman Hezekiah Davis

My dear Mr. President: Washington December 14, 1920.

With reference to your instructions[1] that the Government of Guatemala be requested to recall their Minister[2] here for his breach of etiquette and custom in calling upon Senator Moses,[3] I have felt it necessary, before taking definite action, to confirm the facts as published in the papers.

The Chief of the Latin American Division[4] informs me that Doctor Bianchi called voluntarily to see him Saturday afternoon and stated that he had merely called upon Senator Moses informally in the hope that he might be able to provide him with certain information to refute the statements regarding the present Government of Guatemala previously made by the Senator. No one else was present during his talk with Senator Moses and he read the following day, with surprise and consternation, the press account of his interview.[5] He apologized most profusely, and volunteered to make any possible amends for a well-intentioned, but not well considered act.[6]

I have regretted this incident very much because the Guatemalan Minister is not only honest and intensely pro-American, but he is one of the most popular members of the party now in power in Guatemala, and I am fearful that his dismissal would not be understood in Guatemala and would strengthen the hands of the opposition force, which is the most undesirable element in that Republic. May I ask if, in your judgment, the situation might not be adequately met by sending a formal inquiry as to the accuracy of the press accounts of the interview to the Guatemalan Minister, which would be followed by an official, and possibly published, explanation and apology from him.

I am reluctant to burden you with the consideration of a matter regarding which you have already given instructions, but I feel it my duty to submit the above facts and suggestions for taking final action.   Faithfully yours,   Norman H. Davis

TLS (WP, DLC).
[1] Wilson must have given these orally.
[2] Dr. Julio Bianchi.
[3] That is, George Higgins Moses, Republican of New Hampshire.
[4] That is, Sumner Welles.
[5] In a front-page story in the *Washington Post* on December 11, 1920, Albert W. Fox, an investigative reporter whom Wilson detested, had given a detailed account, based on information received from Moses, of Bianchi's interview with Moses of the previous day. According to Fox, Bianchi had called upon Moses to refute charges against the new Guatemalan government contained in a resolution (S. Res. 395) and an accompanying memorandum introduced by Moses in the Senate on December 8. The resolution called upon the State Department to provide information on the overthrow of Estrada Cabrera. It charged that the leaders of the revolution had violated a solemn agreement signed at the American legation to protect the life and property of the former President, had thrown him in a common jail, deprived him of all legal rights and privileges, and had looted and ransacked his residence. The accompanying memorandum elaborated on these charges and included a sharp indictment of the American Minister, Benton McMillin, for failing to offer protection to Estrada Cabrera and to provide him with the opportunity to leave the country. See *Cong. Record*, 66th Cong., 3d sess., pp. 43-44.
[6] Bianchi did in fact issue a public apology for his alleged transgression of diplomatic niceties. *New York Times*, Dec. 24, 1920.

From Norman Hezekiah Davis, with Enclosure

My dear Mr. President: Washington December 14, 1920.

I have received from Dr. Garo Pasdermadjian, Diplomatic Representative of the Armenian Republic, a letter expressing the gratitude felt by the Armenian people toward yourself as being "their one true champion, the architect of their little State," and requesting me to convey to you his interpretation of the sentiments of his fellow countrymen.

Permit me, accordingly, to enclose a copy of Dr. Pasdermadjian's letter.   Faithfully yours,   Norman H. Davis

TLS (WP, DLC).

E N C L O S U R E

Garo Pasdermadjian to Norman Hezekiah Davis

Sir: Washington, D. C. December 9, 1920.

The Armenian people feel that, without the championship of their cause by the President of the United States, it would have been extremely difficult, if not impossible, for them to secure recognition as a free nation. It is a fact that, without the practical solicitude of the President for the welfare of our people, the great majority of them would have ere long perished from hunger and pestilence and as a result of the sinister schemes of our neighbors.

Today, at the supreme hour of our national crisis, when selfish influences are at work, when a calculated war of extermination is being waged upon us, and when hunger, cold and sickness once more afflict our exhausted people, again the magnanimous utterances and deeds of the President reveal to us rays of hope for a better future. In spite of the physical handicap imposed upon him by cruel fate, he is giving lavishly to Armenia of his thoughts, of his time, and of his energy.

Our people at home, severely shaken by the hostile forces which surround them, may find it expedient to submit to forms or practices which are alien to their character, and abhorrent to their innermost feelings; but I know, that men, women and children of Armenia hope and pray that God may preserve and help their one true champion, the architect of their little State, to carry through to a conclusion his great purpose to bring peace to war-torn Armenia, and also that, in the years to come, he may continue to interest himself in the life of a people whom he has so jealously and steadfastly guarded and defended and made into a free nation.

May I ask you, Mr. Secretary, to be good enough to convey to the President this inadequate expression of the sense of gratitude of the Armenian people which I have tried to interpret.

I have the honor to be, Sir,
　　　　　　　　　　Your humble and most obedient servant,
　　　　　　　　　　　　(Signed) G. Pasdermadjian.

TCL (WP, DLC).

From Josephus Daniels

My dear Mr. President:　　　　　　Washington. December 14, 1920.

We have in type the revision of the regulations of the Navy which we have been working on for months and they are just completed. Under the law they must be approved by the President. They are very long, but we have succeeded in reducing them at least one-fourth from the regulations now in effect. They embody all the general orders and changes which the experience of seven years has justified.

I am enclosing herewith my promulgation letter which I request you to approve if it meets your pleasure.[1]

　　　　　　　　　　　Sincerely yours,　Josephus Daniels

TLS (WP, DLC).
[1] Printed as an Enclosure with WW to JD, Dec. 15, 1920.

From Thomas William Lamont

Dear Mr. President: [New York] December 14th, 1920.

CHINESE FAMINE RELIEF FUND

Your prompt action in making a public appeal for the Chinese famine sufferers and in naming a country-wide committee has, I know from reports received from all over the country, created a most favorable impression. The response in actual dollars and cents, however, is likely to be small, and in these days of business depression and of urgent, repeated demands from many directions this is no wonder. Herbert Hoover's organization for the relief of the children of Europe is very complete throughout the country and, of course, as you indicated in your public statement and as I have said in my initial telegram to committee members, we must do nothing that will interfere with the movement to relieve Europe.

Now, I have discussed the situation carefully with Hoover and the following suggestion occurs to us both as possibly designed to meet this very situation; we hope that it will also appeal to your good judgment: There is in the treasury of the Sugar Equalization Board a profit gained from dealing in sugar to the amount of up-wards of $35,000,000—it may be close to $38,000,000. Why could not this fund be utilized for the relief of starving peoples, to be, in general, distributed within the discretion of the President? I am informed that the capital stock of this Sugar Corporation was sub-scribed from the President's private fund and that the President is of record the sole stockholder. The directors of the Corporation are all men who would be sympathetic to the idea. The Treasury has no claim upon this fund, as I understand it. In effect, it is in the same category as the profit that was made in the United States Grain Corporation—$60,000,000 as I recall it—which, as you will remember, was appropriated by Congress for relief.

If, in the same way, Congress would pass a joint resolution at your request, appropriating such profits as remain in the Sugar Equalization Board for famine relief, then the fund could be promptly distributed and would cover infinitely more ground than we could, by any possibility, hope to cover in collections for China.

As to the division of this fund—I think it would be proper to appropriate $20,000,000 or $25,000,000 for China; perhaps $8,000,000 or $10,000,000 for the starving children of Europe; and something for Armenia, although I understand her case is some-what ameliorated. However, the division should be left to your own discretion and the funds should, I presume, be distributed through the recognized agencies of relief. If we do not accomplish some-thing like this, I am afraid that the response is going to seem very inadequate.

Now as to the *modus operandi*—I myself believe that such an appeal as you might frame to Congress and recommendation along this line, would be likely to meet with the same favorable response that finally came in the case of appropriating the Grain Corporation profits. Certainly in this time of starvation among foreign peoples it is foolish to allow a fund like this to remain idle and unemployed. I should hope that Secretary Houston would favor its use in this way. The fund at present is invested in Treasury Certificates, and I suppose the Treasury is feeling a little hard-up, but, nevertheless, he could hardly offer an objection.

If, upon consideration, you and Secretary Houston favor this plan, then when it comes to the Congress end of it, Hoover is of the judgment that his organization all over the country, made up of influential people, could, severally and as a unit, make such representations to their Congress Representatives that little opposition would be met there. The distress is so appalling that it seems almost a crime to let a valuable fund like this go unutilized. So far as the country is concerned, I do not believe that it is in an ungenerous mood, but it is certainly getting very hard up and our response for China and the rest of the world is likely to be very inadequate.

One great advantage of this plan is that a part of this fund thus released could be used in the purchase of grain and rice held by the farmers in the West and Southwest, who are clamoring very hard now for help through the War Finance Corporation. Such help it may be quite impossible to arrange, but it would be quite proper, at a reasonable market figure, to buy some of their cereal products and help stop the clamoring.

With great respect and hearty appreciation of the honor which you have done me in naming me as Chairman of the Chinese Famine Committee, I am, dear Mr. President,

Sincerely yours,   Thomas W. Lamont

TLS (WP, DLC).

From Charles Zeller Klauder

My dear Mr. President: Philadelphia December 14th, 1920.

The original drawings of the river site scheme have been sent to me at my request that I might have records from which to advance the study of the design as a whole, while considering the rearrangement of rooms.

In order that you may not be without a record of what has been done, we are sending you the enclosed photographs made from these drawings and of a size which we believe will be convenient for your use.[1]

Our further study promises a solution which appears as satisfactory to us as we hope it will appear to you.

Sincerely yours,   Chas Z Klauder

TLS (WP, DLC).
  [1] He enclosed photographs of the floor plans and elevations of a two-story house of some fifteen rooms, including a great hall and a large library, in a monumental Norman-chateau style. The orginal copies of some of these plans and elevations are in the Wilson House in Washington.

To Josephus Daniels, with Enclosure

My dear Mr. Secretary: The White House 15 December, 1920

I return this letter because it seems to me that the last sentence, which I have marked on the margin, gives entirely too wide a field of discretion to men who might or might not know how to act under it. Will you not please reconsider it?

Cordially and faithfully yours,   Woodrow Wilson

TLS (J. Daniels Papers, DLC).

E N C L O S U R E

NAVY DEPARTMENT, Washington, 14 December 1920.

The following Regulations are issued, in accordance with the provisions of section 1547 of the Revised Statutes of the United States, for the government of all persons attached to the naval service.

It is hereby required and directed that all officers and other persons belonging to the Navy, so far as the duties of each are concerned, make themselves acquainted with, observe and comply with the Regulations of the United States Navy contained herein.

These Regulations set forth the duty, responsibility, authority, distinctions and relations of the various bureaus, offices, and individual officers each to the other. Details coming exclusively under the cognizance of a particular bureau or office which might properly be incorporated in a separate manual by the bureau or office concerned have been omitted.

These Regulations are a guide to official conduct. Specific instructions for all circumstances which may arise can not be prepared beforehand. Therefore no person in the naval service must hesitate to assume responsibilities should cases arise requiring immediate action upon which the Regulations are silent.

Josephus Daniels

THE WHITE HOUSE,
14 December 1920.
APPROVED.

TS MS (WP, DLC).

To Norman Hezekiah Davis

My dear Davis: The White House 15 December, 1920

I have your letter of yesterday about the Guatemalan Minister and his call upon Senator Moses, and am quite content that you should follow the course suggested in that letter.

Faithfully yours,   Woodrow Wilson

TLS (SDR, RG 59, 701.1411/108, DNA).

To Frederick Henry Lynch

My dear Doctor Lynch: [The White House] 15 December, 1920

I need hardly assure you of my sincere interest in the purposes of the Church Peace Union, but it is not possible for me to undertake the responsibilities of the kind of connection with it which you propose to me in your letter of December thirteenth. I could not take a working oar, and I have made it a rule all my life to decline connection with any serious undertaking in which I could not take an active and actual part.

With the best wishes,

Sincerely yours,   [Woodrow Wilson]

CCL (WP, DLC).

Two Letters from Norman Hezekiah Davis

My dear Mr. President: Washington December 15, 1920

Dr. Farrand[1] has today informed the Department that he is in receipt of a telegram from the Lord Mayor of Cork[2] appealing to the American Red Cross for assistance to relieve the distressing situation caused by the "burning and sacking of the City of Cork."[3] The Red Cross desires to know whether it would meet with the approval of the American Government for it to send relief in reply to the request from the Lord Mayor. He anticipates that any favorable response by the Red Cross, if made, would take the form of funds or supplies, or both, but would not involve sending Red Cross personnel.

It appears that the Red Cross has, for sometime past, been badgered by demands from many sources in the United States to send relief to Ireland, but not until now has an appeal come from an authoritative quarter. He states that the Red Cross under ordinary circumstances, if its Committee votes to extend aid in a foreign country, would proceed without consulting either the government of that country or the State Department. The case of Ireland, Dr. Farrand feels, however, presents conditions of such a peculiar nature that there is grave risk of the Red Cross involving America in a national controversy foreign to our interests. He is evidently in a quandary, from which he wishes to be extricated by having the State Department assume responsibility for Red Cross action on the Lord Mayor's telegram. In this instance, however, Dr. Farrand intends to make informal inquiry at the British Embassy as to what would be the possible attitude of the British Government should the Red Cross desire to send assistance to Cork; yet he has intimated to the Department that even should the reply of the British Embassy be unfavorable, the Red Cross might still respond favorably to the Lord Mayor provided the Department of State opposed no objection.

This is a matter of great delicacy and importance which I feel should be brought to your attention at once. I will be most grateful, therefore, for any indication as to the course you desire pursued in replying to the Red Cross.

I am, my dear Mr. President,

Faithfully yours,   Norman H. Davis

[1] Livingston Farrand, M.D., of Washington, chairman of the Central Committee of the American Red Cross.

[2] Donal O'Callaghan, who had been elected on November 4, 1920, following the death of Terence J. MacSwiney.

[3] English auxiliaries (former British army officers) of the Royal Irish Constabulary attacked, ransacked, and burned virtually the entire center of Cork on the night of December 11, 1920, in retaliation and rage against recent murderous ambushes of the Irish Republican Army. *New York Times*, Dec. 12-14, 1920, and George Dangerfield, *The Damnable Question: A Study in Anglo-Irish Relations* (Boston and Toronto, 1976), pp. 316-19.

My dear Mr. President: Washington December 15, 1920

I have noted the inquiry in your letter of December 11, 1920, whether I feel certain that the granting of permission to the Cuban-American Telephone and Telegraph Company to lay cables between Key West and Habana is not inconsistent with the attitude taken toward the Western Union Telegraph Company. I believe I can briefly indicate clearly that our action in regard to these two concerns is entirely consistent.

The Western Union Telegraph Company entered into a contract with the Western Telegraph Company, a British concern, under the terms of which the latter agreed to extend its line of cables from Brazil to Barbados, and the former agreed to construct a cable line from Barbados to Miami Beach, Florida. The actual foreign terminus of the line which it is proposed to land at Miami Beach would be Brazil. The Western Telegraph Company, as you are aware, has monopolistic privileges in Brazil from which American concerns are excluded. The permit sought by the Western Union Telegraph Company has been withheld because the cable line which it proposes to lay would be a link in a monopolistic foreign system.

The actual foreign terminus of the Cuban-American Telephone and Telegraph Company is Cuba, where American cable companies are granted satisfactory landing privileges. And traffic arrangements such as the Western Union Company has in contemplation are forbidden by provisions in the permit for the Cuban-American Company which you have just signed.

The granting of the permit to the Cuban-American Company is in line with the policy of the promotion of communication in the interest of American citizens. The refusal of the permit to the Western Union Company is in harmony with the traditional policy of the Government not to grant a permit for the landing of any foreign cable line or any link in any foreign cable line if such foreign line enjoys in a foreign country monopolistic privileges prejudicial to the interests of the United States.

The Cuban-American Company has complied with all of the Government's requirements based on law and national policy. The Western Union Company has refused to meet such requirements and has attempted to land its cable in defiance of them.

Faithfully yours,   Norman H. Davis

TLS (WP, DLC).

From Thomas William Lamont

CHINA FAMINE RELIEF

Dear Mr. President: [New York] December 15th, 1920.

Supplementing my letter to you of the fourteenth, Cleveland
Dodge, who is on our General Committee for Famine Relief and
who of course is head of the Committee on Relief for the Near
East, dropped in for a little chat with me this morning.

He told me of his pleasant call with you the other day snd [and]
of your continued strong improvement in health. He also said that
he had expressed to you the same opinion that I gave in my letter
of Tuesday, namely, that the times were such that we could not
hope for an adequate response from the public, and, therefore, if
there were any device by which unappropriated funds in connection with the government could be considered, it might prove the
way out.

I simply quote this as bearing upon the same suggestion that I
made.   Sincerely yours,   Thomas W. Lamont

TLS (WP, DLC).

From Samuel Gompers

Sir: Washington, D. C. December 15, 1920.

Permit me at this time, when the kindly and considerate spirit of
the Christmastide cannot but be in men's hearts, to appeal to you
in the name of the American labor movement for the performance
of an act which I am convinced will meet with the approval of the
great majority of our people.

I appeal to you for the issuance of a proclamation of amnesty to
those political prisoners whose conviction and imprisonment was
not because of moral turpitude. Especially do I appeal to you for
the granting of a pardon to Eugene V. Debs, now in the Federal
prison at Atlanta, Ga.

During the years that have gone I have had serious differences
with Mr. Debs. It is likely that we shall continue to differ. That,
however, is beside the point. I never have held that Mr. Debs gave
voice to any utterance through insincerity or that he was a traitor
to his country. His was, I firmly believe, a mistaken conviction, but
it was a conviction.

I believe that nothing which it is within your power to do immediately would so ease the tension among so many of our people
or would so breathe over our country the spirit of peace and good
will. A proclamation of amnesty just now would come as a gracious

and forebearing act wholly and properly in keeping with the season. In addition, it would be wholly in keeping with the kind of government and the kind of institutions in which we believe and which our people have so lately made such sacrifice to defend.

The Montreal Convention of the American Federation of Labor, held last June, adopted resolutions urging the granting of amnesty to the prisoners held for political offenses during the war.[1] I believe that the convention acted wisely and I am in hearty accord with the thought expressed in its action. I need not tell you how loyally and sincerely the conventions of the American Federation of Labor in the years just previous had given their support to the cause of freedom and justice. But the war is ended and the danger has passed. Even those who were most perverse in the advocacy of pacifist views during the war can no longer in the least endanger the safety of our Republic. If the object of the confinement of these prisoners was, as I believe it was, to safeguard the nation, then the object has been achieved. The moral strength of our country, as well as the physical strength, has been amply proven. To open the gates to these prisoners now will be no less an example of our moral strength and self-reliance than was their imprisonment in the hour of danger.

I have no thought of asking any kind of clemency for those who have been convicted of crimes or offenses involving moral turpitude, or for those who may be held for trial for such offenses. Quite to the contrary, they should be left to the normal course of the courts of justice.

But in the case of those who were purely political offenders during the war, as was Mr. Debs, I ask a grant of amnesty, that they may have their freedom and the opportunity to enjoy the life of liberty and justice which our land so richly affords even at times to those who are not worthy of it.

Let me say again, that no immediate act of yours would so exemplify the spirit of mercy at this season as the granting of this appeal for amnesty. May I hope this request will find favor in the great heart of a man who has done so much for humanity and who has come to mean so much to those whose faces are turned in hope and aspiration toward the future?

Respectfully yours,   Sam'l. Gompers.

TLS (WP, DLC).
    [1] See the *New York Times*, June 16, 1920.

From Albert George Schmedeman

My dear Mr. President: Christiania, December 15, 1920.

May I not have the honor to inform you that on December tenth, in extraordinary session of the Storting, President Lövland of the Nobel Peace Committee of the Storting announced that the Peace Prizes for 1919 and 1920 had been awarded to you and Léon Bourgeois, respectively. Having been so authorized in the Department's cablegram No. 39 of December eighth, I accepted on your behalf the gold medal and the certificate of award, which will be forwarded in the next pouch. Secretary Moe of the Nobel Committee informs me that he has written you fully regarding the award, and the money award will be sent to you from Stockholm.

In my despatch No. 1720 of December thirteenth to the Secretary of State, I have made a full report of the ceremony which took place, and a summary of expressions from the leading newspapers in Christiania regarding the award. The press and people of Norway are unanimous in their approval of the decision of the Committee.

I may perhaps be permitted to say that this has been one of the most gratifying occasions of my life, and I appreciate unspeakably the honor of receiving on your behalf this token of a nation's recognition of your high purpose towards mankind.

May I also at this time again express to you my appreciation of the honor which you have conferred upon me when you appointed me as your representative in Norway. It has been a great privilege to have been a part of your administration during these trying years, and it is my hope that my work has met with your approval. It is my plan to leave for the United States in the spring and I hope that I may then have the honor of paying my respects in person.

                    Faithfully yours,   A. G. Schmedeman

TLS (WP, DLC).

Norman Hezekiah Davis to Paul Hymans

                    [Washington] December 15, 1920.

The President has directed me to advise you that he has designated the Honorable Henry Morgenthau as his personal representative who is prepared to proceed as soon as practicable to carry out his proffer of good offices and personal mediation in the matter of Armenia. The President, however, is still awaiting advices from the Council of the League as to the avenues through which his proffer should be conveyed and the parties with whom his representative should get in contact, as well as assurances that he may count upon the diplomatic and moral support of the principal powers represented on the Council of the League.   Norman H. Davis

T telegram (N. H. Davis Papers, DLC).

Two Letters to Norman Hezekiah Davis

My dear Davis: The White House 16 December, 1920
I think it would be extremely unwise for the Red Cross to respond to the appeal you refer to in your letter of December fifteenth for the relief of the people of Cork. It would be an international act of the most questionable sort, and I hope that you will express, in my name if you choose, our sense of its unwisdom at this time.
                    Cordially and faithfully yours,   Woodrow Wilson

TLS (SDR, RG 59, 811.142/10239, DNA).

My dear Davis: The White House 16 December, 1920
I do not know what is the proper way to reply to the very delightful and moving message conveyed by you for Doctor Pasdermadjian, the diplomatic representative of the Armenian Republic. I have been deeply moved by the message and would like to have him and those for whom he speaks know it.
                    Faithfully yours,   Woodrow Wilson

TLS (SDR, RG 59, 860j.01/374, DNA).

To Charles Zeller Klauder

My dear Mr. Klauder: [The White House] 16 December, 1920
Will you not be kind enough, so soon as they are ready, to send me the plans of the floors below the main, or library, floor of the river site house, and will you not also be kind enough to include a restudy of the western end of the second floor plan with a view to giving Mrs. Wilson an exclusive bathroom connecting with her dressing room, and of planning a private, if necessary circular, staircase from my study up into her dressing room? In looking over the plans Mrs. Wilson and I agree that it would be just as well to shift my bathroom from the western to the eastern end of my room, but we of course admit our ignorance of structural considerations.

Being where it is, my bathroom shuts off the only view from my bedroom of the pretty part of the river.

We have about settled on a house at last, not the Wyoming Avenue house, but one on S street[1] which we think you will agree with us is much superior, and we may impose still further on your good nature and ask you to come down and advise us with regard to one or two matters that have to be attended to in connection with its prospective use.

Cordially and sincerely yours,   [Woodrow Wilson]

CCL (WP, DLC).

[1] This was a house at 2340 S Street, N.W. A commodious Georgian-style brick house, it was built by Henry Parker Fairbanks, a Boston businessman, and his wife Frances Lewis Fairbanks, as their Washington residence in 1915-1916 at a total cost (not including the cost of the two lots on which it was situated) of $59,639.14. Waddy Butler Wood, an independent architect of Washington, assisted by Wilson's old friend, Benjamin Wistar Morris of New York, designed and oversaw construction of the house.

Mrs. Wilson writes in *My Memoir*, pp. 311-12, that she looked at two houses on S Street and that neither was suitable. Then her agent, Arthur Browne of Randall Hagner Realtors (this information from the news report in the Washington *Evening Star*, Dec. 17, 1920), suggested that she look at another house across the street—the Fairbanks house. She fell in love with it and thought it was almost perfectly suited to her and her husband's needs. Returning to the White House, she told him that this was the house that would qualify in every particular but that she did not think they could get it. As usual, Mrs. Wilson is mistaken or silent about dates, and from this point on her account is quite confabulated.

Mrs. Wilson must have seen the house at 2340 S Street on about December 13. She writes that Wilson took the matter in hand at once, which is undoubtedly true. Wilson (through her brother, Wilmer Bolling, Mrs. Wilson says) on December 15 made a deposit of $5,000 and an agreement to buy the house for $150,000 in cash. A news item in the *Evening Star* of December 17, 1920, reported that Wilson intended to purchase the house and take possession of it on or before February 15, 1921. Mrs. Fairbanks deeded the property to Mrs. Wilson on January 31, 1921. For information about the contributions of a group of friends toward the purchase price, see C. H. Dodge to C. T. Grayson, Feb. 14, 1921.

To Jessie Kennedy Dyer

My dear Jessie: [The White House] 16 December, 1920

Thank you for your letter of December thirteenth. It was pleasant to know how thoroughly you understand the things that I have been going through.

In reply to your question about Jessie Sayre, she will be here on and after the twenty-seventh.

With affectionate messages to you all,

Your affectionate uncle,   [Woodrow Wilson]

CCL (WP, DLC).

From Josephus Daniels

My dear Mr. President: Washington. 16th of December 1920

I thank you for your letter of December 15th with reference to the Regulations, and I agree with you entirely and I am enclosing a renewed draft[1] omitting the paragraph including the sentence you pointed out. It has been in the Regulations for a long time and I had not considered it from the point of view given in your letter. That sentence does indeed give too wide discretion. The Regulations cover almost every point and I am retuning an order for your approval, omitting the paragraph giving too wide discretion.

Faithfully yours,   Josephus Daniels

TLS (WP, DLC).
  [1] T MS, dated Dec. 16, 1920 (J. Daniels Papers, DLC).

From William Bauchop Wilson

My dear Mr. President: Washington December 16, 1920.

During last Session of Congress a bill was passed creating a Women's Bureau in the Department of Labor. During the period of the war this Department organized a Women's Bureau to protect the interests of the large number of women engaged in industrial pursuits, many of them in occupations that had not theretofore been open to women. Congress continued the appropriation for the continuation of this nonstatutory Bureau, and has now given it a statutory existence.

When the Bureau was first organized Miss Mary Van Kleeck, of New York, was made Director, with Miss Mary Anderson as Assistant. Upon the resignation of Miss Van Kleeck, Miss Anderson was promoted to the position of Director, and now occupies that position. She has given very efficient service, and I recommend that she be nominated as Director of the new statutory Bureau, which will take over the organization that she now directs.

I have prepared and am sending herewith the formal nomination papers for the Senate.[1]   Faithfully yours,   W B Wilson

TLS (WP, DLC).
  [1] A note at the bottom of this letter indicates that this nomination was sent to the Senate on December 20.

From Joseph Patrick Tumulty

Dear Governor: The White House, December 16, 1920.

Secretary Meredith asked this morning if you could arrange to see a committee of cattle raisers, who wished to take up with you the question of an embargo. He stated that the situation of the cattle raisers of the country was a desperate one and hoped that you could arrange to see the committee. I told him that I did not think you could see any one at present but that I would bring the matter to your attention.[1]   Faithfully yours,   Tumulty

TLS (WP, DLC).
    [1] "Please tell Meredith I can't arrange this. The President." WW to [JPT], c. Dec. 16, 1920, TL (WP, DLC).

From the Diary of Ray Stannard Baker

Dec. 16 1920.

I got in here this morning & called up Grayson to say howd'y and he told me the president had spoken of me with possible reference to the record at Paris which I feel sure he himself will never write (although Mrs. Wilson told me when I was here 3 weeks ago that a N. Y. publisher had offered him $100000 to do it)[1] So I sat down & wrote to the President & emphasized the need of having *some* record prepared from the American point of view & offered to help in any way I could to bring this about.

    [1] See G. H. Doran to JPT, Nov. 23, 1920, printed as an Enclosure with JPT to EBW, Nov. 24, 1920.

From Ray Stannard Baker

My dear Mr. President: Washington, D. C. December 16 '20.

Ever since my visit to the White House two weeks ago, I have had it strongly in mind to write to you about a subject which has all along lain close to my heart: and that is, the proper and correct account of your immense task in Europe: what your leadership meant to the world before the war, and your achievements at Paris. A flood of books and articles has been appearing upon the Conference, but none that speaks with inside knowledge of what America did there under your leadership: and they are often insidiously unfair to you. I tried to present a hasty outline in my little book[1] (which has had a wide and I think helpful circulation) but no one knows better than I do how utterly inadequate it is. In fact, I made it brief in order that it would be widely bought and read.

I have hoped that you would yourself tell the story in all of its completeness and leave an adequate document upon which history may base its decisions. This seems to me to be of tremendous importance: and I had it strongly in mind when I saw you two weeks ago to raise the subject, but did not have the opportunity of doing it. I have the fear that the testimony will all come from English, French and Italian sources and that the American point of view will fail of proper representation. Indeed, I feel certain that no such punctiliousness regarding the records has been observed over there as here.

Now, it has often occurred to me—though I mention it now with hesitation—that possibly I might be able to help, either now or in the future, to present truly your part there, and to make the record clear. You may remember that I raised the subject once or twice in Paris of being allowed access to the full records. You were considerate enough to let me have the reports of the Council of Ten upon which I drew (with discretion) in preparing my small book: but I have not seen the far more important records of the Council of Four and the many other documents.

I should hesitate even to make this suggestion but for two reasons.

First, the feeling I have of the profound necessity of having the American record set forth from an inside and friendly source.

Second, the feeling that there is perhaps no one outside the actual members of the Council, and your own personal party—at least no American—who was more closely in contact with the whole situation than I was.

You may recall that I was in England, France and Italy for a year before the Peace Conference began, studying conditions there and reporting to Mr. Polk of the State Department. I believe you saw some of my reports. This gave me a wide background of judgment both of conditions and of personalities. I made an especial effort to get at just what the influence of your leadership was in the various countries. I do not think you yourself realize what an immense part you played in the re-moralization of the practically defeated western nations. I saw and felt this at first hand and it will be regarded, certainly, by historians as one of the greatest things you did. I have a mass of concrete material upon this subject.

Other than this, you know what my opportunities were at Paris to have knowledge of the exact situation. I may say I kept copious notes both at Paris and in the year before, upon which I have never yet drawn.

The greatest thing of all of course, is your own complete account of what happened: this ought, above everything, in the interest of history, to be written. But if, for any reason, you do not intend to write it—or write it fully—it might be that I could help—that is, if I could have such an access to the material—and your approval—as would make a really authoritative record.

I make this suggestion with a deep sense of humility, but with a spirit of devoted friendship and admiration. I present the matter in all frankness of spirit.

Faithfully yours,   Ray Stannard Baker
(address: Amherst Mass.)

ALS (WP, DLC).
¹ That is, *What Wilson Did at Paris* (Garden City, N. Y., 1919).

From Alfred Hermann Fried[1]

Translation.

Honored Mr. President: Vienna, Dec. 16, 1920.

As the only subject of the Central Powers, who has the Prize for Peace of the Nobel Endowment, I avail myself of the opportunity of expressing to You, Honored Mr. President, my felicitations for the bestowal of the Nobel Prize.

I am rejoiced that the prize has been given to the man, who, as first Head of a State, promulgated the thought of an international organization as the only remedy and has made the attempt to realize it.

From the bequest of my deceased friend and associate in work, Baroness Suttner,[2] I have a letter, which Alfred Nobel addressed to the Baroness January 7, 1893. In this letter, he expressed for the first time the idea of the establishment of the Peace Prize and declared that he himself considered the putting an end to wars. In the corresponding part the letter has the following text:

"I would like to dispose of a part of my fortune to make of it a prize to be distributed every five years (let us say six times for if in thirty years we have not succeeded in reforming the present system we will inevitably relapse into barbarism).

This Prize should be decreed to the man or to the woman who should have made in Europe the greatest step toward the ideas of general pacification.

I do not speak to you of disarmament, which can be brought about only very slowly; I do not even speak of compulsory arbitration between nations. But one must reach that result soon (and one can reach it) that is that all States pledge themselves jointly and severally to turn against the first aggressor. Then wars will become impossible. And one would have succeeded in forcing even the most quarrelsome State to have recourse to a Court or to keep quiet."

It is interesting that the ideas of Nobel in the Versailles compact (namely Art. 11 and 16) are given for the execution. And You, Honored Mr. President, are the one indeed, who in the acceptation of the Nobel ideas has "had made in Europe the step toward the ideas of General pacification."

To be able to communicate this to You gives me an especial pleasure.

I am, Honored Mr. President,
    Your devoted servant,   (signed) D.h.c. Alfred H. Fried.

TCL (WP, DLC).
  [1] Viennese publicist, founder of the German Peace Society, winner of the Nobel Peace Prize in 1911; in self-imposed exile in Switzerland during the war.
  [2] Bertha Félicie Sophie Kinsky, Baroness von Suttner, a close friend of Nobel and Fried. She was awarded the Nobel Peace Prize in 1905.

From Henry Smith[1]

Dear Mr President,   London, S.E. 15, Dec. 16. 1920.

Only our Conference, which meets annually in July, has authority to speak on behalf of our whole Church; but I am sure that I have the honour to speak in the name of many thousands of my fellow United Methodists when I offer you warm congratulations on your approaching birthday and express the wish that it may have many successors, each of which shall be crowned with abundant blessing.

We remember with deep gratitude the magnificent lead you gave your own people and the world in the formation of the League of Nations; the clarion calls, remarkable alike for their luminous English, their clear vision and their moral and spiritual passion, which you addressed to your own people and through them to the conscience of mankind; the heroism with which you staked all that you might win for the world at large a better way of settling international differences and of adjusting international relations than that which is afforded by war, which one of your own generals described years ago as "hell," and the noble, undaunted persistency with which you still hold to the divine cause to which you have given the best of your brain, your heart and your years. You have builded better than you know, for you have well and truly laid the foundations upon which the Temple of a World Peace shall yet be reared. God inspired, your labour shall endure, and future generations will inscribe your name high on that roll whereon the names of only the world's best and worthiest benefactors are written imperishably.

Mr President, we present to you the assurance of our admiration, our respect, our affection. May the blessing of the God of your father and mother rest upon you abundantly to-day! We know that tomorrow the blessing of thousands saved from the horrors of war through your leadership in the ways of peace will rest upon your memory.

I pray for you, Mr President, and beg to remain,

Always yours very truly,   Henry Smith

ALS (WP, DLC).
¹ President of the United Methodist Conference of England.

From Bernard Mannes Baruch

My dear Mr. President: New York December 16th, 1920.

It is most difficult for me to express to you how deeply touched my associates and myself were by your generous letter commending our activities under your leadership during the war.¹ We shall never fail to be grateful to you for the opportunity you gave us all to be of service.

As for myself, particularly, you have showered so many marks of your approval and friendship upon me, that I feel myself to be the most fortunate of men.

You know, of course, how I feel about the conferment of the Distinguished Service Medal—how I feel that it was the men who served with me who are entitled to it and not myself. I accept it as a mark of your approval, through me, of their services, and as such it has an inestimable value to me.

I shall always be grateful to you not alone for the great opportunities for service which you gave me, but also for your having pointed out to me the finer and better things that men should be happy to live, and if necessary, to suffer for. You will always be to me, as to many millions of others, the leader of unfailing inspiration.

Your last address to Congress has given added courage and cheer to many who were faltering. To me the issue is certain, victory for your ideals is merely deferred. The contemplation of present economic and political difficulties must point to but one solution.

I wish on this occasion to give expression not alone to my admiration of your wonderful accomplishments, but also to my sincere appreciation of your splendid human qualities as a friend. I am looking forward to the time when there will be less crowded days for you, when perhaps I may have more opportunity to enjoy the inspiration of your society.

Again thanking you, Mr. President, for your many official and friendly kindnesses to me, I remain

Sincerely yours,   Bernard M Baruch

TLS (WP, DLC).
    [1] WW to BMB, Dec. 10, 1920.

Cleveland Hoadley Dodge to Bayard Dodge and Mary Williams Bliss Dodge[1]

Dearest Bayard and Mary: [New York] December 16, 1920.

. . . Since I wrote you last week, I have been in Washington, and whilst it was a great effort for me to go, I was more than repaid, and had an exceedingly interesting time. The meetings of the Carnegie Institution were more than usually interesting, and the entire Board, from all over the country, were present. As I wrote you, Mrs. Wilson was very anxious for me to stay at the White House, but with all the meetings I had, I thought it would be difficult, and more or less of an effort, so I arranged to go there to dinner Friday night. Unfortunately it was one of the nights when the President had his masseur, and he took his dinner up stairs early, but as I went early I had a good hour with him before I went down to dinner, and was perfectly delighted to find him in such good form. His voice was clear and natural, and his face looks fuller. He had some new limericks and good stories and was generally in good spirits and cursed out his enemies in grand form. Admiral and Mrs. Grayson were at dinner, and I had a long talk with him afterwards, when he walked back to the Hotel with me, and told me all about the President's condition. He is very much encouraged and is especially pleased that, instead of being knocked out by the elections, he has accepted the situation, and now that the agony is over, has steadily improved. They are looking for a house in Washington, and the President is planning to do a good deal of writing, and I hope will bring out something of very great value and interest. He asked particularly about all of you in the Near East, and sent his warmest love and regards to you. . . .

We think of you all a great deal at this Christmas time, and this letter bears all sorts of good wishes for Christmas and New Year's to you all.   Ever devotedly and affectionately yours,

[Cleveland H. Dodge]

¹ The deleted portions of this letter concern family affairs.

To Josephus Daniels

My dear Daniels: The White House 17 December, 1920

Thank you for the enclosed, which I am very glad to sign. I am very much pleased indeed that you thought me right with regard to the sentence in question.

Cordially and faithfully yours,   Woodrow Wilson

TLS (J. Daniels Papers, DLC).

From Newton Diehl Baker

Dear Mr. President: Washington. December 17, 1920.

When the Army reorganization bill was passed Congress, as the result of prolonged and exhaustive hearings, fixed the size of the Army at about 280,000 men. The language of the act is definite and departs from the previous practice of fixing a minimum peace-time strength with an elastic limit for expansion in emergency by establishing, with definite numbers, the commissioned and enlisted strength of the several arms and staff corps of the service, as, for instance, fixing the strength of enlisted men in the Infantry at 110,000, etc. The appropriation bill passed for the year 1920-21 provided pay and subsistence for only about 175,000 enlisted men, on the theory, expressed at the time in debate and in conference, that judging from previous experience it would not be possible for the War Department to recruit the Army beyond that number during the fiscal year.

The educational advantages now offered in the Army and a number of other circumstances have combined to bring Army recruiting substantially above any previous experience, and there are now about 208,000 enlisted men in the Army. This, of course, will necessitate a deficiency appropriation for pay and subsistence. Such deficiency estimates are authorized by law and are common in practice where recruiting exceeds expectations. There is in my judgment no question that Congress intended the War Department to urge recruiting and, if possible, to bring the Army to the authorized 280,000 enlisted strength, and there is no question of the entire legal right of the War Department to enlist men to the limit authorized under the language of the act.

In view of the serious financial situation which the new Administration faces rigid economies are being urged, and with them I have full sympathy. The Appropriations Committee of the House and the Military Affairs Committee of the House are evidently now disposed to feel that too large an army was authorized by the reorganization act, and that some sort of restriction should be passed by the Congress to prevent further enlistments and fixing a minimum size for the Army of approximately 175,000 enlisted men. For a variety of reasons I have not felt free to discontinue recruiting. The difficulties are—

1. An army smaller than 280,000 men will necessarily be an inefficient army, in view of the lessons of the World War with regard to the necessity for the training of officers in the staff control of substantial numbers of men.

2. An army of 280,000 men is less than the army now maintained by any of the great powers, including England, France, Italy and Japan.

3. The present state of affairs abroad, and particularly America's relations to Germany and to questions growing out of the rejection of the Versailles Treaty, have seemed to me too confused and complicated to justify any acquiescence on my part in the establishment of an army smaller than that directed by the reorganization act.

It seems clear from the present discussions in Congress, in the committees, and the trend being given to newspaper comment by suggestions from the Capitol, that the Republicans intend to pass affirmative legislation reducing the size of the Army. Under these circumstances two courses are open to me—(1) I can continue recruiting, which is now bringing large numbers of men by reason of the industrial depression in the country, or (2) I can have a conference in my office with Senator Wadsworth, Mr. Kahn,[1] and one or two others, lay the whole responsibility frankly on their shoulders as managers for the incoming Administration, and, if they assume the responsibility, discontinue recruiting, which will leave the Army on the 4th of March at about 190,000 men.

My judgment is that it is wiser for me to show a spirit of cooperation by calling such a conference as I have suggested. If I do not call such a conference the result seems quite certain to be legislation reducing the size of the authorized force. If I do call such a conference I shall of course have to say frankly to those who attend it some things which are mere summaries of general information with regard to the European situation, but which run the risk, incident to all such confidential conversations, of being distorted and misrepresented as disclosures on my part of troubling, if not threatening, international complications. With regard to the latter I think I can be discreet and tactful, but before asking for the conference I submit the question to you for advice. If you approve of the conference I will hold it at once; but if you think it unwise, I shall adhere to my present course and continue recruiting until affirmative legislation is passed, which of course I will at once begin to execute.   Respectfully yours,   Newton D. Baker

TLS (WP, DLC).
   [1] That is, James Wolcott Wadsworth, Jr., of New York, Republican, chairman of the Committee on Military Affairs; and Julius Kahn of California, Republican, chairman of the House Committee on Military Affairs.

From David Franklin Houston

Dear Mr. President: Washington December 17, 1920.

I received Mr. Tumulty's letter enclosing a letter dated December 14, 1920, from Mr. Thomas W. Lamont suggesting that the profits of the United States Sugar Equalization Board be made available for relief purposes, in part through the Chinese famine relief fund and in part through the fund for the relief of the starving children of Europe. Mr. Lamont's letter is returned herewith.

I have carefully considered the suggestion and feel clear that you should not recommend to Congress any legislation to make the profits of the Sugar Equalization Board available for these purposes. The United States Government is the sole stockholder in the United States Sugar Equalization Board, whose $5,000,000 of capital stock was purchased out of the fund for the National Security and Defense. The profits resulting from the operations of the Board, amounting to between $35,000,000 and $45,000,000 are not, as Mr. Lamont suggests, lying idle and unemployed at this time. About $40,000,000 of the funds of the Sugar Equalization Board are invested in Treasury certificates of indebtedness and the Board has already officially advised the Treasury that in about two months' time the winding up of its affairs will have progressed sufficiently to permit the payment of its assets into the Treasury on final liquidation. The payment of the assets of the Board into the Treasury will result in a corresponding retirement of the public debt. To divert the profits of the Board for relief purposes would, of course, make this debt retirement impossible and just as truly take money out of the Treasury as if a direct appropriation were made by Congress. The fundamental objection to Mr. Lamont's suggestion is that a joint resolution which took the form of authorizing the use of the profits of the Sugar Equalization Board for relief purposes would conceal both from Congress and from the public the fact that any such action would involve a payment of moneys from the public treasury, and thus tend to secure consideration for the proposition which could not be secured if the matter were presented in its true light as an appropriation of public moneys. Something might be said for a direct appropriation of moneys by Congress as an act of charity toward the suffering peoples of China and Europe, but I think there is nothing whatever to be said for an indirect diversion of public moneys for these purposes. You will recall that in your Annual Message to Congress this year you especially emphasized the importance of avoiding just such action, that is to say, practices which take money out of the Treasury by indirect or indefinite authorizations for expenditures.

Reduced to its simplest terms, the proposal made by Mr. Lamont is not unlike the many other proposals which have been urged during the past few months to give relief to various classes or sections by indirect use of the public funds, as, for example, the agitation by the farmers for legislation taking the earnings of the Federal Reserve Banks which will be paid into the Treasury at the beginning of 1921 and making them available for loans on live stock and staple agricultural products, the proposals by various western agricultural associations to take the profits of the United States Grain Corporation for similar agricultural loans, the insistent requests for Government deposits to assist farmers and others to hold commodities, the repeated suggestions that the December 15th installment of income and profits taxes ought to be postponed in order to assist business, and the proposed revival of the War Finance Corporation. All of these proposals would take money out of the Treasury indirectly without an appropriation, and in the aggregate might have resulted in the expenditure of hundreds of millions of dollars of the public funds.

I ought to add that, from the point of view of the Treasury, I think it would be unfortunate to have to recommend even a direct appropriation of public funds for relief purposes. The burdens already resting upon the Treasury are so great and so many demands for Governmental aid in this country are being pressed upon the Administration and upon Congress at this time, that I should be greatly disturbed if any concerted effort were made to secure public funds to relieve distressing situations of this character abroad, which should properly be met by private contributions or such organizations as the American Red Cross.

Faithfully yours,   D. F. Houston

TLS (WP, DLC).

From Milenko R. Vesnić

Belgrade December 17, 1920.

Never the Nobel prize has been attributed to a more deserving man. I therefore take the liberty of congratulating you most sincerely.[1]   Faithfully yours,   Milenko R. Vesnitch.

T telegram (WP, DLC).
[1] "Please ask the State Department to request our Minister at Belgrade to thank M. Vesnitch for this. The President." WW to [JPT], c. Dec. 17, 1920, TL (WP, DLC).

Joseph Patrick Tumulty to Edith Bolling Galt Wilson, with Enclosure

Dear Mrs. Wilson: The White House 17 December 1920.

I tried this afternoon to reach you by telephone but was informed that you had left for Fort Myer. My purpose was to have you tell the President that I had finally made up my mind with reference to his generous offer of the Chief Justiceship of the Court of Customs Appeals, and that I had decided not to accept it.

I have considered the whole matter of my future and have decided that with all the responsibilities I have, the only fair thing to my family is for me to resume the practice of the law. I had no doubt of my confirmation by the Senate for Senator Harding, through Ray Baker, informed that he would see to it that I was confirmed.

I will drop over tomorrow and tell the President how greatly I appreciate his many kindnesses to me.

With warmest regards,   Sincerely yours,   Tumulty

P.S.—I intend forming no partnership but merely to "hang out my shingle on my own hook."

TLS (C. L. Swem Coll., NjP).

ENCLOSURE

Washington, D. C. 17 December 1920.

STATEMENT BY SECRETARY TUMULTY:

I have just informed the President of my decision not to accept the position of Chief Justice of the Court of Customs Appeals which he so generously tendered me some weeks ago. I had no doubt of my confirmation by the Senate for I had received assurances from leading Republicans that there would be no impedi-

532 DECEMBER 18, 1920

ment placed in the way of it. I have concluded, therefore, to resume on March 5, 1921, the practice of the law in Washington.

T MS (J. P. Tumulty Papers, DLC).

To Newton Diehl Baker

My dear Mr. Secretary: [The White House] 18 December, 1920

I have your letter of December seventeenth about the recruiting quandary, and must admit that I hesitate as to your judgment, but on the whole I so profoundly distrust Wadsworth and Kahn that I hardly believe anything practical could could be made out of a conference with them. It would, of course, quiet feelings and perhaps create sentiments that would be serviceable, but I do not see that it would serve any other purpose. I am inclined to the judgment, therefore, that the best thing for you to do is to act under existing law and proceed with the recruiting. If anything should happen, the country will certainly be grateful to us for having gone as far as we could by way of adequate military preparation.

With warmest regard,
Cordially and faithfully yours,   [Woodrow Wilson]

CCL (WP, DLC).

To Thomas William Lamont

My dear Friend: The White House 18 December, 1920

Thank you for your letter of December fifteenth. As a matter of fact, Dodge did not speak to me about the use of government funds for the famine relief, and I have looked about in vain for any fund that I am at liberty to divert for that purpose. I wish there were such a fund.

With warmest regard,
Cordially yours,   Woodrow Wilson

TLS (T. W. Lamont Papers, MH-BA).

To Ray Stannard Baker

My dear Baker: [The White House] 18 December, 1920

I have read with the deepest interest and appreciation your letter of December sixteenth from the Cosmos Club. It is clear to me that it will not be possible for me to write anything such as you suggest, but I believe that you could do it admirably, and your little book, as you call it, would form an excellent nucleus from which the other could be developed. I would be perfectly willing to give you access to the so-called minutes, though they are not really such, of the "Council of Four," but I am wondering if this is the time that would best afford you an opportunity to examine and work on them. I am going to move, of course, to other premises after the fourth of March, and it occurs to me that I could give you access to material there more readily than I could here. What do you think of that?

With warmest regard and deep affection.

Sincerely and cordially yours,   [Woodrow Wilson]

CCL (WP, DLC).

From the Shorthand Diary of Charles Lee Swem

18 December, 1920

This morning the President replied to a letter from Ray Stannard Baker saying that he himself would never attempt to write "what happened in Paris" at the peace conference but that he hoped Baker himself would do it as he suggests in his letter. I asked the President why he didn't do it himself as nobody else would ever be able adequately to tell just exactly what did happen and he said that he never would; that nothing comes with such bad grace from a man as a narrative of that sort; and besides he would have to fill it too full of acid—it would be as bitter as the memoirs of John [Quincy] Adams. The President has frequently commented upon the acidity of Adams and his memoirs.

JRT transcript (WC, NjP) of CLSsh (C. L. Swem Coll., NjP).

From William Bauchop Wilson

My dear Mr. President: Washington December 18, 1920.

May I suggest to you the advisability of extending clemency to Eugene V. Debbs. In my judgment a sufficient amount of time has now elapsed since the signing of the Armistice to enable sentiment to be created in his favor as a martyr if his incarceration is prolonged. So far as I know no group of his Socialist associates is now pressing for his release, and if he could be promptly pardoned and quietly returned to his home before they were apprised of what had taken place, it would avoid the possibility of disturbing demonstrations.

I sincerely hope that you can see your way clear to grant clemency at this time.   Faithfully yours,   W B Wilson

TLS (WP, DLC).

From Charles Zeller Klauder

My dear Mr. President: Philadelphia December 18th, 1920.

Yesterday Mr. Bolling informed me by telephone of your purchase of a house. This morning I received your letter of the 16th inst.

I may here repeat what I said to Mr. Bolling that I am very glad you have made so satisfactory a purchase. Knowing the character of Mr. Wood's work as I do, I should expect it to be well planned and of good design.

With respect to the changes you contemplate, it is entirely fitting that the Architect who designed the house should have charge of them. Particularly is this so if a garage is to be built, for its style should, manifestly, completely harmonize with that of the house. In the case of alteration work, it is desirable that the Architect be on the spot.

Regarding the suggestions you make in your letter upon the plan of the house, I will write you further in a few days.

Sincerely yours,   Chas Z Klauder

TLS (WP, DLC).

From Jessie Woodrow Wilson Sayre

Darling Father,   [Cambridge, Mass.] Dec. 18, 1920

Many happy returns of today. I am thinking of you all day but especially this evening when dearest Edith became a beautiful and altogether lovely part of our little circle. Give her my love and a kiss from me.

Her dear letters with the precious gifts for us all have just come and we want to thank you so much. I will tell you in a later letter or when I see you all just what we have done with them. I wish you might be here for the children to thank you themselves or rather that you might see their joy in them.

Again with dearest love and thanks to you both and wishing you all a very happy and blessed Christmas

Ever devotedly   Jessie.

ALS (WC, NjP).

To William Bauchop Wilson

My dear Mr. Secretary: The White House 20 December, 1920

I, of course, appreciate the considerations which led you to urge the extension of clemency to Debs, but I am sorry that my judgment differs from yours in the matter and that I do not deem it wise to pardon him. I always differ from you with hesitation and regret, greatly trusting your judgment as I always do.

Cordially and sincerely yours,   Woodrow Wilson

TLS (received from Mary A. Strohecker).

To Bernard Mannes Baruch

My dear Baruch: The White House 20 December, 1920

Your letter of December sixteenth has touched me deeply. You may be sure that it is a delight to me to avail myself of any opportunity to show how much I honor and value you not only as a public servant, but as a friend, one of the best friends I ever had.

Affectionately yours,   Woodrow Wilson

TLS (B. M. Baruch Papers, NjP).

From Norman Hezekiah Davis

My dear Mr. President: Washington December 20, 1920.

On December second our Commissioner at Berlin[1] reported the arrival of a naval lieutenant[2] from the United States with instructions to report to the Commissioner "for duty involving actual flying, in sitting on Aeronautic Commission of Control in Berlin." The Commissioner requested definite confirmation from the Navy Department in view of some doubt raised by the Lieutenant's instructions, and offered the following suggestions:

(1) "In view of our position on the treaty it would appear advisable that (Lieutenant) Culbert's position on the Control Commission should be that of an observer only; that he should take no action and give his approval to no decisions on which he has not previously consulted the American Government. Is such an interpretation approved?

(2) "In order that it may be made clear that the United States is not to be held responsible for decisions taken in Culbert's presence, but to which he has withheld formal adhesion, I suggest the propriety of my giving General Masterman[3] (British Chair-

man) a written statement of Culbert's position as outlined in the foregoing paragraph at the time of his presentation."

It should be stated also that the War Department has detailed two officers to represent it on the Commission.

The Commissioner's telegram has been submitted to Secretaries Daniels and Baker and the enclosed instruction[4] has been prepared, based on the desires expressed by the Navy and War Departments. The Navy and War Departments have felt all along that we should be represented on the Commission, at least by unofficial observers, but in view of your recent instructions concerning future participation of the United States on Treaty commissions in Europe, I have deemed it advisable to consult you before sending the instruction to the Commissioner at Berlin enclosed.

Faithfully yours,   Norman H. Davis

TLS (WP, DLC).
  [1] That is, Ellis Loring Dresel.
  [2] Lt. Frederick Paul Culbert.
  [3] Air Commodore Edward Alexander Dimsdale Masterman, president of the Inter-Allied Aeronautical Commission of Control (Germany) since 1919.
  [4] NHD to Amembassy, Paris, "for Dresel, Berlin," Dec. 15, 1920, T telegram (WP, DLC), saying that the Navy Department requested that efforts be made to obtain for Culbert the privilege of being present in an unofficial capacity at the sittings of the Aeronautic Commission of Control and that Dresel should introduce Culbert to Masterman. Culbert would be only an observer and would take no action nor give his approval of any action except upon the advice of the United States Government.

From Homer Stillé Cummings

Stamford, Connecticut
My dear Mr. President: 20 December 1920.

I have not written you since the election nor was there any need, apart from the pleasure it would give me, that I should do so. To speak temperately of the result was not an altogether simple matter. I got some solace, however, from re-reading John Bright's letter to Richard Cobden[1] written when things, in their latter years, seemed to have gone pretty well to smash.

I am writing to-day to let you know how proud and happy I am that the Nobel Peace Prize has been awarded to you. It is as if the voice of history was already speaking.

I extend to you and to Mrs. Wilson Christmas greetings and best wishes for the New Year.

Sincerely yours,   Homer S. Cummings

TLS (WP, DLC).
  [1] Of April 16, 1857, printed in John Morley, *The Life of Richard Cobden* (2 vols., London and Boston, 1881), II, 194-96.

From the Diary of Ray Stannard Baker

Dec 21.

I had a letter from Mr. Wilson saying that he would like to have me help with the book—& suggesting that I come to Washington after he retires from the White House in March. This is a great chance! I can perhaps write the standard American book upon the Peace Conference.[1]

[1] He did of course write *Woodrow Wilson and World Settlement* (3 vols., Garden City, N. Y., 1922). Subsequent documents in this series will reveal Baker's work on this first history of the peace conference based upon the materials in the Wilson Papers and the degree to which Wilson collaborated with Baker in the project.

From Samuel Gompers, with Enclosure

Sir: Washington, D. C. December 21, 1920.

You are undoubtedly aware of the conditions which prevail in the relations between the government of the United States and of Santo Domingo. I have had the opportunity of information and advice from representative labor men of that Republic, and the anxiety they not only express for themselves but that of a large part of the people of Santo Domingo, and I am informed that there is a fervent desire on the part of the people there for the re-establishment of their own government.

Early in the year I appointed a commission of two labor men to visit Santo Domingo and there make an investigation of affairs. Upon their return they made an exceedingly interesting report which was later submitted to the convention of the American Federation of Labor, which at its session, after deliberate consideration, adopted the resolution urging that everything should be done within our power to "bring about the return of the Dominican government to the Dominican people."

Recently a delegation of labor men from Santo Domingo reached the United States on their way to the Fourth Congress of the Pan American Federation of Labor which is to open at Mexico City, Mexico, January 10, 1921. In turn this commission have stated that the situation has but very little changed, particularly in the desire of the people for the return of the government to the people of Santo Domingo. I asked that the commission should set forth in a letter to me what they have in mind. They have done so and today I am in receipt of a letter of which the enclosed is a true copy.

The American Federation of Labor has selected a delegation of five of which I am to be one, to attend the Pan-American Federation of Labor meeting, and with my associates I shall leave Washington on January 3, 1921.

Inasmuch as the information in the letter conveys the thought that Mr. Francisco Henriquez Carbajal is persona non grata to the American Government, I am acting upon the suggestion made in the letter which is but a reiteration of what was said to me orally, that I might tender myself as a mediator—as one who might be helpful in the solution of the existing situation.

I think you know, Mr. President, that it is not my desire to be an interloper in any matter or to meddle in affairs which do not primarily affect me. Knowing that I endeavor invariably to be of service to my fellows and to my country, and firmly believing that some better understanding may be reached upon this mooted and important question, I make bold to say that I regard myself to be at your disposal in any way which you may deem wise, practical and helpful.

It would have a great moral influence were it possible that something tangible may be done in the premises and that I might be enabled to carry the message to that effect to the delegates who are to assemble from various Pan-American republics at the Pan-American Federation of Labor meeting in Mexico City.

I hold myself in readiness for a conference with you or with such other governmental agent to whom you may prefer to refer the subject.

Wishing you the compliments of the Season, with years of health and happiness in store for you, I have the honor to remain,

Yours very respectfully,   Saml Gompers.

TLS (WP, DLC).

ENCLOSURE

J. E. Kunhardt[1] to Samuel Gompers

Dear Sir and Brother: Washington, D. C., December 21, 1920.

It is our understanding that the American Government is making ready to take the necessary measures toward the restoration of the government of the Dominican Republic to the Dominican people, but that in matters of form and detail an understanding has not been reached between the State Department and the President de jure of the Dominican Republic, Mr. Francisco Henriquez y Carbajal; either because the latter does not feel that he is sufficiently authorized to accept the conditions laid down by the American Government or because the American Government sees a persona non grata in Mr. Henriquez y Carbajal. Therefore, we believe that this is the opportune moment for the President of the American Federation of Labor to act on this matter in behalf of the Dominican people, thus following the instructions of the Montreal Convention to "do everything in its power to being [bring] about the return of the Dominican government to the Dominican people."

For the above reasons, I request in the name of the Dominican Federation of Labor that you offer your services to the Honorable Woodrow Wilson, President of the United States, to the end that an agreement be reached in this matter and the Dominican people be returned their own government according to the principles of justice.

If the American Federation of Labor is able to bring about an understanding between the Dominican people and the United States Government, no better gift could be presented to the Pan-American Labor Congress which convenes in Mexico City next January, for friendship and confidence will be cemented to its greatest magnitude among the peoples of the Western Hemisphere and Pan-Americanism will be firmly established.

Fraternally yours,   (signed) J. E. Kunhardt.

TCL (WP, DLC).
[1] He wrote as a representative of the Dominican Federation of Labor and chairman of the Dominican delegation to the fourth congress of the Pan American Federation of Labor.

To Norman Hezekiah Davis

My dear Mr. Secretary: The White House 22 December, 1920

I have your letter of December twentieth about some sort of representation of the United States on the Aeronautic Commission of Control in Berlin. My judgment in this matter is the same as in other similar ones. I do not think that we ought to be represented in any way or to any extent whatever, and Lieutenant Culbert's authorizations, whatever they are, ought to be cancelled.

Cordially and faithfully yours,   Woodrow Wilson

TLS (SDR, RG 59, 763.72119/10830, DNA).

To Alexander Meiklejohn

My dear Meiklejohn: The White House 22 December, 1920

It was a real pleasure to get your letter of December fifth, and its contents cheered and pleased me mightily. I am glad you are getting a good rest and hope that you will come back refreshed and ready for the most enjoyable kind of work.

With many pleasant recollections of our too infrequent meetings,   Cordially and sincerely yours,   Woodrow Wilson

TLS (WP, DLC).

To Homer Stillé Cummings

My dear Cummings: The White House 22 December, 1920

Your letter of December twentieth pleased and cheered me very much. I think you know, at least I hope you know, how I value your friendship and how highly I estimate your services to the party and to the country, and I shall always follow you with affectionate friendship.

Cordially and faithfully yours,   Woodrow Wilson

TLS (H. S. Cummings Papers, ViU).

From John Spargo, with Enclosure

Old Bennington Vermont
Dear Mr. President: December 22, 1920

It may have been brought to your attention that along with many other forms of hatred and prejudice there is a wave of anti-Semitism surging over the country. Unfortunately, the evidence is all too conclusive that there is an organized propaganda of this vicious and malignant spirit, and, as is always the case, it is linked up with much else that is reactionary and subversive of the best in our national life.

It has seemed to many of us that this un-American propaganda ought to be vigorously rebuked by citizens of Gentile birth and Christian faith; that it should not be left to the Jews alone to make this protest. If the Jews alone are to speak out against it we shall have pro-Semitism as well as anti-Semitism. There ought to be neither in this land of ours.

The annexed protest has been signed by 100 of the leading men and women of the country who are of the Christian faith. They represent all Christian denominations, the leaders in literature, art, the sciences, education, and so on. Since it would not—I suppose—be proper to solicit the signature of the President of the United States to such a document, I am presuming to ask you if you will not be good enough to do the next best thing, that is, to write a letter or brief message, in the spirit of the little protest and let me have it to be given to the press at the same time as the protest is released. I feel quite certain that you will thoroughly approve the spirit of our memorial and our condemnation of anti-Semitism as subversive of our American traditions, ideals and institutions.

Permit me, Mr. President, to avail myself of this opportunity to assure you of my constant confidence and regard, and to wish you the compliments of the season.

Very sincerely yours,   John Spargo.

TLS (WP, DLC).

E N C L O S U R E

The undersigned, citizens of Gentile birth and Christian faith, view with profound regret and disapproval the appearance in this country of what appears to be an organized campaign of anti-Semitism, conducted in close conformity to, and apparent cooperation with, similar campaigns in Europe. We regret exceedingly the publication of a number of books, pamphlets and newspaper articles designed to foster distrust and suspicion of our fellow-citizens of Jewish ancestry and faith—distrust and suspicion of their loyalty and their patriotism.

These publications, to which wide circulation is being given, are thus introducing into our national political life a new and dangerous spirit, one that is wholly at variance with our best traditions and ideals and subversive of our system of government. American citizenship and American democracy are thus challenged aud [and] menaced. We protest against this organized campaign of prejudice and hatred, not only because of its manifest injustice to those against whom it is directed, but also, and especially, because we are convinced that it is wholly incompatible with loyal and intelligent American citizenship. The logical outcome of the success of such a campaign must necessarily be the division of our citizens along racial and religious lines, and, ultimately, the introduction of religious tests and qualifications to determine citizenship.

The loyalty and patriotism of our fellow citizens of the Jewish faith is equal to that of any part of our people, and requires no defense at our hands. From the foundation of this Republic down to the recent World War, men and women of Jewish ancestry and faith have taken an honorable part in building up this great nation and maintaining its prestige and honor among the nations of the world. There is not the slightest justification, therefore, for a campaign of anti-Semitism in this country.

Anti-Semitism is almost invariably associated with lawlessness and with brutality and injustice. It is also invariably found closely intertwined with other sinister forces, particularly those which are corrupt, reactionary and oppressive.

We believe it should not be left to men and women of Jewish faith to fight this evil, but that it is in a very special sense the duty of citizens who are not Jews by ancestry or faith. We therefore make earnest protest against this vicious propaganda, and call upon our fellow citizens of Gentile birth and Christian faith to unite their efforts to ours to the end that it may be crushed. In particular, we call upon all those who are moulders of public opinion—the clergy and ministers of all Christian churches, publicists, teachers, editors and statesmen—to strike at this un-American and un-Christian agitation.[1]   Signed:

Confidential: Please sign above and mail at once to
John Spargo
Old Bennington
Vermont.

Printed copy (WP, DLC).
    [1] This statement was made public on January 16, 1921; it was printed, *inter alia*, in the *New York Times*, January 17, 1921. In addition to Wilson, it was signed, among others, by William Howard Taft, William Cardinal O'Connell, Lyman Abbott, Jane Addams, Newton D. Baker, Ray Stannard Baker, Charles A. Beard, Albert J. Beveridge, W. E. B. DuBois, Mabel T. Boardman, Evangeline C. Booth, William Jennings Bryan, Nicholas Murray Butler, Bainbridge Colby, George Creel, Clarence Darrow, Raymond B. Fosdick, Robert Frost, Harry A. Garfield, Lindley M. Garrison, John Palmer Gavit, Martin H. Glynn, John Grier Hibben, Hamilton Holt, Frederic C. Howe, David Starr Jordan, Paul U. Kellog, Henry Churchill King, Franklin K. Lane, Robert Lansing, Julia C. Lathrop, Frederick Lynch, Edwin T. Meredith, Louis F. Post, Charles Edward Russell, Jacob Gould Schurman, John Spargo, Ida M. Tarbell, and George W. Wickersham.

To Norman Hezekiah Davis

My dear Mr. Secretary: [The White House] 23 December, 1920

You have no doubt heard from George Creel of his anxiety about certain papers connected with the soviet regime in Russia which have been in my custody.[1] I am sending you enclosed what I believe to be those papers. I was not very careful in putting them away and find that during my illness my memory had become very much confused as to what I did with them, but I have gone through such receptacles as I thought might contain them and the result is I am sending you what, as I have said, I suppose to be the papers referred to. They clearly belong in your department, for such disposition as you think wise to make of them.

Cordially and faithfully yours,   Woodrow Wilson

CCL (WP, DLC).
    [1] Wilson had earlier forgotten about these, the so-called Sisson Papers. See JPT to EBW, March 26, 1920 (second letter of that date), Vol. 65.

To Charles Zeller Klauder

My dear Mr. Klauder: The White House 23 December, 1920

I appreciate very much your thoughtful kindness in sending me the little portfolio of reproduced drawings. They were just what I wanted.

Do you remember a picture I showed you of a door with wrought-iron hinges and big nails at Sulgrave Manor?[1] Why would not the entrance from the road to the western cloister be a good place to reproduce that door, or something like it?

We shall be very much interested, when you come down again, to show you the house which we have purchased, and shall hope that your judgment will confirm ours as to its convenience and its excellence as a structure.

With the best wishes of the season from all of us,
          Cordially and sincerely yours,   Woodrow Wilson

TLS (WC, NjP).
[1] Home of George Washington's ancestors from 1539 to 1626, in the village of Sulgrave in southwestern Northamptonshire. It had been purchased by a British committee and presented to the Sulgrave Institution in 1914 to commemorate a century of peace between Great Britain and the United States.

Three Letters from Norman Hezekiah Davis

My dear Mr. President: Washington December 23, 1920.

I beg to enclose a copy of a telegram from the American Embassy at Christiania[1] embodying a message for you to the effect that the Minister has been informed by the Secretary of the Nobel Committee that he has written you fully in regard to the award of the peace prize; that the money award would be sent December 18, from Stockholm; and that the medal and certificate of award were being forwarded by the pouch leaving Christiania the same day.   Faithfully yours,   Norman H. Davis

[1] A. G. Schmedeman to SecState, Dec. 18, 1920, T telegram (WP, DLC).

My dear Mr. President: Washington December 23, 1920

Ambassador Johnson has just informed the Department in a confidential telegram that consideration is being given to the desire of the Duke D'Aosta,[1] cousin of the King, to make a visit of ceremony to the United States. Mr. Johnson reports that he understands that the King and the Prime Minister are in favor of the Duke's visit being made as soon as possible, but the newly appointed Ambassador, Senator Ricci, urges that the visit be delayed.

The Ambassador asks whether the Department has any wishes in the matter.

I hasten to bring this matter to your attention. In view of Mr. Colby's absence, it might be considered that the moment is not entirely opportune for such a visit. If it is your feeling that consideration of the matter should be postponed, I can readily find a suitable excuse for Ambassador Johnson discreetly and informally giving an intimation to this effect. I will be very grateful if you will let me know your wishes in the matter.

I am, my dear Mr. President,

Faithfully yours,   Norman H. Davis

¹ Emanuele Filiberto, Duke of Aosta.

My dear Mr. President: Washington December 23, 1920.

I have not felt like releasing the permits signed by you for the telephone cable from Key West to Habana without knowing whether you felt perfectly comfortable and were satisfied that the granting of the permits would not be inconsistent with the position taken in the Western Union difficulty. As I have not received a reply from you to my letter of December fifteenth I assume that you are now satisfied that everything is all right, but I would appreciate some word from you to that effect.

I have been laid up for a few days but am back on the job again.

Faithfully yours,   Norman H. Davis

TLS (WP, DLC).

From Ray Stannard Baker

Amherst Massachusetts

My dear Mr. President: December 23, 1920.

I am delighted to have your letter of December 18th. Not only because it opens the way to what I believe to be an important and necessary work, but because of the personal confidence which it implies. This means a great deal to me.

I think the plan of delaying the work until after March 4th, is excellent: giving time and space for a really adequate consideration of the material. To develop that great scene from the true American point of view, and in the fundamental American spirit (now unhappily obscured) will, it seems to me, be a great and useful thing to do. I am very keen about it. It seems to me an opportunity not only to describe what happened during one of the most notable conferences in history, the truly dramatic quality of which no one has yet seemed to sense, but to exhibit America to herself (she sadly needs it!) against the vast grim background of European diplomacy and European politics.

Let me wish you and Mrs. Wilson the warmest greetings for this season and for the New Year, which is certain to yield us so much of interest and of beauty.

Cordially yours,   Ray Stannard Baker

TLS (WP, DLC).

From Charles Zeller Klauder

My dear Mr. President: Philadelphia December 23rd, 1920.

Further in answer to your letter of December 16th, I am sending you under a separate cover, plans dated December 23rd[1] which incorporate the changes suggested by you and such improvements as my studies have made possible and perhaps desirable.

The western end of the building has been arranged to provide a stair from the study to the suite of rooms above and, in order to show the full range of such a stair as you mentioned, I have shown the possibility of making it connect your own room with a valet's room in the basement, if you should wish to provide for such an eventuality. To place the door to this stair in the dressing room instead of your own is, of course, equally possible.

The eastern end of the first floor shows a more economical arrangement of kitchen services with the servant's hall placed on an intermediate level between that floor and the basement. The garage has been enlarged to hold two cars, and the chauffeur has been given quarters in the basement, similar to those suggested as possible for the valet at the western end of the house. This would leave separate, the south side of the central portion of the basement for the female help, since access to the furnace rooms can be had down the chauffeur's stair.

On the second floor above the porte cochere, there is now a fair sized sitting room which in its extreme dimensions is 14' x 19'. I suggest that it would be very interesting to enter this room through a wide arch centering exactly on the upper portion of the great hall. This would make it possible for one to stand in the bay of the great hall on the first floor, and look up through this arch to the open timber trusses supporting the roof, which in this case, become the ceiling. This would give a 50' vista to the north wall. The side walls of this room would have low windows in contrast with the higher one in the gable end. In a corner of the sitting room, we propose a rather unusual but most attractive fireplace. Although it can well have another location, I have in this room, tentatively, placed the safe which you mentioned as desirable.

I take this opportunity to acknowledge the receipt of Davies' "Old Cottages etc. in Sussex," Gotch's "Early Renaissance Architecture in England" and Nash's "Mansions in England of the Old Time"[2] which you were so kind as to return a few days since.

With the Compliments of the Season, I am

Sincerely yours,   Chas Z Klauder

TLS (WP, DLC).
[1] These plans and drawings are missing in WP, DLC.
[2] W. Galsworthy Davie, *Old Cottages and Farmhouses in Kent and Sussex* (London, 1900); John Alfred Gotch, *Early Renaissance Architecture in England* (London, 1901); and Joseph Nash, *The Mansions of England in the Olden Time* (4 vols., London, 1839-1849).

William Bauchop Wilson to Joseph Patrick Tumulty, with Enclosure

My dear Mr. Tumulty: Washington December 23, 1920.

Replying to your letter of the 11th instant, asking that I suggest a reply to Mr. Gowan, the Department of Labor has taken the matter of the reinstatement of the men Mr. Gowan is interested in up for consideration with the representatives of the Railway Brotherhoods and the railway management and finds that nothing further can be done towards the reinstatement of these men. I therefore advise that a letter similar to the one herewith inclosed be sent to Mr. Gowan.

Mr. Gowan's letter to the President[1] is herewith returned.

Sincerely yours,   W B Wilson

TLS (WP, DLC).
[1] That is, E. A. Gowen to WW, Dec. 9, 1920.

E N C L O S U R E

Dear Sir:

Referring to the subject matter of your letter of December 9th, I have been advised by the Secretary of Labor that he has interviewed the representatives of the Railway Brotherhoods and railway management relative to securing the reinstatement of the men you represent and he finds that nothing further can be done in that direction.   Respectfully yours,[1]

T MS (WP, DLC).
[1] This letter was typed up and sent as WW to E. A. Gowen, Dec. 27, 1920, TLS (Letterpress Books, WP, DLC).

ADDENDUM

Gilbert Monell Hitchcock to Cary Travers Grayson[1]

My dear Doctor Grayson: [Washington] October 20, 1919

From time to time suggestions are made to me that the President is or may be disturbed over the treaty situation. It occurs to me therefore that it might be wise for you to assure him on my responsibility that there is no occasion at the present time for consulting him and that there probably will not be for a week or ten days. This week will be taken up quite largely with amendments, and even after the fight on reservations begins my judgment is that it will be some time before there is any necessity of submitting any matter to him.   Yours very sincerely,   G M Hitchcock

TLS (received from James Gordon Grayson and Cary T. Grayson, Jr.).
[1] This is the letter referred to as missing in n. 1 to C. T. Grayson to G. M. Hitchcock, Oct. 23, 1919, Vol. 63.

INDEX

NOTE ON THE INDEX

THE alphabetically arranged analytical table of contents at the front of the volume eliminates duplication, in both contents and index, of references to certain documents, such as letters. Letters are listed in the contents alphabetically by name, and chronologically within each name by page. The subject matter of all letters is, of course, indexed. The Editorial Notes and Wilson's writings are listed in the contents chronologically by page. In addition, the subject matter of both categories is indexed. The index covers all references to books and articles mentioned in text or notes. Footnotes are indexed. Page references to footnotes which place a comma between the page number and "n" cite both text and footnote, thus: "418,n1." On the other hand, absence of the comma indicates reference to the footnote only, thus: "59n1"—the page number denoting where the footnote appears.

The index supplies the fullest known form of names and, for the Wilson and Axson families, relationships as far down as cousins. Persons referred to by nicknames or shortened forms of names can be identified by reference to entries for these forms of the names.

All entries consisting of page numbers only and which refer to concepts, issues, and opinions (such as democracy, the tariff, money trust, leadership, and labor problems), are references to Wilson's speeches and writings.

Four cumulative contents-index volumes are now in print: Volume 13, which covers Volumes 1-12, Volume 26, which covers Volumes 14-25, Volume 39, which covers Volumes 27-38, and Volume 52, which covers Volumes 40-49 and 51.

INDEX

Abbott, Lyman, 246n2, 542n1
Abraham Lincoln (play, Drinkwater), 112
Academy of Music (Philadelphia): proposed lecture series at, 31-32, 40, 382n1
Addams, Jane, 542n1
Adee, Alvey Augustus: praised for fifty years of government service, 102, 104
Adelman, H., 421,n1
Adelsburg: and Adriatic settlement, 365
Adriatic question: Lloyd George on, 45; WW on, 307-308; R. U. Johnson on, 322-23; Colby hears of settlement at Rapallo, 364-65; WW on settlement, 367; N. H. Davis on settlement, 377; settlement of, 382, 402; Colby tries to get more information on settlement, 388-89; see also Rapallo, Treaty of
Advancing Hour (Hapgood): WW sent copy of, 28,n1, 30
Aeronautic Commission of Control: see Inter-Allied Aeronautical Commission of Control
After Election (*Springfield Republican*), 258,n2
Aftermath of War: Bainbridge Colby and Wilsonian Diplomacy, 1920-1921 (Smith), 5n2, 19n1, 430n1
agriculture: appeal for federal assistance, 36-38,n2,3; farmers' organization requests hearing with WW, 224; prices and politics, 242-43,n5; and farmers' credit request, 243-45; farm prices discussed at Cabinet, 445; and WW's State of the Union Message, 489; cattle raisers wish to see WW, 521; see also cotton industry
Aharonian, Avetis, 65, 86n1
Alabama: coal strike in, 263-65
Åland Islands, 138n1
Åland Islands Commission: suggestions for and appointment to, 212,n1,2, 229, 230-31, 253, 263, 265, 304
Alaska: J. Daniels and J. B. Payne visit, 4,n1
Albania, 45,n6; WW on, 307-308
Alderman, Edwin Anderson, 234, 258
Alençar, Augusto Cochrane de, 179,n3
Alexander, Henry Eckert, 352n1
Alexander, Joshua Willis, 82n1, 87, 175; wishes to be appointed to Shipping Board, 7, 195; on Jones bill, 60; on European reconstruction and financing of raw materials, 111
Alexandropol, Russia, 422, 437
Aliotti, Baron Carlo Alberto, 339,n3
All-American Cable Company, 221
Allen, Texas, 445
Allenstein (now Olsztyn Province, Poland), 225,n1
Allyn and Bacon Publishers, 242n1
Alvarado, Salvador, 142,n1, 372,n2
Alvord, E. M., 205,n1, 200
Amaral, Silvino Gurgél do, 211-12,n5
American Federation of Labor, 5n3; and general amnesty for "political" prisoners, 120,n1, 231-32, 516; self-government for

Dominican Republic, 537, 539
American Hebrew, 130,n1
Americanization of Edward Bok: The Autobiography of a Dutch Boy Fifty Years After, 131-32,n1
American Legion, 5n1,2; WW's message to, 6
American Monthly, 248n1
American Red Cross, 133n3; relief to Ireland and WW's response, 512-13, 518
Amherst College, 478n1
Anaconda Copper Mining Co., 133n3
Anatolia, 47, 429-30
Anderson, George Weston: on WW resubmitting treaty to Senate, 390,n1, 390-91; WW's reply, 402
Andrews, Charles McLean, 315,n3
Andrews, Philip, 26n1, 59
Angol-French loan of 1915, 166n1
Anthracite Coal Commission, 105-108, 217; majority and minority reports of, 64,n1; W. B. Wilson on report of, 66-69; WW on accepting award with minor changes, 69-70; minority report acceptance urged by United Mine Workers group, 75; W. B. Wilson on WW standing firm on decision by, 75, 76-77
Anthracite Wage Scale Committee, 67, 69-70, 76
anti-Semitism in the U.S.: and H. Ford, 130n1; I. Landman on, 130-31; J. Spargo on, 540-42
Aosta, Duke of (Emanuele Filiberto): proposed visit to U.S., 543-44,n1
Appropriations, Committee on (House of Reps.), 528
Arbe Island (now Rab Island, Yugoslavia), 447,n3
Argentina: and recognition of Bolivia, 135, 480; on U.S. in Santo Domingo, 360; Colby visits, 430n1; issue of invitation to minister to visit U.S., 452, 457
Arias, Desiderio, 361
Arica, 210,n2
Arizona: and copper strike, 125
Armenia, 482; and Russia, 21-22; and Greeks of Euxine Pontus, 29,n1; Lloyd George on, 47; boundary issue and U. S. offer to mediate, 65, 86,n1, 110, 350, 357, 426-28, 436, 450n2, 480; Congress' action on, 421-22,n2; WW's response to League of Nations Council on mediation, 426-28, 443-44,n1; mention of an alleged unpublished speech on, 434,n1; recommended loan to, 448, 449-50, 452,n2, 489-90; Spain and Brazil offer to help, 457, 480; WW on loan to, 489-90; on gratitude to WW, 507-508; Lamont on relief funds for, 509; Morgenthau appointed mediator, 517-18
Armistice Day, 151,n1,2; WW's proclamation on, 204-205
Armour Fertilizer Works, 289n2

WOODROW WILSON